Machine Learning Applications in Seismology

Machine Learning Applications in Seismology

Guest Editors

Shiyong Zhou
Ke Jia

Basel • Beijing • Wuhan • Barcelona • Belgrade • Novi Sad • Cluj • Manchester

Guest Editors

Shiyong Zhou
School of Earth and Space Sciences
Peking University
Beijing
China

Ke Jia
School of Automation
Northwestern Polytechnical University
Xi'an
China

Editorial Office
MDPI AG
Grosspeteranlage 5
4052 Basel, Switzerland

This is a reprint of the Special Issue, published open access by the journal *Applied Sciences* (ISSN 2076-3417), freely accessible at: https://www.mdpi.com/journal/applsci/special_issues/AI_Seismology.

For citation purposes, cite each article independently as indicated on the article page online and as indicated below:

Lastname, A.A.; Lastname, B.B. Article Title. *Journal Name* **Year**, *Volume Number*, Page Range.

ISBN 978-3-7258-2951-4 (Hbk)
ISBN 978-3-7258-2952-1 (PDF)
https://doi.org/10.3390/books978-3-7258-2952-1

© 2025 by the authors. Articles in this book are Open Access and distributed under the Creative Commons Attribution (CC BY) license. The book as a whole is distributed by MDPI under the terms and conditions of the Creative Commons Attribution-NonCommercial-NoDerivs (CC BY-NC-ND) license (https://creativecommons.org/licenses/by-nc-nd/4.0/).

Contents

About the Editors vii

Preface ix

Ke Jia and Shiyong Zhou
Machine Learning Applications in Seismology
Reprinted from: *Appl. Sci.* 2024, 14, 7857, https://doi.org/10.3390/app14177857 1

Xian Lu, Qiong Wang, Xiaodong Zhang, Wei Yan, Lingyuan Meng and Haitao Wang
Machine Learning-Based Precursor Detection Using Seismic Multi-Parameter Data
Reprinted from: *Appl. Sci.* 2024, 14, 2401, https://doi.org/10.3390/app14062401 7

Binghui Zhao, Liguo Han, Pan Zhang, Qiang Feng and Liyun Ma
Randomly Distributed Passive Seismic Source Reconstruction Record Waveform Rectification Based on Deep Learning
Reprinted from: *Appl. Sci.* 2024, 14, 2206, https://doi.org/10.3390/app14052206 22

Lei Li, Xiaobao Zeng, Xinpeng Pan, Ling Peng, Yuyang Tan and Jianxin Liu
Microseismic Velocity Inversion Based on Deep Learning and Data Augmentation
Reprinted from: *Appl. Sci.* 2024, 14, 2194, https://doi.org/10.3390/app14052194 38

Jun Li, Ming Hao and Zijian Cui
A High-Resolution Aftershock Catalog for the 2014 Ms 6.5 Ludian (China) Earthquake Using Deep Learning Methods
Reprinted from: *Appl. Sci.* 2024, 14, 1997, https://doi.org/10.3390/app14051997 52

Mingming Tang, Boyang Huang, Rong Xie and Zhenzhen Chen
A Seismic Inversion Method Based on Multi-Scale Super-Asymmetric Cycle-JNet Network
Reprinted from: *Appl. Sci.* 2024, 14, 242, https://doi.org/10.3390/app14010242 67

Leonidas Agathos, Andreas Avgoustis, Nikolaos Avgoustis, Ioannis Vlachos, Ioannis Karydis and MArkos Avlonitis
Identifying Earthquakes in Low-Cost Sensor Signals Contaminated with Vehicular Noise
Reprinted from: *Appl. Sci.* 2023, 13, 10884, https://doi.org/10.3390/app131910884 80

Junqing Zhu, Ke Sun and Jingye Zhang
Anomalies in Infrared Outgoing Longwave Radiation Data before the Yangbi *Ms*6.4 and Luding *Ms*6.8 Earthquakes Based on Time Series Forecasting Models
Reprinted from: *Appl. Sci.* 2023, 13, 8572, https://doi.org/10.3390/app13158572 99

Jinjun Hu, Yitian Ding, Shibin Lin, Hui Zhang and Chaoyue Jin
A Machine-Learning-Based Software for the Simulation of Regional Characteristic Ground Motion
Reprinted from: *Appl. Sci.* 2023, 13, 8232, https://doi.org/10.3390/app13148232 120

Xi Wang, Zeyuan Zhong, Yuechen Yao, Zexu Li, Shiyong Zhou, Changsheng Jiang and Ke Jia
Small Earthquakes Can Help Predict Large Earthquakes: A Machine Learning Perspective
Reprinted from: *Appl. Sci.* 2023, 13, 6424, https://doi.org/10.3390/app13116424 138

Sergey Agayan, Boris Dzeboev, Shamil Bogoutdinov, Ivan Belov, Boris Dzeranov and Dmitriy Kamaev
Development of the Algorithmic Basis of the FCAZ Method for Earthquake-Prone Area Recognition
Reprinted from: *Appl. Sci.* 2023, 13, 2496, https://doi.org/10.3390/app13042496 157

Shuai Li, Lihua Fang, Zhuowei Xiao, Yijian Zhou, Shirong Liao and Liping Fan
FocMech-Flow: Automatic Determination of P-Wave First-Motion Polarity and Focal Mechanism Inversion and Application to the 2021 Yangbi Earthquake Sequence
Reprinted from: *Appl. Sci.* **2023**, *13*, 2233, https://doi.org/10.3390/app13042233 174

Mouna Merdasse, Mohamed Hamdache, José A. Peláez, Jesús Henares and Tarek Medkour
Earthquake Magnitude and Frequency Forecasting in Northeastern Algeria Using Time Series Analysis
Reprinted from: *Appl. Sci.* **2023**, *13*, 1566, https://doi.org/10.3390/app13031566 187

Bo Liu, Baofeng Zhou, Jingchang Kong, Xiaomin Wang and Chunhui Liu
The Cut-Off Frequency of High-Pass Filtering of Strong-Motion Records Based on Transfer Learning
Reprinted from: *Appl. Sci.* **2023**, *13*, 1500, https://doi.org/10.3390/app13031500 210

Fatema Tuz Johora, Craig J. Hickey and Hakan Yasarer
Predicting Geotechnical Parameters from Seismic Wave Velocity Using Artificial Neural Networks
Reprinted from: *Appl. Sci.* **2023**, *13*, 12815, https://doi.org/10.3390/app122412815 228

Muhammad Atif Bilal, Yanju Ji, Yongzhi Wang, Muhammad Pervez Akhter and Muhammad Yaqub
Early Earthquake Detection Using Batch Normalization Graph Convolutional Neural Network (BNGCNN)
Reprinted from: *Appl. Sci.* **2022**, *12*, 7548, https://doi.org/10.3390/app12157548 244

About the Editors

Shiyong Zhou

Professor at Peking University, primarily engaged in research on seismic activity, machine learning, and seismic data analysis. In 1997, he was selected for the Cross-Century Talent Program by the China Earthquake Administration. From July to December 2002, he was invited to conduct research at the Disaster Prevention Research Institute of Kyoto University, Japan, and from January to October 2003, he was invited to be a visiting scholar at the Faculty of Science, Victoria University of Wellington, New Zealand. He has published a total of 79 papers. In 1997, he received the Third Prize for Scientific and Technological Progress from the China Earthquake Administration, the first Li Shanbang Outstanding Paper Award in 1999, and the Third Prize for Outstanding Postdoctoral Paper in 2000. He has led one key project supported by the Earthquake Joint Fund of the National Natural Science Foundation, one key R&D program project, and eight general projects of the National Natural Science Foundation.

Ke Jia

Associate Professor at the School of Automation, Northwestern Polytechnical University, Head of the Department of Detection Technology and Automation Systems. His research primarily focuses on statistical seismology, machine learning, and geophysical field navigation. He has led several research projects, including the National Natural Science Foundation of China's General Program, Youth Program, Sub-projects of the Earthquake Joint Fund, Key R&D Program Sub-topics, Shaanxi Province Key R&D Program, Postdoctoral General Fund, and Aerospace Fund. He has published over ten papers in journals such as *GRL*, *JGR*, and *SRL*. He serves as a committee member of several professional committees, including the Seismology Committee of the Chinese Seismological Society, the Crustal Stress and Earthquake Committee, the Earthquake Artificial Intelligence Committee, the Youth Work Committee, and the Earthquake Numerical Prediction Committee. He is also a young Editorial Board Member of *Reviews of Geophysics and Planetary Physics and Earthquake Research Advances*. He received the 13th Li Shanbang Young Outstanding Earthquake Science and Technology Paper Award.

Preface

In the ever-evolving field of seismology, the integration of machine-learning-based artificial intelligence represents a groundbreaking advancement. This Special Issue is dedicated to exploring the profound impact of AI on seismic data processing and the development of structured seismic catalogs. Our aim is to delve into the transformative potential of AI technologies, which promise to solve fundamental scientific challenges by identifying signals and patterns that traditional methods often miss. Through this exploration, we seek to enhance our understanding of the physical processes underlying earthquakes and improve our ability to predict and respond to seismic events.

The scope of this Special Issue encompasses a wide array of topics, including seismic data processing, event location and discrimination, early warning systems, forecasting, and the application of machine learning and deep learning in seismology. By presenting innovative ideas and the latest findings, we hope to inspire further research and development in this critical area.

This work is addressed to researchers, practitioners, and students in the field of seismology and related disciplines, who are eager to explore the cutting-edge applications of AI in their work. We are privileged to have contributions from leading experts who share their insights and visions for the future of earthquake monitoring and forecasting.

We extend our heartfelt gratitude to the reviewers whose meticulous evaluations have ensured the quality and rigor of this Special Issue. Special thanks are due to Editor Sonya Qin for her invaluable guidance and support throughout this endeavor. We also express our appreciation to the authors of the included papers, whose pioneering research forms the foundation of this work.

Together, we embark on a journey to unlock the full potential of artificial intelligence in seismology, striving for a future where our understanding of earthquakes is deeper, our predictions more accurate, and our world safer.

Shiyong Zhou and Ke Jia
Guest Editors

Editorial

Machine Learning Applications in Seismology

Ke Jia [1,2,*] and Shiyong Zhou [3,4,*]

1 School of Automation, Northwestern Polytechnical University, Xi'an 710129, China
2 Shanghai Sheshan National Geophysical Observatory, Shanghai 201602, China
3 Department of Artificial Intelligence and Data Science, Guangzhou Xinhua University, Guangzhou 510520, China
4 School of Earth and Space Science, Peking University, Beijing 100871, China
* Correspondence: jk@nwpu.edu.cn (K.J.); zsy@pku.edu.cn (S.Z.)

1. Introduction

The comprehension of earthquakes and natural hazards, including volcanic eruptions and landslides, as well as explosions, through observational data is a pivotal activity within the field of seismology. The rapid advancements in seismogram technology have resulted in the accumulation of extensive seismic datasets, presenting significant opportunities for the exploration of seismicity patterns, the physical processes underlying earthquakes, and the elucidation of earthquake mechanisms [1–8]. The availability of such large-scale seismic data can substantially enhance data-driven research endeavors in seismology [9–13]. These data-rich resources can be employed for a variety of analytical and modeling initiatives, thereby assisting seismologists in gaining insights into earthquake mechanisms, forecasting seismic hazards, and formulating strategies for disaster prevention and mitigation.

Recent progress in seismic data acquisition and processing, particularly through the application of machine learning techniques, has proven beneficial for seismologists in identifying signals or patterns that traditional methodologies may overlook [8,14]. For instance, the automatic detection of seismic events via models such as PhaseNet [15] streamlines the processing of seismic data [16–20]. Additionally, the classification of seismic events utilizing convolutional neural networks (CNN) demonstrates greater efficiency compared to conventional feature-based methods [21–23]. Furthermore, machine learning approaches to earthquake prediction and early warning systems offer alternative strategies for mitigating earthquake hazards [4,24–26]. In summary, machine learning methodologies significantly enhance the capabilities of seismologists in processing seismic data and uncovering the physical mechanisms associated with earthquakes [27].

Over the past two years, we have compiled 15 articles for this Special Issue titled "Machine Learning Applications in Seismology". These contributions encompass topics such as seismic inversion, earthquake detection, ground motion simulation, focal mechanism analysis, and earthquake early warning and forecasting systems. The articles underscore the necessity of integrating machine learning into seismological research and provide illustrative examples of its application within the discipline.

2. Summary of the Published Articles

The following overview of the published articles in this Special Issue is organized chronologically by publication date.

Bilal et al. (Contribution 1) introduce an innovative approach to earthquake detection that integrates batch normalization with graph convolutional neural networks (BNGCNN). This study highlights the significance of hyper-parameter optimization in enhancing model performance and demonstrates that the BNGCNN model effectively amalgamates local and global features from seismic data, resulting in improved earthquake detection capabilities. The experimental findings indicate that the BNGCNN surpasses existing models, suggesting its potential utility in real-time earthquake monitoring systems.

Citation: Jia, K.; Zhou, S. Machine Learning Applications in Seismology. *Appl. Sci.* **2024**, *14*, 7857. https://doi.org/10.3390/app14177857

Received: 1 September 2024
Revised: 3 September 2024
Accepted: 3 September 2024
Published: 4 September 2024

Copyright: © 2024 by the authors. Licensee MDPI, Basel, Switzerland. This article is an open access article distributed under the terms and conditions of the Creative Commons Attribution (CC BY) license (https://creativecommons.org/licenses/by/4.0/).

Johora et al. (Contribution 2) investigate the use of non-destructive seismic wave velocity measurements to predict geotechnical parameters, such as water content and dry density, through artificial neural networks (ANNs). By incorporating seismic wave velocity data, the ANN models exhibit enhanced predictability compared to traditional multilinear regression models, thereby demonstrating the potential for increased efficiency and accuracy in geotechnical evaluations.

Liu et al. (Contribution 3) utilize convolutional neural networks for the automatic classification of filtered displacement time series derived from strong-motion records, thereby improving efficiency over conventional visual inspection techniques. By employing transfer learning with models such as VGG19 and ResNet50, this research work achieves enhanced accuracy in determining high-pass cut-off frequencies, attaining a maximum coefficient of determination (R^2) of 0.82 with minimal prediction errors.

Merdasse et al. (Contribution 4) apply time series analysis to forecast earthquake frequency and magnitude in northeastern Algeria, utilizing both parametric (autoregressive integrated moving average, ARIMA) and non-parametric (singular spectrum analysis, SSA) methodologies. Analyzing data from 1910 to 2019, the findings reveal that the SSA model outperforms the ARIMA model. Their forecasts indicate that between 2020 and 2030, the annual maximum magnitude will range from Mw 4.8 to Mw 5.1, with an expectation of four to six earthquakes of at least Mw 4.0 occurring annually.

Li et al. (Contribution 5) propose FocMech-Flow, an automated workflow designed for determining P-wave first-motion polarity and focal mechanism inversion, applied to the 2021 Yangbi earthquake sequence. Utilizing the deep learning model DiTingMotion, the method achieves an accuracy of 98.49% in polarity detection and provides 112 focal mechanism solutions, thereby enhancing the understanding of fault structures and regional stress fields in small to moderate earthquakes.

Agayan et al. (Contribution 6) present advancements in the FCAZ (fuzzy clustering and zoning) method for identifying earthquake-prone regions through enhancements to its mathematical algorithms and foundational principles. This study focuses on improving the precision and reliability of high-seismicity area identification, exemplified by a case study in California. By refining the FCAZ algorithm, closely linked small zones are consolidated into larger, high-seismicity areas, thereby enhancing the efficacy of earthquake hazard assessments.

Wang et al. (Contribution 7) explore the potential of machine learning techniques, specifically random forest and long short-term memory (LSTM) neural networks, to predict large earthquakes utilizing seismic catalog data from the Sichuan–Yunnan region. The research addresses two critical questions: the likelihood of a significant earthquake occurring within a year and the anticipated maximum magnitude. The results indicate that the random forest method excels in classifying large earthquake occurrences, while LSTM provides reasonable magnitude estimations. The findings suggest that small earthquakes contain valuable predictive information, underscoring the promise of machine learning in improving earthquake prediction accuracy.

Hu Junjun et al. (Contribution 8) propose a novel software application employing machine learning to simulate ground motion by accurately matching amplitude, spectrum, and duration characteristics specific to a region. By utilizing principal component analysis and predictive equations, this software generates simulated ground motions that closely align with the desired attributes, offering a more reliable input for structural design and assessment.

Zhu et al. (Contribution 9) investigate anomalies in outgoing longwave radiation (OLR) data preceding the Yangbi Ms6.4 and Luding Ms6.8 earthquakes using the bidirectional long short-term memory (BILSTM) model. This study predicts OLR values prior to the earthquakes, employing confidence intervals for anomaly detection. The authors suggest that their method effectively captures seismic anomalies and may indicate a correlation between OLR anomalies and earthquake occurrences, advocating for further research involving additional earthquake cases to enhance predictive capabilities.

Agathos et al. (Contribution 10) discuss the application of a specialized deep neural network to identify earthquakes in environments characterized by significant background noise from vehicular activity. To address this challenge, this study proposes utilizing a deep neural network trained on both earthquake and vehicular signals to detect earthquakes within low-cost sensor data contaminated by noise, demonstrating superior effectiveness and efficiency compared to traditional models. This article emphasizes the critical role of earthquake monitoring in disaster management, public safety, and scientific inquiry.

Tang et al. (Contribution 11) present a novel seismic inversion method that employs a multi-scale super-asymmetric network (Cycle-JNet) to enhance the resolution and accuracy of seismic data interpretation. By integrating wavelet analysis with deep learning techniques, the Cycle-JNet model effectively captures multi-scale data characteristics. The model exhibits superior performance in identifying thin sandstone layers compared to conventional approaches, achieving a prediction accuracy of 81.2%. The findings indicate that the Cycle-JNet network serves as a reliable tool for seismic inversion, significantly improving the identification of geological features in complex data environments.

Li et al. (Contribution 12) develop a high-resolution aftershock catalog for the 2014 Ms 6.5 Ludian earthquake in China utilizing deep learning methodologies, specifically the deep learning phase-picking CERP model and seismic-phase association PALM technology. A novel training strategy that combines traditional algorithms with artificial intelligence enhances seismic phase detection and event localization, resulting in the identification of 3286 aftershock events with improved accuracy. This study underscores the effectiveness of the retraining strategy in enhancing the generalization of AI models for seismic analysis in specific tectonic contexts.

Li et al. (Contribution 13) present a deep learning approach for microseismic velocity inversion, employing a Unet model in conjunction with data augmentation and hybrid training strategies. This methodology effectively addresses challenges associated with low signal-to-noise ratios in real microseismic data, enhancing inversion accuracy by integrating synthetic and augmented datasets. The results demonstrate the model's robustness and potential for improved subsurface velocity predictions.

Zhao et al. (Contribution 14) introduce a novel approach for enhancing passive seismic source reconstruction through the use of convolutional neural networks (CNN). The authors tackle the challenges posed by randomly distributed and sparse seismic sources, which often result in artifacts and coherent noise in virtual shot records. By incorporating an adaptive attention mechanism into the CNN architecture, the proposed method effectively suppresses noise and restores valid waveform features. The results demonstrate improved signal clarity and continuity, highlighting the method's applicability in passive seismic exploration, particularly in scenarios characterized by uneven source distributions and limited active sources.

Lu et al. (Contribution 15) investigate the application of machine learning for detecting earthquake precursors through the analysis of seismic multi-parameter data across twelve tectonic regions in western China. This study employs a sliding extreme value relevancy method to analyze various seismic parameters, including the b value, earthquake frequency, and intensity factors. Their findings indicate that significant anomalies frequently precede target earthquakes, with high anomaly rates correlating with earthquake occurrences. The results emphasize the effectiveness of a comprehensive multi-parameter approach in enhancing earthquake prediction accuracy and spatial risk assessment, providing valuable insights for future evaluations of seismic hazards in the investigated regions.

3. Conclusions

The adoption of artificial intelligence in scientific research has gained traction across various disciplines, achieving notable success. The application of machine learning within seismology has also garnered increasing attention. This collection of articles in this Special Issue contribute to the field of seismology by presenting views and research examples that illustrate the integration of machine learning into seismology. The topics covered in these articles include seismic inversion, earthquake detection, focal mechanism analysis, ground motion simulation, earthquake early warning systems, and earthquake forecasting, utilizing a diverse array of machine learning methods.

Moreover, these articles highlight interdisciplinary research that bridges seismology and machine learning, offering innovative solutions to challenges associated with seismic data and advancements in model interpretability. While limitations exist, there is a strong expectation for future work to focus on enhancing model accuracy and generalizability, the development of real-time applications in seismology and the exploration of the physical mechanisms underlying earthquakes through machine learning methodologies.

In conclusion, we extend our heartfelt appreciation to the contributors, reviewers, and the editorial team for their dedicated efforts in bringing this Special Issue to fruition. Their contributions have significantly enriched the discourse on the application of machine learning in seismology, paving the way for future advancements in the field.

Conflicts of Interest: The authors declare no conflict of interest.

List of Contributions:

1. Bilal, M.A.; Ji, Y.; Wang, Y.; Akhter, M.P.; Yaqub, M. Early Earthquake Detection Using Batch Normalization Graph Convolutional Neural Network (BNGCNN). *Appl. Sci.* **2022**, *12*, 7548. https://doi.org/10.3390/app12157548.
2. Johora, F.T.; Hickey, C.J.; Yasarer, H. Predicting Geotechnical Parameters from Seismic Wave Velocity Using Artificial Neural Networks. *Appl. Sci.* **2022**, *12*, 12815. https://doi.org/10.3390/app122412815.
3. Liu, B.; Zhou, B.; Kong, J.; Wang, X.; Liu, C. The Cut-Off Frequency of High-Pass Filtering of Strong-Motion Records Based on Transfer Learning. *Appl. Sci.* **2023**, *13*, 1500. https://doi.org/10.3390/app13031500.
4. Merdasse, M.; Hamdache, M.; Peláez, J.A.; Henares, J.; Medkour, T. Earthquake Magnitude and Frequency Forecasting in Northeastern Algeria using Time Series Analysis. *Appl. Sci.* **2023**, *13*, 1566. https://doi.org/10.3390/app13031566.
5. Li, S.; Fang, L.; Xiao, Z.; Zhou, Y.; Liao, S.; Fan, L. FocMech-Flow: Automatic Determination of P-Wave First-Motion Polarity and Focal Mechanism Inversion and Application to the 2021 Yangbi Earthquake Sequence. *Appl. Sci.* **2023**, *13*, 2233. https://doi.org/10.3390/app13042233.
6. Agayan, S.M.; Dzeboev, B.A.; Bogoutdinov, S.R.; Belov, I.O.; Dzeranov, B.V.; Kamaev, D.A. Development of the Algorithmic Basis of the FCAZ Method for Earthquake-Prone Area Recognition. *Appl. Sci.* **2023**, *13*, 2496. https://doi.org/10.3390/app13042496.
7. Wang, X.; Zhong, Z.; Yao, Y.; Li, Z.; Zhou, S.; Jiang, C.; Jia, K. Small Earthquakes Can Help Predict Large Earthquakes: A Machine Learning Perspective. *Appl. Sci.* **2023**, *13*, 6424. https://doi.org/10.3390/app13116424.
8. Hu, J.; Ding, Y.; Lin, S.; Zhang, H.; Jin, C. A Machine-Learning-Based Software for the Simulation of Regional Characteristic Ground Motion. *Appl. Sci.* **2023**, *13*, 8232. https://doi.org/10.3390/app13148232.
9. Zhu, J.; Sun, K.; Zhang, J. Anomalies in Infrared Outgoing Longwave Radiation Data before the Yangbi Ms6.4 and Luding Ms6.8 Earthquakes Based on Time Series Forecasting Models. *Appl. Sci.* **2023**, *13*, 8572. https://doi.org/10.3390/app13158572.
10. Agathos, L.; Avgoustis, A.; Avgoustis, N.; Vlachos, I.; Karydis, I.; Avlonitis, M. Identifying Earthquakes in Low-Cost Sensor Signals Contaminated with Vehicular Noise. *Appl. Sci.* **2023**, *13*, 10884. https://doi.org/10.3390/app131910884.
11. Tang, M.; Huang, B.; Xie, R.; Chen, Z. A Seismic Inversion Method Based on Multi-Scale Super-Asymmetric Cycle-JNet Network. *Appl. Sci.* **2024**, *14*, 242. https://doi.org/10.3390/app14010242.
12. Li, J.; Hao, M.; Cui, Z. A High-Resolution Aftershock Catalog for the 2014 Ms 6.5 Ludian (China) Earthquake Using Deep Learning Methods. *Appl. Sci.* **2024**, *14*, 1997. https://doi.org/10.3390/app14051997.
13. Li, L.; Zeng, X.; Pan, X.; Peng, L.; Tan, Y.; Liu, J. Microseismic Velocity Inversion Based on Deep Learning and Data Augmentation. *Appl. Sci.* **2024**, *14*, 2194. https://doi.org/10.3390/app14052194.
14. Zhao, B.; Han, L.; Zhang, P.; Feng, Q.; Ma, L. Randomly Distributed Passive Seismic Source Reconstruction Record Waveform Rectification Based on Deep Learning. *Appl. Sci.* **2024**, *14*, 2206. https://doi.org/10.3390/app14052206.

15. Lu, X.; Wang, Q.; Zhang, X.; Yan, W.; Meng, L.; Wang, H. Machine Learning-Based Precursor Detection Using Seismic Multi-Parameter Data. *Appl. Sci.* **2024**, *14*, 2401. https://doi.org/10.3390/app14062401.

References

1. Mousavi, S.M.; Beroza, G.C. Deep-learning seismology. *Science* **2022**, *377*, eabm4470. [CrossRef]
2. Li, Z.; Meier, M.; Hauksson, E.; Zhan, Z.; Andrews, J. Machine Learning Seismic Wave Discrimination: Application to Earthquake Early Warning. *Geophys. Res. Lett.* **2018**, *45*, 4773–4779. [CrossRef]
3. Kong, Q.; Trugman, D.T.; Ross, Z.E.; Bianco, M.J.; Meade, B.J.; Gerstoft, P. Machine Learning in Seismology: Turning Data into Insights. *Seismol. Res. Lett.* **2018**, *90*, 3–14. [CrossRef]
4. Mignan, A.; Broccardo, M. Neural network applications in earthquake prediction (1994–2019): Meta-analytic and statistical insights on their limitations. *Seismol. Res. Lett.* **2020**, *91*, 2330–2342. [CrossRef]
5. Johnson, P.A.; Rouet-Leduc, B.; Pyrak-Nolte, L.J.; Beroza, G.C.; Marone, C.J.; Hulbert, C.; Howard, A.; Singer, P.; Gordeev, D.; Karaflos, D.; et al. Laboratory earthquake forecasting: A machine learning competition. *Proc. Natl. Acad. Sci. USA* **2021**, *118*, e2011362118. [CrossRef] [PubMed]
6. Araya-Polo, M.; Jennings, J.; Adler, A.; Dahlke, T. Deep-learning tomography. *Lead. Edge* **2018**, *37*, 58–66. [CrossRef]
7. Fang, L.; Li, Z. Preface to the special issue of Artificial Intelligence in Seismology. *Earthq. Sci.* **2023**, *36*, 81–83. [CrossRef]
8. Cui, X.; Li, Z.; Hu, Y. Similar seismic moment release process for shallow and deep earthquakes. *Nat. Geosci.* **2023**, *16*, 454–460. [CrossRef]
9. Mousavi, S.M.; Sheng, Y.; Zhu, W.; Beroza, G.C. STanford EArthquake Dataset (STEAD): A global data set of seismic signals for AI. *IEEE Access* **2019**, *7*, 179464–179476. [CrossRef]
10. Zhao, M.; Xiao, Z.; Chen, S.; Fang, L. DiTing: A large-scale Chinese seismic benchmark dataset for artificial intelligence in seismology. *Earthq. Sci.* **2023**, *36*, 84–94. [CrossRef]
11. Michelini, A.; Cianetti, S.; Gaviano, S.; Giunchi, C.; Jozinović, D.; Lauciani, V. INSTANCE–the Italian seismic dataset for machine learning. *Earth Syst. Sci. Data* **2021**, *13*, 5509–5544. [CrossRef]
12. Li, L.; Wang, W.; Yu, Z.; Chen, Y. CREDIT-X1local: A reference dataset for machine learning seismology from ChinArray in Southwest China. *Earthq. Sci.* **2024**, *37*, 139–157. [CrossRef]
13. An, Y. Introduction to a recently released dataset entitled CSNCD: A Comprehensive Dataset of Chinese Seismic Network. *Earthq. Res. Adv.* **2024**, *4*, 100255. [CrossRef]
14. van den Ende, M.P.; Ampuero, J.P. Automated seismic source characterization using deep graph neural networks. *Geophys. Res. Lett.* **2020**, *47*, e2020GL088690. [CrossRef]
15. Zhu, W.; Beroza, G.C. PhaseNet: A deep-neural-network-based seismic arrival-time picking method. *Geophys. J. Int.* **2019**, *216*, 261–273. [CrossRef]
16. Mousavi, S.M.; Ellsworth, W.L.; Zhu, W.; Chuang, L.Y.; Beroza, G.C. Earthquake transformer—An attentive deep-learning model for simultaneous earthquake detection and phase picking. *Nat. Commun.* **2020**, *11*, 3952. [CrossRef]
17. Zhou, Y.; Yue, H.; Kong, Q.; Zhou, S. Hybrid event detection and phase-picking algorithm using convolutional and recurrent neural networks. *Seismol. Res. Lett.* **2019**, *90*, 1079–1087. [CrossRef]
18. Ross, Z.E.; Meier, M.; Hauksson, E.; Heaton, T.H. Generalized seismic phase detection with deep learning. *Bull. Seismol. Soc. Am.* **2018**, *108*, 2894–2901. [CrossRef]
19. Ross, Z.E.; Meier, M.A.; Hauksson, E. P wave arrival picking and first-motion polarity determination with deep learning. *J. Geophys. Res. Solid Earth* **2018**, *123*, 5120–5129. [CrossRef]
20. Zhang, M.; Liu, M.; Feng, T.; Wang, R.; Zhu, W. LOC-FLOW: An End-to-End Machine Learning-Based High-Precision Earthquake Location Workflow. *Seismol. Res. Lett.* **2022**, *93*, 2426–2438. [CrossRef]
21. Perol, T.; Gharbi, M.; Denolle, M. Convolutional neural network for earthquake detection and location. *Sci. Adv.* **2018**, *4*, e1700578. [CrossRef]
22. Kong, Q.; Wang, R.; Walter, W.R.; Pyle, M.; Koper, K.; Schmandt, B. Combining Deep Learning With Physics Based Features in Explosion-Earthquake Discrimination. *Geophys. Res. Lett.* **2022**, *49*, e2022GL098645. [CrossRef]
23. Wang, T.; Bian, Y.; Zhang, Y.; Hou, X. Classification of earthquakes, explosions and mining-induced earthquakes based on XGBoost algorithm. *Comput. Geosci.* **2023**, *170*, 105242. [CrossRef]
24. Wang, Q.; Guo, Y.; Yu, L.; Li, P. Earthquake prediction based on spatio-temporal data mining: An LSTM network approach. *IEEE Trans. Emerg. Top. Comput.* **2017**, *8*, 148–158. [CrossRef]
25. Beroza, G.C.; Segou, M.; Mousavi, S.M. Machine learning and earthquake forecasting—Next steps. *Nat. Commun.* **2021**, *12*, 4761. [CrossRef]

26. Asencio–Cortés, G.; Morales–Esteban, A.; Shang, X.; Martínez–Álvarez, F. Earthquake prediction in California using regression algorithms and cloud-based big data infrastructure. *Comput. Geosci.* **2018**, *115*, 198–210. [CrossRef]
27. Si, X.; Wu, X.; Sheng, H.; Zhu, J.; Li, Z. SeisCLIP: A Seismology Foundation Model Pre-Trained by Multimodal Data for Multipurpose Seismic Feature Extraction. *IEEE Trans. Geosci. Remote Sens.* **2024**, *62*, 5903713. [CrossRef]

Disclaimer/Publisher's Note: The statements, opinions and data contained in all publications are solely those of the individual author(s) and contributor(s) and not of MDPI and/or the editor(s). MDPI and/or the editor(s) disclaim responsibility for any injury to people or property resulting from any ideas, methods, instructions or products referred to in the content.

Article

Machine Learning-Based Precursor Detection Using Seismic Multi-Parameter Data

Xian Lu [1,*], Qiong Wang [2], Xiaodong Zhang [3,4,*], Wei Yan [1], Lingyuan Meng [1] and Haitao Wang [1]

1. China Earthquake Networks Center, Beijing 100045, China; yanwei@seis.ac.cn (W.Y.); menglingyuan@seis.ac.cn (L.M.); wanght@seis.ac.cn (H.W.)
2. Seismological Bureau of Xinjiang Wulumuqi Autonomous Region, Urumqi 830011, China; qiongwang2024@163.com
3. Institute of Earthquake Forecasting, China Earthquake Administration, Beijing 100036, China
4. Shanghai Artificial Intelligence Laboratory, Shanghai 200232, China
* Correspondence: luxian@radi.ac.cn (X.L.); zxd@ief.ac.cn (X.Z.)

Citation: Lu, X.; Wang, Q.; Zhang, X.; Yan, W.; Meng, L.; Wang, H. Machine Learning-Based Precursor Detection Using Seismic Multi-Parameter Data. *Appl. Sci.* **2024**, *14*, 2401. https://doi.org/10.3390/app14062401

Academic Editor: Roberto Scarpa

Received: 6 February 2024
Revised: 7 March 2024
Accepted: 9 March 2024
Published: 13 March 2024

Correction Statement: This article has been republished with a minor change. The change does not affect the scientific content of the article and further details are available within the backmatter of the website version of this article.

Copyright: © 2024 by the authors. Licensee MDPI, Basel, Switzerland. This article is an open access article distributed under the terms and conditions of the Creative Commons Attribution (CC BY) license (https:// creativecommons.org/licenses/by/ 4.0/).

Abstract: The application of certain mathematical–statistical methods can quantitatively identify and extract the abnormal characteristics from the observation data, and the comprehensive analysis of seismic multi-parameters can study and judge the risk of the tectonic regions better than a single parameter. In this study, the machine learning-based detection of seismic multi-parameters using the sliding extreme value relevancy method, based on the earthquake-corresponding relevancy spectrum, was calculated in the tectonic regions in the western Chinese mainland, and the R-value evaluation was completed. Multi-parameter data included the b value, M value (missing earthquakes), η value (the relationship between seismic magnitude and frequency), D value (seismic hazard), Mf value (intensity factor), N value (earthquake frequency), and Rm value (modulation parameter). The temporal results showed that the high-value anomalies appeared before most target earthquakes during the training period. Moreover, some target earthquakes also occurred during the advantageous extrapolation period with high-value anomalies. The spatial results showed that some months before the target earthquakes, there was indeed a significant abnormal enhancement area that appeared near the epicenter, and the anomaly gradually disappeared after the earthquakes. This study demonstrated that machine learning techniques for detecting earthquake anomalies using seismic multi-parameter data were feasible.

Keywords: machine learning; precursor detection; seismic multi-parameter; target earthquake

1. Introduction

Various seismological parameters may exhibit different degrees of precursor anomaly characteristics before major earthquakes and reveal certain laws of earthquake development from different perspectives. There were many studies on the b value within seismological parameters [1–3]. The b value is a critical parameter in seismic hazard studies [4], and a high b value indicates a larger proportion of small earthquakes, and vice versa. In addition, earthquake frequency is also a commonly used seismological parameter internationally [5,6]. What would be the effect of integrating these seismic parameters for analysis? There has been relatively little comprehensive study of seismic parameters, which could solve the limitations of single parameter and method approaches [7]. The comprehensive analysis of multiple methods based on the quantitative description of a single anomaly is of great significance in earthquake research. Based on this idea, the study was conducted on the quantitative identification and extraction of anomalies from observation data using mathematical–statistical methods. For example, Wang Haitao [8] transformed the time series of original data into a probability time series based on the corresponding relevancy spectrum in different investigation durations, and used the multi-point cumulative moving average method to obtain the time curve of average probability; then, the earthquake precursor anomalies were identified, providing quantitative single factor data for the comprehensive method. Bo [9] used the multi-point group slope method and composite information flow method to convert the deformation data into the 'standardized information curve'. Wang [10] quantitatively identified and extracted anomalies from various seismic parameter data in the western section of the southern Tianshan of Xinjiang by using the multi-parameter sliding extreme-value relevancy based on the earthquake-corresponding relevancy spectrum. Lu also conducted a long-term tracking study on the central and southern sections of the Tanlu fault, utilizing the earthquake-corresponding relevancy spectrum of seismic multi-parameters, and found that the earthquake-corresponding efficiency calculated by combining multiple advantageous parameters was indeed better than that of a single parameter [11].

Some studies also found that although some calculated factors and models were different, the regional scales of the predicted earthquake were consistent [12–15]. Perhaps more earthquake factors could more easily predict the spatial–temporal and intensity information of earthquakes. Therefore, it is possible to try combining multiple different factors within a unified and reasonable physical framework for the extraction of seismic anomalies. For example, establishing a physically reasonable framework that combines the pattern informatics (PI) prediction method [16,17] with the load/unload response ratio (LURR), state vector (SV), and accelerating moment release (AMR) method [18] could be considered. Alternatively, the LURR method could be combined with other methods for seismic hazard assessment [19]. Scholars have also attempted to use the LURR method to study the electromechanical coupling process before large earthquakes, using geoelectric data and Benioff strain data from small earthquakes as input [20], and the results were both well. These studies fully demonstrated the advantages of using multiple different factors and models for comprehensive calculation. Recently, there have been many studies on the application of machine learning for earthquake precursor mining and analysis. Possible precursors from the surface to the ionosphere using machine learning techniques were analyzed [21]. And earthquake precursors could be detected by a novel machine learning-based technique with GPS data [22].

The strongest earthquakes in China occur in the western part of the Chinese mainland. This paper focuses on analyzing the characteristics of comprehensive anomalies before and after target earthquakes in the study area through the calculation of the comprehensive probability of seismic multi-parameters in several tectonic areas in the western Chinese mainland. Moreover, the evaluations of the R-value for these tectonic areas were calculated, and the effectiveness of corresponding earthquakes during the advantageous prediction time for the regions with anomalies was tested.

2. Materials and Methods

2.1. Materials

The study areas mainly encompassed 12 tectonic regions in the western Chinese mainland, including the western section of southern Tianshan, the middle of Tianshan, the northwest of Yunnan, the east of the border between Sichuan and Yunnan, the western portions of southern Xizang, Yutian, Xinjiang, and so on (Figure 1). The blue lines in Figure 1 represents the faults. Meanwhile, a completeness analysis and collation of earthquakes since 1991 were carried out. The completeness of earthquake catalogs directly affects the understanding of seismic activity patterns. For a certain tectonic zone, if the earthquake catalog is basically complete in a certain period, the annual frequency of earthquakes in a certain magnitude segment should basically be similar [23]. The seismic data in this study primarily relied on the local magnitude (M_L) and adopted the $\geq M_L 3.0$ earthquake catalog from January 1991 to December 2021 provided by the China Earthquake Networks Center, with good completeness.

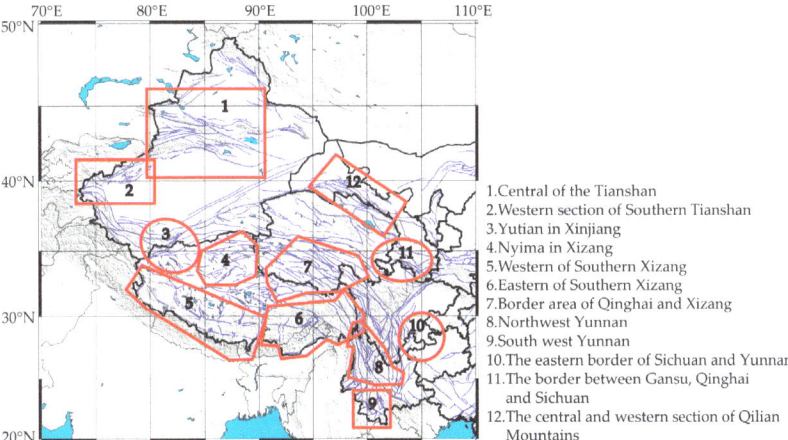

Figure 1. Research regions in the western Chinese mainland.

The appropriate earthquake catalogs for each region in the training database were selected, and the multi-parameter sliding extreme-value relevancy of the training database was calculated, combined with the target earthquakes. Then, the study extrapolated the probability and advantageous time range of target earthquakes in each study area and completed the calculation of the R-value evaluation for each study area.

2.2. Method

Assuming the observation sequence was $x_1, x_2, \ldots, x_n$, $x_{\max}$ was the maximum value in the sequence, $x_{\min}$ was the minimum value. The mean value, $\bar{x}$, and standard deviation, σ, of the sequence x_i ($i = 1, 2, \ldots, n$) could be calculated as follows:

$$\bar{x} = \frac{1}{n}\sum_{i=1}^{n} x_i \tag{1}$$

$$\sigma = \sqrt{\sum_{i=1}^{n}(x_i - \bar{x})^2/(n+1)} \tag{2}$$

Based on the calculation of the mean value and standard deviations, the rules for the value range distribution interval are defined as follows:

$$Dx_0 \in (\bar{x} - k\sigma, \bar{x} + k\sigma)$$

$$Dx_1 \in [\bar{x} + k\sigma, \bar{x} + 2k\sigma)$$

$$Dx_m \in [\bar{x} + mk\sigma, x_{\max}] \tag{3}$$

$$Dx_{-1} \in (\bar{x} - 2k\sigma, \bar{x} - k\sigma]$$

$$Dx_{-m} \in [x_{\min}, \bar{x} - mk\sigma]$$

$Dx_0, Dx_1, \ldots, Dx_{-m}$ in the formula represent the observed values in different value ranges. Formula (3) calculates the frequency of the observed value sequence, x_i, distributed across different intervals, thereby constructing a range spectrum curve to define the distribution interval of the value ranges. Taking the range spectrum curve of the seismic parameter, b, in the western section of southern Tianshan as an example (Figure 2), 0 on the horizontal axis corresponds to the value range of Dx_0, which was near the mean. Value 4 corresponds to the value range Dx_4, -4 corresponds to the value range Dx_{-4}, and so on. The vertical axis represents the frequency of data in the corresponding range.

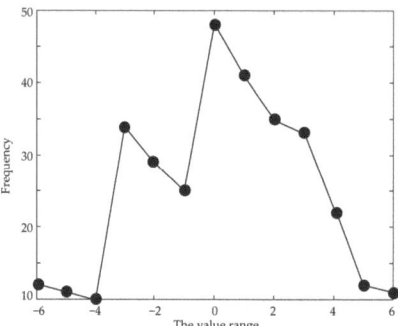

Figure 2. The value range spectrum curve.

The range spectrum curve is similar to a normal distribution, indicating that the range selection is appropriate. k and m are both parameters of the range spectrum curve, where k could adjust the size of each range interval and m could adjust the number of range intervals. This study conducted extensive data calculations and found that the best results were achieved by uniformly using $k = 0.35$ and $m = 6$ to eliminate errors caused by calculating with different parameters of the value range.

Based on the analysis of the value range spectrum, the earthquake-corresponding relevancy spectra (ECRSs) in different value ranges could be solved. By using the ECRS, one can analyze the basic abnormal characteristics of the original observation value sequence and determine the abnormal reliability attributes of data in different value ranges. Firstly, the target earthquakes for retrospective testing in different study areas must be determined. Then, the data falling into the value range from Dx_{-m} to Dx_m (from low to high) are counted, point by point, according to the time series of observation data. At the same time, the method needs to count whether there are target earthquakes in different inspection periods t separately.

According to the above rules, the corresponding number of occurred earthquakes, nDx_m, as well as the total number, NDx_m, in the corresponding value range are determined through the count of the observation value sequence, point by point. Then, the ratio is calculated by $PDx_m = nDx_m/NDx_m$. The ECRSs in different value ranges of the observation value sequence could be obtained by counting the corresponding results of all value ranges.

The time series of different seismic parameters based on the ECRS is x_{ij} ($i = 1, 2, \ldots, n; j = 1, 2, \ldots, k$; k represent the different seismic parameter numbers). The relevancy time sequence, p_{ij}, corresponding to different parameters, j, could be converted from the PDx_m in different value ranges, point-to-point. Then, the sliding average relevancy sequence values, $\bar{p}_{ij}$, of different seismic parameters, according to the lengths of different inspection periods, t, are obtained by the multi-point cumulative average and point-by-point sliding calculation methods.

Setting $t = 12$ (month) represents the different investigation durations. The sliding average relevancy sequence, $\bar{p}_{ij}$, for different seismic parameters is as follows:

$$\bar{p}_{ij} = (p_{ij} + p_{(i+1)j} + \ldots + p_{(i+t-1)j})/t, \ i = 1, 2, \ldots, n-t+1 \tag{4}$$

By analyzing the sliding average relevancy sequences, $\bar{p}_{ij}$, of different seismic parameters, the precursor anomaly characteristics of individual seismic parameters could be quantitatively identified and studied.

Based on the above analysis, we could obtain the multi-point sliding extreme-value relevancy sequence, M_{ij}, of the sliding average relevancy sequence, $\overline{p}_{ij}$, of different parameters, point by point, and finally, calculate the average value of the sliding extreme-value relevancy sequences, M_j, of different parameters to obtain the multi-parameter sliding extreme-value relevancy value, p_c. In order to observe the curve changes more clearly, 6 points are selected as the sliding window lengths in this paper, and the comprehensive results of sliding, point by point, are marked on the time coordinates of the last point.

Suppose that $j = 1, 2, \ldots, k$ (k represents the different seismic parameters), $w = 6$ (w represents the sliding window lengths of different points).

$$M_{ij} = Max\{\overline{p}_{ij}, \overline{p}_{(i+1)j}, \ldots, \overline{p}_{(i+w-1)j}\}, i = 1, 2, \ldots, n - w + 1 \tag{5}$$

$$M_j = \left(M_{1j}, M_{2j}, \ldots, M_{(n-w+1)j}\right), j = 1, 2, \ldots, k \tag{6}$$

In the formula, M_{ij} represents the multi-point sliding extreme-value relevancy for different parameters; M_j represents the multi-point sliding extreme-value relevancy of a single parameter, j.

Then, the multi-parameter sliding extreme-value relevancy value, p_c, is calculated by averaging the values of M_j from different parameters.

$$p_c = \sum_{j=1}^{k} M_j / k \tag{7}$$

3. Results

3.1. Multi-Parameter Relevancy Spectrum Calculation

The most reasonable single parameter and its threshold settings, within the probability spectrum of earthquake occurrence and the value range spectrum in each study area, were analyzed through time scanning with different statistical window lengths and step sizes. After years of analysis and experience summaries, the optimal seven parameters were ultimately selected to participate in the calculation of each research area, namely, the b value, M value (missing earthquake), and η Value—these three parameters could describe the relationship between seismic magnitude and frequency; the D value describes seismic hazard; the Mf value denotes the intensity factor; the N value denotes the earthquake frequency, which describes the intensity changes of seismic activity; and the Rm value is the environmental modulation parameter.

A large portion of the computational analysis was conducted across different research areas. Using the three study areas of border region as examples, e.g., Qinghai and Xizang, the western section of southern Tianshan, and the central and western sections of the Qilian Mountains, different time scanning scales were applied for calculation: 3 months, 6 months, and 12 months. The results showed that the curve did not change much, but the anomaly and earthquake-corresponding rates of the three study areas were relatively high at the 12-month scale (Table 1). Therefore, this study uniformly used a 12-month time scanning scale for all study areas, and the seismic parameters and thresholds used in all study areas were also the same, which could help to avoid errors caused by differences in the time scale and parameters.

Taking the abnormal changes in the border areas of Qinghai and Xizang, where the Maduo M7.4 earthquake occurred on 22 May 2021, as an example, and based on the previous summary and analysis that 12 months was a good sliding window length for calculation, the window lengths of the time calculations for seven parameters were all selected as 12 months, and the calculation step sizes were all 1 month. The 6-point sliding average and 3-point sliding extreme-value algorithms were used to calculate the multi-parameter sliding extreme-value relevancy of earthquake data from January 1991 to December 2021. According to the time distribution of target earthquakes in the study area, it is necessary to ensure that the training period had sufficient sample data and a certain number of target earthquakes to test the extrapolation effect. Therefore, the deadline for the training period here was selected as December 2020, and the target earthquakes in the study area were set as $M_L \geq 6.3$ earthquakes. The results that began in January 2021 were extrapolation values after the machine learning, and the threshold of the probability curve was taken as 0.5 times the standard deviation. The threshold line was obtained through a large number of calculations in 12 study areas in the western Chinese mainland. It was found that when 0.5 times the standard deviation of the multi-parameter probability result was taken as the threshold line, the corresponding effect between the probability value anomaly and the target earthquake was the best. Therefore, in order to eliminate the error caused by using different threshold lines, all study areas uniformly used 0.5 times the standard deviation as the threshold line.

Table 1. Anomaly-corresponding rate and earthquake-corresponding rate of different time scanning scales.

	Name	Anomaly-Corresponding Rate (%)			Earthquake-Corresponding Rate (%)		
	Time scanning scale (month)	3	6	12	3	6	12
Study region	Border regions of Qinghai and Xizang	50.00	66.67	75.00	71.43	100.00	100.00
	Western section of southern Tianshan	50.00	66.67	100.00	71.43	85.71	100.00
	Central and western sections of the Qilian Mountains	77.78	85.71	85.71	80.00	80.00	80.00

Figure 3 shows the study area of the border regions of Qinghai and Xizang. Figure 4 shows the MSER results of the study area. The results show that the earthquake-corresponding rate was good during the training period from January 1991 to December 2020. During the training period, a total of seven target earthquakes occurred, all with high-value anomalies exceeding the threshold line before the earthquakes. The extrapolation period began in January 2021. The probability curve had been in an abnormally high-value state and reached its peak in January 2021. On 19 March 2021, the Xizang Biru $M_L 6.4$ earthquake occurred in the study area, proving that the extrapolation effect was good. According to the retrospective study of earthquakes in this region, there was also an anomaly peak before the Qinghai Yushu $M_L 7.4$ earthquake on 14 April 2010; the anomaly peak occurred in September 2009 and the Xizang Nierong $M_L 6.6$ earthquake occurred on 24 March 2010 (about one month prior). The Maduo $M_L 7.9$ earthquake was similar to the Yushu earthquake. In the process of the curve turning and falling, the Xizang Biru $M_L 6.4$ earthquake first occurred on 19 March, then the Qinghai Maduo $M_L 7.9$ earthquake occurred on 22 May (about two months later).

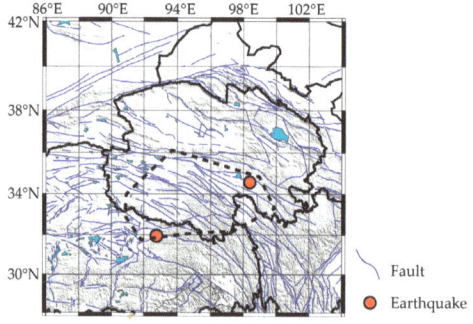

Figure 3. Border regions of Qinghai and Xizang (within the dashed box) and $M_L \geq 6.3$ earthquakes from January 2021 to December 2021.

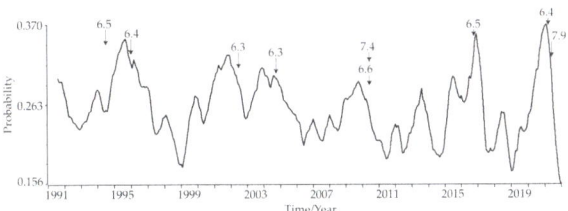

Figure 4. The multi-point sliding extreme-value relevancy (MSER) of the border regions of Qinghai and Xizang.

The spatial scanning calculation of the border regions of Qinghai and Xizang adopted the same seven dominant seismic parameters, which were used in the time scanning. $M_L \geq 3.0$ earthquakes from January 1991 to December 2020 were selected as the training data. The probability spectrum calculation analysis was carried out with a spatial window length of 2° × 2° and a step size of 0.2° × 0.2°, with a duration of 1 year and a step size of 1 month. January 2021 was the starting time for extrapolation testing. The Xizang Biru M_L6.4 earthquake on 19 March 2021 and the Qinghai Maduo M_L7.9 earthquake on 22 May 2021 both occurred in the study area. From the results in Figure 5, it could be seen that there were almost no high-value anomalies in the study area from January to May 2019. In June 2019, sporadic high-value anomalies began to appear near the Xizang Biru region. Afterward, the abnormal area and amplitude gradually expanded and strengthened, reaching their maximum value in December 2020. The Biru M_L6.4 earthquake occurred in the abnormal area in March 2021. At the same time, abnormal high points began to appear between Yushu and Maduo in Qinghai from March 2021 (inside the red dashed box in Figure 5). Although the abnormal points were small, they showed a gradually increasing trend. The Maduo M_L7.9 earthquake occurred to the northeast of the abnormal points in May 2021. Afterward, the abnormal values in both regions gradually weakened, and the high-value abnormal points near the Maduo earthquake completely disappeared in December 2021.

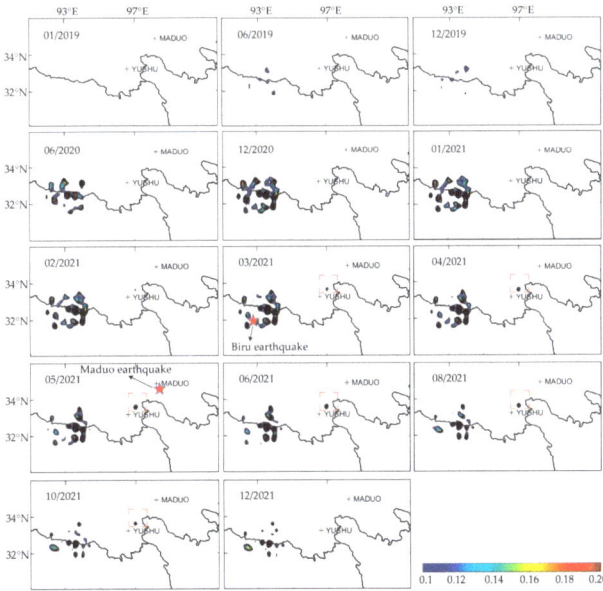

Figure 5. The spatial evolution of the MSER of the border regions of Qinghai and Xizang from January 2019 to September 2021.

It was found that there were similar highly abnormal changes in 2010. From January 2008 to 2009, the anomaly gradually increased, and almost reached its maximum value in December 2009. In March 2010, the Xizang Nierong $M_L6.6$ earthquake occurred near the anomaly concentration area. At the same time, the abnormal high-value points also gradually increased near the Yushu region in December 2009 (inside the red dashed box in Figure 6). In April 2010, the Qinghai Yushu $M_L7.4$ earthquake occurred near the high-value points. Afterward, the abnormal areas gradually weakened, and almost all of them disappeared in December 2010 (Figure 6).

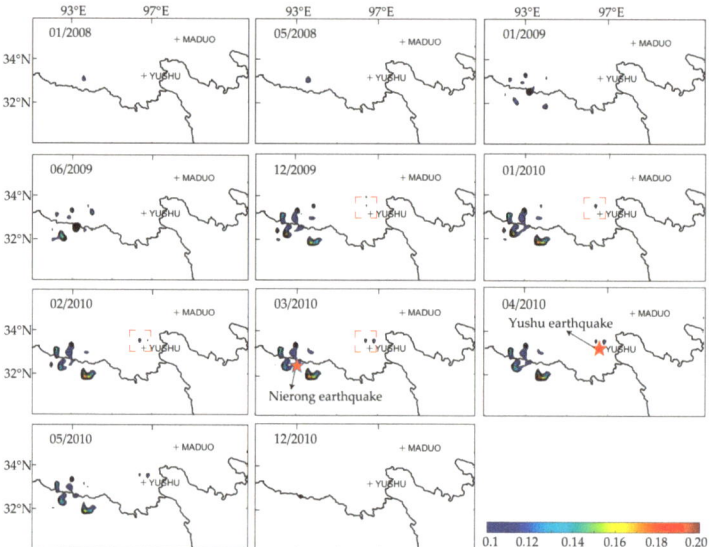

Figure 6. The spatial evolution of the MSER of the border regions of Qinghai and Xizang from January 2008 to September 2010.

3.2. Risk Assessment of the Multi-Parameter Relevancy Spectrum in the Western Chinese Mainland

The R-value evaluation is a widely recognized method used for evaluating the effectiveness of earthquake prediction [24,25]. The R-value evaluation is calculated by the difference between the earthquake prediction accuracy rate and the time occupancy rate of prediction. The specific formula is as follows:

$$R = A - O = \frac{N_a}{N_t} - \frac{S_a}{S_t} \tag{8}$$

A represents the earthquake prediction accuracy rate, O represents the time occupancy rate of the predicted area, N_a represents the number of predicted earthquakes successfully, N_t represents the total number of earthquakes that should be predicted, S_a represents the time occupied by prediction, and S_t represents the total time spent on prediction research.

Assuming that earthquakes occur independently of each other, the number of earthquakes that occur within a certain period should follow the discretization state of the Poisson distribution. The probability of a single earthquake occurring during this period is represented by the time occupancy rate, O, of the predicted area, and the corresponding significance level should be satisfied as follows [26]:

$$\alpha = \sum_{i=N_a}^{N_t} \left[\left(N_{ti} O^i (1-O)^{N_t-i} \right) \right]$$
$$N_{ti} = \frac{N_t!}{i!(N_t-i)!} \tag{9}$$

In the formula, α represents the significance level, taken as 5%. Based on the known A value, the value O is calculated, and the corresponding R score for the significance level α is obtained and represented by R. When $R > R_0$, the predicted result is considered to have high statistical significance [27,28].

In this paper, the R-values of the multi-parameter calculation results of 12 tectonic regions in the western Chinese mainland were evaluated, and finally, 7 tectonic regions passed the test (Table 2), namely, central Tianshan, the western section of southern Tianshan, the border regions of Qinghai and Xizang, Yutian in Xinjiang, Nima in Xizang, the central and western sections of the Qilian Mountains, and the eastern section of southern Xizang. The criterion for determining anomalies was that the relevancy value exceeded the threshold line, and an abnormal peak appeared. The time among the three elements was considered the advantageous extrapolation time when calculating the optimal R-value by different times (Table 2). The extrapolation time period started with the abnormal peak time. Taking central Tianshan in Table 2 as an example, if its relevancy value exceeded the threshold line and reached an abnormal peak in October 2019, its advantageous extrapolation time was 290 days. Therefore, the validity period should be until July 2020. The intensity of the predicted earthquake was based on the minimum magnitude of target earthquakes used for simulation training in the training period. The predicted location refers to the area studied and calculated.

Table 2. Characteristics of multi-parameter relevancy spectrum anomalies in the western Chinese mainland.

No.	Region	Three Elements of Prediction			R-Value
		Time/Day	Intensity/M_L	Location	
1	Central Tianshan	290	$\geq$6.0	Central Tianshan	$R = 0.55$ $R_0 = 0.38$
2	Western section of southern Tianshan	380	$\geq$6.3	Western section of southern Tianshan	$R = 0.44$ $R_0 = 0.29$
3	Border regions of Qinghai and Xizang	260	$\geq$6.3	Border area of Qinghai and Xizang	$R = 0.68$ $R_0 = 0.35$
4	Yutian, Xinjiang	190	$\geq$5.5	Yutian, Xinjiang	$R = 0.58$ $R_0 = 0.29$
5	Nima in Xizang	100	$\geq$5.5	Nyima in Xizang	$R = 0.32$ $R_0 = 0.28$
6	The central and western section of the Qilian Mountains	170	$\geq$5.5	The central and western section of the Qilian Mountains	$R = 0.54$ $R_0 = 0.35$
7	Eastern of Southern Xizang	370	$\geq$6.0	Eastern of Southern Xizang	$R = 0.51$ $R_0 = 0.36$

3.3. Extrapolation Inspection

The research data used in this paper were all up to December 2021. Among the seven areas that passed the R-value evaluation test, in addition to the border regions of Qinghai and Xizang, there were also areas with high anomalies, such as the western section of southern Tianshan and the central and western sections of the Qilian Mountains. The advantageous extrapolation times for the western section of southern Tianshan and the central and western sections of the Qilian Mountains were 380 days and 170 days after the multi-parameter relevancy value exceeded the threshold line and experienced abnormal peaks, respectively (Table 2).

Figure 7 shows the study area of the western section of southern Tianshan. Figure 8 shows that the target earthquakes in the western section of southern Tian Shan had good earthquake-corresponding rates during the training period (January 1991 to October 2016). There were seven target earthquakes during the training period, and all high-value anomalies exceeding the threshold line appeared before the earthquakes. Taking November 2016 as the starting time for extrapolation, the relevancy curve was still at a high value. The Aktao $M_L7.0$ earthquake in Xinjiang occurred in the study area on 25 November 2016, which showed that the extrapolation effect was good. However, there was no high-value anomaly before the Jiashi $M_L6.7$ earthquake in Xinjiang on 19 January 2020, which was considered a missed earthquake. Afterward, the relevancy curve continued to rise, and it exceeded the threshold line, reaching an abnormal peak in February 2021, indicating the possibility of $\geq M_L6.7$ earthquakes within the study area. According to Table 2, the advantageous time for the multi-parameter relevancy spectrum in this region was 380 days. Assuming the peak time of the anomaly in February 2021 as the starting time, the validity period would be until 16 February 2022. On 13 February 2022, the Tajikistan $M_S6.1$ earthquake occurred near the anomaly area, corresponding to this high-value anomaly.

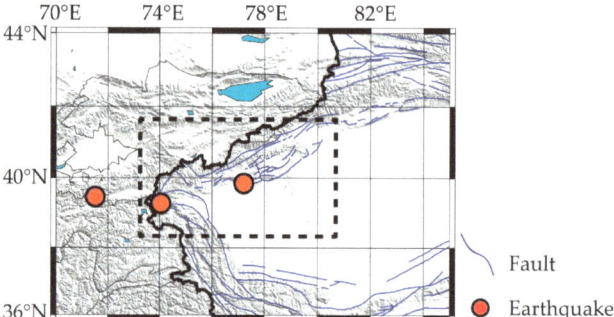

Figure 7. Western section of southern Tianshan (within the dashed box) and $M_L \geq 6.3$ earthquakes from November 2016 to December 2021.

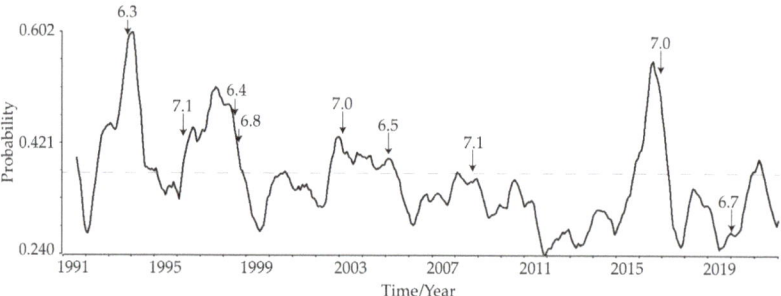

Figure 8. The MSER changes in the western section of southern Tianshan.

The Aktao $M_L7.0$ earthquake in Xinjiang on 25 November 2016 occurred during the extrapolation test period. The spatial evolution of the MSER anomaly in the western section of the southern Tianshan Mountains (Figure 9) showed that the anomaly gradually increased from June 2016, reaching its maximum intensity in September 2016, and the Aktao $M_L7.0$ earthquake occurred near the anomaly area in November. Afterward, the anomaly gradually weakened until it disappeared.

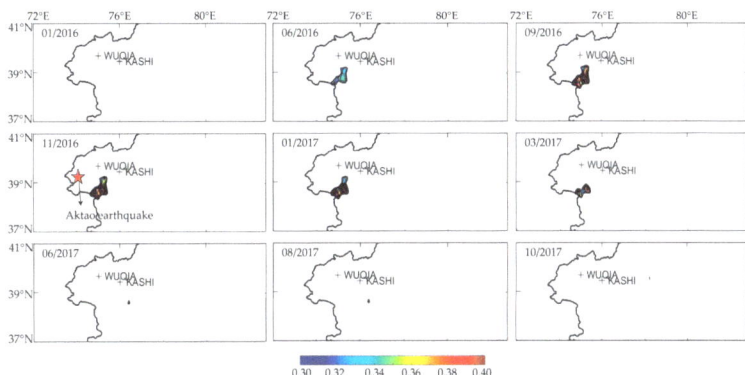

Figure 9. The spatial evolution of the MSER of the western section of southern Tianshan from January 2016 to October 2017.

The training period in the central and western sections of the Qilian Mountains (Figure 10) was from January 1991 to December 2015, during which, a total of 10 target earthquakes occurred. Among them, eight target earthquakes had high-value anomalies exceeding the threshold line before the earthquakes, and two target earthquakes were missed (Figure 11). In January 2016, as the starting time for extrapolation, the relevancy curve continued to decline after reaching the abnormal peak in July 2018, and reached its lowest point in February 2019. During this period, there was no corresponding target earthquake. Afterward, the abnormal curve rose again and reached its peak in July 2019. Two months later, on 16 September 2019, the Gansu Zhangye $M_L 5.5$ earthquake occurred. The relevancy curve had been continuously decreasing and remained below the threshold line after the Zhangye $M_L 5.5$ earthquake in Gansu. The curve began to turn and rise in March 2021, and the Aksai $M_L 6.0$ earthquake in Gansu occurred on 26 August 2021 during the curve ascent process, exceeding the threshold line. The curve reached its peak again in January 2022. Table 2 shows that the advantageous extrapolation time in the central and western sections of the Qilian Mountains was 170 days, so the validity period should be until 20 June 2022. From January 2022 to 20 June 2022, the study region experienced the Qinghai Menyuan $M_L 7.1$ earthquake on 8 January 2022, the Gansu Sunan $M_L 5.5$ earthquake on 17 March 2022, and the Qinghai Delingha $M_L 6.3$ earthquake on 26 March 2022, respectively, proving that the extrapolation effect in this study area was very good.

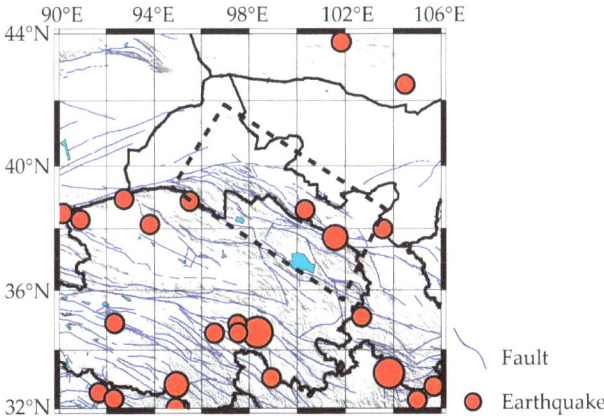

Figure 10. Central and western sections of the Qilian Mountains (within the dashed box) and $M_L \geq$ 5.5 earthquakes from January 2016 to December 2021.

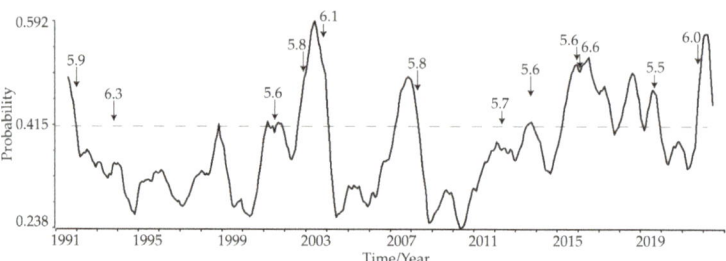

Figure 11. The MSER changes of the central and western sections of the Qilian Mountains.

The extrapolation test period for the central and western sections of the Qilian Mountains began in January 2016. The spatial evolution of the MSER anomaly before the 8 January 2022 Qinghai Menyuan M_L7.1 earthquake showed that the anomaly amplitude in the study area began to increase from August 2020, with the largest anomaly increase in November 2021 (Figure 12). The red pentagram in Figure 12 represents the epicenter position of the Qinghai Menyuan M_L7.1 earthquake in January 2022.

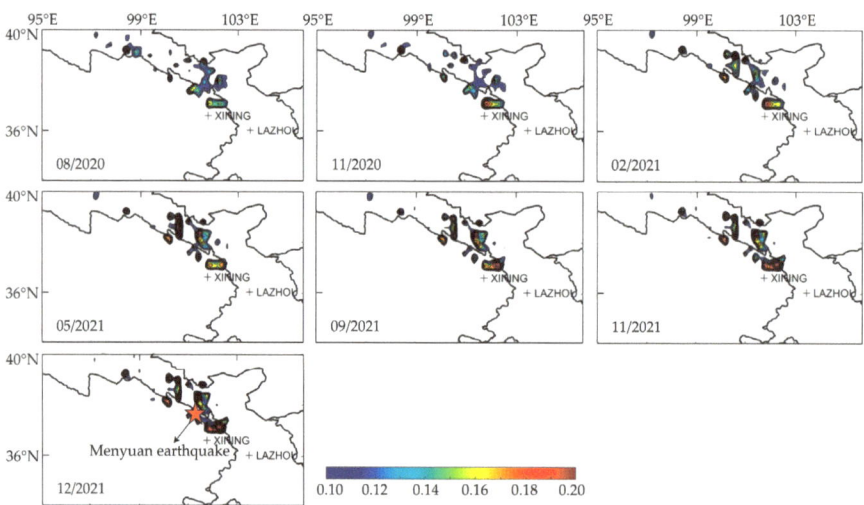

Figure 12. The spatial evolution of the MSER of central and western sections of the Qilian Mountains from June 2020 to September 2021.

4. Discussion

The abnormal patterns of different parameters before the target earthquakes were different. There were differences in the starting times, peak values, and end times of the anomalies. The comprehensive analysis method of seismic parameters can combine single parameters related to physical processes at different stages of earthquake preparation, which could extract the comprehensive abnormal characteristics during the earthquake preparation process more accurately. Wang [10] conducted a comprehensive multi-parameter study on earthquakes from 1979 to 2008 in the western section of southern Tianshan, and the results showed that target earthquakes in the study area exhibited significant high-probability anomalies of multiple parameters 1–2 years prior to the earthquakes. This research conclusion was consistent with the advantageous extrapolation time of 380 days in the western section of southern Tianshan in this paper. In addition, the anomaly-corresponding rate is the ratio of the number of anomalies corresponding to the target earthquake to the total number of anomalies. The earthquake-corresponding rate is the ratio of the number of target earthquakes with anomalies before the earthquake to the number of target earthquakes. By statistically analyzing the anomaly-corresponding rates and earthquake-corresponding rates of single parameters and multiple parameters in different inspection periods and regions of Xinjiang (Table 3), it was found that the anomaly-corresponding rates and earthquake-corresponding rates of multiple parameters were indeed higher than the predictive efficiency of a single parameter.

Table 3. The anomaly-corresponding rates and earthquake-corresponding rates of single parameters and multiple parameters in different regions of Xinjiang [10].

Study Region	Single Parameter		Multi-Parameter	
	Anomaly-Corresponding Rate (%)	Earthquake-Corresponding Rate (%)	Anomaly-Corresponding Rate (%)	Earthquake-Corresponding Rate (%)
West section of Tianshan	54.32	46.88	66.67	68.75
Baicheng-Kuche region	49.66	58.29	70.50	95.00
Korla region	55.64	63.69	70.59	83.33
Keping region	73.12	55.71	100.00	77.50

Related studies had also found that—when combined with methods such as PI, LURR, SV, and AMR—the earthquake prediction performance was better than that of a single method [18]. At present, this study mainly applied different seismological parameters for comprehensive analysis through machine learning. This method could also comprehensively calculate other observation data of earthquake precursors, such as deformation, electromagnetic, and underground fluid anomalies. It was even possible to merge and summarize all seismic observation data to complete a comprehensive probability analysis. At the same time, by analyzing the spatial evolution of the MSER during the extrapolation test periods, it was found that the target earthquakes generally occurred after the maximum amplitude of anomaly enhancement was reached, and the epicenter was located in or near the anomaly concentration area. This indicated that the model obtained by using this method for machine learning of historical earthquakes had a good extrapolation effect, which can provide a reference for the seismic hazard of the study area.

In addition, the R-value in this manuscript is different from the linear correlation coefficient, R, which measures the relationship between two sets of data. The R-value evaluation is calculated by the difference between the earthquake prediction accuracy rate and the time occupancy rate of prediction, as outlined in Formula (8). The best prediction performance corresponds to paying the minimum cost ($O \rightarrow 0$) at the highest accuracy rate ($A \rightarrow 1$), that is, $R \rightarrow 1$. On the contrary, the worst prediction performance corresponds to paying the maximum cost ($O \rightarrow 1$) at the lowest accuracy rate ($A \rightarrow 0$), that is, $R \rightarrow -1$. It is generally believed that when $R > 0$, the success rate of the forecasting is higher than the random probability, and this result has a certain predictive effectiveness [25]. R_0 represents the derived R-value based on the significance level of 5% (95% confidence level). Therefore, when $R > R_0$, the predicted result is considered to have high statistical significance [27,28].

5. Conclusions

Twelve regions in the western Chinese mainland were studied using a comprehensive multi-parameter method, selecting sufficient earthquake events for machine learning to extrapolate and predict the risk of the study areas. The results showed that there were three structural regions with obvious anomalies during the extrapolation period, namely the border regions of Qinghai and Xizang, the western section of southern Tianshan, and the central and western sections of the Qilian Mountains. And the three structural regions all had corresponding target earthquakes within the advantageous extrapolation time. A total of seven advantageous seismological parameters were selected for training and calculation. In order to eliminate errors, all 12 study areas in this paper used the same seismic parameters, parameter thresholds, spatiotemporal scanning scales, and anomaly threshold lines for their calculation data.

In the calculated results, the extrapolation times of the border regions of Qinghai and Xizang started from January 2021, and the results showed that the relevancy curve of extrapolation was in a highly abnormal state. During the advantageous extrapolation time, the Xizang Biru $M_L6.4$ earthquake on 19 March 2021 and the Qinghai Maduo $M_L7.9$ earthquake on 22 May 2021 occurred, which were similar to the change states of the previous Xizang Nierong $M_L6.4$ earthquake on 24 March 2010 and the Qinghai Yushu $M_L7.4$ earthquake on 14 April 2010. Both spatial evolution processes were also very similar, with earthquakes occurring in areas with abnormally high values and their vicinity. This indicated that the seismic activity in this area had a certain regularity. If similar anomalies occur again in the future, it will be necessary to be vigilant about the risk of short-term continuous occurrences of earthquakes in this region.

The extrapolation effects in the western section of southern Tianshan and the central and western sections of the Qilian Mountains were both highly well through the machine learning-based detection of seismic multi-parameters. The anomaly-corresponding rate and earthquake-corresponding rate were all very high in the calculated results. The application of the comprehensive analysis of seismic multi-parameters in the western Chinese mainland could not only infer the urgency of the target earthquakes (in terms of time) but also distinguish the possible areas where the target earthquakes occurred from the spatial distribution of abnormal areas. In all, the results showed that the extrapolation effect using the machine learning method in the western Chinese mainland was very good.

Author Contributions: Conceptualization, H.W. and X.Z.; methodology, X.L. and Q.W.; validation, W.Y. and L.M.; writing—original draft preparation, X.L.; writing—review and editing, X.Z.; supervision, H.W.; project administration, L.M.; funding acquisition, X.Z. All authors have read and agreed to the published version of the manuscript.

Funding: This research was funded by the National Key Research and Development Program of China, grant number 2021YFC3000700, and supported by the Shanghai Artificial Intelligence Laboratory; the Open Fund for Earthquake Prediction, grant number XH24013D; the National Nature Science Youth Fund, grant number 41704062; and the Project of Earthquake Tracking, grant number 2024020509.

Institutional Review Board Statement: Not applicable.

Informed Consent Statement: Not applicable.

Data Availability Statement: The data source of this manuscript is from the China Earthquake Networks Center (https://news.ceic.ac.cn/, accessed on 1 March 2024).

Acknowledgments: Thanks go out to Tao Xie and Xianghua Jiang from the China Earthquake Networks Center for their help in the research process of this paper.

Conflicts of Interest: The authors declare no conflicts of interest.

References

1. Wiemer, S.; Katsumata, K. Spatial variability of seismicity parameters in aftershock zones. *J. Geophys. Res.* **1999**, *104*, 13135–13151. [CrossRef]
2. Ethen, G. Analysis of the b-values before and after the 23 October 2011 Mw7.2 Van-Erciş, Turkey earthquake. *Tectonophysics* **2013**, *603*, 213–221.
3. Laura, G.; Stefan, W. Real-time discrimination of earthquake foreshocks and aftershocks. *Nature* **2019**, *574*, 193–200.
4. Danijel, S.; Stefan, W.; Max, W. Variations in earthquake size distribution across different stress regimes. *Nature* **2005**, *437*, 539–542.
5. Liu, Z.R. Earthquake frequency and prediction. *Bull. Seismol. Soc. Am.* **1984**, *74*, 255–265. [CrossRef]
6. Markus, B. Earthquake frequency and energy in Greece. *Tectonophysics* **1983**, *95*, 233–252.
7. Tang, L.L.; Wang, H.T.; Wang, Q. Anomaly study of ECRS method before mid-strong earthquakes in Xinjiang. *China Earthq. Eng. J.* **2011**, *33*, 159–165.
8. Wang, H.T.; Wang, Q.; Tang, L.L. Comprehensive precursor anomaly research based on earthquake corresponding relevancy spectrum. *Earthq. Sci.* **2009**, *22*, 675–681. [CrossRef]

9. Bo, W.J.; Wu, Y.L. Standardization methods for abnormal information flow and their applications. *Crustal Deform. Earthq.* **1993**, *13*, 9–15.
10. Wang, Q.; Wang, H.T.; Tang, L.L. Research on multi-parameter comprehensive anomaly based on earthquake corresponding probability spectrum. *Earthq. Res. China* **2009**, *25*, 294–302.
11. Lu, X.; Wang, Q.; Li, G.; Li, M.X.; Tang, L.L. Tracking study for earthquakes of the middle-south part of the Tancheng-Lujiang fault zone based on the ECRS method. *Earthq. Res. China* **2016**, *25*, 294–302.
12. Bowman, D.D.; King, G.C.P. Accelerating Seismicity and stress Accumulation Before large earthquake. *Geophys. Res. Lett.* **2001**, *28*, 4039–4042. [CrossRef]
13. Yin, X.C.; Mora, P.; Peng, K.Y.; Wang, Y.C.; Weatherly, D. Load-Unload Response Ratio and Accelerating Moment/Energy Release, Critical Region Scaling and Earthquake prediction. *Pure Appl. Geophys.* **2002**, *159*, 2511–2524.
14. Zhang, Y.X.; Wu, Y.J.; Yin, X.C.; Peng, K.Y.; Zhang, L.P.; Yu, A.Q.; Zhang, X.T. Comparison Between LURR and State Vector Analysis Before Strong Earthquakes in Southern California Since 1980. *Pure Appl. Geophys.* **2008**, *165*, 737–748. [CrossRef]
15. Rhoades, D.A.; Gerstenberger, M.C. Mixture models for improved short-term earthquake forecasting. *Bull. Seismol. Soc. Am.* **2009**, *99*, 636–646. [CrossRef]
16. Rundle, J.B.; Tiampo, K.F.; Klein, W.; Martins, J.S.S. Self-organization in leaky threshold systems: The influence of near-mean field dynamics and its implications for earthquakes, neurobiology, and forecasting. *Proc. Natl. Acad. Sci. USA* **2002**, *99*, 2514–2521. [CrossRef] [PubMed]
17. Rundle, J.B.; Turcotte, D.L.; Shcherbakov, R.; Klein, W.; Sammis, C. Statistical physics approach to understanding the multiscale dynamics of earthquake fault systems. *Rev. Geophys.* **2003**, *41*, 1019. [CrossRef]
18. Yu, H.Z.; Zhu, Q.Y.; Zhou, F.R.; Tian, L.; Zhang, Y.X. An ensemble approach for improved short-to-intermediate-term seismic potential evaluation. *Pure Appl. Geophys.* **2017**, *174*, 2381–2399. [CrossRef]
19. Zakupin, A.S.; Bogomolov, L.M.; Boginskaya, N.V. Using the load/unload response ratio and self-developing processes methods of analyzing seismic sequences to predict earthquakes in Sakhalin. *Izv. Atmos. Ocean. Phys.* **2020**, *56*, 693–705. [CrossRef]
20. Yu, C.; Wang, S.Y.; Yu, H.Z. Study of the electromechanical coupling process before the 2020 M_S6.4 Yutian, China Earthquake. *Sci. Rep.* **2022**, *12*, 17622. [CrossRef]
21. Draz, M.U.; Shah, M.; Jamjareegulgarn, P.; Shahzad, R.; Hasan, A.M.; Ghamry, N.A. Deep machine learning based possible atmospheric and ionospheric precursors of the 2021 M_W7.1 Japan earthquake. *Remote Sens.* **2023**, *15*, 1904. [CrossRef]
22. Akyol, A.A.; Arikan, O.; Arikan, F. A machine learning-based detection of earthquake precursors using ionospheric data. *Radio Sci.* **2020**, *55*, e2019RS006931. [CrossRef]
23. Huang, W.Q.; Li, W.X.; Cao, X.F. Study on Seismic Data Integrity in Chinese Mainland (II). *Acta Seismol. Sin.* **1994**, *16*, 423–432.
24. Xu, S.X. *Scoring of Earthquake Prediction Ability, Collection of Practical Researches on Earthquake Prediction Methods: Seismological Album*, 1st ed.; Academic Book and Journal Publishing House: Beijing, China, 1989; pp. 586–589.
25. Zhang, G.M.; Liu, J.; Shi, Y.L. A scientific evaluation of annual earthquake prediction ability. *Acta Seismol. Sin.* **2002**, *24*, 525–532. [CrossRef]
26. Yuan, Z.Y.; Jiang, X.H.; Liu, Q. Assessment of the number of annual seismic risk areas based on R-value and statistical models. *Earthq. Res. China* **2023**, *39*, 88–97.
27. Zechar, J.D.; Jordan, T.H. Testing alarm-based earthquake predictions. *Geophys. J. Int.* **2008**, *172*, 715–724. [CrossRef]
28. Jiang, C.; Wu, Z. PI forecast for the Sichuan-Yunnan region: Retrospective test after the May 12, 2008, Wenchuan earthquake. *Pure Appl. Geophys.* **2010**, *167*, 751–761. [CrossRef]

Disclaimer/Publisher's Note: The statements, opinions and data contained in all publications are solely those of the individual author(s) and contributor(s) and not of MDPI and/or the editor(s). MDPI and/or the editor(s) disclaim responsibility for any injury to people or property resulting from any ideas, methods, instructions or products referred to in the content.

Article

Randomly Distributed Passive Seismic Source Reconstruction Record Waveform Rectification Based on Deep Learning

Binghui Zhao, Liguo Han *, Pan Zhang, Qiang Feng and Liyun Ma

College of Geo-Exploration Science and Technology, Jilin University, Changchun 130026, China; zbh21@mails.jlu.edu.cn (B.Z.); zhangpan@jlu.edu.cn (P.Z.); fengqiang20@mails.jlu.edu.cn (Q.F.); maly22@mails.jlu.edu.cn (L.M.)
* Correspondence: hanliguo@jlu.edu.cn

Abstract: In passive seismic exploration, the number and location of underground sources are very random, and there may be few passive sources or an uneven spatial distribution. The random distribution of seismic sources can cause the virtual shot recordings to produce artifacts and coherent noise. These artifacts and coherent noise interfere with the valid information in the virtual shot record, making the virtual shot record a poorer presentation of subsurface information. In this paper, we utilize the powerful learning and data processing abilities of convolutional neural networks to process virtual shot recordings of sources in undesirable situations. We add an adaptive attention mechanism to the network so that it can automatically lock the positions that need special attention and processing in the virtual shot records. After testing, the trained network can eliminate coherent noise and artifacts and restore real reflected waves. Protecting valid signals means restoring valid signals with waveform anomalies to a reasonable shape.

Keywords: convolutional neural networks; improved Res-U-net; denoising; passive seismic; reconstruction

Citation: Zhao, B.; Han, L.; Zhang, P.; Feng, Q.; Ma, L. Randomly Distributed Passive Seismic Source Reconstruction Record Waveform Rectification Based on Deep Learning. *Appl. Sci.* **2024**, *14*, 2206. https://doi.org/10.3390/app14052206

Academic Editor: Roberto Scarpa

Received: 25 January 2024
Revised: 2 March 2024
Accepted: 4 March 2024
Published: 6 March 2024

Copyright: © 2024 by the authors. Licensee MDPI, Basel, Switzerland. This article is an open access article distributed under the terms and conditions of the Creative Commons Attribution (CC BY) license (https://creativecommons.org/licenses/by/4.0/).

1. Introduction

In seismic surveys, noise in the subsurface tends to interfere with effective signals. Its signal is weak but widely distributed and haphazard, and we often resort to various techniques to eliminate it. However, waves generated by vibrations from underground sources will carry information about underground tectonics as they propagate. If noise can be used, it can act as a substitute for an active source. In some cases where active source excitation is not possible, such as near cities, it is sufficient to set up geophones to receive passive sources of signals. At the same time, passive acquisition is cost-effective because there is no need to excite seismic sources. Furthermore, due to the rich frequency range of subsurface noise sources, there are a large number of low-frequency signals [1]. Therefore, passive sources are more advantageous than active sources in large-scale, deep seismic surveys.

After acquiring the passive source seismic record, we can use seismic interferometry [2,3] to reconstruct the passive source seismic record into a virtual shot record similar to the active source seismic shot record. However, using seismic interferometry to reconstruct passive seismic data inevitably results in coherent noise and artifacts. The noise has a greater impact on deteriorating the reconstruction of seismic data when the attenuation of the medium is high [4]. Removing the effects of this coherent noise and artifact disturbances is an ongoing effort by geophysicists. The F-K [5] filtering-based processing can suppress the coherent noise to some extent, but it may cause damage to the effective wave. Suppressing the coherent noise in the Radon domain has also been tried several times [6–8], but there is still a problem of low resolution. Rabiner et al. [9] created a median filtering denoising method and later produced many derivative algorithms [10,11]. They can operate on pixels on the image, but their small windows have no effect on coherent noise and artifacts, and large windows will blur effective signals.

The above methods can remove coherent noise and artifacts to some extent. However, they can harm the effective signal or suppress it poorly. The selection of parameters will have a large impact on the processing effect, which is somewhat subjective. In addition, this method cannot effectively recover the effective waveform.

Deep learning learns deep features of images and other information by training neural networks. LeCun [12] and others first invented a convolutional neural network and achieved good results in handwritten digit recognition. The AlexNet, invented by Hinton et al. [13], has achieved good results in image recognition and won the championship in the image recognition contest, setting off an upsurge of in-depth learning. Since then, various deep learning networks have sprung up in the public's view, such as VggNet [14], ResNet [15], FCN [16], DnCNN [17], and UNet [18]. These networks have achieved good results in classification and image segmentation. Based on ensuring the accuracy of manual recognition and conventional methods, they have higher processing efficiency, so they have been widely developed in various fields.

In recent years, thanks to the upgrading of computer hardware resources, deep learning algorithms have been widely used in the geophysical field. Gu et al. [19] realized low-frequency reconstruction in full-waveform inversion based on deep learning. Parasyris et al. [20] synthetic data generation for deep learning-based inversion for velocity model building. Zhang et al. [21] used interactive salt segmentation from 3D seismic images using saltisnet3d. Tao et al. [22] acoustic impedance inversion of seismic imaging profiles using self-attentive U-Net. Xiong et al. [23] use SafeNet to identify seismic disturbances. Sun et al. [24] accomplished low-frequency extrapolation of multicomponent data in Elastic FWI using deep learning. Wang et al. [25] used the MCMC inverse problem method of neural networks to perform numerical simulations in GPR cross-hole full waveform inversion. Liu et al. [26] used fine-tuned FPN to achieve microseismic first-arrival pickup. Lou et al. [27] proposed MCDL to achieve seismic volume dip estimation. Dou et al. [28] used the "MDA GAN" of the adversarial network to realize 3D seismic data interpolation and reconstruction.

In this research, a convolutional neural network is used to identify and suppress the coherent noise and artifacts of the virtual shot record. We obtain passive seismic records with a small number of sources and passive seismic records with a large number of sources through forward simulation. Using seismic interferometry, they are reconstructed as virtual shot records, respectively. The reconstructed records of passive seismic records with fewer sources are used as training data, and the reconstructed records of passive seismic records with more sources are used as training labels. The network is utilized to mine the features of passive data with better passive seismic source effects. Using neural networks to suppress coherent noise and artifacts and restore waveforms in parts where waveforms are not continuous enough. For the virtual shot records with an uneven source distribution, we use the virtual shot records with a wide source distribution as labels. At this time, the task of the network is not only to suppress coherent noise and artifacts and restore the ductility and continuity of the waveform, but also to restore the event of linear intersection to the event of double curvature. Although they are two tasks, we use the same network model to implement them and take a large number of evenly distributed virtual shot records as the training labels for the two tasks. Therefore, if the above two conditions are not ideal when we are collecting passive sources, we can reduce their impact on our seismic records and finally obtain better results, which improves the applicability of passive seismic exploration.

2. Theory and Method

2.1. Cross-Correlation Seismic Interferometry

Seismic interferometry generally includes the cross-correlation method [29], the deconvolution method [30], and the cross-coherence method [31]. Although the multi-dimensional deconvolution method and cross-coherence method can alleviate the impact of fewer sources and uneven source distribution on the virtual shot to a certain extent, they still cannot achieve good results for very extreme source distribution. Here, we used the cross-correlation method, which is the most efficient and stable method, to reconstruct the seismic virtual shot. The reconstruction method of cross-correlation can be expressed as:

$$R(x_B, x_A, t) + R(x_B, x_A, -t) = \delta(x_{H,B}, x_{H,A})\delta(t) - T(x_A, -t) * T(x_B, t)$$

where $R(x_B, x_A, t)$ stands for the seismic response excitation at x_A and received at x_B; $R(x_B, x_A, -t)$ represents its noncausal part; $\delta()$ represents the Dirac function; and $T(x_A, t)$ and $T(x_B, t)$ represent the transmitted wave responses at x_A and x_B, respectively.

When we use the equation for the mutual correlation reconstruction, we keep the x_A channel unchanged and each of the remaining channels as x_B, respectively. Then, we can obtain the reconstruction record with the x_A channel vertex as the excitation point and all channels as the reception points according to the original position of each channel. The reconstruction results here can be divided into two parts: the uncaused part and the causal part. It is a fundamental assumption of seismic interferometry [32] that requires no loss in the medium and a uniform distribution of the sources. Having satisfied these assumptions, we consider the causal part to be symmetrical with the noncausal part. By flipping and summing the causal and non-causal parts, we can obtain a virtual shot record with a higher signal-to-noise ratio. As a result, it is possible to flexibly construct the virtual shot record of a shot point at any detector position when reconstructing passive source seismic data with seismic interferometry without knowing the real source location.

However, when the number of sources is small under not widely distributed conditions, this will lead to spurious reflections and discontinuities in the waveform of the axes. If the source distribution is not uniform, when the virtual source is located on the side where the source distribution is lower, the reflected wave will be anomalous to a straight line. In contrast, the false-shot recordings where the false seismic source is located on the side with more source distribution will have discontinuous reflected waves and artifacts.

2.2. Deep Learning Algorithms

Based on the above problems in the reconstruction process of non-extensive passive source distributions, we hope to restore virtual source records that conform to physical rules, have good continuity, weak coherent noise, and do not contain spurious axes. Here, we propose to use the UNet network for imperfect virtual shot records. Since the direct wave energy in the virtual shot records is strong and the reflected wave energy is weak, we introduced attentional gating (AG) [33] to add multiple attentional layers to the UNet, allowing it to focus more of its learning on the reconstruction of the reflected waves in the lower part of the record.

The AG, first proposed in the medical field, aims to mimic the human attention mechanism by targeting and focusing on salient features in the data, which can make the model more efficient. It enables local regions to receive special attention, automatically learning to focus on the structural features of the target, suppressing irrelevant regions of the input image, and highlighting features useful for a specific task. Validated on a dataset in the medical domain, the results obtained show that not only can it be integrated into a network model with minimal computational overhead, but it will also improve the flexibility and predictive performance of the network. Here, we adopt a lightweight CBAM attention mechanism [34] to make the network more capable of learning. When the network transforms a graph into a feature map, it can simultaneously generate specific feature map information on the channel and spatially. It also performs adaptive operations with the incoming feature maps and finally outputs the feature maps after the action of the attention mechanism. We drew inspiration from residual thinking in ResNet and added residual connections to the network to achieve optimal performance and reduce training difficulty. The network we used is shown in Figure 1.

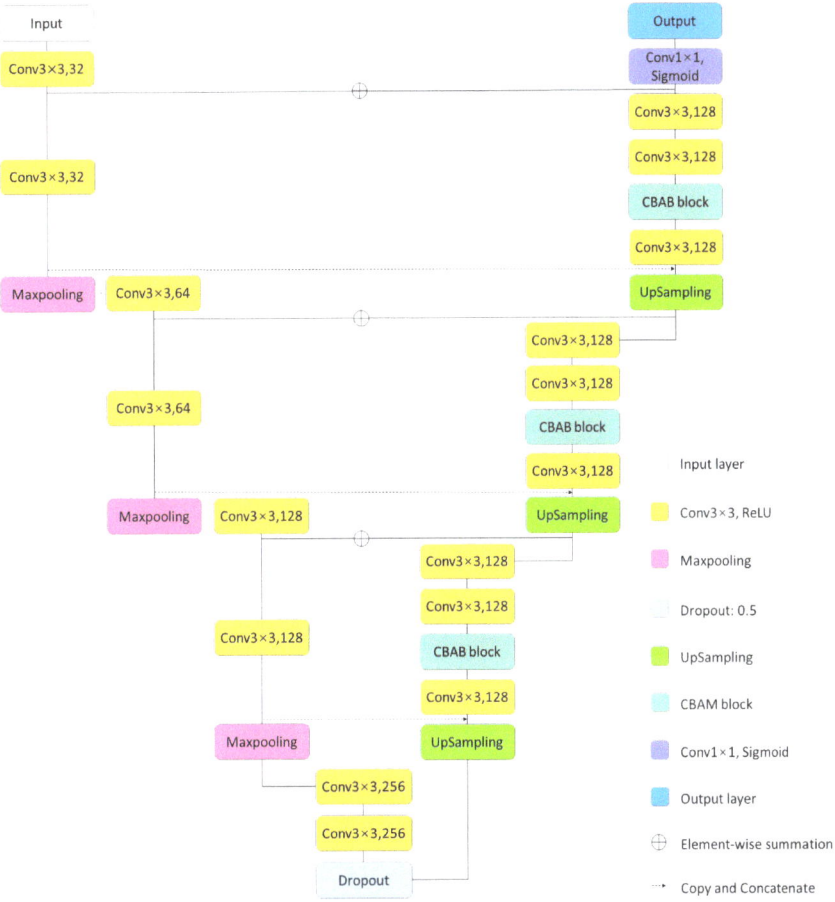

Figure 1. Network structure of improved U-net.

We used virtual shot records with fewer sources and unevenly distributed sources as training datasets, respectively. We used virtual shot records with more sources and randomly distributed in the subsurface as labels. We normalized the virtual shot records with the following equation:

$$x = \frac{x - x_{min}}{x_{max} - x_{min}}$$

where x represents the value of a point in the virtual shot record; x_{min} represents the minimum value in that record; and x_{max} represents the maximum value in that record. Here, we did not normalize the data using the extreme values in the whole data. This is to prevent anomalies in signal strength for some records. We also did not normalize the data using the usual per-track extremes. This is to prevent a blind-like imbalance in the processed data due to differences between seismic traces. We use single record normalization, using the maxima and minima of each virtual shot record to normalize, ensuring high contrast and continuity of pixel points horizontally for each record.

After preprocessing the data, we can then feed the processed dataset into our network. The optimizer is Adam; the activation function is ReLU except for the last layer, which is sigmoid; and the loss function is MSE:

$$loss(y_1, y_2) = \frac{1}{N} \sum_{i=1}^{N} (y_2 - y_1)^2$$

where N represents the sum of the number of pixels in a single seismic record; i represents the number of elements processed by the neural network; and y_2 and y_1 represent the predicted and target values (labels) of the network, respectively.

In general, there are some difficulties in using passive seismic reconstruction records as a dataset. If the active seismic record is chosen as the label, the valuable low frequency information in the passive source data will be lost. If the more effective virtual shot records are chosen as labels, some noise will inevitably be generated. In this paper, we believe that it is more important to protect the low-frequency signal. Therefore, for better, effect virtual shot records are chosen as labels.

3. Numerical Example

3.1. Enhanced Reconstruction Results for a Small Number of Seismic Sources

In this paper, virtual shot records are obtained from twenty velocity models. The velocity model as shown in Figure 2 will be used to obtain passive seismic records, which will be reconstructed into virtual shot records to be used as test data. These velocity models used to generate the training and test sets are randomly generated. To demonstrate the generalizability of the method, the test set is not included in the training set. Here the grid size of the velocity model is 2 m, the geophone spacing is 1 grid spacing, and the sampling interval is set to 1 ms to receive a total of 200 passive seismic records. Random noise sequences were used for the seismic sources. Each velocity model contains 128 seismic traces, and since the intercorrelation method allows the construction of shot points at any geophone point, 128 virtual shot point seismic records can be generated. To address the poor results of reconstructed records due to the small number of sources, we used them as training data and used reconstructed records with a large number of evenly distributed sources as labels. To compress the training cost and reduce unnecessary training, we only show the virtual shot records of the first 800 sampling points after reconstruction. We show the two source distributions as training sets and training labels under the velocity model (see Figure 3). The virtual shot records used as training data are obtained by reconstructing the passive source seismic records under the source distribution shown in Figure 3a. Under the distribution of seismic sources shown in Figure 3b, we reconstructed the virtual shot records as training labels. By inputting training data and training labels into the network, we can obtain a trained network. This network can process the waveforms of the virtual shot records.

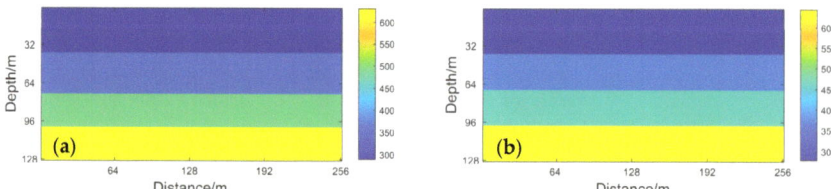

Figure 2. Velocity models used for the test data. (**a**) Test model 1; (**b**) test model 2.

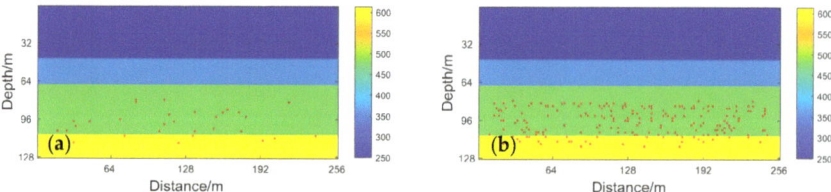

Figure 3. Completely randomized distribution of passive seismic sources. The red dots represent where the sources are located. (**a**) Distribution of a small number of sources. (**b**) Distribution of a large number of sources.

Our computing device was a Nvidia Quadro RTX 4000, and our neural network framework was TensorFlow-GPU 2.6.0 with 8 GB of video memory. To improve the generalization of the network, we set the batch size to 4, the learning rate to 0.00001, and gave a large dropout value of 0.5. We selected 2560 seismic records as training data and 256 seismic records as test data. After 1000 iterations, the loss of the network converges, and training is complete. The loss and decline of the network are shown in Figure 4. We fed the test data into the network, and the results are shown in Figures 5 and 6.

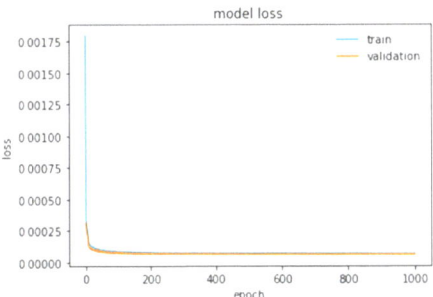

Figure 4. The loss convergence of the network.

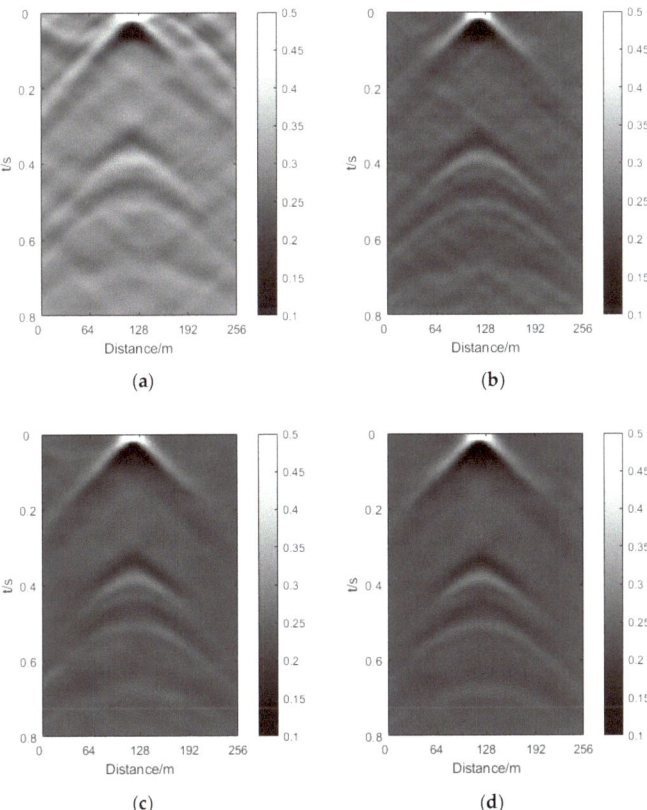

Figure 5. The processing results display virtual shot records with a small number of seismic sources under test model1. (**a**) A virtual shot of a small number of sources and input data. (**b**) A virtual shot of a large number of sources, labeled. (**c**) Processing result of attention mechanism UNet, prediction. (**d**) Processing result of improved network prediction.

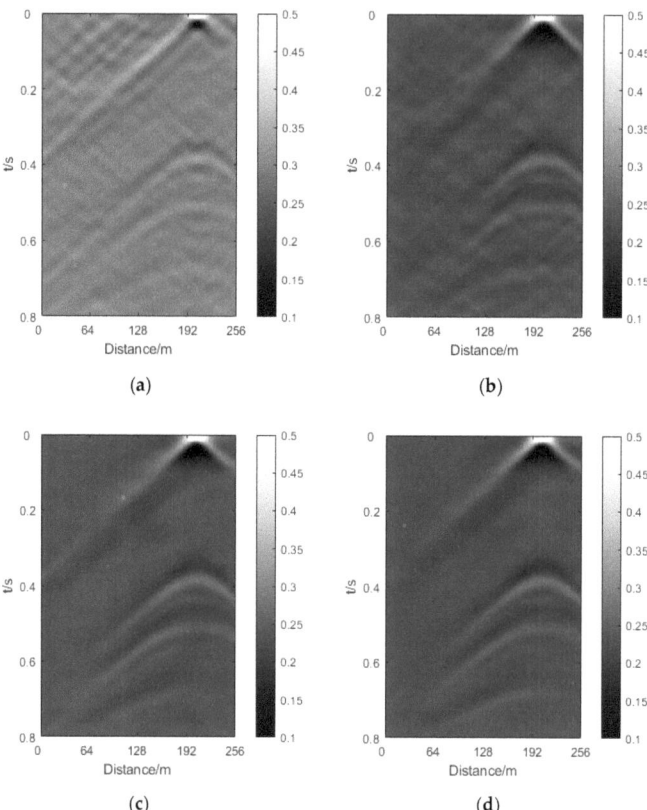

Figure 6. The processing results display virtual shot records with a small number of seismic sources under test model2. (**a**) A virtual shot of a small number of sources and input data. (**b**) A virtual shot of a large number of sources, labeled. (**c**) Processing result of attention mechanism UNet, prediction. (**d**) Processing result of improved network prediction.

To test whether the performance of our designed network is enhanced compared to the original network, we set the UNet neural network with attention mechanisms as the control group to test the improvement effect. By comparison, we can see that the coherent noise is effectively suppressed by the processing of the neural network. To solve the above problem that passive virtual shot records as labels may still be noisy, we found that both the training set and its labels contain a certain amount of coherent noise during the training process. However, due to the differences in objective factors such as their source locations and numbers, the training data and labels corresponding to the same virtual shot recordings under the same velocity model are similar in terms of effective waveforms when reconstructed, whereas the coherent noise in the virtual shot recordings is unmatchable. This also leads to the fact that our neural network does not learn the invalid features of the relevant noise during training. Although the labels also inevitably contain some coherent noise, which is an interesting finding in our suppression of coherent noise. Similarly, it is difficult for the neural network to learn the features of the artifacts because the features recorded by the virtual shot vary in each training data, and the corresponding virtual shot labels contain few or no artifacts in the same position. As a result, the artifacts are eliminated. In contrast, since the effective signals on the training data and corresponding labels are similar, our neural network can learn their features. Therefore, the weaker effective waveforms in the virtual shot records of a small number of sources are better protected and enhanced. In addition, where waveform discontinuities are present, our network complements them, restoring waveforms with good continuity.

Although these networks can suppress coherent noise and artifacts effectively, they also extract effective signals. However, it can be clearly seen that the improved network can suppress noise more thoroughly. The continuity of the same waveform axis is better and clearer, which also proves that our improvement of the network is effective.

In this section, we experiment with neural networks to reconstruct records of unevenly distributed seismic sources. Using the velocity model from the previous section, we can concentrate the subsurface seismic sources in a small region for numerical simulation. The resulting passive seismic source records are reconstructed into unevenly distributed virtual shot records. The distribution of seismic sources is shown in Figure 7.

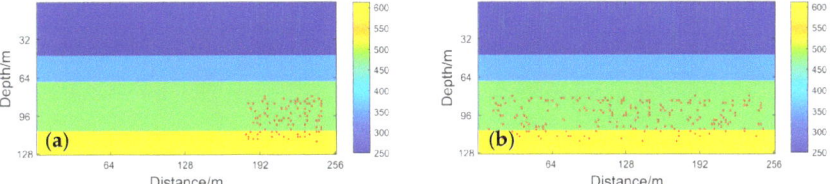

Figure 7. Schematic diagram of source distribution. The red dots represent where the sources are located. (**a**) Schematic diagram of inhomogeneous source distribution. (**b**) Schematic diagram of homogeneous source distribution.

After 400 iterations, our network was trained, and we fed the test data into the network, which was processed as shown in the figure. To test the generalizability of our network under different models and the processing performance for virtual shots located at different positions, we selected records of virtual shots located in multiple locations for display (see Figures 8 and 9).

Similar to the previous section, we can still use both of our neural networks to suppress coherent noise and artifacts. We can revert to a reasonable hyperbolic homogeneous axis in the virtual shot records on the side without the source distribution; we suppress the spurious homogeneous axis on the side with the source distribution. At the same time, the problem of insufficient continuation of the waveform is well resolved. We analyze that since there are many linear intersecting homography features in the training set corresponding to the hyperbolic homography axes in the training labels, it is possible to learn the corresponding features. The reason that coherent noise with artifacts can be suppressed is also similar to the previous section. In the tracts with the right side of the seismic distribution, our neural network recovers its waveform even though the training data are broken waveforms.

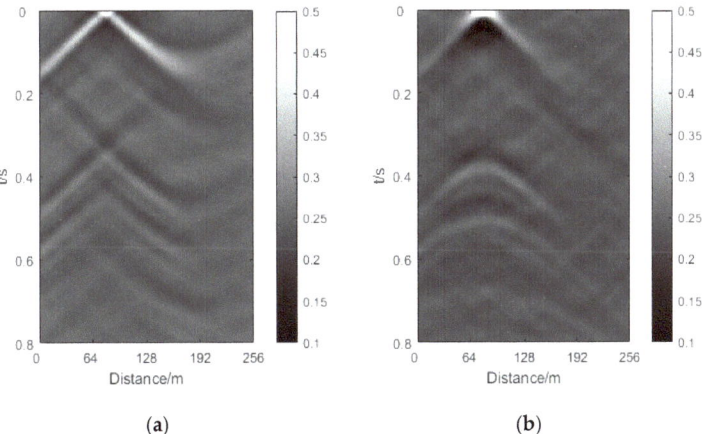

(**a**)   (**b**)

Figure 8. *Cont.*

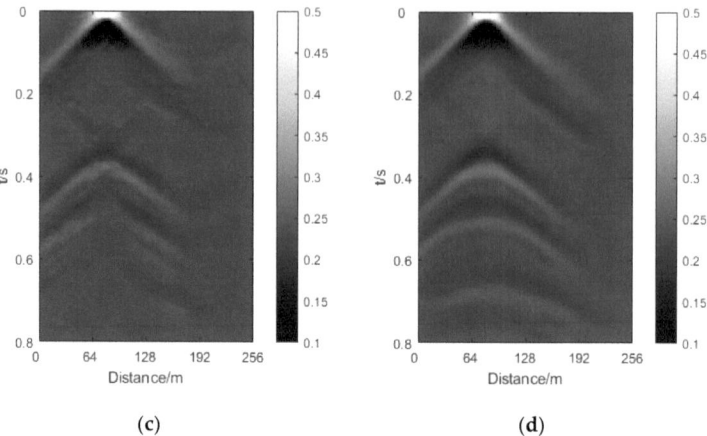

(c)   (d)

Figure 8. The processing results display virtual shot records with uneven seismic sources under test model1. (**a**) A virtual shot of uneven seismic sources and input data. (**b**) A virtual shot of uniformly distributed sources, labeled. (**c**) Processing result of attention mechanism UNet prediction. (**d**) Processing result of improved network prediction.

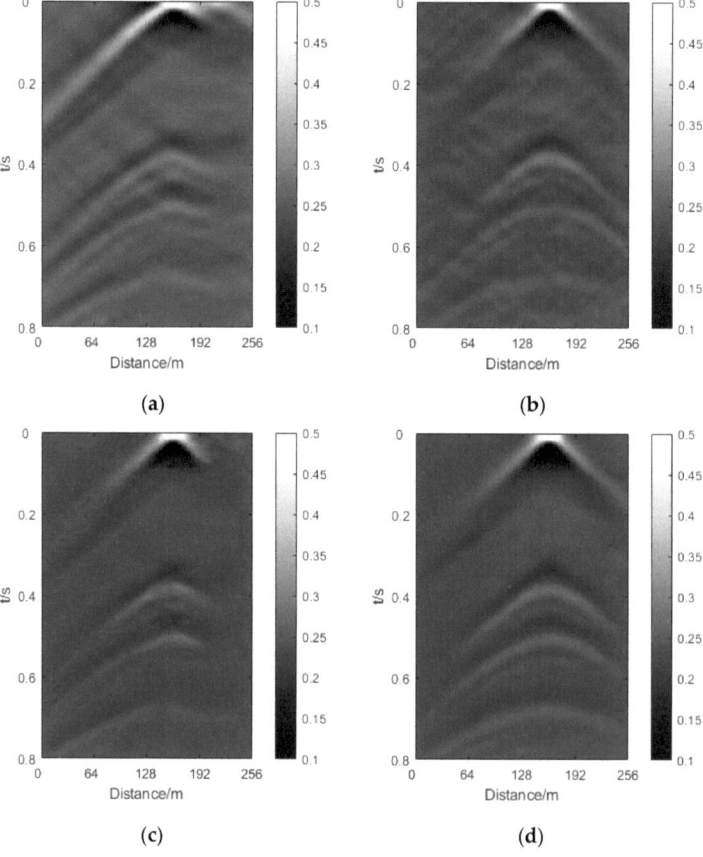

Figure 9. The processing results display virtual shot records with uneven seismic sources under test model2. (**a**) A virtual shot of uneven seismic sources and input data. (**b**) A virtual shot of uniformly

distributed sources, labeled. (**c**) Processing result of attention mechanism UNet prediction. (**d**) Processing result of improved network prediction.

In the testing of uneven source distribution, we can see that both networks can effectively suppress coherent noise and artifacts. However, when carefully comparing the processed waveforms, we found that the virtual records processed by the improved network showed clearer and more continuous waveforms.

3.2. Virtual Shot Record Processing under a Complex Model

In the experiment with the simple layered model, we have achieved good processing results for simple seismic records. When the velocity model becomes complex, the seismic record will inevitably become complex. In order to test the effect of our method on processing complex seismic records, we used the virtual shot record generated by the complex velocity models to train the neural network. The complex velocity models are shown in Figure 10, and their processing results are shown in Figures 11 and 12.

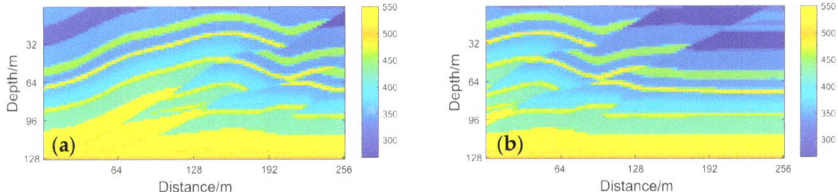

Figure 10. Complex velocity model of test data. (**a**) Test model 1; (**b**) test model 2.

Through the above comparison before and after processing, we can find that in the face of complex models, even if the number of sources is sufficient and the distribution is uniform, the virtual shot record is not perfect. In the face of imperfect processing tasks, the network processing effect is still good.

In the case of a small number of sources, our network can still remove a large number of virtual events and coherent noise from the virtual shot record and effectively restore the discontinuous events to continuous events.

In the case of dealing with unevenly distributed sources, the network also removes a large number of spurious events and coherent noise from the virtual shot recordings. It will also effectively reduce linear intersection events to hyperbolic events that conform to physical laws.

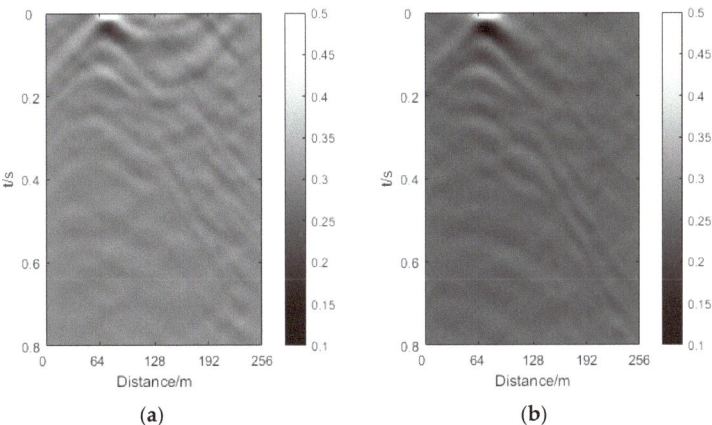

Figure 11. *Cont.*

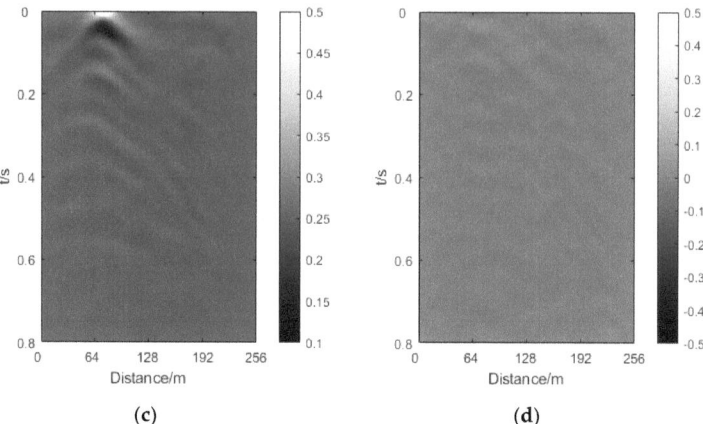

Figure 11. The processing results display virtual shot records with a small number of seismic sources under test model1. (**a**) A virtual shot of a small number of sources. (**b**) A virtual shot of a large number of sources, labeled. (**c**) Processing result of improved network prediction. (**d**) The residual between the processing result and the test label.

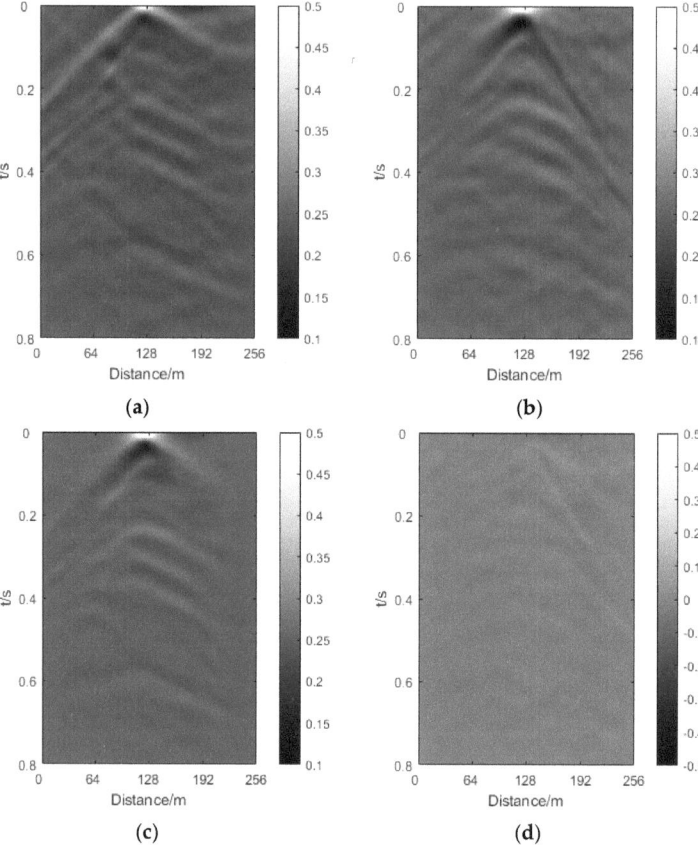

Figure 12. The processing results display virtual shot records with uneven seismic sources under test model2. (**a**) A virtual shot of uneven seismic distributed sources and input data. (**b**) A virtual shot of

uniformly distributed sources, labeled. (**c**) Processing result of improved network prediction. (**d**) The residual between the processing result and the test label.

It can be seen that our method has achieved good results not only in the simple layered model but also in the complex model. This result also proves that this method has wide applicability.

We can see that the waveforms in the wavefield become more complex in spite of the fact that the velocity model becomes complex, resulting in the waveforms in the wavefield becoming more complex. Our network still suppresses the coherent signal at a low level. For the virtual shot records of a small number of sources, the waveforms are clearer with our network processing. For the virtual shot records of sources distributed only on one side, the waveform anomalies are restored to a reasonable shape by our network processing.

After achieving good results in the processing of virtual shot records for conventionally small numbers of sources and for conventionally unevenly distributed sources, we tried to process the virtual shot records for extremely distributed sources. The two extremely distributed sources are shown in Figure 13. They are the sources located in the shallow space and the sources located in the narrow range, respectively.

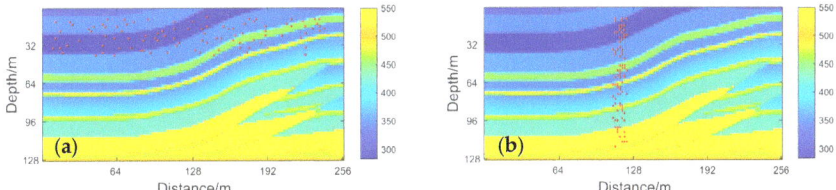

Figure 13. Schematic diagram of two extreme distributions of seismic sources. The red dots represent where the sources are located. (**a**) The sources are located in a shallow space. (**b**) The sources are located in a narrow range.

After processing using neural networks, the results are shown in Figures 14 and 15. It can be seen from the comparison figure that the virtual shot records corresponding to these two extreme signal source distributions contain a large number of spurious events and coherent noise. Moreover, the false reflections are stronger in the reconstructed records, and the ductility of the effective signal reflection waveform is not enough.

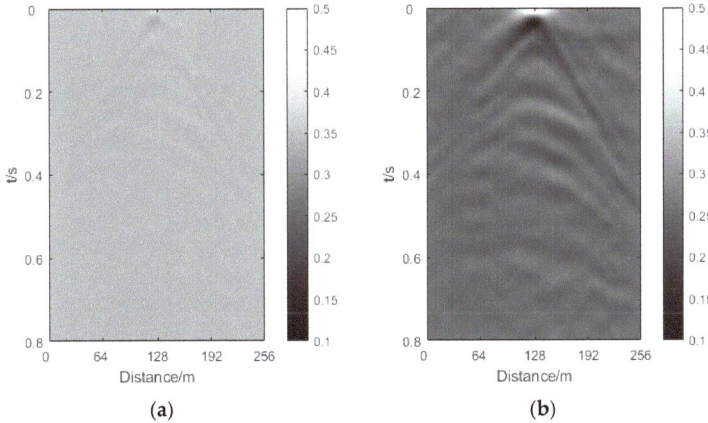

Figure 14. *Cont.*

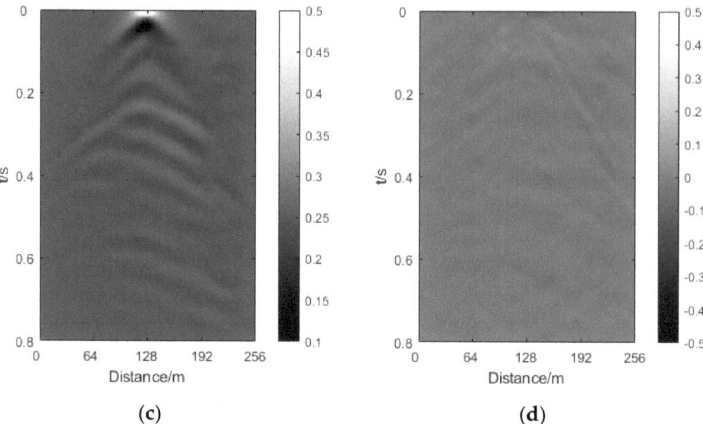

Figure 14. The processing results display virtual shot records with uneven seismic sources under test model1. (**a**) A virtual shot of shallow spaces distributed sources and input data. (**b**) A virtual shot of uniformly distributed sources, labeled. (**c**) Processing result of improved network prediction. (**d**) The residual between the processing result and the test label.

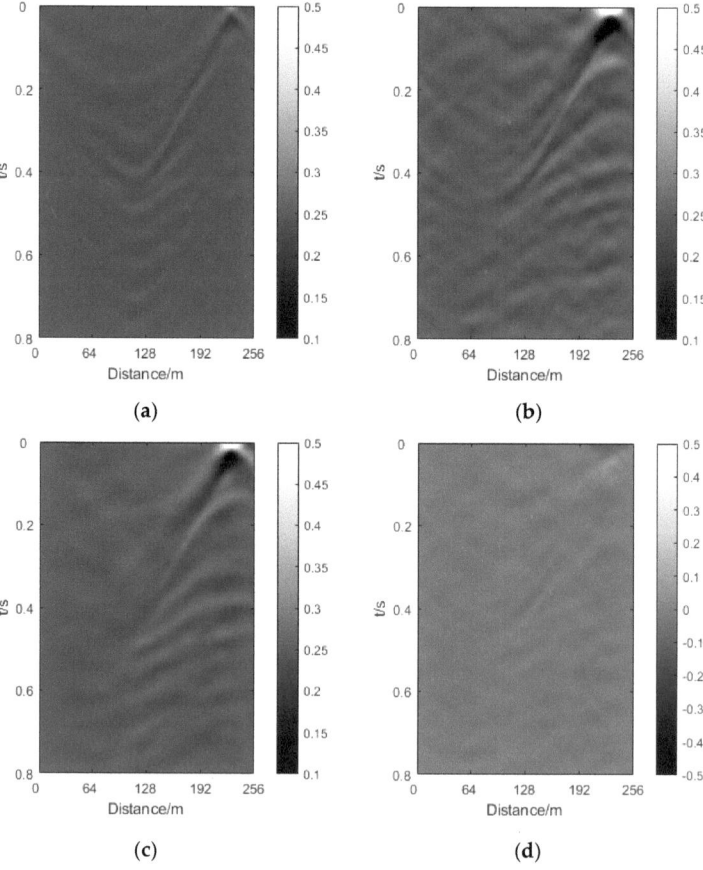

Figure 15. The processing results display virtual shot records with uneven seismic sources under test model1. (**a**) A virtual shot of narrow spaces distributed sources and input data. (**b**) A virtual shot of

uniformly distributed sources, labeled. (**c**) Processing result of improved network prediction. (**d**) The residual between the processing result and the test label.

After processing with the neural network, we successfully restored the waveform of the effective signal to a reasonable level. We can see from Figures 13 and 14 that the effective signal in the processed wavefield is stronger. It can be seen that our network can still recover effective signals from the artifacts and coherent noise.

4. Discussion

In passive-source seismic exploration, the number and distribution of subsurface sources are very random. The traditional seismic interferometry needs to satisfy the uniform distribution of the sources and be at a certain depth to reconstruct a high-quality virtual shot record. And the number and distribution location of undesirable seismic sources have a great impact on the virtual shot record.

Some conventional classical interferometric methods, such as inverse convolutional seismic interferometry [30], and algorithms developed on this basis, such as multidimensional deconvolutional seismic interferometry [35], can mitigate the effect of the inhomogeneous distribution of sources on the virtual seismic recordings to some extent. However, all of these methods require strict constraints on the uniform distribution of the geophones and the excision of the direct waves (which is very difficult to achieve for the noise sources). On this basis, the inverse is applied to the records received by all geophones. This operation is not only computationally huge, but the process is extremely unstable. These methods also do not give good results for specific source distributions (such as sources distributed in a narrow range on the survey line). In the method using deep learning, Sun et al. [36] used neural networks to make the virtual seismic record under uneven source distribution and learn the signal of the active source. Not only were a lot of artifacts eliminated, but the waveforms were also clearer. However, there is no discussion of the extreme case of distributed sources or the case of a small number of sources. And the use of active source records for labeling may cause some loss of low-frequency signals.

Compared with the improved seismic interferometry of the inverse convolution class, the cross-correlation-based seismic interferometry has fewer limitations, is computationally stable, and does not require strict uniform arrangement of geophones, cumbersome resection of direct waves, or computationally unstable inverse operations. And using the virtual seismic records of passive sources as labels for the training of the network can not only retain the low-frequency signals better but also train better due to the higher degree of similarity. Therefore, this method can improve the application effect of passive source seismic exploration to a certain extent on the basis of no additional requirements on the observation system and no loss of low-frequency signals. In this paper, we only show four of these cases of seismic source inactivity. After processing according to our network, the influence of the number and distribution of sources on the virtual seismic record can be reduced to some extent.

Only four of these inactive cases are shown in this paper. After the processing based on our network, the influence of the distribution of the seismic sources on the virtual shot records can be reduced to a certain extent. Therefore, this method can improve the application of passive source seismic exploration to some extent.

In the future development trend, with the future development of computing equipment and deep learning technology, there will be neural networks with better processing effects, which can solve the influence of the distribution of more complex seismic sources on the virtual shot record.

5. Conclusions

In this paper, a wavefield enhancement technique based on a convolutional neural network for passive seismic reconstruction records is proposed. The reconstructed virtual source records with a small number of sources and uneven source distribution are fed into the trained convolutional neural network, and the virtual source records with suppressed artifacts and coherent noise are obtained. The unphysical axes are restored to hyperbolic axes, and the low-frequency advantage of passive seismic surveys is retained.

Compared with reconstructed virtual shot recordings with a better number and distribution of sources, we retain accurate waveform information and low-frequency features with a lower proportion of noise. The network also has good generalization ability.

For passive sources that are not active in the subsurface, including the case where the number of sources is small and unevenly distributed, we provide a technical approach that ensures the effectiveness of passive seismic survey methods. It ensures high quality passive seismic reconstruction records when the sources are not widely distributed. The actual processing efficiency is high, and real-time monitoring can be realized.

Author Contributions: Methodology and manuscript writing, B.Z.; project administration and review, L.H.; experiments design guidance and review, P.Z.; investigation, Q.F.; validation, L.M. All authors have read and agreed to the published version of the manuscript.

Funding: This research was funded by the National Natural Science Foundation of China, grant numbers 42130805, 42074154, 42374147, and 42004106, the Natural Science Foundation of Jilin Province (no. YDZJ202101ZYTS020), and the Lift Project for Young Science and Technology Talents of Jilin Province (no. QT202116).

Data Availability Statement: The data presented in this study are available on request from the corresponding author.

Conflicts of Interest: The authors declare no conflicts of interest.

References

1. Bouchaala, F.; Vavryčuk, V.; Fischer, T. Accuracy of the master-event and double-difference locations: Synthetic tests and application to seismicity in West Bohemia, Czech Republic. *J. Seismol.* **2013**, *17*, 841–859. [CrossRef]
2. Draganov, D.; Wapenaar, K.; Thorbecke, J. Seismic interferometry: Reconstructing the earth's reflection response. *Geophysics* **2006**, *71*, SI61–SI70. [CrossRef]
3. Wapenaar, K.; Fokkema, J. Green's function representations for seismic interferometry. *Geophysics* **2006**, *71*, SI33–SI46. [CrossRef]
4. Bouchaala, F.; Ali, M.Y.; Matsushima, J.; Bouzidi, Y.; Takougang, E.T.; Mohamed, A.A.; Sultan, A.A. Scattering and intrinsic attenuation as a potential tool for studying of a fractured reservoir. *J. Pet. Sci. Eng.* **2019**, *174*, 533–543. [CrossRef]
5. Hale, D.; Claerbout, J.F. Butterworth dip filters. *Geophysics* **1983**, *48*, 1033–1038. [CrossRef]
6. Foster, D.J.; Mosher, C.C. Suppression of multiple reflections using the Radon transform. *Geophysics* **1992**, *57*, 386–395. [CrossRef]
7. Sacchi, M.D.; Porsani, M. Fast high resolution parabolic Radon transform. In Proceedings of the 1999 SEG Annual Meeting, Houston, TX, USA, 31 October–5 November 1999; OnePetro: Richardson, TX, USA, 1999.
8. Akerberg, P.; Hampson, G.; Rickett, J.; Martin, H.; Cole, J. Simultaneous source separation by sparse Radon transform. In Proceedings of the 2008 SEG Annual Meeting, Las Vegas, NV, USA, 9–14 November 2008; OnePetro: Richardson, TX, USA, 2008.
9. Rabiner, L.; Sambur, M.; Schmidt, C. Applications of a nonlinear smoothing algorithm to speech processing. *IEEE Trans. Acoust. Speech Signal Process.* **1975**, *23*, 552–557. [CrossRef]
10. Brownrigg, D.R.K. The Weighted Median Filter. *Commun. Assoc. Comput. Mach.* **1984**, *27*, 807. [CrossRef]
11. Liu, C.; Wang, D.; Liu, Y.; Wang, P.M.; Li, Q.X. Preliminary study of using 2D multi-level median filtering technique to eliminate random noises. *Oil Geophys. Prospect.* **2005**, *40*, 163–167.
12. LeCun, Y.; Boser, B.; Denker, J.S.; Henderson, D.; Howard, R.E.; Hubbard, W.; Jackel, L.D. Backpropagation applied to handwritten zip code recognition. *Neural Comput.* **1989**, *1*, 541–551. [CrossRef]
13. Krizhevsky, A.; Sutskever, I.; Hinton, G.E. Imagenet classification with deep convolutional neural networks. *Commun. ACM* **2017**, *60*, 84–90. [CrossRef]
14. Kataoka, H.; Iwata, K.; Satoh, Y. Feature evaluation of deep convolutional neural networks for object recognition and detection. *arXiv* **2015**, arXiv:1509.07627.
15. He, K.; Zhang, X.; Ren, S.; Sun, J. Deep residual learning for image recognition. In Proceedings of the IEEE Conference on Computer Vision and Pattern Recognition, Las Vegas, NV, USA, 27–30 June 2016; pp. 770–778.
16. Long, J.; Shelhamer, E.; Darrell, T. Fully convolutional networks for semantic segmentation. In Proceedings of the IEEE Conference on Computer Vision and Pattern Recognition, Boston, MA, USA, 7–12 June 2015; pp. 3431–3440.
17. Zhang, K.; Zuo, W.; Chen, Y.; Meng, D.; Zhang, L. Beyond a Gaussian Denoiser: Residual Learning of Deep CNN for Image Denoising. *arXiv* **2016**, arXiv:1608.03981. [CrossRef]
18. Ronneberger, O.; Fischer, P.; Brox, T. U-net: Convolutional networks for biomedical image segmentation. In *Medical Image Computing and Computer-Assisted Intervention–MICCAI 2015, Proceedings of the 18th International Conference, Munich, Germany, 5–9 October 2015*; Proceedings, Part III 18; Springer International Publishing: Berlin/Heidelberg, Germany, 2015; pp. 234–241.

19. Gu, Z.; Chai, X.; Yang, T. Deep-Learning-Based Low-Frequency Reconstruction in Full-Waveform Inversion. *Remote Sens.* **2023**, *15*, 1387. [CrossRef]
20. Parasyris, A.; Stankovic, L.; Stankovic, V. Synthetic Data Generation for Deep Learning-Based Inversion for Velocity Model Building. *Remote Sens.* **2023**, *15*, 2901. [CrossRef]
21. Zhang, H.; Zhu, P.; Liao, Z. SaltISNet3D: Interactive Salt Segmentation from 3D Seismic Images Using Deep Learning. *Remote Sens.* **2023**, *15*, 2319. [CrossRef]
22. Tao, L.; Ren, H.; Gu, Z. Acoustic Impedance Inversion from Seismic Imaging Profiles Using Self Attention U-Net. *Remote Sens.* **2023**, *15*, 891. [CrossRef]
23. Xiong, P.; Marchetti, D.; De Santis, A.; Zhang, X.; Shen, X. SafeNet: SwArm for Earthquake Perturbations Identification Using Deep Learning Networks. *Remote Sens.* **2021**, *13*, 5033. [CrossRef]
24. Sun, H.; Demanet, L. Deep Learning for Low-Frequency Extrapolation of Multicomponent Data in Elastic FWI. *IEEE Trans. Geosci. Remote Sens.* **2022**, *60*, 5909511. [CrossRef]
25. Wang, S.; Han, L.; Gong, X.; Zhang, S.; Huang, X.; Zhang, P. MCMC Method of Inverse Problems Using a Neural Network—Application in GPR Crosshole Full Waveform Inversion: A Numerical Simulation Study. *Remote Sens.* **2022**, *14*, 1320. [CrossRef]
26. Liu, N.; Chen, J.; Wu, H.; Li, F.; Gao, J. Microseismic First-Arrival Picking Using Fine-Tuning Feature Pyramid Networks. *IEEE Geosci. Remote Sens. Lett.* **2022**, *19*, 7505105. [CrossRef]
27. Lou, Y.; Li, S.; Li, S.; Liu, N.; Zhang, B. Seismic Volumetric Dip Estimation via Multichannel Deep Learning Model. *IEEE Trans. Geosci. Remote Sens.* **2022**, *60*, 4511014. [CrossRef]
28. Dou, Y.; Li, K.; Duan, H.; Li, T.; Dong, L.; Huang, Z. MDA GAN: Adversarial-Learning-Based 3-D Seismic Data Interpolation and Reconstruction for Complex Missing. *IEEE Trans. Geosci. Remote Sens.* **2023**, *61*, 5905014. [CrossRef]
29. Roux, P.; Sabra, K.G.; Gerstoft, P.; Kuperman, W.A.; Fehler, M.C. P-waves from cross-correlation of seismic noise. *Geophys. Res. Lett.* **2005**, *32*. [CrossRef]
30. Snieder, R.; Sheiman, J.; Calvert, R. Equivalence of the virtual-source method and wave-field deconvolution in seismic interferometry. *Phys. Rev. E* **2006**, *73*, 066620. [CrossRef] [PubMed]
31. Nakata, N.; Snieder, R.; Tsuji, T.; Larner, K.; Matsuoka, T. Shear wave imaging from traffic noise using seismic interferometry by cross-coherence. *Geophysics* **2011**, *76*, SA97–SA106. [CrossRef]
32. Wapenaar, K.; Van Der Neut, J.; Ruigrok, E.; Draganov, D.; Hunziker, J.; Slob, E.; Thorbecke, J.; Snieder, R. Seismic interferometry by crosscorrelation and by multidimensional deconvolution: A systematic comparison. *Geophys. J. Int.* **2011**, *185*, 1335–1364. [CrossRef]
33. Oktay, O.; Schlemper, J.; Folgoc, L.L.; Lee, M.; Heinrich, M.; Misawa, K.; Mori, K.; McDonagh, S.; Hammerla, N.Y.; Kainz, B.; et al. Attention u-net: Learning where to look for the pancreas. *arXiv* **2018**, arXiv:1804.03999.
34. Woo, S.; Park, J.; Lee, J.Y.; Kweon, I.S. CBAM: Convolutional Block Attention Module. In Proceedings of the European Conference on Computer Vision (ECCV), Munich, Germany, 8–14 September 2018.
35. Wapenaar, K.; van der Neut, J.; Ruigrok, E. Passive seismic interferometry by multidimensional deconvolution. *Geophysics* **2008**, *73*, A51–A56. [CrossRef]
36. Sun, H.; Demanet, L. Beyond Correlations: Deep Learning for Seismic Interferometry. *IEEE Trans. Neural Netw. Learn. Syst.* **2023**, *34*, 3385–3396. [CrossRef]

Disclaimer/Publisher's Note: The statements, opinions and data contained in all publications are solely those of the individual author(s) and contributor(s) and not of MDPI and/or the editor(s). MDPI and/or the editor(s) disclaim responsibility for any injury to people or property resulting from any ideas, methods, instructions or products referred to in the content.

Article

Microseismic Velocity Inversion Based on Deep Learning and Data Augmentation

Lei Li [1,2], Xiaobao Zeng [1,2], Xinpeng Pan [1,2,*], Ling Peng [1,2], Yuyang Tan [3] and Jianxin Liu [1,2]

[1] Key Laboratory of Metallogenic Prediction of Nonferrous Metals and Geological Environment Monitoring (Central South University), Ministry of Education, Changsha 410083, China; leileely@126.com (L.L.); zengxiaobao@csu.edu.cn (X.Z.); pengling2022@163.com (L.P.); ljx6666@126.com (J.L.)

[2] School of Geosciences and Info-Physics, Central South University, Changsha 410083, China

[3] Frontiers Science Center for Deep Ocean Multispheres and Earth System, Key Lab of Submarine Geosciences and Prospecting Techniques MOE, College of Marine Geosciences, Ocean University of China, Qingdao 266100, China; tanyuyang@ouc.edu.cn

* Correspondence: panxinpeng1990@gmail.com

Abstract: Microseismic monitoring plays an essential role for reservoir characterization and earthquake disaster monitoring and early warning. The accuracy of the subsurface velocity model directly affects the precision of event localization and subsequent processing. It is challenging for traditional methods to realize efficient and accurate microseismic velocity inversion due to the low signal-to-noise ratio of field data. Deep learning can efficiently invert the velocity model by constructing a mapping relationship from the waveform data domain to the velocity model domain. The predicted and reference values are fitted with mean square error as the loss function. To reduce the feature mismatch between the synthetic and real microseismic data, data augmentation is also performed using correlation and convolution operations. Moreover, a hybrid training strategy is proposed by combining synthetic and augmented data. By testing real microseismic data, the results show that the Unet is capable of high-resolution and robust velocity prediction. The data augmentation method complements more high-frequency components, while the hybrid training strategy fully combines the low-frequency and high-frequency components in the data to improve the inversion accuracy.

Keywords: microseismic velocity inversion; deep learning; data augmentation; hybrid training; Unet

Citation: Li, L.; Zeng, X.; Pan, X.; Peng, L.; Tan, Y.; Liu, J. Microseismic Velocity Inversion Based on Deep Learning and Data Augmentation. *Appl. Sci.* **2024**, *14*, 2194. https://doi.org/10.3390/app14052194

Academic Editor: Roberto Scarpa

Received: 20 February 2024
Revised: 1 March 2024
Accepted: 4 March 2024
Published: 6 March 2024

Copyright: © 2024 by the authors. Licensee MDPI, Basel, Switzerland. This article is an open access article distributed under the terms and conditions of the Creative Commons Attribution (CC BY) license (https://creativecommons.org/licenses/by/4.0/).

1. Introduction

Microseismic monitoring plays an important role for both fault/fracture characterization and seismic risk analysis in unconventional reservoirs and rock masses [1–5]. Most current microseismic inversion procedures require realistic velocity models. For example, the reliability of microseismic inversion and interpretation depends heavily on the accuracy of the velocity model [6,7]. However, most microseismic velocity models used in production are directly adapted from the well-logging curves, which are generally approximate to simplified models and may be contaminated by noise. Various velocity model calibration methods have been proposed based on traveltime (difference)-based inversion [8–10]. Additionally, full waveform inversion (FWI), as a strong inversion tool, has also been introduced to microseismic inversion [11,12]. However, FWI usually involves a higher computational demand and is also affected by cycle skipping due to the sinusoidal nature of the wavefield and complex scattering [13]. Cycle skipping can lead convergence at local minima and thus yield incorrect velocity models.

Traditional traveltime-based velocity inversion and full-waveform inversion rely on data quality, such as signal-to-noise ratio (SNR) [14]. However, the real microseismic data are usually of low SNR, which largely affects the accuracy of the inversion. In addition, traditional velocity inversion methods rely on the accuracy of the initial velocity.

Recently, deep learning (DL) has shown excellent capabilities for nonlinear mapping function approximation in computer vision, especially in the tasks of reconstructing models and high-resolution images [15,16]. The development of DL has also brought new opportunities to seismic and microseismic data processing and inversion [17], such as signal denoising [18], signal identification and classification [19,20], first-arrival picking [21–23], source location [24], and velocity model building and calibration [25]. Using seismic waveforms as the feature input and velocity models as the labels, the trained models with the nonlinear mapping capability of neural networks can effectively predict velocity models from seismic waveforms. There are already several studies on using DL algorithms to invert velocity models. Araya-Polo et al. [26] extracted features from the acquired seismic data and proposed using deep convolutional neural networks (DCNNs), instead of seismic tomography, to reconstruct velocity models. Yang et al. [27] proposed a supervised deep fully convolutional neural network (FCN) approach to build velocity models directly from raw seismic data.

However, there are only a few studies on DL-based downhole microseismic velocity inversion to take advantage of the nonlinear mapping ability of deep neural networks (DNNs) to carry out velocity inversion tasks [28,29]. Unlike velocity model inversion in active seismology, there is generally only one velocity model corresponding to hundreds, possibly even thousands, of microseismic events. The combination of abundant microseismic events within restricted regions and limited velocity model information hinders dataset construction and network performance. Additionally, microseismic processing and interpretation is dependent on activities and geology in the region of interest, which may limit the availability of past microseismic events for DL algorithms. In this sense, the training data play a vital role to ensure the learning performance of the network. FWI in active seismology relies heavily on low-frequency components [30], while field microseismic data generally contain higher frequency contents than active seismic data, and the high-frequency information might be missing in synthetic data considering the computational expense. Yang et al. [31] found that integrating physical information with synthetic data can improve the effectiveness of the training data and network performance. Alkhalifah et al. [32] employed the domain adaptation approach to introduce real signal features into the synthetic data by correlation and convolution operations. They demonstrated the effectiveness of domain adaptation by applying it to seismic imaging problems. Wu et al. [33] proposed to integrate domain knowledge to impose prior constraints for geophysical problems, which can improve the generalizability and interpretability of DNN models.

In this study, we adopt the Unet model to construct a mapping relationship between microseismic waveform data and the velocity model. The data augmentation is implemented by correlation and convolution operations to alleviate the feature differences between the training and real data. We also propose a hybrid training strategy to better integrate the low-frequency feature in synthetic data and high-frequency feature in augmented data. By testing real data of downhole microseismic monitoring, we demonstrate that the proposed data augmentation and hybrid training strategy is reliable and effective in predicting microseismic velocity models.

2. Methodology

2.1. Velocity Inversion and Network Architecture

The velocity inversion can be expressed as the minimization of the following objective function:

$$J = \left\| d^{syn} - d^{obs} \right\|_2 \quad (1)$$

where J is the objective function, $\| \ \|_2$ denotes the Euclidean norm, d^{syn} is the synthetic data vector, and d^{obs} is the recorded data vector.

Conventional methods for velocity inversion include seismic tomography and full-waveform inversion, which are based on travel time and waveform, respectively. As mentioned before, the two methods rely on the data quality and the setting of the initial velocity model, both of which cannot be well satisfied in microseismic monitoring. In this paper, we use neural networks to solve this nonlinear function. Neural networks can create strongly nonlinear mappings between microseismic gathers and velocities by building multiple hidden layers:

$$v = Net(\boldsymbol{d}; \boldsymbol{\theta}) \qquad (2)$$

where $v \equiv [v_p, v_s]$ denotes the predicted velocity value, and $\boldsymbol{\theta}$ indicates the total weight in the network. The training process of the network is realized through forward propagation and back propagation in the network models to update the $\boldsymbol{\theta}$. The testing process involves directly predicting the velocity model by inputting waveform data to the trained model.

We adopt the Unet (Figure 1), as it has shown great potential for many geophysical inversion tasks [34,35]. We make microseismic data and the associated velocity model $\{\boldsymbol{d}, \boldsymbol{v}\}$ in pairs as the network input. We use the leaky rectified linear unit (LeakyReLU) activation function, which alleviates the problems of gradient vanishing and allows for a better fitting of the model [36].

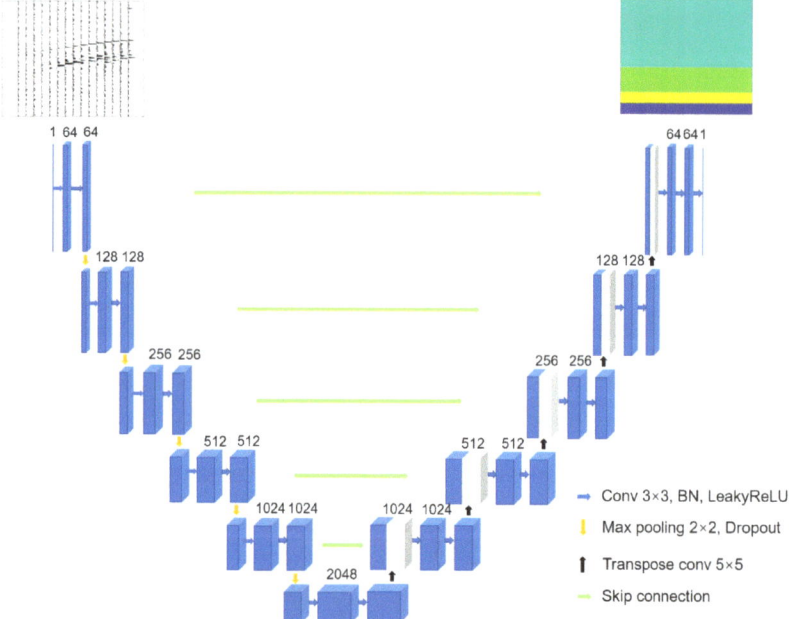

Figure 1. Unet network architecture. Gathers are input features, and the outputs are velocity models. Each box represents the output feature map of the convolutional layer. The number at the top of each box indicates the channel number in the corresponding feature map. The encoder consists of a convolution layer with a 3×3 convolution kernel size (blue arrow), a batch normalization (BN) layer, a leaky rectified linear unit (LeakyReLU), and a 2×2 maximum pooling layer and the Dropout layer (yellow arrow). Each decoder replaces the maximum pooling layer with a 5×5 transposed convolution layer (black arrows). Skip connections indicate the corresponding channel feature maps connecting the encoder and decoder sections (green arrows).

2.2. Data Augmentation

Domain adaptation refers to learning when the feature distributions of the source and target domains are inconsistent [37]. It aims to narrow the distribution gap between the two domains to achieve a better learning performance in the target domain. Based on the idea of domain adaptation, data augmentation is achieved by linear operations of correlation and convolution operations between synthetic and real data [38]:

$$\overline{d_s^i}(t) = d_s^i(t) \otimes d_s^k(t) * d_r^{ij}(t) \otimes d_r^{ij}(t) \tag{3}$$

where i is the index of the single trace, j is the index of an arbitrary event of the real data, k is the index of the reference trace and we set $k = 1$, $\overline{d_s^i}(t)$ is the new augmented data, $d_s^i(t)$ is the single trace of the synthetic data, $d_s^k(t)$ is the reference trace of the synthetic data, $d_r^{ij}(t)$ is the single trace of the real data, $\otimes$ is the correlation operator, and $*$ is the convolution operator.

Here, we randomly select one reference field event for each synthetic event corresponding to each stage and set the first trace as the reference trace. The high-frequency information in the real data can be implicitly introduced through the operations in Equation (3). The correlation operation can eliminate the effects of recording time delays between the synthetic and real data. The data augmentation operation can reduce the feature difference between the training (source) synthetic data and the (target) real data and will finally contribute to enhancing the performance of the neural network model when applying to the real data.

2.3. Loss Functions and Quantitative Metrics

Deep learning-based microseismic velocity inversion is a regression problem. We use MSE as the loss function to fit the reference velocity model and the predicted values:

$$L_{MSE}(x_i, \overline{x}_i) = \frac{1}{N}\sum_{i=1}^{N}(x_i - \overline{x}_i)^2 \tag{4}$$

where N is the total number of pixels in a single velocity image; x_i and $\overline{x}_i$ are a reference velocity value and a predicted value, respectively.

We use the regression metrics peak signal-to-noise ratio ($PSNR$), structural similarity ($SSIM$), and mean absolute error (MAE) to quantify the prediction results and evaluate the inversion performance [39–41]. $PSNR$ reflects the degree of global reconstruction of the velocity image. The $PSNR$ unit is dB, and the larger the value, the better the inversion performance:

$$PSNR(\mathbf{x}, \overline{\mathbf{x}}) = 20 \times \log_{10}\left(\frac{Max(\mathbf{x})}{\sqrt{MSE(\mathbf{x}, \overline{\mathbf{x}})}}\right) \tag{5}$$

where $\mathbf{x}$ and $\overline{\mathbf{x}}$ denote the velocity label and inverted velocity, respectively.

Local structure and detail are important factors when recovering a velocity model. To evaluate the performance of the network model in reconstructing the local details, we use $SSIM$ to characterize the similarity between the predicted velocity model and the reference velocity model. The values range from 0 to 1. The higher the value, the lower the image distortion, indicating that the predicted velocity model is closer to the ground truth:

$$SSIM(\mathbf{x}, \overline{\mathbf{x}}) = \frac{(2\mu_x\mu_{\overline{x}} + G_1)(2\sigma_{x\overline{x}} + G_2)}{(\mu_x^2 + \mu_{\overline{x}}^2 + G_1)(\sigma_x^2 + \sigma_{\overline{x}}^2 + G_2)} \tag{6}$$

where μ_x and $\mu_{\overline{x}}$ represent the mean values of x_i and $\overline{x}_i$ values, respectively, σ_x and $\sigma_{\overline{x}}$ are their standard deviations, $\sigma_{x\overline{x}}$ denotes their covariance, and G_1 and G_2 represent the constants to avoid a zero denominator.

MAE is utilized to evaluate the variation in velocity across the stratigraphic interface. The lower the value, the lower the error:

$$MAE(x_i, \bar{x}_i) = \frac{1}{N} \sum_{i=1}^{N} |x_i - \bar{x}_i| \qquad (7)$$

2.4. Training Procedure

We investigate three different training strategies, training only the synthetic dataset, training only the augmented dataset, and the hybrid training strategy:

$$loss = \begin{cases} loss\_syn, & epoch < epochs\_syn \\ w \times loss\_aug, & else \end{cases} \qquad (8)$$

where $epochs\_syn$ is the number of epochs when training the synthetic data, and w is a weight coefficient that indicates the smoothness of the loss curve, enabling the loss value to have a smooth transition from the synthetic data training stage to the augmented data training stage.

In our single-stage and multi-stage examples, we use different parameter settings. The optimizers are Adam. After many rounds of parameter tuning and tests, we finally select the following hyperparameters: the batch sizes are 32, and w values are 0.1, while the learn rates are 0.001 and 0.0001, training epochs are 200 and 300, and $epochs\_syn$ has values of 80 and 140, respectively.

We work with a PyTorch implementation of the neural network [42]. All network training and testing in this study was performed on a CPU with a frequency of 2.90 GHz and 512 GB RAM.

3. Data

To generate more training data, we prepare a horizontally layered model adapted from a field downhole monitoring of five-stage hydraulic fracturing [10], as shown in Figures 2 and 3a. There are 395 events in total and the event numbers from stage 1 to stage 5 are 105, 116, 48, 66, and 60, respectively. The field microseismic data contain three components and we consider only the Z component to reduce the number of operations. The acquisition system consists of 15 receivers (black reverse triangles) placed at a constant spacing of 20 m in a vertical linear array. Each trace has 1201 samples with a time interval of 0.5 ms. Four-layer velocity models are constructed referring to the velocity model from traveltime inversion with eight ball-hit events [10]. We obtain 200 velocity models by adding random ±10% perturbations to the P- and S-wave velocities with fixed layer depths. We randomly set 30 source locations in the source region (Figure 3a) for each velocity model. The velocity model has a size of 64 × 200, with a grid spacing of 5 m. A Ricker wavelet with a peak frequency of 100 Hz is used as the source function. We use 6000 synthetic gathers (200 models × 30 sources) as the initial training dataset. The testing dataset included 105 field microseismic events from stage 1 (corresponding to a single reference velocity model).

Figure 3b shows the results of the power spectra comparison. The augmented data approaches the real data in terms of energy distribution by retaining more high-frequency contents of the real data. The exemplary synthetic and real microseismic waveform data are shown in Figure 3c–f.

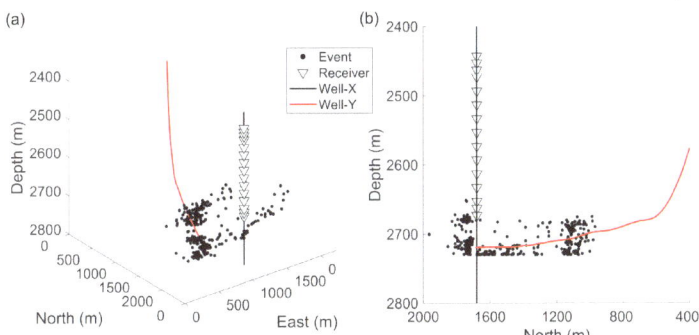

Figure 2. The layout of a real downhole microseismic monitoring project. (**a**) Three-dimensional view. (**b**) Side view of (**a**). Black reverse triangles indicate the receivers and the dots are microseismic events.

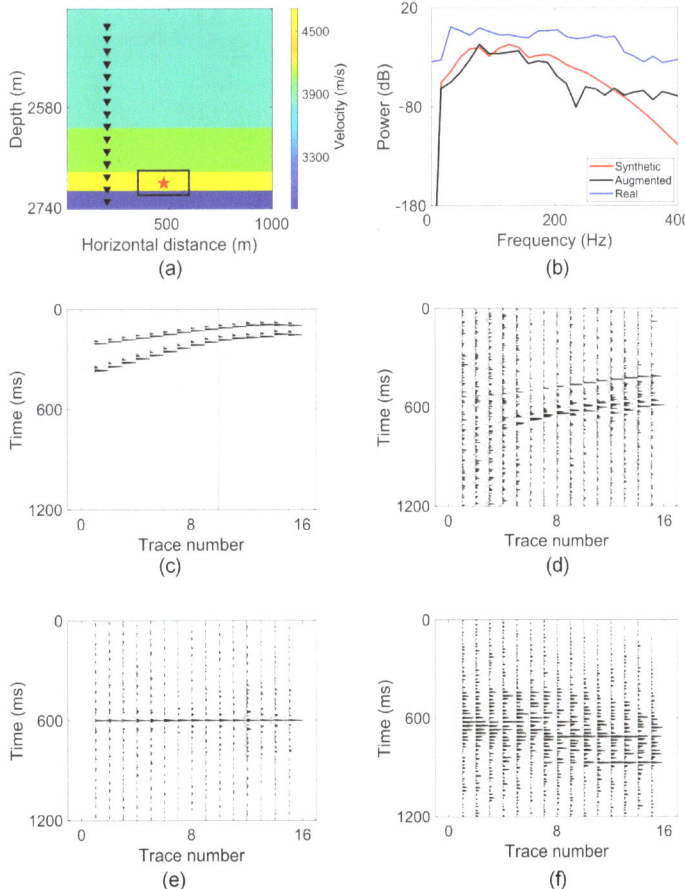

Figure 3. Model and data. (**a**) A horizontally layered model for downhole microseismic monitoring. The black rectangle indicates the region where the sources are located, the red pentagram indicates an arbitrary source, and black reverse triangles indicate the receivers. (**b**) Power spectra comparison. (**c**) The original noise-free synthetic waveforms generated by ray-tracing. (**d**) Real microseismic data. (**e**) Result of the real data autocorrelation. (**f**) The augmented data for the synthetic waveforms in (**c**).

4. Result

4.1. Single-Stage Examples

For single-stage examples, we focus on the feasibility of the network and training strategy. The overall quantitative metrics are listed in Table 1. As indicated in Equation (8), the hybrid dataset here denotes a hybrid strategy involving both synthetic and augmented data. It shows that the hybrid training strategy outperforms the other two training strategies for almost all metrics in the velocity inversion task under the same conditions.

Table 1. The mean values of quantitative metrics for single-stage examples.

Training Dataset	Phase	PSNR	SSIM	MAE
Synthetic	P	19.88	0.7097	272.243
	S	19.92	0.8139	133.958
Augmented	P	27.90	0.8644	113.514
	S	27.71	0.8912	57.431
Hybrid	P	30.04	0.8591	93.143
	S	29.60	0.8911	48.308

The predicted one-dimensional velocity profiles of the Unet model using the three training strategies are shown in Figure 4. The displayed velocity values correspond to two arbitrary events and are averaged along the horizontal direction. We can find that augmented data and the hybrid training strategy yield better fittings to the reference velocity model. Figure 5 shows the two-dimensional profiles corresponding to Figure 4b by the hybrid training strategy. Training with the synthetic data involves first learning the low-frequency information in the data, and then it can provide an initial velocity model (Figure 5c,d). The model obtained by training the synthetic data (low frequency) may also predict high-frequency velocity components with the real data (with high frequency), but the results have a large error since the model did not learn these high-frequency features. After training with the augmented data containing high-frequency information, the model improves the precision of the predicted velocity models (Figure 5e,f).

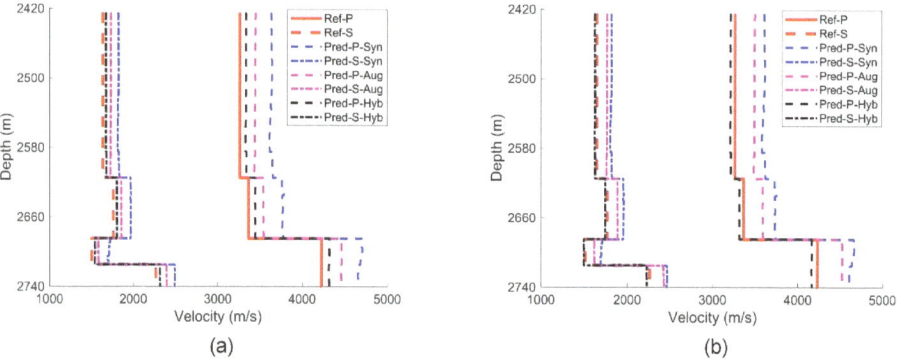

Figure 4. One-dimensional profiles of the reference and predicted velocity values of two arbitrary events from the first stage. (**a**) Velocity curves of one sample event. The red solid and dashed lines indicate the reference velocity for P- and S-wave, respectively, and the blue, magenta, and black dashed lines indicate the results of training with synthetic, augmented, and hybrid dataset. (**b**) Velocity curves of another sample event. The meanings of the symbols and colors are the same with (**a**).

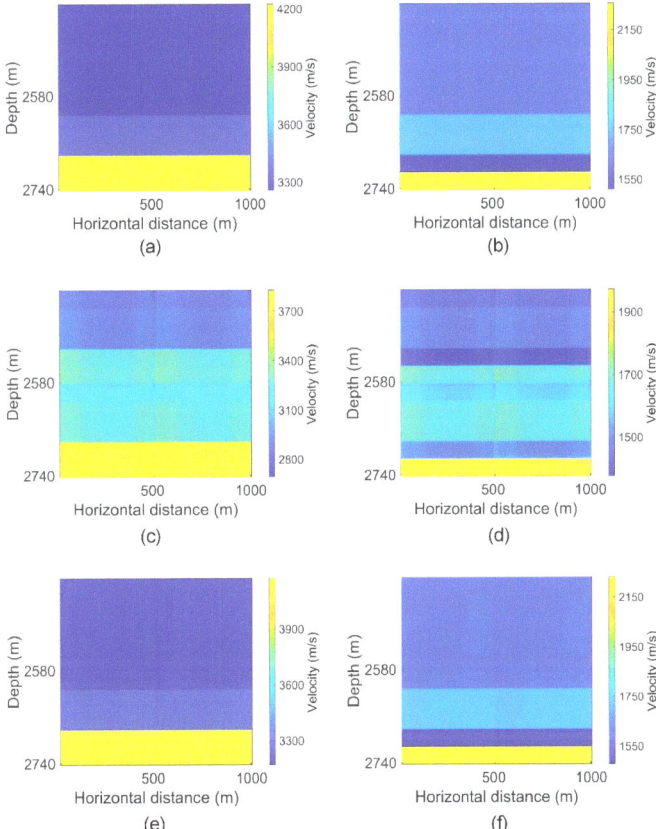

Figure 5. Two-dimensional profiles of the reference and predicted velocity values of an arbitrary event from the first stage. (**a**,**b**) The reference P- and S-wave velocities. (**c**,**d**) Predictions of P- and S-wave velocities trained with the synthetic dataset (when the epoch is 80). (**e**,**f**) Predictions of P- and S-wave velocities trained with both the synthetic and the augmented dataset (when the epoch is 200).

4.2. Robustness Testing

In order to further evaluate the superiority of the proposed data augmentation method and hybrid training strategy, we carry out robustness tests on the real data of the first stage. We denoise the real data by wavelet filtering to obtain the clean signals, and then calculate the SNR of the real data [43]:

$$S/N = 10 \times \log_{10}\left(\frac{S_c}{S_n}\right) = 10 \times \log_{10}\left(\frac{S_c}{S_r - S_c}\right) \quad (9)$$

where S/N is the SNR, S_r is the real data signal, S_c is the clean signal after denoising the real data signal, and S_n is the noise of the real data signal.

The distribution of the SNRs for all events in the first stage is shown in Figure 6. Most of the SNRs of the real events are lower than 5 dB. We select a sample event ($S/N = 3.44$) to quantitatively evaluate the stability and robustness of the network. The predicted two-dimensional and one-dimensional velocity profiles of the Unet model using the three training strategies are shown in Figures 7 and 8. The detailed values of quantitative metrics are listed in Figure 7. The results suggested that the data augmentation method can significantly improve the prediction accuracy of purely synthetic data by introducing real data information. Moreover, the hybrid training strategy effectively utilizes the useful information of the synthetic data in the low-frequency components and yields the best inversion results.

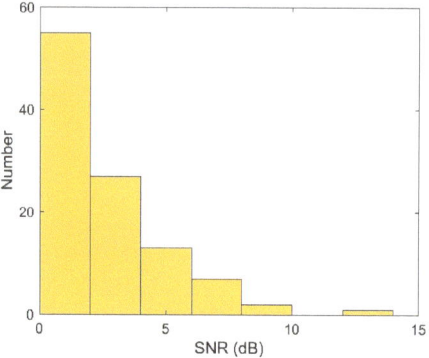

Figure 6. The distribution of SNRs of the events of the first stage.

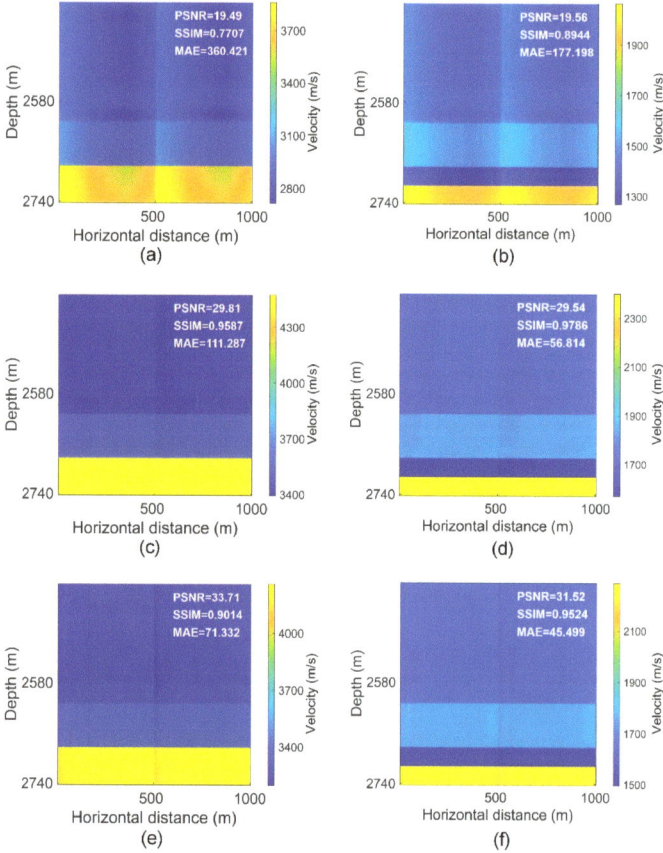

Figure 7. Two-dimensional profiles of the predicted velocity values of the sample event. (**a**,**b**) Predictions of P- and S-wave velocities trained with the synthetic dataset only. (**c**,**d**) Predictions of P- and S-wave velocities trained with the augmented dataset only. (**e**,**f**) Predictions of P- and S-wave velocities trained with the hybrid strategy involving both synthetic and augmented data. The reference velocity models are shown in Figure 5a,b.

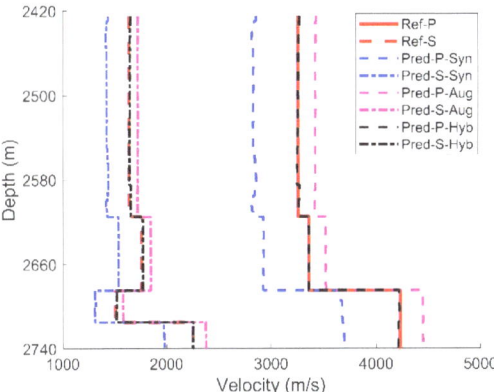

Figure 8. One-dimensional profiles of the reference and predicted velocity values of the sample event. The meanings of the symbols and colors are the same as Figure 4.

4.3. Multi-Stage Examples

From the results of single-stage examples, we believe that the augmented data and hybrid training strategy have higher accuracies for efficient velocity inversion. Therefore, we try to expand the research area to consider more fracturing stages. We consider all five stages, corresponding to five reference velocity models. We generate 12,000 gathers (1000 models × 12 sources) as the initial training dataset. The quantitative metrics are shown in Table 2. Compared to single-stage examples, the predictions are generally worse due to the combined effects of increased area and characteristics and limited field samples. Please also note that these metrics are mean values for all the predictions in five stages. The one-dimensional velocity profiles and the loss curves are shown in Figures 9 and 10, respectively. The predictions for the first stage (Figure 9a) are better than other stages (Figure 9b), especially for the two deep layers, mainly due to the largest number and best coverage of the microseismic events in the first stage. The hybrid training strategy can achieve slightly faster convergence rates than the other two strategies.

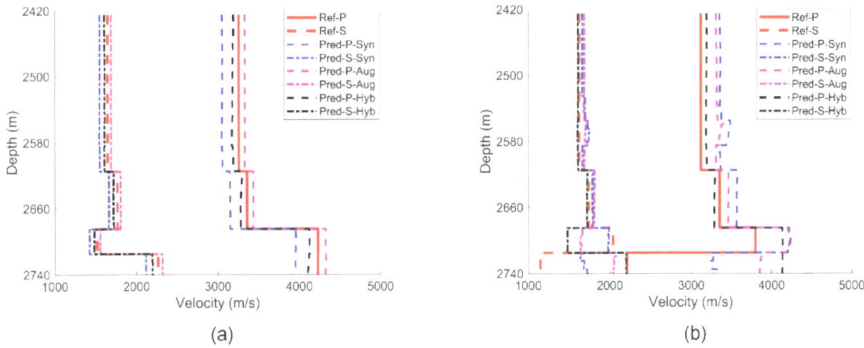

Figure 9. One-dimensional profiles of the reference and predicted velocity values of two arbitrary events from two stages. (**a**) Velocity curves of one sample event. The red solid and dashed lines indicate the reference velocity for the P- and S-wave, respectively, and the blue, magenta, and black dashed lines indicate the results of training with synthetic, augmented, and hybrid dataset. (**b**) Velocity curves of another sample event. The meanings of the symbols and colors are the same as Figure 4.

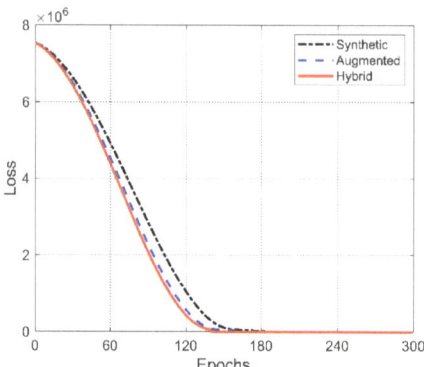

Figure 10. The loss curves for three different training strategies.

Table 2. The mean values of quantitative metrics for multi-stage examples.

Training Dataset	Phase	PSNR	SSIM	MAE
Synthetic	P	18.75	0.7094	314.843
	S	19.16	0.7209	155.461
Augmented	P	21.50	0.7030	228.985
	S	17.89	0.6759	152.441
Hybrid	P	22.24	0.7478	221.382
	S	18.46	0.6369	165.114

5. Discussion and Conclusions

We attempt to directly invert the velocity models from microseismic waveforms in this study. The testing results with purely synthetic data demonstrate the Unet model can predict the layered velocity model quite well and in an efficient manner. Since the predicted velocity models are almost the same as the real ones and thus do not contain much information, we do not show those simple results in this manuscript. Zhou et al. [29] demonstrated the effectiveness of a modified Attention Unet in predicting complex synthetic velocity models with microseismic records. They did not consider field microseismic data and adopted Gaussian noise to evaluate the robustness of the model, while we used field data to enhance the synthetic data by data augmentation operations. We also investigate and test many other scenarios by considering different SNRs, source locations, source mechanisms, and model numbers and sizes to mimic the field cases. Specially, the number and coverage of real microseismic events largely determine the features and constraints that can be extracted by the network model. However, these cases just introduce more complicated features which require a larger training dataset and computation expense. Further investigation of the influential factors on deep learning-based microseismic velocity inversion is out of the scope of the current study.

The disadvantage of most current deep learning algorithms is the heavy dependence on the training dataset and weak generalization capability. The introduced data augmentation method and hybrid training strategy proved to be effective in alleviating the feature gap in data domains and improving the generalization ability of the network model, which may provide guidance for other deep learning-based seismic inversion tasks. Transfer learning is also helpful to fill the feature gap, but also relies on the scale of the training data. Another feasible approach to realize seismic inversion with a limited training dataset is combing data-driven algorithms with the physical laws of seismic wave propagation, to provide more physical constraints and optimize the learning performance. In this work, we only consider a horizontally layered model, which is the most-commonly used model in microseismic processing. We will investigate the performance of the proposed method on heterogeneous models and compare it with conventional velocity inversion methods (e.g., FWI method). One of the advantages of deep learning methods is the weak dependence on the raypath coverage since we can train the model with a large and complete dataset.

In this paper, we propose an improved deep learning method for microseismic velocity inversion. The synthetic data are augmented to incorporate the features of the real data, and a hybrid training strategy that integrates the synthetic and augmented data is introduced. The Unet model can directly predict the layered velocity model from microseismic waveforms. Training the synthetic data involves first learning the low-frequency information in the data, and then it can provide an initial velocity model. Then, the augmented data are trained to learn the high-frequency information, which can improve the precision of the predicted velocity model. The hybrid training strategy makes better use of the data and enables the model to learn more imbedded connections between the waveforms and velocity models. Field downhole microseismic examples demonstrate the feasibility and superiority of the proposed method for efficient inversion of microseismic velocity models.

Author Contributions: Formal analysis, L.L. and X.Z.; Investigation, L.L., X.Z. and Y.T.; Methodology, L.L., X.Z. and L.P.; Supervision, X.P. and J.L.; Writing—original draft, L.L. and X.Z.; Writing—review and editing, X.P., L.P., Y.T. and J.L. All authors have read and agreed to the published version of the manuscript.

Funding: This work was supported the National Natural Science Foundation of China, grant number 42374076; Natural Science Foundation for Excellent Young Scholars of Hunan Province, China, grant number 2022JJ20057; Central South University Innovation-Driven Research Programme, grant number 2023CXQD063.

Institutional Review Board Statement: Not applicable.

Informed Consent Statement: Not applicable.

Data Availability Statement: The dataset for this research is available by contacting the corresponding author. The data are not publicly available due to privacy.

Conflicts of Interest: The authors declare no conflicts of interest.

References

1. Eaton, D.W. *Passive Seismic Monitoring of Induced Seismicity: Fundamental Principles and Application to Energy Technologies*, 1st ed.; Cambridge University Press: Cambridge, UK, 2018; ISBN 978-1-107-14525-2.
2. Li, L.; Tan, J.; Wood, D.A.; Zhao, Z.; Becker, D.; Lyu, Q.; Shu, B.; Chen, H. A Review of the Current Status of Induced Seismicity Monitoring for Hydraulic Fracturing in Unconventional Tight Oil and Gas Reservoirs. *Fuel* **2019**, *242*, 195–210. [CrossRef]
3. Meng, X.-B.; Chen, H.-C.; Niu, F.-L.; Du, Y.-J. Master Event Based Backazimuth Estimation and Its Application to Downhole Microseismic Monitoring. *Pet. Sci.* **2022**, *19*, 2675–2682. [CrossRef]
4. Li, L.; Tan, J.; Tan, Y.; Pan, X.; Zhao, Z. Chapter Eight: Microseismic Analysis to Aid Gas Reservoir Characterization. In *Sustainable Natural Gas Reservoir and Production Engineering*; Wood, D.A., Cai, J., Eds.; Elsevier: Amsterdam, The Netherlands, 2022; pp. 219–242.
5. Tomassi, A.; Milli, S.; Tentori, D. Synthetic Seismic Forward Modeling of a High-Frequency Depositional Sequence: The Example of the Tiber Depositional Sequence (Central Italy). *Mar. Pet. Geol.* **2024**, *160*, 106624. [CrossRef]
6. Jansky, J.; Plicka, V.; Eisner, L. Feasibility of Joint 1D Velocity Model and Event Location Inversion by the Neighbourhood Algorithm. *Geophys. Prospect.* **2010**, *58*, 229–234. [CrossRef]
7. Li, L.; Tan, J.; Schwarz, B.; Staněk, F.; Poiata, N.; Shi, P.; Diekmann, L.; Eisner, L.; Gajewski, D. Recent Advances and Challenges of Waveform-based Seismic Location Methods at Multiple Scales. *Rev. Geophys.* **2020**, *58*, e2019RG000667. [CrossRef]
8. Warpinski, N.R.; Sullivan, R.B.; Uhl, J.E.; Waltman, C.K.; Machovoe, S.R. Improved Microseismic Fracture Mapping Using Perforation Timing Measurements for Velocity Calibration. *SPE J.* **2005**, *10*, 14–23. [CrossRef]
9. Pei, D.; Quirein, J.A.; Cornish, B.E.Q.; Quinn, D.; Warpinski, N.R. Velocity Calibration for Microseismic Monitoring: A Very Fast Simulated Annealing (VFSA) Approach for Joint-Objective Optimization. *Geophysics* **2009**, *74*, WCB47–WCB55. [CrossRef]
10. Tan, Y.; He, C.; Mao, Z. Microseismic Velocity Model Inversion and Source Location: The Use of Neighborhood Algorithm and Master Station Method. *Geophysics* **2018**, *83*, 1JA-Z18. [CrossRef]
11. Igonin, N.; Innanen, K.A. Analysis of Simultaneous Velocity and Source Parameter Updates in Microseismic FWI. In Proceedings of the SEG Technical Program Expanded Abstracts 2018, Anaheim, CA, USA, 27 August 2018; Society of Exploration Geophysicists: Houston, TX, USA, 2018; pp. 1033–1037.

12. Wang, H.; Alkhalifah, T. Microseismic Imaging Using a Source Function Independent Full Waveform Inversion Method. *Geophys. J. Int.* **2018**, *214*, 46–57. [CrossRef]
13. Virieux, J.; Operto, S. An Overview of Full-Waveform Inversion in Exploration Geophysics. *Geophysics* **2009**, *74*, WCC1–WCC26. [CrossRef]
14. Guitton, A.; Díaz, E. Attenuating Crosstalk Noise with Simultaneous Source Full Waveform Inversion. *Geophys. Prospect.* **2012**, *60*, 759–768. [CrossRef]
15. LeCun, Y.; Bengio, Y.; Hinton, G. Deep Learning. *Nature* **2015**, *521*, 436–444. [CrossRef] [PubMed]
16. Mousavi, S.M.; Beroza, G.C. Deep-Learning Seismology. *Science* **2022**, *377*, eabm4470. [CrossRef] [PubMed]
17. Anikiev, D.; Birnie, C.; bin Waheed, U.; Alkhalifah, T.; Gu, C.; Verschuur, D.J.; Eisner, L. Machine Learning in Microseismic Monitoring. *Earth-Sci. Rev.* **2023**, *239*, 104371. [CrossRef]
18. Zhang, H.; Ma, C.; Pazzi, V.; Zou, Y.; Casagli, N. Microseismic Signal Denoising and Separation Based on Fully Convolutional Encoder–Decoder Network. *Appl. Sci.* **2020**, *10*, 6621. [CrossRef]
19. Shang, G.; Li, L.; Zhang, L.; Liu, X.; Li, D.; Qin, G.; Li, H. Research on Automatic Classification of Coal Mine Microseismic Events Based on Data Enhancement and FCN-LSTM Network. *Appl. Sci.* **2023**, *13*, 11158. [CrossRef]
20. Ma, C.; Ran, X.; Xu, W.; Yan, W.; Li, T.; Dai, K.; Wan, J.; Lin, Y.; Tong, K. Fine Classification Method for Massive Microseismic Signals Based on Short-Time Fourier Transform and Deep Learning. *Remote Sens.* **2023**, *15*, 502. [CrossRef]
21. Liu, N.; Chen, J.; Wu, H.; Li, F.; Gao, J. Microseismic First-Arrival Picking Using Fine-Tuning Feature Pyramid Networks. *IEEE Geosci. Remote Sens. Lett.* **2022**, *19*, 7505105. [CrossRef]
22. Yuan, S.-Y.; Zhao, Y.; Xie, T.; Qi, J.; Wang, S.-X. SegNet-Based First-Break Picking via Seismic Waveform Classification Directly from Shot Gathers with Sparsely Distributed Traces. *Pet. Sci.* **2022**, *19*, 162–179. [CrossRef]
23. Zhang, Y.; Leng, J.; Dong, Y.; Yu, Z.; Hu, T.; He, C. Phase Arrival Picking for Bridging Multi-Source Downhole Microseismic Data Using Deep Transfer Learning. *J. Geophys. Eng.* **2022**, *19*, 178–191. [CrossRef]
24. Wamriew, D.; Dorhjie, D.B.; Bogoedov, D.; Pevzner, R.; Maltsev, E.; Charara, M.; Pissarenko, D.; Koroteev, D. Microseismic Monitoring and Analysis Using Cutting-Edge Technology: A Key Enabler for Reservoir Characterization. *Remote Sens.* **2022**, *14*, 3417. [CrossRef]
25. Wamriew, D.; Pevzner, R.; Maltsev, E.; Pissarenko, D. Deep Neural Networks for Detection and Location of Microseismic Events and Velocity Model Inversion from Microseismic Data Acquired by Distributed Acoustic Sensing Array. *Sensors* **2021**, *21*, 6627. [CrossRef] [PubMed]
26. Araya-Polo, M.; Jennings, J.; Adler, A.; Dahlke, T. Deep-Learning Tomography. *Lead. Edge* **2018**, *37*, 58–66. [CrossRef]
27. Yang, F.; Ma, J. Deep-Learning Inversion: A next-Generation Seismic Velocity Model Building Method. *Geophysics* **2019**, *84*, R583–R599. [CrossRef]
28. Wamriew, D.; Charara, M.; Pissarenko, D. Joint Event Location and Velocity Model Update in Real-Time for Downhole Microseismic Monitoring: A Deep Learning Approach. *Comput. Geosci.* **2022**, *158*, 104965. [CrossRef]
29. Zhou, Y.; Han, L.; Zhang, P.; Zeng, J.; Shang, X.; Huang, W. Microseismic Data-Direct Velocity Modeling Method Based on a Modified Attention U-Net Architecture. *Appl. Sci.* **2023**, *13*, 11166. [CrossRef]
30. Xu, X.; Guo, P.; Yang, J.; Xu, W.; Tong, S. Compensating Low-Frequency Signals for Prestack Seismic Data and Its Applications in Full-Waveform Inversion. *IEEE Trans. Geosci. Remote Sens.* **2023**, *61*, 5920814. [CrossRef]
31. Yang, Y.; Zhang, X.; Guan, Q.; Lin, Y. Enhancing Data-Driven Seismic Inversion Using Physics-Guided Spatiotemporal Data Augmentation. In Proceedings of the First International Meeting for Applied Geoscience & Energy Expanded Abstracts, Denver, CO, USA, 1 September 2021; Society of Exploration Geophysicists: Houston, TX, USA, 2021; pp. 1395–1399.
32. Alkhalifah, T.; Wang, H.; Ovcharenko, O. MLReal: Bridging the Gap between Training on Synthetic Data and Real Data Applications in Machine Learning. *Artif. Intell. Geosci.* **2022**, *3*, 101–114. [CrossRef]
33. Wu, X.; Ma, J.; Si, X.; Bi, Z.; Yang, J.; Gao, H.; Xie, D.; Guo, Z.; Zhang, J. Sensing Prior Constraints in Deep Neural Networks for Solving Exploration Geophysical Problems. *Proc. Natl. Acad. Sci. USA* **2023**, *120*, e2219573120. [CrossRef]
34. Ronneberger, O.; Fischer, P.; Brox, T. U-Net: Convolutional Networks for Biomedical Image Segmentation. In *Medical Image Computing and Computer-Assisted Intervention—MICCAI 2015*; Navab, N., Hornegger, J., Wells, W.M., Frangi, A.F., Eds.; Lecture Notes in Computer Science; Springer International Publishing: Cham, Switzerland, 2015; Volume 9351, pp. 234–241. ISBN 978-3-319-24573-7.
35. Zhang, S.-B.; Si, H.-J.; Wu, X.-M.; Yan, S.-S. A Comparison of Deep Learning Methods for Seismic Impedance Inversion. *Pet. Sci.* **2022**, *19*, 1019–1030. [CrossRef]
36. Xu, B.; Wang, N.; Chen, T.; Li, M. Empirical Evaluation of Rectified Activations in Convolutional Network. *arXiv* **2015**, arXiv:1505.00853.
37. Glorot, X.; Bordes, A.; Bengio, Y. Domain Adaptation for Large-Scale Sentiment Classification: A Deep Learning Approach. In Proceedings of the 28th International Conference on Machine Learning (ICML-11), Bellevue, WA, USA, 28 June–2 July 2011; pp. 513–520.
38. Wang, H.; Alkhalifah, T. Direct Microseismic Event Location and Characterization from Passive Seismic Data Using Convolutional Neural Networks. *Geophysics* **2021**, *86*, KS109–KS121. [CrossRef]
39. Zhang, Z.; Lin, Y. Data-Driven Seismic Waveform Inversion: A Study on the Robustness and Generalization. *IEEE Trans. Geosci. Remote Sens.* **2020**, *58*, 6900–6913. [CrossRef]

40. Li, F.; Guo, Z.; Pan, X.; Liu, J.; Wang, Y.; Gao, D. Deep Learning with Adaptive Attention for Seismic Velocity Inversion. *Remote Sens.* **2022**, *14*, 3810. [CrossRef]
41. Li, S.; Liu, B.; Ren, Y.; Chen, Y.; Yang, S.; Wang, Y.; Jiang, P. Deep-Learning Inversion of Seismic Data. *IEEE Trans. Geosci. Remote Sens.* **2020**, *58*, 2135–2149. [CrossRef]
42. Paszke, A.; Gross, S.; Massa, F.; Lerer, A.; Bradbury, J.; Chanan, G.; Killeen, T.; Lin, Z.; Gimelshein, N.; Antiga, L.; et al. PyTorch: An Imperative Style, High-Performance Deep Learning Library. In Proceedings of the 33rd Conference on Neural Information Processing Systems, Vancouver, BC, Canada, 8–14 December 2019; pp. 1–12.
43. Zhao, R.; Cui, H. Improved Threshold Denoising Method Based on Wavelet Transform. In Proceedings of the 7th International Conference on Modelling, Identification and Control (ICMIC 2015), Sousse, Tunisia, 18–20 December 2015; p. 1.

Disclaimer/Publisher's Note: The statements, opinions and data contained in all publications are solely those of the individual author(s) and contributor(s) and not of MDPI and/or the editor(s). MDPI and/or the editor(s) disclaim responsibility for any injury to people or property resulting from any ideas, methods, instructions or products referred to in the content.

Article

A High-Resolution Aftershock Catalog for the 2014 *Ms* 6.5 Ludian (China) Earthquake Using Deep Learning Methods

Jun Li [1], Ming Hao [1,*] and Zijian Cui [2]

1. The Second Monitoring and Application Center, China Earthquake Administration, Xi'an 710054, China
2. Institute of Earthquake Forecasting, China Earthquake Administration, Beijing 100036, China
* Correspondence: ha_mg@163.com

Abstract: A high-resolution catalog for the 2014 *Ms* 6.5 Ludian aftershocks was constructed based on the deep learning phase-picking model (CERP) and seismic-phase association technology (PALM). A specific training strategy, which combines the advantages of the conventional short–long window average energy ratio algorithm (STA/LTA) and AI algorithms, is employed to retrain the CERP model. The P- and S-wave phases were accurately detected and picked on continuous seismic waveforms by the retained AI model. Hypoinverse and HypoDD were utilized for the precise location of 3286 events. Compared to the previous results, our new catalog exhibits superior performances in terms of location accuracy and the number of aftershock events, thereby enabling a more detailed depiction of the deep-seated tectonic features. According to the distribution of aftershocks, it can be inferred that (1) the seismogenic fault of the Ludian earthquake is the NW-trending Baogunao–Xiaohe Fault, (2) the Ludian aftershocks interconnected with the discontinuous NW-trending Baogunao–Xiaohe Fault, and they also intersected with the Zhaotong–Ludian Fault. (3) This suggests that the NE-trending Zhaotong–Ludian Fault may have been intersected by the NW-trending Baogunao–Xiaohe Fault, indicating that the Baogunao–Xiaohe Fault is likely a relatively young Neogene fault.

Keywords: deep learning; 2014 Ludian earthquake; aftershock catalog

1. Introduction

The earthquake catalog is a crucial foundation for seismic research. A high-resolution regional catalog includes a large number of highly precisely located earthquakes. The greater the number of precisely located earthquake events, the more it helps to clearly reveal the physical structure of the underground media. This is crucial for various seismological research fields, such as seismic tomography, fault zone structures, stress states of the Earth's interior, and seismic hazard assessments [1–3]. Generally, the process of constructing a seismic catalog involves multiple steps, including earthquake detection, seismic phase picking, phase association, and earthquake localization. Since the inception of seismology, seismologists have been dedicated to detecting more events from noise-rich continuous seismic waveforms, more precisely picking seismic phase arrivals, and more precisely locating earthquakes to construct high-resolution catalogs [4–13]. However, manual phase-picking methods are not only inefficient but also susceptible to picking errors. Moreover, traditional rule-based automated algorithms face challenges in balancing efficiency, accuracy, and completeness. For instance, a class of automated algorithms based on energy characteristic functions struggles to correctly identify seismic signals characterized by impulsive noise [13]. On the other hand, algorithms based on waveform similarity principles heavily rely on the diversity of prior template events, with low computational efficiency, making them less suitable for scenarios involving large datasets [11,12]. The key challenge encountered when using traditional automated algorithms to address seismic phase recognition issues lies in the inherent difficulty of mathematically describing these problems [14]. Deep learning technology allows computational models composed of multiple processing layers to learn mathematical representations with multiple abstraction levels. Its advantage lies in employing a data-driven learning approach to find solutions to problems [15]. This characteristic is particularly suitable for addressing phase-picking issues.

In recent years, the technology used to construct seismic catalogs based on deep learning has experienced rapid development. This includes not only deep learning-based techniques for earthquake detection [16–18], seismic phase-picking [18,19], phase association [20], and automatic earthquake location workflows [21,22], but also the gradual improvement of AI earthquake benchmark datasets [23,24]. Perol et al. [16] first trained a deep convolutional neural network (CNN) with eight hidden layers and used it to detect roughly located earthquakes in the Oklahoma area. Mousavi et al. [17] first designed a hybrid model integrating a CNN with a recurrent neural network (RNN). This model utilized a CNN to classify earthquake events and noise, while an RNN was employed for the phase-picking of P- and S-waves within the time windows of the seismic events. For regression-based solutions, Zhu and Beroza [19] designed a U-shaped deep neural network with four downsampling and four upsampling processes. This network (PhaseNet) treated the phase-picking of seismic waves as a probability distribution of P, S, and noise at each point within a time series window, achieving pixel-level identification in seismic waveform data for the first time. They trained their PhaseNet with over 700,000 earthquake events from California, enabling the high-precision picking of P and S wave arrivals across different instrument types. Mousavi et al. [18] first introduced the attention mechanism into the problem of phase detection in seismology and presented a global deep learning model (EQtransformer, Stanford, CA, USA) for simultaneous earthquake detection and phase-picking. These four AI models represent the four types of neural network structures commonly used in seismology. Compared to traditional methods, they all showed improvements in detection accuracy, completeness, and computational efficiency. However, they shared a common issue: significant variation in generalizability across different tectonic regions. In the field of AI earthquake datasets, Mousavi et al. [23] published the Stanford Earthquake Dataset (STEAD), the first publicly released benchmark dataset for training AI seismic models, which contains approximately 3 million global seismic and noise records. However, most seismic data in STEAD originated from Europe and the USA, with only a small portion originating from mainland China. Later, Zhao et al. [24] launched the DiTing dataset, which primarily features seismic benchmark AI data from mainland China, including about 780,000 earthquake events. Additionally, phase association technology was a crucial aspect following phase detection that impacted earthquake localization. Zhu et al. [20] developed a Bayesian-based hybrid model for this purpose, enhancing the accuracy and efficiency of seismic phase association. Furthermore, to enhance the efficiency of the earthquake location workflow, Zhang et al. [21] and Zhou et al. [22] developed comprehensive workflow frameworks called LOC-FLOW and PALM (Phase picking, Association, Location and Matched Filter), respectively. Both frameworks offered flexible interfaces to overcome format barriers between multiple processing steps and employed traditional methods for earthquake association. The main difference between these frameworks was that LOC-FLOW used a grid search for association and localization, which had lower computational efficiency, while PALM achieved association based on temporal and spatial differences between different stations, resulting in improved computational efficiency.

Despite significant progress over the past years, data-driven deep learning technology still encounters big challenges when confronted with complex regional structures and observation conditions in the real world. Jiang et al. highlighted that, when the EQTransformer and PhaseNet were simultaneously utilized for detecting the aftershock sequences of the 2021 Yangbi earthquake and the 2021 Maduo earthquake, the catalogs produced by the two AI models exhibited significant differences. This inconsistency between the two catalogs indicated that the regional tectonic structures exerted a significant influence on the generalization of AI models.

In this study, we designed a novel training strategy by retraining the AI model on a small sample set to improve its generalization in specific regional tectonic structural scenarios. This retraining strategy combined the advantages of AI algorithms and the traditional short-long window algorithm (STA/LTA) [13]. We utilized the PALM method to obtain seismic/noise sample sets specific to the local region, which were then used to train a CNN model. Simultaneously, a manually picked P and S phases dataset was employed to train an RNN model. The CNN model was employed for detecting seismic events, while the RNN model was dedicated to picking seismic phases. Finally, the retrained AI model was applied to the 2014 Ludian aftershocks, resulting in a high-resolution catalog. Our results not only offer essential foundational data for the study of small seismic activities in the Ludian region but also provide a viable solution to the current challenges of generalization in AI phase detection.

2. Tectonic Background

The 2014 Ms 6.5 Ludian earthquake occurred along the southeastern margin of the Qinghai–Tibet Plateau (Figure 1). This region, experiencing the influence of compressional force between the Qinghai–Tibet Plateau and the South China Block, is known for its complex and diverse geological structures, marked by active tectonic features. Historically, this area has been the location of intense seismic activity in mainland China, with a recorded history of 17 earthquakes greater than Ms 6.0, the most notable being the Ms 7.1 Yongshan–Daguan earthquake in 1974 [25]. The 2014 Ludian earthquake was closely associated with several active faults, including the Xiaojiang Fault, the Lianfeng Fault, and the Zhaotong–Ludian Fault. This seismogenic fault zone is a part of the boundary separating the Sichuan–Yunnan block and the South China block, and also the transition zone from the actively deforming sub-block of the Dalianshan to the relatively stable South China block [26]. In addition, the region encompasses other important fault zones such as the Anninghe Fault, the Zemuhe Fault, the Daliangshan Fault, and the Mabian–Yanjin Fault. Many moderate earthquakes have occurred along these faults in the past decades, including the 2003 Ludian Ms 5.0 and Ms 5.2 earthquakes, the 2004 Ludian Ms 5.6 earthquake, the 2006 Yanjin Ms 5.1 earthquake, and the 2012 Yiliang Ms 5.7 and Ms 6.5 earthquakes. These seismic activities underscore the active characteristics of the region's tectonics. He et al. [27] and Xu et al. [28] suggest that the Daliangshan and Mabian fault zones, previously disjointed, represent emerging neo-seismic tectonic belts. Currently, these zones are undergoing a phase of structural connectivity, with the precise location of this recent linkage yet to be determined. Situated at the southern end of the Daliangshan Fault's tail, the Ludian region provides a critical vantage point for understanding the structural connectivity of this fault and for assessing related seismic hazards. The 2014 Ludian earthquake thus offers valuable insights into the dynamics of tectonic activities in this seismically active region.

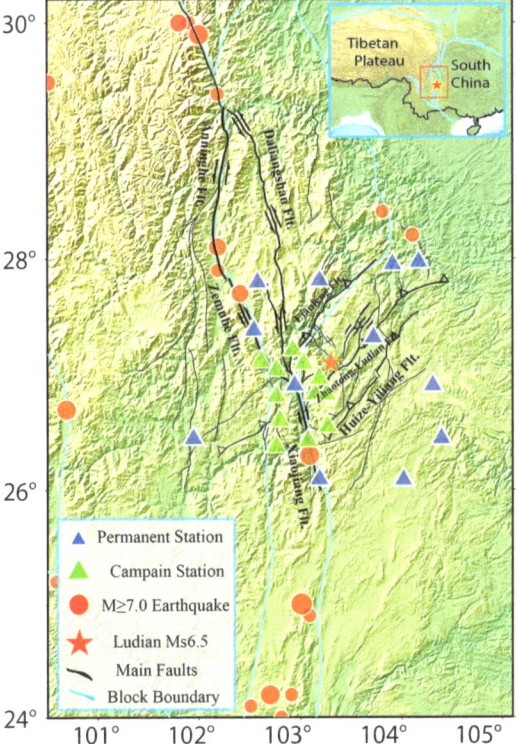

Figure 1. The tectonic background, seismic station distribution and historical large earthquakes in the study area. Blue triangles and green triangles represent the permanent stations and campaign stations, respectively. The red circles represent the historical earthquakes greater than 7.0. The red star represents the 2014 Ms 6.5 Ludian earthquake. The black solid curves represent the primary active faults, and the blue solid curves represent the block boundary in China's mainland.

3. Data and Methods

3.1. Seismic Data

In this research, we gathered comprehensive seismic data to construct a high-resolution aftershock catalog of the 2014 Ludian earthquake. The data collection involved continuous waveform and manually picked phase data from the Sichuan Seismic Network, the Yunnan Seismic Network, and the Qiaojia–Ludian seismic station network. The Qiaojia–Ludian network consisted of 12 permanent stations and 12 campaign stations, which were deployed near the Xiaojiang–Zhaotong–Ludian Fault Zone, allowing for a robust coverage of the 2014 Ludian earthquake. The campaign stations used Güralp CMG-3T seismometers (Güralp Systems Ltd., Aldermaston, UK) and Reftek 130S data loggers (Trimble Navigation Ltd., Sunnyvale, CA, USA), with a frequency range of 120 s–50 Hz. The permanent stations used Güralp CMG-3ESPC seismometers (Güralp Systems Ltd.) and EDAS-24I data loggers (Beijing Gangzhen Technology Development Co., Ltd., Beijing, China), with a frequency range of 60 s–50 Hz, and the seismometers are mostly installed on bedrock. The initial step in data handling was a rigorous assessment of data quality from all seismic stations. This involved evaluating the continuity of waveform data and excluding stations with consistently poor data quality. Then, we meticulously selected 12 campaign stations and 12 regional permanent stations to locate Ludian aftershocks, considering data quality and geographical significance. The selection criteria aimed to achieve an optimal balance between station quality and location to enhance aftershock location effectiveness. The observation period for these 24 seismic stations spanned from 1 August 2014 to 31 December

2015, with data continuity exceeding 90%. To verify the consistency of instrument responses, especially in campaign stations, we conducted comparative analyses using instrument responses to surface waves from global earthquakes greater than Ms 7.0. This comparison, which involved examining recordings from different stations for the same global seismic events, focused particularly on the response to long-distance seismic surface waves. This procedure confirmed the consistency of instrument responses across stations, which was crucial for the accurate determination of earthquake magnitudes.

The construction of the seismic AI training dataset was a crucial step in the development of a reliable and effective deep learning model for seismic event detection and phase picking. Our dataset was structured into three distinct sets: seismic event samples (positive), noise samples (negative), and seismic phase-picking samples. The CNN model was tailored to learn from the event and noise samples, while the RNN model was specifically trained using the seismic phase-picking samples.

For the generation of phase-picking samples, 55 regional permanent stations from the Sichuan Seismic Network were selected to create sample datasets for training the RNN model. These seismic records, encompassing continuous waveforms and P- and S-wave phase data, were collected from 1 January 2008 to 31 December 2012. The accuracy of the P- and S-wave phase arrivals was ascertained using the theoretical travel time versus epicentral distance relationship. We extracted earthquake events from 24 h continuous waveforms based on the arrival times of P- and S-wave phases. These events were then represented as 30 s seismic waveform segments, with the P- and S-wave arrival times annotated on each segment. To ensure the quality of the data, the signal-to-noise ratio (SNR) for all samples was calculated, and samples with exceptionally high or low SNR were excluded. Ultimately, this meticulous process yielded a dataset comprising 121,507 event samples annotated with manual phase labels, providing a rich and reliable foundation for the subsequent deep learning training and aftershock cataloging. For the generation of positive (seismic event) and negative (noise) samples, we employed a multifaceted approach integrating the STA/LTA, Kurtosis [29], and seismic association algorithms embedded within the PALM framework. This approach was applied to waveform data from the Ludian region to extract both event and noise samples efficiently. The Kurtosis algorithm was an automatic S-wave onset-picker, which used kurtosis-derived characteristic functions and eigenvalue decompositions on three-component seismic data. The Kurtosis algorithm outperformed the STA/LTA (short-term average/long-term average) algorithm in terms of accuracy and the number of picks, especially for S-wave. The detection of P and S arrival pairs for seismic events was accomplished using both the STA/LTA picker and the Kurtosis picker. Once all P and S arrival pairs were detected, the seismic association algorithm was employed to associate phase arrivals across all stations, thus forming distinct seismic events. These detected events constituted our event sample dataset. Noise samples were randomly extracted from 24 h continuous waveform recordings. A 30 s window was deemed a noise sample if it lacked any P or S phase arrivals. This method ensures the inclusion of diverse noise characteristics in the training dataset. In the end, we obtained 15,833 event samples. To augment the event samples, we added noise and randomly shifted time windows, resulting in a fivefold increase. A total of 75,327 noise samples were obtained through random selection. Since noise data were abundant and diverse, we did not perform data augmentation on the noise data to maintain its original complexity and diversity. After assembling all sample sets, we conducted a thorough analysis of various attributes within the dataset. This included assessing the distribution of signal-to-noise ratios, epicentral distances, azimuths, and the relationship between travel time and epicentral distance (see Figure 2). Such an analysis is essential to understand the dataset's diversity and to ensure that the deep learning models are trained on a representative and comprehensive sample of seismic data. For a visual understanding of these distributions, refer to Figure 2 in the paper. This figure illustrates the range and variability of the aforementioned attributes within the dataset, offering insights into the data's complexity and the challenges it poses for AI-based seismic analysis. This comprehensive preparation and analysis of the seismic

AI training dataset lay the groundwork for the effective training of deep learning models, enabling them to accurately discern between seismic events and noise and to proficiently identify seismic phases, thereby contributing to the advancement of seismic research and aftershock analysis.

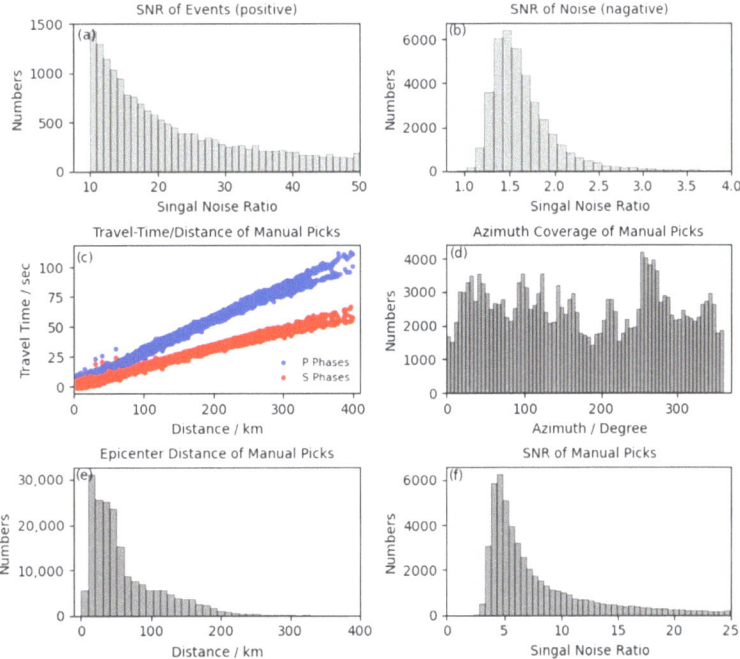

Figure 2. Histograms of signal-to-noise ratio, epicentral distance, azimuth coverage, and travel time-to-epicentral distance relationship in the training dataset. (**a**,**b**) depict the distribution of signal-to-noise ratio for earthquake events and noise samples in the CNN training set. (**c**–**f**) represent histograms of the travel time-to-epicentral distance relationship, azimuth coverage, epicentral distance, and signal-to-noise ratio in the RNN training set.

3.2. Methods

The comprehensive AI detection workflow is depicted in Figure 3. Unlike the procedural framework presented in Zhou et al. [30], the seismic phase data used in training the RNN model were manually picked by experts. In contrast, the sample dataset in Zhou et al. [30] was obtained through detection by the PAL-picker. The AI model in this study integrates a hybrid CNN and RNN structure, an approach previously developed by Zhou et al. [14]. Within this combined CNN and RNN model, the CNN deep neural network is composed of eight convolutional layers, Rectified Linear Unit (ReLU) non-linear activation functions, Max Pooling layers, and fully connected layers. The forward propagation procedure is defined by a loss function based on the L1 norm, while the backward propagation utilizes the Adam optimizer. The RNN features two bidirectional Gated Recurrent Unit (GRU) layers, which process data both forward and backward in time. In the RNN, each layer's current state is influenced by both the input at the present time step and the hidden state from the preceding time step.

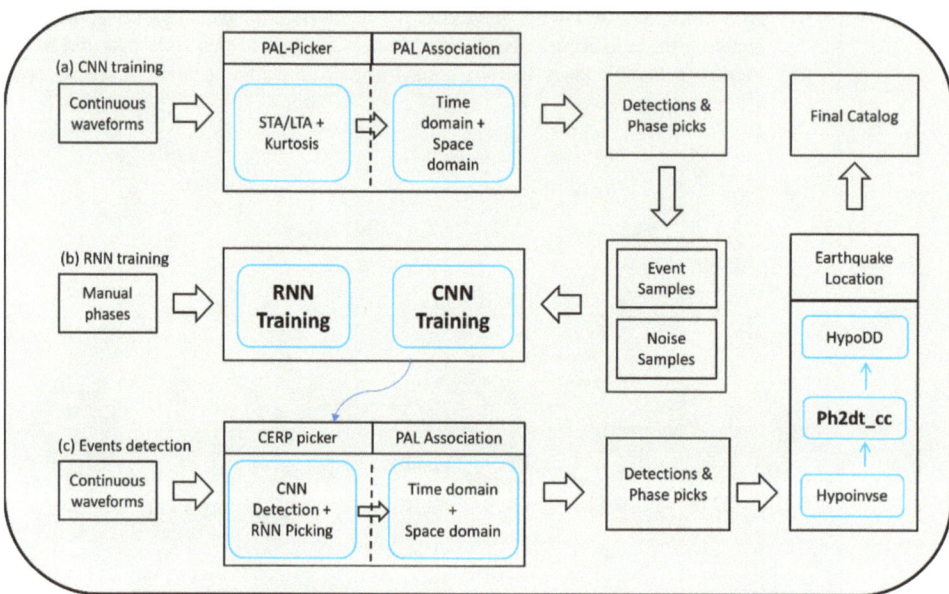

Figure 3. The workflow of earthquake detection and location. The blue boxes represent important processing steps, while the black boxes indicate input and output data.

Phase association incorporates clustering analysis in both time and space domains [22]. Temporal association is achieved by searching for clusters of earthquake occurrence times. Spatial association is accomplished through grid searching for the hypocenter position with the minimum travel time residual. The phase association procedure ensures the detection of the same seismic signal by a minimum of four stations, thereby reducing the likelihood of misidentified signals. The magnitude estimation is determined by calculating the body wave magnitude using the S-wave amplitude. The earthquake localization utilizes Hypoinverse [7] for absolute location and HypoDD [10,31] for relative relocation.

3.3. AI Model Training

To improve the performance of the AI model under specific tectonic and observation conditions, we rapidly constructed a sample dataset for the local region and retrained the AI model. The methodology for curating the AI training dataset has been delineated in the preceding section. Before feeding samples into the AI model, data augmentation techniques were employed on the original dataset to enhance its robustness. This included temporal adjustments of the sampling window and the infusion of varying degrees of white noise. Specifically, the P-wave arrival served as the temporal anchor around which five random shifts within a 15 s interval were executed, each accompanied by the introduction of white noise ranging from 0 to 40%.

The hyperparameters, notably the learning rate and batch size, are pivotal in the AI training process, influencing model convergence, the risk of overfitting, and computational efficiency. An inordinately high learning rate can precipitate non-convergence, while an excessively low learning rate may unduly protract the convergence timeline. Similarly, a minuscule batch size could prove inadequate in counterbalancing the stochastic influence on gradient estimation, whereas an excessively large batch size could lead to protracted iteration durations. For the training executed in this study, we utilized hardware equipped with a GeForce RTX 3090 GPU, boasting 24 GB of memory (Nvidia Corporation, Santa Clara, CA, USA). A learning rate of 0.001 was established for both CNN and RNN training, with a batch size of 512. The training dataset was apportioned into training, validation, and test sets following a 7:2:1 ratio.

Detection accuracy was quantified as the proportion of correct predictions derived from the training dataset during the CNN training epoch, while validation accuracy was ascertained using the validation dataset. An observed increment in detection accuracy concomitant with a decrement in validation accuracy typically denotes the phenomenon of overfitting within the AI training regime. The 30 s sampling window was dissected into multiple time steps with a granularity of 0.5 s. The accuracy of these time steps, along with the validation rate, was defined as the likelihood of accurately predicting the P- and S-wave phases within these temporal increments during the RNN training phase. The picking uncertainty is characterized as the temporal precision in identifying the P- and S-wave arrivals within the training/validation datasets during the RNN training phase. The trajectories of detection/validation accuracy, picking uncertainty, and time step accuracy are graphically represented in Figure 4.

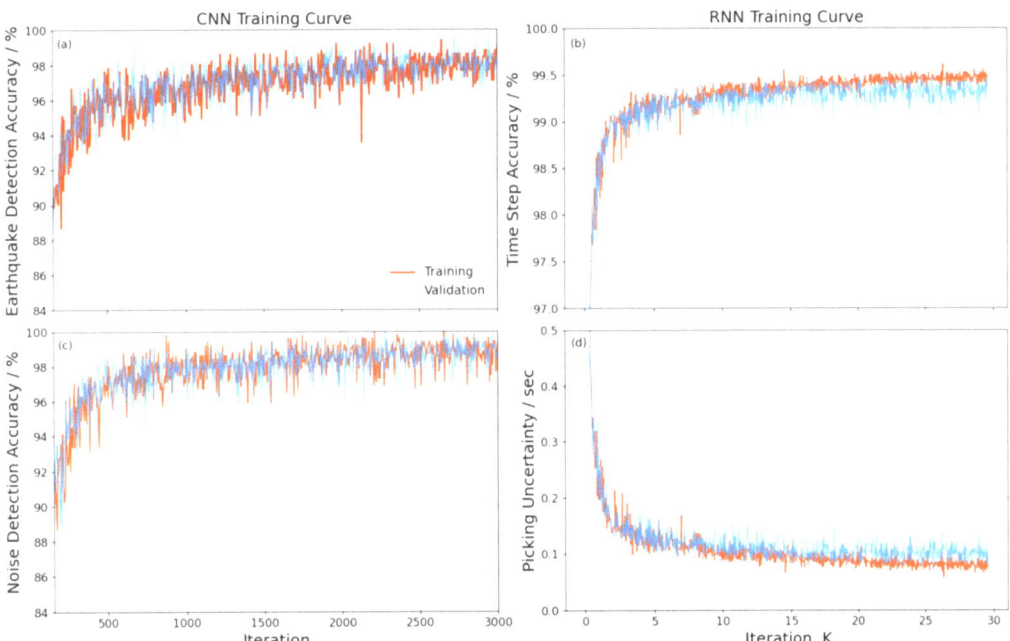

Figure 4. Detection accuracy and picking uncertainty over the course of CNN and RNN training iterations. (**a**,**c**) The training accuracy and validation accuracy, respectively, for event samples and noise samples during the iteration process of the CNN model. Here, the red curve denotes the training accuracy, while the blue curve represents the validation accuracy. (**b**,**d**) The time step accuracy and picking uncertainty, respectively, during the iteration process of the RNN model, where the red curve indicates the accuracy on the training set, and the blue curve signifies the accuracy on the validation set.

3.4. Earthquake Detection, Phase Picking, Association and Location

Utilizing the retrained CNN and RNN models on continuous waveform data, we conducted earthquake detection over a 30 s window with a 15 s sliding step, applying a 1–20 Hz bandpass filter to 24 h three-component waveforms. P- and S-wave phases were concurrently picked within this framework, and surface wave amplitudes were quantified within an amplitude window extending from 1 s pre P-wave to 5 s post S-wave. After obtaining the P- and S-wave phases for all stations, clustering of phase arrival times is achieved using a threshold of 2.0 s for grid search travel time residual, and a requirement of at least 4 stations simultaneously recording the same seismic signal. This process culminated in initial detections comprising 3624 seismic events and 25,125 P- and S-wave phase arrivals. A juxtaposition of the AI-determined arrival times with those manually picked revealed an average temporal discrepancy for P-waves of 0.02 s (standard deviation of 0.32 s), and for S-waves, an average discrepancy of 0.11 s (standard deviation of 0.44 s).

For absolute earthquake localization, the Hypoinverse software (Version 1.40) was harnessed. We adopted an average strategy for the initial velocity model, utilizing an averaged three-layer model of Fang et al. (Figure 5) [25]. Throughout the iterative inversion process, station weights were modulated based on the root mean square of the travel time residuals and epicentral distance. A residual cutoff threshold was established, affording full weight to stations with residuals under 0.3 s, nullifying weights for residuals exceeding three times the cutoff residual (0.9 s), and implementing weighted interpolation for intermediate values according to a cosine function curve. A distance cutoff was set at 40 km, with a cutoff range spanning 40–120 km.

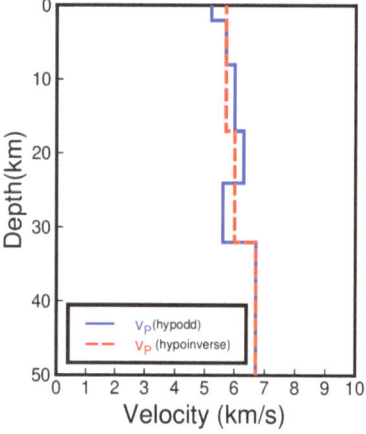

Figure 5. The velocity model used in the Ludian region. The red dashed line represents the averaged P-wave velocity from Fang et al. [25], which is used for absolute localization with Hypoinverse, while the blue solid line indicates the P-wave velocity model from Fang et al. [25], used for relative localization with HypoDD.

Subsequent to the absolute localization, relative localization was performed employing the HypoDD algorithm (Version 1.3). The double-difference method incorporates an initial relative location derived from travel time measurements, further refined by cross-correlation to correct temporal disparities, thereby augmenting the precision of the relative locations. The parameters included a maximum station-event distance of 150 km, an event-pair distance constraint of 6 km, and a minimum of 8 phases per event pair. After two cycles and eight iterations, the inversion parameters, inclusive of travel time residuals and horizontal and vertical discrepancies, were stabilized. During the cross-correlation for travel time difference calculations (cc), the maximum distance between events pairs was set to 4 km, and the maximum epicentral distance for stations was 120 km. Template windows are defined as a P-wave before 0.5 s and after 3.5 s, and S-wave before 0.3 s and after 4.5 s, using a 2–15 Hz bandpass filter. The velocity model is the same as the one used by Fang et al. (Figure 5). Finally, we obtained high-precision location results for 3286 events.

The Frequency–Magnitude Distribution (FMD) between the AI catalog of this study and those compiled by Fang et al. and the China Earthquake Network Center (CENC) was contrasted (Figure 6). This comparative analysis indicated that the AI-generated catalog exhibits superior detection capabilities relative to the catalogs by Fang et al. [25] and CENC.

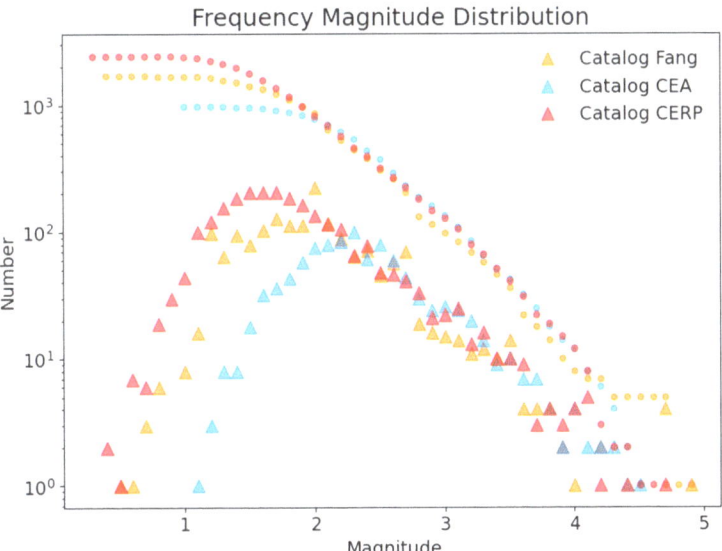

Figure 6. Comparison of frequency magnitude distribution. The solid circles and solid triangles represent the cumulative and non-cumulative distribution, respectively. These indicate the relationship between the number of earthquakes equal to or greater than a certain magnitude. The red symbols represent the CERP catalog in this study, the orange symbols represent the earthquake catalog by Fang et al. [25], and the blue symbols represent the earthquake catalog from the China Earthquake Administration's station network, which overlaps with the fixed stations used in this study.

4. Results

4.1. Aftershocks Space Distribution, Temporal Evolution and Focal Mechanism

The analysis of the aftershock sequence following the 2014 Ludian Ms 6.5 earthquake elucidates a distinct L-shaped conjugate distribution, suggesting a compound fracture orientation primarily along the east–west (E–W) and northwest–southeast (NW–SE) axes. The E–W oriented section spans approximately 23 km in length and 5 km in breadth, while the NW–SE extension measures about 18 km in length and similarly 5 km across. In terms of depth, the aftershocks predominantly clustered within a stratum extending from 5 to 15 km beneath the surface. The intersection of the conjugate faults marks the zone of maximal hypocentral depth, where the concentration of aftershocks is notably dense. Moving laterally from this central intersection, there is a discernible gradation towards more superficial seismic events (Figure 7).

The aftershocks also exhibited distinct spatiotemporal variation characteristics. Initially, within the first 2 to 5 h post-main shock, the aftershocks predominantly aligned in a northwest–southeast (NW–SE) orientation, forming a strip-like distribution. This pattern underwent a notable shift approximately 5 h later, with the emergence of a northeast–southwest (NE–SW) directional trend in the aftershock distribution. This NE–SW orientation became increasingly pronounced over the subsequent 24 h. Remarkably, after five days, the aftershock sequence evolved to display an asymmetric conjugate distribution, further illustrating the dynamic nature of the seismic event's aftershock activity.

The focal mechanism solutions for the two nodal planes, as published by the Global Centroid Moment Tensor (GCMT) [32,33], were consistent with the dominant orientations of the L-shaped conjugate distribution of aftershocks. On the other hand, this spatiotemporal patterning of the Ludian aftershock sequence concurred with the observations presented in the works of Fang et al. [25] and Wang et al. [34]. The consistency of these findings across independent studies lends credence to the interpretation of the tectonic behavior in the aftermath of the Ludian earthquake and reinforces the understanding of seismic dynamics in conjugate fault systems.

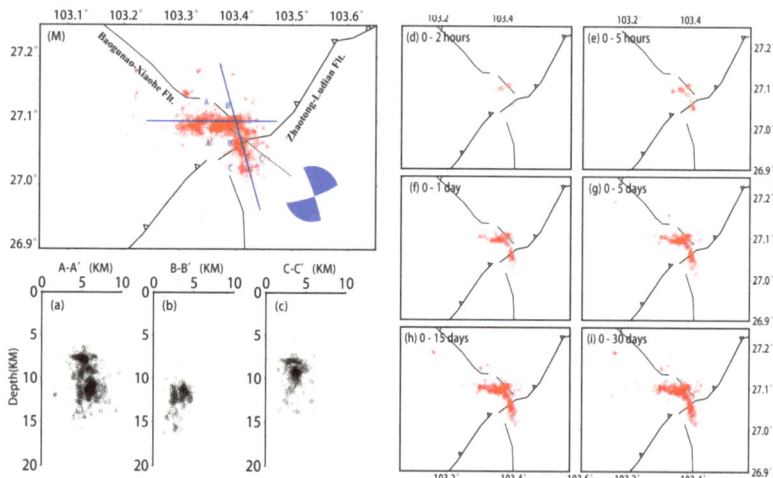

Figure 7. The space distribution and temporal evolution of the Ludian aftershocks. (**M**) The spatial horizontal distribution of the Ludian aftershocks. (**a–c**) The depth of aftershocks along three profiles shown in (**M**). A-A′, B-B′, and C-C′ represent three different depth profiles corresponding to subfigures (**a–c**), respectively. Insert figures (**d–i**) illustrate the temporal evolution of aftershocks within 30 days after the main shock. The focal mechanism is from the Global Centroid Moment Tensor Project (https://www.globalcmt.org/) (accessed on 5 February 2024) [32,33].

4.2. Seismic Rate Evolution

The seismic rate, defined as the frequency of earthquakes occurring per hour, peaked within the initial day following the main shock, and thereafter exhibited a general diminishing trend. This decay in seismic rate over time is a typical characteristic of aftershock sequence, as postulated by established seismic laws, such as Omori's law for aftershock temporal decay. The observed magnitude-time relationship and seismic rate for the aftershocks also presented conspicuous diurnal patterns. These patterns were discerned to be linked to the diurnal variations in the ambient noise level, which in turn affected the earthquake detection capability of the monitoring system. During periods of heightened daily noise—such as human activity during daytime hours—the ability to detect smaller seismic events is often compromised. Conversely, the relative quietude of nighttime generally corresponds to higher detection rates of smaller aftershocks.

Furthermore, the seismic detection capability is also temporally affected by the 'tail waves' of larger seismic events. These trailing seismic waves generate a transient increase in the noise floor, which can substantially diminish the detection efficiency for smaller magnitude earthquakes in the period following significant aftershocks. The impact of these larger events on detection capability is visually represented in Figure 8, which likely includes a time series plot showing the variation in seismic rate alongside the occurrence of larger aftershocks. Such fluctuations in detection capability necessitate careful consideration when analyzing seismicity rates and the corresponding magnitude distributions. These variations underscore the importance of incorporating noise level assessments and potential detection biases into the seismic analysis to ensure the accurate interpretation of seismicity patterns and the underlying physical processes driving the aftershock sequence.

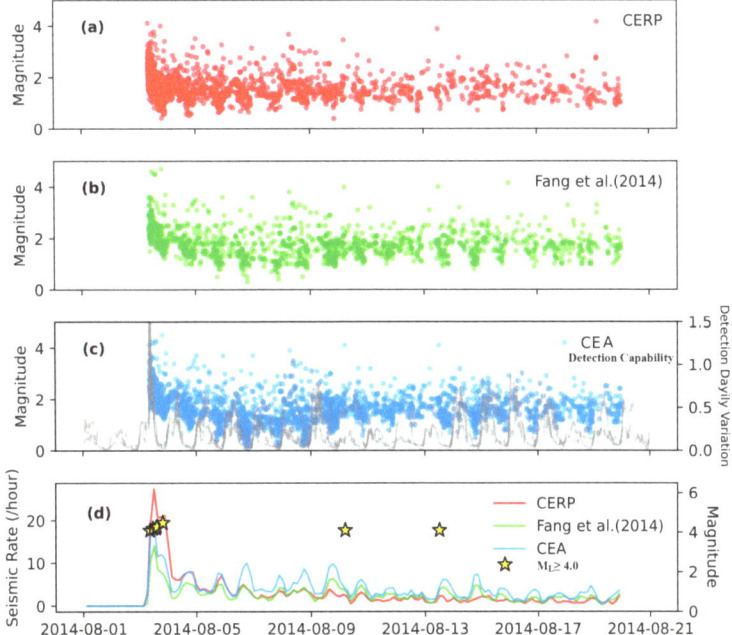

Figure 8. Seismicity–time distribution of the Ludian aftershock catalog. (**a–c**) The earthquake catalogs obtained in this study (CERP), the earthquake catalog by Fang Lihua et al. [25] and the earthquake catalog from the China Earthquake Administration (CEA) regional seismic network, respectively. Panel (**d**) shows the seismicity rate calculated from the three earthquake catalogs between 1 August 2014 and 21 August 2014. The seismicity rate is defined as the number of earthquakes occurring per hour in the region.

5. Discussion

5.1. The 2014 Ludian Earthquake's Seismogenic Fault and Its Tectonic Implications

Within the vicinity of the epicenter, the NE-oriented Zhaotong–Ludian fault is primarily recognized for its thrust faulting. However, the focal mechanism of strike–slip and the spatial-temporal pattern of aftershocks, which align predominantly along NW–SE and near E–W directions, imply that the Zhaotong–Ludian fault may not be the only seismogenic fault. The presence of the NW-oriented Baogunao–Xiaohe fault, noted for its left-lateral strike–slip movement, provides an alternative tectonic feature that corresponds more closely with the aftershock distribution and focal mechanism. Particularly within the first 5 h following the main shock, the predominance of aftershocks in the NW–SE direction, coupled with their depth characteristics consistent with a strike–slip fault, suggested that the Baogunao–Xiaohe Fault may have been the seismogenic fault for the Ludian earthquake. Synthesizing the aftershocks' spatial-temporal pattern, the focal mechanism, and the intrinsic characteristics of the regional faults, we inferred that the seismogenic fault responsible for the Ludian earthquake is the NW-oriented Baogunao–Xiaohe fault.

The distribution of the NW-trending Ludian aftershocks, intersecting the NE-trending Zhaotong–Ludian fault, suggests that the former may be transecting the latter. This intersection could imply that the Zhaotong–Ludian fault, despite its longstanding geological presence, has been intersected and possibly offset by the younger Baogunao–Xiaohe fault, a tectonic feature that may have developed during the Cenozoic era [25]. Furthermore, geological structural maps indicate that the Baogunao–Xiaohe Fault is a minor and less distinct fault located north of the Zhaotong–Ludian Fault. On the south side of the Zhaotong–Ludian Fault lies another small fault, with both minor faults being separated by the Zhaotong–Ludian Fault. Based on these, we assumed that the 2014 Ludian earthquake may have interconnected the Baogunao–Xiaohe Fault across the north and south sides of the Zhaotong–Ludian Fault.

5.2. The Future Application of This Retraining Strategy

Previous researchers have attempted to train high-generalization AI models using large-scale global datasets to address phase-picking challenges [18,19,35]. However, these efforts have fallen short of achieving the desired results in complex real-world scenarios. This suggests that the approach of relying on massive global datasets to solve the generalization problem may not be feasible. In contrast, this study explores the use of small, easily obtainable datasets to retrain AI models for specific scenarios, aiming to improve model applicability in those specific contexts. We employed both traditional automated algorithms, STA/LTA and Kurtosis, for P and S phase detection, applying multi-station constraints to eliminate erroneous data. Data augmentation techniques were applied to expand the dataset for training precise AI models. Therefore, this re-training strategy is highly adaptable and flexible, theoretically applicable to different earthquake events and tectonic regions. Our successful results further demonstrated that this AI re-training strategy can generate a high-performance AI model suitable for specific scenarios. However, it relies on a well-distributed network. The well-distributed network influences the accuracy of the phase association process and further affects the generation of high-accuracy event samples.

6. Conclusions

A high-resolution catalog for the 2014 Ms 6.5 Ludian aftershocks is constructed based on an AI-picker model. During the AI model training process, we designed a specific training strategy that combines the advantages of the STA/LTA and AI algorithms. Our successful retraining and detection results indicate that this training strategy for building a sample set in a specific tectonic region to retrain the AI model can improve the generalization performance of the AI model in the specific region. Compared to the previous results from the Fang et al. [25] and China Earthquake Networks Center (CENC), our result exhibits superior performance in location accuracy and the number of aftershock events. According to the accurate distribution of aftershocks, we conclude that (1) the seismogenic fault of the Ludian earthquake is the NW-trending Baogunao–Xiaohe Fault; (2) the Ludian aftershocks interconnected with the discontinuous NW-trending Baogunao–Xiaohe Fault, and intersected with the Zhaotong–Ludian Fault; and (3) this suggests that the NE-trending Zhaotong–Ludian Fault may have been intersected by the NW-trending Baogunao–Xiaohe Fault, indicating that the Baogunao–Xiaohe Fault is likely a relatively young Neogene fault.

Author Contributions: Conceptualization, J.L. and M.H.; methodology, J.L.; software, J.L.; validation, M.H. and Z.C.; formal analysis, J.L.; investigation, J.L.; resources, M.H.; data curation, J.L.; writing—original draft preparation, J.L.; writing—review and editing, M.H. and Z.C.; visualization, J.L. and Z.C.; project administration, M.H.; funding acquisition, M.H. All authors have read and agreed to the published version of the manuscript.

Funding: This research was jointly funded by the National Natural Science Foundation of China (NSFC) projects (grant numbers: U2139205 and 42374140), National Observation and Research Station, Institute of Geology, China Earthquake Administration (NORSLS23-05), the Natural Science Basic Research Program of Shaanxi (Program numbers: 2024JC-YBQN-0313, 2024JC-YBQN-0334 and 2022JQ-235), and the Special Key Project of the Basic Research Service Fee of the Institute of Earthquake Forecasting, China Earthquake Administration (CEAIEF2022030100).

Institutional Review Board Statement: Not applicable.

Informed Consent Statement: Not applicable.

Data Availability Statement: Seismic waveform data can be applied for and downloaded from the International Earthquake Science Data Center (http://www.esdc.ac.cn/). Fault data can be download from the China Seismic Experimental Site (http://www.cses.ac.cn/).

Acknowledgments: The authors thank Zhou Yijian and Fang Lihua for their guidance and assistance in the methods and conceptualization of this study and thank Xu Lisheng for providing mobile seismic data in the Ludian region. The authors also thank Wang Qingliang for his valuable contributions to this research.

Conflicts of Interest: All of the authors declare no conflict of interest.

References

1. Shelly, D.R. A High-Resolution Seismic Catalog for the Initial 2019 Ridgecrest Earthquake Sequence: Foreshocks, Aftershocks, and Faulting Complexity. *Seismol. Res. Lett.* **2020**, *91*, 1971–1978. [CrossRef]
2. Ross, Z.E.; Idini, B.; Jia, Z.; Stephenson, O.L.; Zhong, M.Y.; Wang, X.; Zhan, Z.W.; Simons, M.; Fielding, E.J.; Yun, S.H.; et al. Hierarchical interlocked orthogonal faulting in the 2019 Ridgecrest earthquake sequence. *Science* **2019**, *366*, 346–351. [CrossRef]
3. Ross, Z.E.; Trugman, D.T.; Hauksson, E.; Shearer, P.M. Searching for hidden earthquakes in Southern California. *Science* **2019**, *364*, 767–771. [CrossRef]
4. Geiger, L. Probability method for the determination of earthquake epicentres from the arrival time only. *Bull. St. Louis Univ.* **1912**, *8*, 60.
5. Lee, W.H.K.; Lahr, J.C. *HYPO71: A Computer Program for Determining Hypocenter, Magnitude, and First Motion Pattern of Local Earthquakes*; US Department of the Interior, Geological Survey, National Center for Earthquake Reasearch: Reston, VA, USA, 1972.
6. Klein, F.W. *Hypocenter Location Program HYPOINVERSE: Part I. Users Guide to Versions 1, 2, 3, and 4. Part II. Source Listings and Notes*; US Geological Survey: Reston, VA, USA, 1978.
7. Klein, F.W. *User's Guide to HYPOINVERSE-2000, a Fortran Program to Solve for Earthquake Locations and Magnitudes*; Open-File Report; US Geological Survey: Reston, VA, USA, 2002.
8. Lienert, B.R.; Berg, E.; Frazer, L.N. HYPOCENTER: An earthquake location method using centered, scaled, and adaptively damped least squares. *Bull. Seismol. Soc. Am.* **1986**, *76*, 771–783. [CrossRef]
9. Nelson, G.D.; Vidale, J.E. Earthquake locations by 3-D finite-difference travel times. *Bull. Seismol. Soc. Am.* **1990**, *80*, 395–410. [CrossRef]
10. Waldhauser, F.; Ellsworth, W. A double-difference earthquake location algorithm: Method and application to the northern Hayward fault, California. *Bull. Seismol. Soc. Am.* **2000**, *90*, 1353–1368. [CrossRef]
11. Gibbons, S.J.; Ringdal, F. The detection of low magnitude seismic events using array-based waveform correlation. *Geophys. J. Int.* **2006**, *165*, 149–166. [CrossRef]
12. Zhang, M.; Wen, L. An effective method for small event detection: Match and locate (M&L). *Geophys. J. Int.* **2015**, *200*, 1523–1537.
13. Allen, R.V. Automatic earthquake recognition and timing from single traces. *Bull. Seismol. Soc. Am.* **1978**, *68*, 1521–1532. [CrossRef]
14. Zhou, Y.J.; Yue, H.; Kong, Q.K.; Zhou, S.Y. Hybrid Event Detection and Phase-Picking Algorithm Using Convolutional and Recurrent Neural Networks. *Seismol. Res. Lett.* **2019**, *90*, 1079–1087. [CrossRef]
15. LeCun, Y.; Bengio, Y.; Hinton, G. Deep learning. *Nature* **2015**, *521*, 436–444. [CrossRef]
16. Perol, T.; Gharbi, M.; Denolle, M. Convolutional neural network for earthquake detection and location. *Sci. Adv.* **2018**, *4*, e1700578. [CrossRef]
17. Mousavi, S.M.; Zhu, W.Q.; Sheng, Y.X.; Beroza, G.C. CRED: A Deep Residual Network of Convolutional and Recurrent Units for Earthquake Signal Detection. *Sci. Rep.* **2019**, *9*, 10267. [CrossRef]
18. Mousavi, S.M.; Ellsworth, W.L.; Zhu, W.Q.; Chuang, L.Y.; Beroza, G.C. Earthquake transformer—An attentive deep-learning model for simultaneous earthquake detection and phase picking. *Nat. Commun.* **2020**, *11*, 3952. [CrossRef] [PubMed]
19. Zhu, W.Q.; Beroza, G.C. PhaseNet: A Deep-Neural-Network-Based Seismic Arrival Time Picking Method. *Geophys. J. Int.* **2018**, *216*, 261–273. [CrossRef]
20. Zhu, W.; McBrearty, I.W.; Mousavi, S.M.; Ellsworth, W.L.; Beroza, G.C. Earthquake Phase Association Using a Bayesian Gaussian Mixture Model. *J. Geophys. Res. Solid Earth* **2022**, *127*, e2021JB023249. [CrossRef]
21. Zhang, M.; Liu, M.; Feng, T.; Wang, R.; Zhu, W. LOC-FLOW: An End-to-End Machine Learning-Based High-Precision Earthquake Location Workflow. *Seismol. Res. Lett.* **2022**, *93*, 2426–2438. [CrossRef]
22. Zhou, Y.J.; Yue, H.; Fang, L.H.; Zhou, S.Y.; Zhao, L.; Ghosh, A. An Earthquake Detection and Location Architecture for Continuous Seismograms: Phase Picking, Association, Location, and Matched Filter (PALM). *Seismol. Res. Lett.* **2021**, *93*, 413–425. [CrossRef]
23. Mousavi, S.M.; Sheng, Y.X.; Zhu, W.Q.; Beroza, G.C. STanford EArthquake Dataset (STEAD): A Global Data Set of Seismic Signals for AI. *IEEE Access* **2019**, *7*, 179464–179476. [CrossRef]
24. Zhao, M.; Xiao, Z.W.; Chen, S.; Fang, L.H. DiTing: A large-scale Chinese seismic benchmark dataset for artificial intelligence in seismology. *Earthq. Sci.* **2023**, *36*, 84–94. [CrossRef]
25. Fang, L.H.; Wu, J.P.; Wang, W.L.; Lv, Z.Y.; Wang, C.Z.; Yang, T.; Zhong, S.J. Relocation of the aftershock sequence of the M S 6.5 Ludian earthquake and its seismogenic structure. *Seismol. Geol.* **2014**, *36*, 1173–1185.
26. Wen, X.Z.; Du, F.; Yi, G.X.; Long, F.; Fan, J.; Yang, F.X.; Xiong, R.W.; Liu, Q.X.; Liu, Q. Earthquake potential of the Zhaotong and Lianfeng fault zones of the eastern Sichuan-Yunnan border region. *Chin. J. Geophys.* **2013**, *56*, 3361–3372.

27. He, H.L.; Ikeda, Y.; He, Y.L.; Togo, M.; Chen, J.; Chen, C.Y.; Tajikara, M.; Echigo, T.; Okada, S. Newly-generated Daliangshan fault zone—Shortcutting on the central section of Xianshuihe-Xiaojiang fault system. *Sci. China Ser. D Earth Sci.* **2008**, *51*, 1248–1258. [CrossRef]
28. Xu, X.W.; Wen, X.Z.; Zheng, R.Z.; Ma, W.T.; Song, F.M.; Yu, G.H. Pattern of latest tectonic motion and its dynamics for active blocks in Sichuan-Yunnan region, China. *Sci. China Ser. D Earth Sci.* **2003**, *46*, 210–226. [CrossRef]
29. Baillard, C.; Crawford, W.C.; Ballu, V.; Hibert, C.; Mangeney, A. An Automatic Kurtosis-Based P- and S-Phase Picker Designed for Local Seismic Networks. *Bull. Seismol. Soc. Am.* **2013**, *104*, 394–409. [CrossRef]
30. Zhou, Y.Y.; Ghosh, A.; Fang, L.H.; Yue, H.; Zhou, S.Y.; Su, Y.J. A high-resolution seismic catalog for the 2021 MS6.4/MW6.1 Yangbi earthquake sequence, Yunnan, China: Application of AI picker and matched filter. *Earthq. Sci.* **2021**, *34*, 390–398. [CrossRef]
31. Waldhauser, F.; Ellsworth, W.L. Fault structure and mechanics of the Hayward Fault, California, from double-difference earthquake locations. *J. Geophys. Res. Solid Earth* **2002**, *107*, ESE 3-1–ESE 3-15. [CrossRef]
32. Dziewonski, A.M.; Chou, T.A.; Woodhouse, J.H. Determination of earthquake source parameters from waveform data for studies of global and regional seismicity. *J. Geophys. Res. Solid Earth* **1981**, *86*, 2825–2852. [CrossRef]
33. Ekström, G.; Nettles, M.; Dziewoński, A.M. The global CMT project 2004–2010: Centroid-moment tensors for 13,017 earthquakes. *Phys. Earth Planet. Inter.* **2012**, *200–201*, 1–9. [CrossRef]
34. Wang, W.; Wu, J.; Fang, L.; Juan, L. Double difference location of the Ludian MS6.5 earthquake sequences in Yunnan province in 2014. *Chin. J. Geophys.* **2014**, *57*, 3042–3051. (In Chinese)
35. Ross, Z.E.; Meier, M.A.; Hauksson, E.; Heaton, T.H. Generalized Seismic Phase Detection with Deep Learning. *Bull. Seismol. Soc. Am.* **2018**, *108*, 2894–2901. [CrossRef]

Disclaimer/Publisher's Note: The statements, opinions and data contained in all publications are solely those of the individual author(s) and contributor(s) and not of MDPI and/or the editor(s). MDPI and/or the editor(s) disclaim responsibility for any injury to people or property resulting from any ideas, methods, instructions or products referred to in the content.

Article

A Seismic Inversion Method Based on Multi-Scale Super-Asymmetric Cycle-JNet Network

Mingming Tang [1,2,*], Boyang Huang [1,2], Rong Xie [1,2] and Zhenzhen Chen [1,2]

1. Key Laboratory of Deep Oil and Gas, China University of Petroleum (East China), Qingdao 266580, China; z21010028@s.upc.edu.cn (B.H.); z22010093@s.upc.edu.cn (R.X.); z21010029@s.upc.edu.cn (Z.C.)
2. School of Geosciences, China University of Petroleum (East China), Qingdao 266580, China
* Correspondence: tangmingming@upc.edu.cn

Abstract: In order to improve the resolution and accuracy of seismic inversion, this study constructs a multi-scale super-asymmetric network (Cycle-JNet). In this model, wavelet analysis is used to capture the multi-scale data characteristics of well-seismic data, thereby improving the machine's ability to learn details. Using the UNet neural network from Convolutional Neural Network (CNN), we modified the network structure by adding several convolution kernel layers at the output end to expand generated data, solving the problem of mismatched resolutions in well-seismic data, thus improving the resolution of seismic inversion and achieving the purpose of accurately identifying thin sandstone layers. Meanwhile, a cycle structure of Recurrent Neural Network (RNN) was designed for the secondary learning of the seismic data generated by JNet. By comparing the data transformed through inverse wavelet transform with the original data again, the accuracy of machine learning can be improved. After optimization, the Cycle-JNet model significantly outperforms traditional seismic inversion methods in terms of resolution and accuracy. This indicates that this method can provide more precise inversion results in more complex data environments, providing stronger support for seismic analysis.

Keywords: seismic; inversion; wavelet transform; deep learning; Cycle-JNet

Citation: Tang, M.; Huang, B.; Xie, R.; Chen, Z. A Seismic Inversion Method Based on Multi-Scale Super-Asymmetric Cycle-JNet Network. *Appl. Sci.* **2024**, *14*, 242. https://doi.org/10.3390/app14010242

Academic Editor: Jong Wan Hu

Received: 9 November 2023
Revised: 15 December 2023
Accepted: 21 December 2023
Published: 27 December 2023

Copyright: © 2023 by the authors. Licensee MDPI, Basel, Switzerland. This article is an open access article distributed under the terms and conditions of the Creative Commons Attribution (CC BY) license (https://creativecommons.org/licenses/by/4.0/).

1. Introduction

Seismic inversion, as a crucial reservoir characterization technique, has received extensive research attention over the past decades. Seismic inversion takes seismic data as input and converts the observed data into rock physics parameters by a mapping model. However, most existing seismic inversion methods, which are largely model-based, often exhibit lower accuracy and resolution when faced with complex seismic information. With the recent widespread application of deep learning across various domains, the technology has also begun to have a significant impact on seismic inversion. Many researchers are now utilizing diverse neural networks to establish inversion mapping models and achieve the mapping of seismic data to wave impedance, aiming to enhance the precision and resolution of seismic inversion.

Conventional seismic inversion theories mainly rely on convolutional modeling, initially proposed by Cooke et al. in 1983 [1]. Later, Debe and Van in 1990 presented an iterative sparse pulse inversion method [2], and Hass and Dubrule introduced the concept of geostatistical inversion using sequential simulation algorithms based on seismic data in 1994 [3]. Combining recursive inversion, constrained sparse pulse inversion, and neural network inversion, Zhang et al. achieved highly accurate results reflecting reservoir properties in 2009 [4]. Recently, Sheng et al. proposed Seisminc Motion Inversion (SMI) in 2015 [5]. Traditional seismic inversions typically involve establishing target equations based on assumptions about inversion equations and imposing certain constraints to solve them, yet real geological conditions and data complexity render it difficult to express these problems in a single explicit manner. There are great challenges in both the creation of inverse equations and the solution of such equations.

In recent years, deep learning has developed rapidly in many fields [6]. Compared with traditional seismology and seismic engineering methods, the machine learning method has the advantages of processing large numbers of data, a diversity in processing data types, and high precision prediction ability. Therefore, many researchers use machine learning methods to deal with the problems of processing seismic wave equations, seismic detection and phase selection, seismic early warning (EEW), ground motion prediction, seismic tomography and seismic geodesy, etc. [7–10]. Meanwhile, in the study of seismic inversion, through various deep learning frameworks and model examples [11–13], researchers have found that neural networks can be used to construct inversion mapping models and realize the mapping of seismic data to wave impedance. The advantage of this method is that it can avoid complex mathematical equation modeling and solving and can complete feature learning, extraction, and prediction in one iteration. By jointly optimizing all parameters, errors are expected to be reduced and the entire processing process simplified. Therefore, many researchers have begun to explore seismic wave impedance inversion methods based on deep learning [14–21].

At present, the main types of networks applicable to the inversion of seismic wave impedance include Convolutional Neural Networks (CNN) [22] and Recurrent Neural Networks (RNN) [23]. UNet is a network structure commonly used in CNN. U-Net was first proposed by Ronneberger in 2015 and successfully applied to medical image segmentation [24]. UNet is named for its simple and elegant network structure and U-shaped architecture. UNet is a network structure evolved from convolutional neural networks, which can combine the deep and shallow information in the network structure to achieve pixel-level image semantic segmentation. However, due to the mismatch between the resolution of well curve data and seismic data, as well as an insufficient ability to integrate and learn global information [25], learning seismic data solely by relying on the network structure of UNet is not conducive to the identification of sand bodies of different thickness. Therefore, a structural improvement in the UNet network is carried out to improve its accuracy and resolution by adding the Cycle network.

In order to process and interpret complex seismic data and improve the learning efficiency of the machine, this study uses wavelet analysis to capture multi-scale data features of seismic data. Previously, the method based on wavelet transform has been widely used in seismic time–frequency analysis [26,27]. Compared with the traditional time–frequency decomposition method for processing seismic data, wavelet transform overcomes the fixed spectral resolution of Fourier Transform (STFT) for time–frequency analysis [28] and has a rather high spectral resolution.

Current intelligent seismic inversion usually uses various simple networks to directly train various seismic data sets, and the characteristics of frequent frequency changes and an insufficient resolution of seismic data are ignored [14–21]. Compared with the current intelligent seismic inversion methods, this study uses wavelet analysis to capture data characteristics, realize the separation of seismic data of different frequencies, and learn them separately to improve learning efficiency and accuracy. At the same time, the UNet network is taken as the main structure, and its structure is designed and improved according to the particularity of seismic data, so as to improve its learning ability and resolution. In this paper, a new and reliable prediction model for seismic inversion is established, namely a multi-scale super-asymmetric single-attribute Cycle-JNet network simulation model. This article is structured as follows. Section 2 introduces wavelet transform and the construction of the Cycle-JNet network. Section 3 explains the data used and the exploratory analysis of the data. In Section 4, the structure and prediction accuracy of the model are evaluated.

2. Multi-Scale Superasymmetric Network (Cycle-JNet) Method

In order to solve the problem that the traditional inversion method has poor processing ability for complex seismic data and a low recognition accuracy for the thin sand body interface, the Cycle-JNet network simulation model used in this study combines wavelet transform with a variety of deep learning methods to build a multi-scale super-asymmetric network (Cycle-JNet) seismic intelligent inversion method.

2.1. Wavelet Transform

Wavelet transform plays an important role in various signal processing applications [29–31]. Among them, discrete wavelet transform (DWT) can decompose the signal into several wavelets, which is an ideal tool to map the change characteristics of unsteady signals. As shown in Figure 1, this is the basic principle of DWT. Seismic data processed by DWT will show the characteristics of multi-scale and high resolution, which helps in improving the accuracy of machine learning and thus improving the accuracy and resolution of inversion results.

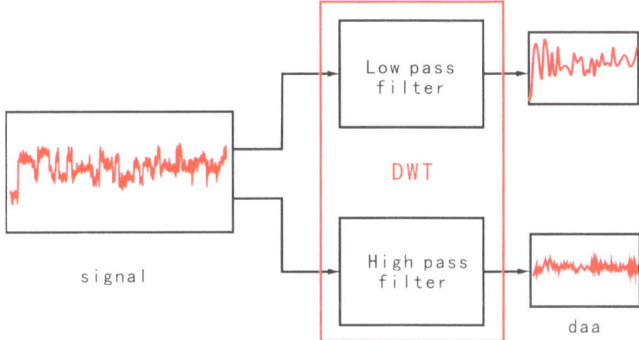

Figure 1. DWT working diagram.

DWT is the convolution between the data sequence and the parent wavelet. The mother wavelet ψ is:

$$\psi_{a,b}(t) = |a|^{-1/2} \psi\left(\frac{t-b}{a}\right), \ a, b \in R, \ a \neq 0 \quad (1)$$

where a is the scaling factor and b is the translation factor. The inversion target of seismic inversion body P(t) is the mud content, and its DWT is defined as:

$$P(a,b) = |a|^{-1/2} \int P(t) \overline{\psi}\left(\frac{t-b}{a}\right) dt = \langle P(t), \psi_{a,b}(t) \rangle \quad (2)$$

where P(a,b) is the wavelet coefficient. Common mother wavelet functions include Mexican-hat wavelet, Morlet wavelet, and so on. This paper focuses on the wavelet decomposition of well vibration curve data. In the curve data, the sand value is 0, and the mud value is 1; the composition of sand and mud changes frequently and complicatedly. The db 1 wavelet in Daubechies wavelet [32] is selected to analyze the characteristics of well seismic data, because it has low complexity and strong mutation detection ability, which can improve the calculation efficiency and accurately identify the frequently changing mud. However, the decomposition of other wavelets in Daubechies wavelet, such as db 2 and db 4, is too complex and too computationally intensive to be suitable for a large number of well vibration data. The permissible conditions for Daubechies wavelets used in this study are:

$$C_\psi = \int \frac{|\hat{\psi}(\omega)|}{|\omega|} d\omega < \infty \quad (3)$$

In Equation (3), $\hat{\psi}(\omega)$ is obtained after the Fourier transform of $\psi(t)$. After the inverse transformation of Equation (2), the following equation is obtained:

$$P(t) = C_\psi^{-1} \iint \frac{P(a,b)\psi_{a,b}(t)}{a^2} da db \tag{4}$$

The negative frequency of $\hat{\psi}(\omega)$ has no meaning; therefore, Equation (4) can be written as Equation (5):

$$P(t) = 2C_\psi^{-1} \int_0^\infty \int_0^\infty \frac{P(a,b)\psi_{a,b}(t)}{a^2} da db \tag{5}$$

In order to improve calculation speed and reduce data redundancy, the scale and displacement parameters of DWT are amplified. The discrete mother wavelet function can be defined as

$$\psi_{j,k}(t) = a_0^{-j/2} \psi\left(a_0^{-j/2} t - kb_0\right), \, j, k \in Z \tag{6}$$

In a J level decomposition, $j = 1 + 2 + \ldots + J$.

The dilated and translated basis functions at different resolution levels are described by the scaling function, which is called the father wavelet $\Phi_{j,k}(t)$ and is given by

$$\Phi_{j,k}(t) = a_0^{-j/2} \Phi\left(a_0^{-j/2} t - kb_0\right), \, j, k \in Z \tag{7}$$

where a_0 and b_0 are the scale factors and J is the scale level. By using these two basic wavelet functions, the DWT approximation of the well shock data can be extended to the following:

$$P(t) \approx \sum_j \sum_k x_{j,k} \Phi_{j,k}(t) \approx \sum_k S_{J,K} \Phi_{J,K}(t) + \sum_k dS_{J,K} \psi_{J,K}(t) + \ldots + \sum_k dS_{1,K} \psi_{1,K}(t) \approx \sum_k S_{J,K} \Phi_{J,K}(t) + \sum_j \sum_k d_{j,k} \psi_{J,K}(t) \tag{8}$$

where $S_{J,K}$ and $d_{j,k}$ are smooth and detailed component coefficients representing the trend and random component of the seismic data, respectively, and have:

$$S_{J,K} = \int \Phi_{j,k}(t) P(t) dt, \, d_{J,K} = \int \psi_{j,k}(t) P(t) dt \tag{9}$$

To enable the effective decomposition of seismic data features at different frequencies and increase machine learning efficiency and accuracy, it is necessary to determine a reasonable number of decomposition layers. In the actual wavelet decomposition, although eight results can be obtained from the well vibration data, there are only two different resolutions in fact, and the other six results are the mappings of the two results in different dimensions. This is because the decomposition object is the well curve and has one dimension, so the number of decomposition layers for each dimension is 2. Figure 2 shows the seismic data and well curve data after DWT. The high and low frequency data of seismic data and well curve after DWT are separated, which is conducive to machine learning.

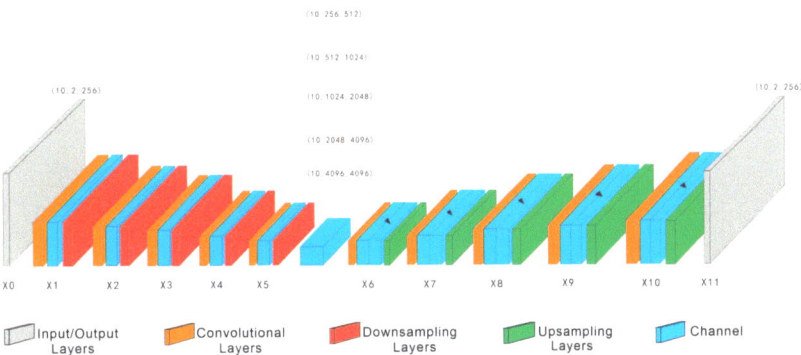

Figure 2. Schematic diagram of the UNet neural network.

2.2. Cycle-JNet

The UNet network is called UNet because of its symmetrical structure, which resembles the letter U. The structure is shown in Figure 2: the gray layer is Input/Output Layers, the orange layer is Convolution Layers, the red layer is Downsampling Layers, the green layer is Upsampling Layers, and the red layer is Channel (channel is one of the dimensions of the input data or feature map, which is different types of features in the same spatial position). The network mainly extracts the detailed feature information of the data by using Encoder and decodes and restores the size of the original data by using Decoder, which can effectively extract the details in the seismic data after wavelet transform.

Although the resolution of well curve data (about 0.625 ms) is much higher than that of seismic data (2 ms), the resolution of the well curve data generated is actually consistent with that of seismic data due to the symmetry of its structure when using the UNet network for training. It not only reduces the accuracy of machine learning, but the seismic resolution of Vsh properties produced by the trained network inversion is also low, which is not conducive to the identification of sand bodies of different thickness. In this study, several layers of convolution kernel are added to the output end of the UNet network to expand the data generated by the machine, so that the resolution of the output end is greatly increased, which is consistent with the well data. Because its structure is like the letter "J", it is named JNet. The structure is shown in Figure 3; the legend in the figure is consistent with that in Figure 2. The original network is called "thick sand identification network (TSIN)", which can distinguish and learn the thick sand body and muddy layers in seismic data. The convolution kernel expanded at the output end is called "super-resolution thin sand identification network (SR-TSIN)", and it can distinguish and learn the details of high-resolution seismic data after wavelet transform, so as to improve the data learning and output seismic body resolution.

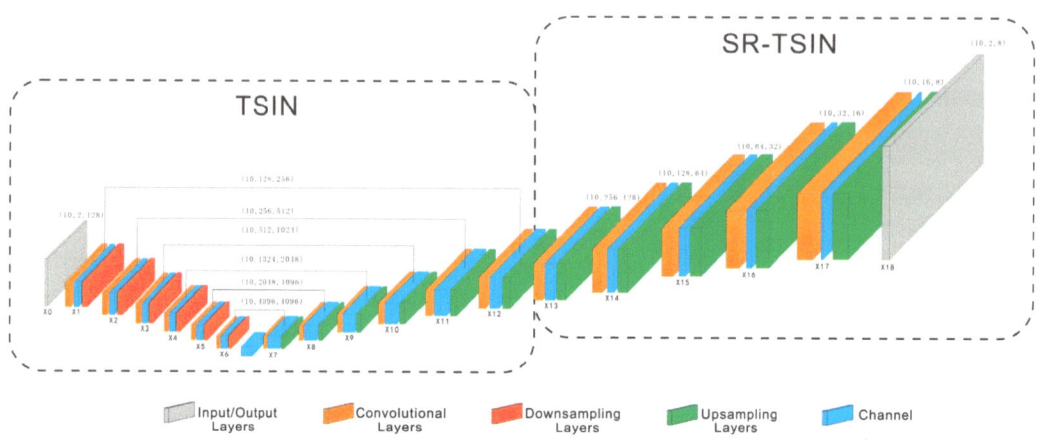

Figure 3. Schematic diagram of the JNet neural network structure.

The Cycle-JNet network built in this study uses the following hyperparameters: The batch size of samples processed at one time is 10; the sample size (well vibration data) is $128 \times 4 \times 4$; the sampling interval was 8; learning factor lr = 0.001; initial channel = 2, convolution kernel size = 4, stride = 2, padding = 1. There are seven convolution layers in the discriminant network and 11 deconvolution layers in the generative network (seven in TSIN; SR-TSIN has five layers). The input channel of the first layer X_0 is 2, and the output channel is 128. The input channel of the second layer X_1 of the discriminant network is 128, and the output channel is 256. The input channel and output channel of the third layer X_2 of discriminant network are 256 and 512, respectively. The input channel of the fourth layer X_3 is 512 and the output channel is 1024. The input channel of the fifth layer X_4 is 1024, and the output channel is 2048. The input channel and output channel of X_5 of the sixth layer of the discriminant network are 2048 and 4096, respectively. The input channel and output channel of the seventh layer X_6 of the discriminant network are 4096 and 4096, respectively. The input channel and output channel of the first layer X_7 of the generation network are 4096 and 4096, respectively. The input channel of the second layer X_8 of the generation network is 8192, and the output channel is 2048. The input channel of the third layer X_9 of the generation network is 4096, and the output channel is 1024. The input channel of the fourth layer X_{10} of the generation network is 2048, and the output channel is 512. The input channel of Layer 5 X_{11} of the generation network is 1024, and the output channel is 256. The input channel of X_{12} of the sixth layer of the generation network is 512, and the output channel is 128. The input channel of the seventh layer X_{13} of the generation network is 256, and the output channel is 128. The input channel of the eighth layer X_{14} of the generation network is 128, and the output channel is 64. The input channel of X_{15} at layer 9 of the generation network is 64, and the output channel is 32. The input channel of X_{16} of the tenth layer of the generation network is 32, and the output channel is 16. The input channel of X_{17} of the eleventh layer of the generation network is 16, and the output channel is 8. The input channel of Layer 12 X_{18} of the generation network is 8, and the output channel is 2. The optimization function is Adam, the loss function is MCEloss, the activation function of layers X_0 to X_{17} is LeakyReLU, layer X_{18} is Sigmoid, and the epoch is 200.

Since JNet is a convolution-based inversion network, the learning ability of the global information correlation of seismic data is defective [25], which affects the accuracy of inversion results. Therefore, a Cycle network is introduced to improve the accuracy of machine learning. In actual network operation, due to the 1D nature of well curve data, there are only two scales of effective information when db1 wavelet transform is performed. Therefore, the well shock data will be decomposed into eight results after DWT. However, due to the 1D nature of well shock data, there are only two effective results, namely low-resolution well shock data (aaa) and high-resolution well shock data (daa), and the other results are the mapping of them in different dimensions.

Based on the two-resolution information, in order to improve efficiency and accuracy, the Cycle-JNet network is designed as two parallel aaa networks and daa networks; the structure is shown in Figure 4. Take the aaa network as an example, where "real" is defined as actual well shock data, "fake" is defined as machine-generated fake well shock data, and "R" and "F" are short for "real" and "fake". In the process of network operation, the low-frequency seismic data of real seismic data Segy (real) after DWT are called Segy (R-aaa), and the high-frequency seismic data are called Segy (R-daa). Segy (R-aaa) is input into the forward convolution network JNet (S1-aaa) of the aaa network to obtain Vsh (F-aaa), which is a false well curve corresponding to Segy (R-aaa), that is, the Vsh curve considered by the machine in the aaa network. The purpose of forward training is to let the network learn the correspondence between seismic data and well data, and linearly add the residuals obtained by the two aaa networks and daa networks to obtain the residual Loss1 (S1) of the JNet (S1) network, that is, the weight of the S1 network under the network. Then, Vsh (F-aaa) output from JNet (S1-aaa) is reversely input into the JNet (S2) of the aaa network to convolve Vsh (F-aaa) and generate false seismic data Segy (F-aaa) generated according to Vsh (F-aaa) under the aaa network. At the same time, the daa network generates the corresponding false seismic data Segy (F-daa), and the purpose of reverse training is to let the network learn the correspondence between well data and seismic data, carry out inverse wavelet transform (IWT) on Segy (F-aaa) and Segy (F-daa), and combine the seismic data of the two scales into one. By comparing the fake seismic data SegY (fake) with the real seismic data SegY (real), the residual Loss2 (S2) of the JNet (S2) network can be obtained, that is, the weight of the S2 network under the network. Total residual Loss (S) is the linear addition of Loss1 (S1) and Loss2 (S2). Using Loss (S) to optimize JNet (S1) and JNet (S2), the machine is then allowed to enter the next round of training and learning. Thus, the forward training network JNet (S1-aaa) and JNet (S1-daa) with ideal results can be obtained in multiple samples and long training time. In actual seismic inversion generation, select the ideal network JNet (S1-aaa) and JNet (S1-daa) to generate two seismic inversions with different resolutions, and they will finally be output as a complete seismic inversion through inverse wavelet transform. Then, reverse input Vsh (F-aaa) into the reverse convolution network JNet (S2) of the aaa network for convolution.

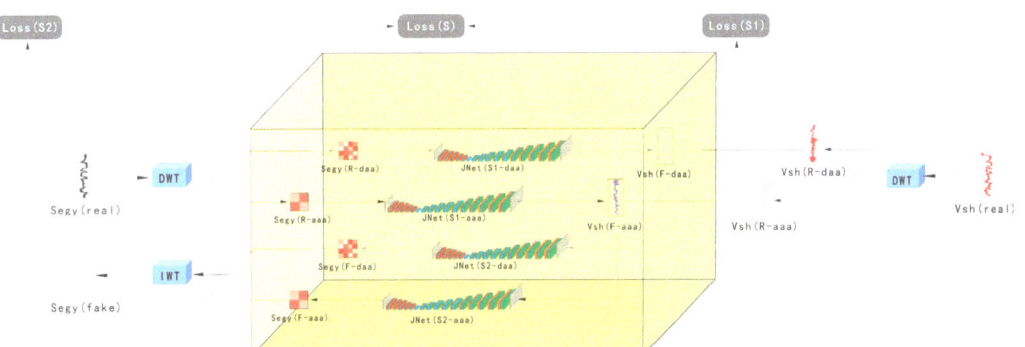

Figure 4. Multi-scale super-asymmetric Cycle-JNet network design.

3. Discussion of the Analysis Results

To address the limitations of traditional inversion methods in processing complex seismic data and accurately identifying thin sand body interfaces [14–21], we constructed a multi-scale super-asymmetric network (Cycle-JNet) seismic intelligent inversion method in this study. In order to verify the feasibility of the method, we analyzed and evaluated the data of artificial intelligence seismic training and results, intelligent seismic inversion and other inversion methods, and the section comparison of different inversion methods.

3.1. Artificial Intelligence Seismic Analysis

In the intelligent seismic training, the JNet network randomly selects ten $1 \times 1 \times 128$ seismic data samples from seismic data for learning. Each seismic data sample contains a section of seismic curve and a Vsh curve of equal length, in which the input wave of seismic data is seismic wave. The seismic waves were input into JNet (S1) for training, and the training results were recorded, as shown in Figure 5. The vertical axis on the left of the figure represents the value of Vsh curve (that is the sand–mud ratio, the value ranging from 0 to 1. The smaller the value, the higher the sand body composition and the better the sand body, and the larger the value, the higher the mud composition). The vertical axis on the right represents the amplitude of the seismic curve (−56,053~67,456 Hz), and the horizontal axis represents the depth of the curve (1350~1600 ms). The artificial intelligence Vsh curve generated by the generator (the green curve in Figure 5), the real Vsh curve (the red curve in Figure 5), and the input seismic curve (the blue curve in Figure 5) were compared, and some typical curves of one training round, 50 training rounds, 100 training rounds, and 200 training rounds were selected for comparison. The artificial intelligence Vsh curve generated by the generator (the green curve in Figure 5) and the well Vsh curve (the red curve in Figure 5) were compared to obtain the coincidence rate of the generator generation curve under different training rounds. When comparing the three curves, it was found that the resolution of the seismic curve was much lower than that of the well Vsh curve, but the artificial intelligence Vsh curve successfully expanded the resolution through the unique structure of JNet and was consistent with the well Vsh curve.

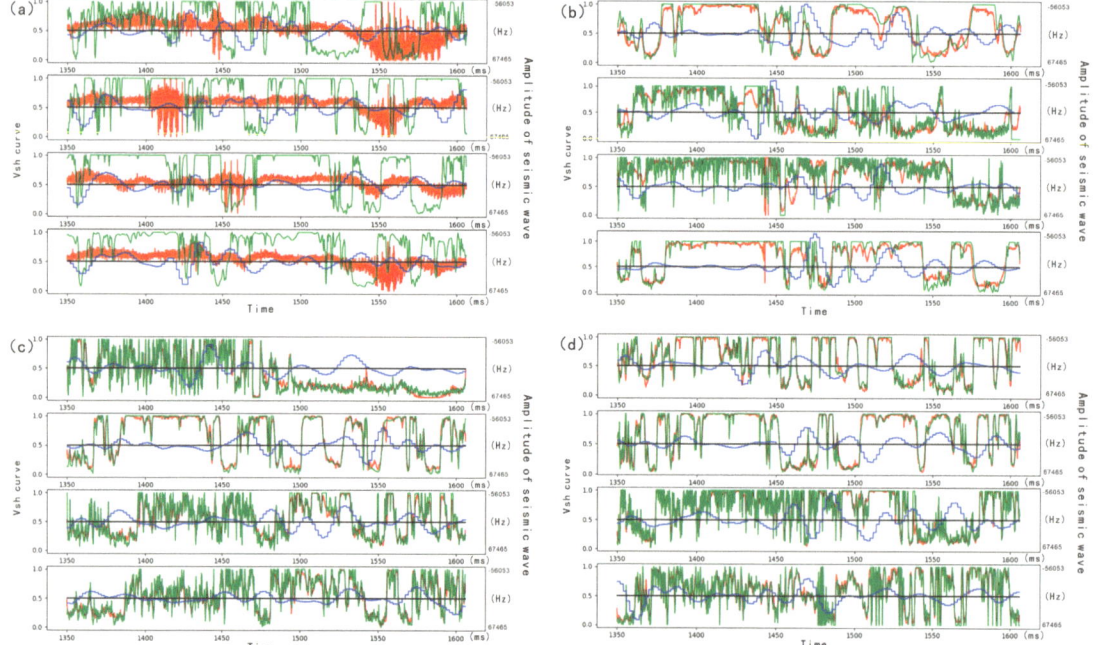

Figure 5. Single well curve analysis for different training rounds. The green line is the well Vsh curve, the blue line is the seismic curve, and the red line is the artificial intelligence Vsh curve: (**a**) Partial single-well curves after one round of training; (**b**) Partial single-well curves after 50 rounds of training; (**c**) Partial single-well curves after 100 rounds of training; (**d**) Partial single-well curves after 200 rounds of training.

As can be seen from Figure 5a, during the first training of the machine, the Vsh curve generated by the generator was irregular with great fluctuation, poor coincidence rate with the well Vsh curve, almost no correlation with the seismic curve, and an insufficient learning of the characteristics of the well seismic relationship. After 50 rounds of learning, the artificial intelligence Vsh curve in Figure 5b began to show certain rules and had a certain coincidence rate with the well Vsh curve, and it showed a certain correlation with the seismic curve. After 100 rounds of training, the Vsh curve generated by the generator in Figure 5c had a 90% coincidence rate with the well Vsh curve, which was strongly correlated with the seismic curve and had an obvious learning effect, indicating that the neural network is sensitive to changes in well seismic data and has strong learning ability. However, as shown in Figure 5d, after 200 rounds of training, the efficiency improved slightly compared to after 100 rounds of training. Both of them showed the high efficiency and accuracy of the training, with the Vsh curves generated by the two generators having a very high coincidence rate with the well Vsh curves and the differences in the coincidence rate between the two being small. If the training continues, the network conformity rate increases very little, so the training rounds are set at 200 rounds, which reflects the high efficiency and accuracy of the training.

3.2. Comparative Analysis of Intelligent Seismic Inversion and Other Inversion Methods

The JNET trained for 200 rounds was selected to generate seismic inversion, and a small piece of the seismic inversion body in the well-dense area was obtained by using the method of write-by-track inversion. The 1450~1485 ms sections of well A8 and well A14 in the well density area were selected, and the traditional seismic inversion method (SMI) and AI were used to compare the sand prediction ability of these two methods. It can be seen from Figure 6 that for the thick sand body in the lower half, both AI seismic inversion and SMI inversion can identify the sand body, but the resolution of AI seismic inversion is higher, clearly depicting the distribution and stack of the sand body in the thick sand body. For the strata with complex geological conditions in the upper part of the formation, SMI inversion is almost difficult to identify, and only large sections of fuzzy sand layer can be seen. However, AI seismic inversion can identify thinner sand layers and predict and characterize their morphological distribution. In general, the sand body obtained by SMI inversion can only show rough rules, the characterization of sand body interface is not clear, the recognition and processing ability of complex strata is weak, and the prediction accuracy reached 62.7%. While the recognition of thin sand obtained by AI seismic inversion is quite accurate and detailed, with strong correspondence with lithology, a high coincidence rate with the VSH curve, and the clear characterization of the sand body boundary, the prediction accuracy reached 81.3%.

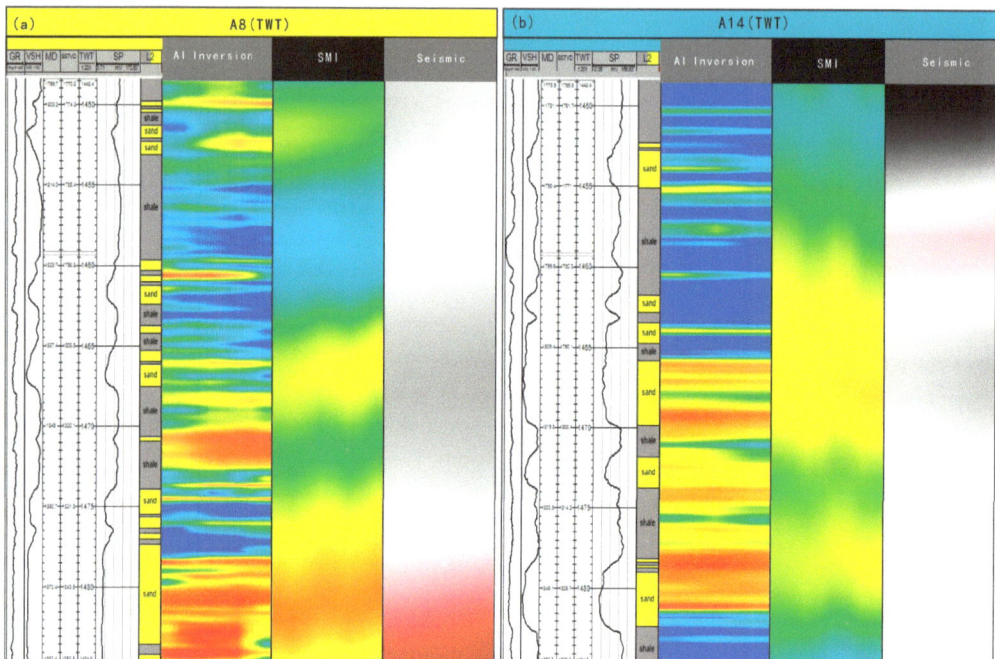

Figure 6. Comparison between artificial intelligence seismic inversion intelligent prediction and other inversion prediction: (**a**) Well A8 is the test well; (**b**) Well A14 is the test well.

By comparing the AI seismic inversion results of Figure 6a,b, the prediction accuracy for sand bodies in well A14 and well A8 is 72.1% and 85.5% respectively. It is found that the prediction accuracy for sand bodies in well A14 is slightly lower than that in well A8, while the prediction accuracy of the traditional inversion method (SMI) was 63.4% and 62.1%, respectively, because the number of AI seismic inversion training datasets is not large enough and the feature learning of well A14 is not complete, indicating that the AI seismic inversion results have some instability.

3.3. Intelligent Seismic Inversion Profile Analysis

The JNet-generated seismic inversion body after 200 rounds of training was used to discretely model the 1350~1580 ms interval to obtain the intelligent seismic inversion. Then, we used two-point stochastic modeling and the traditional inversion method SMI to obtain two inversions and discretely modeled them to obtain the stochastic modeling inversion and SMI inversion, and the thin sand body prediction and comparison were performed. Taking well A8 as the test well, after removing the influence of well A8 on the inversion, the profiles of this segment under different inversion modeling methods were obtained, as shown in Figure 7. Thus, the accuracy of prediction by different inversion methods was tested. Figure 7a shows the random modeling inversion modeling profile. The sand bodies have too strong continuity, which is not in line with the actual situation, and the corresponding degree with the lithology of the test well is poor. The prediction of the sand body depends entirely on the curve and stratification of the adjacent Wells, which is very inaccurate. Figure 7b shows the SMI inversion modeling profile. Compared with the random thin sand modeling, the sand body continuity is slightly reduced, but the corresponding degree with the lithology of the test well is improved. However, the recognition and resolution of the thin sand body on the well are poor, and the prediction of the thin sand body is not accurate enough. Figure 7c shows the AI seismic inversion profile, which has a very high coincidence rate for lithology, reaching 85% on the test well.

It has good identification and high resolution for thin layer sand bodies on the well, and the continuity of sand bodies is higher than that of SMI modeling inversion, and the prediction of sand bodies is accurate and of high resolution.

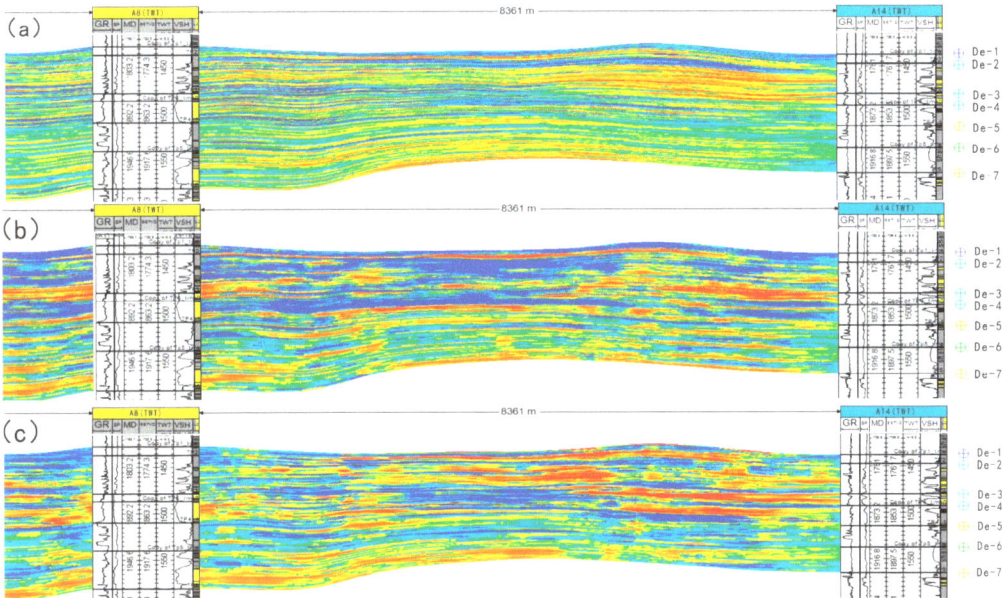

Figure 7. Seismic inversion profiles of sand bodies by each method: (**a**) random modeling inversion; (**b**) SMI; (**c**) AI seismic inversion.

4. Conclusions

In this paper, a seismic intelligent inversion method based on the multi-scale super-asymmetric Cycle-JNet network is proposed to predict seismic inversion. The network includes many technologies such as CNN, RNN, and wavelet transform. Through about 100 rounds of machine learning, the coincidence rate of well vibration curve reached 92.1%, which proves that the neural network is sensitive to changes in well vibration data and has strong learning ability. Compared with traditional seismic inversion prediction, it can easily identify and predict the thin sand layer. During the pumping test, the profile of sand bodies was uniform and continuous, and the coincidence rate of sand prediction in the test well reached 81.2%, which proves the accuracy of the proposed method in predicting sand bodies and also proves that the Cycl-JNet network is a new and reliable seismic inversion prediction model. The prediction model can realize the identification and prediction of sand bodies of different thickness, which greatly improves the accuracy and resolution of seismic inversion.

In practical applications, since the method completely relies on the network of machine learning to generate the inversion body, it will not be able to make accurate predictions in the face of the types of seismic data that are not learned, and the accuracy will be greatly reduced. However, in the face of problematic data, the network cannot judge its correctness and will still output seismic inversion bodies based on wrong data. It is necessary to continuously carry out a large amount of seismic data training to improve the network and train its ability to identify the wrong data.

Author Contributions: Conceptualization, M.T. and B.H.; methodology, M.T. and B.H.; validation, M.T., B.H., Z.C. and R.X. All authors have read and agreed to the published version of the manuscript.

Funding: This research was funded by the National Natural Science Foundation (grant numbers. 42072163, 41972250), and the Foundation of Shandong Province (grant number ZR2019MD006), and the Foundation of CNPC (grant number 2021DJ3302), and the National Natural Science Foundation of China (62305196), and the National Postdoctoral Researcher Program (GZC20231498).

Informed Consent Statement: Not applicable.

Data Availability Statement: The data presented in this study are available on request from the corresponding author. The data are not publicly available due to privacy.

Conflicts of Interest: The authors declare no conflict of interest.

References

1. Cooke, D.A.; Schneider, W.A. Generalized linear inversion of reflection seismic data. *Geophysics* **1983**, *48*, 665. [CrossRef]
2. Debeye, H.W.J.; Riel, P.V. Lp-NORM DECONVOLUTION1. *Geophys. Prospect.* **1990**, *38*, 381–403. [CrossRef]
3. Haas, A.; Dubrule, O. Geostatistical inversion: A sequential method of stochastic reservoir modeling constrained by seismic data. *First Break* **1994**, *12*, 561–569. [CrossRef]
4. Zhang, H.; Yang, F.; Chang, Z.; Ren, J.Z.; Wu, G.S. Joint application of post-stack seismic inversion method. *J. Oil Gas Technol.* **2009**, *31*, 4.
5. Sheng, C.; Bi, J.; Li, Z.; Zhang, M.; Sun, X. Research on SMI method for seismic waveform indication inversion. *Inn. Mong. Petrochem. Ind.* **2015**, *5*, 147–151. [CrossRef]
6. Krizhevsky, A.; Sutskever, I.; Hinton, G. ImageNet Classification with Deep Convolutional Neural Networks. *Adv. Neural Inf. Process. Syst.* **2012**, *25*, 2. [CrossRef]
7. Kong, Q.; Trugman, D.T.; Ross, Z.E.; Bianco, M.J.; Meade, B.J.; Gerstoft, P. Machine learning in seismology: Turning data into insights. *Seismol. Res. Lett.* **2019**, *90*, 3–14. [CrossRef]
8. Karimzadeh, S.; Mohammadi, A.; Hussaini, S.M.S.; Caicedo, D.; Askan, A.; Lourenço, P.B. ANN-based ground motion model for Turkey using stochastic simulation of earthquakes. *Geophys. J. Int.* **2024**, *236*, 413–429. [CrossRef]
9. Mousavi, S.M.; Beroza, G.C. Deep-learning seismology. *Science* **2022**, *377*, eabm4470. [CrossRef]
10. Karimpouli, S.; Tahmasebi, P. Physics informed machine learning: Seismic wave equation. *Geosci. Front.* **2020**, *11*, 1993–2001. [CrossRef]
11. Szegedy, C.; Liu, W.; Jia, Y.; Sermanet, P.; Reed, S.; Anguelov, D.; Erhan, D.; Vanhoucke, V.; Rabinovich, A. Going deeper with convolutions. In Proceedings of the 2015 IEEE Conference on Computer Vision and Pattern Recognition (CVPR), Boston, MA, USA, 7–12 June 2015. [CrossRef]
12. He, K.; Zhang, X.; Ren, S.; Sun, J. Deep Residual Learning for Image Recognition. In Proceedings of the IEEE Conference on Computer Vision and Pattern Recognition, Las Vegas, NV, USA, 27–30 June 2016. [CrossRef]
13. Huang, G.; Liu, Z.; Van Der Maaten, L.; Weinberger, K.Q. Densely Connected Convolutional Networks. In Proceedings of the IEEE Conference on Computer Vision and Pattern Recognition, Las Vegas, NV, USA, 27–30 June 2016. [CrossRef]
14. Das, V.; Pollack, A.; Wollner, U.; Mukerji, T. Convolutional neural network for seismic impedance inversion. *Geophysics* **2019**, *84*, R869–R880. [CrossRef]
15. Wang, K.; Bandura, L.; Bevc, D.; Cheng, S.; DiSiena, J.; Halpert, A.; Osypov, K.; Power, B.; Xu, E. End-to-end deep neural network for seismic inversion. In Proceedings of the SEG International Exposition and Annual Meeting, San Antonio, TX, USA, 15–20 September 2019; p. D043S152R002.
16. Wang, Y.Q.; Wang, Q.; Lu, W.K.; Ge, Q.; Yan, X.F. Seismic impedance inversion based on cycle-consistent generative adversarial network. *Pet. Sci.* **2022**, *19*, 147–161. [CrossRef]
17. Phan, S.; Sen, M.K. Hopfield networks for high-resolution prestack seismic inversion. In Proceedings of the SEG International Exposition and Annual Meeting, Anaheim, CA, USA, 14–19 October 2018; p. SEG-2018-2996244.
18. Biswas, R.; Sen, M.K.; Das, V.; Mukerji, T. Prestack and poststack inversion using a physics-guided convolutional neural network. *Interpretation* **2019**, *7*, SE161–SE174. [CrossRef]
19. Alfarraj, M.; AlRegib, G. Semi-supervised learning for acoustic impedance inversion. In *SEG Technical Program Expanded Abstracts 2019*; Society of Exploration Geophysicists: Tulsa, OK, USA, 2019; pp. 2298–2302.
20. Alfarraj, M.; AlRegib, G. Semisupervised sequence modeling for elastic impedance inversion. *Interpretation* **2019**, *7*, SE237–SE249. [CrossRef]
21. Zheng, Y.; Zhang, Q.; Yusifov, A.; Shi, Y. Applications of supervised deep learning for seismic interpretation and inversion. *Lead. Edge* **2019**, *38*, 526–533. [CrossRef]
22. Bouvrie, J. Notes on Convolutional Neural Networks. *Procedia Technology.* **2006**, 47–60. [CrossRef]
23. Zaremba, W.; Sutskever, I.; Vinyals, O. Recurrent neural network regularization. *arXiv* **2014**, arXiv:1409.2329.
24. Ronneberger, O.; Fischer, P.; Brox, T. U-net: Convolutional networks for biomedical image segmentation. In Proceedings of the Medical Image Computing and Computer-Assisted Intervention–MICCAI 2015: 18th International Conference, Munich, Germany, 5–9 October 2015; Proceedings, Part III 18. Springer International Publishing: Berlin/Heidelberg, Germany, 2015; pp. 234–241.

25. Liu, J.; Zhang, Y.; Xie, J.; Wei, Y.; Wang, Z.; Niu, M. Head detection based on dr feature extraction network and mixed dilated convolution module. *Electronics* **2021**, *10*, 1565. [CrossRef]
26. Allen, J. Short term spectral analysis, synthesis, and modification by discrete Fourier transform. *IEEE Trans. Acoust. Speech Signal Process.* **1977**, *25*, 235–238. [CrossRef]
27. Chakraborty, A.; Okaya, D. Frequency-time decomposition of seismic data using wavelet-based methods. *Geophysics* **1995**, *60*, 1906–1916. [CrossRef]
28. Mallat, S. *A Wavelet Tour of Signal Processing*; Elsevier: Amsterdam, The Netherlands, 1999.
29. Burrus, C.S.; Gopinath, R.A.; Guo, H.; Hall, P. *Introduction to Wavelets and Wavelet Transforms: A Primer*; Pearson Schweiz AG: London, UK, 1998.
30. Morlet, J. *Sampling Theory and Wave Propagation*; Springer: Berlin/Heidelberg, Germany, 1983. [CrossRef]
31. Thuillard, M. *Wavelets in Soft Computing*; World Scientific Series in Robotics and Intelligent Systems: Basel, Switzerland, 2001; p. 320.
32. Maleknejad, K.; Derili, H. The collocation method for Hammerstein equations by Daubechies wavelets. *Appl. Math. Comput.* **2006**, *172*, 846–864. [CrossRef]

Disclaimer/Publisher's Note: The statements, opinions and data contained in all publications are solely those of the individual author(s) and contributor(s) and not of MDPI and/or the editor(s). MDPI and/or the editor(s) disclaim responsibility for any injury to people or property resulting from any ideas, methods, instructions or products referred to in the content.

Article

Identifying Earthquakes in Low-Cost Sensor Signals Contaminated with Vehicular Noise

Leonidas Agathos, Andreas Avgoustis, Nikolaos Avgoustis, Ioannis Vlachos, Ioannis Karydis and Markos Avlonitis *

Department of Informatics, Ionian University, 49132 Kerkyra, Greece; inf.bdn2203@ionio.gr (L.A.); inf.bdn2202@ionio.gr (A.A.); avgoustis@ionio.gr (N.A.); gvlachos@ionio.gr (I.V.); karydis@ionio.gr (I.K.)
* Correspondence: avlon@ionio.gr; Tel.: +30-266187766

Abstract: The importance of monitoring earthquakes for disaster management, public safety, and scientific research can hardly be overstated. The emergence of low-cost seismic sensors offers potential for widespread deployment due to their affordability. Nevertheless, vehicular noise in low-cost seismic sensors presents as a significant challenge in urban environments where such sensors are often deployed. In order to address these challenges, this work proposes the use of an amalgamated deep neural network constituent of a DNN trained on earthquake signals from professional sensory equipment as well as a DNN trained on vehicular signals from low-cost sensors for the purpose of earthquake identification in signals from low-cost sensors contaminated with vehicular noise. To this end, we present low-cost seismic sensory equipment and three discrete datasets that—when the proposed methodology is applied—are shown to significantly outperform a generic stochastic differential model in terms of effectiveness and efficiency.

Keywords: low-cost sensors; deep neural networks; vehicular noise; earthquake measurement; earthquake signal contamination; seismometer

1. Introduction

Earthquakes are sudden movements along fault lines that release stored elastic energy in rocks, generating seismic waves that propagate throughout the Earth [1]. Seismology is a field abundant with data and is heavily reliant on data analysis. Each day witnesses numerous earthquakes worldwide with magnitudes exceeding 2.5, which can be felt locally. Additionally, every few days, earthquakes capable of causing structural damage occur [2]. Moreover, there is a continuous occurrence of numerous smaller earthquakes, typically with magnitudes below 2.5, which are too weak to be perceptible but are consistently recorded by modern instruments [3]. These minor seismic events offer valuable insights into the mechanisms of earthquakes [4].

Monitoring earthquakes is important for disaster management, public safety, and scientific research. It enables determining preparatory activities such as timely warnings, evacuation plans, and response strategies in order to mitigate the impact of seismic events, in addition to studying earthquake patterns to accrue valuable insights into Earth's dynamics. To this end, sensor networks, comprising mostly of seismometers and accelerometers placed throughout the globe, play a pivotal role in this effort by continuously collecting seismic data. These networks facilitate real-time monitoring, data analysis, and the development of earthquake prediction models, ultimately enhancing the ability to protect lives and infrastructure, and advance the scientific understanding of earthquake behavior.

The emergence of low-cost sensors represents a significant advancement in environmental monitoring [5], in general, and earthquake monitoring [6], specifically, as their affordability allows for widespread deployment. These sensors offer a plethora of advantages, including increased spatial coverage and dense monitoring networks that allow for

Citation: Agathos, L.; Avgoustis, A.; Avgoustis, N.; Vlachos, I.; Karydis, I.; Avlonitis, M. Identifying Earthquakes in Low-Cost Sensor Signals Contaminated with Vehicular Noise. *Appl. Sci.* **2023**, *13*, 10884. https://doi.org/10.3390/app131910884

Academic Editors: Shiyong Zhou and Ke Jia

Received: 13 September 2023
Revised: 25 September 2023
Accepted: 27 September 2023
Published: 30 September 2023

Copyright: © 2023 by the authors. Licensee MDPI, Basel, Switzerland. This article is an open access article distributed under the terms and conditions of the Creative Commons Attribution (CC BY) license (https://creativecommons.org/licenses/by/4.0/).

a more comprehensive understanding of environmental conditions. Moreover, their cost-effectiveness allows for easier replacement in the event of malfunction or damage, ensuring continuous data collection without substantial financial burdens. This democratization of sensor technology not only enhances our ability to gather data across vast geographical areas but also empowers communities, researchers, and organizations to address critical environmental and societal challenges with greater precision and efficiency.

Vehicular noise contamination poses a significant challenge in urban environments, where the deployment of low-cost sensors is common. This challenge stems from the ubiquitous presence of vehicles on roads and highways, generating a continuous stream of noise that can impact various aspects of urban life [7]. The deployment of low-cost sensors, while advantageous for monitoring purposes, can also exacerbate the problem by providing a platform for capturing and transmitting this noise. As urban areas continue to grow and traffic congestion increases, the issue of vehicular noise becomes more pronounced, affecting the well-being of residents, wildlife habitats, and overall quality of life [8]. The task of effectively using sensor data to monitor and analyze while accounting for noise contamination presents a complex problem that requires innovative solutions and advanced earthquake signal processing and deep learning techniques [9].

Earthquake identification is of paramount importance due to its significant impact on public safety, emergency response efforts, and disaster preparedness. Earthquakes are natural disasters that can cause widespread destruction, loss of life, and disruption to communities. The accurate and timely identification of earthquakes allows a variety of critical actions that can mitigate their effects and save lives [10]. It is thus fundamental to effective disaster management and empowers individuals, communities, and authorities with the information needed to make informed decisions, take swift actions, and allocate resources efficiently. The consequences of false positives, and negatives, underscore the critical nature of reliable seismic monitoring systems in ensuring public safety and disaster preparedness [11].

Motivation and Contribution

The aforementioned importance of accurate earthquake identification can hardly be overstated, given the effect of earthquakes on so many aspects of life. Moreover, the emergence of low-cost sensory equipment for such identification, and its widespread adoption nowadays, calls for research on the effectiveness and efficiency of this use. This is further exacerbated by the high density of such sensors that frequently are adjacent to publicly accessible road infrastructure which in turn contaminates the signals received by the sensors with vehicular noise. It is, thus, the lack of comprehensive studies addressing the impact of vehicular noise on earthquake signals captured by low-cost sensors that this work aims to address.

In order to address these challenges, this work proposes the use of an amalgamated deep neural network (DNN) composed of (i) a DNN trained on earthquake signals from professional sensory equipment, as well as (ii) a DNN trained on vehicular signals from low-cost sensors, for the purpose of earthquake identification in signals from low-cost sensors contaminated with vehicular noise. The key contributions of this work can be summarised as follows:

- Creation and dissemination of a dataset of vehicular noise measured with low-cost seismic sensor;
- Collection and dissemination of ground truth data from professional seismic measurement equipment;
- Creation of DNNs for the aforementioned dataset approaches and experimentation on their performance;
- Creation and dissemination of a two-fold synchronized dataset: seismic data from a low-cost seismic sensor, and seismic data from a professional seismic sensor. Both sensors are in very close proximity; and

- Amalgamation of the aforementioned DNNs for the identification of earthquakes in signals from low-cost sensors contaminated with vehicular noise and experimentation on the DNN.

The rest of this paper is organized as follows: Section 2 discusses the key recent relevant studies about seismology, seismic waves, sensors for measuring and removing noise from seismic waves, and deep learning for earthquake and vehicle classification. Section 3 presents the proposed methodology and the deep learning classification algorithm utilized in this work. Section 4 details the pre-processing techniques applied to the datasets and the experiments conducted, wherein their respective results are presented and discussed. Finally, this paper is concluded in Section 5.

2. Background and Related Work

In seismology, the foundation of knowledge lies in data analysis, with significant breakthroughs often stemming from the examination of fresh datasets or the creation of novel data analysis techniques [12]. Seismology focuses on the study of earthquakes and associated phenomena, primarily applying the principles of continuous medium mechanics, specifically the theory of elasticity. In contrast, seismic engineering is an applied science concerned with understanding how earthquake-induced motion impacts man-made structures, including buildings and other constructions [13].

Earthquake impacts on both natural and human-made structures are primarily driven by the transfer of energy through seismic waves originating from the earthquake's source. Seismic waves propagate through the Earth and are detected at distant locations using sensitive seismographs. Interpreting seismic records requires an understanding of how seismic waves are generated and propagated, and how recording processes affect them. Advances in seismic instrumentation now allow for accurate digital representation of particle motion across a wide frequency range. However, this necessitates careful consideration of seismic noise, the background irregular ground motion caused by various factors, including human activities and natural phenomena. Occasionally, this background noise is interrupted by organized energy patterns generated by seismic waves from natural or artificial sources. These wave-trains, characterized by distinct arrivals associated with specific propagation paths, become more pronounced with increasing distance from the source. Following the initial body-wave phases, like P (compressional waves) and S (shear waves), there is an increase in record amplitude as surface-guided waves arrive [14].

Over the centuries, seismology has evolved significantly. From Zhang Heng's ancient seismograph in 132 AD to the late 1800s when scientific research on seismology began, progress was slow. It was not until around 1900 that precise measuring instruments, like geophones and seismometers, emerged. These early devices were large, costly, and had limited sensitivity. However, recent advances in micro-electro-mechanical system (MEMS) technology have drastically reduced size and cost while improving sensitivity, making MEMS-based seismic sensors highly promising for their ability to provide reliable measurements across a wide bandwidth [15]. Modern seismographs produce digitized information at varying regular time intervals sent to be analyzed on computers. Many concepts of time series analysis, including filtering and spectral methods, are valuable in seismic analysis [16].

The identification of noise (seismic included) depends on a plethora of parameters and usually requires data analysis while depending on the domain or application, a part of the information may be be treated as noise or useful signal [17]. Seismic noise monitoring systems have been proposed [18] that address continuous traffic noise utilizing raw noise records as well as shear-wave velocity profiles. Prior to seismic wave measurement and identification, noise removal is another important factor that has been addressed [19]. Periodic noise poses a well-documented challenge in the context of seismic wave removal, often originating from sources such as power lines, pump jacks, engine operations, or other forms of interference. It introduces contamination to seismic data and has a notable impact on subsequent data processing and interpretation. The proposed denoising approach hinges on the sparse representation of periodic noise, enabling its estimation without being influenced by seismic reflections. Consequently, this method effectively reduces periodic noise without compromising the integrity of seismic events. Similarly, the utilization of machine learning algorithms for eliminating random noise in seismic data has emerged as a crucial aspect of seismic analysis [20]. In this work, the authors emphasize that the elimination of random noise from seismic data significantly affects the accuracy of subsequent data processing. They achieve an enhancement in the signal-to-noise ratio of seismic data through the application of a convolutional neural network trained on noise. This not only results in a higher signal-to-noise ratio but also preserves more valuable information.

Given the previously discussed importance of earthquake identification, and thus, early warning systems, the prohibitive cost of high-end ground motion sensors often leaves earthquake-prone areas unable to implement such systems for measuring seismic waves. Low-cost MEMS-based ground motion sensors present a promising solution for creating affordable, yet reliable and sturdy, seismometers. Traditional high-end monitoring systems are highly dedicated measuring systems with high to very high precision of measurement, usually significantly above the monitoring scenario's requirements. The low-cost approach in such monitoring systems attempts to minimize the cost (usually at the level of one to, hopefully, two orders of magnitude) while preserving the precision of measurements within acceptable [21]. The lower cost allows for a higher number of deployed systems and a lower cost per system unit replacement, leading to a denser network of interconnected systems compared to high-end solutions, offering redundancy, expansive spatial measurements, and—utilizing AI methods—the capacity for collective extraction of information. This collective approach yields insights unattainable by unique systems, achieving significantly higher levels of precision compared to unique low-cost systems and rivaling those of non-low-cost systems. The advancements in utilizing low-cost sensors for detecting earthquakes and issuing warnings have shown remarkable progress in recent years. This progress is evident in the expansion of station coverage, the enhancement of data quality, and the broadening scope of applications related to earthquake detection [22]. Real-time seismic signal waves are available to be plotted using ShakeMaps, helping to assess the damage patterns and directivity of rupture. These ShakeMaps plots have proven [23] helpful in establishing the peak ground velocity indicator of damage, and the peak ground acceleration.

Similar to our proposed work for earthquake identification, some research efforts have also been made for the event detection of earthquakes with machine learning algorithms, applying time wave series data analogous to those used for different vehicle types. The implementation of different machine learning algorithms determines the class of automobiles [24] for distinguishing between earthquake and non-earthquake, vandalism vibrations [25], even for event detection, phase identification, and the onset picking time [26]. In all such cases, the results indicate that the use of deep neural networks was superior in distinguishing and provided high classification accuracy during training, as well as in the event and phase detection of earthquakes.

3. Proposed Methodology

Our work proposes the use of an amalgamated deep neural network constituent of a deep neural network trained on earthquake signals from professional sensory equipment, as well as a deep neural network trained on vehicular signals from low-cost sensors. These sensors were placed at points with vehicular activity, enabling them to record passing vehicles for model training. On the other hand, the professional sensory equipment used consisted of high-end seismographs, which are used to record seismic events. The key purpose is to convey the amalgamated deep neural network with the capability to effectively discern earthquakes in signals from low-cost sensors that are contaminated with vehicular noise, thereby avoiding false positives caused by vehicles. The proposed low-cost sensors could be used in bulk and placed in different areas so they can record an upcoming seismic event. This could benefit researchers and give them the ability to record the events from different sensors and extract valuable information. In addition, the low-cost sensors are easy to maintain or replace, given their affordability in comparison to professional equipment, and could be placed near roads for easier access to them. Finally, the model we propose could be very useful when it comes to earthquake recognition, as it has the ability to recognize the seismic event from a passing vehicle; our model is trained to discern the difference between them. This model supports our proposal of placing the low-cost sensors near roads for easier access, as passing vehicles will not affect the recognition process of the model. A bird's-eye view of the key pillars of this work is presented in Figure 1.

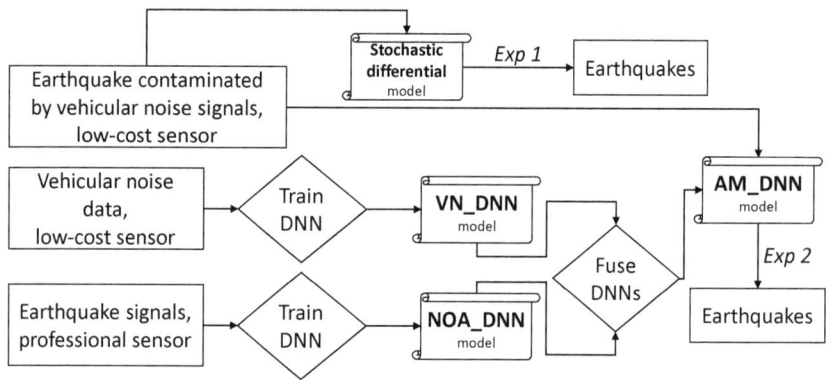

Figure 1. Architectural diagram of the proposed methodology.

The online availability of the programming code and data in the scientific research offers numerous benefits, i.e., it improves transparency, collaboration, and accountability by enabling independent verification of the findings. To this end, all data and code of this work are available online (https://github.com/LeonidasAgathos/Identifying_earth quakes_in_low_cost_sensors_signals_contaminated_with_vehicular_noise, accessed on 13 September 2023).

3.1. A Stochastic Approach

A very common scenario used to detect earthquake events involves signals from low-cost sensors, placed in several areas near roads and a methodology that allows the identification of earthquake events in such data. In our context, a seismic event is defined as the transition from a state of pure noise to a seismic signal. The current methodology we use to detect earthquake events, as presented in [27], is a stochastic differential model that employs a sliding window technique on the time-series data of the sensor. This window is incrementally moved through the dataset at predefined intervals. Within each window, the data undergo a transformation process, the variance function of the transformed data is computed, and its shape is assessed in relation to a power law distribution.

If the shape of the variance function closely aligns with the characteristics of a power law distribution, it is postulated that this is indicative of the data window predominantly representing noise. In this case, the model proceeds to the next window. However, when the shape of the variance function diverges significantly from the expected power law shape, the algorithm terminates and signals the detection of a seismic event.

In our case, we applied this algorithm to a dataset obtained from our low-cost seismic monitoring system. The successful detection of a seismic event was determined based on the algorithm's ability to identify an outbreak near the initiation of the seismic event, while not focusing on the detection of the whole event.

It is worth noting that, although this method demonstrated competency in identifying seismic events in its original presentation, it faced challenges in distinguishing between seismic events and events triggered by external factors, such as passing vehicles. This limitation was discussed as a key factor in the interpretation of the results.

3.2. Low-Cost Seismic Sensory Equipment

The low-cost sensor mentioned in Section 3.1 was created in the CMODLab of Ionian University, Corfu, Greece; it consists of low-cost hardware and a data logger system. Originally, it was created for detecting seismic events and was placed in various areas, mostly near traffic roads. This placement is a part of the low-cost concept, so the sensors are easily accessible and replaceable in case of malfunction.

The system employs a 3-axis geophone, operating at 4.5 Hz and 380 Ohm, serving as the main data logger to record signals. A sampling rate of 225 Hz is archived from the data logger and an accurate timestamp is added to each sample from a precise real-time clock circuit. This clock is checked and corrected every hour by using internet information. The recorded data are stored internally at the system in 5 min chunks (coinciding with files); subsequently, these are transmitted to the database server every 5 min by using internet connectivity.

The low-cost system consists of low-cost hardware and open-source software. The system uses Raspberry Pi 3 B+, which is a credit-card-sized microcomputer board (see Figure 2). In addition, the system uses an analog-to-digital board with 24-bit high speed (ADS1256) precision, specialized for interconnection with the microcomputer and the real-time clock circuit breakout board DS3231. To support the system's energy needs, it uses a step-down converter with +5Volt power, up to 3 Amps. The system is also fitted with a solar panel, battery, and a solar charger controller to make the system autonomous. Moreover, the system utilized additional accessories, such as a USB GSM–GPRS 4G modem to support the system's internet connection, a 3-axis geophone sensor with a cutoff frequency *fc* set at 4.5 Hz, and a micro-SD 32 GB memory card that functions as the hard disk of the microcomputer board and stores all the necessary software needed to support the system (e.g., Python, data, etc.). The operating system used in the sensor is a Linux-based operational system for Raspberry Pi. We also used Python and C++ to write and execute scripts, depending on the needs of the task. The microcomputer board Raspberry Pi 3 B+, is the heart of the data logger system, and was selected for its high adaptability to integrate with various additional boards, like (I2c Bus, UART, SPI, GPIO, etc.), and it provides the data logger with multiple capabilities.

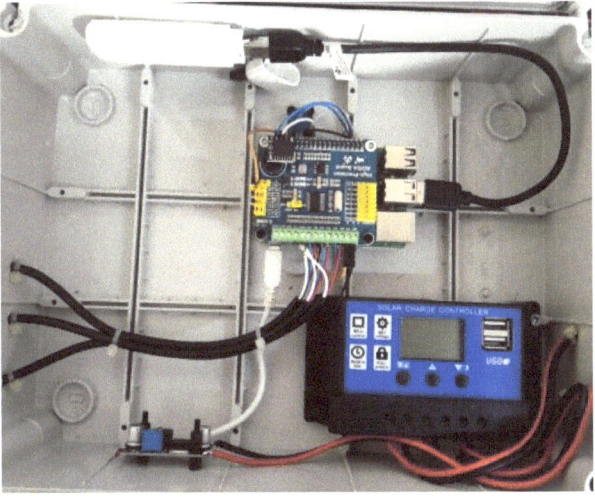

Figure 2. Full data logger system setup with housing in a plastic waterproof IP67 box.

In addition, as mentioned above, a 24-bit A/D high-speed analog-to-digital precision board (ADS1256), as shown in Figure 3, is connected to the microcomputer board using the 40-pin GPIO connector.

Figure 3. Raspberry Pi 3 B+ in combination with the 24 bit high precision A/D board—ADS1256.

The A/D board has 24 bits of accuracy and has a quantization error 1/2 LSB of 2^{24}/max input voltage. It can be adjusted to operate with a max input voltage of 3.3 or 5 volts. In our case, the max input voltage is 5 volts, which means we have a quantization error of 1/2 of 5 volts/2^{24}. The board has 8 analog inputs, which can work in a simple mode (8 input channels) or in a differential mode (4 input channels), similar to our data logger. It can accommodate sample rates of up to 30K samples per second (in a single channel—simple mode) and features an internal amplifier with an amplification factor of up to 64. In the proposed system, it uses a sampling rate of 3750 Hz and an amplification factor of 64. As per the datasheet (https://www.ti.com/lit/ds/symlink/ads1256.pdf, accessed on 13 September 2023) of the ADS1256, the noise level is up to 6 bits, while the effective number of bits (ENOB) with the buffer off is essentially the remaining 18 bits. The output of the A/D card is given in counts. According to the amplification factor of 64, the differential max input voltage that can be measured from the A/D card cannot be higher than ± 78.125 mV. Each count has a value of $2^{24} \pm -78.125$ mV, so that means that each count has a value of 0.000009312 mVolts (minimum count step).

The system's 3-axis 4.5 Hz geophone, as shown in Figure 4, is a SEIS (https://www.seis-tech.com/4-5hz-3c-geophone/, accessed on 13 September 2023) 4.5 Hz 3C geophone, and it is connected to our data logger via inputs of the A/D high-speed analog-to-digital precision board. The geophone is connected in differential mode (A0–A1 input for X-Axis, A2–A3 input for Y-Axis, A4–A5 input for Z-Axis, while A6–A7 is not used). The sensitivity of the geophone for each axis, as per the datasheet (https://www.seis-tech.com/wp-content/uploads/2022/01/3c-geophone-4.5hz.pdf, accessed on 13 September 2023), is about 28.8 Volt/m/s (in open circuit) or 0.0288 Volt/mm/s. Finally, according to the maximum input voltage of the A/D card and the geophone output voltage, we can see that our system has an area to collect the ground velocity data of almost ± 2.71 mm/s.

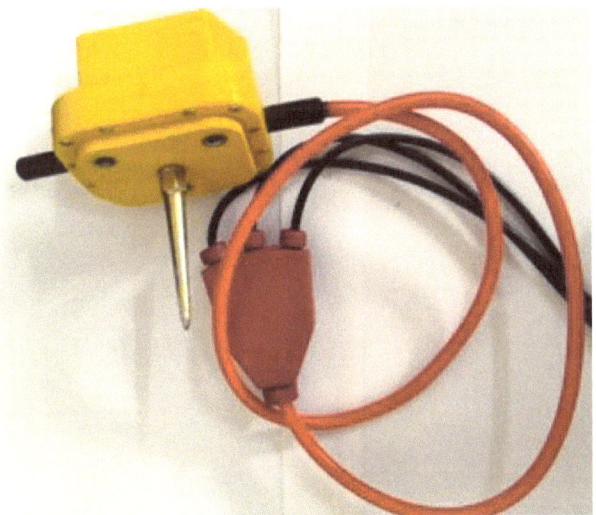

Figure 4. Three-axis geophone with cutoff frequency fc = 4.5 Hz.

3.3. Vehicular Noise

The acquisition of data originating from vehicular noise, utilizing the aforementioned geophone system in Section 3.2, constituted a crucial phase of our experiments. The key requirement was to identify a location to place the sensor on a major road with a gap close to the road for the positioning of the sensor. Additionally, in order to be able to monitor the collection process, the location had to be opportune for human operators tasked with recording the passing vehicles so that we could confirm the ground truth and align it with the signals captured by the geophone. To fulfill all these requirements, we selected a frequently accessed road in close proximity to our laboratory in the Garitsa area in Corfu, Greece. For all the above constraints, we collected the signals of passing cars via the geophone of the sensor, along with the audio recording, in order to assist in the labeling phase of ground truth later on. Using these recordings, we created an annotated dataset containing vehicular noise. In the post-collection process, to create the final dataset for vehicular noise, we cleaned and labeled the data by selecting the most representative axes of the geophone data containing the records from the movement of the ground. For the labeling process, the timestamps were labeled manually using the synchronous audio mentioned previously, collected concurrently with the geophone data, each time a vehicle passed. In order to further support the reproducibility of our work, the data of this dataset are available online (https://drive.google.com/drive/folders/1_H72gqp2ObBizB_YHRI0u53yTSHRiLqc?usp=drive_link, accessed on 13 September 2023).

3.4. Ground Truth Earthquake Dataset

After collecting the vehicular dataset, we also had to collect a dataset about earthquake events that would act as the ground truth. To complete this task, a data pipeline was created using the Obspy framework [28], which extracts waveform events from the European Integrated Data Archive in the National Observatory of Athens (NOA) [29] and saves the value of data and the timestamp of each signal wave in raw format. The seismic events were recorded and downloaded from the station *VLS* in Valsamata, Kefalonia, Greece, which is part of the NOA network. After collecting data for 773 seismic events from NOA for the VLS station, data cleaning was applied. All earthquakes were visually inspected for anomalies during their recording process. Earthquake signals that displayed irregular patterns in their recording before or after the main event were discarded. Figure 5 shows examples of regular and irregular earthquake signals. After the above phase, a total of 503 seismic events remained in our training dataset. To label the data and find the timestamps of the start time and end time of each event, we used the STA/LTA Z-Detect [30] algorithm. This task was conducted using Obspy, which also features libraries for this task. Finally, and in preparation for feeding these data to the neural network, we created data frames for all the seismic events with their original values, and their values normalized in the range of $(-1, 1)$. In order to further support the reproducibility of our work, the data of this dataset are available online (https://drive.google.com/drive/folders/1AgB4aC3yI7axPM9Jp4RhvkwORBjOK5ST?usp=drive_link, accessed on 13 September 2023).

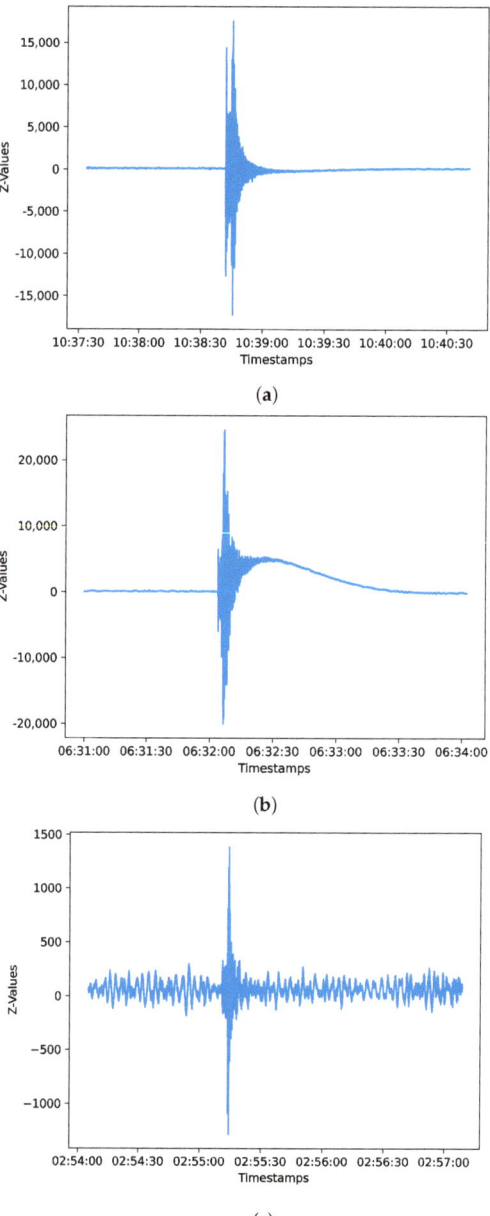

Figure 5. (**a**) Regular earthquake signal; (**b**) irregular earthquake signal; (**c**) irregular earthquake signal.

3.5. Training Process and Creation of DNNs

In order to train the models discussed herein, the following tasks were performed:
- Data preparation included several format conversion tasks aimed at converting the data into a proper form;
- Data normalization, wherein data were linearly normalized in the range of $[-1, 1]$;
- Class imbalance handling, dealt with the imbalance of the dataset using the NearMiss method [31];
- Train–test split, where the available data were split in training and testing by means of a generic approach of an 80–20% split, so we could use enough data to train the models.

In order to create the classification models based on each of the aforementioned datasets (Sections 3.3 and 3.4), we utilized the TensorFlow [32] and Keras [33] frameworks. Both these frameworks are renowned for their high performance. In detail, the used classification model is a long short-term memory model [34], which contains five layers for training and validation:

- A hidden LSTM (long short-term memory neural network) [35] layer with 64 units and a *return_sequences = True* parameter, which returns the full sequence of outputs for each input sequence and allows stacking additional recurrent layers;
- A 'flatten' layer [2], which flattens the 3D output from the LSTM layer into a 2D tensor; this is typically done to connect the LSTM layer to a standard feed-forward neural network;
- Two dense layers [36]: The first layer comprises 32 units and the second of 16 units, which are fully connected, and each neuron is connected to every neuron in the previous layer. Both dense layers use the ReLU (rectified linear unit) [37] as activation functions;
- An output layer, which is also a dense layer that represents the output of the model. The activation function used in this case is the sigmoid function [38], which outputs a probability score between 0 and 1.

3.6. Two-Fold Synchronized Dataset

The final seismic signal dataset consists of time-series data collected from our low-cost system, described in Section 3.2, strategically placed in a region prone to seismic activity. This dataset primarily comprises seismic signals associated with earthquake events. These signals exhibit a wide spectrum of characteristics, encompassing various magnitudes and frequencies. Of particular significance is the inclusion of ambient noise originating from passing vehicular traffic. This environmental noise component, stemming from the dataset's proximity to a roadway, introduces a distinctive dimension to our dataset. While seismic signals provide insights into genuine ground motion events, the presence of vehicular noise poses a challenge that reflects real-world scenarios and presents a challenge to our machine learning model.

To ensure the dataset's reliability, we cross-referenced our recorded signals with data from established seismographs from NOA, known for their accuracy and trustworthiness. The purpose of this dataset is to test both the stochastic and amalgamated models, in order to verify their ability to distinguish between earthquake signals against vehicular noise signals. The dataset was recorded and saved into 84 distinct csv files, which then were visually inspected, and each data point was labeled either as an earthquake or noise (irrespective of being vehicular or otherwise). Later, the same procedure as with the previous datasets was performed to prepare it for the testing phase. In order to further support the reproducibility of our work, the data of this dataset are available online (https://drive.google.com/drive/folders/16uKG9eq1kkf9Xpk39Tt96HHBtZ06N6qq?usp=drive_link, accessed on 13 September 2023).

4. Experimental Evaluation

This section details the setup that was used for performing the experimental evaluation of the proposed methodology, as well as the results received.

4.1. Experimental Setup

For the experimental part of our research, we utilized the datasets previously described: the dataset for vehicular noise (Section 3.3), the ground truth earthquake dataset (Section 3.4), as well as the two-fold synchronized dataset (Section 3.6). The former aims at providing information on vehicular noise, as perceived by the proposed low-cost sensory equipment. The second dataset aims to act as the ground truth point of reference, given its provenance from the European Integrated Data Archive in the National Observatory of Athens, and the fact that the sensory equipment used to collect these data is of very high accuracy. The latter dataset is the combined and synchronized dataset of seismic data from the low-cost seismic sensor in addition to seismic data from the professional seismic sensor, while both sensors were in very close proximity. All these datasets are also available (https://github.com/LeonidasAgathos/Identifying_earthquakes_in_low_cost_sensors_signals_contaminated_with_vehicular_noise/blob/main/Data_Availability, accessed on 13 September 2023). For the training part of the process, as extensively discussed in Section 3.5, the TensorFlow and Keras frameworks were utilized to create the classification models. The creation of DNNs was based on the LSTM classification model (see Section 3.5 for more details) using five layers for training and validation. The hardware configuration used was a computer with an i7-9700k CPU, featuring 8 cores and 16 gigabytes of RAM, along with an MSI GTX 1660 Ti GPU, equipped with a 6-gigabyte memory card. In order to evaluate the results received, the metrics used herein were accuracy, precision, recall, F1 score, and the area under the curve (AUC) [39], as per the following equations:

$$\text{Accuracy} = \frac{TP + TN}{TP + TN + FP + FN} \quad (1)$$

$$\text{Precision} = \frac{TP}{TP + FP} \quad (2)$$

$$\text{Recall or Sensitivity} = \frac{TP}{TP + FN} \quad (3)$$

$$\text{F1 score} = \frac{2 * Precision * Recall}{Precision + Recall} \quad (4)$$

where TN, FN, FP, and TP are true negative, false negative, false positive, and true positive, respectively.

4.2. Training Model 1

In this training model, we trained a DNN (https://github.com/LeonidasAgathos/Identifying_earthquakes_in_low_cost_sensors_signals_contaminated_with_vehicular_noise/blob/main/Model_for_Car.ipynb, accessed on 13 September 2023) to identify vehicular signals so that the model can predict when we have a signal from a passing vehicle or pure noise. To achieve that, we had to normalize the data in the range (1, −1) and additionally balance the data. The balancing was done by undersampling the majority class (noise class) using the method NearMiss (version1), so we have the same amount of data on both classes. After the pre-processing of the data, we created the DNN, which contained four layers (as per Section 3.5). We used one LSTM layer followed by a 'flatten' layer and three dense layers. LSTM layers are widely used for time series predictions as they can learn patterns and correlations within the time series, crucial for earthquake detection. The other layers are simple ones that assist in transforming the data. The data were allocated with 80% for training and 20% for testing. The results of the training are shown in Table 1 while the ROC curve is shown in Figure 6.

Table 1. Performance metrics for training model 1.

Accuracy	Precision	Recall	F1 Score	AUC Curve
68%	77%	52%	69%	73%

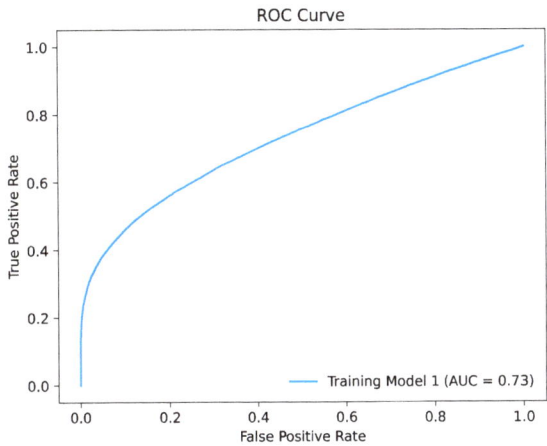

Figure 6. AUC for Model 1.

The results, despite being promising, are far from optimal because of the complexity of the data we used for training. Also, signals were labeled manually using the synchronized audio files as ground truth, which means that minor discrepancies between the audio and the file may have occurred.

4.3. Training Model 2

The second model (https://github.com/LeonidasAgathos/Identifying_earthquakes_in_low_cost_sensors_signals_contaminated_with_vehicular_noise/blob/main/Model_for_Eartquake.ipynb, accessed on 13 September 2023) was trained to identify earthquake events. To perform this task, the NOA data were used, which, as mentioned above in Section 3.4, includes 502 seismic events. After collecting the data, during the pre-processing phase, normalization was applied in the (−1, 1) range. After that, we performed the balancing of the data and the creation of the DNN. As mentioned before, the balancing method we used was NearMiss (version 1) and the DNN contained the same layers as the prior training model 1 (Section 4.2) for the same reasons mentioned above. In this model, samples were classified as either noise or earthquake. Table 2 shows the training and test results while the ROC curve is shown in Figure 7.

Table 2. Performance metrics for training model 2.

Accuracy	Precision	Recall	F1 Score	AUC Curve
75%	83%	63%	72%	82%

The training was conducted in 10 epochs, selected to avoid over-fitting, and lasted approximately 2 min. The results received from the training and testing phase were better than the previous model but again far from optimal.

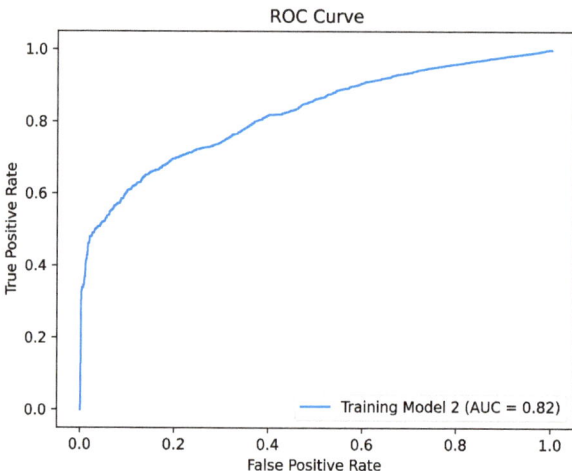

Figure 7. AUC for Model 2.

4.4. Experiment 1

The first experiment in this study employed the stochastic differential model, as described in Section 3.1. The primary objective of this model was to identify the onset of seismic events within an arbitrary time-series dataset. To do that, the two-fold synchronized dataset was fed to the stochastic differential model. Then, we extracted the actual starting point of every earthquake event and compared it to the true labels held on the two-fold synchronized dataset files. Finally, we had to evaluate the results and extract the metrics of the results.

The results obtained from this experiment can be seen in Table 3 and Figure 8. The metrics received from the first experiment show us a moderate performance of the model; the accuracy and precision reached 46% while the F1 score was 63%. Also, the AUC curve (shown in Figure 9) was 50% and the recall was at 100%.

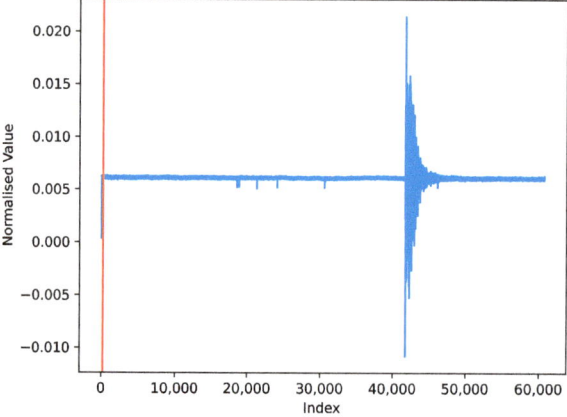

Figure 8. *Cont.*

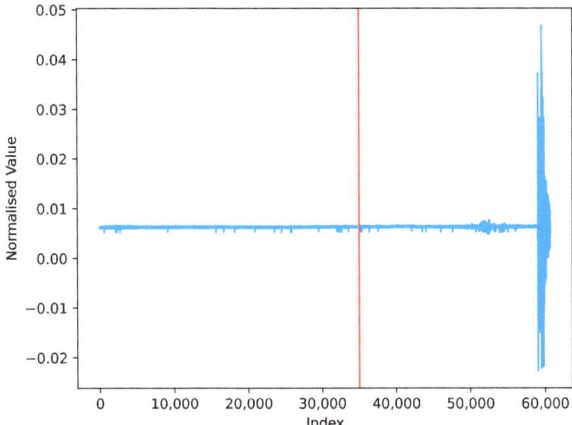

Figure 8. Results of the stochastic algorithm's performance.

Table 3. Performance metrics for experiment 1.

Accuracy	Precision	Recall	F1 Score	AUC Curve
46%	46%	100%	63%	50%

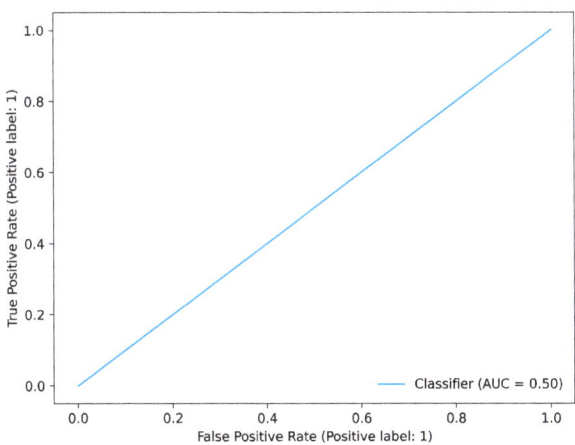

Figure 9. AUC for the stochastic model.

4.5. Experiment 2

In our second experiment, we created an amalgamated DNN model (https://github.com/LeonidasAgathos/Identifying_earthquakes_in_low_cost_sensors_signals_contaminated_with_vehicular_noise/blob/main/Model_Concatenation.ipynb, accessed on 13 September 2023), which includes the two models from Sections 4.2 and 4.3. The purpose of this experiment is for our model to be able to classify the starting point of an earthquake event without confusion from car signals and to perform better than the current methodology used by the stochastic model. This was achieved by combining the two different trained models and concatenating them, thus resulting in a single tensor that is the concatenation of all inputs. Initially, the pre-trained models of noise–cars and noise–earthquakes were loaded, and we applied the concatenation process. After that, we had to load the two-fold synchronized dataset and pre-process the data, which pertained to dropping the unnecessary columns and normalizing the data. With our two models in the same shape and the two-fold synchronized dataset in the proper form, our final model was ready to classify the two-fold synchronized dataset. We set a dense layer with the activation function "sigmoid", as we needed to differentiate between noise and earthquakes. We considered car signals and noise in the same class, as the task was to find the earthquake events and separate them from any noise signals. To compare the results, we had to classify the two-fold synchronized dataset based on the final model we created. After that, we had to find the first point of every file in the two-fold synchronized dataset, which was classified as an earthquake in order to determine the starting point of the event. This would also be the point where we would assess proper metrics and compare the two experiments. We saved the classified labels along with the true labels, so we could derive the metrics from this experiment. The results of the metrics can be seen in Table 4.

Table 4. Performance metrics for experiment 2.

Accuracy	Precision	Recall	F1 Score	AUC Curve
78%	78%	100%	88%	51%

As we can see, the accuracy is 78%, which means that we see a big improvement when compared to the results of the experiment in Section 4.4, and our model was able to classify the start of the event, in a much more efficient way. Also, the precision of this experiment is 78%, which means our model performed well in finding the actual start of the earthquake events (the positive class). The recall was found to be at 100% due to the one class we have in the predicted labels (we only kept the positive class, which indicates the earthquake). Finally, the F1 score was found to be at 88%, which is likely the most important metric to consider in this experiment, as our target was to classify as many true positives as possible and the AUC curve (shown in Figure 10) was at 51%, which is probably caused by the lack of the negative class in the given dataset.

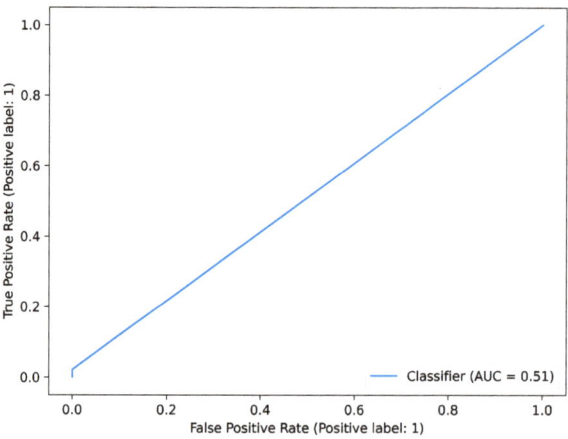

Figure 10. AUC for the proposed model.

In summary, the results, as illustrated in Figure 11, firmly validate the efficacy of our proposed methodology when compared to the stochastic approach. Our proposed model exhibits notably superior performance, emphasizing its potential in practical applications. Specifically, our proposed model achieves comparable results in the recall metric when contrasted with the stochastic model. However, it significantly outperforms the latter by achieving a precision score exceeding 30%, underscoring its capacity to accurately identify positive instances (true positives) while mitigating the occurrence of false positive errors. Moreover, our model attains a substantially improved F1 score, surpassing the stochastic model by more than 20%. This superior F1 score attests to our model's ability to strike an optimal balance between precision and recall, making it a promising choice for various real-world scenarios.

As shown in Figure 12, we can see how our model performed in real-world scenarios. The red color presents the space between the first point predicted as the earthquake to the last point predicted as the earthquake. The two vertical lines show the actual start and end of the earthquake (ground truth). When it comes to the start of the event, our model classifies the starting point exactly at the onset. As we can also observe, the model classifies the whole earthquake event, not only the starting point. The ending part of an earthquake is always a complex task so the model performs decently (regarding classification) on that as well. When comparing these results with the stochastic methodology (Section 4.4), we can see a big improvement in finding the earthquake events, not only on the metrics, but also in the actual usage of a model like this, which detects an earthquake event.

While our cost-effective system, built on open hardware and software, offers an attractive alternative to pricier traditional seismographs, it comes with inherent limitations in the sampling rate, bit precision, and amplification. Our dataset, a combination of high-quality and low-cost recordings, presents an imbalance issue due to the significantly smaller proportion of low-cost data. This imbalance affects our model's outcomes. Additionally, the constraints tied to our DNN's architecture were expected, given its off-the-shelf nature. However, this architecture can be enhanced through increased parameterization.

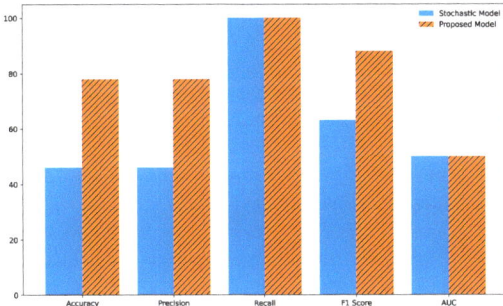

Figure 11. Comparison of metric scores.

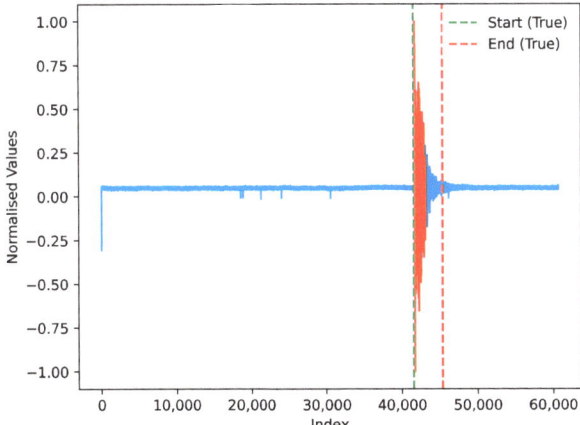

Figure 12. *Cont.*

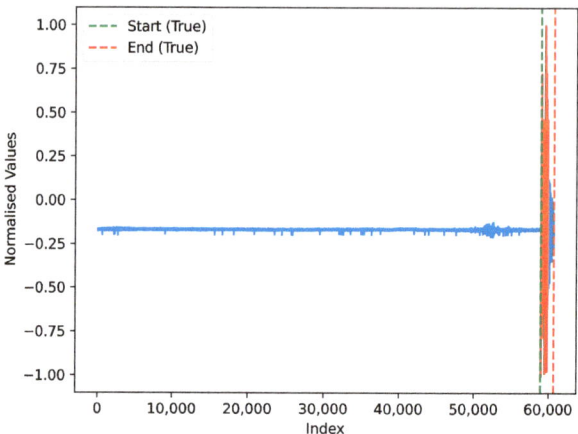

Figure 12. Results of the amalgamated DNN model's performance.

5. Conclusions

This paper underscores the profound significance of earthquake monitoring for the purposes of disaster management, public safety, and scientific research. Moreover, the pivotal role of sensor networks in amassing seismic data is presented, forming the cornerstone of current earthquake detection capabilities. In that context, the advent of low-cost sensors has unlocked the potential for their extensive deployment in the field, despite their susceptibility to vehicular noise pollution. Low-cost seismic sensors present a formidable challenge, necessitating innovative solutions for accurate signal extraction. Since the importance of precise earthquake identification cannot be overstated, as it holds the key to timely alerts and informed decision-making, herein, we propose the use of an amalgamated deep neural network (DNN) composed of (i) a DNN trained on earthquake signals from professional sensory equipment, as well as (ii) a DNN trained on vehicular signals from low-cost sensors, for the purpose of earthquake identification in signals from low-cost sensors contaminated with vehicular noise.

Our proposal includes a detailed presentation of a low-cost seismic sensory equipment, which is designed to be approximately two orders of magnitude less expensive than typical professional seismic measurement equipment. Still, the low-cost seismic sensory equipment was shown to be prone to vehicular noise contamination. Accordingly, the proposed amalgamated deep neural network underwent evaluation through experimentation and has manifested significant performance improvements compared to a generic stochastic differential model. The superiority of the proposed methodology addresses the need of effectiveness, as it identifies both the beginning and the end of a seismic event, as well as the need of efficiency, as indicated by the performance measures. Future plans will include customizing the generic DNNs deployed in this study for the task at hand, in order to address the necessities of the work's scenario and achieve even higher efficiency in the end identification process. Moreover, we plan to expand the two training datasets (vehicular noise and ground truth from professional seismometers) provided herein to ensure more generality and to better train the DNN, accordingly obtaining more general results. Finally, we plan to extend our low-cost network of sensors in locations near the professional seismometers in order to enhance the two-fold synchronized dataset and to test even more diverse scenarios.

Author Contributions: Conceptualization, L.A., A.A., N.A., I.V., I.K. and M.A.; Methodology, L.A., A.A., N.A., I.V., I.K. and M.A.; Software, L.A., A.A., N.A., I.V., I.K. and M.A.; Validation, L.A., A.A., N.A., I.V., I.K. and M.A.; Formal analysis, L.A., A.A., N.A., I.V., I.K. and M.A.; Investigation, L.A., A.A., N.A., I.V., I.K. and M.A.; Resources, L.A., A.A., N.A., I.V., I.K. and M.A.; Data curation, L.A., A.A., N.A., I.V., I.K. and M.A.; Writing—original draft, L.A., A.A., N.A., I.V., I.K. and M.A.; Writing—review & editing, L.A., A.A., N.A., I.V., I.K. and M.A.; Visualization, L.A., A.A., N.A., I.V., I.K. and M.A.; Supervision, L.A., A.A., N.A., I.V., I.K. and M.A.; Project administration, L.A., A.A., N.A., I.V., I.K. and M.A.; Funding acquisition, L.A., A.A., N.A., I.V., I.K. and M.A. All authors have read and agreed to the published version of the manuscript.

Funding: This research received no external funding.

Institutional Review Board Statement: Not applicable.

Informed Consent Statement: Not applicable.

Data Availability Statement: Not applicable.

Conflicts of Interest: The authors declare no conflict of interest.

References

1. Lim, J.; Jung, S.; JeGal, C.; Jung, G.; Yoo, J.H.; Gahm, J.K.; Song, G. LEQNet: Light Earthquake Deep Neural Network for Earthquake Detection and Phase Picking. *Front. Earth Sci.* **2022**, *10*, 848237. [CrossRef]
2. Ji, L.; Zou, Y.; He, K.; Zhu, B. Carbon futures price forecasting based with ARIMA-CNN-LSTM model. *Procedia Comput. Sci.* **2019**, *162*, 33–38. [CrossRef]
3. Murti, M.; Junior, R.; Najah, A.M.; Elshafie, A. Earthquake multi-classification detection based velocity and displacement data filtering using machine learning algorithms. *Sci. Rep.* **2022**, *12*, 21200. [CrossRef]
4. Mousavi, S.M.; Sheng, Y.; Zhu, W.; Beroza, G.C. STanford EArthquake Dataset (STEAD): A Global Data Set of Seismic Signals for AI. *IEEE Access* **2019**, *7*, 179464–179476. [CrossRef]
5. Mao, F.; Khamis, K.; Krause, S.; Clark, J.; Hannah, D.M. Low-cost environmental sensor networks: Recent advances and future directions. *Front. Earth Sci.* **2019**, *7*, 221. [CrossRef]
6. D'Alessandro, A.; Scudero, S.; Vitale, G. A review of the capacitive MEMS for seismology. *Sensors* **2019**, *19*, 3093. [PubMed]
7. Arora, N.; Kumar, Y. Automatic vehicle detection system in Day and Night Mode: Challenges, applications and panoramic review. *Evol. Intell.* **2023**, *16*, 1077–1095. [CrossRef]
8. Mondal, B. Pandemic COVID-19, Reduced Usage of Public Transportation Systems and Urban Environmental Challenges: Few Evidences from India and West Bengal. In *Environmental Management and Sustainability in India: Case Studies from West Bengal*; Springer: Berlin/Heidelberg, Germany, 2023; pp. 341–368.
9. Yu, Q.; Wang, C.; Li, J.; Xiong, R.; Pecht, M. Challenges and outlook for lithium-ion battery fault diagnosis methods from the laboratory to real world applications. *eTransportation* **2023**, *17*, 100254. [CrossRef]
10. Bhatia, M.; Ahanger, T.A.; Manocha, A. Artificial intelligence based real-time earthquake prediction. *Eng. Appl. Artif. Intell.* **2023**, *120*, 105856. [CrossRef]
11. Kassa, A.B.; Dugda, M.T.; Lin, Y.; Seifu, A. Earthquake Aftershocks Pattern Prediction. In Proceedings of the AGU Fall Meeting, Chicago, IL, USA, 12–16 December 2022; Volume 2022, p. S42C–0177. Available online: https://ui.adsabs.harvard.edu/abs/2022AGUFM.S42C0177D (accessed on 13 September 2023).
12. Shearer, P.M. *Introduction to Seismology: The Wave Equation and Body Waves*; Institute of Geophysics and Planetary Physics, Scipps Institution of Oceanography, University of California: San Diego, CA, USA, 2010; unpublished.
13. Udias, A.; Buforn, E. *Principles of Seismology*; Cambridge University Press: Cambridge, UK, 2017.
14. Kennett, B.L.N. *The Seismic Wavefield: Volume 1, Introduction and Theoretical Development*; Cambridge University Press: Cambridge, UK, 2001; Volume 1.
15. Hou, Y.; Jiao, R.; Yu, H. MEMS based geophones and seismometers. *Sens. Actuators Phys.* **2021**, *318*, 112498. [CrossRef]
16. Bullen, K.E.; Bolt, B.A. *An Introduction to the Theory of Seismology*; Cambridge University Press: Cambridge, UK, 1985.
17. Kumar, D.; Ahmed, I. Seismic Noise. In *Encyclopedia of Solid Earth Geophysics*; Gupta, H.K., Ed.; Springer International Publishing: Cham, Switzerland, 2021; pp. 1442–1447.
18. Dou, S.; Lindsey, N.; Wagner, A.M.; Daley, T.M.; Freifeld, B.; Robertson, M.; Peterson, J.; Ulrich, C.; Martin, E.R.; Ajo-Franklin, J.B. Distributed acoustic sensing for seismic monitoring of the near surface: A traffic-noise interferometry case study. *Sci. Rep.* **2017**, *7*, 11620. [CrossRef] [PubMed]
19. Sun, L.; Qiu, X.; Wang, Y.; Wang, C. Seismic Periodic Noise Attenuation Based on Sparse Representation Using a Noise Dictionary. *Appl. Sci.* **2023**, *13*, 2835. [CrossRef]
20. Du, R.; Liu, W.; Fu, X.; Meng, L.; Liu, Z. Random noise attenuation via convolutional neural network in seismic datasets. *Alex. Eng. J.* **2022**, *61*, 9901–9909. [CrossRef]

21. Prasanna, R.; Chandrakumar, C.; Nandana, R.; Holden, C.; Punchihewa, A.; Becker, J.S.; Jeong, S.; Liyanage, N.; Ravishan, D.; Sampath, R.; et al. "Saving Precious Seconds"—A novel approach to implementing a low-cost earthquake early warning system with node-level detection and alert generation. *Informatics* **2022**, *9*, 25. [CrossRef]
22. Wu, Y.M.; Mittal, H. A review on the development of earthquake warning system using low-cost sensors in Taiwan. *Sensors* **2021**, *21*, 7649. [CrossRef]
23. Lee, J.; Khan, I.; Choi, S.; Kwon, Y.W. A smart iot device for detecting and responding to earthquakes. *Electronics* **2019**, *8*, 1546. [CrossRef]
24. Ahmad, A.B.; Saibi, H.; Belkacem, A.N.; Tsuji, T. Vehicle Auto-Classification Using Machine Learning Algorithms Based on Seismic Fingerprinting. *Computers* **2022**, *11*, 148. [CrossRef]
25. Nie, T.; Wang, S.; Wang, Y.; Tong, X.; Sun, F. An effective recognition of moving target seismic anomaly for security region based on deep bidirectional LSTM combined CNN. *Multimed. Tools Appl.* **2023**. [CrossRef]
26. Münchmeyer, J.; Woollam, J.; Rietbrock, A.; Tilmann, F.; Lange, D.; Bornstein, T.; Diehl, T.; Giunchi, C.; Haslinger, F.; Jozinović, D.; et al. Which Picker Fits My Data? A Quantitative Evaluation of Deep Learning Based Seismic Pickers. *J. Geophys. Res. Solid Earth* **2022**, *127*, e2021JB023499.
27. Avlonitis, M. On the problem of early detection of users interaction outbreaks via stochastic differential models. *Eng. Appl. Artif. Intell.* **2016**, *51*, 92–96.
28. Krischer, L.; Megies, T.; Barsch, R.; Beyreuther, M.; Lecocq, T.; Caudron, C.; Wassermann, J. ObsPy: A bridge for seismology into the scientific Python ecosystem. *Comput. Sci. Discov.* **2015**, *8*, 014003. [CrossRef]
29. Evangelidis, C.P.; Triantafyllis, N.; Samios, M.; Boukouras, K.; Kontakos, K.; Ktenidou, O.; Fountoulakis, I.; Kalogeras, I.; Melis, N.S.; Galanis, O.; et al. Seismic Waveform Data from Greece and Cyprus: Integration, Archival, and Open Access. *Seismol. Res. Lett.* **2021**, *92*, 1672–1684.
30. Choubik, Y.; Mahmoudi, A.; Himmi, M.; El Moudnib, L. STA/LTA trigger algorithm implementation on a seismological dataset using Hadoop MapReduce. *Iaes Int. J. Artif. Intell. (IJ-AI)* **2020**, *9*, 269. [CrossRef]
31. Mani, I.; Zhang, I. kNN approach to unbalanced data distributions: A case study involving information extraction. In Proceedings of the Workshop on Learning from Imbalanced Datasets, Washington, DC, USA, 21 August 2003; Volume 126, pp. 1–7.
32. Abadi, M.; Barham, P.; Chen, J.; Chen, Z.; Davis, A.; Dean, J.; Devin, M.; Ghemawat, S.; Irving, G.; Isard, M.; et al. TensorFlow: A System for Large-Scale Machine Learning. In Proceedings of the 12th USENIX Conference on Operating Systems Design and Implementation, OSDI'16, Savannah, GA, USA, 2–4 November 2016; pp. 265–283.
33. Chollet, F. Keras. 2015. Available online: https://keras.io (accessed on 13 September 2023).
34. Hochreiter, S.; Schmidhuber, J. Long short-term memory. *Neural Comput.* **1997**, *9*, 1735–1780. [CrossRef]
35. Kowsher, M.; Tahabilder, A.; Islam Sanjid, M.Z.; Prottasha, N.J.; Uddin, M.S.; Hossain, M.A.; Kader Jilani, M.A. LSTM-ANN & BiLSTM-ANN: Hybrid deep learning models for enhanced classification accuracy. *Procedia Comput. Sci.* **2021**, *193*, 131–140.
36. Abualhaol, I.; Falcon, R.; Abielmona, R.; Petriu, E. Data-Driven Vessel Service Time Forecasting using Long Short-Term Memory Recurrent Neural Networks. In Proceedings of the 2018 IEEE International Conference on Big Data (Big Data), Seattle, WA, USA, 10–13 December 2018; Volume 12, pp. 2580–2590. [CrossRef]
37. Agarap, A.F. Deep Learning using Rectified Linear Units (ReLU). *arXiv* **2018**, arXiv:1803.08375.
38. Dubey, S.R.; Singh, S.K.; Chaudhuri, B.B. A Comprehensive Survey and Performance Analysis of Activation Functions in Deep Learning. *arXiv* **2021**, arXiv:2109.14545.
39. Yang, T.; Ying, Y. AUC Maximization in the Era of Big Data and AI: A Survey. *arXiv* **2022**, arXiv:2203.15046.

Disclaimer/Publisher's Note: The statements, opinions and data contained in all publications are solely those of the individual author(s) and contributor(s) and not of MDPI and/or the editor(s). MDPI and/or the editor(s) disclaim responsibility for any injury to people or property resulting from any ideas, methods, instructions or products referred to in the content.

Article

Anomalies in Infrared Outgoing Longwave Radiation Data before the Yangbi *Ms*6.4 and Luding *Ms*6.8 Earthquakes Based on Time Series Forecasting Models

Junqing Zhu, Ke Sun * and Jingye Zhang

Institute of Earthquake Forecasting, CEA, Beijing 100036, China
* Correspondence: sunke@cea-ies.ac.cn

Abstract: Numerous scholars have used traditional thermal anomaly extraction methods and time series prediction models to study seismic anomalies based on longwave infrared radiation data. This paper selected bidirectional long short-term memory (BILSTM) as the research algorithm after analyzing and comparing the prediction performance of five time series prediction models. Based on the outgoing longwave radiation (OLR) data, the time series prediction model was used to predict the infrared longwave radiation values in the spatial area of 5° × 5° at the epicenter for 30 days before the earthquake. The confidence interval was used as the evaluation criterion to extract anomalies. The examples of earthquakes selected for study were the Yangbi *Ms*6.4-magnitude earthquake in Yunnan on 21 May 2021 and the Luding *Ms*6.8-magnitude earthquake in Sichuan on 5 September 2022. The results showed that the observed values of the Yangbi earthquake 15 to 16 days before the earthquake (5 May to 6 May) exceeded the prediction confidence interval over a wide area and to a large extent. This indicates a strong and concentrated OLR anomaly before the Yangbi earthquake. The observations at 27 days (9 August), 18 days (18 August), and 8 days (28 August) before the Luding earthquake exceeded the prediction confidence interval in a local area and by a large extent, indicating a strong and scattered OLR anomaly before the Luding earthquake. Overall, the method used in this paper extracts anomalies in both spatial and temporal dimensions and is an effective method for extracting infrared longwave radiation anomalies.

Keywords: time series forecasting models; infrared longwave radiation data; seismic anomaly; confidence interval; BILSTM

Citation: Zhu, J.; Sun, K.; Zhang, J. Anomalies in Infrared Outgoing Longwave Radiation Data before the Yangbi *Ms*6.4 and Luding *Ms*6.8 Earthquakes Based on Time Series Forecasting Models. *Appl. Sci.* **2023**, *13*, 8572. https://doi.org/10.3390/app13158572

Academic Editor: José A. Peláez

Received: 15 May 2023
Revised: 21 July 2023
Accepted: 22 July 2023
Published: 25 July 2023

Copyright: © 2023 by the authors. Licensee MDPI, Basel, Switzerland. This article is an open access article distributed under the terms and conditions of the Creative Commons Attribution (CC BY) license (https:// creativecommons.org/licenses/by/ 4.0/).

1. Introduction

Since the 1980s, when the Soviet scientist Gornyy [1] first discovered anomalies in thermal infrared remote sensing images before earthquakes in Central Asia, researchers in various countries have been using thermal infrared data to study seismic activity and to attempt to predict earthquakes. Many scholars have used various methods to study pre-earthquake anomalies based on outgoing longwave radiation data, including wavelet variation methods [2], the robust satellite techniques (RST) algorithm [3], and the eddy field method [4], and to analyze pre-earthquake precursor patterns based on the spatial and temporal evolution of the anomalies. Time series studies of longwave radiation data could also demonstrate pre-earthquake anomalies from a single time dimension. Many scholars have used various methods to study changes in temporal OLR values, such as the geometric moving average martingale (GMAM) change detection method used by Kong et al. [5], the background field difference method and the mean value method used by Mahmood et al. [6], and the flux method used by Natarajan et al. [7], after processing the OLR data and displaying them on a two-dimensional image with time as the horizontal coordinate. The images showed anomalies that exceeded the thresholds. Many studies have shown that some thermal infrared anomalies may exist before earthquakes. However, some scientists have argued against this. For example, Prakash et al. [8] found no significant thermal anomalies before earthquakes in and around India after studying earthquakes in the region. Although there is no consensus on the mechanism of pre-earthquake infrared anomalies, it is generally accepted that a certain range of thermal anomalies can occur at some time before an earthquake. Significantly, Chinese seismologists introduced their research results of seismic infrared remote sensing into daily earthquake forecasting practice and obtained a good correspondence in the prediction of earthquake risk areas in 2008, 2009, and 2013 [9].

The Earth's outgoing longwave radiation is the primary driver of the Earth's climate. This energy's reflection, absorption, and emission occur through a complex system of clouds, aerosols, atmospheric constituents, oceans, and land surfaces [10]. By definition, longwave radiation is the energy density of electromagnetic waves of all wavelengths radiated into outer space by the Earth's atmospheric system. It can reflect the energy radiation of the Earth's atmospheric system [11]. The outgoing longwave radiation data used were acquired by the High-Resolution Infrared Radiation Sounder (HIRS) carried by the National Oceanic and Atmospheric Administration's (NOAA) polar-orbiting weather satellites. The NOAA satellite series has been continuously collecting longwave radiation data since the 1970s. These data have been used in a variety of applications due to the long accumulation of data and open-source access.

The rapid development of society has led to the generation of vast amounts of time series data in economics, meteorology, geology, and the environment. The correct application of time series data and forecasting models has been of great value to social activities. Classical time series forecasting models mainly include autoregressive moving average (ARMA) and autoregressive integrated moving average (ARIMA) models. Machine learning has a regression function that has been adapted to the characteristics of time series data. Various machine learning-based forecasting methods have been applied to time series data, including support vector machines, Bayesian networks, and Gaussian processes. With the development of deep learning, convolutional neural networks based on time series data, long short-term memory models, and multi-model hybrid models have been widely used and have achieved excellent performance [12]. Large amounts of data are required for data training of time series prediction models. The early deployment of seismic monitoring equipment and advances in observational monitoring techniques have facilitated the development of multiple types and long-time series of seismic data. These have provided favorable conditions for the application of time series forecasting models in the field of seismology. Saqib et al. [13,14] used the ARIMA algorithm for the short-term prediction of total electron content (TEC) and detected several pre-earthquake anomalies. In another paper published in the same year, the authors reported a better performance of the long short-term memory (LSTM) model than the ARIMA model in detecting seismic ionospheric anomalies. Some researchers have made improvements to the LSTM algorithm. A multi-network-based hybrid long and short-term memory (N-LSTM) model was proposed by Senturk et al. [15]; Yue et al. [16] combined the LSTM model and the relative power spectrum method for TEC anomaly detection; Xiong et al. [17] proposed an encoder–decoder extended short-term memory expansion model; all these improved models obtained better performance in their article applications.

In radon time series studies, Mohammed et al. [18] used the ARIMA model and Monte Carlo prediction model to find a good correlation between soil radon and micro-seismicity in the study area; Mir et al. [19] used different sets of algorithms to predict time series and detect anomalies for real-time soil radon time series of different scenarios; Feng et al. [20] studied groundwater radon and used an empirical mode decomposition–long short-term memory (EMD–LSTM) model to find multiple possible radon anomalies before earthquakes. In addition to TEC data and radon data, surface temperature, geoelectric seismic signal, seismic energy release, b-value (Gutenberg–Richter law's b-value), groundwater level, OLR, and geomagnetic data with time series properties have all been used by scholars and based on time prediction models to study pre-earthquake sequence anomalies.

This paper first describes traditional methods for studying longwave radiation data and analyzing seismic sequence data based on different time series prediction models. The data section presents the data sources and data processing methods used and selects the Yangbi Ms6.4 earthquake of 21 May 2021 and the Luding Ms6.8 earthquake of 5 September 2022 as research cases. Conventional anomaly extraction methods were able to detect pre-seismic OLR anomalies for both earthquakes. The Methods section describes time series prediction models and anomaly assessment methods. The Discussion section discusses the strengths and weaknesses of this experiment, how the results compare with those of previous studies, and future directions for improvement. Finally, conclusions were drawn for the whole text.

2. Data

2.1. HIRS OLR Data

The HIRS sensor is an atmospheric sounding instrument that has been in operation on the NOAA series of satellites since 1978, with three types of HIRS instruments in use since 1982, namely HIRS/2 for NOAA 1–14, HIRS/3 for NOAA 15–17, and HIRS/4 for NOAA-18 and Metop-B [21]. The High-Resolution Infrared Radiation Sounder/4 (HIRS/4) comprises 19 infrared channels. A total of 12 thermal infrared channels (6.7–15 μm) were defined as the longwave band, 7 near-infrared channels (3.7–4.6 μm) were defined as the short-wave band, and 1 channel (0.69 μm) was identified as visible [22]. Compared to HIRS/3, the latest HIRS/4 has a 10 km instantaneous field of view (IFOV) and a 20 km ground sample distance (GSD), facilitating increased instrument observations in cloud-free conditions. The HIRS instrument has a rich set of objects and is capable of acquiring data on ocean surface temperature, total atmospheric ozone, cloud top height, and coverage, water vapor distribution, and surface radiance [23].

The HIRS OLR product was developed in the 1980s by Ellingson et al. The unit of OLR values is W/m^2. If radiance data were available from several spectral intervals encompassing the entire spectrum at a given viewing angle, a first-order estimate of the OLR could be obtained by summing the radiance for each spectral interval. The estimation equation for the flux (OLR) was, therefore, chosen as a weighted sum of the HIRS radiance observations, given as:

$$OLR = a_0 + \sum_k a_k(\theta) N_k(\theta) \tag{1}$$

where the a's are regression coefficients, θ is the satellite zenith angle, and N is the observed radiance which is related to the specific intensity I at wavenumber v and the instrument responsivity ϕ. $N_k(\theta)$ is defined as:

$$N_k(\theta) = \int_{\Delta v} I(v,\theta) \phi_k dv \tag{2}$$

The outgoing flux for an axisymmetric atmosphere is related to the specific intensity as:

$$OLR = 2\pi \int_0^\infty dv \int_0^{\pi/2} I(v,\theta) \cos\theta \sin\theta d\theta \tag{3}$$

The spectral intervals and the regression coefficients for (1) were determined with a stepwise regression analysis of calculations from a theoretical radiation model using 1600 soundings as input data. Ellingson et al. [24] used multispectral regression technology to evaluate OLR values from four HIRS channels (channels: 3, 7, 10, and 12). The outgoing flux error of this method was about 4 times smaller than the error of NOAA using AVHRR to estimate flux. Because the spectral response function for channel 10 has changed in the HIRS instruments developed after HIRS/2, the algorithm used channels 3, 10, 11, and 12 [25].

The 1° × 1° OLR data from the NOAA-18 satellite used can be downloaded from the National Centers for Environmental Prediction (NCEP) FTP server. The downloaded data were in a binary ASCII format with "1" for daytime data and "2" for nighttime data, and the daytime and nighttime data were in a 180 × 360 array. We chose nighttime data for the study to minimize interference from solar radiation and human activity [23]. NOAA-18 satellite 1° × 1° OLR data can be downloaded via NCEP's FTP server (ftp://ftp.cpc.ncep.noaa.gov/precip/noaa18_1x1/) (accessed on 20 December 2022).

2.2. Data Processing

In studying the spatial dimension of pre-earthquake thermal infrared anomalies, Sun et al. [9] found that the most significant thermal anomaly of the 25 April 2015 $Ms8.1$ earthquake occurred about 100 km west of the epicenter, and the most significant thermal anomaly of the 12 May 2015 $Ms7.5$ earthquake occurred about 200 km east of the epicenter. Lu et al. [2] used the wavelet variation method to study the Tibet Shigatse 26 February 2010 $Ms5.0$ earthquake, the Tibet Nierong 4 March 2010 $Ms5.7$ and $Ms5.5$ earthquakes, and the Yushu 14 April 2010 $Ms7.1$ earthquake. After observing the spatial and temporal evolution maps of the seismic thermal anomalies, we found that the anomalies were mainly distributed near the epicenter. Most of the anomaly distribution was in the spatial range of 5° × 5°. The range of effects of different earthquake magnitudes was also provided by the "SERIES OF EARTHQUAKE CASES IN CHINA": $Ms \geq 7.0$ earthquake, within 500 km; $6.0 \leq M_S < 7.0$ earthquake, within 300 km; $5.0 \leq Ms < 6.0$ earthquake, within 200 km [26–28].

In order to study the temporal dimension of the pre-earthquake thermal infrared anomalies, Jing et al. [29] chose a 5° × 5° area centered on the epicenter as the study area after considering that the thermal anomalies usually reflected an extensive range and took two months as the study time dimension. It was found that the pre-earthquake high OLR value anomalies appeared within one month in the study of the Zhongba $Ms6.8$ earthquake on 25 August 2008 and the Yutian $Ms7.3$ earthquake on 21 March 2008. In another paper, Jing et al. [30] found a thermal anomaly in the fault zone near the epicenter of the 25 April 2015 $Ms8.1$ earthquake in Nepal six months before its occurrence. Song et al. [31] used the RST algorithm to study the 12 May 2008 Wenchuan $Ms8.0$ earthquake, which showed that thermal anomalies began to accumulate spatially three months before the quake, with anomalies of different intensities and distribution ranges appearing multiple times over time. Based on existing studies, the following could be concluded: the distribution of anomaly ranges extracted by the thermal infrared anomaly extraction algorithm was irregular but generally distributed near the epicenter; and pre-earthquake thermal anomalies occurred irregularly, usually within six months before the earthquake.

The examples of earthquakes selected for study in this paper were the Yangbi $Ms6.4$ earthquake of 21 May 2021 and the Luding $Ms6.8$ earthquake of 5 September 2022. The epicenter of the Yangbi earthquake was located near the southwest edge of the Sichuan–Yunnan rhombic block, which is a channel for material extrusion from the Qinghai–Tibet Plateau to the southeast and belongs to the area with the strongest extrusion deformation. Within 100 km of the epicenter, there were five Holocene active fractures: the Honghe Fault, the Lijiang-Xiaojinhe Fault, the Heqing-Eryuan Fault, the Chenghai-Binchuan Fault, and the Longban-Qiaohou Fault. The Yangbi earthquake was the result of a shallow fault slip, and the regional geologic structure is consistent with the spatial characteristics of dextral strike-slip movement [32]. The epicenter of the Luding earthquake was located near the Moxi Fault in the southeast section of the Xianshuihe Fault Zone on the southeastern edge of the Tibetan Plateau. The Xianshuihe Fault Zone has a total length of about 350 km and is a large sinistral strike-slip fault zone with strong activity, high seismic development, and geological disaster risk [33]. Table 1 shows the information for the two studied earthquakes.

Due to the moderate magnitude of the earthquake, the experimental area selected was a 5° × 5° area close to the center. In this paper, we mainly wanted to study close-proximity anomalies, so we chose the 30 days before the earthquake as the prediction days. The study area shown in Figure 1 and the nearest grid data to the epicenter were chosen to represent the data at the epicenter.

Table 1. Detailed information of earthquake examples.

Time (UTC + 8)	Longitude/° E	Latitude /° N	Depth/KM	Magnitude/M_S	Location
21 May 2021 21:48	99.87	25.67	8	6.4	Yangbi County, Yunnan Province
5 September 2022 12:52	102.08	29.59	16	6.8	Luding County, Sichuan Province

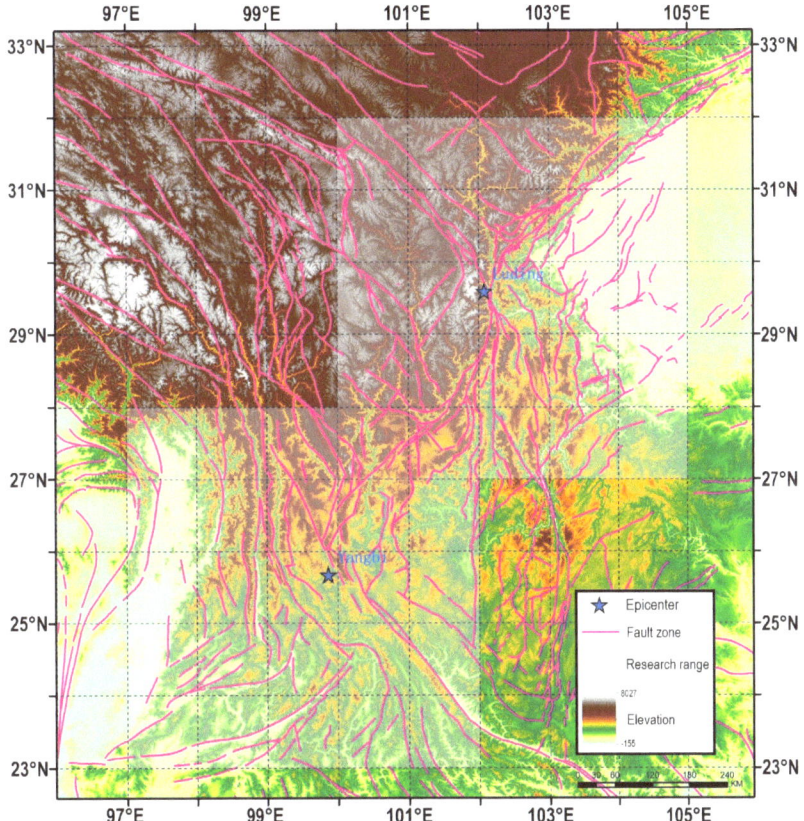

Figure 1. Research region. The pentagrams indicate the locations of epicenters, the gray area indicates the 5° × 5° study area, and the pink lines represent the fault zones.

The original OLR data were organized in an array of 180 × 360 pixels. The time dimension was continuous. The a-plot in Figure 2 shows the OLR values for the region of China from 22 April 2022 to 21 May 2022. The b-plot in Figure 2 shows the Yangbi earthquake in the 5° × 5° area (5 × 5 pixels). Figure 2 was drawn in MATLAB. Extracting the experimental area from the original data was the main pre-processing method in this experiment.

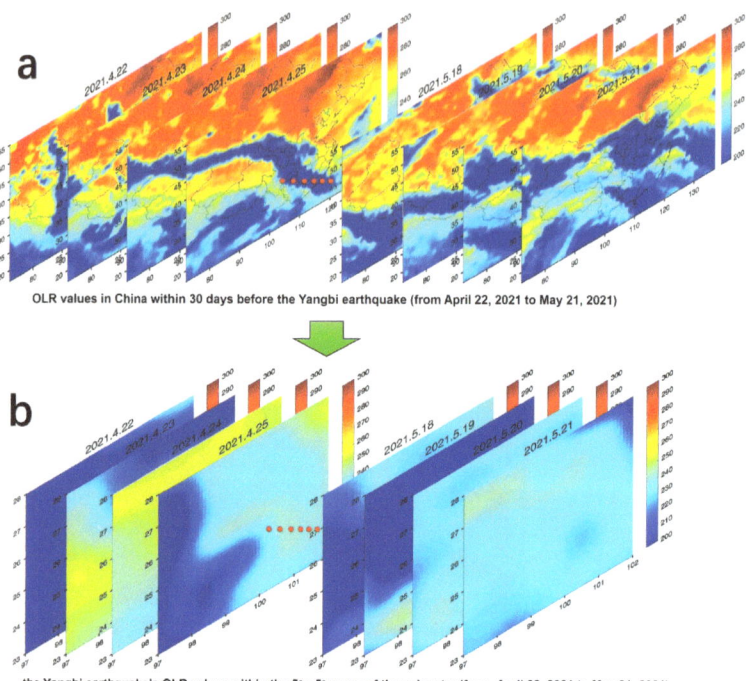

Figure 2. (**a**) OLR values in China in the 30 days before Yangbi Ms6.4 earthquake (from 22 April 2021 to 21 May 2021). The red box indicates the study area of the Yangbi earthquake. (**b**) The Yangbi Ms6.4 earthquake's OLR values within the 5° × 5° range of the epicenter (from 22 April 2021 to 21 May 2021).

3. Methods

The existence of pre-earthquake thermal infrared anomalies has been demonstrated in many studies. Most traditional studies were based on different algorithms to extract the intensity and distribution range of thermal infrared anomalies in pre-earthquake time and spatial dimensions, such as the RST algorithm, wavelet vorticity method, and eddy field method [2–4]. The experiment was based on time series data of outgoing longwave infrared radiation and used a time series prediction model to predict the values of longwave infrared radiation at different time ranges before the earthquake within a specific spatial coverage of the epicenter. Data preparation involved downloading the data and selecting seismic examples and spatial and temporal scales. The data were cropped to the corresponding temporal and spatial scales to generate the dataset. By comparing and analyzing the prediction performance of different time series prediction models for different prediction periods, we selected the best performing model for the earthquake example study in the algorithm evaluation phase. In the anomaly extraction phase, the confidence interval was used as the evaluation criterion to extract the magnitude of the range outside the confidence interval and the corresponding date. Finally, the anomalies were analyzed based on the spatiotemporal dimension. Figure 3 shows the entire process of this experiment.

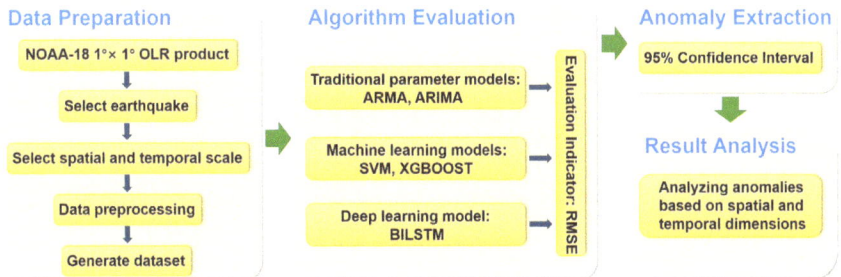

Figure 3. Experimental flowchart. The experimental process is divided into four parts: Data Preparation, Algorithm Evaluation, Anomaly Extraction, and Result Analysis.

3.1. Time Series Forecasting Models

3.1.1. ARMA/ARIMA

ARMA and ARIMA models were obtained from a combination of autoregressive and moving average models [34]. When the time series is smooth, given a time series $t = 0, t = 1, t = 2 \ldots$, ARMA(p, q) can be expressed as

$$z_t = m_1 z_{t-1} + \cdots + m_p z_{t-p} + c_t + n_1 c_{t-1} + \cdots + n_q c_{t-q} \tag{4}$$

where $m_p \neq 0, n_q \neq 0$, z_t is a stationary sequence, c_t is a white noise sequence, p is the autoregressive parameter, and q is the moving average parameter. If the mean of z_t is non-zero, then $\delta = \mu(1 - \eta_1 - \cdots - \eta_p)$ is set and (1) is rewritten as [35,36]:

$$z_t = \delta + m_1 z_{t-1} + \cdots + m_p z_{t-p} + c_t + n_1 c_{t-1} + \cdots + n_q c_{t-q} \tag{5}$$

When the time series is not smooth, the difference term can be introduced to smooth the series, where ARMA(p, q) becomes ARMA(p, d, q). The "d" in ARMA(p, d, q) is called the difference order, and is usually differenced once or twice for an unsteady time series. The difference separates out the noise in the time series and replaces the time series value with the difference between the original and previous values [37].

3.1.2. SVM

Since Vapnik [38] developed support vector machines in 1995, the machine learning model has been widely used in pattern recognition, object classification, and time series regression tasks. Support vector regression models differ from traditional parametric models in that the former uses training data to obtain regression results [39]. Suppose that we have training data $(x_1, y_1), (x_2, y_2), \ldots (x_l, y_l)$, where x_i is the input value and y_i is the output value corresponding to it. Optimization problems in support vector regression are as follows:

$$\min_{\omega, b, \xi, \xi^*} \frac{1}{2} \omega^T \omega + C \sum_{i=1}^{l} (\xi_i + \xi_i^*) \tag{6}$$

$$\text{subject to} \quad \begin{array}{l} y_i - (\omega^T \varphi(x_i) + b) \leq \epsilon + \xi_i^*, \\ (\omega^T \varphi(x_i) + b) - y_i \leq \epsilon + \xi_i \\ \xi_i, \xi_i^* \geq 0, \quad i = 1, \ldots, l \end{array}$$

where ω is the normal vector, b is the intercept distance, x_i is mapped by the function to a high-dimensional space, and ξ_i^* and ξ_i are the upper and lower errors of the training respectively. The parameters controlling the regression quality are the cost error C, the width of the dimension ϵ, and the mapping function φ. SVR avoids under- and overfitting training data by minimizing the error and the canonical term. The dual problem of the function is treated next.

$$\min_{\alpha,\alpha^*} \frac{1}{2}(\alpha-\alpha^*)^T Q(\alpha-\alpha^*) + \epsilon \sum_{i=1}^{l}(\alpha_i + \alpha_i^*) + \sum_{i=1}^{i} y_i(\alpha - \alpha_i^*) \qquad (7)$$

subject to $\sum_{i=1}^{l}(\alpha_i - \alpha_i^*) = 0 \quad Q_{ij} = \varphi(x_i)^T \varphi(x_j) \quad 0 \leq \alpha_i, \quad \alpha_i^* \leq C, \quad i = 1, \ldots, l$

Faced with the problem of computing functions, we can introduce polynomial kernels or RBF kernels for efficient computation [40].

3.1.3. XGBoost

XGBoost is a machine learning model proposed by Tianqi Chen et al. [41]. It is an improvement on the gradient-boosting decision tree, which gives full play to the calculator's parallel computing power and improves the algorithm's accuracy. Suppose we have training data $(c_1,d_1),(c_2,d_2),\ldots(c_s,d_s), x_r \in X \subseteq R^o, y_r \in Y \subseteq R$, where X is the input space and Y is the output space corresponding to it. The optimization objective function $L(u)$ of the XGBoost algorithm is:

$$L(u) = \sum_{r=1}^{s} l\left(d_r, \widetilde{d}_r(u-1)\right) + f_u(c_r)) + H(f_u) \qquad (8)$$

where $\widetilde{d}_r(u-1)$ is expressed as the predicted value of the model at the $(u-1)$th iteration of the sample; $f_u(c_s)$ is described as the predicted value of the model at the tth iteration of the sample; and $H(f_u)$ is the canonical term of the objective function. A Taylor expansion of the above equation gives:

$$\widetilde{L}(u) \cong \sum_{j=1}^{v}\left[e_j \sum_{r \in K_j} g_r + \frac{1}{2}e_j^2\left(\sum_{r \in K_j} h_r + \lambda\right)\right] + \gamma T \qquad (9)$$

where g_r and h_r are the first- and second-order gradients of sample c_r, respectively; e_j is the output value of the jth node; λ and γ are the regular term coefficients; and K_j is the subset of samples in the jth leaf node. The training process of the XGBoost model is the process of solving the above equation and finding the optimal solution [42].

3.1.4. BILSTM

Recurrent neural networks (RNNs) are a sequence-to-sequence model where the model does not change depending on the length of the sequence. However, when dealing with long sequences, it forgets information from further back in time, leading to problems such as gradient loss and overfitting. The long short-term memory (LSTM) model improves on the RNN by adding "forgetting gates", "input gates", and "output gates" to control the retention and rejection of information through the function of gates. This optimizes the shortcomings of RNN's short-term memory and can effectively handle the transfer of information in long-time sequences [43,44]. Figure 4 shows a structural diagram of the LSTM model.

The BILSTM model, a bidirectional long short-term memory neural network, consists of two independent LSTM models, a forward model and a backward model. The output combines the results of both models. To some extent, the BILSTM model can compensate for information that may be missed by the unidirectional LSTM [45]. Figure 5 shows a structural diagram of the BILSTM model.

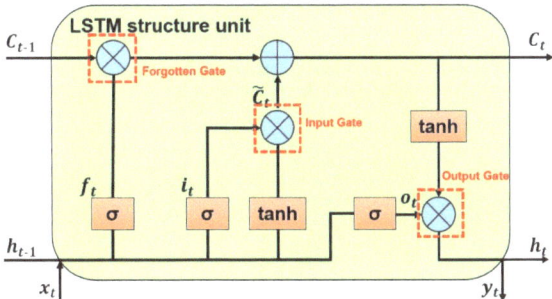

Figure 4. LSTM unit structure diagram. h_{t-1} and h_t are the hidden information of the previous cell output and this cell output, respectively; x_t and y_t are the input and output of this cell, respectively; C_{t-1} and C_t are the cell states of the previous cell output and this cell output, respectively; f_t, i_t, and o_t are the objective functions; σ is the sigmoid function.

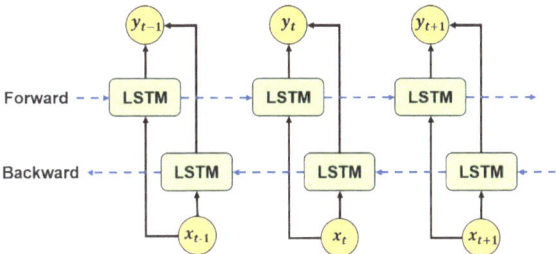

Figure 5. BILSTM structure diagram. x_t and y_t are the input and output of the model, respectively.

3.2. Anomaly Assessment Method

The confidence level, which belongs to statistics, has also been widely used in the earthquake field. Yu et al. [46] studied the load/unload response ratio (LURR) time series before earthquakes and found that the confidence level of LURR anomalies was highly correlated with the occurrence of large earthquakes. LURR precursor anomalies preceded most earthquakes with a probability higher than 90%. Alam et al. [47] used a confidence interval of 95% for anomaly selection in a statistical analysis of radon data from the Wenchuan earthquake in their analysis of the global seismic activity in 12 scenarios by magnitude and period. Yin et al. [48] found a significant activity cycle of about 50 years with a confidence level well above 95%. Kutoglu et al. [49] used the 95% confidence level as an anomaly test in their analysis of aerosol optical depth (AOD) time series data. Zhang et al. [50] proposed a new method for pre-seismic TEC detection using the time series method, in which the difference between the predicted and actual values of the time series prediction model was presented. The upper and lower limits were the residual values with a statistical ratio above 95%. The range was obtained by adding and subtracting from the predicted value, and any actual value outside this range was considered an anomaly. Zhai et al. [23] also applied this method to detect anomalies in a pre-earthquake longwave radiation time series and successfully detected significant anomalies. We have made improvements to the above methods. We trained several days of data and predicted OLR values for the corresponding number of days. Then, we calculated the residual value of the original data and obtained the 95% confidence interval of the predicted value. When the true value exceeded the upper or lower bound of the confidence interval, the datapoint was determined as an anomaly. Figure 6 shows the detailed anomaly extraction method process.

Using the Luding earthquake 31.5° N 102.5° E grid data as an example, 95% confidence intervals were calculated for the predicted values after the use of the time series to predict the longwave radiation values. The red curve shows the predicted value 30 days before the earthquake, and the blue curve shows the upper 95% confidence interval, the light blue curve shows the lower 95% confidence interval, and the green curve shows the true value of the grid. In the graphs, we considered the longwave radiation values to be anomalous if the actual values were below the lower bound of the interval or above the upper bound of the interval. For the 31.5° N 102.5° E grid of the Luding earthquake, Figure 7 shows the predicted OLR values and the anomaly performance.

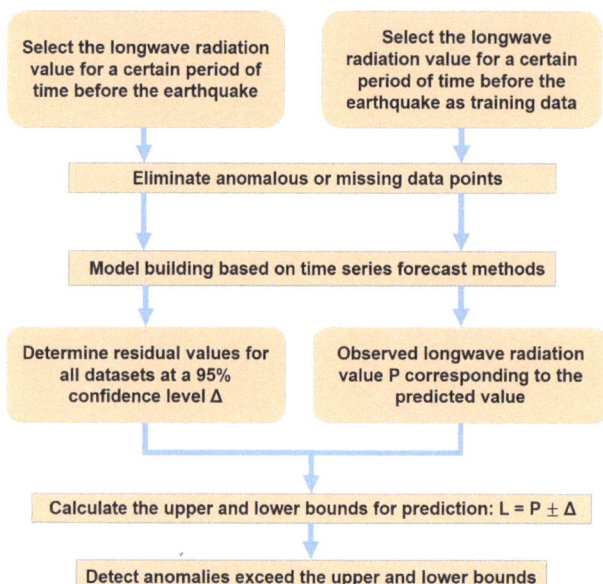

Figure 6. Anomaly extraction method flowchart. The flowchart was modified based on the anomaly extraction method proposed by Zhai et al. [23] and Zhang et al. [50] in their articles.

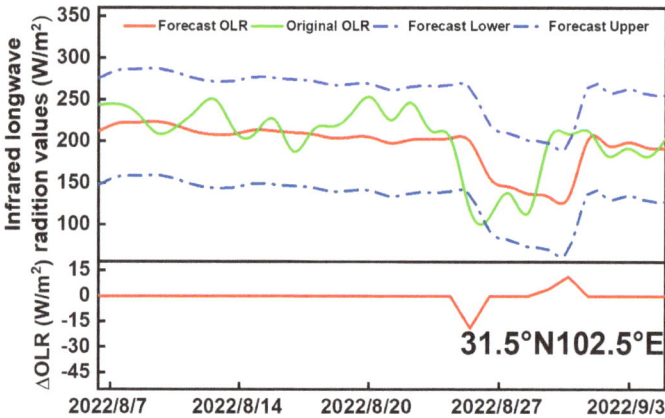

Figure 7. Prediction and anomaly performance of the 31.5° N 102.5° E grid OLR values of the Luding earthquake. The red curve is the predicted OLR value, and the blue and light blue curves are the upper and lower bounds of the confidence interval, respectively. The green curve is the actual OLR value; ΔOLR indicates how much the true value exceeds the prediction interval.

4. Results

4.1. Analysis of Algorithm Evaluation Results

We have chosen the Yangbi earthquake as a study earthquake example. Different training and test data were selected to predict and calculate the error on the grid data within

$5° \times 5°$ for this earthquake example. For the evaluation of the performance of the different algorithms, the data need to be divided into training data and test data. Based on previous conclusions, the time of occurrence of pre-seismic thermal anomalies is irregular. In general, they occur within six months prior to the earthquake. We aimed to study close-proximity anomalies, so we chose the 30 days before the earthquake as the prediction days. Due to the lag in data acquisition and our desire to obtain the long time series distribution of the anomalies for future practical applications, our test data were sourced from 5, 10, 15, 20, 25, and 30 days before the earthquake. The OLR data are seasonal. A training period of one year was found to work best when Zhai et al. [23] investigated the predictive performance of OLR based on different algorithms. Data from the year before the earthquake can reduce the disturbance of seismic anomalies to some extent. Therefore, we chose the training data in this experiment to be one year (360 days) ahead of the test data. Taking the Yangbi earthquake on 21 May 2021, for example, 5-day training data: 22 May 2020–16 May 2021, test data: 17–21 May 2021, 10-day training data: 17–11 May 2021, test data: 12–21 May 2021, and so on. The study area of the algorithm is shown in Figure 1. As the original data provided data located at a $1° \times 1°$ centroid, the location was recorded in the form of $25.5°$ N $99.5°$ E. The root mean square error is a common error test and has been widely used in earthquake prediction research [13–15,19,51]. The experiment uses the root mean square error (RMSE) to assess the error between the predicted and actual values. The total error is calculated for the same number of days tested.

Table 2 shows the error results of the BILSTM algorithm for different days and grid points. The remaining ARMA, ARIMA, SVM, and XGBoost algorithms were evaluated separately, and the total error of the different algorithms was analyzed following the same steps as described above; not all values are shown in the paper for the sake of brevity. Table 3 shows the total RMSE for all grids of the five algorithms for different forecast days.

Table 2. Error results for different days and different grids points based on time series BILSTM prediction model.

BILSTM	5 Days	10 Days	15 Days	20 Days	25 Days	30 Days
23.5° N 97.5° E	35.8714	44.4602	40.7788	44.0537	41.95	44.4664
23.5° N 98.5° E	21.17	24.7485	26.7656	33.1145	33.2425	39.824
23.5° N 99.5° E	24.1076	24.4975	30.2064	37.9868	37.9291	42.8743
23.5° N 100.5° E	16.7314	18.9341	23.4452	42.1087	43.1239	41.4841
23.5° N 101.5° E	31.0999	27.5695	31.9941	50.9161	49.8469	47.2746
24.5° N 97.5° E	9.9734	24.9584	26.6236	33.5992	38.2924	36.2921
24.5° N 98.5° E	13.3886	34.8646	35.2853	38.5706	37.172	40.8611
24.5° N 99.5° E	15.065	25.6253	34.2971	40.8797	38.0604	40.7207
24.5° N 100.5° E	15.0526	24.6202	27.0864	41.9177	42.5833	41.4012
24.5° N 101.5° E	22.1425	26.9378	29.9275	44.0822	44.73	42.7893
25.5° N 97.5° E	42.6918	41.4088	38.9593	40.4864	43.8695	41.0631
25.5° N 98.5° E	48.6846	39.9932	37.4426	39.5021	40.3489	41.4182
25.5° N 99.5° E	22.459	22.2276	29.1774	42.9795	39.9472	38.9058
25.5° N 100.5° E	22.459	22.2276	29.1774	42.9795	39.9472	38.9058
25.5° N 101.5° E	23.2545	22.5681	30.5917	43.7706	44.0704	41.7547
26.5° N 97.5° E	25.8453	26.5048	25.9652	32.772	33.1736	31.2204
26.5° N 98.5° E	42.6866	34.406	31.3593	31.8476	34.0241	32.3093
26.5° N 99.5° E	24.1937	25.337	25.5326	32.002	31.4707	30.8233
26.5° N 100.5° E	12.9577	13.9075	25.1652	38.3288	37.1007	36.8696
26.5° N 101.5° E	16.4933	19.1507	25.8206	38.2982	38.8576	37.6009
27.5° N 97.5° E	16.3102	14.6956	19.9246	26.974	34.2035	32.8196
27.5° N 98.5° E	16.2189	13.5482	18.7207	28.0452	27.5518	26.2956
27.5° N 99.5° E	42.1547	32.8008	29.7843	31.8504	30.7415	28.9882
27.5° N 100.5° E	22.2848	30.6576	29.3146	32.4005	30.3714	29.3901
27.5° N 101.5° E	35.9955	31.3212	31.2098	38.7217	35.2332	33.7072
Total RMSE	619.292	667.9708	734.5553	948.2177	947.8418	940.0596

Table 3. Total RMSE error of different time prediction models.

	5 Days	10 Days	15 Days	20 Days	25 Days	30 Days
ARMA	625.0028	647.0955	835.6342	871.0932	882.8587	941.6699
ARIMA	718.1327	738.4042	2060.7494	1034.0422	1542.7989	928.8650
SVM	775.9093	784.3109	806.0665	1025.3715	1034.8680	1026.3374
XGBoost	640.0953	670.1815	773.8258	930.6856	964.0494	946.3818
BILSTM	619.2920	667.9708	734.5553	948.2177	947.8418	940.0596

Table 3 shows that the total sum of root mean square errors for all algorithms was the smallest for the 5-day prediction time; the BILSTM algorithm had the smallest sum of root mean square errors for the 5-day prediction time. Therefore, BILSTM was selected as the research algorithm for this experiment. Five days was chosen as the prediction time. Five days was a short prediction time, and we used the sliding time window method [51] in this specific experiment to achieve a prediction of thirty days.

4.2. Analysis of Anomaly Results of Earthquake Cases

The best performing BILSTM prediction model was selected as the prediction algorithm after the error analysis of different algorithms and different prediction days. We then used the anomaly assessment method to study the Yangbi *M*s6.4-magnitude earthquake on 21 May 2021 and the Luding *M*s6.8-magnitude earthquake on 5 September 2022. The following graphs show the predicted results for two examples of earthquakes.

The green curve shows the actual value; the red curve shows the predicted value; the blue curve shows the upper bound of the confidence interval; the light blue curve shows the lower bound of the confidence interval; and the red dashed line in the subplots indicates the difference between exceeding the upper bound and falling below the lower bound. Figure 8 shows that within the $5° \times 5°$ area, 22 grid points, excluding grids points 23.5° N 98.5° E, 24.5° N 101.5° E, and 26.5° N 98.5° E, provided one to three cases of varying amounts outside the confidence interval in the month before the earthquake. Of these, 24 grid points were below the lower bound of the confidence interval, with the exception of the 23.5° N 101.5° E point, which was above the upper bound. The maximum value below the lower confidence interval was found at grid point 27.5° N 101.5° E, northeast of the epicenter. Therefore, we speculated that in the month before the Yangbi earthquake, anomalies of varying sizes were prevalent in the $5° \times 5°$ area near the epicenter, dominated by those below the lower confidence interval.

Figure 8 shows that most of the anomalies are below the lower bound of the confidence interval. To better illustrate how much the range was exceeded, the vertical coordinates in Figure 9 are negative upwards and positive downwards. Figure 9 shows that smaller-scale and smaller-range anomalies were observed during the two time periods from 25 April to 26 April and from 11 May to 12 May. A large-scale and more robust anomaly was observed from 5 May to 6 May, with the anomaly covering 17 grids, and the radiative energy of individual grid points was exceeded by up to 42.27 W/m^2, 27.52 W/m^2, 23.58 W/m^2, and 23.11 W/m^2. Therefore, we speculated that a strong and concentrated OLR anomaly existed 15 to 16 days before the Yangbi earthquake (5–6 May).

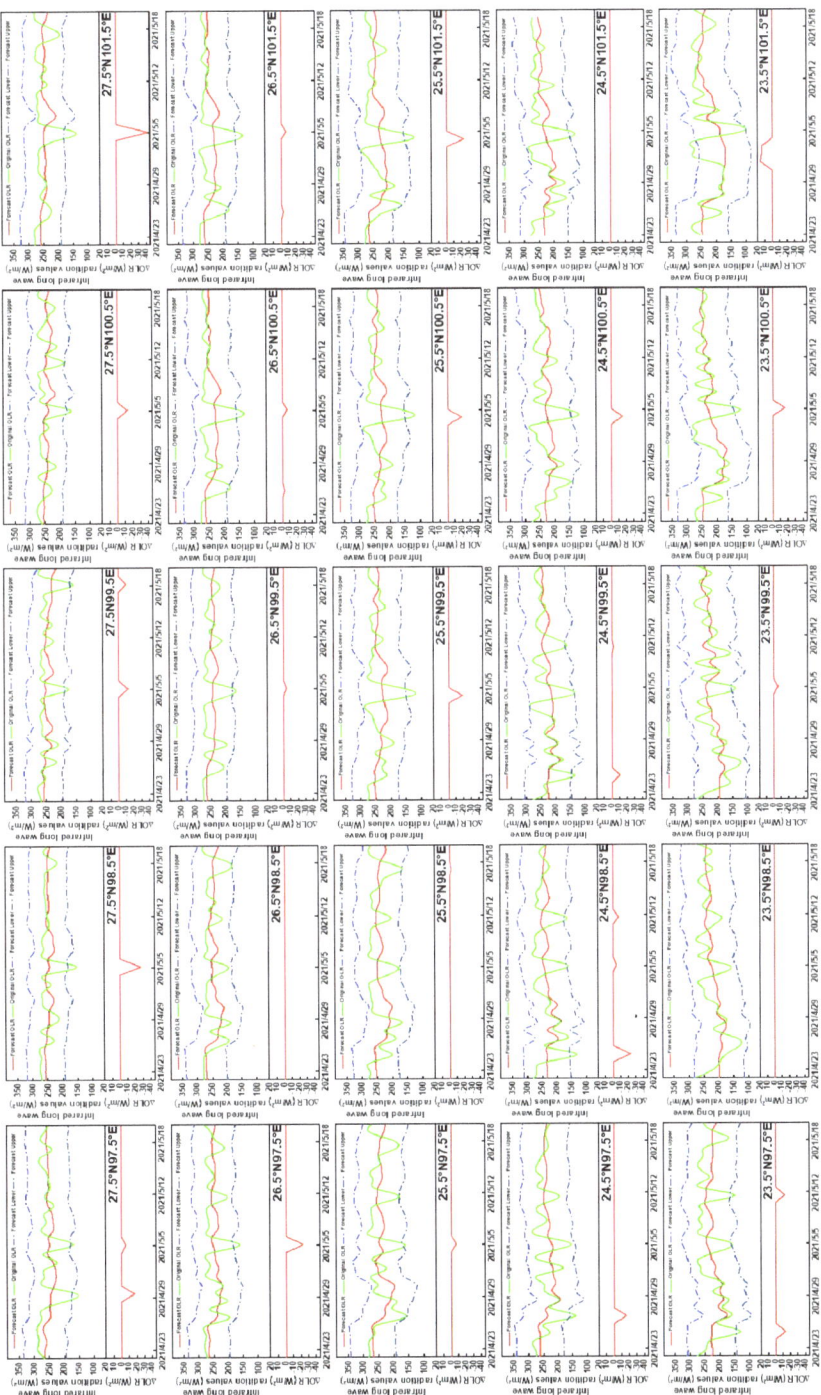

Figure 8. Pre-earthquake OLR prediction and anomalies of the Yangbi *M*s6.4 earthquake–spatial dimension.

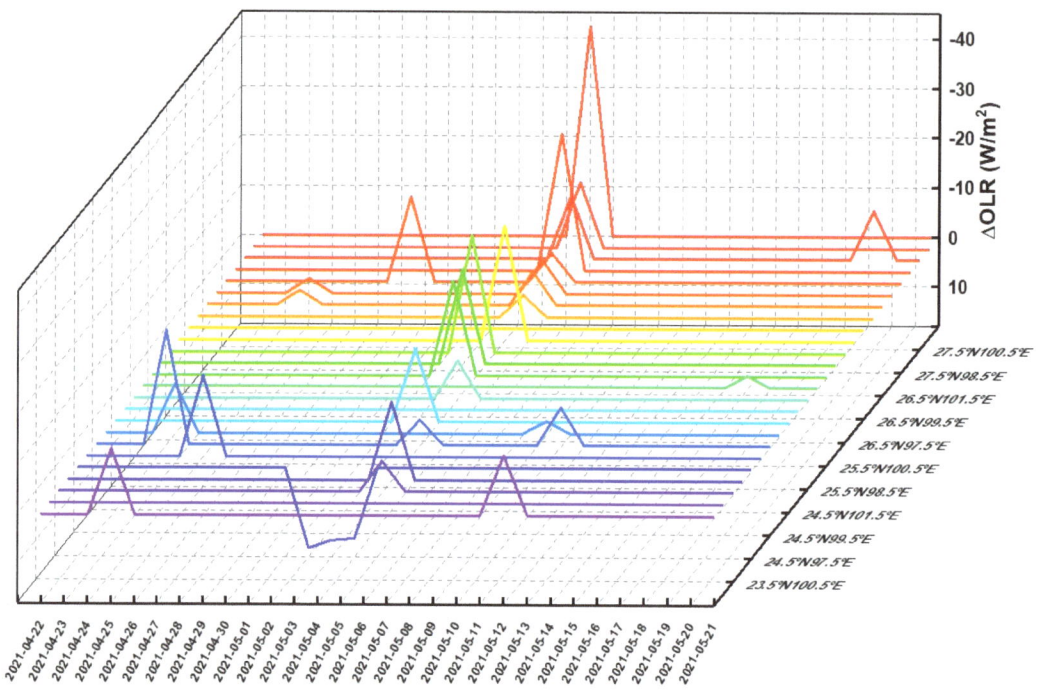

Figure 9. Pre-earthquake anomalies of the Yangbi Ms6.4 earthquake—temporal dimension. The X axis indicates the time, the Y axis indicates the grid position, and the Z axis indicates the degree of anomaly.

Figure 10 shows that nine grid points did not exceed the confidence interval and were mainly located near the epicenter and to the east. Combined with Figure 1, it can be seen that the eastern part of the epicenter is the Chengdu Plain, which is at a lower elevation and has relatively inactive fault zone activity with fewer anomalies. The coexistence of anomalies above and below confidence intervals occurred at several grid points. The maximum value below the lower boundary occurs at the 28.5° N 100.5° E grid point southwest of the epicenter. Therefore, we speculated that the anomalies near the epicenter one month before the Luding earthquake were mainly distributed southwest and northwest of the epicenter. Both anomaly types below the lower confidence interval and above the upper confidence interval occurred.

As shown in Figure 11, anomalies of different intensity, type, and extent were present on 9 August, 11 August, 18 August, 20 August to 21 August, 25 August to 26 August, 28 August, and 31 August. The maximum radiation exceedance on 9 August, 18 August, and August 28 reached 40.08 W/m^2, 34.08 W/m^2, and 51.52 W/m^2, respectively. We, therefore, speculated that there were several OLR anomalies of high intensity in the month before the Luding earthquake.

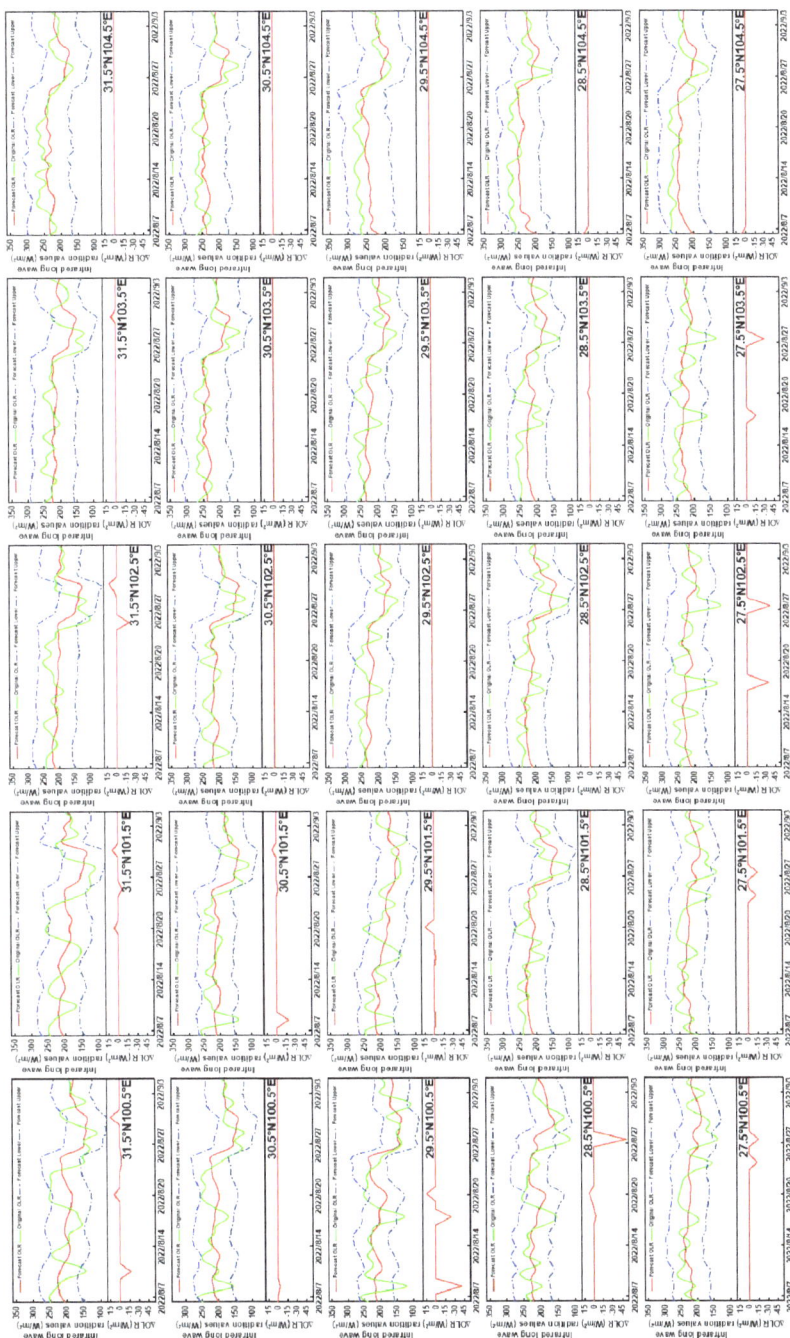

Figure 10. Pre-earthquake OLR prediction and anomalies of the Luding Ms6.8 earthquake—spatial dimension.

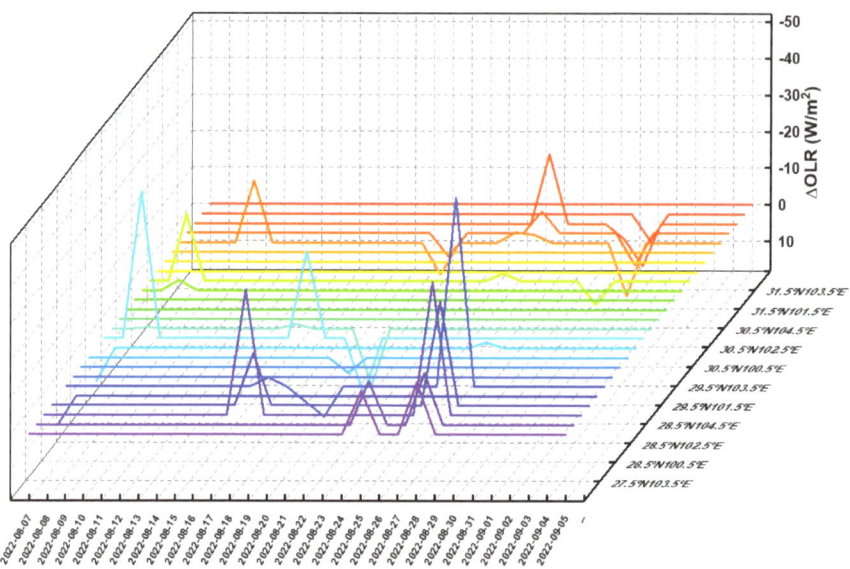

Figure 11. Pre-earthquake anomalies of the Luding Ms6.8 earthquake—temporal dimension. The X axis indicates the time, the Y axis indicates the grid position, and the Z axis indicates the degree of anomaly.

5. Discussion

Many studies have shown the presence of infrared longwave anomalies before earthquakes, but these studies have limitations. Researchers have obtained good anomaly predictions in different case studies using different methods and data, but similar results may not be obtained with a different method, data, or case. Xie et al. [52] used the two-year relative wavelet power spectrum method, and Wei et al. [53] used the wavelet power spectrum method based on FY-2E bright temperature data to study the 14 April 2010 Yushu Ms7.1 earthquake in China. The spatial distribution and intensity of the anomaly spatiotemporal evolution results obtained by the two differed significantly. Sun et al. [9] found no significant anomalies when they studied the 25 April 2015 Ms8.1 earthquake in Nepal using the RST algorithm and OLR data. However, Zhang et al. [54] obtained good anomaly prediction performance near the epicenter when studying the same earthquake case using the power spectrum method and bright temperature data. In addition, traditional methods for studying anomalies in longwave radiation data have been biased towards the representation of thermal anomalies, such as the RST algorithm, where values less than zero are ignored in the calculation of the Alice index [55].

Addressing the two limitations mentioned above, the method of this paper is innovative in two ways. The traditional thermal anomaly extraction model is only a model. In contrast, the BILSTM time series prediction model used is a deep learning model with the ability to train data and learn data, which is a data-driven approach. The training process does not change the original data for earthquake cases and data sources. The model can learn the data trend in the period before the earthquake. In the prediction process, the model parameters are modified to make the predicted value as close to the actual value as possible to achieve a better prediction result. The anomaly detection method used calculates 95% confidence intervals for the OLR, forming several ranges with upper and lower bounds. True values falling within this range are considered to be free of anomalies, while true values above the upper bound or below the lower bound are considered to be anomalous. This approach implies that there are two different types of anomalies. If the anomaly is above the upper bound, we consider it to be a hot anomaly, and if the anomaly is below the lower bound, we consider it to be a cold anomaly. While traditional methods can only show anomalies of high longwave radiation values, our method has both hot and cold anomalies, subdividing the types of anomalies that exist before the earthquake [2,3]. We have tried to explain cold anomalies at a physical level. According to the results of the rock experiments, compression leads to an increase in temperature, and tension leads to a decrease in temperature. The location of the Yangbi earthquake and the results of a multi-period GNSS strain rate field based on GPS data indicate that the Yangbi earthquake is located in a tension zone; the Luding earthquake is in a zone of weakness at the high-value edge of the shear strain of a large strike-slip fault zone and a zone of tensor strain perpendicular to the fault direction.

Lithosphere–Atmosphere–Ionosphere Coupling (LAIC) was used to explain the physical and chemical mechanisms of the various anomalies that appear at the surface, in the atmosphere, and in the ionosphere during the gestation and occurrence of earthquakes [56]. It was found that there was a relationship between pre-earthquake OLR and ionospheric anomalies, which can be explained by LAIC [57–59]. Fu et al. studied strong earthquakes with magnitudes greater than 6 in Taiwan and concluded that seismic OLR anomalies may originate from electromagnetic radiation as well as gas emissions [60]. We tried to compare anomalous the OLR results of the two earthquakes with the anomalous results of TEC obtained by other scholars. Zhai et al. [23] used the ARMA model to predict the longwave radiation values of the 8 August 2017 Jiuzhaigou Ms7.0 earthquake and found OLR anomalies at the epicenter on 27 July and 5 August; Zhu et al. [61] used the sliding quartile to detect ionospheric TEC anomalies for the same earthquake and found TEC anomalies on 28 July, 4 August, and 6 August; the timing of OLR anomalies and of ionospheric anomalies were close. Du et al. [62] used Chinese seismo-electromagnetic satellite data to detect electron density anomalies of the Yangbi Ms6.4 earthquake in Yunnan on 21 May 2021 and found anomalies on 5 May and 8 May; Dong et al. [63] used ionospheric TEC data to study the same earthquake case and detected the strongest anomaly near the epicenter on 5 May. We found strong and concentrated OLR anomalies from 5 May to 6 May before the Yangbi earthquake. The timing of the OLR anomalies is also very close to that of the ionospheric anomalies detected before the Yangbi Ms6.4 earthquake. Therefore, we believe that there is a specific link exists between the OLR anomaly and the ionospheric anomaly that existed before the earthquake.

In this paper, we only selected the Yangbi Ms6.4 earthquake of 21 May 2021 and the Luding Ms6.8 earthquake of 5 September 2022 for study. The number of earthquake cases was too low to form a statistical analysis of the method. We detected significant anomalies within a $5° \times 5°$ area of the epicenter and a month before the earthquake with the parameters of the earthquake case study determined with reference to the summary of previous works. It was not possible to determine whether such anomalies existed beyond this range and time period. The distribution and timing of pre-earthquake anomalies varied between different-magnitude earthquakes, and specific study areas and times need to be delineated based on specific earthquake examples. The rapid development of deep learning has led to more and better time series prediction models, such as the Transformer algorithm [64,65], a complex time series algorithm that can better predict OLR values and reduce errors. In addition, the parameter setting of the model was also an important factor affecting good and bad errors, and different parameters give different results. The experiment needed to establish the optimal set of model parameters. In future research, we need to improve and refine the above-mentioned drawbacks.

6. Conclusions

This paper used OLR data to predict 30-day values before the Yangbi Ms6.4-magnitude earthquake on 21 May 2021 and the Luding Ms6.8-magnitude earthquake on 5 September 2022 based on a time series prediction model and the sliding time window method and assessed the anomalies using 95% confidence intervals. Five time series prediction models were used to calculate the RMSE for 5, 10, 15, 20, 25, and 30 days in 25 grids using the

Yangbi earthquake as an evaluation example. The total RMSE of the BILSTM model for the 5-day prediction time was 619.2920, which was smaller than any other combination of model and number of days. The following conclusions can be drawn:

(1) The anomaly distributions of the Yangbi and Luding earthquakes were large. There was a correspondence between the anomaly distribution area and the distribution of fault zones. The magnitude of the anomalies of the two earthquakes was significant, and both earthquakes had showed anomaly values above 40. The anomalies of the two earthquakes showed different characteristics in the time dimension. The Yangbi earthquake anomaly appeared 15 to 16 days before the earthquake (5–6 May) with a higher intensity and more concentrated temporal distribution. The Luding earthquake showed stronger anomalies 27 (9 August), 18 (18 August), and 8 (28 August) days before the earthquake. The temporal distribution was more scattered. Overall, OLR data based on time series could effectively detect apparent pre-earthquake anomalies and analyze the possibility of earthquake generation by the characteristics presented by the anomalies, which was a promising method for earthquake prediction.

(2) Based on the time series prediction model to study the seismic anomalies in the $5° \times 5°$ area and within one pre-earthquake time period, we found that the Yangbi and Luding earthquakes have specific anomaly characteristics and show similar but not identical anomaly distributions. However, we may find anomalies with the same characteristics in different cases by studying many earthquake cases. This experimental anomaly extraction method used a 95% confidence interval, and there were many small and heterogeneous distribution characteristics in the results of the studied earthquake anomalies. These anomalies were minor in degree and in terms of indicative features, which may affect the interpretation of the overall seismic anomaly and need to be eliminated. Overall, the study of multiple cases based on time series prediction models is a direction for future anomaly research. The best confidence interval setting must be found in numerous cases and studies to summarize the potential patterns between the characteristics of the OLR anomaly distribution and earthquake occurrence.

Author Contributions: Conceptualization, J.Z. (Junqing Zhu) and K.S.; methodology, J.Z. (Junqing Zhu); software, J.Z. (Junqing Zhu); validation, J.Z. (Junqing Zhu), J.Z. (Jingye Zhang), and K.S.; formal analysis, J.Z. (Jingye Zhang); investigation, J.Z. (Jingye Zhang); resources, J.Z. (Junqing Zhu); writing—original draft preparation, J.Z. (Junqing Zhu); writing—review and editing, J.Z. (Junqing Zhu); visualization, J.Z. (Jingye Zhang); supervision, K.S.; project administration, K.S.; funding acquisition, K.S. All authors have read and agreed to the published version of the manuscript.

Funding: This work was funded by the National Natural Science Foundation of China under Grant No. U2039202, and the National Key Research and Development Program of China under Grant No. 2019YFC1509202.

Institutional Review Board Statement: Not applicable.

Informed Consent Statement: Not applicable.

Data Availability Statement: This study uses NOAA-18 satellite $1° \times 1°$ OLR data that can be downloaded via NCEP's FTP server (ftp://ftp.cpc.ncep.noaa.gov/precip/noaa18_1x1/) (accessed on 20 December 2022).

Acknowledgments: We thank the National Natural Science Foundation of China and the National Key Research and Development Program of China for funding this study. We thank NOAA for providing the OLR data and Sha Yin for guidance in producing the figures.

Conflicts of Interest: The authors declare no conflict of interest.

References

1. Gornyy, V.; Sal'man, A.; Tronin, A.; Shilin, B. Outgoing terrestrial infrared radiation as an indicator of seismic activity. *Dokl. Akad. Nauk USSR* **1988**, *301*, 67–69. (In Russian)
2. Lu, X.; Meng, Q.; Gu, X.; Zhang, X.; Xie, T.; Geng, F. Thermal infrared anomalies associated with multi-year earthquakes in the Tibet region based on China's FY-2E satellite data. *Adv. Space Res.* **2016**, *58*, 989–1001. [CrossRef]

3. Zhang, Y.; Meng, Q. A statistical analysis of TIR anomalies extracted by RSTs in relation to an earthquake in the Sichuan area using MODIS LST data. *Nat. Hazards Earth Syst. Sci.* **2019**, *19*, 535–549. [CrossRef]
4. Xiong, P.; Shen, X.H.; Bi, Y.X.; Kang, C.L.; Chen, L.Z.; Jing, F.; Chen, Y. Study of outgoing longwave radiation anomalies associated with Haiti earthquake. *Nat. Hazards Earth Syst. Sci.* **2010**, *10*, 2169–2178. [CrossRef]
5. Kong, X.; Bi, Y.; Glass, D.H. Detecting seismic anomalies in outgoing long-wave radiation data. *IEEE J. Sel. Top. Appl. Earth Obs. Remote Sens.* **2014**, *8*, 649–660. [CrossRef]
6. Mahmood, I.; Iqbal, M.F.; Shahzad, M.I.; Qaiser, S. Investigation of atmospheric anomalies associated with Kashmir and Awaran Earthquakes. *J. Atmos. Sol.-Terr. Phys.* **2017**, *154*, 75–85. [CrossRef]
7. Natarajan, V.; Philipoff, P.; Sreedharan, V.W.; Venkatachalapathy, H. Observation of pre-earthquake thermal signatures using geostationary satellites: Implications for earthquake forecasting. *J. Appl. Remote Sens.* **2016**, *10*, 46004. [CrossRef]
8. Prakash, R.; Srivastava, H. Diurnal variations of outgoing long wave radiation (OLR) vis a vis 4 January, 2016 Manipur earthquake (Mw: 6.7): An earthquake precursor? *Mausam* **2017**, *68*, 475–486. [CrossRef]
9. Sun, K.; Shan, X.-J.; Ouzounov, D.; Shen, X.-H.; Jing, F. Analyzing long wave radiation data associated with the 2015 Nepal earthquakes based on Multi-orbit satellite observations. *Chin. J. Geophys.* **2017**, *60*, 3457–3465.
10. Ouzounov, D.; Liu, D.; Chunli, K.; Cervone, G.; Kafatos, M.; Taylor, P. Outgoing long wave radiation variability from IR satellite data prior to major earthquakes. *Tectonophysics* **2007**, *431*, 211–220. [CrossRef]
11. Ohring, G.; Gruber, A. Satellite radiation observations and climate theory. In *Advances in Geophysics*; Elsevier: Amsterdam, The Netherlands, 1983; Volume 25, pp. 237–304.
12. Yang, H.M.; Pan, Z.S.; Wei, B.; Of, S. Review of Time Series Prediction Methods. *Comput. Sci.* **2019**, *46*, 21–28.
13. Saqib, M.; Senturk, E.; Sahu, S.A.; Adil, M.A. Ionospheric anomalies detection using autoregressive integrated moving average (ARIMA) model as an earthquake precursor. *Acta Geophys.* **2021**, *69*, 1493–1507. [CrossRef]
14. Saqib, M.; Senturk, E.; Sahu, S.A.; Adil, M.A. Comparisons of autoregressive integrated moving average (ARIMA) and long short term memory (LSTM) network models for ionospheric anomalies detection: A study on Haiti (M-w=7.0) earthquake. *Acta Geod. Geophys.* **2022**, *57*, 195–213. [CrossRef]
15. Senturk, E.; Saqib, M.; Adil, M.A. A Multi-Network based Hybrid LSTM model for ionospheric anomaly detection: A case study of the M-w 7.8 Nepal earthquake. *Adv. Space Res.* **2022**, *70*, 440–455. [CrossRef]
16. Yue, Y.; Koivula, H.; Bilker-Koivula, M.; Chen, Y.; Chen, F.; Chen, G. TEC Anomalies Detection for Qinghai and Yunnan Earthquakes on 21 May 2021. *Remote Sens.* **2022**, *14*, 4152. [CrossRef]
17. Xiong, P.; Zhai, D.; Long, C.; Zhou, H.; Zhang, X.; Shen, X. Long short-term memory neural network for ionospheric total electron content forecasting over China. *Space Weather.* **2021**, *19*, e2020SW002706. [CrossRef]
18. Mohammed, D.H.K.; Kulahci, F.; Muhammed, A. Determination of possible responses of Radon-222, magnetic effects, and total electron content to earthquakes on the North Anatolian Fault Zone, Turkiye: An ARIMA and Monte Carlo Simulation. *Nat. Hazards* **2021**, *108*, 2493–2512. [CrossRef]
19. Mir, A.A.; Celebi, F.V.; Alsolai, H.; Qureshi, S.A.; Rafique, M.; Alzahrani, J.S.; Mahgoub, H.; Hamza, M.A. Anomalies Prediction in Radon Time Series for Earthquake Likelihood Using Machine Learning-Based Ensemble Model. *IEEE Access* **2022**, *10*, 37984–37999. [CrossRef]
20. Feng, X.; Zhong, J.; Yan, R.; Zhou, Z.; Tian, L.; Zhao, J.; Yuan, Z. Groundwater radon precursor anomalies identification by EMD-LSTM model. *Water* **2022**, *14*, 69. [CrossRef]
21. Roebeling, R.; Schulz, J.; Hewison, T.; Theodore, B. Inter-calibration of METEOSAT IR and WV channels using HIRS. *AIP Conf. Proc.* **2013**, *1531*, 288–291.
22. Turner, E.C.; Tett, S.F. Using longwave HIRS radiances to test climate models. *Clim. Dyn.* **2014**, *43*, 1103–1127. [CrossRef]
23. Zhai, D.; Zhang, X.; Xiong, P. Detecting thermal anomalies of earthquake process within outgoing longwave radiation using time series forecasting models. *Ann. Geophys.* **2020**, *63*, PA548. [CrossRef]
24. Ellingson, R.G.; Yanuk, D.J.; Lee, H.-T.; Gruber, A. A technique for estimating outgoing longwave radiation from HIRS radiance observations. *J. Atmos. Ocean. Technol.* **1989**, *6*, 706–711. [CrossRef]
25. Lee, H.-T.; Ellingson, R.G. HIRS OLR climate data record–production and validation updates. *AIP Conf. Proc.* **2013**, *1531*, 420–423.
26. Chen, Q.F.; Zheng, D.L.; Che, S. *Earthquake Cases in China (1992–1994)*; Seismological Press: Beijng, China, 2002.
27. Chen, Q.F.; Zheng, D.L.; Liu, G.P.; Li, M. *Earthquake Cases in China (1995–1996)*; Seismological Press: Beijing, China, 2002.
28. Jiang, H.K.; Fu, H.; Yang, M.L.; Ma, H.S. *Earthquake Cases in China (2003–2006)*; Seismological Press: Beijing, China, 2014.
29. Jing, F.; Shen, X.; Kang, C.; Meng, Q.; Xiong, P. Anomalies of outgoing longwave radiation before some medium to large earthquakes. *Earthquake* **2009**, *29*, 117–122.
30. Feng, J.; Xuhui, S.; Hui, W.; Chunli, K.; Pan, X. Infrared characteristics analysis of the 2015 Nepal M S 8.1 earthquake. *Acta Seismol. Sin.* **2016**, *38*, 429–437.
31. Song, D.; Zang, L.; Shan, X.; Yuan, Y.; Cui, J.; Shao, H.; Shen, C.; Shi, H. A study on the algorithm for extracting earthquake thermal infrared anomalies based on the yearly trend of LST. *Seismol. Geol.* **2016**, *38*, 680–695.
32. He, S.; Zhou, Q.; Liu, Z. Seismogenic Structure of the 2021 Yangbi, Yunnan MS6.4 Earthquake and Earthquake Risk Analysis in the Epicenter Area. *J. Seismol. Res.* **2021**, *44*, 380–390.
33. Fan, X.; Wang, X.; Dai, L.; Fang, C.; Deng, Y.; Zou, C.; Tang, M.; Wei, Z.; Dou, X.; Zhang, J. Characteristics and spatial distribution pattern of M S 6.8 Luding earthquake occurred on September 5, 2022. *J. Eng. Geol.* **2022**, *30*, 1504–1516.

34. Valipour, M.; Banihabib, M.E.; Behbahani, S.M.R. Comparison of the ARMA, ARIMA, and the autoregressive artificial neural network models in forecasting the monthly inflow of Dez dam reservoir. *J. Hydrol.* **2013**, *476*, 433–441. [CrossRef]
35. Kumar, U.; Jain, V. ARIMA forecasting of ambient air pollutants (O 3, NO, NO 2 and CO). *Stoch. Environ. Res. Risk Assess.* **2010**, *24*, 751–760. [CrossRef]
36. Shumway, R.H.; Stoffer, D.S.; Stoffer, D.S. *Time Series Analysis and Its Applications*; Springer: Berlin/Heidelberg, Germany, 2000; Volume 3.
37. Zhang, H.; Zhang, S.; Wang, P.; Qin, Y.; Wang, H. Forecasting of particulate matter time series using wavelet analysis and wavelet-ARMA/ARIMA model in Taiyuan, China. *J. Air Waste Manag. Assoc.* **2017**, *67*, 776–788. [CrossRef] [PubMed]
38. Vapnik, V. *The Nature of Statistical Learning Theory*; Springer Science & Business Media: Berlin/Heidelberg, Germany, 1999.
39. Sapankevych, N.I.; Sankar, R. Time series prediction using support vector machines: A survey. *IEEE Comput. Intell. Mag.* **2009**, *4*, 24–38. [CrossRef]
40. Chen, B.-J.; Chang, M.-W. Load forecasting using support vector machines: A study on EUNITE competition 2001. *IEEE Trans. Power Syst.* **2004**, *19*, 1821–1830. [CrossRef]
41. Chen, T.; Guestrin, C. Xgboost: A scalable tree boosting system. In Proceedings of the 22nd ACM Sigkdd International Conference on Knowledge Discovery and Data Mining, San Francisco, CA, USA, 13–17 August 2016; pp. 785–794.
42. LI, H.; ZHU, Y. Xgboost algorithm optimization based on gradient distribution harmonized strategy. *J. Comput. Appl.* **2020**, *40*, 1633.
43. Hochreiter, S.; Schmidhuber, J. Long short-term memory. *Neural Comput.* **1997**, *9*, 1735–1780. [CrossRef]
44. Yan, X.; Shi, Z.; Wang, G.; Zhang, H.; Bi, E. Detection of possible hydrological precursor anomalies using long short-term memory: A case study of the 1996 Lijiang earthquake. *J. Hydrol.* **2021**, *599*, 126369. [CrossRef]
45. Lin, H.; Zhang, S.; Li, Q.; Li, Y.; Li, J.; Yang, Y. A new method for heart rate prediction based on LSTM-BiLSTM-Att. *Measurement* **2023**, *207*, 112384. [CrossRef]
46. Yu, H.Z.; Zhu, Q.Y. A probabilistic approach for earthquake potential evaluation based on the load/unload response ratio method. *Concurr. Comput. Pract. Exp.* **2010**, *22*, 1520–1533. [CrossRef]
47. Alam, A.; Wang, N.; Zhao, G.; Barkat, A. Implication of radon monitoring for earthquake surveillance using statistical techniques: A case study of Wenchuan earthquake. *Geofluids* **2020**, *2020*, 2429165. [CrossRef]
48. Yin, J.; Song, Z.; Xue, Y.; Liu, J.; Zhang, G.; Zhu, Y. Analysis on global huge earthquake activity. *Acta Seismol. Sin.* **2012**, *34*, 191–201.
49. Kutoglu, S.H.; Ghasempour, F.; Sekertekin, A. Investigation of Possible MODIS AOD Anomalies as Earthquake Precursors for Global Earthquakes. *Adv. Space Res.* **2021**, *68*, 3531–3545. [CrossRef]
50. Zhang, X.; Ren, X.; Wu, F.; Chen, Y. A New Method for Detection of Pre-Earthquake Ionospheric Anomalies. *Chin. J. Geophys.* **2013**, *56*, 213–222.
51. Xiong, P.; Tong, L.; Zhang, K.; Shen, X.; Battiston, R.; Ouzounov, D.; Iuppa, R.; Crookes, D.; Long, C.; Zhou, H. Towards advancing the earthquake forecasting by machine learning of satellite data. *Sci. Total Environ.* **2021**, *771*, 145256. [CrossRef]
52. Xie, T.; Kang, C.L.; Ma, W.Y. Thermal infrared brightness temperature anomalies associated with the Yushu (China) Ms = 7.1 earthquake on 14 April 2010. *Nat. Hazards Earth Syst. Sci.* **2013**, *13*, 1105–1111. [CrossRef]
53. Wei, C.; Zhang, Y.; Guo, X.; Qin, M.; Ning, Y.-L.; Gao, J. Thermal infrared and long-wave radiation anomalies of Yushu MS 7.1 earthquake. *Prog. Geophys.* **2013**, *28*, 2444–2452.
54. Zhang, X.; Zhang, Y.; Guo, X.; Wei, C.; Zhang, L. Analysis of thermal infrared anomaly in the Nepal MS8.1 earthquake. *Earth Sci. Front.* **2017**, *24*, 227–233.
55. Tramutoli, V. Robust AVHRR Techniques (RAT) for environmental monitoring: Theory and applications. In *Earth Surface Remote Sensing II*; SPIE: Bellingham, WA, USA, 1998; pp. 101–113.
56. Pulinets, S.; Ouzounov, D.; Karelin, A.; Davidenko, D. Lithosphere-atmosphere-ionosphere-magnetosphere coupling-a concept for pre-earthquake signals generation. In *Pre-Earthquake Processes: A Multidisciplinary Approach to Earthquake Prediction Studies*; American Geophysical Union: Washington, DC, USA, 2018; pp. 77–98.
57. Parrot, M.; Tramutoli, V.; Liu, T.J.; Pulinets, S.; Ouzounov, D.; Genzano, N.; Lisi, M.; Hattori, K.; Namgaladze, A. Atmospheric and ionospheric coupling phenomena associated with large earthquakes. *Eur. Phys. J. Spec. Top.* **2021**, *230*, 197–225. [CrossRef]
58. Conti, L.; Picozza, P.; Sotgiu, A. A critical review of ground based observations of earthquake precursors. *Front. Earth Sci.* **2021**, *9*, 676766. [CrossRef]
59. Lu, J.; Hu, Y.; Jiang, C.; Zhao, Z.; Zhang, Y.; Ma, Z. Analysis of Pre-Earthquake Ionospheric Anomalies in the Japanese Region Based on DEMETER Satellite Data. *Universe* **2023**, *9*, 229. [CrossRef]
60. Fu, C.-C.; Lee, L.-C.; Ouzounov, D.; Jan, J.-C. Earth's outgoing longwave radiation variability prior to M≥ 6.0 earthquakes in the Taiwan area during 2009–2019. *Front. Earth Sci.* **2020**, *8*, 364. [CrossRef]
61. Zhu, J.; Zhao, M.; Gong, C.; Wang, L. Ionosphere abnormalities before the 2017 MS7. 0 Jiuzhai Valley earthquake. *J. Guilin Univ. Technol.* **2020**, *40*, 372–378.
62. Du, X.; Zhang, X. Ionospheric Disturbances Possibly Associated with Yangbi Ms6. 4 and Maduo Ms7. 4 Earthquakes in China from China Seismo Electromagnetic Satellite. *Atmosphere* **2022**, *13*, 438. [CrossRef]
63. Dong, L.; Zhang, X.; Du, X. Analysis of Ionospheric Perturbations Possibly Related to Yangbi Ms6. 4 and Maduo Ms7. 4 Earthquakes on 21 May 2021 in China Using GPS TEC and GIM TEC Data. *Atmosphere* **2022**, *13*, 1725. [CrossRef]

64. Jaderberg, M.; Simonyan, K.; Zisserman, A. Spatial transformer networks. In *Advances in Neural Information Processing Systems*; MIT Press: Cambridge, MA, USA, 2015; Volume 28.
65. Liu, Z.; Lin, Y.; Cao, Y.; Hu, H.; Wei, Y.; Zhang, Z.; Lin, S.; Guo, B. Swin transformer: Hierarchical vision transformer using shifted windows. In Proceedings of the IEEE/CVF International Conference on Computer Vision, Montreal, BC, Canada, 11–17 October 2021; pp. 10012–10022.

Disclaimer/Publisher's Note: The statements, opinions and data contained in all publications are solely those of the individual author(s) and contributor(s) and not of MDPI and/or the editor(s). MDPI and/or the editor(s) disclaim responsibility for any injury to people or property resulting from any ideas, methods, instructions or products referred to in the content.

Article

A Machine-Learning-Based Software for the Simulation of Regional Characteristic Ground Motion

Jinjun Hu [1,*], Yitian Ding [1], Shibin Lin [2], Hui Zhang [1] and Chaoyue Jin [1]

[1] Key Laboratory of Earthquake Engineering Vibration, Institute of Engineering Mechanics, China Earthquake Administration, Harbin 150080, China; dingyt1998@163.com (Y.D.)
[2] Hubei (Wuhan) Institute of Explosion Science and Blasting Technology, Jianghan University, Economic and Technological Development Zone, Wuhan 430056, China
* Correspondence: hujinjun@iem.ac.cn

Featured Application: Earthquake Detection, Earthquake Early Warning System (EEWS), Processing of Seismic data.

Abstract: Ground-motion simulations provide input time history data required for designing and assessing structures; however, the simulations conducted by the currently available tools only match the design spectrum without verifying if the statistical characteristics of the spectrum and duration are satisfied. A ground-motion simulation software was developed to resolve these issues. The developed software employs machine learning methods to match the amplitude, spectrum, and duration features of the target region. Principal component analysis is employed to extract features from the actual ground-motion database to detect characteristic ground motions and predict the target acceleration amplitude, response spectrum, and duration, based on the response spectrum and duration prediction equations. The results show that the simulated ground motion can match the amplitude, spectrum, and duration characteristics well. Therefore, the simulated ground motion can provide more reasonable input for the structure. Moreover, the developed software provides visualization functions that enable the user to determine the target area and obtain the amplitude field intuitively.

Keywords: reginal characteristic ground motion; ground motion; ground-motion field simulation; principal component analysis; genetic algorithms; MATLAB-based simulator

1. Introduction

The time-history analysis method is an important tool for calculating the response of structures under earthquakes. However, time-history analysis relies on reliable ground-motion inputs. In general, there are two types of ground motion—the real ground-motion records obtained by seismic stations in the advent of earthquakes, and synthetic ground motion. Real ground motions are obtained from the ground-motion database [1], whereas several methodologies are employed to obtain synthetic ground motions [2,3]. Many factors affect the structural response (e.g., load uncertainty, structural material, and construction quality), among which load uncertainty has the highest influence [4,5], and ground-motion input (as an important part of the structural load input) has a considerable effect.

In practice, recorded ground motions are preferred over synthetic ground motions [6]. This is because the synthetic ground motions according to some criteria (e.g., control spectra, etc.) are different from the recorded ground motions to some extent. However, the lack of recorded ground motion makes it impossible to select a suitable record. Therefore, it is important to synthesize reliable and reasonable ground motion for time-history analysis [2].

Ground-motion-synthesis methodologies have been developed for many years, and several researchers have proposed different methods to simulate ground motions based on different principles. Currently, ground-motion-simulation methods are divided into three categories: (1) Ground-motion simulation based on the stochastic method; (2) physics-based ground-motion-simulation methods; and (3) hybrid simulated ground motions [3,7–11]. Numerous techniques for simulating ground motion are currently under investigation [12–17]. For example, Ref. [18] simulated ground-motion time series at uninstrumented sites using a gaussian process regression. They estimated the time series at a site based on observed ground motions at surrounding sites, and the method can be used for estimating and understanding causes of earthquake damage at uninstrumented sites. The amplitude, spectrum, and duration simultaneously constrain the ground motions. Currently, the most widely used method in engineering is ground-motion synthesis with matching target response spectrum. However, this synthesis method cannot obtain a unique ground-motion time history. Therefore, a multicriteria objective function for ground motion is proposed. Seismic event parameters, target spectra (Sa, haz(T)), target intensity measures (IMs) for a specific site, structure of interest, and other conditions are investigated to simulate more reasonable ground motion [19–31]. The energy of seismic waves recorded at a station is related to the strong motion part of the recorded ground motion. For a given acceleration a(t), velocity v(t), or displacement d(t), Ref. [29] defined the strong motion part of the recorded ground motion as the fast-growing region of the integral, where f(t) is any of a(t), v(t), or d(t). The time interval at which the maximum contribution of this integral occurs is defined as the strong motion duration. Ref. [29] defined the 5–95% time interval as the ground-motion duration. Therefore, it is commonly used in seismic hazard analysis [18,19]. However, this is not reflected in the simulation method. In addition, there are regional differences in the amplitude, spectrum, and duration of ground motions due to geological formations [26]. When simulating ground motions using the machine learning method, it is essential to consider the regional characteristics of the location of interest. To ensure accurate results, it becomes necessary to constrain the amplitude, spectrum, and duration as the main control factors. By carefully adjusting these parameters, the simulation can better capture the specific ground-motion characteristics relevant to the location under study.

Thus far, researchers have developed ground-motion-selection software or frameworks based on different methods [27–29]; however, procedures for developing ground motion simulations using advanced methodologies are lacking. Although some methods have been proposed for synthesizing ground-motion records that meet some of the statistical characteristics, the current theoretical approach does not consider user-oriented applications [31]. The current user-oriented ground-motion simulation records cannot meet user requirements for more accurate acceleration time history records. The user-friendly interface and visualization allows users to focus on other aspects of their research, and software or plug-ins have been developed to facilitate their use [32]. Thus, it is necessary to develop user-friendly software that provides a graphical user interface (GUI) with visualization functions and applies a more rational and advanced ground-motion methodology [33–35].

Machine learning methods have been successfully applied in various fields in recent years [36]. The proposed software employs a machine learning synthesis method based on an actual ground-motion database that not only matches the target response spectrum, but also ensures constraints on the duration using constraints. This resolves the significant variations in the input response caused by the diversity of the matching results mentioned above. This method first extracts the characteristic ground motions from the actual ground-motion database using principal component analysis (PCA), and then matches the amplitude, spectrum, and duration. To determine the most reasonable ground motions, the extracted characteristic ground motions are combined using a multi-objective genetic algorithm known for its successful application in numerous studies [37]. This algorithm efficiently determines the optimal solution by considering multiple constraints, enabling the linear combination of the extracted characteristic ground motions. The software is a MATLAB-based application that clearly identifies target areas based on engineering parameters provided by researchers and engineers, obtains amplitude fields visualized at different periods, and generates acceleration time history records on demand, which enables researchers to focus on subsequent research. This paper introduces ground-motion simulation methodology used by the software and demonstrates its application.

2. Methods for Ground-Motion Simulation

Ref. [38] was the first to carry out the work on ground-motion simulation. Subsequently, there has been long-term development of ground-motion simulation methods and theories. Deterministic methods are mainly applied to simulate the low-frequency components of ground motion, and stochastic methods are proposed to simulate the high-frequency components of ground motion [39]. Hybrid simulation methods combine the advantages of both deterministic and stochastic simulations, and can simulate a wide range of earthquakes [40]. However, the deterministic approach requires a hypocenter model [41]. The stochastic and hybrid simulation methods also require parameters specific to the target region, such as stress drop, local site effects, etc. [9]. Therefore, simulating ground motion remains a huge challenge. With the increasing number of modern seismic stations and the development of seismic monitoring and ground motion databases—which are now becoming increasingly abundant—a large amount of data is bound to provide a wealth of information for research. Owing to the large amount of data, it is important to determine how to use these data. A regional ground motion field is obtained by applying machine learning methods with user-requested scenario parameters (e.g., magnitude, epicenter distance, latitude, and longitude).

The program applies a ground-motion simulation method based on the database of actual time-history records by applying machine learning PCA for extracting characteristic ground motions and combining them with a genetic algorithm to determine the optimal solution. First, ground motion records in the database are extracted by PCA to obtain the characteristic ground motions that represent the characteristics in the target area. The extracted characteristic ground motions are independent of each other, and they are linearly combined to simulate ground motions. The linear combination coefficients are unknown. The synthesized ground motions require the simultaneous matching of the response spectrum with both the target response spectrum and the target duration characteristics. A multi-objective genetic algorithm is applied for using these two matching relationships as constraints to solve for the combination coefficients that meet the evaluation criteria. The simulation process is illustrated in Figure 1.

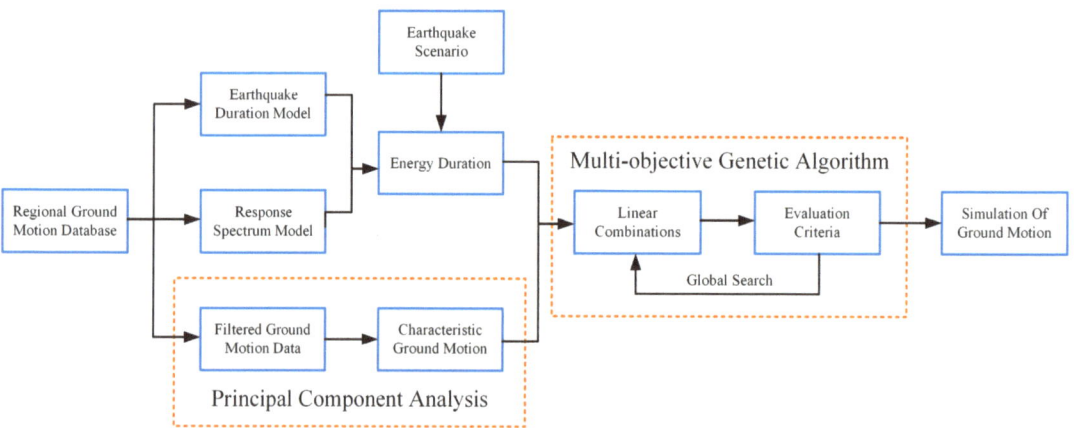

Figure 1. Framework of the proposed ground-motion simulation method.

2.1. PCA for Extracting Ground Motions

The sheer volume of data in the ground-motion database and the potential correlation between individual datum makes the data difficult to process. First, the characteristics of the ground-motion data in the database need to be extracted and processed (i.e., dimensionality reduction of the data). There are many methods of data dimensionality reduction in machine learning: PCA, linear discriminant analysis (LDA), locally linear embedding (LLE), and so on. However, LDA is a supervised dimensionality reduction algorithm; the stream shape learned by LLE can only be unclosed, and the sample set is dense and uniform. PCA, as an unsupervised dimensionality reduction algorithm, is easier to use and less demanding on data.

We use PCA to obtain the reduced-dimensional characteristics from the ground-motion database, calling them characteristic ground motions. Specifically, we use PCA to reduce the dimensionality of the entire accelerated ground-motion record and to obtain a time series of data similar to the accelerated ground motion. It should be noted that PCA uses the ground shaking database of the target region to reflect the regional characteristics of the synthetic ground motion. For areas lacking ground-motion records, ground motion from areas with similar earthquake sources, propagation paths, and site conditions can be selected as ground-motion data.

The application of the PCA algorithm for dimensionality reduction of the ground-motion dataset involves the following process:

Dataset X needs to be reduced to k dimensions, where X is a matrix of n rows and m columns. The m represents the ground-motion durations, and 'n' stands for the number of ground motions. $X = \begin{Bmatrix} x_{11}, x_{12}, x_{13}, \ldots, x_{1m}; \\ x_{21}, x_{22}, x_{23}, \ldots, x_{2m} \\ \ldots \\ x_{n1}, x_{n2}, x_{n3}, \ldots, x_{nm} \end{Bmatrix}$

(1) Centralize all samples according to Equation (1); i.e., each bit of the feature minus its respective mean.

$$x_{nm} = x_{nm} - \frac{1}{k} \sum_{i=1}^{k} x_{nm}, \tag{1}$$

(2) Calculate the covariance matrix of sample C, $C = \frac{1}{n} X^T X$

(3) Determine the eigenvalues and eigenvectors of the covariance matrix via the eigenvalue decomposition of the matrix covariance matrix.

The eigenvalues are sorted from the largest to the smallest, and the largest k values are selected. The corresponding k eigenvectors are used as row vectors to form the eigenvector matrix P. $P = \begin{Bmatrix} \lambda_1 \\ \lambda_2 \\ \ldots \\ \lambda_k \end{Bmatrix}$.

The centralized data matrix is transformed into a new space constructed by k eigenvectors, i.e., $Y = PX$, which in turn yields new orthogonal feature ground motion data.

$$1 - \frac{\sum_{i=1}^{K} S_{ii}}{\sum_{i=1}^{N} S_{ii}} \leq t, \tag{2}$$

The selection of dimension K, representing the number of characteristic ground motions after dimensionality reduction, can be determined based on the scatter matrix S generated during singular value decomposition. Equation (2) can be used to calculate the minimum value of K that satisfies the error condition. If the value of t is 0.15, then it indicates that the PCA algorithm retains 85% of the main information from the original data. Consequently, the minimum number of characteristic ground-shaking that can be extracted under this allowable error can be determined. The specific value of t can be determined according to the requirements for the error; therefore, different K values can be selected.

Multiple characteristic ground motions that are independent of each other can be obtained by applying the abovementioned PCA method to the actual ground-motion records. The characteristic ground motions and actual ground-motion records in the database shared the same sampling rate. As a result, it is possible to synthesize the target ground motions by combining the characteristic ground motions in a linear manner and determining the combination coefficients that dictate their blending. The linear combination is a vector synthesis of the characteristic ground-motion vectors multiplied by scaling coefficients. The characteristic ground motions are linearly combined as Equation (3)

$$a(t) = \sum_{i=1}^{q} k_i a_i, \qquad (3)$$

where k_i, a_i, and q denote the coefficient, extracted characteristic ground motion, and number of extracted characteristic ground motions, respectively. The characteristic ground motions are eigenvectors composed of data matrices, which are then sorted according to the size of the eigenvalues.

2.2. Optimization of Coefficients Using NSGA-II

A genetic algorithm is applied because it is necessary to determine the combination coefficients in Equation (3). The simulating method employed in this procedure takes into account both the matching of the target response spectrum and the target duration, which are obtained from the ground-motion-duration model. This approach differs from the traditional method that only considers matching the target response spectrum based on the prediction equation of the ground-motion-response spectrum. Since it involves multiple constraints and requires solving multiple equations, the conventional single-objective optimization algorithm is no longer applicable, and the computational effort becomes significant. Therefore, the elitist nondominated sorting genetic algorithm NSGA-II is utilized [42]. This algorithm effectively balances the relationship between each objective function, resulting in an optimal solution set that maximizes the performance of each subobjective function. This approach differs from single-objective optimization and offers a unique solution. Consequently, the solution to the multi-objective optimization problem comprises a set of equilibrium solution sets.

The algorithm uses fast dominant sorting to minimize the complexity of the algorithm and volume of operations. Furthermore, it replaces the fitness-sharing strategy via crowding and crowding comparison operators to perform a peer comparison of the results after fast sorting such that the individuals in the Pareto solution can be evenly extended to the whole domain, and the diversity of the population is preserved. Among them, the banded elite strategy expands the sample by combining the parent and child populations to ensure that better individuals can be retained.

2.3. Control Conditions of the Synthesis Coefficient

A well-matched ground motion is defined as a ground motion with a minimum error in the response spectrum constraint and a minimum error in the duration constraint. The mean absolute error (MAE) is used to match the response spectra of the synthesized ground motions with the target spectrum. We used MAE as the error because it is a more common and straightforward error compared to other errors [43]. Equation (4) introduces the constraint equation for the response spectrum.

$$E_1 = \sum_{j=1}^{m} \left[\left| S_a\left(\sum_{i=1}^{n} k_i a_i, T_j \right) - S_a^*(T_j) \right| \right], \qquad (4)$$

where E_1 refers to the MAE between the response spectra of the synthesized ground motions and the target spectrum, $S_a^*(T_j)$ represents the target response spectrum obtained from the ground-motion prediction equation in the target area, and T_j indicates the selected self-oscillation period control point in the spectral matching process. m is the number of response spectrum period points. Furthermore, $S_a\left(\sum_{j=1}^n k_i a_i, T_i\right)$ represents the response spectrum calculated from the new time-history records obtained by a linear combination of the extracted characteristic ground motions, where $\sum_{i=1}^n k_i a_i$ represents the new time-history record obtained by multiplying the extracted N characteristic ground motions by their respective coefficients.

The simulating method applied by the software considers not only the amplitude and frequency spectrum reflected by the ground-motion response spectrum, but also the parametric characteristics of the duration, which is an important parameter of ground motions. As the structure undergoes nonlinearization, the probability of permanent deformation increases with longer durations due to the cumulative effect of earthquakes. Therefore, ground-motion duration is a very important constraint. It is necessary to obtain a reasonable prediction of the ground-motion duration and select the ground-motion duration prediction equation suitable for the target area. The constraint equation for the duration is introduced as Equation (5).

$$E_2 = [|D_{5-95} - d_{5-95}|], \tag{5}$$

where d_{5-95} denotes the target ground-motion duration time (different types of duration definitions can be selected, and this paper considers a 5–95% significant duration as an example to introduce the method). The new synthetic ground-motion duration is recorded as D_{5-95}.

3. Results

3.1. Validation of Methods

An earthquake of magnitude Ms6.0 occurred at 28.34° N 104.90° E, located in Changning County, Yibin City, southeastern Sichuan Province, China, on 17 June 2019. In this study, the ground-motion database was created by collecting the mainshock of the Changning earthquake and aftershock records of magnitude 4 or higher that occurred between June 17 and 24. The specific earthquake information is summarized in Table 1. The epicenter, station locations, and the intensity distribution of the mainshock in Changning are illustrated in Figure 2a; the epicenter and source mechanism of the selected main aftershock are illustrated in Figure 2b. The database contains 9 earthquakes with a total of 286 horizontally oriented seismic records, and raw ground-motion data are filtered and baseline adjusted [44]. The feasibility of the synthesis method is verified by simulating the Changning earthquake. The Changning earthquake was selected as the scenario, and the target response spectrum and duration were calculated to validate the method.

Table 1. Selected Changning mainshock–aftershock events.

Name	Date	Latitude	Longitude	Depth (km)	Magnitude (Ms)
Mainshock	June 17	28.34° N	104.9° E	16	6
Aftershock	June 17	28.43° N	104.769° E	16	5.1
Aftershock	June 18	28.389° N	104.849° E	10	4.1
Aftershock	June 18	28.389° N	104.87° E	10	4.2
Aftershock	June 18	28.379° N	104.87° E	14	4.5
Aftershock	June 18	28.37° N	104.889° E	17	5.3
Aftershock	June 22	28.43° N	104.769° E	10	5.4
Aftershock	June 23	28.389° N	104.819° E	14	4.6
Aftershock	June 24	28.44° N	104.8° E	10	4.1

Note: Information on seismic events listed in the table comes from the China Earthquake Network Center (CENC).

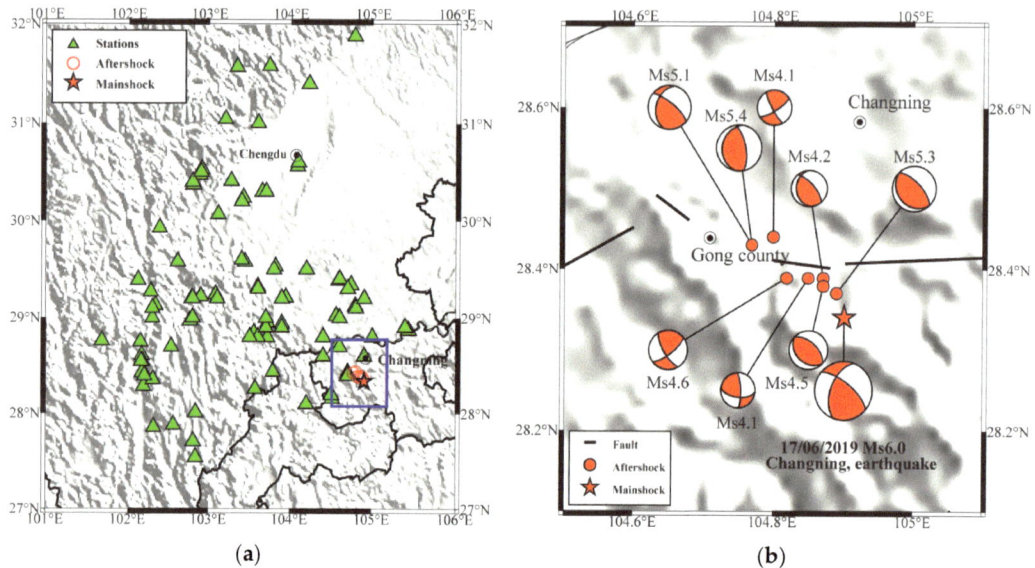

Figure 2. Epicenters, station distribution, and focal mechanism parameters of the selected Changning mainshock and aftershocks. (**a**) Location of epicenter and stations, and the intensity distribution map. (**b**) Epicenter and source mechanism.

3.1.1. Extraction of Characteristic Ground Motion

The PCA was applied to extract the characteristic ground motion in the mainshock and aftershock databases of Changning. The number of extracted characteristic ground motions was calculated according to Equation (2) to determine the number of extracted characteristic ground motions. In this study, t is set to 0.05, i.e., we expect the obtained extracted characteristic ground motion to retain 95% of the main information in the dataset. The minimum K value that satisfied the error condition was 11. The top 11 waves were extracted from the database and ranked according to the percentage of retained information for the subsequent synthesis of ground motion. Table 2 summarizes the percentage of information retained in the original database for each extracted ground motion, and Figure 3 shows the time and frequency analysis of the top eight characteristic ground motions. The extracted ground motion has similar nonstationary characteristics to the actual ground-motion recordings in the time and frequency domains, which makes the characteristic ground motions suitable as a set of basis vectors for ground-motion synthesis.

Table 2. Proportion of information retained by the extracted ground motion mother waves.

Number	1	2	3	4	5	6	7	8	9	10	11
S_{ii}	0.363	0.203	0.104	0.097	0.069	0.039	0.030	0.025	0.010	0.007	0.004
$\sum_{i=1}^{K} S_{ii}$	0.363	0.566	0.670	0.767	0.836	0.875	0.905	0.930	0.940	0.947	0.951

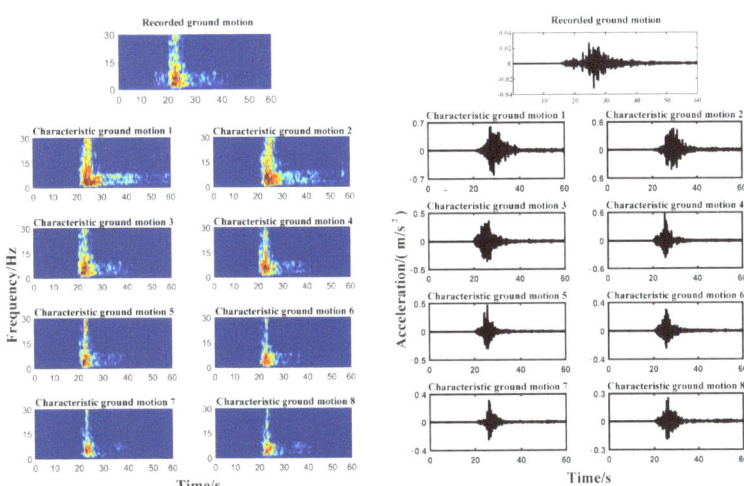

Figure 3. Top eight time histories and time-frequency analyses of characteristic ground motion.

3.1.2. Validation of Ground-Motion Prediction Equation and Constraints

The Changning earthquake in Sichuan occurred in the western part of China; therefore, it is necessary to select a ground-motion model for western China that is suitable for this region and a ground-motion duration prediction equation based on a strong ground-motion database in China [45]. The target response spectrum and target duration ground-motion models were calculated using the response spectrum and duration, respectively, as the constraints for ground-motion synthesis of the Changning earthquake by setting the earthquake scenario. The specific forms of the selected response spectrum ground-motion model and the ground-motion duration model are shown as Equations (6) and (7).

$$lgS_a(T) = C_1 + C_2 M_s + C_4 lg[R_{rup} + C_5 exp(C_6 M_s)], \qquad (6)$$

$$lnD_{5-95} = 0.1561 + 0.3647 M_s + (0.4958 - 0.0145 M_s) ln\sqrt{R_{rup}^2 + 2.5} - 0.1784 ln v_s 30, \quad (7)$$

where $Sa(T)$ is the response spectrum, M_s is the surface wave magnitude, R_{rup} is the rupture distance, and D_{5-95} is the ground-motion duration. $V_s 30$ is the shear wave velocity at 30 m below ground, representing the site conditions, and the value of our target site $V_s 30$ is 302 m/s.

Figure 4a–d shows the comparison of the response spectra of the Changning earthquake records at three period points (0.01 s, 0.20 s, and 1.00 s) with the attenuation curves obtained from the corresponding ground-motion models. The figures also show the comparison of the 5–95% significant duration of the actual ground-motion data with the predicted values obtained from the duration prediction equation. The two chosen ground-motion models have the capability to predict the actual ground-motion characteristics of the region and demonstrate the validity of the selected synthetic constraints, including the target response spectrum and duration. It is important to mention that two independent GMPEs are used in this paper. However, it is more reasonable to use the generalized conditioning intensity measure (GCIM) or generalized ground-motion prediction model (GGMPM) models, which can provide realistic targets to validate the simulation.

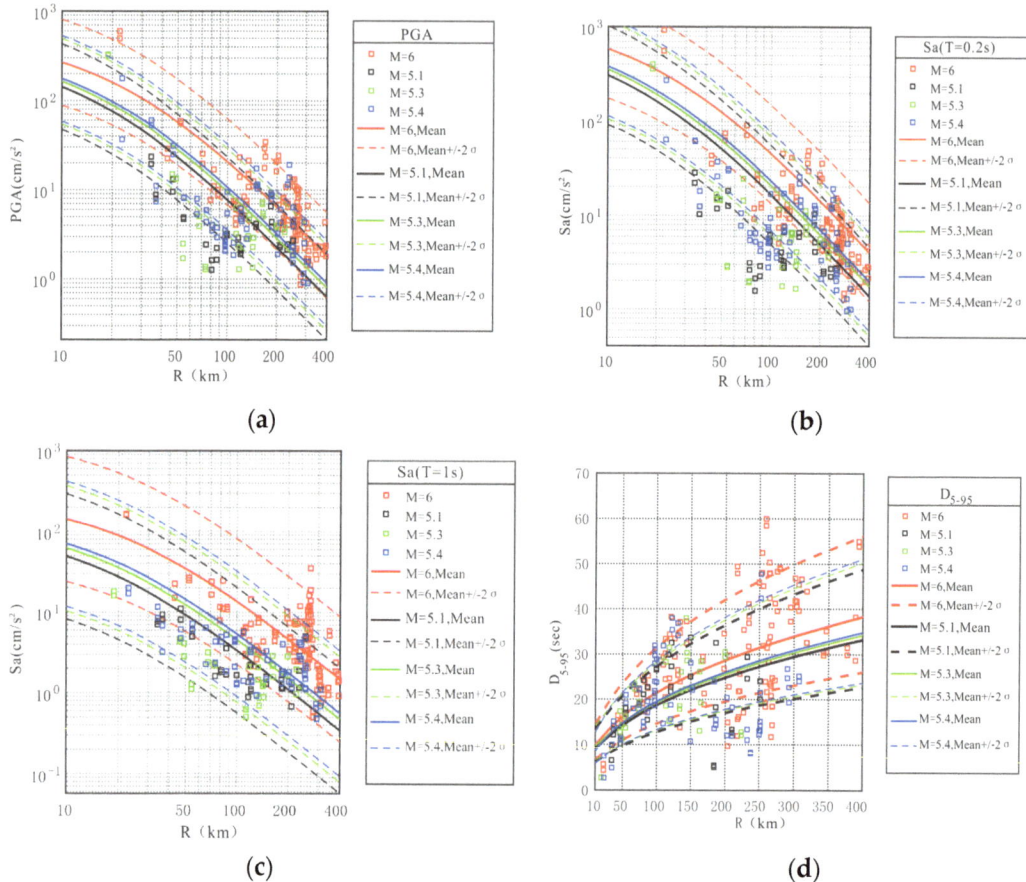

Figure 4. Comparison between the response spectra and durations of Changning ground motions and ground-motion models: (**a**) PGA; (**b**) Sa (T = 0.2 s); (**c**) Sa (T = 1 s); (**d**) D_{5-95}.

3.1.3. Validation of Synthetic Ground Motion

We used the method in this study to synthesize a ground motion and match it with a record selected from the real ground-motion database to verify the feasibility of the synthesis method and to verify if the matching results are reasonable. One station in the Changning earthquake, i.e., 51NXT, was arbitrarily selected, and the specific ground-shaking information is as listed in Table 3. The synthesis was conducted based on this method, and the matching effect of the synthesized peak ground acceleration, response spectrum, and duration with the real ground-motion records, is also summarized in Table 3. The matching effect and error distribution of the synthesized ground motion and actual seismic records are illustrated in Figure 5. In Figure 5b, the horizontal and vertical axes represent the error values between the response spectrum and the holding time of the synthetic ground shaking, and between the response spectrum and the target values obtained from the ground-shaking model, respectively. These error values are calculated using Equations (4) and (5). Each scatter in the distribution of the figure represents a set of linear combination coefficients of waves in the optimal solution set, whereas the red scatter represents the finalized combination coefficients under the judging criteria. The synthetic ground motion in Figure 5a,c shows the result of the linear combination of waves obtained using the corresponding combination coefficients of the scatter. Peak ground accelerations and response spectra of the synthetic ground motion are well matched with the actual records; more importantly, 90% of the significant duration of the synthetic ground shaking is matched perfectly with the actual records, and the duration of synthetic earthquakes is controlled to the target level of the regional duration prediction model. This method allows the synthesis of ground motion considering constraints of the regional ground-motion prediction model; they can be used for the construction of a regional set and a ground-shaking time field for engineering structure input.

Table 3. Basic parameters required for the synthetic ground motion and match of the duration.

-	Magnitude (Ms)	Depth (km)	Distance (km)	PGA (g)	Significant Duration D_{5-95}(s)	Response Spectrum Error (g)
Recorded ground motion	5.4	10	46.92	0.0318	11.045	-
Simulated ground motion	5.4	10	46.92	0.0333	11.060	0.0784

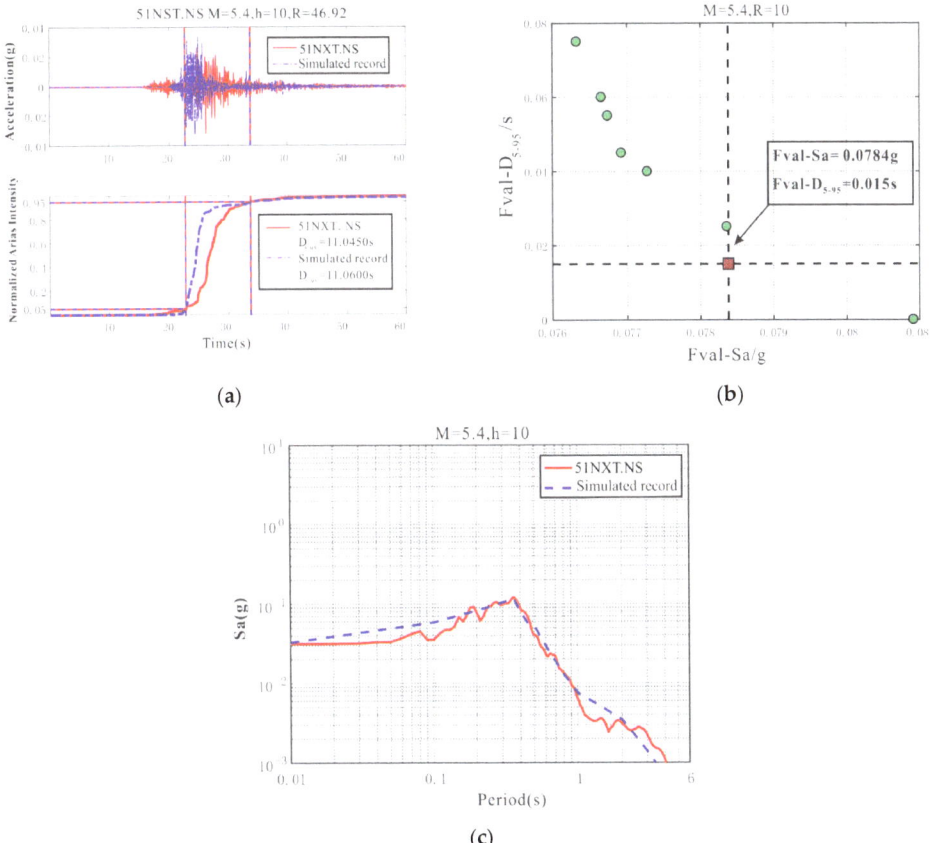

Figure 5. Comparison with real ground motions: (**a**) Comparison of the time-history and duration of real ground-motion records and synthetic ground motion; (**b**) Error distribution of the optimal solution set for multi-objective optimization; (**c**) Matching of response spectrum.

3.2. Architecture of Software

The software has three modules: (1) parameter input, (2) visualization, and (3) calculation history time record. Simulating ground motions require the user to provide parameters for engineering demand. The program functions as a black box, requiring only user-provided parameters to yield results. For instance, regional ground-motion time-history records that meet the user's requirements can be input into the program. This eliminates the need for users to delve into the program's execution details, allowing them to concentrate on other aspects. Initially, users can utilize the software's area module to mark the epicenter and target area accurately and distinctly on the map, facilitating quick determination of the target area and enhancing user experience. Subsequently, within the field simulation module, users can swiftly obtain the amplitude field for each period in the target area by inputting parameters, enabling clear observation of period amplitudes and intuitive judgments. Ultimately, the program can be employed to precisely calculate historical time records for further research. Figure 6 shows the architecture of the proposed procedure.

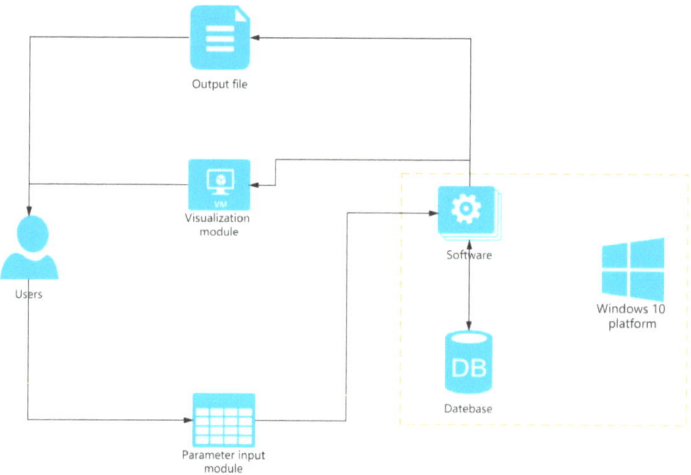

Figure 6. Framework of the ground-motion simulation software.

3.3. Parameter Input Module

Scenario construction for the ground motion needs the user to propose requirements and determine the demand parameters. The user is first required to determine the magnitude of the earthquake and the location of the epicenter, and then to determine other parameters such as latitude and longitude, Vs30, and rupture angle of the target area. The input parameter module was entered through the panel in Figure 7a. The specific meanings of the parameters are listed in Table 4.

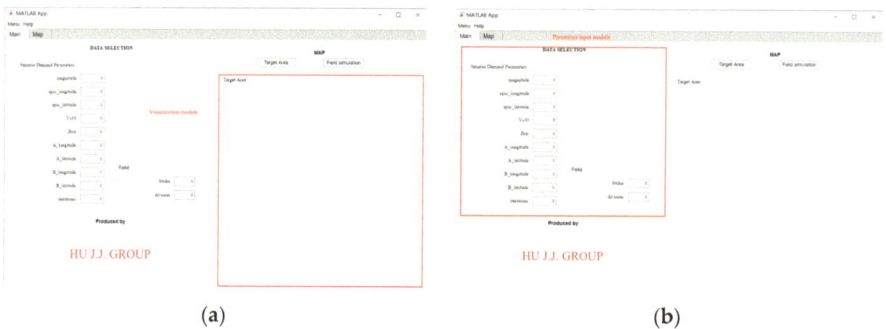

(a)   (b)

Figure 7. (a) Input parameter module in the panel; (b) area module in the panel.

Table 4. Meanings of parameters in the software.

Parameters	Description
Magnitude	Moment magnitude
epic_longitude	Epicenter longitude (e.g., enter 112 for 112° East)
epic_latitude	Epicenter latitude (e.g., enter 27 for 27° North)
Vs30	Equivalent shear-wave velocity within 30 m
Ztor	Depth to the top of the co-seismic rupture plane
A_longitude	Specify the longitude of the lower left corner of the rectangular area
A_latitude	Specify the latitude of the lower left corner of the rectangular area
B_longitude	Specify the longitude of the upper right corner of the rectangular area
B_latitude	Specify the latitude of the upper right corner of the rectangular area
Strike	Fault rupture angle 0–180, e.g., 45
Division	Interval for gridding the ground-motion field, e.g., 5 km

3.4. Visualization Module

In the past, the command line format was poorly interactive and costly to learn; GUI is the trend of modern program development, which makes it easy for users to use the software without having to pay a high learning cost. Data visualization is an efficient form of presenting data that allows users to observe data results clearly and intuitively, and helps users use the software better.

3.4.1. Target Area

The target area visualization module allows the user to clearly determine if the area is their desired area and easily adjust it to their needs; this results in a better interactive experience. Based on parameters entered in the previous subsection, the epic_longitude and epic_latitude—which are the location of the epicenter—were determined. Then, the target area was determined based on the information provided by the user about the target area (latitude and longitude of the specified area); these are displayed in the area module panel, as shown in Figure 7b.

3.4.2. Field Simulation

Under the action of the same ground-motion record, a single-degree-of-freedom system with the same damping and different periods will exhibit different structural responses. The maximum acceleration of the single-degree-of-freedom system represents the damage force of the ground motion. Hence, visually depicting the amplitude field—specifically the maximum acceleration field—of the ground motion within the target area aids in assessing the destructive force of the ground motion. After determining the target area according to the target area module, the target area amplitude field should be drawn in the panel under the MAP according to the location information, magnitude, strike, division, etc., as shown in Figure 7. In the left panel, IMMAP draws the amplitude field based on all amplitude values, and users can obtain the corresponding location information based on the latitude and longitude of the horizontal and vertical coordinates. The values of the amplitude field are marked by contour lines in the panel so that users can better understand the amplitude size. The GEOMAP on the right shows a geographic map which serves as the base map, and the amplitude field is drawn with itself as the base to ensure convenience for users to compare geographic information.

Furthermore, it is necessary to provide the amplitude fields for different periods. IMMAP and GEOMAP provide amplitude fields for shorter to longer periods, as illustrated in Figure 8a,b. This provides the user with a visual reference to obtain the degree of damage to the target area caused by this earthquake.

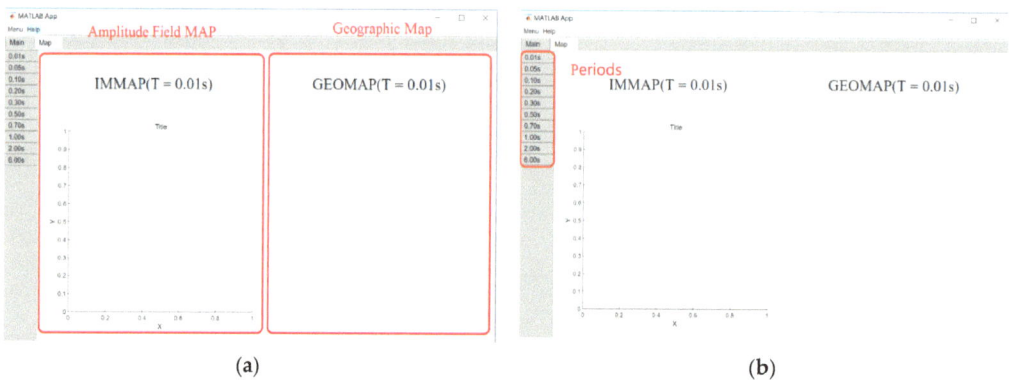

Figure 8. Different period field simulation in the panel: (**a**) MAP's module in the panel; (**b**) Different period button.

3.5. Calculation History Time Record Module

Within the visualization module, the user-provided parameters for scenario requirements serve as inputs. As shown in Figure 9, the RUN button in the menu is clicked to generate a series of acceleration time history records denoted by latitude and longitude coordinates in the "data" folder under the installation directory.

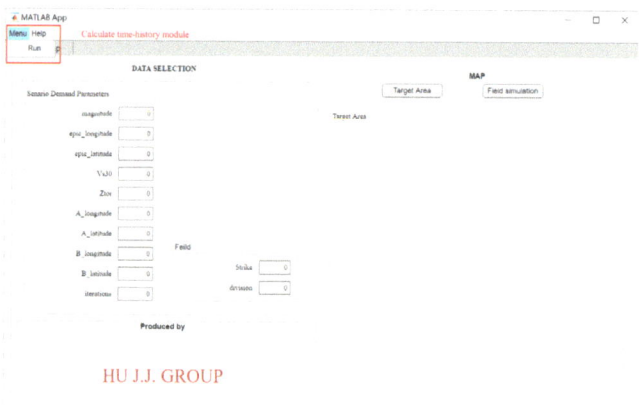

Figure 9. Acquiring time-history module in the panel.

3.6. Properties and Usage of Software

The parameter input module allows us to enter scenarios that the user needs to build. The visualization module is a visualization function that provides the user-defined epicenter and the range of the target area while providing the amplitude fields of the main periods of the response spectrum. The calculation history time record module provides the time-history records.

Demand parameters are entered into the software, and the demand scenarios are determined by entering the magnitude, epicenter, and target area. Figure 10 shows the settings for the Changning earthquake.

After entering the parameters, the epicenter and target area (blue area) were illustrated by clicking on the AREA button in the visualization module to determine if the set area matches the demanded scenario and if adjustments are required. The epicenter is indicated by a red star, and the target area is indicated by a blue box. The base map is provided by the Map Toolkit in MATLAB (MATLAB Basemap Data, colorterrain); the map indicates important cities and roads, which enables better user experience, as indicated in Figure 10.

After determining the target area, another visualization feature of the software is drawing the amplitude field based on the input parameters. After clicking on the field simulation button, the amplitude field is drawn in the panel under the MAP, as indicated in Figure 11.

Figure 10. Example of MAPs in the panel.

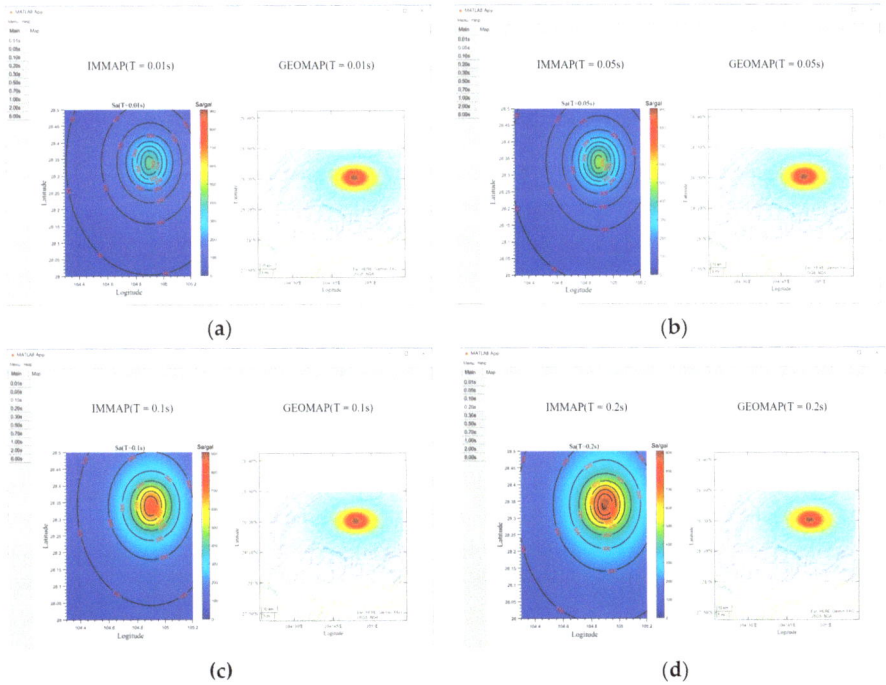

Figure 11. *Cont.*

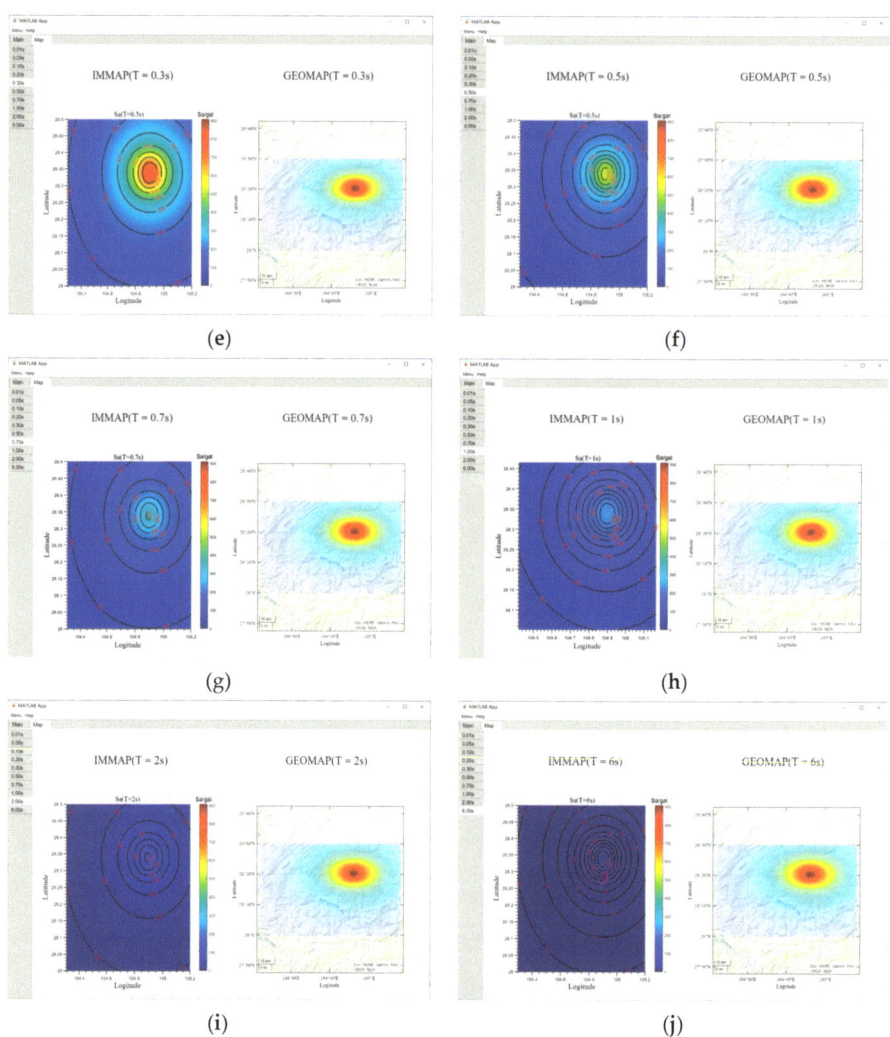

Figure 11. Visualization example of ground motion fields for different periods in the panel: (**a**) Sa (T = 0.01 s); (**b**) Sa (T = 0.05 s); (**c**) Sa (T = 0.1 s); (**d**) Sa (T = 0.2 s); (**e**) Sa (T = 0.3 s); (**f**) Sa (T = 0.5 s); (**g**) Sa (T = 0.7 s); (**h**) Sa (T = 1 s); (**i**) Sa (T = 2 s); (**j**) Sa (T = 6 s).

Finally, one feature of the software is the provision of ground-motion records. After clicking the RUN button, time course files are generated in the data folder and named latitude and longitude for easy selection and use. One file is opened; the header of the file describes the number of samples, sampling rate, set magnitude, epicenter, and sampling points. Subsequently, the time record is provided for the next use.

4. Discussion

The trigonometric series method is a widely used method for simulating ground motion in engineering. To compare the results of this paper with those of this method, the ground-motion synthesis is carried out using the trigonometric series method. The set of seismic information required for synthesizing ground motion and the matching of duration and response spectrum are shown in Table 5. Figure 5 shows the ground-motion time history and duration curves, and the matching error of the response spectrum synthesized by the two methods.

Table 5. The time and response spectrum matching of two synthetic methods.

Method	Ms	Hypocenter (km)	Epicentral Distance (km)	Vs30	D_{5-95}	Duration Error	Response Spectrum Error
Trigonometric series	5	10	10	360	8.469	0.239	0.0739
Method in the paper	5	10	10	360	8.469	6.334	0.3204

The ground motions synthesized by the software In this paper can match the spectrum and duration well, compared to the traditional methods. However, the method based on PCA and multi-objective genetic algorithm has some limitations. Therefore, it is necessary to discuss the scope of application in this software here. Firstly, for areas with real records, the ground-motion database of the software can be updated to apply to the target area, while the method has some limitations for areas lacking records. For areas lacking records, ground motions from areas with similar sources, propagation paths, and site conditions can be selected as the database of the software, which is of some significance for areas lacking data. Secondly, because the synthetic ground-motion field needs to depend on the ground-motion model, areas lacking records should first establish the ground-motion model, which is out of the scope of this study. Thirdly, due to the regional characteristic ground motions of the method in this study, only a small sample was selected for testing because of the limited number of records currently available in a specific small area.

The synthesis results of this paper's method and the trigonometric series method can be seen in the comparison; the trigonometric series method considered by matching with the spectrum can achieve the ground-motion amplitude and spectrum constraints, but cannot be bound to the duration. In contrast, the ground-motion synthesis method of this paper can well-reflect the regional ground-motion characteristics reflected by the regional ground-motion prediction equation in the synthesis results under the control of the constraint conditions and evaluation criteria.

5. Conclusions

A regional ground-motion synthesis software was developed in this study. The software extracts characteristic ground motions using PCA and a linear combination of algorithms that perform genetic algorithm optimization for obtaining time history records, satisfying real requirements and verifying their accuracy.

Combined with the machine learning method, the synthesis method of this procedure considers matching both the target response spectrum and target duration compared to the traditional simulation method, and it satisfies engineering demands for achieving reasonable ground motions. The software also offers regional amplitude fields and time history records for larger scenarios.

The software was designed entirely in a MATLAB GUI environment. A clear target area can be drawn via the visualization interface and provided parameters (such as seismic magnitude, site, and latitude and longitude of the target area) to improve the user's understanding; furthermore, amplitude intensity fields of the main periods are provided, while the time-history records are generated in the target folder. In addition, the software provides a user-friendly interface for users to obtain artificial regional ground-motion fields as per their requirements.

Amplitude, spectrum, and duration are the three most important features of ground motion. Amplitude and spectrum are usually matched in engineering. Therefore, we introduce duration as a matching restriction. However, other intensity metrics like Arias intensity, CAV, and PGV are also significant, and we will continue to investigate them in the next works.

Author Contributions: Conceptualization, J.H. and Y.D.; methodology, H.Z.; software, Y.D.; validation, C.J., H.Z. and S.L.; formal analysis, Y.D.; investigation, J.H.; resources, C.J.; data curation, H.Z.; writing—original draft preparation, Y.D.; writing—review and editing, J.H.; visualization, J.H.; funding acquisition, J.H. All authors have read and agreed to the published version of the manuscript.

Funding: This research was funded by Scientific Research Fund of Institute of Engineering Mechanics, China Earthquake Administration, grant number 2020D08; 2021EEEVL0103, National Key R&D Program of China, grant number 2018YFC1504401, and the National Natural Science Foundation of China, grant number U1939210.

Institutional Review Board Statement: Not applicable.

Informed Consent Statement: Not applicable.

Data Availability Statement: Data for this study were provided by the China Strong Motion Networks Center (CSMNC) at the Institute of Engineering Mechanics, China Earthquake Administration.

Conflicts of Interest: The authors declare no conflict of interest.

References

1. Amiri, G.G.; Abdolahi Rad, A.; Aghajari, S.; Khanmohamadi Hazaveh, N. Generation of Near-Field Artificial Ground Motions Compatible with Median-Predicted Spectra Using PSO-Based Neural Network and Wavelet Analysis. *Comput. Civ. Infrastruct. Eng.* **2012**, *27*, 711–730. [CrossRef]
2. Iervolino, I.; Cornell, C.A. Record Selection for Nonlinear Seismic Analysis of Structures. *Earthq. Spectra* **2005**, *21*, 685–713. [CrossRef]
3. Mir, R.R.; Parvez, I.A. Ground Motion Modelling in Northwestern Himalaya Using Stochastic Finite-Fault Method. *Nat. Hazards* **2020**, *103*, 1989–2007. [CrossRef]
4. Elnashai, A.S.; McClure, D.C. Effect of Modelling Assumptions and Input Motion Characteristics on Seismic Design Parameters of RC Bridge Piers. *Earthq. Eng. Struct. Dyn.* **1996**, *25*, 435–463. [CrossRef]
5. Jamie Ellen Padgett, M.A.; Reginald DesRoches, M.A. Sensitivity of Seismic Response and Fragility to Parameter Uncertainty. *J. Struct. Eng.* **2007**, *133*, 1710–1718. [CrossRef]
6. Fayaz, J.; Zareian, F. Reliability Analysis of Steel SMRF and SCBF Structures Considering the Vertical Component of Near-Fault Ground Motions. *J. Struct. Eng.* **2019**, *145*, 04019061. [CrossRef]
7. Motazedian, D.; Atkinson, G.M. Stochastic Finite-Fault Modeling Based on a Dynamic Corner Frequency. *Bull. Seismol. Soc. Am.* **2005**, *95*, 995–1010. [CrossRef]
8. Dabaghi, M.; Der Kiureghian, A. Simulation of Orthogonal Horizontal Components of Near-Fault Ground Motion for Specified Earthquake Source and Site Characteristics. *Earthq. Eng. Struct. Dyn.* **2018**, *47*, 1369–1393. [CrossRef]
9. Heidari, R. Stochastic Finite-Fault Simulation of Ground Motion from the August 11, 2012, M w 6.4 Ahar Earthquake, Northwestern Iran. *J. Seismol.* **2016**, *20*, 463–473. [CrossRef]
10. Maechling, P.J.; Silva, F.; Callaghan, S.; Jordan, T.H. SCEC Broadband Platform: System Architecture and Software Implementation. *Seismol. Res. Lett.* **2015**, *86*, 27–38. [CrossRef]
11. Graves, R.; Jordan, T.H.; Callaghan, S.; Deelman, E.; Field, E.; Juve, G.; Kesselman, C.; Maechling, P.; Mehta, G.; Milner, K.; et al. CyberShake: A Physics-Based Seismic Hazard Model for Southern California. *Pure Appl. Geophys.* **2011**, *168*, 367–381. [CrossRef]
12. Douglas, J.; Aochi, H. A survey of techniques for predicting earthquake ground motions for engineering purposes. *Surv. Geophys.* **2008**, *29*, 187–220. [CrossRef]
13. Causse, M.; Laurendeau, A.; Perrault, M.; Douglas, J.; Bonilla, L.F.; Guéguen, P. Eurocode 8-compatible synthetic time-series as input to dynamic analysis. *Bull. Earthq. Eng.* **2013**, *12*, 755–768. [CrossRef]
14. Cui, X.Z.; Hong, H.P. Use of Discrete Orthonormal S-Transform to Simulate Earthquake Ground Motions. *Bull. Seism. Soc. Am.* **2020**, *110*, 565–575. [CrossRef]
15. Laurendeau, A.; Cotton, F.; Bonilla, L.F. Nonstationary stochastic simulation of strong ground motion time histories: Application to the Japanese database. *arXiv* **2012**, arXiv:1212.3938.
16. Pousse, G.; Bonilla, L.F.; Cotton, F.; Margerin, L. Nonstationary stochastic simulation of strong ground motion time histories including natural variability: Application to the K-net Japanese database. *Bull. Seism. Soc. Am.* **2006**, *96*, 2103–2117. [CrossRef]
17. Sabetta, F.; Pugliese, A.; Fiorentino, G.; Lanzano, G.; Luzi, L. Simulation of non-stationary stochastic ground motions based on recent Italian earthquakes. *Bull. Earthq. Eng.* **2021**, *19*, 3287–3315. [CrossRef]
18. Tamhidi, A.; Kuehn, N.; Ghahari, S.F.; Rodgers, A.J.; Kohler, M.D.; Taciroglu, E.; Bozorgnia, Y. Conditioned Simulation of Ground-Motion Time Series at Uninstrumented Sites Using Gaussian Process Regression. *Bull. Seism. Soc. Am.* **2022**, *112*, 331–347. [CrossRef]
19. Tsioulou, A.; Taflanidis, A.A.; Galasso, C. Hazard-Compatible Modification of Stochastic Ground Motion Models. *Earthq. Eng. Struct. Dyn.* **2018**, *47*, 1774–1798. [CrossRef]

20. Tsioulou, A.; Taflanidis, A.A.; Galasso, C. Modification of Stochastic Ground Motion Models for Matching Target Intensity Measures. *Earthq. Eng. Struct. Dyn.* **2018**, *47*, 3–24. [CrossRef]
21. Fayaz, J.; Azar, S.; Dabaghi, M.; Zareian, F. An Efficient Algorithm to Simulate Hazard-Targeted Site-Based Synthetic Ground Motions. *Earthq. Spectra* **2021**, *37*, 876–902. [CrossRef]
22. Fayaz, J.; Zareian, F. An Efficient Algorithm to Simulate Site-Based Ground Motions That Match a Target Spectrum. *Earthq. Eng. Struct. Dyn.* **2021**, *50*, 3532–3549. [CrossRef]
23. Trifunac, M.D. A Study on Duration of Strong Earthquake Ground Motion. *Bull. Seismol. Soc. Am.* **1975**, *65*, 581–626.
24. Bommer, J.J.; Marytínezpereira, A. The Effective Duration of Earthquake Strong Motion. *J. Earthq. Eng.* **1999**, *3*, 127–172. [CrossRef]
25. Cabanas, L.; Benito, B.; Herraiz, M. An Approach To the Measurement of the Potential Structural. *Earthq. Eng. Struct. Dyn.* **1997**, *26*, 79–92. [CrossRef]
26. Atkinson, G.M.; Boore, D.M. Earthquake Ground-Motion Prediction Equations for Eastern North America. *Bull. Seismol. Soc. Am.* **2006**, *96*, 2181–2205. [CrossRef]
27. Macedo, L.; Castro, J.M. SelEQ: An Advanced Ground Motion Record Selection and Scaling Framework. *Adv. Eng. Softw.* **2017**, *114*, 32–47. [CrossRef]
28. Katsanos, E.I.; Sextos, A.G. ISSARS: An Integrated Software Environment for Structure-Specific Earthquake Ground Motion Selection. *Adv. Eng. Softw.* **2013**, *58*, 70–85. [CrossRef]
29. Klinc, R.; Šebenik, Ž.; Dolšek, M.; Brozovič, M.; Dolenc, M. A Web-Based System for the Selection of Characteristic Ground Motions. *Adv. Eng. Softw.* **2019**, *135*, 102688. [CrossRef]
30. Kayhan, A.H.; Demir, A.; Palanci, M. Multi-functional solution model for spectrum compatible ground motion record selection using stochastic harmony search algorithm. *Bull. Earthq. Eng.* **2022**, *20*, 6407–6440. [CrossRef]
31. Alimoradi, A.; Beck, J.L. Machine-Learning Methods for Earthquake Ground Motion Analysis and Simulation. *J. Eng. Mech.* **2015**, *141*, 04014147. [CrossRef]
32. Guo, Z.; Torra, O.; Hürlimann, M.; Abancó, C.; Medina, V. FSLAM: A QGIS Plugin for Fast Regional Susceptibility Assessment of Rainfall-Induced Landslides. *Environ. Model. Softw.* **2022**, *150*, 105354. [CrossRef]
33. Grelle, G.; Sappa, G.; Madiai, C. SHAKER: A selector of consistent and energetically equalized natural ground motions using the Italian earthquake database. *Eng. Geol.* **2023**, *316*, 107046. [CrossRef]
34. Iervolino, I.; De Luca, F.; Cosenza, E. Spectral shape-based assessment of SDOF nonlinear response to real, adjusted and artificial accelerograms. *Eng. Struct.* **2010**, *32*, 2776–2792. [CrossRef]
35. Gabriele, F. SIGMA: A software tool to simulate non-stationary ground motions for engineering applications. In Proceedings of the 3rd European Conference on Earthquake Engineering and Seismology, Bucharest, Romania, 4–9 September 2022.
36. Medina, V.; Hürlimann, M.; Guo, Z.; Lloret, A.; Vaunat, J. Fast Physically-Based Model for Rainfall-Induced Landslide Susceptibility Assessment at Regional Scale. *Catena* **2021**, *201*, 105213. [CrossRef]
37. Ji, K.; Wen, R.; Zong, C.; Ren, Y. Genetic Algorithm-Based Ground Motion Selection Method Matching Target Distribution of Generalized Conditional Intensity Measures. *Earthq. Eng. Struct. Dyn.* **2021**, *50*, 1497–1516. [CrossRef]
38. Hartzell, S.H. Earthquake Aftershocks as Green's Functions. *Geophys. Res. Lett.* **1978**, *5*, 1–4. [CrossRef]
39. Boore, D.M. Simulation of Ground Motion Using the Stochastic Method. *Pure Appl. Geophys.* **2003**, *160*, 635–676. [CrossRef]
40. Wang, G.; Ding, Y.; Borcherdt, R. *Simulation of Acceleration Field of the Lushan Earthquake (Ms7.0, April 20, 2013, China)*; Elsevier B.V.: Amsterdam, The Netherlands, 2015; Volume 189, ISBN 8604118470.
41. Lu, X.; Cheng, Q.; Tian, Y.; Huang, Y. Regional Ground-Motion Simulation Using Recorded Ground Motions. *Bull. Seismol. Soc. Am.* **2021**, *111*, 825–838. [CrossRef]
42. Deb, K.; Pratap, A.; Agarwal, S.; Meyarivan, T. A Fast and Elitist Multiobjective Genetic Algorithm: NSGA-II. *IEEE Trans. Evol. Comput.* **2002**, *6*, 182–197. [CrossRef]
43. Demir, A.; Palanci, M.; Kayhan, A.H. Evaluation of supplementary constraints on dispersion of EDPs using real ground motion record sets. *Arab. J. Sci. Eng.* **2020**, *45*, 8379–8401. [CrossRef]
44. Boore, D.M.; Watson-Lamprey, J.; Abrahamson, N.A. Orientation-Independent Measures of Ground Motion. *Bull. Seismol. Soc. Am.* **2006**, *96*, 1502–1511. [CrossRef]
45. Yu, Y.X.; Wang, S.Y. Attenuation Relations for Horizontal Peak Ground Acceleration and Response Spectrum in Eastern and Western China. *Technol. Earthq. Disaster Prev.* **2006**, *1*, 206–217.

Disclaimer/Publisher's Note: The statements, opinions and data contained in all publications are solely those of the individual author(s) and contributor(s) and not of MDPI and/or the editor(s). MDPI and/or the editor(s) disclaim responsibility for any injury to people or property resulting from any ideas, methods, instructions or products referred to in the content.

Article

Small Earthquakes Can Help Predict Large Earthquakes: A Machine Learning Perspective

Xi Wang [1], Zeyuan Zhong [1], Yuechen Yao [1], Zexu Li [1], Shiyong Zhou [2], Changsheng Jiang [3] and Ke Jia [1,4,*]

[1] School of Automation, Northwestern Polytechnical University, Xi'an 710129, China
[2] School of Earth and Space Science, Peking University, Beijing 100871, China
[3] Institute of Geophysics, China Earthquake Administration, No. 5 Minzu Daxue Nan Road, Haidian District, Beijing 100086, China
[4] Shanghai Sheshan National Geophysical Observatory, Shanghai 201602, China
* Correspondence: jk@nwpu.edu.cn

Abstract: Earthquake prediction is a long-standing problem in seismology that has garnered attention from the scientific community and the public. Despite ongoing efforts to understand the physical mechanisms of earthquake occurrence, there is no convincing physical or statistical model for predicting large earthquakes. Machine learning methods, such as random forest and long short-term memory (LSTM) neural networks, excel at identifying patterns in large-scale databases and offer a potential means to improve earthquake prediction performance. Differing from physical and statistical approaches to earthquake prediction, we explore whether small earthquakes can be used to predict large earthquakes within the framework of machine learning. Specifically, we attempt to answer two questions for a given region: (1) Is there a likelihood of a large earthquake (e.g., M $\geq$ 6.0) occurring within the next year? (2) What is the maximum magnitude of an earthquake expected to occur within the next year? Our results show that the random forest method performs best in classifying large earthquake occurrences, while the LSTM method provides a rough estimation of earthquake magnitude. We conclude that small earthquakes contain information relevant to predicting future large earthquakes and that machine learning provides a promising avenue for improving the prediction of earthquake occurrences.

Keywords: earthquake prediction; machine learning; random forest; long short-term memory neural network

Citation: Wang, X.; Zhong, Z.; Yao, Y.; Li, Z.; Zhou, S.; Jiang, C.; Jia, K. Small Earthquakes Can Help Predict Large Earthquakes: A Machine Learning Perspective. Appl. Sci. 2023, 13, 6424. https://doi.org/10.3390/app13116424

Academic Editor: Roberto Zivieri

Received: 6 April 2023
Revised: 7 May 2023
Accepted: 22 May 2023
Published: 24 May 2023

Copyright: © 2023 by the authors. Licensee MDPI, Basel, Switzerland. This article is an open access article distributed under the terms and conditions of the Creative Commons Attribution (CC BY) license (https://creativecommons.org/licenses/by/4.0/).

1. Introduction

The prediction of earthquakes has long been a formidable challenge [1–3], owing to several factors. Firstly, seismic events are the result of intricate interactions between tectonic plates, faults, and other geological factors [4], rendering the accurate forecasting of their timing and magnitudes exceedingly challenging. Secondly, the paucity of long-term and extensive data poses a significant hurdle in earthquake prediction. Large earthquakes often recur at lengthy intervals (hundreds to thousands of years) [5], making it arduous to identify trends and patterns over a prolonged time frame [6]. Owing to the intricate geological interplay, the variability of seismic activity, the inadequacy of comprehensive data, and the current technological limitations, the prediction of earthquakes remains a complex and formidable field.

Moreover, conventional prediction methods based on empirical (physical or statistical) models are often oversimplified and fallacious when applied to real-life scenarios [7]. With the rapid development of artificial intelligence (AI) in recent years, many research fields have been benefited, including earthquake prediction. At the core of AI lies machine learning, which plays an essential role in driving this transformation. Machine learning's ability to identify the corresponding functional relationships between vast amounts of data and corresponding labels is its primary advantage. These relationships can be high-dimensional and nonlinear, making it challenging for humans to comprehend, as is the case with earthquake prediction [8,9]. Traditionally, experts' experiences formed the basis of earthquake prediction, which led to random and uncertain outcomes. However, the application of machine learning to earthquake prediction provides a promising approach to achieving more accurate and reliable results.

As early as the 1990s, some scholars proposed the use of machine learning in the area of research in seismology [10]. Currently, various machine learning methods have been applied to seismic classification and location [11–14], seismic event prediction [15–17], seismic early warning [18], seismic exploration [19], slow slip event detection [20], and tomography [21], achieving promising preliminary results in these research fields. Meanwhile, the rapid deployment of long-term seismic monitoring, providing a huge amount of seismic dataset information, accelerates the application of machine learning methods in seismology [8,9,22].

In the research of time series and magnitude prediction, neural networks, including LSTM and convolution neural networks, have been widely used in recent years [23,24]. In [25], the authors proposed a novel approach to earthquake prediction using LSTM networks to capture spatiotemporal correlations among earthquakes in different locations. Their simulation results demonstrate that their method outperforms traditional approaches.

The use of seismicity indicators as inputs in machine learning classifiers has been shown to improve accuracy in earthquake prediction [26]. Results from applying this methodology to four cities in Chile demonstrate that robust predictions can be made by exhaustively exploring how certain parameters should be set up. In [27], a proposed methodology based on the computation of seismic indicators and GP-AdaBoost classification has been trained and tested for three regions: the Hindu Kush, Chile, and Southern California. The obtained prediction results for these regions exhibit improvement when compared with already available studies.

The application of artificial neural networks (ANNs) to earthquake prediction is explored in [28]. The results from the application of ANNs to Chile and the Iberian peninsula are presented, along with a comparative analysis with other well-known classifiers. The conclusion is that the use of a new set of inputs improved all classifiers, but the ANN obtained better results than any other classifier.

A methodology for discovering earthquake precursors by using clustering, grouping, constructing a precursor tree, pattern extraction, and pattern selection has been applied to seven different datasets from three different regions [29]. Results show a remarkable improvement in terms of all evaluated quality measures compared to the former version. The authors suggest that this approach could be further developed and applied to other regions with different geophysical properties to improve earthquake prediction.

In [30], the authors use machine learning techniques to detect signals in a correlation time series corresponding to future large earthquakes. The overall quality is measured by decision thresholds and receiver operating characteristic (ROC) methods together with Shannon information entropy. They hope that the deep learning approach will be more general than previous methods and not require prior guesswork as to what patterns are important.

The seismic activity parameters constructed based on seismic catalogs are typically used as the input data set for earthquake prediction. However, it is still debatable whether the information about small earthquakes (typically with a magnitude smaller than 4.0), such as foreshocks and aftershocks, contained in these seismic features can predict large earthquakes (typically with a magnitude larger than 6.0). In fact, the ability to successfully predict earthquakes has been the subject of controversy [1,3] among researchers. Some studies have shown that information about small earthquakes can indicate the occurrence of large earthquakes, while others have drawn opposite conclusions [31,32].

To clarify this debate, a study was conducted by using seismic features based on seismic catalogs containing small earthquakes to test whether this information can help predict large earthquakes. Additionally, the possibility of using machine learning in earthquake prediction was explored. The study focused on two important questions:

1. Will there be a strong earthquake (M $\geq$ 6.0, 7.0, or 8.0) in the next year?
2. What will be the maximum magnitude of the earthquake in the next year?

The Sichuan–Yunnan region, as shown in Figure 1, was chosen as the research area and seismic features were extracted from the seismic catalog to predict earthquakes.

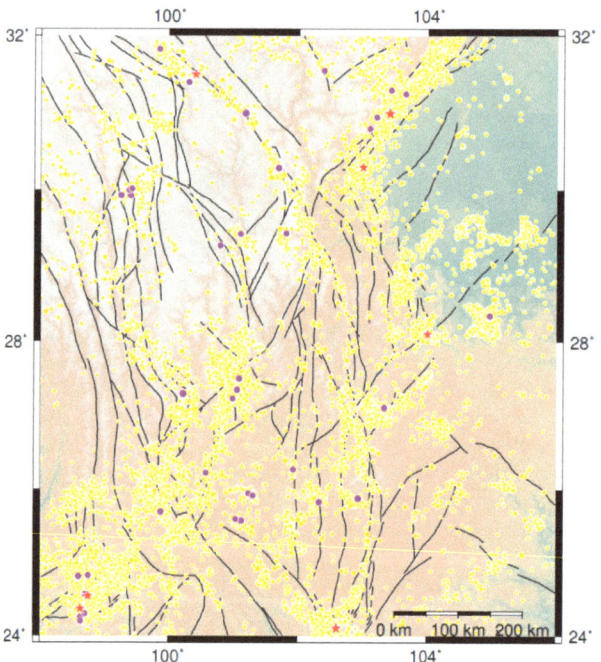

Figure 1. Spatial distribution of seismicity in Chuandian region from 1970 to 2021. The black lines represent active faults [33]. The yellow circles represent earthquakes larger than 3.0, the purple circles show earthquakes larger than 6.0, and the red stars are earthquakes larger than 7.0.

The traditional machine learning methods were used to classify whether there would be strong earthquakes in the next year, and the LSTM network was used to estimate the maximum magnitude of the earthquake in the next year. In this way, we explored the potential applications of machine learning methods in earthquake prediction and provided a possible solution for seismic hazard evaluation.

2. Dataset and Feature Engineering

The seismic catalog used in this study was obtained from the China Earthquake Data Center (CEDC, http://data.earthquake.cn/index.html, last accessed on 23 May 2022) and includes earthquake events with a magnitude greater than 3.0 in the Sichuan–Yunnan region from 1970 to 2021. By means of feature engineering, seismic activity parameters were generated based on several statistical laws. These parameters were derived from the seismic catalog and were used as the input features for earthquake prediction, rather than the original catalog itself.

To test these methods, the Chuandian region of Southwestern China (98.0° E–106.0° E, 24.0° N–32.0° N) was selected due to its abundant earthquakes. The time range for analysis was from 1 January 1970 to 23 May 2021. While there were several sudden large increases in earthquake activity due to large earthquakes during this time period, the completeness magnitude was estimated to be approximately 3.0 using the maximum curvature technique [34,35] (Figure 2). Therefore, the cutoff magnitude was set at 3.0 for this study.

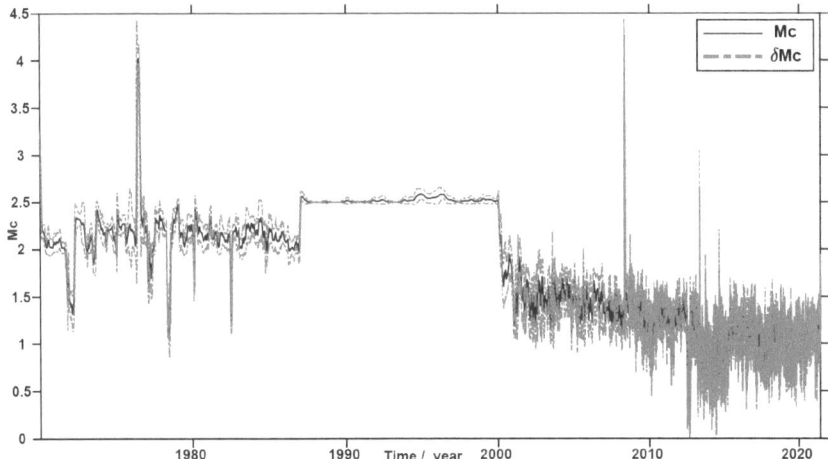

Figure 2. The temporal completeness magnitude from 1970 to 2021 in the Chuandian region based on the maximum curvature technique [34,35].

Prior research has demonstrated that many seismic features derived from earthquake catalogs can be used to predict earthquakes [36–38]. These features include an 'a' value and a 'b' value in the Gutenberg–Richter law, the number and maximum/mean magnitude of past earthquakes, seismic energy release, magnitude deficit, seismic rate changes, and elapsed time since the last large earthquake. In addition, the standard deviation of the estimated b value, the deviation from the Gutenberg–Richter law, and the probability of earthquake occurrence are also calculated as seismic features. The formulas used to calculate these seismic features are listed in Table 1.

Table 1. Details of seismic features and mathematical expressions.

Seismic Features	Description	Mathematical Expressions
N.O.	Number of earthquakes in observation window	
Mag_max	Maximum magnitude in observation window	$\max\{M_i\}$, when $t \in [t_j, t_j + t\_obs]$
Mag_mean	Mean magnitude in observation window	$\frac{\sum_i M_i}{n}$
b_lsq	b value using least square regression analysis	$\frac{n\sum (M_i \log N_i) - \sum M_i \sum \log N_i}{(\sum M_i)^2 - n\sum M_i^2}$
a_lsq	a value using least square regression analysis	$\frac{\sum (\log N_i + b\_lsq \cdot M_i)}{n}$
b_std_lsq	Standard deviation of b_lsq	$2.3(b\_lsq)^2 \sqrt{\frac{\sum_{i=1}^{n}(M_i - Mag\_mean)^2}{n(n-1)}}$
std_gr_lsq	Deviation from Gutenberg–Richter law (b_lsq, a_lsq)	$\frac{\sum (\log N_i - a\_lsq - b\_lsq \cdot M_i)^2}{n-1}$
b_mlk	b value using maximum likelihood method	$\frac{\log e}{Mag\_mean - M_c}$
a_mlk	a value using maximum likelihood method	$\log N + b\_mlk \cdot M_c$
b_std_mlk	Standard deviation of b_mlk	$2.3(b\_mlk)^2 \sqrt{\frac{\sum_{i=1}^{n}(M_i - Mag\_mean)^2}{n(n-1)}}$

Table 1. Cont.

Seismic Features	Description	Mathematical Expressions
std_gr_mlk	Deviation from Gutenberg–Richter law (b_mlk, a_mlk)	$\frac{\sum(\log N_i - a\_mlk - b\_mlk \cdot M_i)^2}{n-1}$
dM_lsq	Magnitude deficit (b_lsq, a_lsq)	$Mag\_max - a\_lsq/b\_lsq$
dM_mlk	Magnitude deficit (b_mlk, a_mlk)	$Mag\_max - a\_mlk/b\_mlk$
Energy	Seismic energy release	$\sqrt{\sum(10^{12+1.8M_i})}$
x7_lsq	Probability of earthquake occurrence using b_lsq	$e^{\frac{-3b\_lsq}{\log e}}$
x7_mlk	Probability of earthquake occurrence using b_mlk	$e^{\frac{-3b\_mlk}{\log e}}$
zvalue	Seismic rate change	$\frac{R_1 - R_2}{\sqrt{\frac{S_1}{n_1} + \frac{S_2}{n_2}}}$, where R_1 and R_2 are seismic rate for the first and second half interval in the observation window. S_1 and S_2 represent the standard deviation of seismic rate R_1 and R_2. n_1 and n_2 are the number of earthquakes in those two intervals.
beta	Seismic rate change	$\frac{M(t,\delta) - n\delta}{\sqrt{n\delta(1-\delta)}}$, where n is the number of earthquakes of the whole seismic catalog, t is the time duration, and δ is the normalized duration of interest. $M(t,\delta)$ represents the observed number of earthquakes by defining end time t and interval of interest δ.
T_elaps6	Days since the last M6.0 earthquake	
T_elaps65	Days since the last M6.5 earthquake	
T_elaps7	Days since the last M7.0 earthquake	
T_elaps75	Days since the last M7.5 earthquake	

The temporal variations of all 22 seismic features listed in Table 1. were calculated for the Chuandian region from 1970 to 2021 using a sliding window process, similarly to previous studies [39]. To predict earthquakes on a mid-term basis, the observation window, the prediction window, and the sliding window were set to be 2 years, 1 year, and 30 days, respectively (Figure 3). This resulted in 591 time steps with 22 seismic features at each step. For earthquake classification, labels were marked with either 0 or 1, and observed magnitudes were used for earthquake magnitude prediction.

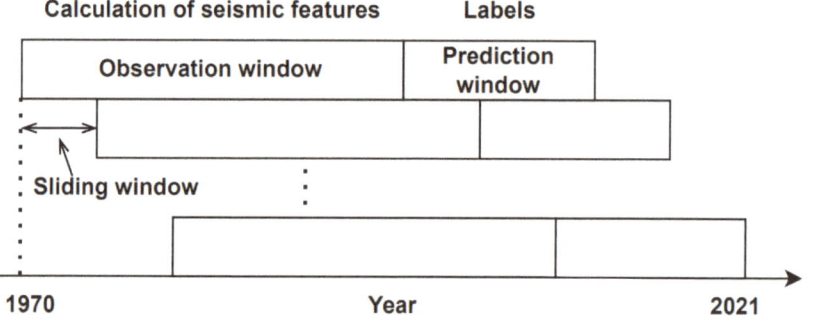

Figure 3. Schematic diagram of seismic feature generation and labels using sliding window approach. The observation window, the prediction window, and the sliding window are set to be 2 years, 1 year, and 30 days, respectively.

3. Methods

In this study, both traditional machine learning algorithms and LSTM neural networks are employed to investigate the occurrence of strong earthquakes and predict their magnitudes, respectively. In the following sections, a brief introduction to these two approaches will be provided. Additionally, the complete earthquake prediction process is illustrated in Figure 4.

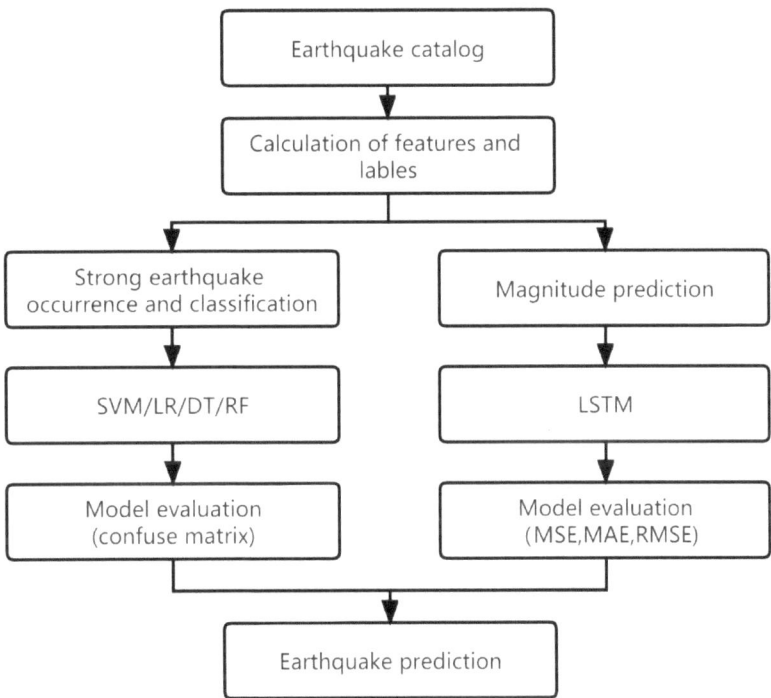

Figure 4. Flow chart of earthquake prediction.

3.1. Traditional Machine Learning Algorithms

Support vector machine (SVM) is a widely used machine learning algorithm for classification and regression problems. It constructs a decision boundary defined by a hyperplane in the feature space, which maximizes the distance between the hyperplane and the nearest training samples, thereby improving the generalization performance of the model. In high-dimensional space, SVM can efficiently handle nonlinear problems, and it performs well for data with small sample size but high dimensionality.

Logistic regression (LR) is a commonly used binary classification algorithm, mainly used to predict the probability of an output variable given an input variable. It calculates the weighted sum of the input variables and passes it through a sigmoid function to map the result to the [0, 1] interval, representing the probability. Logistic regression can use optimization algorithms such as gradient descent for parameter estimation and supports extended forms such as polynomial regression.

Decision tree (DT) is a commonly used machine learning algorithm, which makes decisions by constructing a tree-shaped model. In a decision tree, each node represents a feature, each branch represents a feature value, and each leaf node represents a decision result. By partitioning the data and selecting features, decision trees can effectively perform classification and regression tasks.

Random forest is an ensemble learning algorithm that combines multiple decision trees for classification and regression tasks. In random forests, each decision tree is trained using randomly selected samples and features, and the final result is obtained by voting or averaging. Due to its ability to reduce overfitting and improve prediction performance, random forest is widely used in various machine learning problems.

3.2. Long Short-Term Memory Neutral Network

LSTM is a special kind of recurrent neural network (RNN) proposed in 1997, mainly to solve the problem of gradient disappearance and gradient explosion in the long time series training process. In comparison to RNNs, LSTM performs better for longer time series data. In recent years, LSTM has been widely used in various fields, such as traffic flow prediction [40], stock yield forecast [41], trajectory prediction [42,43], and earthquake forecasting [37].

The memory unit structure of LSTM, consisting of the forget gate, the input gate, and the output gate, is illustrated in Figure 5. At the current time step, the memory unit takes in the hidden variable h_{t-1}, the memory variable C_{t-1}, and the input x_t. Then, the calculation of the forget gate, the input gate, and the output gate yields the output variables h_t and C_t, which are then fed to the next unit.

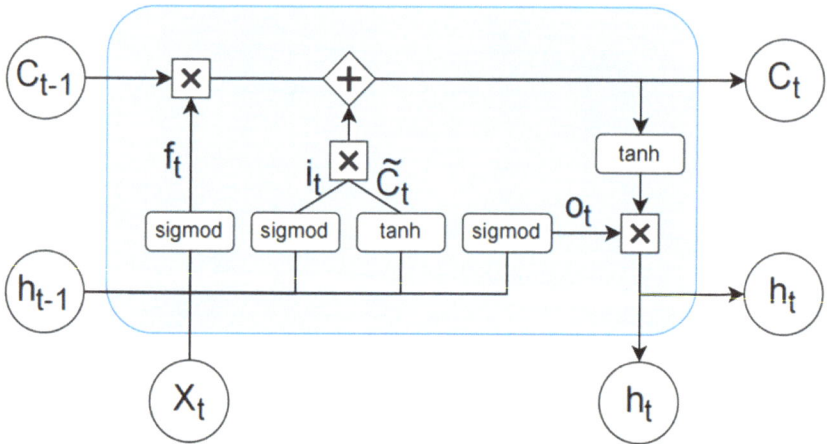

Figure 5. The structure of one memory block in LSTM neural network.

The forget gate first adds h_{t-1} and x_t and passes the result through a sigmoid function to obtain the forget factor, which is then multiplied with C_{t-1}. The forget factor is calculated as follows:

$$f_t = \sigma\left(W_f \cdot [h_{t-1}, x_t] + b_f\right) \quad (1)$$

Similarly, the input gate firstly adds h_{t-1} and x_t, and passes the result through a sigmoid function and a tanh function to obtain i_t and $\widetilde{C}_t$, respectively. The input gate then multiplies the results of the two functions and adds the results with the output of the forget gate to obtain C_t. The calculation formula of i_t, $\widetilde{C}_t$, and C_t is as follows:

$$i_t = \sigma(W_i \cdot [h_{t-1}, x_t] + b_i) \quad (2)$$

$$\widetilde{C}_t = tanh(W_C \cdot [h_{t-1}, x_t] + b_C) \quad (3)$$

$$C_t = f_t \times C_{t-1} + i_t \times \widetilde{C}_t \quad (4)$$

Finally, the output gate adds h_{t-1} and x_t, and passes the result through a sigmoid function to obtain the forget factor. The cell state is then passed into the tanh function and multiplied by the forget factor to obtain the new hidden state, which is then passed into the next unit. The calculation formula of o_t and h_t is as follows:

$$o_t = \sigma(W_o \cdot [h_{t-1}, x_t] + b_o) \quad (5)$$

$$h_t = o_t \times tanh(C_t) \quad (6)$$

Here, W_f, W_i, W_C, and W_o are weight parameters and b_f, b_i, b_C, and b_o are bias parameters.

4. Results
4.1. Evaluation Metrics

The prediction of the occurrence of strong earthquakes involves a two-class classification problem, and the evaluation of its prediction results typically employs a confusion matrix (Table 2).

Table 2. Confusion matrix of binary classification problem.

	Predicted Condition Is Positive	Predicted Condition Is Negative
Actual condition is positive	True Positive (TP)	False Negative (FN)
Actual condition is negative	False Positive (FP)	True Negative (TN)

Specific judgments regarding the performance of earthquake occurrence prediction models are typically made by calculating four evaluation indicators based on the confusion matrix:

$$Accuracy = \frac{TP + TN}{TP + TN + FP + FN} \quad (7)$$

$$Precision = \frac{TP}{TP + FP} \quad (8)$$

$$Recall = \frac{TP}{TP + FN} \quad (9)$$

$$F1 = \frac{2 * Precision * Recall}{Precision + Recall} \quad (10)$$

Additionally, ROC curves and area under curve (AUC) are used to illustrate the relationship between the aforementioned indicators and present the results.

For magnitude prediction, mean square error (*MSE*), mean absolute error (*MAE*), and root mean square error (*RMSE*) are calculated to evaluate the prediction accuracy of the model. *MSE* represents the prediction error, *MAE* represents the average absolute error between the predicted value and the observed value, and *RMSE* reflects the degree of deviation between the predicted value and the true value. The formula to calculate each index is as follows:

$$MSE = \frac{1}{n} \sum_{i=1}^{n} (y_i - \hat{y}_i)^2 \quad (11)$$

$$MAE = \frac{1}{n} \sum_{i=1}^{n} |y_i - \hat{y}_i| \quad (12)$$

$$RMSE = \sqrt{\frac{1}{n} \sum_{i=1}^{n} (y_i - \hat{y}_i)^2} \quad (13)$$

where n is the number of predicted values, y_i is the true value, and $\hat{y}_i$ is the predicted value.

4.2. Forecast Results

4.2.1. Strong Earthquake Occurrence and Classification

Figure 6 illustrates the evaluation results of four traditional machine learning models (random forest (RF), decision tree (DT), support vector machine (SVM), and logistic regression (LR)) for the classification of large earthquake occurrence, namely, accuracy, precision, recall, and F1 score. The four models were implemented by calling the respective functions of SVM in the sklearn toolkit, LogisticRegression, tree in the ensemble, and RandomForestClassifier in the ensemble. For SVM, the kernel function was set to rbf, and the penalty relaxation variable was set to 1.0, with other parameters adopting default values. Pandas and NumPy were called here to read the dataset file and generate the corresponding array, respectively. Finally, matplotlib.pyplot was used to visualize the predicted results. The four evaluation indicators were calculated using Formulas (7)–(10). All tasks were completed using Python 3.9.6.

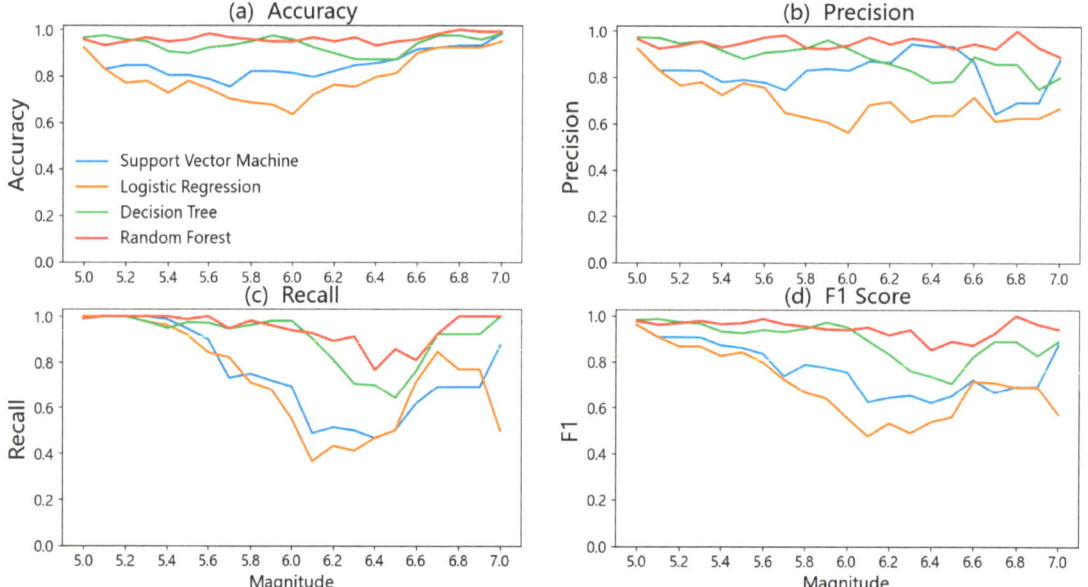

Figure 6. Results of large earthquake occurrence classification: accuracy, precision, recall, and F1 score. A magnitude range of 5.0 to 7.0 is used to represent magnitude threshold of prediction.

The vertical axis of each subgraph in Figure 6 represents the respective evaluation metric value, while the horizontal axis represents the magnitude threshold based on the magnitude range of the catalog. For the experiment's training and test sets, the entire dataset was divided using a 7:3 ratio by calling the function train_test_split in the model_selection of the sklearn package.

During the experiment, it was observed that using the dataset directly as input data for support vector machine and logistic regression resulted in poor classification indicators at certain magnitude thresholds. This was mainly due to the fact that the test data points, which were not of the same class at these thresholds, were only divided into one class. To address this issue, the dataset was standardized and normalized before being used as input. After comparing the experiment's results before and after normalization, it was found that the classification results had been improved to some extent.

Figure 7 displays the ROC curves for the classification of large earthquake occurrences. Unlike the four evaluation indicators, the ROC curve can evaluate the model without requiring a threshold to be set, providing results that better reflect the true performance of the model. Moreover, the ROC curve remains unaffected even when the distribution proportion of positive and negative samples in the test set changes. This feature is particularly important when dealing with category imbalances in actual datasets, as the ROC curve is able to effectively eliminate the impact of such imbalances on the evaluation results.

An important measure derived from the ROC curve is the area under the curve (AUC). The closer the AUC value is to 1, the better the classification performance of the model. When the AUC is 0.5, the classification result is no better than random guessing. As depicted in Figure 7, the RF classifier achieved the highest AUC value of 0.98, indicating its superior performance in earthquake prediction. In contrast, the LR classifier had the lowest AUC value of 0.72, indicating the weakest performance among the four classifiers.

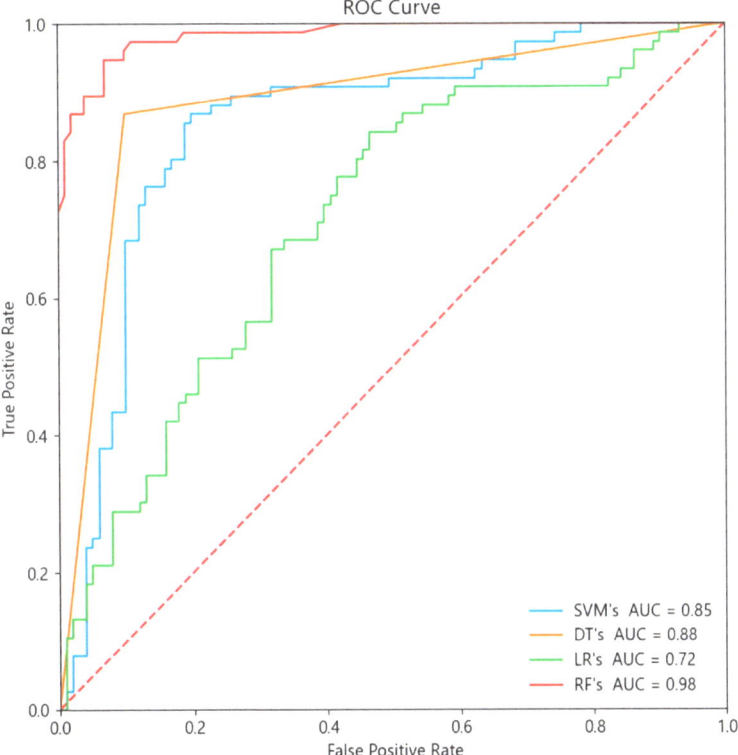

Figure 7. ROC curves of the large earthquake occurrence classification using SVM, DT, LR, RF.

4.2.2. Magnitude Prediction

In the magnitude prediction process, the same 22 feature parameters were utilized as input to the LSTM model, which then outputted the maximum magnitude of the next forecast window. The training set, validation set, and test set were divided in an 8:1:1 ratio. Given the small size of the data set, we needed to be cautious of overfitting. Therefore, we performed multiple optimizations using the validation set and determined the optimal configuration of the LSTM model. Specifically, the number of hidden layers was set as 1, the number of neurons as 16, the initial learning rate as 0.01, and the number of epochs as 200, to prevent overfitting. Pandas and NumPy were also called here to read the dataset file and generate the corresponding array, respectively. Torch was imported to build the LSTM model. All figures were obtained using matplotlib.

In the data preprocessing stage, the MinMaxScaler function was utilized to normalize the data, which was then fed into the model for training. The denormalized prediction results were obtained after the model had made its predictions. The MinMaxScaler function of sklearn was called in this section. The magnitude prediction results are presented in Figures 8 and 9.

Figures 8 and 9 present the outcomes of the maximum magnitude prediction. The LSTM model can effectively capture the temporal variations of the maximum magnitudes in the training and validation sets, with most of the predicted magnitudes oscillating within a range of ±0.5 of the observed magnitude. However, on the test set, the model can only grasp the trend of the magnitude and tends to overestimate the maximum magnitude for actual events with magnitude <= 5.0 and underestimate the maximum magnitude for actual events with magnitude >= 6.0. This suggests that although the LSTM model can detect the general pattern, it tends to produce oversimple predictions for the maximum magnitude.

Figures 10 and 11 illustrate the dispersion of errors using boxplot and histogram. Notably, the error distribution of the training set is centered around 0, whereas the error distribution of the test set is much wider, centered around 0.5. In the test set, the model produces a higher quantity of positive errors than negative ones, as is evident from the histograms in Figure 11.

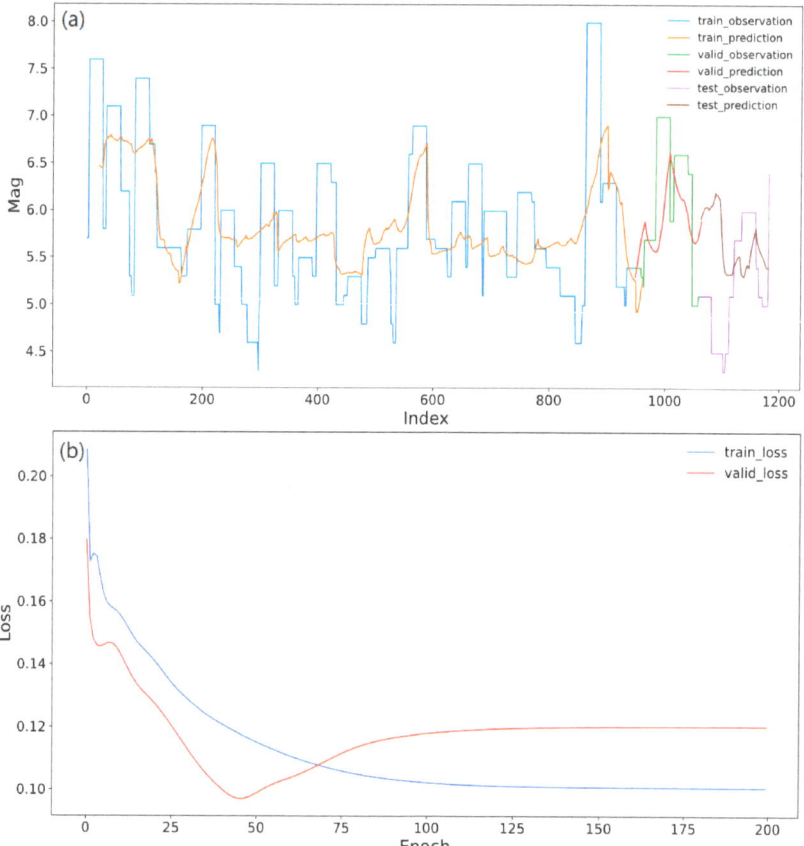

Figure 8. (**a**) Retrospective test of prediction of the maximum magnitude earthquake. The blue, green, and purple curves represent training, validation, and test period of the observations, respectively. The yellow, red, and brown curves represent training, validation, and test period of the predictions, respectively. (**b**) Loss curves of prediction of the maximum magnitude earthquake. The blue and red curves represent the loss of training set and test set, respectively.

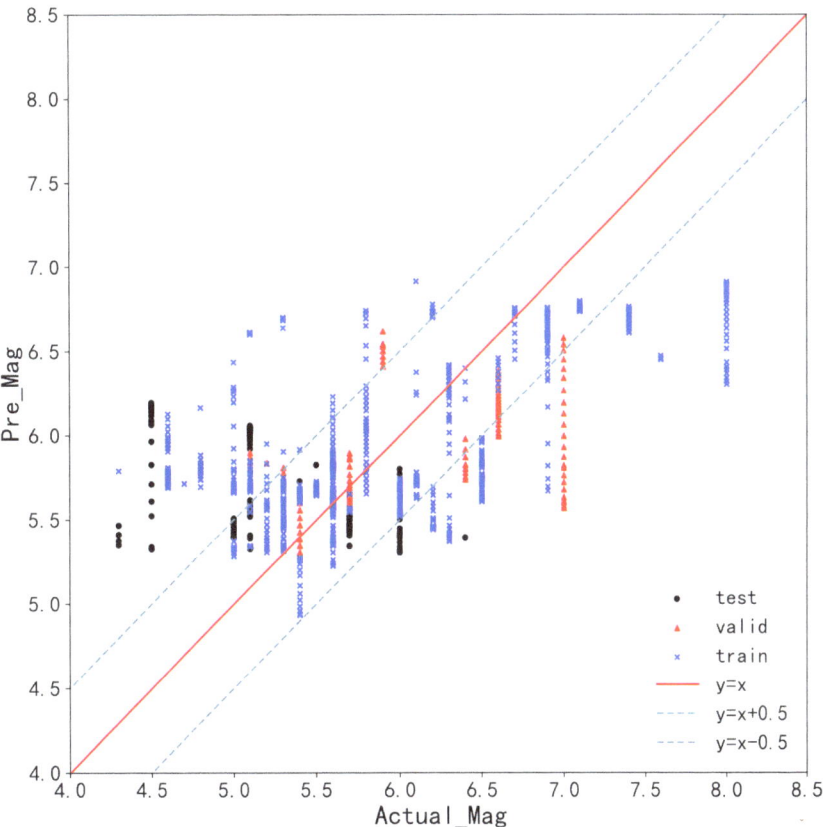

Figure 9. Comparison of the predicted and observed maximum magnitudes. The black dots, red triangles, and blue crosses represent test, validation, and training dataset, respectively.

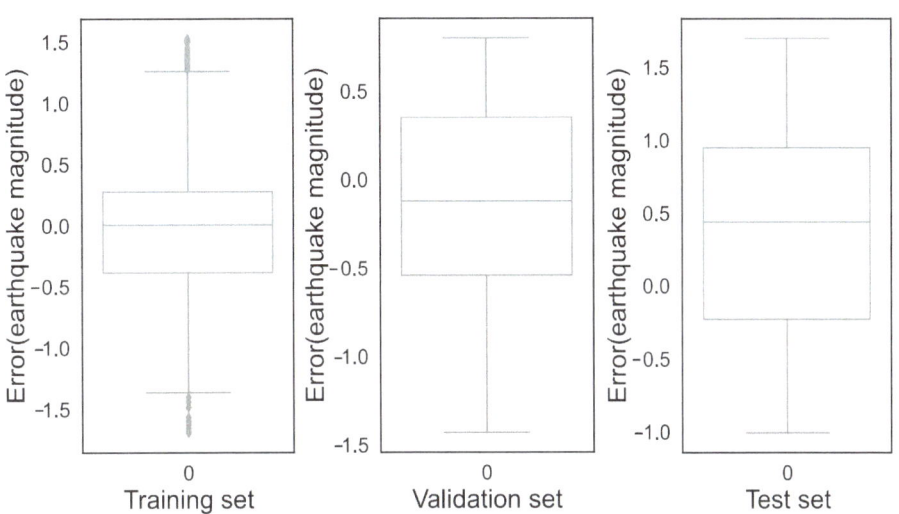

Figure 10. Boxplot of the errors of training set, validation set, and test set.

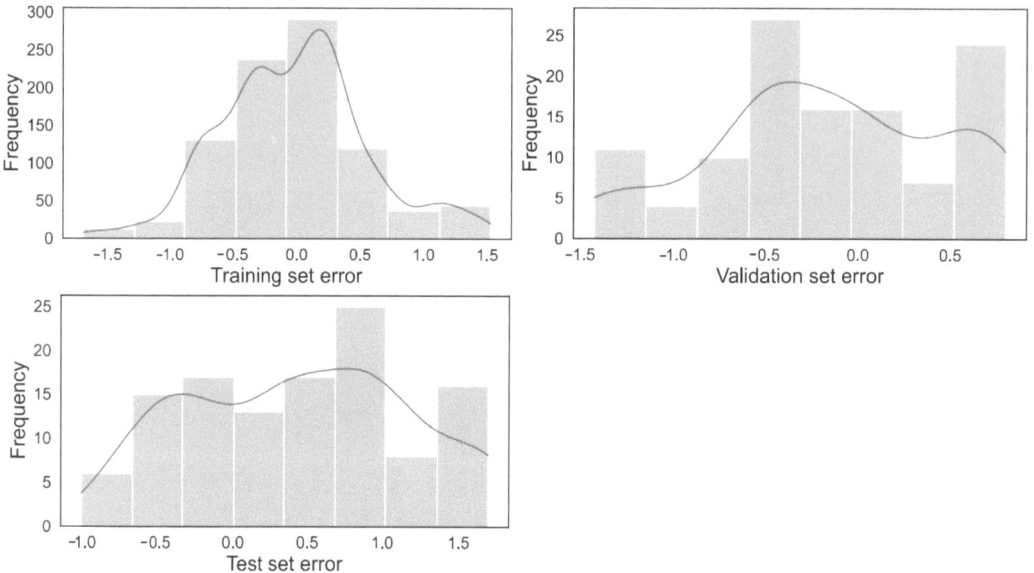

Figure 11. Histograms of the errors of training set, validation set, and test set in earthquake magnitude prediction using LSTM.

Table 3 presents the evaluation indicators of our model and compares them with those of other studies. The results are better than that of [36], but worse than [37]. The reasons for these differences will be discussed in the Section 5.

Table 3. Comparison of prediction results by different researchers.

Evaluation Index	This Study	[37]	[36]		
			DL	RF	GLM
MSE	0.7347	0.015192			
MAE	0.7252	0.097173	1.15	0.74	1.03
RMSE	0.8571	0.123256			

To evaluate the importance of different features, the permutation importance method was used. This method measures the importance of features by calculating the increase of model prediction error after shuffling the time series of each feature. The advantage of this method is that it can compare the importance of different features and save more time compared to other methods.

Figure 12 shows the feature importance of our model, where the length of the bar chart represents the error of the model after shuffling the order. Longer bars indicate more important features, while the orange line represents the MAE of the model as the reference line.

Figure 12 reveals that nearly all the features used have a positive effect on the model's performance. Among them, b_std_mlk, x7_mlk, and T_elaps7 are less important, while dM_mlk, x7_lsq, N.O., and T_elaps6 are the top four most important features. These results demonstrate that magnitude deficit, probability of earthquake occurrence, number of earthquakes, and the days since the last large earthquake are crucial factors for earthquake magnitude prediction, which is consistent with physical understanding.

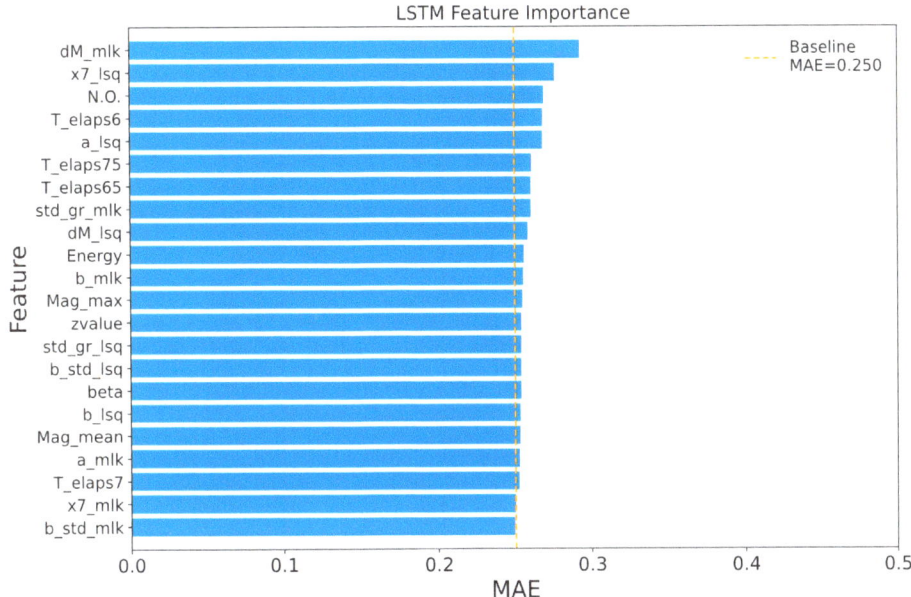

Figure 12. Feature importance obtained by the permutation importance method.

5. Discussion

5.1. Sample Number Issue and Feature Importance

Based on the classification results presented above, it is evident that RF outperforms LR and SVM in terms of several evaluation indicators and is also marginally better than DT. However, it should be noted that the classification results may be affected by the different proportions of positive and negative samples in the dataset, which is determined by the setting of the strong earthquake threshold and can impact the prediction outcomes. To investigate this further, we experimented with several magnitudes which were shown in Table 4 as the classification threshold and analyzed the number of positive and negative samples, as well as the difference in classification metrics. It is important to exercise caution when interpreting the accuracy score in cases where there is an imbalance in the number of positive and negative samples. Newer models that are insensitive to class imbalance [44] may help overcome this problem, but this is out of the scope of this study.

Table 4. Evaluation results and sample numbers of the random forest method.

Magnitude	Accuracy	Precision	Recall	F1 Score	Positive Samples	Negative Samples
5.0	0.975	0.982	0.991	0.986	549	41
5.5	0.958	0.949	0.987	0.967	386	204
6.0	0.949	0.922	0.959	0.940	258	332
6.5	0.958	0.96	0.857	0.906	141	449
7.0	0.992	0.889	1.0	0.941	60	530

At the same time, the impact of the small number of overall samples on the classification results should also be taken into consideration. Although the evaluation metric of RF is relatively the highest among the four classification methods, indicating that it is the best classifier in the prediction of strong earthquakes, further verification is necessary to determine its reliability on different datasets due to the small number of samples in the test set and the uneven distribution of positive and negative samples. To better interpret the classification results of RF, the feature quantity was ranked from high to low based on their weights in the classification, as illustrated in Figure 13. The top three most important features are T_elaps75, T_elaps7, and dM_lsq, which is consistent with the feature importance of earthquake magnitude prediction and confirms the important role of the number of days since the last large earthquake and the magnitude deficit.

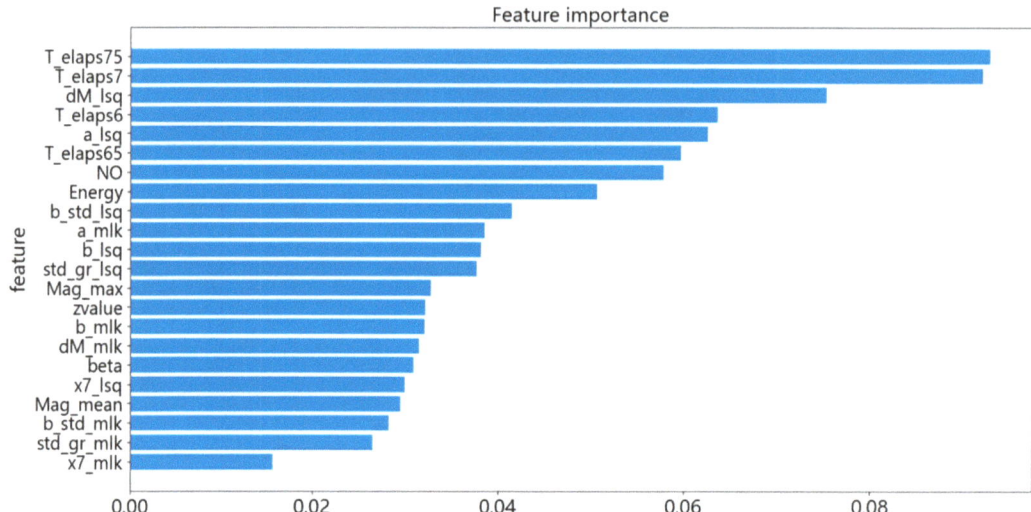

Figure 13. Feature importance ranking by the random forest method.

The poor classification results of LR and SVM in this experiment also suggest the need for further investigation into the potential impact of dataset size and feature distribution on the classification performance. To address this issue, the feature values were standardized and normalized in the dataset, and the classifier parameters were adjusted accordingly. This approach led to an improvement in the overall classification performance.

5.2. Comparison with Previous Studies

From the prediction results, it can be seen that the LSTM model only trended in the prediction results, but the predicted values were significantly larger than the observed values. Upon comparison with two other articles in Table 3, the results were inferior to those reported in [37]. However, after conducting replication experiments, we discovered that this disparity could be attributed to differences in the input features used in those two studies. Using the same input approach as in [37], a similar performance was obtained, as shown in Figures 14 and 15.

In the replication experiment, the MSE was found to be 0.2289, while MAE was 0.4193, and RMSE was 0.4784. The prediction results obtained using the approach of [29] are shown in Figures 14 and 15 and appear to be better than the results obtained previously. However, we identified a potential data leakage issue in their approach due to the overlap between input features and output labels. Specifically, the feature "Mag_max_obs" dominated other features, as confirmed by the feature importance shown in Figure 16. Upon careful examination of the approach of [37], we found that they input the maximum magnitude of the first few windows for training and then obtain the maximum magnitude for the several windows that follow. As these windows have overlapping parts, the maximum magnitudes of the first several windows contain some characteristics of the maximum magnitudes of the following several windows. This data leakage problem resulted in the information of the test set being leaked to the training set, leading to a too-low error and a too-high feature importance of Mag_max_obs.

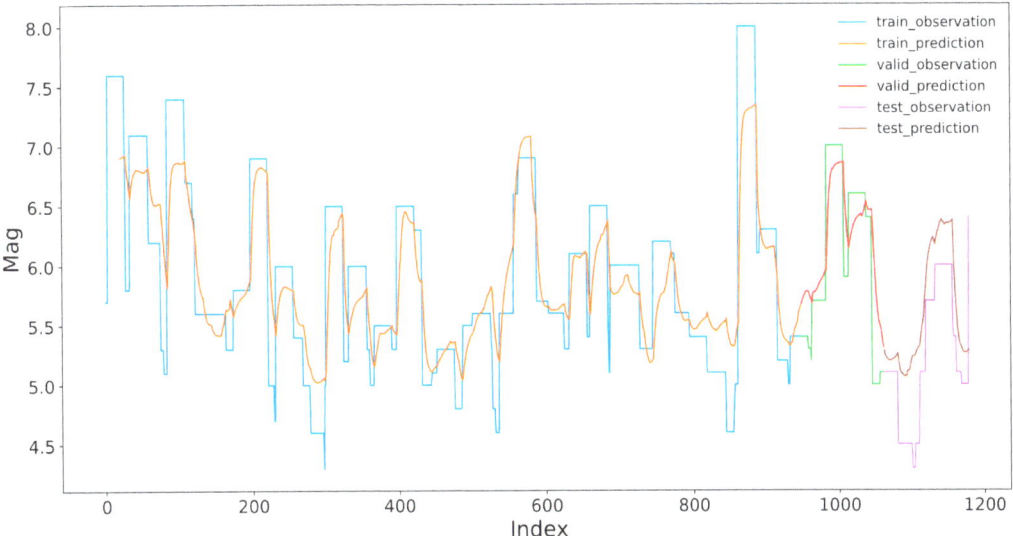

Figure 14. Retrospective test of prediction of the maximum magnitude earthquake using the similar input with [37]. The blue, green, and purple curves represent training, validation, and test period of the observations, respectively. The yellow, red, and brown curves represent training, validation, and test period of the predictions, respectively.

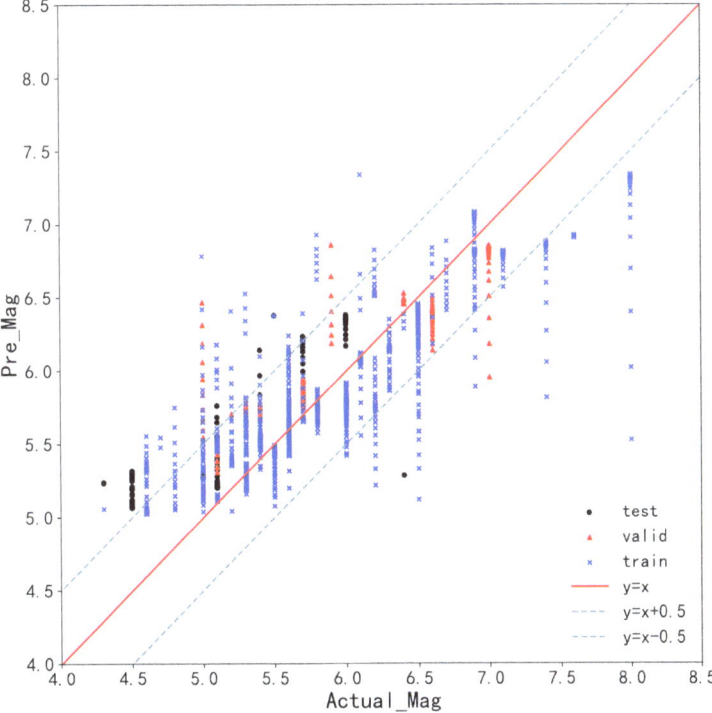

Figure 15. Comparison of the predicted and observed maximum magnitudes using the same input with [37]. The black dots, red triangles, and blue crosses represent test, validation, and training data set, respectively.

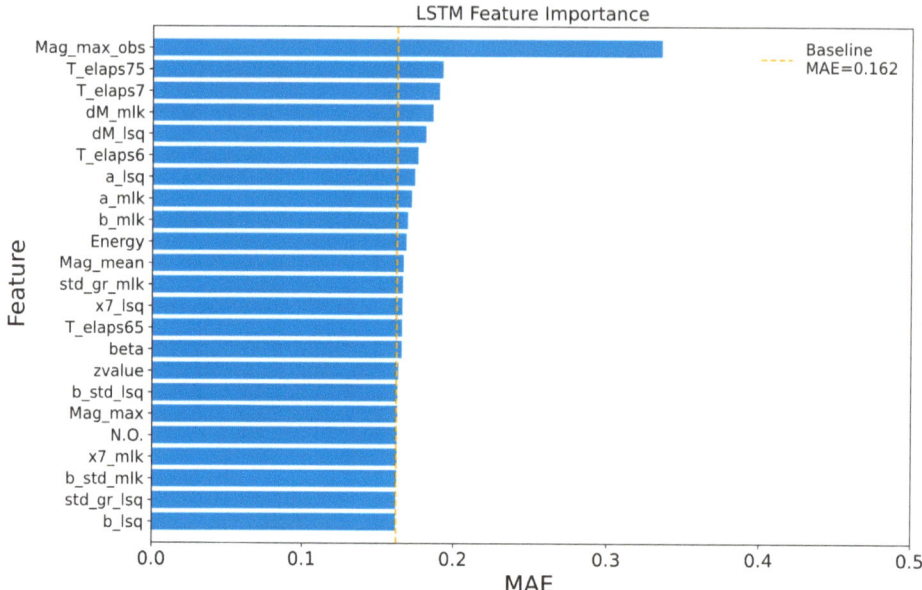

Figure 16. Feature importance for the retrospective experiment with [37].

Meanwhile, in Table 3, a comparative analysis of the results with those presented in [36] is conducted. The authors of this paper employ generalized linear models (GLM), random forest (RF), and deep neural network (DNN) to predict the maximum magnitude of future earthquakes. Unlike this study, their work benefits from sufficient training data. Remarkably, their predicted magnitudes are smaller than the observed values. Notably, the LSTM model outperforms the predictions reported in [36], underscoring the effectiveness of the model construction.

6. Conclusions

In this study, we explored the possibility of using machine learning for earthquake prediction by applying four traditional machine learning methods and the LSTM neural network to predict the occurrences and maximum magnitudes of earthquakes in the Sichuan–Yunnan region. We calculated and extracted seismicity parameters related to earthquake occurrence from the earthquake catalog as input features. The results showed that the random forest method was the most effective at classifying large earthquake occurrences, and the LSTM method provided a reasonable estimation of earthquake magnitude.

The findings support the idea that small earthquakes contain information relevant to predicting future large earthquakes and offer a promising way to predict the occurrence of large earthquakes. Additionally, the findings provide useful information on which features that are consistent with physical interpretation are important for earthquake prediction.

While the limitations of this study should be noted, they also represent the next steps for future work. First, under this framework, earthquake swarms, which are statistically very rare [45], are difficult to predict due to the small differences between their magnitudes. Second, longer-term seismic monitoring is needed for the further application of more complex models (e.g., transformer) to improve the performance of predictions. Third, the spatial locations of earthquakes are not considered in this study but are important for earthquake prediction. New models which can address spatial information (e.g., graph neural networks) may be useful to tackle this problem in the future. Although limitations and difficulties exist, we are trying to explore the nonlinear relations of earthquake prediction, which is one of the most difficult problems in seismology, by applying machine learning methods. This study presents a potential avenue for improving the accuracy of earthquake prediction in the future.

Author Contributions: Methodology, X.W., Z.Z. and K.J.; Software, X.W., Z.Z., Y.Y. and K.J.; Validation, X.W., Z.Z. and Z.L.; Formal analysis, S.Z., C.J. and K.J.; Resources, K.J.; Data curation, C.J.; Writing—original draft, X.W. and Z.Z.; Writing—review & editing, S.Z. and K.J.; Visualization, X.W. and Z.Z.; Supervision, K.J.; Project administration, K.J.; Funding acquisition, S.Z. and K.J. All authors have read and agreed to the published version of the manuscript.

Funding: This research was funded by the Special Fund of the Institute of Geophysics, China Earthquake Administration (Grant No. DQJB 22Z01-09), the National Natural Science Foundation of China (Grant Nos. 42274068, U2039204), the Key Research and Development Project in Shaanxi Province (Grant No. 2023-YBSF-237), and the Shanghai Sheshan National Geophysical Observatory (Grant No. SSOP202207).

Institutional Review Board Statement: Not applicable.

Informed Consent Statement: Not applicable.

Data Availability Statement: The dataset of this research can be found from the China Earthquake Data Center (CEDC, http://data.earthquake.cn/index.html, last accessed on 23 May 2022).

Acknowledgments: We benefit from helpful discussions with Naidan Yun, Han Yue and Xiaoyan Cai. Comments and suggestions from Editor and two anonymous reviewers are appreciated.

Conflicts of Interest: The authors declare no conflict of interest.

References

1. Geller, R.J.; Jackson, D.D.; Kagan, Y.Y.; Mulargia, F. Earthquakes cannot be predicted. *Science* **1997**, *275*, 1616. [CrossRef]
2. Knopoff, L. Earthquake prediction: The scientific challenge. *Proc. Natl. Acad. Sci. USA* **1996**, *93*, 3719–3720. [CrossRef]
3. Wyss, M. Cannot earthquakes be predicted? *Science* **1997**, *278*, 487–490. [CrossRef]
4. Sibson, R.H. Crustal stress, faulting and fluid flow. *Geol. Soc. Lond. Spec. Publ.* **1994**, *78*, 69–84. [CrossRef]
5. Liu, M.; Stein, S. Mid-continental earthquakes: Spatiotemporal occurrences, causes, and hazards. *Earth-Sci. Rev.* **2016**, *162*, 364–386. [CrossRef]
6. Field, E.H. How Physics-Based Earthquake Simulators Might Help Improve Earthquake Forecasts. *Seismol. Res. Lett.* **2019**, *90*, 467–472. [CrossRef]
7. Shi, Y.; Sun, Y.; Luo, G.; Dong, P.; Zhang, H. Roadmap for earthquake numerical forecasting in China—Reflection on the tenth anniversary of Wenchuan earthquake. *Chin. Sci. Bull.* **2018**, *63*, 1865–1881. [CrossRef]
8. Bergen, K.J.; Johnson, P.A.; de Hoop, M.V.; Beroza, G.C. Machine learning for data-driven discovery in solid Earth geoscience. *Science* **2019**, *363*, eaau0323. [CrossRef]
9. Beroza, G.C.; Segou, M.; Mostafa Mousavi, S. Machine learning and earthquake forecasting-next steps. *Nat. Commun.* **2021**, *12*, 4761. [CrossRef]
10. Shimshoni, Y.; Intrator, N. Classification of seismic signals by integrating ensembles of neural networks. *IEEE Trans. Signal Process.* **1998**, *46*, 1194–1201. [CrossRef]
11. Li, Z.; Meier, M.-A.; Hauksson, E.; Zhan, Z.; Andrews, J. Machine Learning Seismic Wave Discrimination: Application to Earthquake Early Warning. *Geophys. Res. Lett.* **2018**, *45*, 4773–4779. [CrossRef]
12. Malfante, M.; Dalla Mura, M.; Metaxian, J.-P.; Mars, J.I.; Macedo, O.; Inza, A. Machine Learning for Volcano-Seismic Signals Challenges and perspectives. *IEEE Signal Process. Mag.* **2018**, *35*, 20–30. [CrossRef]
13. Tang, L.; Zhang, M.; Wen, L. Support Vector Machine Classification of Seismic Events in the Tianshan Orogenic Belt. *J. Geophys. Res. Solid Earth* **2020**, *125*, e2019JB018132. [CrossRef]
14. Titos, M.; Bueno, A.; Garcia, L.; Benitez, C. A Deep Neural Networks Approach to Automatic Recognition Systems for Volcano-Seismic Events. *IEEE J. Sel. Top. Appl. Earth Obs. Remote Sens.* **2018**, *11*, 1533–1544. [CrossRef]
15. Asim, K.M.; Martinez-Alvarez, F.; Basit, A.; Iqbal, T. Earthquake magnitude prediction in Hindukush region using machine learning techniques. *Nat. Hazards* **2017**, *85*, 471–486. [CrossRef]
16. Mousavi, S.M.; Beroza, G.C. A Machine-Learning Approach for Earthquake Magnitude Estimation. *Geophys. Res. Lett.* **2020**, *47*, e2019GL085976. [CrossRef]
17. Rouet-Leduc, B.; Hulbert, C.; Lubbers, N.; Barros, K.; Humphreys, C.J.; Johnson, P.A. Machine Learning Predicts Laboratory Earthquakes. *Geophys. Res. Lett.* **2017**, *44*, 9276–9282. [CrossRef]
18. Li, Z.; Tian, K.; Wang, F.; Zheng, X.; Wang, F. Home damage estimation after disasters using crowdsourcing ideas and Convolutional Neural Networks. In Proceedings of the 5th International Conference on Measurement, Instrumentation and Automation (ICMIA), Shenzhen, China, 17–18 September 2016; pp. 857–860.

19. Shahnas, M.H.; Yuen, D.A.; Pysklywec, R.N. Inverse Problems in Geodynamics Using Machine Learning Algorithms. *J. Geophys. Res. Solid Earth* **2018**, *123*, 296–310. [CrossRef]
20. Provost, F.; Hibert, C.; Malet, J.P. Automatic classification of endogenous landslide seismicity using the Random Forest supervised classifier. *Geophys. Res. Lett.* **2017**, *44*, 113–120. [CrossRef]
21. Araya-Polo, M.; Jennings, J.; Adler, A.; Dahlke, T. Deep-learning tomography. *Lead. Edge* **2018**, *37*, 58–66. [CrossRef]
22. DeVries, P.M.R.; Viegas, F.; Wattenberg, M.; Meade, B.J. Deep learning of aftershock patterns following large earthquakes. *Nature* **2018**, *560*, 632–634. [CrossRef] [PubMed]
23. Moustra, M.; Avraamides, M.; Christodoulou, C. Artificial neural networks for earthquake prediction using time series magnitude data or Seismic Electric Signals. *Expert Syst. Appl.* **2011**, *38*, 15032–15039. [CrossRef]
24. Panakkat, A.; Adeli, H. Neural network models for earthquake magnitude prediction using multiple seismicity indicators. *Int. J. Neural Syst.* **2007**, *17*, 13–33. [CrossRef] [PubMed]
25. Wang, Q.; Guo, Y.; Yu, L.; Li, P. Earthquake Prediction Based on Spatio-Temporal Data Mining: An LSTM Network Approach. *IEEE Trans. Emerg. Top. Comput.* **2020**, *8*, 148–158. [CrossRef]
26. Asencio-Cortes, G.; Martinez-Alvarez, F.; Morales-Esteban, A.; Reyes, J. A sensitivity study of seismicity indicators in supervised learning to improve earthquake prediction. *Knowl.-Based Syst.* **2016**, *101*, 15–30. [CrossRef]
27. Asim, K.M.; Idris, A.; Iqbal, T.; Martinez-Alvarez, F. Seismic indicators based earthquake predictor system using Genetic Programming and AdaBoost classification. *Soil Dyn. Earthq. Eng.* **2018**, *111*, 1–7. [CrossRef]
28. Martinez-Alvarez, F.; Reyes, J.; Morales-Esteban, A.; Rubio-Escudero, C. Determining the best set of seismicity indicators to predict earthquakes. Two case studies: Chile and the Iberian Peninsula. *Knowl.-Based Syst.* **2013**, *50*, 198–210. [CrossRef]
29. Florido, E.; Asencio Cortes, G.; Aznarte, J.L.; Rubio-Escudero, C.; Martinez-Alvarez, F. A novel tree-based algorithm to discover seismic patterns in earthquake catalogs. *Comput. Geosci.* **2018**, *115*, 96–104. [CrossRef]
30. Rundle, J.B.; Donnellan, A.; Fox, G.; Crutchfield, J.P. Nowcasting Earthquakes by Visualizing the Earthquake Cycle with Machine Learning: A Comparison of Two Methods. *Surv. Geophys.* **2022**, *43*, 483–501. [CrossRef]
31. Rundle, J.B.; Donnellan, A.; Fox, G.; Ludwig, L.G.; Crutchfield, J. Does the Catalog of California Earthquakes, With Aftershocks Included, Contain Information About Future Large Earthquakes? *Earth Space Sci.* **2023**, *10*, e2022EA002521. [CrossRef]
32. Alexandridis, A.; Chondrodima, E.; Efthimiou, E.; Papadakis, G.; Vallianatos, F.; Triantis, D. Large Earthquake Occurrence Estimation Based on Radial Basis Function Neural Networks. *IEEE Trans. Geosci. Remote Sens.* **2014**, *52*, 5443–5453. [CrossRef]
33. Deng, Q.D.; Zhang, P.Z.; Ran, Y.K.; Yang, X.P.; Min, W.; Chu, Q.Z. Basic characteristics of active tectonics of China. *Sci. China Ser. D-Earth Sci.* **2003**, *46*, 356–372.
34. Wiemer, S. A Software Package to Analyze Seismicity: ZMAP. *Seismol. Res. Lett.* **2001**, *72*, 373–382. [CrossRef]
35. Wiemer, S.; Wyss, M. Minimum magnitude of completeness in earthquake catalogs: Examples from Alaska, the western United States, and Japan. *Bull. Seismol. Soc. Am.* **2000**, *90*, 859–869. [CrossRef]
36. Asencio-Cortes, G.; Morales-Esteban, A.; Shang, X.; Martinez-Alvarez, F. Earthquake prediction in California using regression algorithms and cloud-based big data infrastructure. *Comput. Geosci.* **2018**, *115*, 198–210. [CrossRef]
37. Li, L.; Shi, Y.; Cheng, S. Exploration of long short-term memory neural network in intermediate earthquake forecast: A case study in Sichuan-Yunnan region. *Chin. J. Geophys. Chin. Ed.* **2022**, *65*, 12–25. [CrossRef]
38. Reyes, J.; Morales-Esteban, A.; Martinez-Alvarez, F. Neural networks to predict earthquakes in Chile. *Appl. Soft Comput.* **2013**, *13*, 1314–1328. [CrossRef]
39. Hochreiter, S.; Schmidhuber, J. Long short-term memory. *Neural Comput.* **1997**, *9*, 1735–1780. [CrossRef]
40. Fu, R.; Zhang, Z.; Li, L. Using LSTM and GRU Neural Network Methods for Traffic Flow Prediction. In Proceedings of the 31st Youth Academic Annual Conference of Chinese-Association-of-Automation (YAC), Wuhan, China, 11–13 November 2016; pp. 324–328.
41. Chen, K.; Zhou, Y.; Dai, F. A LSTM-based method for stock returns prediction: A case study of China stock market. In Proceedings of the 2015 IEEE international conference on big data (big data), Santa Clara, CA, USA, 29 October–1 November 2015; pp. 2823–2824.
42. Altché, F.; de La Fortelle, A. An LSTM network for highway trajectory prediction. In Proceedings of the 2017 IEEE 20th international conference on intelligent transportation systems (ITSC), Yokohama, Japan, 16–19 October 2017; pp. 353–359.
43. Xue, H.; Huynh, D.Q.; Reynolds, M. SS-LSTM: A hierarchical LSTM model for pedestrian trajectory prediction. In Proceedings of the 2018 IEEE Winter Conference on Applications of Computer Vision (WACV), Lake Tahoe, NV, USA, 12–15 March 2018; pp. 1186–1194.
44. Peng, C.; Cheng, Q. Discriminative Ridge Machine: A Classifier for High-Dimensional Data or Imbalanced Data. *IEEE Trans. Neural Netw. Learn. Syst.* **2021**, *32*, 2595–2609. [CrossRef]
45. Scislo, L. High Activity Earthquake Swarm Event Monitoring and Impact Analysis on Underground High Energy Physics Research Facilities. *Energies* **2022**, *15*, 3705. [CrossRef]

Disclaimer/Publisher's Note: The statements, opinions and data contained in all publications are solely those of the individual author(s) and contributor(s) and not of MDPI and/or the editor(s). MDPI and/or the editor(s) disclaim responsibility for any injury to people or property resulting from any ideas, methods, instructions or products referred to in the content.

Article

Development of the Algorithmic Basis of the FCAZ Method for Earthquake-Prone Area Recognition

Sergey M. Agayan [1,*], Boris A. Dzeboev [1], Shamil R. Bogoutdinov [1,2], Ivan O. Belov [1], Boris V. Dzeranov [1] and Dmitriy A. Kamaev [3]

1 Geophysical Center of the Russian Academy of Sciences, 119296 Moscow, Russia
2 Schmidt Institute of Physics of the Earth of the Russian Academy of Sciences, 123995 Moscow, Russia
3 Research and Production Association "Typhoon", 249038 Obninsk, Russia
* Correspondence: s.agayan@gcras.ru

Abstract: The present paper continues the series of publications by the authors devoted to solving the problem of recognition regions with potential high seismicity. It is aimed at the development of the mathematical apparatus and the algorithmic base of the FCAZ method, designed for effective recognition of earthquake-prone areas. A detailed description of both the mathematical algorithms included in the FCAZ in its original form and those developed in this paper is given. Using California as an example, it is shown that a significantly developed algorithmic FCAZ base makes it possible to increase the reliability and accuracy of FCAZ recognition. In particular, a number of small zones located at a fairly small distance from each other but having a close "internal" connection are being connected into single large, high-seismicity areas.

Keywords: FCAZ; DPS; earthquake-prone areas; density; finite metric spaces; connectivity; isolation

Citation: Agayan, S.M.; Dzeboev, B.A.; Bogoutdinov, S.R.; Belov, I.O.; Dzeranov, B.V.; Kamaev, D.A. Development of the Algorithmic Basis of the FCAZ Method for Earthquake-Prone Area Recognition. *Appl. Sci.* **2023**, *13*, 2496. https://doi.org/10.3390/app13042496

Academic Editors: Shiyong Zhou and Ke Jia

Received: 8 November 2022
Revised: 9 February 2023
Accepted: 12 February 2023
Published: 15 February 2023

Copyright: © 2023 by the authors. Licensee MDPI, Basel, Switzerland. This article is an open access article distributed under the terms and conditions of the Creative Commons Attribution (CC BY) license (https://creativecommons.org/licenses/by/4.0/).

1. Introduction

The aim of seismic hazard assessment is to analyze and predict the parameters of seismic impact for future strong earthquakes. The first methods for finding solutions to this problem were deterministic (deterministic seismic hazard analysis (DSHA)) [1,2]. In DSHA, a seismic hazard is assessed for the maximum possible earthquake magnitude in each zone of seismic source occurrence over the shortest distance. A disadvantage of DSHA is that the timing (earthquake frequency and associated uncertainty) is often neglected. Only one scenario is used which describes the maximum possible earthquake [1–5].

In the 1970s, the development of probabilistic seismic hazard maps at the national, regional, and urban (microzonation) scales began [6–9]. In the 1990s, probabilistic methods began to prevail over deterministic ones. Currently, there are two main directions in research on seismic hazard assessment: probabilistic (probabilistic seismic hazard assessment (PSHA)) [10] and neodeterministic (neodeterministic seismic hazard assessment (NDSHA)) [11,12].

NDSHA allows a deterministic description of the seismic ground motion caused by an earthquake with a given epicentral or hypocentral distance and magnitude [13]. NDSHA methods are based on modeling in terms of detailed knowledge of the earthquake source [14–16] and the scenario of seismic wave propagation [17].

One of the key conditions for the successful application of NDSHA is the availability of adequate information about the areas prone to strong earthquakes in the studied region. The flexibility of NDSHA makes it possible to successfully incorporate additional information about areas prone to strong earthquakes obtained using independent methods and calculations. This reduces the existing gaps in knowledge about seismicity obtained from earthquake catalogs [18]. It was demonstrated in [19,20] that the use in NDSHA of additional knowledge about the areas prone to strong earthquakes, obtained by applying pattern recognition methods [21–24], makes it possible to create effective preventive seismic hazard maps.

The fundamental possibility of using methods and algorithms of pattern recognition for earthquake-prone area recognition was first substantiated by the eminent mathematician I.M. Gelfand et al. in 1972 [25]. The formalized approach developed by them was subsequently called earthquake-prone areas (EPA) [21–23]. Over the past 50 years, since its inception, EPA has been used to recognize strong earthquake-prone areas in a number of mountainous countries in the world. A posteriori estimates of the recognition reliability that were obtained based on the analysis of the locations of the epicenters of strong earthquakes that occurred in the considered regions after receiving results for them became a confirmation of the effectiveness of using pattern recognition to identify territories with potentially high seismicity [24].

The authors of [21,26] described in detail the still-existing significant difficulties of applying EPA in practice. The latter served as the fundamental basis for the beginning of research at the Geophysical Center of the Russian Academy of Sciences, dedicated to the development of the ideological, system-mathematical, and computational base for earthquake-prone area recognition. As part of these studies, the algorithmic system of formalized clustering and zoning (FCAZ) [27,28] was developed, which is an unsupervised pattern recognition method. FCAZ is based on the classification of recognition objects by clustering. The epicenters of weak earthquakes are used as recognition objects.

Note that clustering is an important tool in the mining of geophysical data [29]. Clustering studies on earthquake epicenters [30–35] have been actively developed since the early 1990s [36]. As a rule, they are aimed at achieving two goals: revealing the characteristics of clusters and their relationship with the physical properties of the Earth's crust [37–40] and the declustering [29,31] of earthquake catalogs [41].

The analysis of earthquake epicenters with classical clustering algorithms is associated with difficulties [29,36]. It turns out that algorithms that take into account the "density" of the locations of objects are effective due to their ability to find clusters of an arbitrary shape even with significant data noise [29]. Within the framework of the scientific direction of discrete mathematical analysis (DMA) [42–44], created and developed at the Geophysical Center of the Russian Academy of Sciences, based on fuzzy mathematics and fuzzy logic under the general name DPS clustering, a complex of topological filtering algorithms is being developed that takes into account the density of the objects being classified [45–47]. It should be noted that DPS clustering algorithms are actively and effectively used in various geological and geophysical studies (analysis of earthquake catalogs, searching for signals on geophysical records, the problem of radioactive waste disposal, etc. [26,47–50]). DPS clustering is the algorithmic core of the FCAZ method [28].

FCAZ makes it possible to effectively recognize earthquake-prone areas (with a magnitude $M \geq M_0$) based on the clustering study of the catalog of seismic events [21]. In its original form, FCAZ was a sequential application of DPS clustering algorithms and the Ext algorithm [26]. The fundamental difference between FCAZ and its predecessors, particularly EPA, is the presence of a formalized block (algorithm) Ext. This implements the transition from the classification of point objects into high- and low-seismicity zones to the original flat high-seismicity zones. Ext formalizes the construction of a unique mapping of DPS clusters into flat zones of nonzero measure inside and on the boundary of which an earthquake with $M \geq M_0$ may occur [28]. FCAZ made it possible to move from simple pattern recognition to system analysis in the problem of earthquake-prone area recognition. In particular, with the help of FCAZ, it was possible to uniquely distinguish a subsystem of high-seismicity zones from a non-empty complement using an exact boundary.

Previously, FCAZ was used to successfully recognize earthquake-prone areas in the Andean mountain belt of South America, on the Pacific coast of the Kamchatka Peninsula and the Kuril Islands in California, in the Baikal-Transbaikal and Altai-Sayan regions, in the Caucasus, and in the Crimean Peninsula and northwestern Caucasus. A detailed description of the FCAZ method, its mathematical apparatus, and the results obtained is given in [26].

It should be noted that at present, in parallel with the mathematical tools described here by the authors of earthquake-prone area recognition, methods for seismic hazard and subsequent seismic risk assessment are being created and developed based on other ideological foundations and mathematical solutions [2,51–57]. Most of them are still part of PSHA, although in recent years, there have been more and more publications in which PSHA has been criticized [2].

Returning to DPS clustering, it should be noted that, conceptually, its initial concept is a fuzzy model of the fundamental mathematical "limit" property. It is called the density and is a non-negative function that depends on an arbitrary subset and any point in the initial space in which clustering is assumed. The value of the density should be understood as the strength of the connection between a subset and a point, as the degree of influence of a subset on a point, or dually as the degree of limiting a point to a subset.

Nontrivial densities always exist in finite metric spaces (FMS). By fixing the density level α and interpreting it as a limit level, we can introduce the notion of discrete perfection with a level α. The set in the initial space is called discretely perfect with a level α (α-DPS set or just DPS set) if it consists of all points of the original space's α limit.

A rigorous theory of DPS sets (DPS theory) was constructed within the framework of DMA, in which, in particular, it is shown that DPS sets have the properties of clusters. The currently developed DPS clustering algorithms (DPS algorithms) operate in finite metric spaces and depend on a number of parameters, the main ones of which are the density P, its level α, and the local survey radius r, and they have three stages [43,46].

In the first stage, topological filtering of the original space is carried out, and its noise is cleared. DPS algorithms iteratively cut out from the original space the maximum α-perfect subset, the existence and uniqueness of which is guaranteed by the DPS theory.

In the second stage, the DPS algorithm splits the result of the first stage into r-connected components, which according to the DPS theory will be DPS sets. These are local DPS clusters. Due to the locality of the viewing radius, the division into r-connected components of the maximum α-perfect subset at the second stage is often small, detailed, and needs to be enlarged. This is the essence of the third and final stage of DPS clustering. Its result will be the representation of the maximum DPS subset in the form of a disjunct union of groups of local DPS clusters, each of which is a fragmentary manifestation (edge) of the global anomalous entity behind it in the original FMS. A detailed description of all DPS stages will be given below using the example of the SDPS algorithm, which is the most famous of the DPS algorithms.

This article is devoted to the further development of both DPS clustering and, in general, the mathematical apparatus of the FCAZ method. In the example of California, the advantages of strong earthquake-prone area recognition based on the developed algorithmic tools of the FCAZ method are shown.

2. Materials and Methods: SDPS Algorithm

Historically, the first in a series of DPS algorithms was the set theoretic SDPS algorithm [26,47,58]. It is based on the density S, which conveys the degree of concentration of the initial FMS X around each of its points x (the most natural understanding of the density X in x) (Figure 1). The result of SDPS is condensed groups in $X \leftrightarrow$ sets that locally contain "many X" and formally correspond best to empirical clusters.

Let us move on to a precise presentation of the SDPS algorithm.

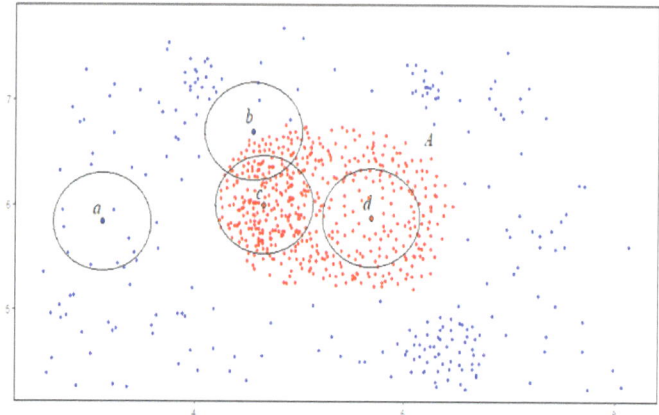

Figure 1. The concept of density relative to a set. Four points (*a*, *b*, *c*, and *d*) are selected in the initial array X. The density S in them relative to the subset A (red dots) is equal to the number of points from A that fall into the balls indicated in the figure. Point c will be densest with respect to A, followed by points b, d, and a.

2.1. Density S

Let X be a finite subset in the Euclidean plane Π with a distance d. The density S is a non-negative functional relationship between an arbitrary subset $A \subset X$ and any point $x \in X$: $S(A, x) \leftrightarrow S_A(x)$. Thus, the density $S_A(x)$ is also defined in the case where $x \notin A$.

S is determined by two parameters: the localization radius r and the center parameter $p \geq 0$, which takes into account the distance to x in the ball $D_A(x, r) = \{a \in A : d(x, a) \leq r\}$:

$$S_A(x) = S_A(x|r, p) = \sum_{y \in D_A(x,r)} \left(1 - \frac{d(x, y)}{r}\right)^p. \tag{1}$$

With $p = 0$, we obtain the usual number of points in $D_A(x, r)$:

$$S_A(x|r, 0) = |D_A(x, r)|.$$

2.2. First Stage

Set the level α of the density S, let $X^0(\alpha) = X$, and define the sequence of sets $X^{i+1}(\alpha) = \{x \in X^i(\alpha) : S_{X^i(\alpha)}(x) \geq \alpha\}, i = 0, 1, \ldots$. This does not increase $X^i(\alpha) \supseteq X^{i+1}(\alpha)$, and therefore, due to the finite nature of X, it will necessarily stabilize from some moment i^*:

$$X = X^0(\alpha) \supset X^i(\alpha) \supset \cdots \supset X^{i^*}(\alpha) = X^{i^*+1}(\alpha) = \cdots \leftrightarrow X(\alpha). \tag{2}$$

By replacing in the equality $X^{i^*+1}(\alpha) = \{x \in X^{i^*}(\alpha) : P_{X^{i^*}(\alpha)}(x) \geq \alpha\}$ the sets $X^{i^*}(\alpha)$ and $Xi^* + 1(\alpha)$ on $X(\alpha)$, we obtain the equality

$$X(\alpha) = \{x \in X(\alpha) : P_{X(\alpha)}(x) \geq \alpha\},$$

which indicates the α density of the set $X(\alpha)$ in the space X even at its points. Such a set in X is called α discretely perfect:

Definition 1. *A subset A in X is α discretely perfect if*

$$A = \{x \in X : S_A(x) \geq \alpha\}. \tag{3}$$

The first stage (SDPS$_1$) of the SDPS algorithm is to build $X(\alpha)$ (i.e., transition from the entire set X to a subset $X(\alpha)$: SDPS$_1$: $X \to X(\alpha)$). The result ($X(\alpha)$) of the first stage of the SDPS algorithm will also be referred to as SDPS(X) or SDPS(α, r, p)(X). The cutting process (Equation (2)) is shown in Figure 2, from which, in particular, it can be seen that the first stage of SDPS is a topological filtering of the space X (i.e., clearing it of noise).

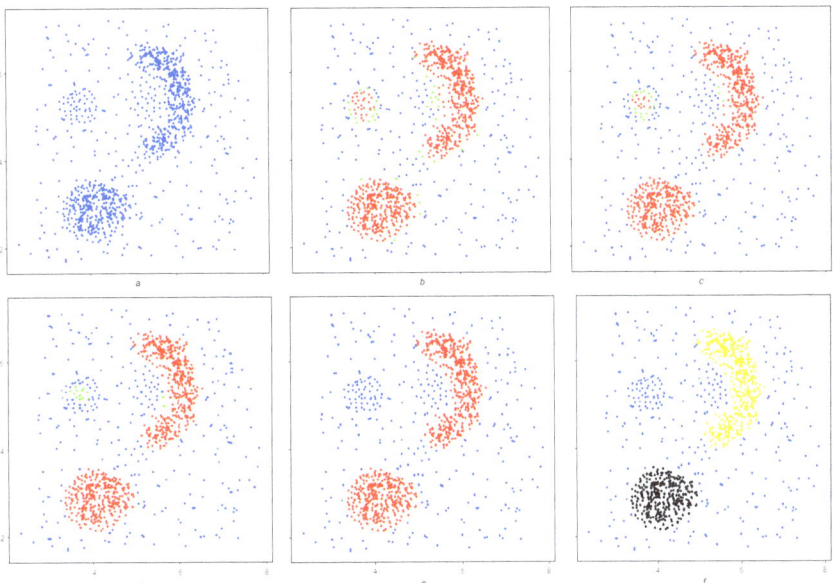

Figure 2. Application of the SDPS algorithm to the array X (**a**). Four iterations are shown in (**b**–**e**). The result is a local α-perfect subset of $X(\alpha)$ in X (**e**). The green points in figures (**b**–**d**) show the points that did not pass the next iteration in SDPS. SDPS further split $X(\alpha)$ into connected components (yellow and black subsets (**f**)).

The examples below illustrate the general nature of the dependence of the SDPS algorithm on the parameters at the first stage: the smaller the radius r, and the larger the parameters p and α, the more rigorous the SDPS was, and the denser and smaller its resulting SDPS$_1(X)$ was:

Example 1. *The initial array X (Figure 3a) shows the inverse nature of the dependence of the SDPS algorithm on the density level α. By raising it, we went inside the condensations, finding dense nuclei already in them (Figure 3b,c)*

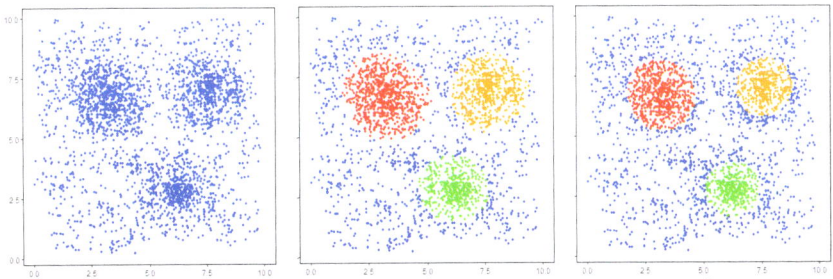

Figure 3. The inverse character of the dependence of the first stage of SDPS on the density level, where (**a**) is the initial array X and (**b**,**c**) have sets shown in red, yellow, and green for SDPS(α, r, p)(X) and SDPS($\bar{\alpha}, r, p$)(X) for $\alpha < \bar{\alpha}$.

Example 2. *Under the conditions of Example 1, the direct nature of the dependence of the SDPS algorithm on the vision radius r is shown. By lowering it by passing from r to $\bar{r} < r$, we made the SDPS algorithm more local with the aim of finding smaller condensations (Figure 4). All small condensations in Figure 4b are shown in black.*

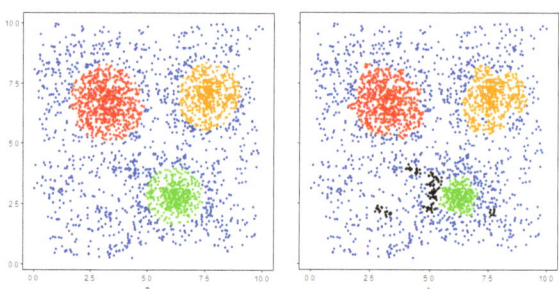

Figure 4. Direct dependence on the radius of localization of the first stage of SDPS when moving from SDPS$(\alpha, r, p)(X)$ (**a**) to SDPS$(\alpha, \bar{r}, p)(X)$ (**b**) with $r > \bar{r}$ on the array X (Figure 3a). Finer black condensations were added to the red, yellow and green ones.

Example 3. *In the conditions in Example 1, the inverse nature of the dependence of the SDPS algorithm on the parameter p was shown. By increasing it by going from p to $\bar{p} > p$, we made the SDPS algorithm more rigorous (Figure 5).*

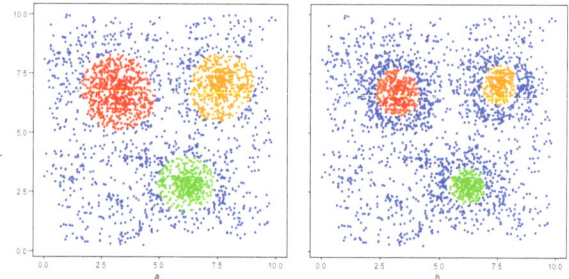

Figure 5. The inverse nature of the dependence of the first stage of SDPS on the center parameter. For $\bar{p} > p$, the result of SDPS$(\alpha, r, \bar{p})(X)$ (**b**) was more rigorous than the result of SDPS$(\alpha, r, p)(X)$ (**a**) on array X (Figure 3a).

2.3. Second Stage

Figure 6b shows the result of the first stage SDPS$_1(X)$ for the array X shown in Figure 6a. It is clear that it needed "reasonable" partitioning. In the SDPS algorithm, the second and third stages are devoted to this.

At the second stage, the set $X(\alpha)$ is partitioned into non-intersecting r-connected components (Figure 6c) which, of course, must be included in any reasonable partition of $X(\alpha)$. There are two reasons for this, and they are given below:

Definition 2. *Points x and y in $X(\alpha)$ are called r-connected if in $X(\alpha)$, there is a chain of r close-to-each-other points $x_0, \ldots, x_n$ with a start $x = x_0$, end $y = x_n$, and distances $d(x_i, x_{i+1}) \leq r, i = 0, \ldots, n-1$.*

The r connectivity relation is an equivalence that splits $X(\alpha)$ into disjunctive r connectivity components which, depending on the context, will be denoted below as c or c_k, $k = 1, \ldots, k^* = k^*(X(\alpha), r)$.

The second stage of the SDPS algorithm, which we will denote as SDPS$_2$, consists of constructing the c components. Their collection, as well as the partition $X(\alpha)$ associated with them, will be denoted identically as $C_r(X(\alpha))$, and thus

$$C_r(X(\alpha)) = \{c_k|_1^{k^*}\} \text{ and } C_r(X(\alpha)) \leftrightarrow X(\alpha) = \vee_{k=1}^{k^*} c_k. \quad (4)$$

This is the result of the second stage of the SDPS algorithm: SDPS$_2(X) = C_r(\text{SDPS}(X))$.

Rationale (first reason): r is the localization radius in the SDPS algorithm, and therefore any points that are r close to each other are considered close and must necessarily be included in the same partition component $X(\alpha)$ (the partition should not break close points).

Rationale (second reason): the components of the r connectivity are separated from each other by more than r, so the density S of each of them at any point from the other component is equal to zero. Hence, the conclusion is that each component of the r connection in $X(\alpha)$ is itself discretely perfect, since it independently provides the necessary level α of the density S at each of its points and is equal to zero at other points.

Figure 6 shows that the result of cutting (red dots in Figure 6b) was split in the second stage into 24 r-connected components, shown in Figure 6c with different colors.

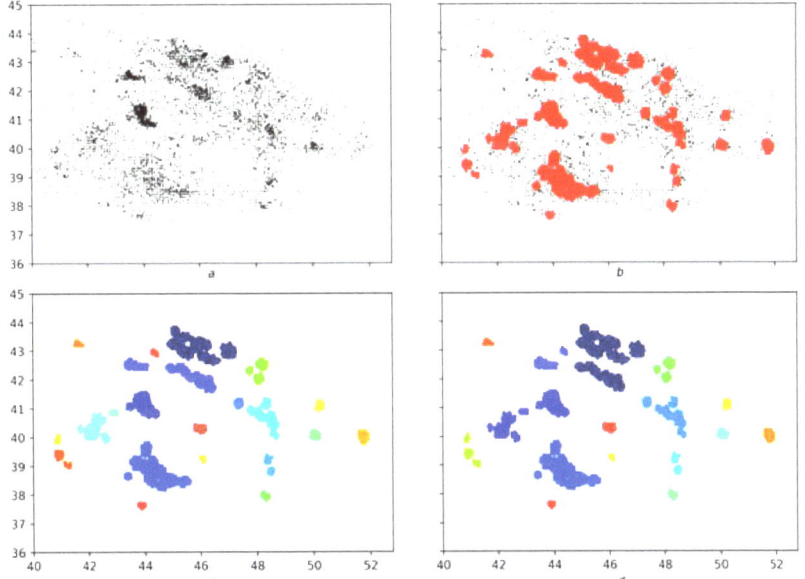

Figure 6. (**a**) Initial array X. (**b**) Result of the first stage of the SDPS algorithm. (**c**) Result of the second stage of the SDPS algorithm with r connectivity components (uniform in color sets). (**d**) Result of the third stage of the SDPS algorithm with edges and quasi-edges (uniform in color sets).

2.4. The Third Stage

The results of the second stage may be enough (Figures 3–5) or may not (Figure 6c). The expert E decides. He or she perceives the second stage SDPS$_2(X)$ as a given that is not subject to further internal transformation, considering each component of the r connectivity $c \in \text{SDPS}_2(X)$ to be a single and indivisible spot (big point).

The spots $c = cX(\alpha)$ are interpreted by the expert E as single exits (manifestations) of global anomalous entities in X. To understand their true scale, additional connection of spots, if possible, may be needed. This is the third and final stage of the SDPS algorithm.

The expert E considers a set of spots $C \subset \text{SDPS}_2(X)$ to be one whole if any two spots in it can be connected by a chain of close (in his or her opinion) intermediate transitions.

This gives the expert a reason to conclude that C is not random and that the set of spots (r components of connectivity) included in C is a collective but fragmentary manifestation (edge) of some global anomalous entity in X.

We denote with χ_E the partition of the spot space $\text{SDPS}_2(X)$ into such "non-random" sets C_i:

$$\chi_E \leftrightarrow \text{SDPS}_2(X) = \vee_{i=1}^{i^*(E)} C_i, C_i = \left\{ C_{ij}|_{j=1}^{j^*(i)} \right\}. \tag{5}$$

This is the third stage of the SDPS algorithm ($\text{SDPS}_3(X) = \chi_E$), and it depends on the expert E's analysis of the initial space X and the first and second SDPS stages of it:

$$\chi_E = \chi_E(X, \text{SDPS}_1(X), \text{SDPS}_2(X)). \tag{6}$$

With such an analysis, for each set C_i, the question of proximity within it is generally solved individually.

In this paper, the simplest Boolean version of the third stage is presented where, based on the analysis of the space X only, the expert E develops its proximity threshold r_E, which is weaker than r ($r < r_E$) and splits the spot space $\text{SDPS}_2(X)$ into r_E connectivity components ($\chi_E = C_{r_E} X(\alpha)$).

The parameters r and r_E are constructed using power law averaging of non-trivial distances in X:

$$r = \left(\frac{\sum_{x \neq y \in X} d(x,y)^{q(r)}}{|X|(|X|-1)} \right)^{1/q(r)},$$

$$r_E = \left(\frac{\sum_{x \neq y \in X} d(x,y)^{q(E)}}{|X|(|X|-1)} \right)^{1/q(E)}.$$

For the parameter r, numerous tests of the SDPS algorithm have established that the choice of $q(r) \in [-3, -2]$ can be considered optimal. The studies carried out in the framework of this work show that $q(E) \in [-2.5, -1.5]$. The intersection of the areas of parameters r and r_E is explained both by the fuzzy perception of proximity by the expert and by the diversity in construction of X.

Figure 6c shows the 24 r connectivity components (spots) obtained in the second stage, which combined into 15 r_E connectivity components (Figure 6d). Note that, in this case, $q(r) = -3.0$, and $q(r_E) = -2.3$.

2.5. SDPS and DBSCAN Algorithms

The cutting process (Equation (2)) was also valid for other density constructions, particularly for the derivative of S of the construction $\tilde{S}$: $\tilde{S}_A(x) = \max S_A(\tilde{x}), \tilde{x} \in D_A(x, r)$. The related ŠDPS algorithm was less rigorous than the SDPS algorithm. For the same parameters r, p, and α, $\text{SDPS}(X) \subseteq \text{ŠDPS}(X)$) always held and coincided with the well-known DBSCAN algorithm.

Figure 7b,c shows the results of the second stage of the SDPS and ŠDPS = DBSCAN algorithms, and Figure 7a shows traditional k-means clustering. All this gives grounds for the following conclusion: the SDPS algorithm in its first two stages, as in the well-known algorithms DBSCAN, OPTICS, and RSC [59,60], represents a new stage in cluster analysis, where modern cluster analysis algorithms first filter the initial space, clearing it of noise (first stage), and then the result is divided into homogeneous parts (second stage).

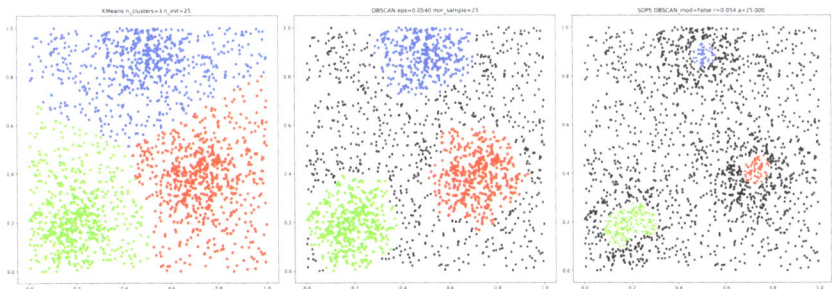

Figure 7. Comparison of the results of the algorithms. (**a**) Results of clustering with the k-means algorithm. (**b**) SDPS algorithm. (**c**) DBSCAN algorithm.

3. Immersion of a Finite Set into a Domain of Euclidean Space under DMA Methods

The results for the operation of the SDPS algorithm in its pure form were of little use for practical conclusions. Therefore, discrete expansions needed to be immersed in Euclidean domains, finding a compromise between the economy (scanability) and connectivity (smoothness) of such immersion. The resulting disjunctive regions would be areas of increased interest for the reasons that prompted the operation of the SDPS algorithm.

DMA methods help to solve the problem of immersing a finite set into the domain of a Euclidean space in the two-dimensional case. The solution is the result of the joint work of the Ext and Int algorithms. Ext was developed earlier, and it is responsible for the ability to scan the embedding. It is a component of FCAZ [26,50]. Int is responsible for the connectivity of the embedding. It is presented here for the first time and is the main theoretical result of this paper.

The initial data were a domain B in the Euclidean plane Ξ and a finite set A in B. The task was to construct a Euclidean shell $H(A)$ for A in B that satisfied the ability to scan and connectivity requirements formulated above.

3.1. Ext and Int Algorithms

Let us choose an orthonormal coordinate system xOy in Ξ so that $\Xi = \mathbb{R}^2(x,y)$ and also a regular pixel cover Π of the plane Ξ, consistent with the xOy coordinates.

The shell $\text{Ext}(A)$ for A in B is obtained as the union of all pixels π from Π that intersect B and are close to A:

$$\text{Ext}(a) = \cup\{\pi \in \Pi : ((\pi \cap B) \neq \varnothing) \wedge (\pi \text{ close to } A)\}. \tag{7}$$

Thus, it is necessary to determine the proximity π to A. There are several ways to accomplish this in DMA, namely quantiles, fuzzy comparisons, and Kolmogorov averages. Let us present the last option.

Let $c(\pi)$ denote the center of the pixel π, and define the distance $\rho(A, \pi)$ from A to π as the Kolmogorov averaging M_ν of the nontrivial distances between elements A and $c(\pi)$ with a negative index ν:

$$\rho(A, \pi) = M_\nu\{\rho(a, c(\pi)) : a \in A \wedge \rho(a, c(\pi)) \neq 0\}, \; \nu < 0.$$

The proximity threshold $\rho(A|B)$ to A in B is also obtained using Kolmogorov averaging in the general case with another negative index ω:

$$\rho(A|B) = M_\omega\{\rho(A, \pi) : \pi \cap B \neq \varnothing\}, \; \omega < 0.$$

The shell $\text{Ext}(A)$ is formed by all pixels close to A in B:

$$\text{Ext}(A) = \cup\{\pi : \rho(A, \pi) \leq \rho(A|B)\}.$$

Next, we turn to the Int. Let us fix any point b from B and, for any a from A other than b, denote with $\Theta_b(a)$ the angle in $[0, 2\pi)$ corresponding to the direction of $e_b(a)$ from b to a:

$$e_b(a) = \frac{b-a}{||b-a||} = (\cos \Theta_b(a), \sin \Theta_b(a)).$$

Let us properly order the set of angles $\Theta_b(A) = \{\Theta_b(a), a \in A \setminus b\}$ in $[0, 2\pi)$:

$$\Theta_b(A) \to \{\Theta_1 < \Theta_2 < \cdots < \Theta_n\}, \ n = n(b, A)$$

and assume $\Theta_{n+1} = \Theta_1$.

The extended set $\overline{\Theta_b(A)} = \{\Theta_i|_1^{n+1}\}$ is responsible for the environment of the point b by the set A and helps to express it formally. If, for the chosen environment threshold $\Theta \in [0, \pi]$, all successive differences $\Theta_{i+1} - \Theta_i$ are less than Θ ($i = 1, \ldots, n$), then the point b is considered to be environed by the set A (internal for A). Otherwise, the point b is considered external to A:

$$b \leftrightarrow \begin{array}{c} \text{internal} \\ \text{external} \end{array} \text{ for } A, \text{ if } \max\{\Theta_{i+1} - \Theta_i|_1^n\} \begin{array}{c} < \\ \geq \end{array} \Theta. \qquad (8)$$

The connection (Equation (8)) with the locality threshold R makes the environing criterion more flexible by making it local, where b is locally internal (external) for A if b is internal (external) for the ball $D_A(b, R)$ according to Equation (8).

The shell $\text{Int}(A)$ is formed by all pixels whose centers are internal to A:

$$\text{Int}(A) = \{\pi \in \Pi : c(\pi) \text{ locally internal } A\}.$$

The shell $H(A)$ for A in B with the ability to scan and connectivity conditions is obtained by the union of $\text{Ext}(A)$ and $\text{Int}(A)$:

$$H(A) = (\text{Ext} + \text{Int})(A) = \text{Ext}(A) \cup \text{Int}(A).$$

Its construction depends on four parameters: two negative indices ν, ω for Ext, and the environing and locality thresholds Θ and R for Int.

Figure 8 shows the set A for which Figure 9 presents all the stages of constructing the shell $H(A)$. The final result is shown in two ways: $H(A) = \text{Ext}(A) \cup (\text{Int}(A) \setminus \text{Ext}(A))$ (Int against the background of Ext (Figure 9c)) and $H(A) = \text{Int}(A) \cup (\text{Ext}(A) \setminus \text{Int}(A))$ (Ext against the background of Int (Figure 9d)).

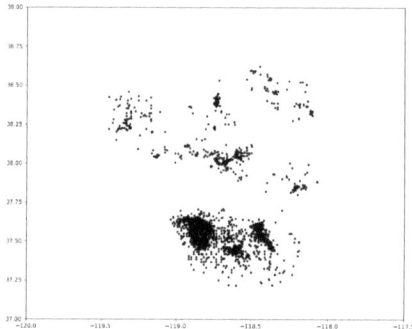

Figure 8. Initial array X for constructing the shell $H(A)$.

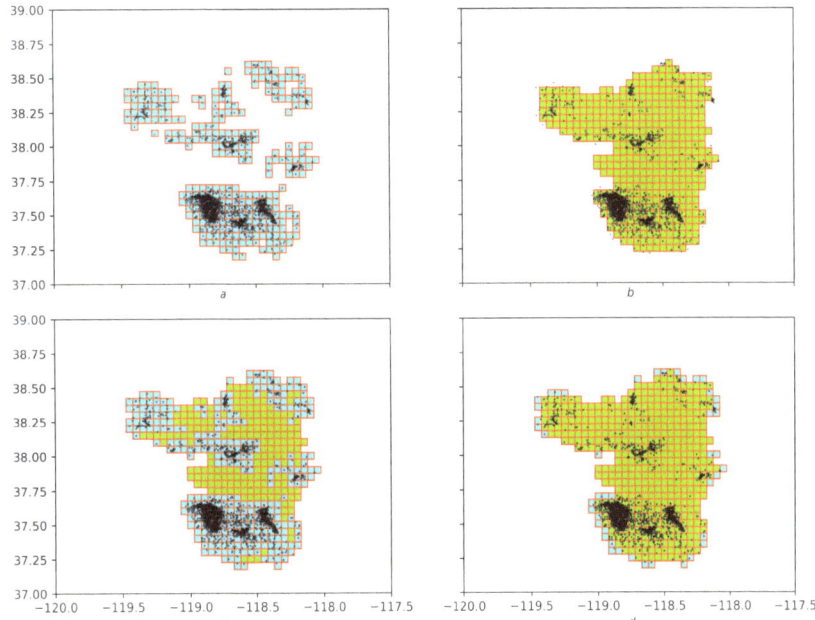

Figure 9. (**a**) Ext shell for the set A. (**b**) Shell of Int for the set A. (**c**) Shell $H(A) = \text{Ext}(A) \cup (\text{Int}(A) \setminus \text{Ext}(A))$ (Int against the background of Ext). (**d**) Shell $H(A) = \text{Int}(A) \cup (\text{Ext}(A) \setminus \text{Int}(A))$ (Ext against the background of Int).

3.2. FCAZ Method

FCAZ in its original version was a sequential combination of only the first stage of the SDPS algorithm and the Ext algorithm [28]:

$$\text{FCAZ}(X) = \text{Ext}(\text{SDPS}(X)).$$

The additional stages in the SDPS algorithm presented in this article, as well as Int algorithm, allowed us to continue the development of FCAZ. We propose a new variant of FCAZ associated with the Boolean version of SDPS, namely the joint use of Ext and Int algorithms, resulting in the SDPS algorithm on X in the form of decomposition:

$$\text{FCAZ}(X) = (\text{Ext} + \text{Int})(\text{SDPS}(X)).$$

Figure 10 shows an example of constructing FCAZ zones based on a developed mathematical apparatus.

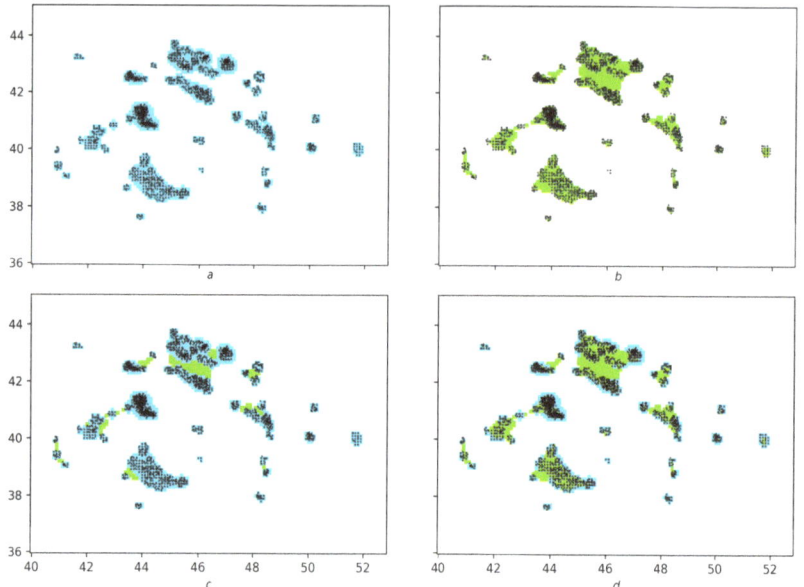

Figure 10. FCAZ zones constructed for the results from running the first stage of the SDPS algorithm on the array X (Figure 6b). (**a**) Extzones. (**b**) Int zones. (**c**) Int against the background of Ext. (**d**) Ext on the background of Int.

4. Discussion

As mentioned above, the FCAZ method in its initial form, which has been used to date to recognize the areas prone to the strongest, strong, and significant earthquakes in a number of mountainous countries of the world [26], is a sequential application of the first stage of the SDPS algorithm (in the papers devoted to FCAZ recognition, it is just the DPS algorithm) and the Ext algorithm, where $FCAZ(X) = Ext(DPS(X))$ [28]. In the present work, the algorithmic base of the FCAZ method was substantially developed. Thus, in particular, its algorithmic base was expanded.

Using California as an example, let us consider the contribution of the Int algorithm developed in this paper to the mapping of potential high-seismicity zones (i.e., contouring of the recognized DPS clusters of epicenters of weak earthquakes). In Figure 11, the green and red colors show the results of FCAZ recognition of strong earthquake-prone areas with magnitudes $M \geq 6.5$ in California from [26]. Earthquake epicenters from the ANSS catalog (http://www.ncedc.org/anss/catalog-search.html, accessed on 1 January 2020) with $M \geq 3.0$ that occurred over the period of 1960–2012 were used as recognition objects (DPS clustering). The choice of the magnitude threshold $M = 3.0$ was carried out based on theoretical and practical analysis of the magnitude–frequency graphs for the entire considered region. The green color in Figure 11 shows the DPS clusters, while red shows the high-seismicity zones mapped by the Ext algorithm based on the clusters within which earthquakes with $M \geq 6.5$ can occur. In [26], the arguments in favor of the reliability of the performed recognition are presented in detail. In turn, it was shown in [50] that the result of FCAZ recognition in California depended little on the presence or absence of foreshock and aftershock sequences in the earthquake catalog, which is the source of recognition objects.

The black stars in Figure 11 show the epicenters of 33 earthquakes with $M \geq 6.5$ that occurred over the period of 1836–2010. The blue and white stars show the epicenters of events with $M \geq 6.5$ that occurred in 2014 and 2019 (i.e., after the end of the instrumental catalog, which made up a set of recognition objects). These events formed the material of a pure experiment. Thus, the consistency of the recognized FCAZ zones with the locations of the epicenters of strong earthquakes that occurred more than 180 years ago, including the ones before and after the beginning of the instrumental catalog used in recognition, was checked.

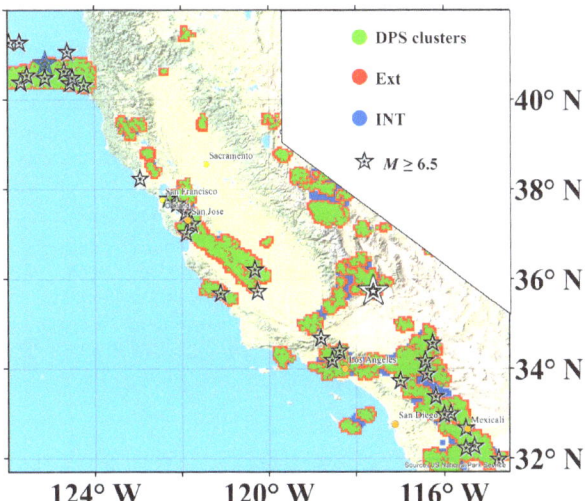

Figure 11. New FCAZ zones prone to earthquakes with $M \geq 6.5$ in California and earthquake epicenters with $M \geq 6.5$.

Out of 35 events with $M \geq 6.5$, only 5 (14.3%) epicenters did not fall into the recognized FCAZ-zones (Figure 11). At the same time, it should be noted that three epicenters located in the northwest of the region are located in the Pacific Ocean at a fairly large distance from the coast. Additionally, two epicenters of historical earthquakes did not fall into the FCAZ zones: near Fort Tehon (1857) and in San Francisco (1906). These earthquakes occurred long before the start of systematic instrumental observations of seismicity in California. Thus, for various reasons, there were not enough objects (earthquake epicenters with $M \geq 3.0$) to recognize the areas of these five strong earthquakes.

The positive result of the pure experiment should be noted: both epicenters fell strictly inside the FCAZ zones (Figure 11). At the same time, we emphasize that the epicenter of the earthquake on 6 July 2019 with $M = 7.1$ (white star in Figure 11) [61], being inside the FCAZ zones, was located outside the areas determined for the magnitude threshold $M = 6.5$ being high seismicity under the EPA method [21]. The latter once again emphasizes the modernity and reliability of the obtained FCAZ results.

The result of applying the new computational component Int in the FCAZ structure is shown in Figure 11 in blue against the background of red zones mapped by the Ext algorithm. Thus, we have a new shell Ext(DPS) $\cup$ (Int(DPS) \ Ext(DPS)) of high-seismicity DPS clusters in California, which we will consider in this paper as new FCAZ zones prone to strong earthquakes.

The new FCAZ zones had the same number of "miss target" errors. As before, five earthquake epicenters were outside the recognized zones. However, it should be noted that the development of the FCAZ algorithmic basis, including the expansion of the algorithmic base of the method, could not directly lead to a decrease in the number of target misses. The contribution of the updated mathematical toolkit of the method which significantly develops FCAZ-seismic zoning is as follows. At the second (described in detail above) stage of the application of the DPS algorithm in California, clusters were formed that were r-connected components (Equation (4)). According to the mathematical construction embedded in the third DPS stage, some of these connected components need to be combined into large clusters that have a close internal connection against the background of all recognized dense condensations. However, the Ext algorithm does not always allow building a single FCAZ zone for clusters that are united at the third DPS stage. The Int algorithm effectively solves this problem.

From Figure 11, it can be seen that the result of the operation of the Int algorithm made it possible to combine several zones mapped by the Ext algorithm into individual high-seismicity areas. This was especially well observed in the south and east of the Sierra Nevada mountains, in the ocean area south of Los Angeles, as well as northeast of the city of San Diego. In the last location, Int made it possible to connect the edges of a large FCAZ zone mapped by the Ext algorithm. Thereby, the degree of falling into this zone of two strong earthquake epicenters increased. Before the application of the Int algorithm, these epicenters were located on the very edge of the recognized FCAZ zones.

From Figure 11, it can be concluded that the FCAZ recognition result obtained in California using the updated algorithmic base, which presented more interconnected potential high-seismicity zones, has a greater degree of reliability. Thus, based on the developed mathematical apparatus, the reliability and accuracy of the FCAZ recognition of areas prone to earthquakes were significantly increased. This in turn contributes to the prediction of damage from earthquakes and, for the first time, can be directly used to update seismic zoning maps.

5. Conclusions

Discrete mathematical analysis is a discrete data analysis method that uses scenarios of classical continuous mathematics, in which the fundamentals are replaced by fuzzy models of their discrete analogs. From a practical point of view, DMA is a new approach to data analysis focused on an expert and occupying an intermediate position between rigorous mathematical methods and soft combinatorial ones.

The solution to the problem within the DMA framework consists of two parts. The first one is informal, as it analyzes the logic of the expert, introduces the necessary concepts, and explains the scenarios and principles of the solution. The second has a formal characteristic. With the help of the DMA apparatus, all concepts receive rigorous definitions within the framework of fuzzy mathematics and fuzzy logic, and the schemes and principles become algorithms.

This article provides three such solutions:

- The SDPS algorithm is a DMA response to the empirical definition of a cluster as a connected set, the measure of the presence of which at each of its points is higher than at any other.
  The answer is a rigorous DPS set theory and DPS clustering based on it.
- The Ext algorithm is a DMA formalization of the scanning ability and proximity based on an empirical understanding with the help of Kolmogorov means (one of the main technical means of DMA).
- The Int algorithm is a DMA formalization of smoothness (insideness) based on the empirical logic of the circle with the help of Kolmogorov means and standard linear algebra.

It should be noted that DMA has all the necessary tools to generate unsupervised topological filtering and classification algorithms. Based on fuzzy sets and fuzzy logic, DMA can convey expert ideas about the spatial distributions of objects. DMA makes it possible to implement a system approach to the analysis of geophysical data in the problem of adequate seismic hazard assessment studied in the article.

In conclusion, we emphasize that based on the mathematical apparatus of the FCAZ method, which has been substantially developed based on DMA, in this work, new zones prone to earthquakes with $M \geq 6.5$ in California were constructed. A distinctive feature of the new FCAZ recognition system is the combination of a number of smaller zones located at a relatively small distance from each other into large, single, connected potential high-seismicity zones. Note that after applying the Int algorithm, the area of the FCAZ zones increased by only 6%.

The results presented in the present and previous works indicate the high reliability of the interpretation of FCAZ zones as earthquake-prone areas. The FCAZ method makes it possible to effectively recognize possible locations of future earthquakes solely from seismological data. We also note that the results of the FCAZ studies indicate that weak seismicity can actually "manifest" the properties of geophysical fields, which are used directly in the form of characteristics of recognition objects in other (similar to FCAZ) methodologies.

Author Contributions: All authors contributed to the study's conception and design. Conceptualization and original draft preparation, S.M.A., B.A.D. and S.R.B.; conceptualization, methodology, review and editing and validation, D.A.K. and B.V.D.; material preparation, formal analysis, data curation, and algorithm development, S.R.B. and I.O.B. All authors have read and agreed to the published version of the manuscript.

Funding: This work was conducted in the framework of budgetary funding of the Geophysical Center of RAS, adopted by the Ministry of Science and Higher Education of the Russian Federation.

Institutional Review Board Statement: Not applicable.

Informed Consent Statement: Informed consent was obtained from all subjects involved in the study.

Data Availability Statement: Not applicable.

Conflicts of Interest: The authors declare no conflict of interest.

Abbreviations

The following abbreviations are used in this manuscript:

DSHA	Deterministic seismic hazard analysis
PSHA	Probabilistic seismic hazard assessment
NDSHA	Neodeterministic seismic hazard assessment
EPA	Earthquake-prone areas
FCAZ	Formalized clustering and zoning
DMA	Discrete mathematical analysis
DPS	Discrete perfect sets
FMS	Finite metric space
SDPS	Sets discrete perfect sets

References

1. Mualchin, L. History of Modern Earthquake Hazard Mapping and Assessment in California Using a Deterministic or Scenario Approach. *Pure Appl. Geophys.* **2010**, *168*, 383–407. [CrossRef]
2. Wang, Z. Seismic Hazard Assessment: Issues and Alternatives. *Pure Appl. Geophys.* **2010**, *168*, 11–25. [CrossRef]
3. Atkinson, G.M. The Integration of Emerging Trends in Engineering Seismology. In Proceedings of the 13th World Conference on Earthquake Engineering, Lisbon, Portugal, 24–28 September 2012.
4. Kijko, A. Seismic Hazard. In *Encyclopedia of Solid Earth Geophysics*; Springer: Dordrecht, The Netherlands, 2011; pp. 1107–1121. [CrossRef]
5. Krinitzsky, E.L. How to combine deterministic and probabilistic methods for assessing earthquake hazards. *Eng. Geol.* **2003**, *70*, 157–163. [CrossRef]
6. Bommer, J.J.; Abrahamson, N.A. Why Do Modern Probabilistic Seismic-Hazard Analyses Often Lead to Increased Hazard Estimates? *Bull. Seismol. Soc. Am.* **2006**, *96*, 1967–1977. [CrossRef]
7. Ulomov, V.I. Seismic hazard of Northern Eurasia. *Ann. Geophys.* **1999**, *42*, 1023–1038. [CrossRef]
8. Zaalishvili, V.B.; Dzeranov, B.V.; Gabaraev, A.F. Seismic hazard assessment of the territory and construction of probability maps. *Geol. Geophys. Russ. South* **2011**, *1*, 48–58. (In Russian)
9. Shibaev, S.V.; Kozmin, B.M.; Imaev, V.S.; Imaeva, L.P.; Petrov, A.F.; Starkova, N.N. The February 14, 2013 Ilin-Tas (Abyi) earthquake (Mw=6.7), Northeast Yakutia. *Ross. Seismol. Zhurnal Russ. J. Seismol.* **2020**, *2*, 92–102. [CrossRef]
10. Cornell, C.A. Engineering seismic risk analysis. *Bull. Seismol. Soc. Am.* **1968**, *58*, 1583–1606. [CrossRef]
11. Panza, G.F.; Bela, J. NDSHA: A new paradigm for reliable seismic hazard assessment. *Eng. Geol.* **2020**, *275*, 105403. [CrossRef]
12. Panza, G.F.; Mura, C.L.; Peresan, A.; Romanelli, F.; Vaccari, F. Seismic Hazard Scenarios as Preventive Tools for a Disaster Resilient Society. In *Advances in Geophysics*; Elsevier: Amsterdam, The Netherlands, 2012; pp. 93–165. [CrossRef]
13. Skorkina, A.A. Scaling of two corner frequencies of source spectra for earthquakes of the Bering fault. *Russ. J. Earth Sci.* **2020**, *20*, 1–9. [CrossRef]

14. Dziewonski, A.M.; Chou, T.A.; Woodhouse, J.H. Determination of earthquake source parameters from waveform data for studies of global and regional seismicity. *J. Geophys. Res. Solid Earth* **1981**, *86*, 2825–2852. [CrossRef]
15. Mäntyniemi, P.; Tatevossian, R.E.; Tatevossian, T.N. Uncertain historical earthquakes and seismic hazard: Theoretical and practical considerations. *Geomat. Nat. Hazards Risk* **2013**, *5*, 1–6. [CrossRef]
16. Rebetsky, Y.L.; Tatevossian, R. Rupture propagation in strong earthquake sources and tectonic stress field. *Bull. De La Société Géologique De Fr.* **2013**, *184*, 335–346. [CrossRef]
17. Parvez, I.A.; Rosset, P. The Role of Microzonation in Estimating Earthquake Risk. In *Earthquake Hazard, Risk and Disasters*; Elsevier: Amsterdam, The Netherlands, 2014; pp. 273–308. [CrossRef]
18. Karapetyan, J.K.; Gasparyan, A.S.; Shakhparonyan, S.R.; Karapetyan, R.K. Registration and spectral analysis of waveforms of 10.24.2019 earthquake in the Caucasus using the new IGES-006 seismic sensor. *Russ. J. Earth Sci.* **2020**, *20*, 1–8. [CrossRef]
19. Peresan, A. The Contribution of Pattern Recognition of Seismic and Morphostructural Data to Seismic Hazard Assessment. *arXiv* **2015**, arXiv:1406.2932. [CrossRef]
20. Rugarli, P.; Vaccari, F.; Panza, G. Seismogenic nodes as a viable alternative to seismogenic zones and observed seismicity for the definition of seismic hazard at regional scale. *Vietnam. J. Earth Sci.* **2019**, *41*, 289–304. [CrossRef]
21. Gvishiani, A.D.; Soloviev, A.A.; Dzeboev, B.A. Problem of Recognition of Strong-Earthquake-Prone Areas: A State-of-the-Art Review. *Izv. Phys. Solid Earth* **2020**, *56*, 1–23. [CrossRef]
22. Gorshkov, A.I.; Soloviev, A.A. Recognition of earthquake-prone areas in the Altai-Sayan-Baikal region based on the morphostructural zoning. *Russ. J. Earth Sci.* **2021**, *21*, 1–16. [CrossRef]
23. Kossobokov, V.G.; Soloviev, A.A. Pattern recognition in problems of seismic hazard assessment. *Chebyshevskii Sb.* **2018**, *19*, 55–90. [CrossRef]
24. Soloviev, A.A.; Gvishiani, A.D.; Gorshkov, A.I.; Dobrovolsky, M.N.; Novikova, O.V. Recognition of earthquake-prone areas: Methodology and analysis of the results. *Izv. Phys. Solid Earth* **2014**, *50*, 151–168. [CrossRef]
25. Gelfand, I.M.; Guberman, S.I.; Izvekova, M.L.; Keilis-Borok, V.I.; Ranzman, E.J. Criteria of high seismicity, determined by pattern recognition. *Tectonophysics* **1972**, *13*, 415–422. [CrossRef]
26. Dzeboev, B.A.; Gvishiani, A.D.; Agayan, S.M.; Belov, I.O.; Karapetyan, J.K.; Dzeranov, B.V.; Barykina, Y.V. System-Analytical Method of Earthquake-Prone Areas Recognition. *Appl. Sci.* **2021**, *11*, 7972. [CrossRef]
27. Gvishiani, A.D.; Dzeboev, B.A.; Agayan, S.M. A new approach to recognition of the strong earthquake-prone areas in the Caucasus. *Izv. Phys. Solid Earth* **2013**, *49*, 747–766. [CrossRef]
28. Gvishiani, A.D.; Dzeboev, B.A.; Agayan, S.M. FCaZm intelligent recognition system for locating areas prone to strong earthquakes in the Andean and Caucasian mountain belts. *Izv. Phys. Solid Earth* **2016**, *52*, 461–491. [CrossRef]
29. Vijay, R.K.; Nanda, S.J. Seismicity analysis using space-time density peak clustering method. *Pattern Anal. Appl.* **2020**, *24*, 181–201. [CrossRef]
30. Zaliapin, I.; Ben-Zion, Y. Earthquake clusters in southern California I: Identification and stability. *J. Geophys. Res. Solid Earth* **2013**, *118*, 2847–2864. [CrossRef]
31. Zaliapin, I.; Gabrielov, A.; Keilis-Borok, V.; Wong, H. Clustering Analysis of Seismicity and Aftershock Identification. *Phys. Rev. Lett.* **2008**, *101*, 018501. [CrossRef]
32. Telesca, L.; Golay, J.; Kanevski, M. Morisita-based space-clustering analysis of Swiss seismicity. *Phys. A Stat. Mech. Its Appl.* **2015**, *419*, 40–47. [CrossRef]
33. Rehman, K.; Burton, P.W.; Weatherill, G.A. K-means cluster analysis and seismicity partitioning for Pakistan. *J. Seismol.* **2013**, *18*, 401–419. [CrossRef]
34. Peresan, A.; Gentili, S. Identification and characterization of earthquake clusters: A comparative analysis for selected sequences in Italy and adjacent regions. *Boll. Geofis. Teor. Ed Appl.* **2020**, *61*, 57–80.
35. Melnikova, V.; Seredkina, A.; Gileva, N. Spatio-Temporal Patterns of the Development of Strong Seismic Activations (1999–2007) in the Northern Baikal Area. *Russ. Geol. Geophys.* **2020**, *61*, 96–109. [CrossRef]
36. Shang, X.; Li, X.; Morales-Esteban, A.; Asencio-Cortés, G.; Wang, Z. Data Field-Based K-Means Clustering for Spatio-Temporal Seismicity Analysis and Hazard Assessment. *Remote Sens.* **2018**, *10*, 461. [CrossRef]
37. Telesca, L.; Alcaz, V.; Burtiev, R.; Sandu, I. Time-clustering analysis of the 1978–2008 sub-crustal seismicity of Vrancea region. *Nat. Hazards Earth Syst. Sci.* **2011**, *11*, 2335–2340. [CrossRef]
38. Aslam, B.; Naseer, F. A statistical analysis of the spatial existence of earthquakes in Balochistan: Clusters of seismicity. *Environ. Earth Sci.* **2020**, *79*, 1–12. [CrossRef]
39. Matoza, R.S.; Shearer, P.M.; Lin, G.; Wolfe, C.J.; Okubo, P.G. Systematic relocation of seismicity on Hawaii Island from 1992 to 2009 using waveform cross correlation and cluster analysis. *J. Geophys. Res. Solid Earth* **2013**, *118*, 2275–2288. [CrossRef]
40. Al-Ahmadi, K.; Al-Amri, A.; See, L. A spatial statistical analysis of the occurrence of earthquakes along the Red Sea floor spreading: Clusters of seismicity. *Arab. J. Geosci.* **2013**, *7*, 2893–2904. [CrossRef]
41. Gvishiani, A.D.; Vorobieva, I.A.; Shebalin, P.N.; Dzeboev, B.A.; Dzeranov, B.V.; Skorkina, A.A. Integrated Earthquake Catalog of the Eastern Sector of the Russian Arctic. *Appl. Sci.* **2022**, *12*, 5010. [CrossRef]
42. Agayan, S.M.; Bogoutdinov, S.R.; Krasnoperov, R.I. Short introduction into DMA. *Russ. J. Earth Sci.* **2018**, *18*, 1–10. [CrossRef]
43. Agayan, S.M.; Bogoutdinov, S.R.; Dobrovolsky, M.N. Discrete Perfect Sets and Their Application in Cluster Analysis. *Cybern. Syst. Anal.* **2014**, *50*, 176–190. [CrossRef]

44. Bogoutdinov, S.R.; Odintsova, A.A.; Pirogova, A.S. Search for extremity zones with discrete mathematical analysis algorithms to identify risks when drilling based on geophysical data. *Russ. J. Earth Sci.* **2022**, *22*, 1–9. [CrossRef]
45. Agayan, S.; Bogoutdinov, S.; Kamaev, D.; Kaftan, V.; Osipov, M.; Tatarinov, V. Theoretical Framework for Determination of Linear Structures in Multidimensional Geodynamic Data Arrays. *Appl. Sci.* **2021**, *11*, 11606. [CrossRef]
46. Agayan, S.M.; Bogoutdinov, S.R.; Dzeboev, B.A.; Dzeranov, B.V.; Kamaev, D.A.; Osipov, M.O. DPS Clustering: New Results. *Appl. Sci.* **2022**, *12*, 9335. [CrossRef]
47. Agayan, S.M.; Tatarinov, V.N.; Gvishiani, A.D.; Bogoutdinov, S.R.; Belov, I.O. FDPS algorithm in stability assessment of the Earth's crust structural tectonic blocks. *Russ. J. Earth Sci.* **2020**, *20*, 1–14. [CrossRef]
48. Agayan, S.M.; Losev, I.V.; Belov, I.O.; Tatarinov, V.N.; Manevich, A.I.; Pasishnichenko, M.A. Dynamic Activity Index for Feature Engineering of Geodynamic Data for Safe Underground Isolation of High-Level Radioactive Waste. *Appl. Sci.* **2022**, *12*, 2010. [CrossRef]
49. Agayan, S.; Bogoutdinov, S.; Soloviev, A.; Sidorov, R. The Study of Time Series Using the DMA Methods and Geophysical Applications. *Data Sci. J.* **2016**, *15*. [CrossRef]
50. Dzeboev, B.A.; Karapetyan, J.K.; Aronov, G.A.; Dzeranov, B.V.; Kudin, D.V.; Karapetyan, R.K.; Vavilin, E.V. FCAZ-recognition based on declustered earthquake catalogs. *Russ. J. Earth Sci.* **2020**, *20*, 1–9. [CrossRef]
51. Işık, E.; Harirchian, E. A Comparative Probabilistic Seismic Hazard Analysis for Eastern Turkey (Bitlis) Based on Updated Hazard Map and Its Effect on Regular RC Structures. *Buildings* **2022**, *12*, 1573. [CrossRef]
52. Işık, E.; Harirchian, E.; Büyüksaraç, A.; Ekinci, Y.L. Seismic and Structural Analyses of the Eastern Anatolian Region (Turkey) Using Different Probabilities of Exceedance. *Appl. Syst. Innov.* **2021**, *4*, 89. [CrossRef]
53. Buyuksarac, A.; Isik, E.; Harirchian, E. A case study for determination of seismic risk priorities in Van (Eastern Turkey). *Earthq. Struct.* **2021**, *20*, 445–455. [CrossRef]
54. Bülbül, M.A.; Harirchian, E.; Işık, M.F.; Aghakouchaki Hosseini, S.E.; Işık, E. A Hybrid ANN-GA Model for an Automated Rapid Vulnerability Assessment of Existing RC Buildings. *Appl. Sci.* **2022**, *12*, 5138. [CrossRef]
55. Gupta, I. Probabilistic seismic hazard analysis method for mapping of spectral amplitudes and other design specific quantities to estimate the earthquake effects on manmade structures. *ISET J. Earthq. Technol.* **2007**, *44*, 127–167.
56. Robinson, T.R. Scenario ensemble modelling of possible future earthquake impacts in Bhutan. *Nat. Hazards* **2020**, *103*, 3457–3478. [CrossRef]
57. Tehseen, R.; Farooq, M.S.; Abid, A. Earthquake Prediction Using Expert Systems: A Systematic Mapping Study. *Sustainability* **2020**, *12*, 2420. [CrossRef]
58. Gvishiani, A.D.; Agayan, S.M.; Losev, I.V.; Tatarinov, V.N. Geodynamic hazard assessment of a structural block holding an underground radioactive waste disposal facility. *Min. Inform. Anal. Bull.* **2021**, 5–18. [CrossRef]
59. Ester, M.; Kriegel, H.P.; Sander, J.; Xu, X. A density-based algorithm for discovering clusters in large spatial databases with noise. In Proceedings of the Second International Conference on Knowledge Discovery and Data Mining (KDD-96), Portland, OR, USA, 2–4 August 1996; AAAI Press: Washington, DC, USA, 1996; pp. 26–231.
60. Ankerst, M.; Breunig, M.; Kriegel, H.P.; Sander, J. OPTICS: Ordering Points To Identify the Clustering Structure. In Proceedings of the ACM SIGMOD International Conference on Management of Data, Philadelphia, PA, USA, 31 May–3 June 1999; ACM Press: New York, NY, USA, 1999; pp. 49–60.
61. Bondur, V.; Gokhberg, M.; Garagash, I.; Alekseev, D. Features of the modelled stress-strain state dynamics prior to the M7.1 2019 Ridgecrest earthquake in Southern California. *Russ. J. Earth Sci.* **2022**, 1–19. [CrossRef]

Disclaimer/Publisher's Note: The statements, opinions and data contained in all publications are solely those of the individual author(s) and contributor(s) and not of MDPI and/or the editor(s). MDPI and/or the editor(s) disclaim responsibility for any injury to people or property resulting from any ideas, methods, instructions or products referred to in the content.

Article

FocMech-Flow: Automatic Determination of P-Wave First-Motion Polarity and Focal Mechanism Inversion and Application to the 2021 Yangbi Earthquake Sequence

Shuai Li [1], Lihua Fang [1,2,*], Zhuowei Xiao [3], Yijian Zhou [4], Shirong Liao [5] and Liping Fan [1]

[1] Institute of Geophysics, China Earthquake Administration, Beijing 100081, China
[2] Key Laboratory of Earthquake Source Physics, China Earthquake Administration, Beijing 100081, China
[3] Institute of Geology and Geophysics, Chinese Academy of Sciences, Beijing 100029, China
[4] Department of Earth and Planetary Sciences, University of California, Riverside, CA 92521, USA
[5] Fujian Earthquake Agency, Fuzhou 350003, China
* Correspondence: flh@cea-igp.ac.cn

Featured Application: P-wave first-motion detection; focal mechanism inversion.

Abstract: P-wave first-motion polarity is important for the inversion of earthquake focal mechanism solutions. The focal mechanism solution can further contribute to our understanding of the source rupture process, the fault structure, and the regional stress field characteristics. By using the abundant focal mechanism solutions of small and moderate earthquakes, we can deepen our understanding of fault geometry and the seismogenic environment. In this paper, we propose an automatic workflow, FocMech-Flow (Focal Mechanism-Flow), for identifying P-wave first-motion polarity and focal mechanism inversion with deep learning and applied it to the 2021 Yangbi earthquake sequence. We use a deep learning model named DiTingMotion to detect the P-wave first-motion polarity of 2389 waveforms, resulting in 98.49% accuracy of polarity discrimination compared with human experts. The focal mechanisms of 112 earthquakes are obtained by using the CHNYTX program, which is 3.7 times more than that of the waveform inversion method, and the results are highly consistent. The analysis shows that the focal mechanisms of the foreshock sequence of the Yangbi earthquake are highly consistent and are all of the strike-slip type; the focal mechanisms of the aftershock sequence are complex, mainly the strike-slip type, but there are also reverse and normal fault types. This study shows that the deep learning method has high reliability in determining the P-wave first-motion polarity, and FocMech-Flow can obtain a large number of focal mechanism solutions from small and moderate earthquakes, having promising application in fine-scale stress inversion.

Keywords: P-wave first-motion; focal mechanism; Yangbi earthquake; deep learning

1. Introduction

The focal mechanism solution reflects the seismogenic fault structure and regional stress field information, which is essential for understanding the regional geological structure and seismicity analysis [1–5]. Compared with moderate and strong earthquakes, small earthquakes (M < 3.0) are more numerous, occur more frequently, and have a wider distribution. The focal mechanisms of small and moderate earthquakes contain a wealth of fault structure information, which is of great significance for the simulation of the earthquake rupture process, the analysis of fault zone characteristics and fault properties, and the inversion of stress fields [4,6–8].

The inversion methods of focal mechanism solutions can be divided into two categories: waveform fitting and P-wave first-motion polarity. For moderate and strong earthquakes (M > 3.5), the waveform inversion method is commonly used to determine the focal mechanism [9–12]. This method uses information carried in the waveform and

Citation: Li, S.; Fang, L.; Xiao, Z.; Zhou, Y.; Liao, S.; Fan, L. FocMech-Flow: Automatic Determination of P-Wave First-Motion Polarity and Focal Mechanism Inversion and Application to the 2021 Yangbi Earthquake Sequence. *Appl. Sci.* **2023**, *13*, 2233. https://doi.org/10.3390/app13042233

Academic Editor: Nicholas Vassiliou Sarlis

Received: 19 January 2023
Revised: 5 February 2023
Accepted: 6 February 2023
Published: 9 February 2023

Copyright: © 2023 by the authors. Licensee MDPI, Basel, Switzerland. This article is an open access article distributed under the terms and conditions of the Creative Commons Attribution (CC BY) license (https://creativecommons.org/licenses/by/4.0/).

can give a good focal mechanism solution even when there are few stations. However, most of the earthquakes recorded by the regional seismic network are small earthquakes below M3.0, with short propagation distances and high-frequency components, making their waveforms difficult to fit and their focal mechanism solutions difficult to obtain. On the other hand, because the rupture of small earthquakes is relatively simple, the results based on the P-wave first-motion polarity are generally consistent with the results based on waveform fitting. Therefore, for small earthquakes (M < 3.0), the first-motion polarity of P-wave inversion is often used to retrieve focal mechanism solutions [1,6,13–16]. Manually identifying the first-motion polarity of a P-wave is stable, reliable, and easy to operate, and it was the earliest method used to study the source mechanism of earthquakes [17]. With the continuous advancement of technology, many focal mechanism inversion methods have been developed, such as [18,19], combining P-wave first-motion polarity and the S/P wave amplitude ratio to determine focal mechanisms, which was called the HASH method. Moreover, [20] used a high-frequency full waveform combined with P-wave first-motion and the S/P wave amplitude ratio to invert the focal mechanism of small earthquakes in a sparse network, and the GPAT [21] method combines P-wave first-motion polarity and generalized maximum amplitude to invert the focal mechanism of earthquakes.

The identification of the P-wave first-motion polarity was performed manually in the past. In recent years, with the construction of the National Intensity Rapid Report and Earthquake Early Warning Project, the number of seismic stations in China has increased from ~1200 to more than 15,000. Manual processing can no longer meet the needs for the development of earthquake monitoring. In order to quickly identify the polarity of a P-wave, seismologists have developed a variety of methods. For example, [22,23] proposed an autoregressive model to automatically determine P-wave first-motion polarity, [24] used the Bayesian probability density function to identify the polarity of a P-wave, and [25] focused on mutual information and maximum order statistics in information theory to determine the P-wave first-motion polarity. However, when the signal-to-noise ratio of the waveform is low, these automatic algorithms based on rules are unable to achieve reliable first-motion polarity discrimination, and manual review is required. In addition, these algorithms only use limited discriminant parameters, and it is difficult to reflect the complete waveform characteristics, which restricts the accuracy of the algorithm.

With the rise of deep learning, data-driven algorithms have made breakthroughs in tasks such as object detection and classification, and have been widely used not only in image recognition [26,27] and speech recognition [28,29], but also developed rapidly in the field of seismology, such as earthquake detection [30,31], seismic phase picking [32–35], earthquake classification [36,37], and focal mechanism inversion [38,39]. The P-wave first-motion polarity is usually divided into three categories: upward, downward, and uncertain. Therefore, the discrimination of incipient polarity can be regarded as a classification problem, and the automatic identification of first-motion polarity can be realized by using a large number of known labels for supervised learning. Specifically, Refs. [40–43] used data from Southern California, Japan, and Taiwan, China, and used a convolutional neural network to try to realize the automatic determination of the first-motion polarity of P-waves, and they achieved good results.

In this paper, based on a deep-learning P-wave first-motion picking model named DiTingMotion [44,45], we detected the P-wave first motions of the 2021 Yangbi Ms6.4 earthquake sequence and compared them with the manual picking results and the rule-based automatic algorithm. The P-wave first-motion polarity discriminative effect of the model was evaluated using 2389 P-wave first-motion polarities detected by DiTingMotion; the focal mechanisms of 112 earthquakes were retrieved by the CHNYTX program [16]. The FocMech-Flow process for the automatic inversion of focal mechanisms using P-wave first-motion was established. Compared to the results of other methods, the feasibility of automatic inversion of the focal mechanism solution was analyzed.

2. FocMech-Flow Workflow

The workflow of FocMech-Flow for focal mechanism inversion is shown in Figure 1. The main steps consist of four parts:

1. Seismic Event Screening. Seismic events satisfying focal mechanism inversion are selected from the observation report. Seismic events recorded by at least 10 stations and with a maximum gap angle less than 70° are selected.
2. Data Preprocessing. According to the P-wave arrival time in the observation report picked by analysts, we take the P-wave arrival time as the center, cut a 4-s waveform window, and carry out de-mean, de-trend, and amplitude normalization processing.
3. Determination of the P-Wave First-Motion Polarity. The preprocessed vertical component waveform is centered on the P-wave arrival time; we cut a 1.28-s waveform window, detected by DiTingMotion, and the polarity of the P-wave is given.
4. Focal Mechanism Inversion. According to the earthquake location, station location, and regional velocity model, we calculate the takeoff angle, combined with the first-motion polarity, and invert the focal mechanism with the CHNYTX program.

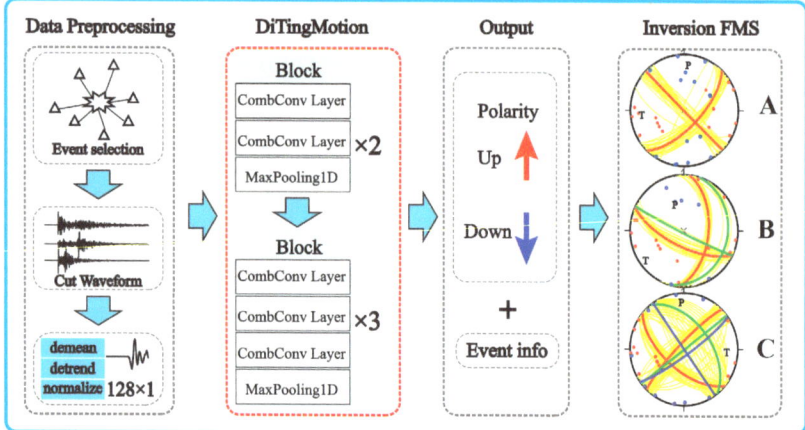

Figure 1. FocMech-Flow flow chart for focal mechanism inversion. A, B and C represent three levels of reliability of the focal mechanism solution. A is the best, B is the second, and C is the worst. P and T are the pressure axis and tension axis, respectively.

The first-motion polarity of the P-wave is detected automatically by DiTingMotion. DiTingMotion was trained by [45,46] using the DiTing dataset [44] and the first-motion dataset from the Southern California Seismic Network [40]. DiTingMotion is a deep learning model based on a convolution neural network. The model consists of five convolution modules. The first two convolution modules contain two one-dimensional convolution layers and one maximum pooling layer, respectively. The last three convolution modules contain three one-dimensional convolution layers and one maximum pooling layer, respectively. In the last three convolution modules, each module outputs a set of polarity predictions and then determines the P-wave polarity as "Up" or "Down" by comparing the probability threshold. See Ref. [45] for details about the network structure, training process, and test results of DiTingMotion.

The CHNYTX program [16] is used for focal mechanism inversion, which is based on the grid research method [6,14]. By improving the calculation of the weight factor of the data points and the dynamic clustering of solution areas, the reliability of the focal mechanism is evaluated according to the number of clustering centers, the lowest weighted contradiction ratio, and the minimum root mean square (RMS) of the rotation angle.

3. Yangbi Earthquake Sequence

At 21:48 on 21 May 2021 (Beijing time), a Ms 6.4 earthquake occurred in Yangbi, Yunnan (Figure 2). The epicenter was located at 25.63° N, 99.92° E, with a focal depth of 8 km. Around 27 min before the mainshock, an M_L 5.4 foreshock occurred. The foreshock activity of this earthquake was very obvious, and more than 4600 aftershocks occurred two weeks after the mainshock [47–51]. There were 88 seismic stations around the mainshock, with good azimuthal coverage. The phase arrivals and P-wave first-motion polarity were picked manually by experienced analysts, which provided good observation data to study the focal mechanisms of this sequence and compare different methods for the automatic determination of the P-wave first-motion polarity [52–57].

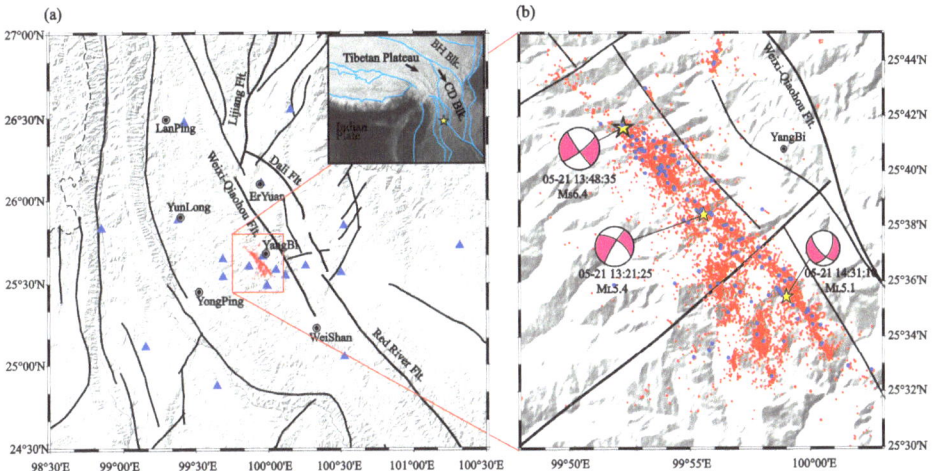

Figure 2. Seismic stations, faults, and epicenters of the Yangbi earthquake sequence. (**a**) The tectonic setting of the Yangbi earthquake. Black lines indicate faults [58], blue triangles indicate seismic stations, and red dots represent the epicenters of the sequence. The blue line in the inset indicates the boundary of the active block, and the yellow five-pointed star indicates the mainshock. (**b**) The distribution of the Yangbi earthquake sequence (red dots), the epicenters of 112 earthquakes used for focal mechanism inversion (blue dots), and the focal mechanism solutions of large earthquakes.

The observation report and earthquake waveforms were provided by the Yunnan Earthquake Agency. We selected events with at least ten first-motion polarities [42]. There were 112 events with 2389 P-wave first-motion polarities that met the requirements. The magnitude range of 112 events was $1.6 \leq M_L \leq 5.7$, of which 50 earthquakes were below $M_L 3.0$.

4. The Detection Results of P-Wave First-Motion Polarity

The experts from the Yunnan Earthquake Agency processed 2389 P-wave first-motion polarities of 112 earthquakes, of which 1360 polarities were upward and 1029 polarities were downward. To ensure the reliability of the first-motion polarities, we conducted a review and corrected 13 polarities with obvious errors. The detection results of DiTingMotion showed that 2353 polarities were consistent and 36 polarities were inconsistent, with an accuracy rate of 98.49% (Table 1). Among them, there were 1376 polarities detected as upward, with an accuracy rate of 99.19%; there were 1013 polarities recognized as downward, with an accuracy rate of 97.38%. After visual inspection, the 36 waveforms that were identified incorrectly were mainly due to the low signal-to-noise ratio and difficulty in distinguishing first-motion polarity, which led to the inconsistency between DiTingMotion and manual picks (Supplementary Figure S1).

Table 1. Comparison of polarity classification results obtained with different methods.

Method	Up	Down	Uncertain	TP	FP	TP/ALL
DiTingMotion (This Study)	1376	1013	0	2353	36	98.49%
PhasePApy [23]	768	509	1112	1275	2	53.37%
NPC [59]	1366	1023	0	2261	128	94.64%

Note: Uncertain indicates the number of polarities that cannot be determined; TP and FP represent the numbers of consistent and inconsistent polarities between automatic methods and manual discrimination; ALL represents 2389 P-wave first-motion polarities used for test; TP/ALL represents the accuracy.

In order to compare the advantages and disadvantages of different methods for identifying the first-motion polarity of the P-wave, we selected the PhasePApy [23] and the Network for Polarity Classification (NPC) [59] model, and compared the detection results with DiTingMotion (Table 1). PhasePApy uses a rule-based automatic algorithm to distinguish P-wave first-motion polarities and divides them into three categories: upward, downward, and uncertain. The NPC model is developed on the basis of a convolutional neural network and attention mechanism, and outputs upward and downward results. The NPC model used in this study was trained with data from Southern California and Oklahoma, Japan, Italy, and Taiwan, Chinese Mainland.

It can be seen from Table 1 that the two models trained by deep learning have accuracy higher than 90% in the classification of the P-wave polarity. DiTingMotion used 641,025 P-wave first-motion polarity data from the Chinese Mainland in the past 10 years for training. It had the highest accuracy and was more suitable for detecting earthquakes in China. The NPC model used only part of the DiTing dataset, and the detection accuracy was slightly lower than that of DiTingMotion. However, PhasePApy discriminated the polarity according to the threshold given manually, and its ability to distinguish the characteristics of different waveforms was weak, which led to misdetection in nearly half of all cases. It can be seen that the deep learning models have obvious advantages over traditional rule-based methods in the detection of the P-wave first-motion polarity.

5. Robustness of P-Wave First-Motion Polarity

In Ref. [15], the authors calibrated the polarity error rate for the handmade first-motion polarities with similar events and found that ~10% of the impulsive polarities and ~20% of the emergent polarities were wrong. In order to test the robustness of the DiTingMotion, we flipped the amplitudes of 2389 waveforms and detected their polarities with DiTingMotion again. The test showed that for 2389 reversed waveforms, 56 polarities were misidentified. The detection accuracy was 97.66%, which was similar to that before the waveform flip. This test indicated that DiTingMotion has good robustness in determining the first-motion polarity.

The precision of the P-wave arrival time will affect the discrimination of first-motion polarity, especially when there is strong noise before the P-wave, which may cause the opposite sign of the first motion. To investigate whether the detection results were affected by the P-wave arrival time, we added a random shift to the P-wave arrival times of 2389 waveforms to simulate the picking error. The predominant P-wave period of the local earthquakes recorded by the regional network was generally 0.1–0.2 s. We applied a random error within ± 0.1 s to the arrival time of the P-wave, and cut the waveforms with the shifted arrival times. Then, we detected the polarities with DiTingMotion again. Tests showed that when the arrival time of the P-wave was incorrectly marked, the detection accuracy of P-wave first-motion polarities decreased by 5.61–22.1% (Table 2).

Table 2. Detection accuracy of P-wave first-motion polarity before and after shifting the arrival time.

Random Error	0	±0.1 s	+0.1 s	−0.1 s
Accuracy (all)	98.49%	84.26%	76.39%	92.88%
Accuracy (SNR ≥ 30 dB)	99.60%	87.69%	82.85%	95.58%
Accuracy (SNR < 30 dB)	97.57%	81.12%	71.96%	92.22%

To further analyze the reason for the drop in accuracy, we calculated the signal-to-noise ratio (SNR) of the waveform. The formula for calculating SNR is as follows:

$$\text{SNR} = 10 \times \log_{10}\left(\frac{\text{signal}}{\text{noise}}\right)^2 \tag{1}$$

where signal is the maximum absolute value of the amplitude in the signal window, noise is the root mean square of the waveform amplitude in the noise window, and the unit of SNR is dB. The signal window is taken as 0.5 s after the arrival time of the P-wave, and the noise window is taken as 0.5–1.5 s before the arrival time of the P-wave.

We take the SNR of 30 dB as the boundary, divide the data into two categories— high SNR and low SNR—and calculate the detection accuracy at different SNRs (Table 2). When the SNR is high, the arrival deviation has less influence on the accuracy of polarity detection; however, when the picked arrival time is earlier, the false detection rate is higher. It can be seen that when using DiTingMotion to detect the P-wave first-motion polarities, the picking accuracy of the P-wave arrival time should be as accurate as possible. For the manually picked arrival times, one can use deep learning-based methods, such as Refs. [32,34], etc., to detect the event waveform again, and select the waveform that is manually and automatically marked at the same time (the residual less than 0.1 s) to detect its first-motion polarities. On the one hand, this can ensure the reliability of the first-motion polarities. On the other hand, it can also improve the waveform utilization. In some cases, only the arrival time is picked manually, but the initial movement symbol is not given.

6. Focal Mechanism Solutions of the Yangbi Earthquake Sequence

Using 2389 P-wave first-motion polarities of the above 112 earthquakes, the focal mechanism solutions of 112 earthquakes were inverted by the CHNYTX program [16]. Referring to the evaluation metrics in [16] (Table 3), the inversion results were divided into three classes, A, B, and C. There were 43 in Class A, 9 in Class B, and 60 in Class C. The detailed parameters of the focal mechanism solutions are shown in Supplementary Table S1.

Table 3. Focal mechanism solution quality evaluation [16].

Classes	Evaluation Threshold
A	$\Psi_{min} \leq 0.15$, and $N_C = 1$, and RMS $\leq 15°$
B	Each parameter is between Class A and Class C
C	$\Psi_{min} \geq = 0.30$, or $N_C \geq 2$

Note: Ψ_{min} denotes the minimum weighted contradiction ratio; N_C denotes the number of clustering centers; RMS denotes the minimum root mean square of the rotation angle.

The focal mechanism solutions of approximately 30 earthquakes with $M_L \geq 3.5$ have been obtained by using the waveform inversion method [52–55,57]. In this study, we determined 112 focal mechanism solutions using the P-wave first-motion polarity, which is 3.7 times that of the waveform inversion method (Figure 3). Among the 112 earthquakes, there are 40 earthquakes with $M_L \geq 3.5$ and 50 earthquakes with $M_L < 3.0$, and the minimum magnitude is $M_L 1.6$. This shows that when the stations are well distributed, the focal mechanism of a large number of small earthquakes can be retrieved using the P-wave first-motion data.

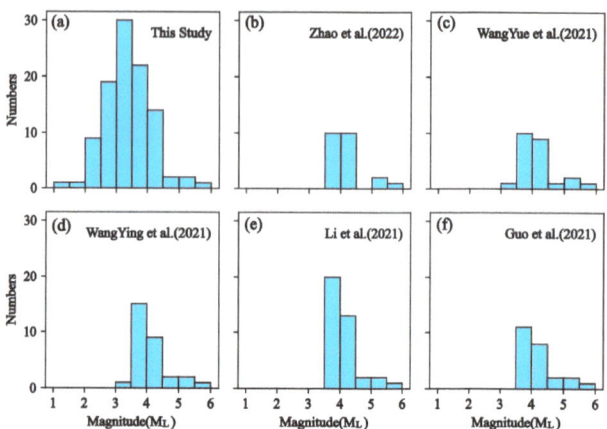

Figure 3. Statistics of the focal mechanism solutions for $1 \leq M_L \leq 6.4$. (**a**–**f**) denotes the magnitude distribution of the focal mechanisms obtained in this study and Refs. [52–55,57].

To verify the reliability of the new inversion results, we selected 10 earthquakes with focal mechanism solutions from published articles that have been commonly studied (Figure 4). We measured the consistency of the focal mechanism solutions [60] using the Kagan angle (*KA*). We calculated *KA* with the FMcenter program [61]. When *KA* is less than 25°, it can be considered that the focal mechanism solutions are consistent [62]. Figure 4 is the comparison result. The standard deviation of the *KA* obtained in this paper is less than 24°, which is in good agreement with previous results. It shows that the focal mechanism solution obtained by FocMech-Flow inversion is reliable.

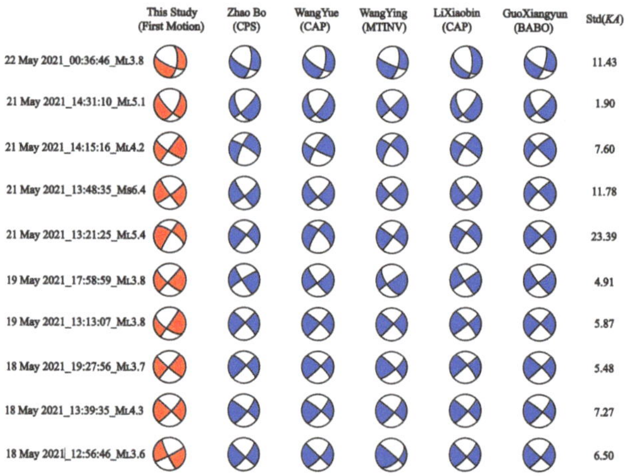

Figure 4. Comparison of focal mechanism solutions between different studies.

The leftmost column is the earthquake information; the rightmost column is the standard deviation of the Kagan angle.

Previous studies have shown that the Yangbi earthquake sequence occurred on a secondary fault parallel to the Weixi-Qiaohou fault [52,53,55,56]. This right-lateral strike-slip fault can be regarded as the northward extension of the Red River fault zone [63]. We used the FMC program [64] to classify the focal mechanisms (Figure 5). The results showed that there were 31 strike-slip events (SS), 35 strike-slip types with normal fault components (SS-N), 17 normal fault types with strike-slip components (N-SS), 15 strike-slip types with reverse components (SS-R), 9 normal fault types (N), 2 reverse fault types (R), and 3 reverse fault types with strike-slip components (R-SS).

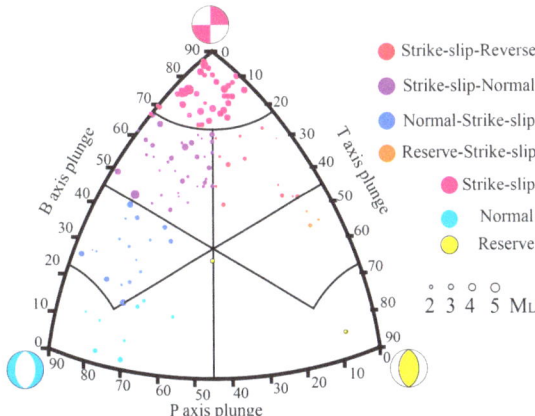

Figure 5. Types of focal mechanism solutions of the Yangbi earthquake sequence.

We divided the magnitude–time (M-T) diagram of the Yangbi earthquake sequence from 18 to 28 May into two phases: foreshock and aftershock sequences. Figure 6 shows the focal mechanism solutions of this study for some large earthquakes ($M_L \geq 3.5$). We found that the focal mechanisms of the foreshocks were consistent, and they were all strike-slip-type events. The earthquakes were distributed along the NW-SE direction, and the largest $M_L 5.4$ foreshock occurred at the southeast end of the foreshock sequence. The focal mechanisms of the aftershocks were complex. The focal mechanism of the mainshock was the strike-slip type, and the focal mechanism of the largest aftershock $M_L 5.1$ was the strike-slip type with a normal fault component. Earthquakes at the periphery of the source region had prominent normal fault components, and very few of them had normal fault events. The focal mechanisms with the strike-slip and normal-fault components accounted for more than 92% of the total inversion results in this study, which was consistent with the regional tectonic background (Figures 5 and 6). In particular, the focal mechanism solutions for the foreshock sequence were not only highly consistent, but their nodal planes had an NW-SE orientation (Figure 6b), which is consistent with the seismogenic tectonics of this earthquake, as suggested by previous studies. Although the focal mechanisms of the aftershocks were relatively complex, the orientation of the nodal planes of the source mechanism solution for most aftershocks was also consistent with the seismogenic tectonics. This indicates that the focal mechanisms obtained in this study are highly credible.

It was found that there were differences in the consistency of the focal mechanisms between foreshocks and aftershocks [65–67], which was proposed to describe the seismicity with parameter K ($K \in [-1, 1]$) using the consistency of the focal mechanisms. High K means high consistency of the focal mechanism. In addition, KA can also reflect the consistency of the focal mechanisms. Except for the largest foreshock ($M_L 5.4$) whose KA was more than 30°, the KA values of other foreshocks were all less than 25°, indicating that the focal mechanisms were consistent (Figure 7c). On the contrary, the KA of the aftershocks has a wide distribution range and low consistency. The seismicity parameter K and the KA of the foreshock and aftershock changed before and after the mainshock. The focal mechanisms of the foreshock sequence were consistent, all of which were of the strike-slip type with high K values, which reflects that the stress in the source area accumulated continuously before the mainshock, resulting in the stress field tending to be uniform. This is consistent with the previous research that considered that the foreshocks were controlled by a unified stress field, and the focal mechanism solutions had high similarity [8,65,68,69]. After the mainshock, the number of aftershocks with different types of focal mechanisms increased, the K value decreased, and the KA increased, all of which reflected the adjustment process of the stress field in the source area [8,70–72].

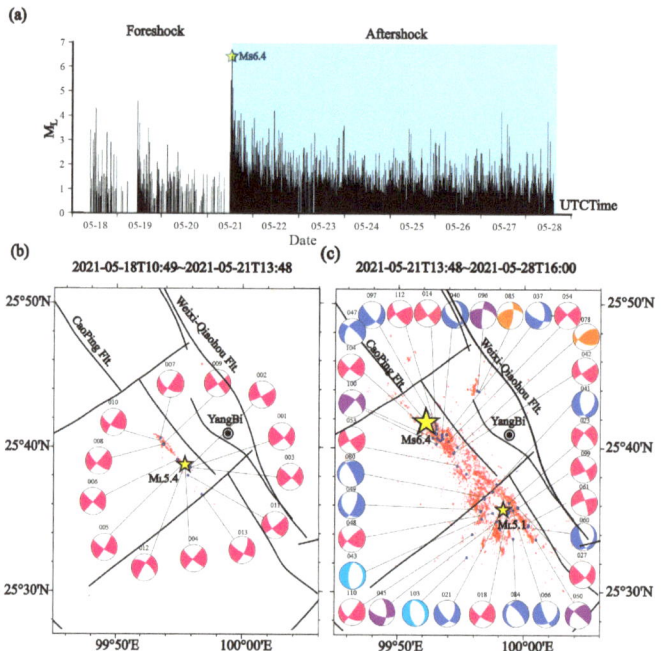

Figure 6. M-T diagram, earthquake distribution, and focal mechanism solutions for foreshocks and aftershocks. (**a**) M-T diagram of the Yangbi earthquake sequence. The yellow star indicates the mainshock. (**b**) Focal mechanism solutions of the foreshock sequence. (**c**) Focal mechanisms of the mainshock and aftershocks. The color of the beach ball represents different types of focal mechanisms (see Figure 5).

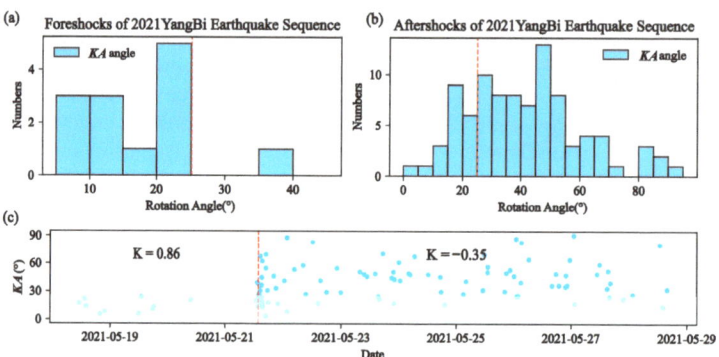

Figure 7. Temporal variation in KA angle and K value in the Yangbi earthquake sequence. (**a**) KA angle of the foreshock sequence. (**b**) KA angle of the aftershock sequence. (**c**) K value for the consistency of the foreshock and aftershock (light green indicates $KA \leq 25°$), and the red dotted line separates the foreshock and aftershock. The red dotted lines in (**a**,**b**) indicate $25°$ KA angle.

7. Conclusions

Taking the Yangbi earthquake sequence in 2021 as an example, this paper discusses the feasibility of the automatic discrimination of the polarity of P-wave first motion and its application in focal mechanism inversion and establishes a workflow named FocMech-Flow for automatic focal mechanism inversion by using P-wave first motion. The main conclusions are as follows.

(1) Compared with manual and rule-based methods, deep learning-based methods have high accuracy in determining P-wave first-motion polarity. Even if there is a 0.1-s error in the P-wave arrival time, the recognition accuracy of the P-wave first-motion polarity is still over 80%.

(2) Focal mechanism solutions of 112 earthquakes in the Yangbi earthquake sequence were determined with FocMech-Flow, which were in good agreement with previous results. FocMech-Flow can reduce the lower limit of focal mechanism inversion to approximately $M_L 2.0$, and can obtain a large number of focal mechanism solutions for small and moderate earthquakes ($M_L \leq 3.0$), which provides extensive data to depict the fine fault geometry and stress field inversion.

(3) The Yangbi earthquake sequence is mainly strike-slip. A few earthquakes have normal fault components. The focal mechanisms with strike-slip and normal fault components account for more than 92% of events. The focal mechanisms of the Yangbi foreshock sequence are highly similar to that of the mainshock. The consistency of focal mechanism solutions decreases for the aftershock sequence, which reflects the stress field adjustment after the earthquake.

Supplementary Materials: The following supporting information can be downloaded at: https://www.mdpi.com/article/10.3390/app13042233/s1, Figure S1: Inconsistent discrimination between DiTingMotion and analysts. The red dotted line indicates P-wave arrival time. Light blue shading region indicates the DiTingMotion detection window (± 0.64 s centered at the P-wave arrival time); Figure S2: Consistent discrimination between DiTingMotion and analysts. The red dashed line indicates the arrival time of P-wave. Light blue shading indicates the DiTingMotion detection window (± 0.64 s centered at the P-wave arrival time); Table S1: The source parameters of 112 earthquakes in this paper.

Author Contributions: Conceptualization, S.L. (Shuai Li), L.F. (Lihua Fang) and Y.Z.; Data curation, S.L. (Shuai Li), S.L. (Shirong Liao) and L.F. (Liping Fan); Formal analysis, S.L. (Shuai Li); Funding acquisition, L.F. (Lihua Fang); Investigation, S.L. (Shuai Li); Methodology, L.F. (Lihua Fang) and Z.X.; Project administration, L.F. (Lihua Fang); Resources, L.F. (Lihua Fang), Z.X., Y.Z., S.L. (Shirong Liao) and L.F. (Liping Fan); Software, S.L. (Shuai Li), Z.X. and L.F. (Liping Fan); Supervision, S.L. (Shuai Li), L.F. (Lihua Fang), Z.X., Y.Z. and S.L. (Shirong Liao); Validation, S.L. (Shuai Li); Writing—original draft, S.L. (Shuai Li); Writing—review and editing, L.F. (Lihua Fang), Z.X., Y.Z. and S.L. (Shirong Liao). All authors have read and agreed to the published version of the manuscript.

Funding: National Key R & D Plan: 2021YFC3000702 and Basic Research Project of the Institute of Geophysics, China Earthquake Administration: DQJB22X08.

Institutional Review Board Statement: Not applicable.

Informed Consent Statement: Not applicable.

Data Availability Statement: The data and code are available upon request.

Acknowledgments: We would like to thank the Yunnan Earthquake Agency for providing high-quality observation reports and waveform data, Qiushi Zhai for providing the NPC model, and Shuzhong Sheng, Xiangyun Guo, ZhaoMing, and Zhe Zhang for the suggestions in preparing the manuscript. This research was supported by the National Key Research and Development Program of China (2021YFC3000702) and the Special Fund of the Institute of Geophysics, China Earthquake Administration (DQJB22X08). The figures were plotted with GMT6 (https://www.generic-mapping-tools.org, accessed on 15 January 2022) and Matplotlib (https://matplotlib.org, accessed on 15 January 2022).

Conflicts of Interest: The authors declare no conflict of interest.

References

1. Xu, Z.; Liu, Y.; Zhang, Y. On the characteristic of direction of the earthquake stress field around the Beijing aera. *Acta Seismol. Sin.* **1979**, *1*, 121–132.
2. Gephart, J.W.; Forsyth, D.W. An Improved Method for Determining the Regional Stress Tensor Using Earthquake Focal Mechanism Data: Application to the San Fernando Earthquake Sequence. *J. Geophys. Res.* **1984**, *89*, 9305–9320. [CrossRef]
3. Wan, Y.; Sheng, S.; Huang, J.; Li, X.; Chen, X. The Grid Search Algorithm of Tectonic Stress Tensor Based on Focal Mechanism Data and Its Application in the Boundary Zone of China, Vietnam and Laos. *J. Earth Sci.* **2016**, *27*, 777–785. [CrossRef]
4. Sheng, S.; Chen, G.; Xu, X.; Wan, Y.; Li, H.; Gong, M.; Wang, X.; Zhang, X.; Zhang, X. Identification of seismogenic faults between focal nodal planes based on tectonic stress fields with applications to the Yingjiang area. *Chin. J. Geophys.* **2022**, *65*, 4273–4283. (In Chinese) [CrossRef]
5. Jia, K.; Zhou, S. Inference of source parameters of historical major earthquakes from 1900 to 1970 in southwestern China and analysis of their uncertainties. *Chin. J. Geophys.* **2012**, *55*, 2948–2962. (In Chinese) [CrossRef]
6. Xu, Z.; Yan, M.; Zhao, Z. Evaluation of the direction of tectonic stress in north China from recorded data of a large number of small earthquakes. *Acta Seismol. Sin.* **1983**, *5*, 268–279.
7. Luo, Y.; Ni, S.; Zeng, X.; Zheng, Y.; Chen, Q.; Chen, Y. A shallow aftershock sequence in the north-eastern end of the Wenchuan earthquake aftershock zone. *Sci. China Earth Sci.* **2010**, *40*, 677–687. [CrossRef]
8. Cheng, Y.; Ben-Zion, Y. Variations of Earthquake Properties Before, During, and After the 2019 M7.1 Ridgecrest, CA, Earthquake. *Geophys. Res. Lett.* **2020**, *47*, e2020GL089650. [CrossRef]
9. Zhao, L.; Helmberger, D.V. Source Estimation from Broadband Regional Seismograms. *Bull. Seismol. Soc. Am.* **1994**, *84*, 91–104.
10. Zhu, L.; Helmberger, D.V. Advancement in Source Estimation Techniques Using Broadband Regional Seismograms. *Bull. Seismol. Soc. Am.* **1996**, *86*, 1634–1641. [CrossRef]
11. Zhu, L.; Zhou, X. Seismic Moment Tensor Inversion Using 3D Velocity Model and Its Application to the 2013 Lushan Earthquake Sequence. *Phys. Chem. Earth Parts ABC* **2016**, *95*, 10–18. [CrossRef]
12. Wang, X.; Zhan, Z. Moving from 1-D to 3-D Velocity Model: Automated Waveform-Based Earthquake Moment Tensor Inversion in the Los Angeles Region. *Geophys. J. Int.* **2020**, *220*, 218–234. [CrossRef]
13. Li, Q.; Zhang, Z.; Jin, Y.; Yu, X.; Li, Z. Focal mechanisms of tangshan earthquakes. *Seismol. Geol.* **1980**, *2*, 59–67.
14. Xu, X.; Xu, Z.; Zhang, D. A probabilistic grid test method of determining earthquake focal mechanisms using P-wave onset polarity data. *Seismol. Geomagn. Obs. Res.* **1995**, *16*, 34–42.
15. Hardebeck, J.L.; Shearer, P.M. A New Method for Determining First-Motion Focal Mechanisms. *Bull. Seismol. Soc. Am.* **2002**, *92*, 2264–2276. [CrossRef]
16. Yu, C.; Tao, K.; Cui, X.; Hu, X.; Ning, J. P-wave first-motion focal mechanism solutions and their quality evaluation. *Chin. J. Geophys.* **2009**, *52*, 1402–1411. (In Chinese) [CrossRef]
17. Chen, Y.; Liu, R. The use of the first P motion data for earthquake focal mechanism determination: A tutorial(1). *Seismol. Geomagn. Obs. Res.* **2021**, *42*, 1–14. [CrossRef]
18. Hardebeck, J.L.; Shearer, P.M. Using S/P Amplitude Ratios to Constrain the Focal Mechanisms of Small Earthquakes. *Bull. Seismol. Soc. Am.* **2003**, *93*, 2434–2444. [CrossRef]
19. Hardebeck, J.L. HASH: A FORTRAN Program for Computing Earthquake First-Motion Focal Mechanisms. 2008. Available online: https://www.geo.uib.no/seismo/SOFTWARE/SEISAN/OLDER_VERSIONS/SEISAN_10.4.1/alpha/PCWIN/INF/hash.pdf (accessed on 15 January 2021).
20. Li, J.; Zhang, H.; Kuleli, H.S.; Toksoz, M.N. Focal Mechanism Determination Using High-Frequency Waveform Matching and Its Application to Small Magnitude Induced Earthquakes: Focal Mechanism by Waveform Matching. *Geophys. J. Int.* **2011**, *184*, 1261–1274. [CrossRef]
21. Yan, C.; Xu, L. An inversion technique for the mechanisms of local and regional earthquakes: Generalized polarity and amplitude technique (I)—Principle and numerical tests. *Chin. J. Geophys.* **2014**, *57*, 2555–2572. (In Chinese) [CrossRef]
22. Nakamura, M. Automatic Determination of Focal Mechanism Solutions Using Initial Motion Polarities of P and S Waves. *Phys. Earth Planet. Inter.* **2004**, *146*, 531–549. [CrossRef]
23. Chen, C.; Holland, A.A. PhasePApy: A Robust Pure Python Package for Automatic Identification of Seismic Phases. *Seismol. Res. Lett.* **2016**, *87*, 1384–1396. [CrossRef]
24. Pugh, D.J.; White, R.S.; Christie, P.A.F. Automatic Bayesian Polarity Determination. *Geophys. J. Int.* **2016**, *206*, 275–291. [CrossRef]
25. Pei, W.; Zhou, S. Automatic P-wave polarity determination and focal mechanism inversion based on maximum order statistics and its application in Xiaojiang Fault Zone, Yunnan. *Chin. J. Geophys.* **2022**, *65*, 992–1005. (In Chinese) [CrossRef]
26. Farabet, C.; Couprie, C.; Najman, L.; LeCun, Y. Learning Hierarchical Features for Scene Labeling. *IEEE Trans. Pattern Anal. Mach. Intell.* **2013**, *35*, 1915–1929. [CrossRef] [PubMed]
27. Tompson, J.; Jain, A.; LeCun, Y.; Bregler, C. Joint training ofa convolutional network and a graphical model for human poseestimation. *Adv. Neural Inf. Process. Syst.* **2014**, *2*, 1799–1807.
28. Mikolov, T.; Deoras, A.; Povey, D. Strategies for training large scale neural network language models. In Proceedings of the 2011 IEEE Workshop on Automatic Speech Recognition & Understanding, Waikoloa, HI, USA, 11–15 December 2012; pp. 11–15.

29. Sainath, T.N.; Mohamed, A.; Kingsbury, B.; Ramabhadran, B. Deep Convolutional neural networks for LVCSR. In Proceedings of the 2013 IEEE International Conference on Acoustics, Speech and Signal Processing, Vancouver, BC, Canada, 26–31 May 2013; pp. 8614–8618.
30. Perol, T.; Gharbi, M.; Denolle, M. Convolutional neural network for Earthquake Detection and Location. *Sci. Adv.* **2018**, *4*, e1700578. [CrossRef]
31. Meier, M.; Ross, Z.E.; Ramachandran, A.; Balakrishna, A.; Nair, S.; Kundzicz, P.; Li, Z.; Andrews, J.; Hauksson, E.; Yue, Y. Reliable Real-Time Seismic Signal/Noise Discrimination with Machine Learning. *J. Geophys. Res. Solid Earth* **2019**, *124*, 788–800. [CrossRef]
32. Zhu, W.; Beroza, G.C. PhaseNet: A Deep-Neural-Network-Based Seismic Arrival Time Picking Method. *Geophys. J. Int.* **2018**, *216*, 261–273. [CrossRef]
33. Zhou, Y.; Yue, H.; Kong, Q.; Zhou, S. Hybrid Event Detection and Phase-Picking Algorithm Using Convolutional and Recurrent Neural Networks. *Seismol. Res. Lett.* **2019**, *90*, 1079–1087. [CrossRef]
34. Mousavi, S.M.; Ellsworth, W.L.; Zhu, W.; Chuang, L.Y.; Beroza, G.C. Earthquake Transformer—An Attentive Deep-Learning Model for Simultaneous Earthquake Detection and Phase Picking. *Nat. Commun.* **2020**, *11*, 3952. [CrossRef] [PubMed]
35. Zhu, J.; Li, Z.; Fang, L. USTC-Pickers: A Unified Set of Seismic Phase Pickers Transfer Learned for China. *Earthq. Sci.* **2022**, *36*, 1–11.
36. Li, Z.; Meier, M.-A.; Hauksson, E.; Zhan, Z.; Andrews, J. Machine Learning Seismic Wave Discrimination: Application to Earthquake Early Warning. *Geophys. Res. Lett.* **2018**, *45*, 4773–4779. [CrossRef]
37. Miao, F.; Carpenter, N.S.; Wang, Z.; Holcomb, A.S.; Woolery, E.W. High-Accuracy Discrimination of Blasts and Earthquakes Using Neural Networks With Multiwindow Spectral Data. *Seismol. Res. Lett.* **2020**, *91*, 1646–1659. [CrossRef]
38. Kuang, W.; Yuan, C.; Zhang, J. Real-Time Determination of Earthquake Focal Mechanism via Deep Learning. *Nat. Commun.* **2021**, *12*, 1432. [CrossRef]
39. Kuang, W.; Yuan, C.; Zhang, J.; Zhang, W. Relative Focal Mechanism Inversion and Its Application to Ridgecrest Sequence. *Seismol. Res. Lett.* **2022**, *13*, 305–317. [CrossRef]
40. Ross, Z.E.; Meier, M.; Hauksson, E. P Wave Arrival Picking and First-Motion Polarity Determination With Deep Learning. *J. Geophys. Res. Solid Earth* **2018**, *123*, 5120–5129. [CrossRef]
41. Hara, S.; Fukahata, Y.; Iio, Y. P-Wave First-Motion Polarity Determination of Waveform Data in Western Japan Using Deep Learning. *Earth Planets Space* **2019**, *71*, 127. [CrossRef]
42. Uchide, T. Focal Mechanisms of Small Earthquakes beneath the Japanese Islands Based on First-Motion Polarities Picked Using Deep Learning. *Geophys. J. Int.* **2020**, *223*, 1658–1671. [CrossRef]
43. Zhai, Q.; Peng, Z.; Chuang, L.Y.; Wu, Y.; Hsu, Y.; Wdowinski, S. Investigating the Impacts of a Wet Typhoon on Microseismicity: A Case Study of the 2009 Typhoon Morakot in Taiwan Based on a Template Matching Catalog. *J. Geophys. Res. Solid Earth* **2021**, *126*, e2021JB023026. [CrossRef]
44. Zhao, M.; Xiao, Z.; Chen, S.; Fang, L. DiTing: A Large-Scale Chinese Seismic Benchmark Dataset for Artificial Intelligence in Seismology. *Earthq. Sci.* **2022**, *35*, 1–11.
45. Zhao, M.; Xiao, Z.; Zhang, M.; Yang, Y.; Tang, L.; Chen, S. DiTingMotion: A Deep-Learning First- Motion-Polarity Classifier and Its Application to Focal Mechanism Inversion. **2022**; *in review*.
46. Xiao, Z. *Deep-Learning for Data Processing in Seismology*; Institute of Geology and Geophysics, Chinese Academy of Sciences (CAS): Beijing, China, 2022.
47. Zhou, Y.; Ghosh, A.; Fang, L.; Yue, H.; Zhou, S.; Su, Y. A High-Resolution Seismic Catalog for the 2021 M_S6.4/M_W6.1 Yangbi Earthquake Sequence, Yunnan, China: Application of AI Picker and Matched Filter. *Earthq. Sci.* **2021**, *34*, 390–398. [CrossRef]
48. Zhou, Y.; Ren, C.; Ghosh, A.; Meng, H.; Fang, L.; Yue, H.; Zhou, S.; Su, Y. Seismological Characterization of the 2021 Yangbi Foreshock-Mainshock Sequence, Yunnan, China: More than a Triggered Cascade. *J. Geophys. Res. Solid Earth* **2022**, *127*, e2022JB024534. [CrossRef]
49. Liu, M.; Li, H.; Li, L.; Zhang, M.; Wang, W. Multistage Nucleation of the 2021 Yangbi M_S 6.4 Earthquake, Yunnan, China and Its Foreshocks. *J. Geophys. Res. Solid Earth.* **2022**, *127*, e2022JB024091. [CrossRef]
50. Yang, T.; Li, B.; Fang, L.; Su, Y.; Zhong, Y.; Yang, J.; Qin, M.; Xu, Y. Relocation of the Foreshocks and Aftershocks of the 2021 Ms 6.4 Yangbi Earthquake Sequence, Yunnan, China. *J. Earth Sci.* **2022**, *33*, 892–900. [CrossRef]
51. Zhu, G.; Yang, H.; Tan, Y.J.; Jin, M.; Li, X.; Yang, W. The Cascading Foreshock Sequence of the Ms 6.4 Yangbi Earthquake in Yunnan, China. *Earth Planet. Sci. Lett.* **2022**, *591*, 117594. [CrossRef]
52. Li, X.; Jin, M.; Huang, Y.; Cha, W.; Wang, J.; Li, S. Staged Characteristics on the Consistency Parameters of the Focal Mechanisms of the 2021 Yangbi MS6.4 Earthquake Sequence in Yunnan. *Earthq. Res. Adv.* **2021**, *34*, 100061. [CrossRef]
53. Wang, Y.; Hu, S.; He, X.; Guo, K.; Xie, M.; Deng, S.; Ma, Y. Relocation and focal mechanism solutions of the 21 May 2021 Ms6.4 Yunnan Yangbi earthquake sequence. *Chin. J. Geophys.* **2021**, *64*, 4510–4525. (In Chinese) [CrossRef]
54. Wang, Y.; Zhao, T.; Hu, J.; Liu, C. Relocation and Focal Mechanism Solutions of the 2021 Yangbi, Yunnan M_s6.4 earthquake sequence. *Seismol. Geol.* **2021**, *43*, 847–863.
55. Guo, X.; Yin, H.; Wang, Z.; Yang, H. Earthquake centroid, seismic moment tensor and dynamic environment analysis of the Ms6.4 earthquake sequence in Yangbi, Yunnan on May 21, 2021. *Seismol. Geol.* **2021**, *43*, 806–826.
56. Lei, X.; Wang, Z.; Ma, S.; He, C. A preliminary study on the characteristics and mechanism of the May 2021 MS6.4 Yangbi earthquake sequence, Yunnan, China. *Acta Seismol. Sin.* **2021**, *43*, 261–286. [CrossRef]

57. Zhao, B.; Gao, Y.; Ma, Y. Relocations, focal mechanisms and stress inversion of the May 21th 2021 Yangbi Ms6.4 earthquake sequence in Yunnan, China. *Chin. J. Geophys* **2022**, *65*, 1006–1020. (In Chinese) [CrossRef]
58. Wang, G.; Wu, Z.; Peng, G.; Liu, Z.; Luo, R.; Huang, X.; Chen, H. Seismogenic fault and it's rupture characteristics of the 21 May, 2021 Yangbi Ms 6.4 earthquake: Analysis results from the relocation of the earthquake sequence. *J. Geomech.* **2021**, *27*, 662–678. [CrossRef]
59. Zhai, Q. *Understanding Microseismicity Behavior and Their Response to Earth Processes by Improving Earthquake Catalogs*; Georgia Institute of Technology: Atlanta, GA, USA, 2022.
60. Kagan, Y.Y. 3-D Rotation of Double-Couple Earthquake Sources. *Geophys. J. Int.* **1991**, *106*, 709–716. [CrossRef]
61. Wan, Y. Determination of Center of Several Focal Mechanisms of the Same Earthquake. *Chin. J. Geophys.* **2019**, *62*, 4718–4728. (In Chinese) [CrossRef]
62. Zheng, J.; Chen, Y. Regional deviatoric moment tensor inversion based on Langston's decomposition and Hilbert transform constraints and its application. *Acta Seismol. Sin.* **2012**, *34*, 171–190.
63. Chang, Z.; Chang, H.; Zang, Y.; Dai, B. Recent active features of Weixi-Qiaohou fault and its relationship with the honghe fault. *J. Geomech.* **2016**, *22*, 517–530.
64. Álvarez-Gómez, J.A. FMC—Earthquake Focal Mechanisms Data Management, Cluster and Classification. *SoftwareX* **2019**, *9*, 299–307. [CrossRef]
65. Chen, Y. Consistency of Focal Mechanism as a New Parameter in Describing Seismic Activity. *Chin. J. Geophys.* **1978**, *21*, 142–159. (In Chinese)
66. Wilding, J.D.; Ross, Z.E. Aftershock Moment Tensor Scattering. *Geophys. Res. Lett.* **2022**, *49*, 14. [CrossRef]
67. Rodkin, M.V. Patterns of Seismicity Found in the Generalized Vicinity of a Strong Earthquake: Agreement with Common Scenarios of Instability Development. In *Extreme Events and Natural Hazards: The Complexity Perspective*; Geophysical Monograph Series; Sharma, A.S., Bunde, A., Dimri, V.P., Baker, D.N., Eds.; American Geophysical Union: Washington, DC, USA, 2012; Volume 196, pp. 27–39. ISBN 978-0-87590-486-3.
68. Wang, J.; Diao, G. Consistent CMT Solutions from Harvard University before the Great Earthquakes in Kurile Islands and its Significance for Earthquake Prediction. China. *Acta Seismol. Sin.* **2005**, *27*, 178–183.
69. Wan, Y. Study on Consistency of Focal Mechanism of Mainshock and That of Preshocks in Landers and Hector Mine Earthquake in United States. *Earthq. Res. China* **2008**, *24*, 216–225.
70. Ickrath, M.; Bohnhoff, M.; Bulut, F.; Dresen, G. Stress Rotation and Recovery in Conjunction with the 1999 Izmit Mw 7.4 Earthquake. *Geophys. J. Int.* **2014**, *196*, 951–956. [CrossRef]
71. Sheng, S.; Meng, L. Stress Field Variation During the 2019 Ridgecrest Earthquake Sequence. *Geophys. Res. Lett.* **2020**, *47*, e2020GL087722. [CrossRef]
72. Trugman, D.T.; Ross, Z.E.; Johnson, P.A. Imaging Stress and Faulting Complexity Through Earthquake Waveform Similarity. *Geophys. Res. Lett.* **2020**, *47*, e2019GL085888. [CrossRef]

Disclaimer/Publisher's Note: The statements, opinions and data contained in all publications are solely those of the individual author(s) and contributor(s) and not of MDPI and/or the editor(s). MDPI and/or the editor(s) disclaim responsibility for any injury to people or property resulting from any ideas, methods, instructions or products referred to in the content.

Article

Earthquake Magnitude and Frequency Forecasting in Northeastern Algeria Using Time Series Analysis

Mouna Merdasse [1], Mohamed Hamdache [2], José A. Peláez [3,*], Jesús Henares [4] and Tarek Medkour [5]

1. Department of Probability and Statistics, Faculty of Mathematics, University of Sciences USTHB, Algiers 16111, Algeria
2. Seismological Survey Department, CRAAG, Algiers 16032, Algeria
3. Department of Physics, University of Jaén, 23071 Jaén, Spain
4. International University of La Rioja, 26006 La Rioja, Spain
5. Department of Intelligent Systems Engineering, National School of Artificial Intelligence, Algiers 16309, Algeria
* Correspondence: japelaez@ujaen.es

Abstract: This study uses two different time series forecasting approaches (parametric and non-parametric) to assess a frequency and magnitude forecasting of earthquakes above Mw 4.0 in Northeastern Algeria. The Autoregressive Integrated Moving Average (ARIMA) model encompasses the parametric approach, while the non-parametric method employs the Singular Spectrum Analysis (SSA) approach. The ARIMA and SSA models were then used to train and forecast the annual number of earthquakes and annual maximum magnitude events occurring in Northeastern Algeria between 1910 and 2019, including 287 main events larger than Mw 4.0. The SSA method is used as a forecasting algorithm in this case, and the results are compared to those obtained by the ARIMA model. Based on the root mean square error (RMSE) criterion, the SSA forecasting model appears to be more appropriate than the ARIMA model. The consistency between the observation and the forecast is analyzed using a statistical test in terms of the total number of events, denoted as N-test. As a result, the findings indicate that the annual maximum magnitude in Northeastern Algeria between 2020 and 2030 will range from Mw 4.8 to Mw 5.1, while between four and six events with a magnitude of at least Mw 4.0 will occur annually.

Keywords: earthquake magnitude forecasting; time series analysis; singular spectrum analysis (SSA); autoregressive integrated moving average (ARIMA) model

Citation: Merdasse, M.; Hamdache, M.; Peláez, J.A.; Henares, J.; Medkour, T. Earthquake Magnitude and Frequency Forecasting in Northeastern Algeria Using Time Series Analysis. *Appl. Sci.* **2023**, *13*, 1566. https://doi.org/10.3390/app13031566

Academic Editor: Shiyong Zhou

Received: 12 January 2023
Revised: 23 January 2023
Accepted: 24 January 2023
Published: 26 January 2023

Copyright: © 2023 by the authors. Licensee MDPI, Basel, Switzerland. This article is an open access article distributed under the terms and conditions of the Creative Commons Attribution (CC BY) license (https://creativecommons.org/licenses/by/4.0/).

1. Introduction

Earthquakes are one of the most challenging natural disasters for populations to manage. Even though earthquakes are unpredictable and typically occur without warning, a detailed analysis of the seismic hazard and risk-reduction measures can help to reduce subsequent economic and social losses after the occurrence of an earthquake.

The north of Algeria is located on the border of the Nubian Plate, which is in a compressional movement with the Eurasian Plate [1–3] (Figure 1a). The origin of the seismicity in this region is the compressional movement between these two plates. Known seismic activity (Figure 1b) includes several damaging earthquakes, especially in the last 50 years, where severe earthquakes have been recorded in the El Asnam region (now Chleff), including the earthquakes of 9 September 1954 (Mw 6.8) and 10 October 1980 (Ms 7.3) (see [4]). The most recent significant event was the Zemmouri/Algiers earthquake 21 May 2003 (Mw 6.9), occurring roughly 50 km offshore from the northeast of Algiers (e.g., [5,6]). In addition, in this period, several earthquakes affected regions close to important cities and caused some damages, such as the Constantine (northeast Algeria) earthquake (Ms 5.9) of 27 October 1985.

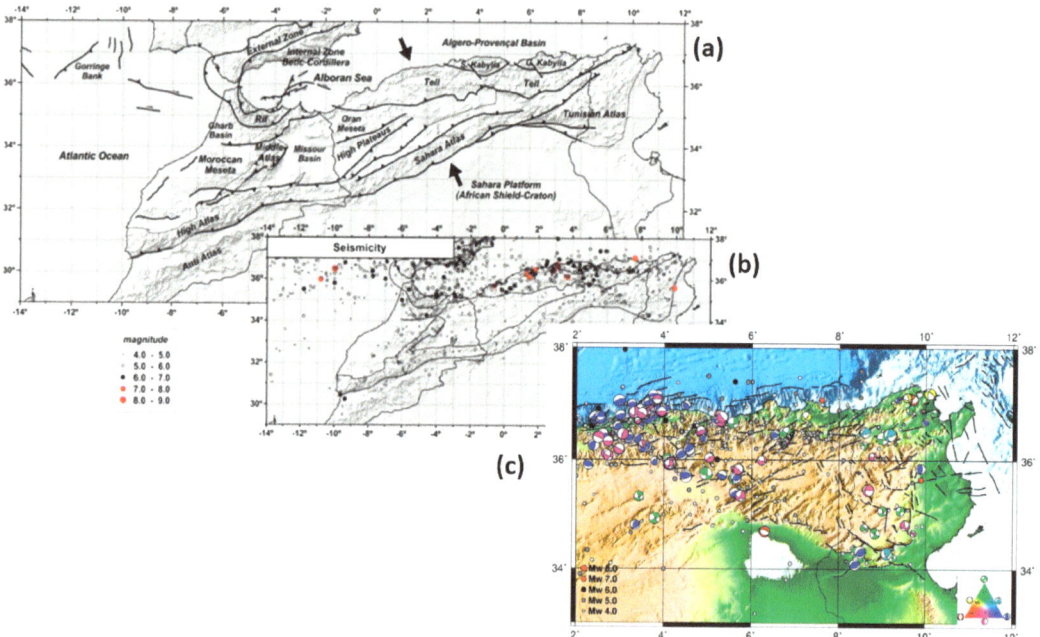

Figure 1. Tectonic and seismicity frame. (**a**) Tectonic sketch for the studied region. (**b**) Sha-low seismicity with depth less than 30 km and magnitude above magnitude Mw 4.0. (**c**) Distribution of seismicity with magnitude above Mw 4.0 and distribution of focal mechanism solutions.

The interest of the scientific community in approaches to reduce the risk of damaging earthquakes and related seismic risk assessments of urban areas in Northern Algeria is steadily growing in response to this seismic activity. There is always a pressing need for studies on earthquake forecasting, the implementation of building regulations, and safe constructions, especially in developing countries like Algeria, due to the severity of large earthquakes and the damage they produce. The resulting improvement in earthquake risk assessment and hazard management leads to significant savings in human life and properties.

The effects of the earthquakes previously mentioned in Northern Algeria [7] indicate the importance of improving estimates of the forecasting from different source zones. Due to its complex tectonics, the Northeastern region of Algeria was chosen as the studied area.

On both short- and long-term time periods, earthquake forecasting has significant social and economic consequences. In addition, it plays a main role in earthquake preparedness. On the basis of the quantification of patterns in seismicity data, a wide range of forecasting methods have been proposed with varied degrees of effectiveness [8–17]. For instance, Mignan [17] develops an analysis of the steady increase in seismic activity around a potential earthquake epicenter, known as the accelerating moment release (AMR) approach, while Keilis–Borok [8] presents and analyses step-by-step the topic of the earthquake prediction. A significant advance in this research field is the earthquake forecasting method based on Regional Earthquake Likelihood Models (RELM) [14,18–21]. Nowadays, a new algorithm known as pattern informatics (PI) is also emerging as an advanced method [14]. In addition, new methods based on deep learning are being developed to find a static-stress-based criterion predicting the location of aftershocks [22], as well as the interest in real-time post-seismic forecasting based on ground velocity recorded within the first hour after the mainshock by means of the perceived magnitude [23].

Several studies have been conducted from the perspective of seismic hazard assessment and forecasting. The Gutenberg Richter (GR) model [24] is widely used and states that the logarithm of the cumulative number of events is linearly proportional to the magnitude.

It is worth noting that several authors [25–27] suggested that the extreme value distribution is a more suitable analytical model and should be employed for the distribution of the magnitude set rather than the GR model. Stochastic processes, particularly Poisson processes, are also used to forecast earthquake frequencies by taking the earthquake occurrence time into account. The Poisson model is characterized by a constant hazard function and an exponential recurrence time distribution. This assumption leads to the unsatisfying result of only time-independent seismic hazard or seismic forecasting estimates, suggesting that the probability of an earthquake at any given time is independent of its magnitude and the time since the last one, respectively. Additionally, compared to the Poisson law, the distribution of earthquakes is over-dispersed, since the events are grouped in time and location. Various other models based on stochastic processes have also been investigated to predict the number of events, such as compound Poisson [28,29], branching [15,30] and stochastic point processes [31,32]. These stochastic procedures made predicting the magnitude of the earthquake challenging. In addition, these approaches are ineffective for determining earthquake seasonality and patterns.

Recently, a few studies attempted to use forecasting models based on time series, such as the Auto-Regressive Integrated Moving Average (ARIMA) and the generalized autoregressive conditional heteroscedasticity (GARCH) models [33,34], to forecast earthquake magnitudes by considering the seasonality and trends of earthquake series. Another model, the singular spectrum analysis model, or SSA [35–37], is becoming more attractive in order to forecast earthquake magnitudes in a specific seismic zone. It is a reliable and advanced non-parametric time series analysis method combining dynamical systems, signal processing, multivariate statistics and traditional forecasting analysis. According to several authors [35–37], this approach is useful for determining the magnitude of earthquakes in a given area. The SSA model can identify significant seismic time series components exhibiting typical irregular behavior and provide accurate forecasts for them. Despite the fact that a few studies on earthquake magnitude forecasting using the SSA approach have been conducted [37], the primary goal of our study is to apply this method in Northeastern Algeria to predict earthquake magnitudes with time effects, which are frequently missed in estimates, while also capturing the dynamics of earthquake occurrences. Subsequently, the ARIMA and SSA models provided the annual maximum earthquake magnitudes for the first time in the studied area.

The root mean square error approach, usually denoted as RMSE, is a common tool for comparing different models and/or methodologies in time series [38,39]. In this study, the estimated RMSE values show that the SSA is the best model for describing the number of earthquakes and the annual maximum magnitude in this region. The seismicity in this area is continuous, and it is characterized by low-to-moderate seismic activity. Despite the interest of the scientific community in regional seismology and seismic hazards, the studied area remains of great interest due mainly to the tectonic complexity, which resulted in the identification of several active faults, the characteristics of which are still under investigation [40]. Then, this study is the first one in this region to address the issue of forecasting using time series, and it is part of the scientific community's efforts to manage and reduce seismic risk. It is worth noting that, previously, a model has been developed for Northern Morocco and Algeria to assess the probability of exceeding magnitudes Mw 5.0 and 6.0 in 10 years [41], but assuming a Poissonian process on a spatially smoothed seismicity model. This study enabled for the spatial variation of such results.

In the current study, the consistency between the observation and the forecast is analyzed using the CSEP (Collaborative for the Study of Earthquake Predicability) test [42] in terms of the total number of events, also denoted as N-test. The results are presented as quantile scores, δ_1 and δ_2 indices. According to Nanjo et al. [43], the forecast rate is too high (an overestimation) if δ_2 is very small, and too low (an underestimation) if δ_1 is very small for the N-test. Furthermore, according to the original CSEP testing framework, a model fails the test if its score is below a significance level of 2.5%, indicating an inconsistency between the forecast and the observation.

2. Seismicity and Earthquake Database

The study area is situated in the Tell Atlas in Northeastern Algeria (Figure 1a). This important geological formation resulted from a collision caused by the Algero–Provençal Basin opening within the Nubia Plate in the Early Miocene. Furthermore, it is most likely related to the Nubian Plate subduction, which is dipping to the north [44,45].

Onshore and offshore folds and thrust faults extending from NE–SW and from E–W represent the majority of the current tectonic features (e.g., [46,47]). The compressional movement between the Nubian and Eurasian Plates causes considerable seismicity, which is mostly represented in a moderately diffused seismic area in Northern Africa in its western domain (Figure 1b). This collision zone includes Northern Algeria, where recent geodetic studies reveal an actual plate convergence rate of about 5 ± 1 mm/yr in a N60°W direction, as illustrated in Figure 1a [2,3,48–50]. Earthquakes with a magnitude above Mw 5.0 frequently occur in the area [7,51], sometimes causing significant damage and casualties [52,53].

Most well-studied thrusting earthquakes occur on land, including the largest-recorded Ms 7.3 10 October 1980, El Asnam earthquake [54–56]. Examples of destructive earthquakes in the past include the 3 January 1365, and 5 May 1716 earthquakes, both felt with intensity X (European Macroseismic Scale, EMS-98) [57]. The earthquake that struck on 2 March 1825, with a felt intensity of X–XI on the Modified Mercalli Intensity Scale (MMI), was another historical occurrence. The Mw 6.9 earthquake that struck the area under consideration on 21 May 2003 was the most recent destructive earthquake [7]. The seismicity of the studied area displayed in Figure 1b has been the subject of various studies, both on historical and instrumental seismicity. For instance, Harbi et al. [51] performed a clear and comprehensive analysis of the historical seismicity, proposing the re-appraisal of several historical events located in the region. On the other hand, recent instrumental seismicity recorded by the Algerian seismic network has also been the subject of several works [58–62]. Figure 1c depicts the shallow depth ($h \leq 30$ km) focal mechanism data compiled in the region [44,45]; the Frohlich diagram [63] is displayed, and the Zoback classification [64] is used. In previous studies [44,45], a detailed analysis of the inversion of the focal mechanism solutions and the inferred stress pattern was performed. The tectonic framework of the Ibero–Maghrebian region is detailed from these data, and the results are found to be in agreement with more recent studies (e.g., [50]). Similar horizontal maximum principal stress directions can be seen throughout the area, and they almost exactly coincide with the previously identified horizontal P axis in the NW–SE direction, as previously established by Henares et al. [65]. Additional tectonic stress regimes have been identified, including extensional, compressional, transpressional and strike-slip schemes.

The earthquake data file considered in this analysis was obtained from a seismic catalog previously compiled [7] for Northern Algeria, which has been updated until December 2019. It is well recognized that having an up-to-date Poissonian earthquake data file is a prerequisite for any seismic hazard assessment [66–69]. A combination of available published studies, bulletins and original data was used to produce the early earthquake data file. This led to the development of a unified earthquake data file, including information on magnitude, regional extent (between 32° and 38° latitudes and between 3°W and 10°E longitude), and date range (between AD 856 and June 2008) [7].

Specifically, for the current study, this initial earthquake data file has been updated to December 2019, with data coming from the Spanish Instituto Geográfico Nacional (IGN) and the Algerian Centre de Recherche en Astronomie, Astrophysique et Geophysique (CRAAG). It is important to note that in order to maintain the magnitude homogenization, this process was performed using the same relationships between reported magnitudes and moment magnitude that were used to generate the initial catalog [7]. The initial recorded events were described using several scales (surface-wave Ms, body wave m_b, body wave from Lg phase amplitude m_{bLg} and local duration M_L magnitudes). The next stage was to identify and remove any dependent event or non-Poissonian earthquake (foreshocks, aftershocks and swarms). In the present study, the method of Gardner and Knopoff [70] was applied using the particular temporal and spatial window introduced in the initial catalog [7]. Figure 1b shows the spatial distribution of shallow seismicity for earthquakes with magnitudes greater than Mw 4.0 using the declustered dataset. Figure 1c, on the other hand, shows the distribution of focal mechanism solutions and seismicity with magnitudes greater than Mw 4.0.

Finally, the completeness of this catalog is performed at the base of a visual approach [71] in order to evaluate the threshold magnitude of the earthquake data file. Following previous studies [7,72], this approach is applied to our data above different magnitude values: if the cumulative annual number of earthquakes over this magnitude is approximately linear, then the seismic catalog is complete and Poissonian for a given threshold magnitude during a specific period of time. The cumulative number of events with a magnitude above Mw 4.0, 4.5, 5.0, 5.5, 6.0 and 6.5 is depicted in Figure 2. It shows that magnitudes above Mw 4.0 and 4.5 appear roughly complete and Poissonian since 1920 and 1910, with rates of 7.7 and 4.2 events/year, respectively. However, approximately since 1870 and 1885, with rates of 2.1 and 0.81 events/year, magnitudes exceeding Mw 5.5 and 5.0 can be considered complete and Poissonian, respectively. For magnitudes greater than Mw 6.0 and 6.5, they are likely complete and Poissonian since 1860 and 1700, respectively, with rates of 0.21 and 0.08 events/year.

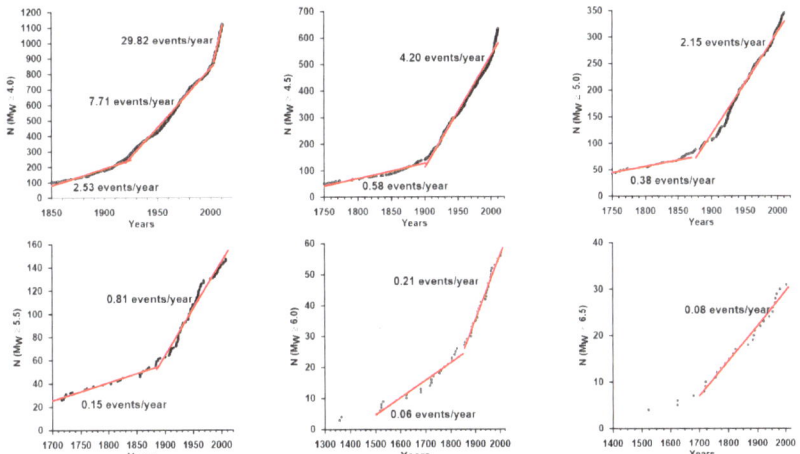

Figure 2. Cumulative number of earthquakes above magnitudes Mw 4.0, 4.5, 5.0, 5.5, 6.0 and 6.5 vs. time (black circles). The straight lines (in red) show linear fits.

3. Methodology Outline

The annual earthquake number series, denoted as $\{N_k; k \geq 0\}$, and the annual maximum magnitude in Northeastern Algeria that occurred during the period from 1910 to 2019, named $\{m_k, k \geq 0\}$, have been modelled using two different approaches. Initially, a parametric approach, abbreviated as ARIMA, was based on the Autoregressive Integrated Moving Average model, and a non-parametric approach was based on the Singular Spectrum Analysis model, abbreviated as SSA. ARIMA models [73], also known as Box–Jenkins models, are powerful tools in time series analysis aiming to describe the autocorrelations in the data and forecast values in the univariate time series that are non-stationaries, which are the time series with a trend component [74]. Usually, the notation *ARIMA (p,d,q)* is used, where *q* is the parameter of the moving average (MA) model, *p* is the parameter of the autoregression (AR) model, and d is the number of the differentiation procedure necessary to ensure the stationarity in the series. The extensions to ARIMA models are the Seasonal Box–Jenkins models [75], which support the direct modelling of the seasonal component of the non-stationaries time series exhibiting both the trend and seasonal fluctuations [74]. For seasonal series of a given period *S*, a Seasonal Autoregressive Integrated Moving Average (SARIMA, or

Seasonal ARIMA) is introduced with the notation $SARIMA(p,d,q) \times (P,D,Q)_S$, with P and Q being the orders of the seasonal autoregressive and seasonal moving average polynomials. Let $(X_t)_{t \geq 0}$ be a time series. The $ARIMA(p,d,q)$ equation model takes the form

$$\Phi_p(B)\nabla^d X_t = \Theta_p(B)\varepsilon_t \tag{1}$$

where ε_t is the error series representing the white noise of mean 0 and variance σ_ε^2, and

$$\nabla^d = (1-B)^d \tag{2}$$

represents the difference operator of order d, being d, the order of integration required to achieve the stationarity in the data. The polynomial

$$\Phi_p(B) = 1 - \varphi_1 B^1 - \varphi_2 B^2 - \ldots - \varphi_p B^p \tag{3}$$

corresponds to the AR term at the pth order and

$$\Phi_p(B) = 1 - \varphi_1 B^1 - \varphi_2 B^2 - \ldots - \varphi_p B^p \tag{4}$$

is the MA polynomial at the qth order [76].

The first stage in the Box–Jenkins analysis procedure is to ensure that the analyzed series is stationary; that is, free of trend and seasonal terms. The plot of the autocorrelation (ACF) and partial autocorrelation functions (PACF) are used to determine the parameters p and q, which control substantially the model. According to Cowpertwait and Metcalfe [77], for a second-order stationary time series, the autocovariance function of the lag k is given by

$$\gamma_k = E[(x_t - \mu)(x_{t+k} - \mu)] \tag{5}$$

noticing that the number of time steps between the variables is known as the lag.

The lag k autocorrelation function (ACF) ρ_k, is defined as

$$\rho_k = \frac{\gamma_k}{\sigma^2} \tag{6}$$

being μ and σ^2 the mean and the variance of the time series, respectively, where $\rho_0 = 1$. In general, the partial autocorrelation function (PACF) of stationary time series at lag k is the k-th coefficient of a fitted AR(k) model; if the underlying process is AR(p), then the coefficients will be zero for all $k > p$. It measures the correlation between observations that are separated by k time units (e.g., x_t and x_{t-k}) after removing the effect of any correlation resulting by the terms at shorter lags (e.g., $x_{t-1}, \ldots \ldots, x_{t-k-1}$). The Akaike information criterion [78] and the Bayesian information criterion [79], denoted as AIC and BIC, respectively, are used to select the best model, the one with minimum information criterion values and white noise error series. According to Fabozzi et al. [80], it is worth noting that the AIC criterion represents the relationship between the Kullback–Leibler measure [81] and the maximum likelihood estimation method. The Kullback–Leibler measure is developed to capture the lost information in the estimation, which means that this measure selects the good model minimizing the loss of information. Usually, the AIC criterion is given by the equation

$$AIC = -2 \log L(\widetilde{\theta}) + 2K \tag{7}$$

where θ is the set of model parameters, $L(\widetilde{\theta})$ is the likelihood of the candidate model given the data when evaluated at the maximum likelihood estimate of θ, and K is the number of the estimated parameters in the candidate model.

For small samples, the corrected Akaike information criterion, denoted as AIC_c, should be used instead of the AIC criterion described previously. The relation giving the AIC_c is

$$AIC_c = -2\log L(\widetilde{\theta}) + 2K + \frac{2K+1}{N-K-1} \qquad (8)$$

where N is the number of observations. Hurvich and Tsai [82] define a small sample size as one that is less than 40. It is noteworthy that, as N increases, the third term in AIC_c approaches zero, producing the same result as the AIC criterion.

The Bayesian information criterion [79], denoted as BIC, is another model selection criterion based on the information theory but set within a Bayesian context. The difference between the BIC and the AIC criteria is that the former puts a greater penalty for the number of parameters than the latter. It is computed using the following relation

$$BIC = -2\log L(\widetilde{\theta}) + K\log N \qquad (9)$$

where the terms are the same as described in the definition of the AIC criterion. As in the previous criterion, the best model is the one providing the minimum BIC value.

The Single Spectrum Analysis (SSA) model is a time series forecasting method commonly used to analyze time series with periodic oscillations. The application of the SSA method is advantageous because it encompasses decomposing a time series into simpler components, such as a gradually changing trend, oscillations and noise. Various disciplines have implemented the SSA method, including signal processing [83], nonlinear dynamics [84,85], climate data [86–88], medical science [89] and mathematical statistics [90]. Furthermore, when combined with neural networks or other comparable techniques, it is a powerful pre-processing tool for time series forecasting [91,92]. Decomposition and reconstruction are the two complementary processes that make up the SSA implementation algorithm.

According to Golyandina and Zhigljavsky [93], we consider a real-valued time series $X = (x_1, \ldots, x_N)$ with length N ($N > 2$), satisfying $x_j \neq 0$ for at least one j. The first step in the decomposition stage, named the embedding step, consists in transforming the original time series into a sequence of L-dimensional vectors, $X_i = (x_i, \ldots, x_J)^T$, where $J = N - L + 1$, and L is the window length. The J-formed vectors are called L-lagged vectors and present the columns of the trajectory matrix (or L-trajectory matrix) of the series X ($L \times J$) given by

$$X = \begin{pmatrix} x_1 & x_2 & \cdots & x_J \\ x_2 & x_3 & \cdots & x_{J+1} \\ \vdots & \vdots & \ddots & \vdots \\ x_L & x_{L+1} & \cdots & x_N \end{pmatrix} \qquad (10)$$

The window length L is obtained through experimentation, and the appropriate L parameter is determined according to the problem being considered and some preliminary information from the time series [94]. It is worth noting that there are no general rules for the determination of this parameter. However, it is advised that for time series exhibiting seasonality, the window length can be chosen as common multiples of 12 [95].

The second step in this stage, called the singular value decomposition, consists of performing a singular value decomposition method to the trajectory matrix X. Here, we will define the matrix $S = X.X^T$, and denote by $\lambda_1, \lambda_2, \ldots, \lambda_L$ the eigenvalues of S that are taken in the decreasing order ($\lambda_1 \geq \lambda_2 \geq \ldots \geq \lambda_L \geq 0$), and by $U_1, U_2, \ldots, U_L$ the orthonormal system corresponding to the eigenvalues of S. Let $d = rank(X)$, which is equal to $\max\{i, \text{ such that } \lambda_i > 0\}$ and

$$V_i = X^T U_i / \sqrt{\lambda_i} \text{ for } i = 1, \ldots, d \qquad (11)$$

Using this notation, the singular value decomposition of the trajectory matrix X can be written as

$$X = X_1 + X_2 + \ldots + X_d \qquad (12)$$

with
$$X_i = \sqrt{\lambda_i} U_i V_i^T \qquad (13)$$

The matrices X_i, called elementary matrices, with the rank equal to one, and the set of triplets $(\sqrt{\lambda_i}, U_i, V_i)$ are called the ith eigen-triplet of the singular values decomposition.

The second stage of the algorithm implementation corresponding to the reconstruction stage includes two other steps: the eigentriple grouping and the diagonal averaging steps. The eigentriple grouping step consists of dividing the elementary matrices X_i ($i = 1, \ldots, L$) into r groups, $1 \leq r \leq d$ [94]. The resulting matrices are then produced by adding the r eigen-triples in each group.

Whereas, the diagonal averaging step is based on the reconstruction of the one-dimensional series of length N, that can be considered as an approximation of the original series, by applying the diagonal averaging method on the grouped matrices that are resulted in the previous step [93,96].

In order to compare between the different approaches applied, an important convention is widely used and based on the root mean square error (RMSE) criterion [38,39], which is calculated by

$$RMSE = \sqrt{\frac{1}{N} \sum_{k=1}^{N} (x_k - \hat{x}_k)^2} \qquad (14)$$

where x_k indicates the actual value and $\hat{x}_k$ represents the kth forecasted value based on the previous data. Therefore, the optimum model is the one presenting the smallest RMSE value.

4. Earthquake Magnitude Forecasting

The magnitude forecasting analysis for earthquakes with magnitudes equal to or greater than Mw 4.0 is implemented in this section using the previously described models. The data file used in this section includes the main shocks that occurred between 1910 and 2019 in Northeastern Algeria.

Figure 2 shows that the occurrence process during this time period can be approximated by a Poisson process. In this section, we will focus on two time series that represent the annual number of earthquakes and the annual maximum magnitudes in this region.

Here, we denote for $j = 1, \ldots, N$ by $m_j^{(k)}$ the magnitudes above Mw 4.0 of events occurred during the k-th year and define m_k as the annual maximum magnitude $\max_{0 \leq j \leq N} m_j^{(k)}$ during the k-th year, whereas the number of earthquakes during the considered year, the k-th year, is denoted as N_k.

Figure 3a displays the $\{N_k; k \geq 0\}$ and $\{m_k, k \geq 0\}$ plots covering the considered time period using a threshold magnitude equal to Mw 4.0. The ARIMA and SSA time series models are then employed to forecast both the frequency and annual maximum magnitude of earthquakes using the R-packages [97] RSSA and FORECAST [98,99]. By comparing the observed and predicted values, it is critical to identify the fitting models [74]. To increase the accuracy and reduce the rate of uncertainty, we have divided the dataset into training and testing data. We have identified that between 1910 and 2000, nearly 80% of the total events in the series $\{N_k; k \geq 0\}$ and $\{m_k, k \geq 0\}$ are included, corresponding to 70 observations. As a result, we estimate that 80% of the data are composed of training data, while the remaining 20% are events that were recorded between 2001 and 2019.

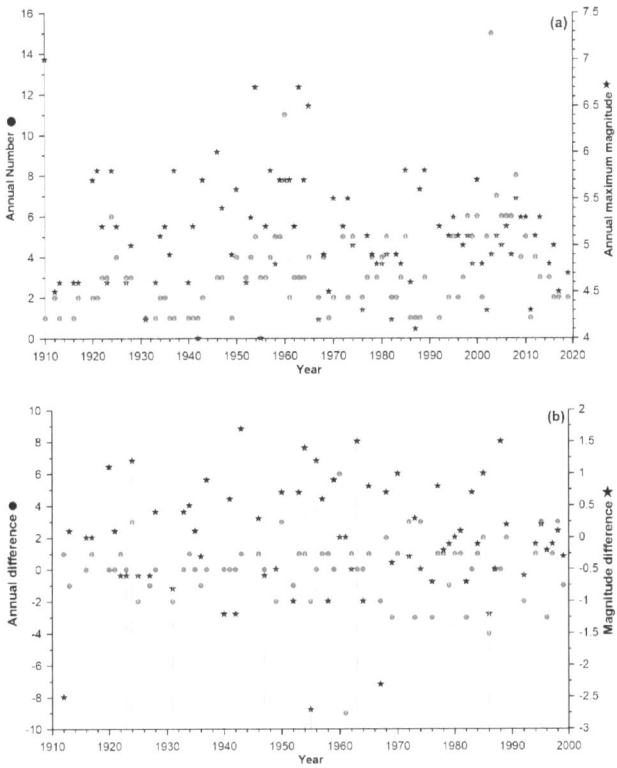

Figure 3. (**a**) Annual number of earthquakes (circles) and maximum annual magnitude (stars) in the period 1910–2019. (**b**) Differential time series for annual earthquake number (circles) and for maximum annual magnitude (stars) in the period 1910–2000.

Figure 3a shows two significate peaks in the $\{N_k; k \geq 0\}$ plot that refer to the high number of earthquakes that occurred between 1960 and 2003, and an important peak in the $\{N_k; k \geq 0\}$ plot corresponding to the biggest earthquakes that occurred in the studied region during this period.

The stationarity and the normality of the studied series are tested using the Augmented Dickey Fuller (ADF) [100] and the Shapiro–Wilk (SW) tests [101]. The obtained results are shown in Table 1. The ADF test indicates the non-stationarity in $\{N_k; k \geq 0\}$ and $\{m_k, k \geq 0\}$ time series with a p-value greater than 5%, and according to SW test (Table 1), the normality hypothesis is rejected for both series (p-value less than 5%). Thus, the $\{N_k; k \geq 0\}$ and $\{m_k, k \geq 0\}$ series are not normally distributed variables with non-stationary behaviour, which means that these non-parametric methods can be more appropriate for our study.

The stationarity of the data is an important hypothesis in ARIMA modelling. As a result, the first order differentiated series of $\{N_k; k \geq 0\}$ and $\{m_k, k \geq 0\}$ are computed. Figure 3b shows the differentiated resultant time series, with the two plots indicating a clear stationarity in the data. Thus, the integration parameter d is fixed in this study to 1. The p and q parameters of the ARIMA model are determined from the ACF and PACF plots of the differentiated series of $\{N_k; k \geq 0\}$ and $\{m_k, k \geq 0\}$, respectively, which are shown in Figure 4. In the set of candidate ARIMA models, the optimum models for $\{N_k; k \geq 0\}$ and $\{m_k, k \geq 0\}$ are the ones that minimize the AIC and BIC criteria and have a normally uncorrelated residual. Hence, according to Table 1, the ARIMA (2,1,1) and ARIMA (2,1,2) models are the selected ones for $\{N_k; k \geq 0\}$ and $\{m_k, k \geq 0\}$ time series, respectively. Figure 5 illustrates the residuals analysis of the two models, where Figure 5a shows the residuals of the selected models. Figure 5b shows the ACF residual plots, indicating that the residuals of the two models are uncorrelated. Finally, Figure 5c shows that the residuals are normally distributed according to the residuals Quantile-Quantile plots (Q-Q plot) statistical test [102,103].

Table 1. Annual earthquake number and annual maximum magnitude time series stationarity (ADF) and normality (SW) tests results. ARIMA model selection using the AIC and BIC criteria are also showed.

Series	ADF Test	SW Test	Model	AIC	BIC
Eartq_Num	0.345	7.21×10^{-7}	ARIMA (2,1,2)	4.061	4.255
			ARIMA (2,1,1)	3.995	4.175
			SARIMA (2,1,2) (1,0,1)$_{(S=12)}$	4.068	4.294
Max_Mag	0.063	0.029	ARIMA (2,1,2)	2.169	2.364
			ARIMA (2,1,1)	2.191	2.425
			SARIMA (2,1,2) (1,0,1)$_{(S=12)}$	2.198	2.425

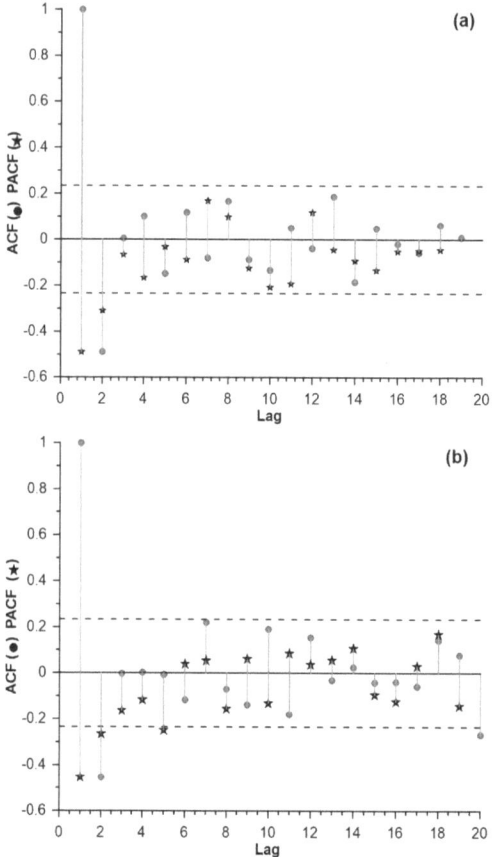

Figure 4. ACF (circles) and PACF (stars) values (**a**) for the differential annual earthquake number and (**b**) for the differential annual maximum magnitude.

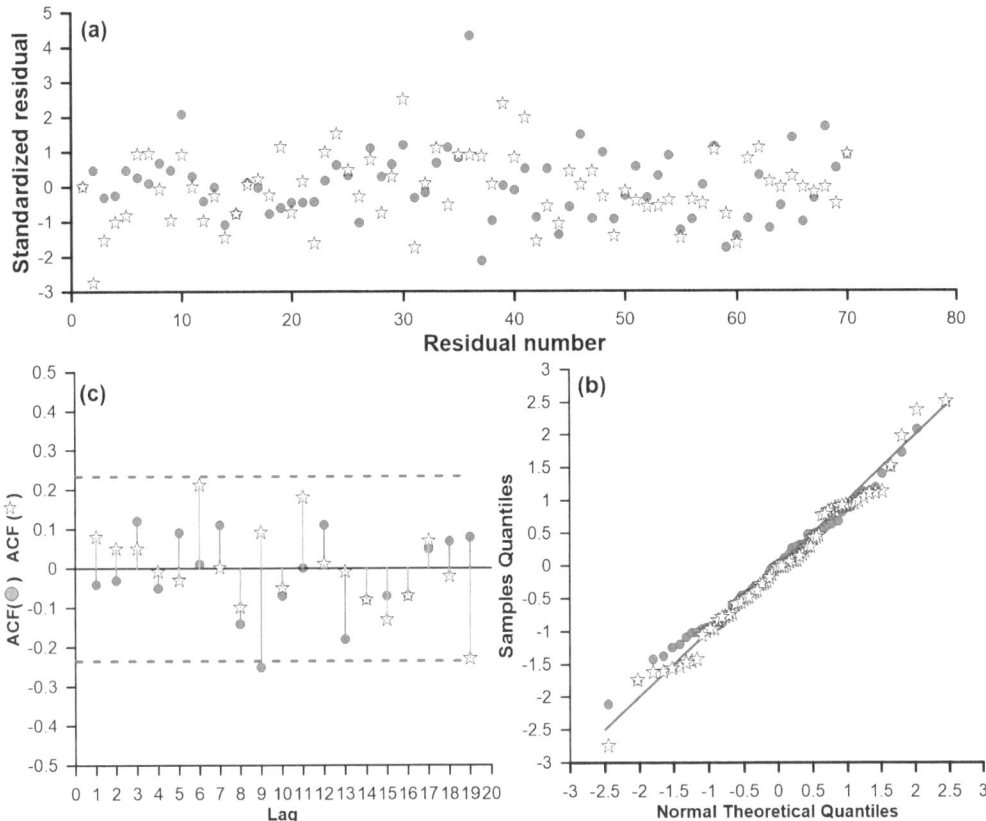

Figure 5. Residual analysis of the selected ARIMA model for earthquakes number time series (circles) and for annual maximum magnitudes time series (stars). (**a**) residuals of the selected models; (**b**) ACF residual plots, indicating that the residuals of the two models are uncorrelated; (**c**) residuals are normally distributed according to the residuals Quantile-Quantile plots (Q-Q plot).

The second approach considered in our study is based on the SSA method. The first stage of the SSA method consists of decomposing the $\{N_k; k \geq 0\}$ and $\{m_k, k \geq 0\}$ time series into principal independent components, which are the trend, the seasonality and the noise. The second stage consists of reconstructing the original series using only the trend and the seasonality. Figure 6 indicates that the seasonality and trend components used together (blue line) describe the observed earthquake number and the annual maximum magnitude in the studied region better than the trend component alone (red line).

The parameters of the SSA model were empirically chosen based on a visual presentation and clear separability of the main independent components. According to Hassani [104], a window length less than half of the sample size is considered adequate. According to Golyandina et al. [94], for seasonal time series, this parameter must be a common multiple of the seasonality period. Several window lengths (12, 24 and 36 samples) were thus evaluated to select the best one, which has been chosen using the RMSE criterion. The reconstruction stage parameter (see Section 3), denoted r, is determined using the eigenvalues plot of the $\{N_k; k \geq 0\}$ and $\{m_k, k \geq 0\}$ series presented in Figure 7, where the slow decrease in these plots suggests the beginning of the noise component. Then, according to Figure 7, two components are used both in the reconstruction process of the $\{N_k; k \geq 0\}$ series and in the reconstruction of the $\{m_k, k \geq 0\}$ series. These results can be confirmed using the w-correlation matrices shown in Figure 8. The w-correlation matrices indicate that the first three components are uncorrelated in the $\{N_k; k \geq 0\}$ series (Figure 8a), and two components in the $\{m_k, k \geq 0\}$ series (Figure 8b). Therefore, from the w-correlation matrices, the reconstruction parameter is fixed to 3 and 2 for the $\{N_k; k \geq 0\}$ and $\{m_k, k \geq 0\}$ time series, respectively.

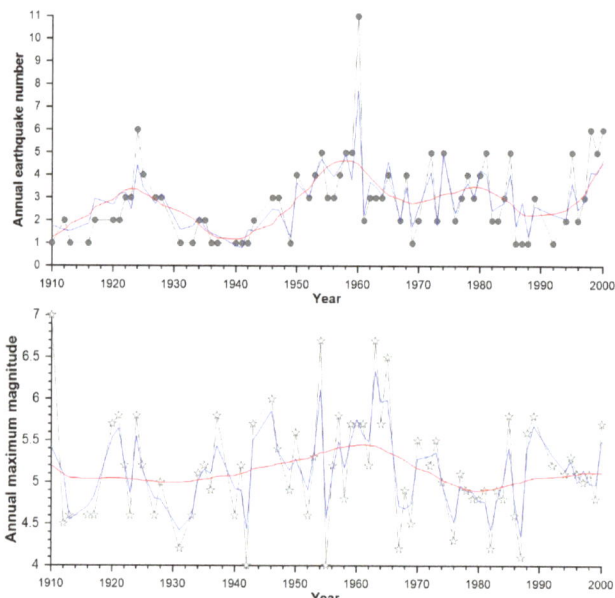

Figure 6. Fit of the recorded annual number and the annual maximum earthquake magnitude (grey line) by the seasonality and trend components combined (blue line) and by the trend component alone (red line).

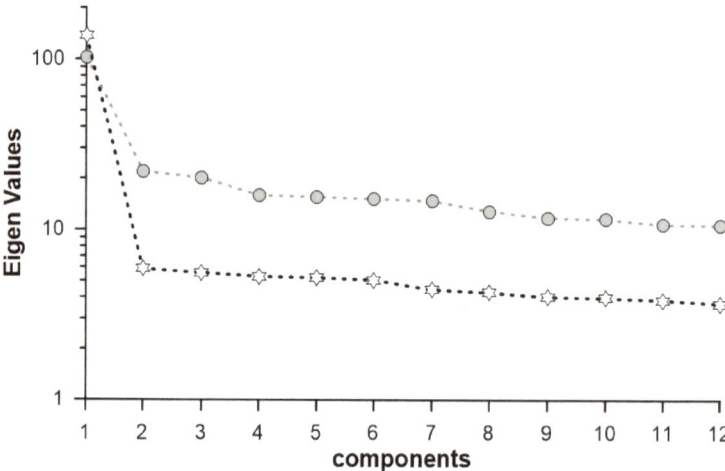

Figure 7. Eigenvalues plots of the first 12 components for the annual earthquake number series (circles) and for the annual maximum magnitudes series (stars).

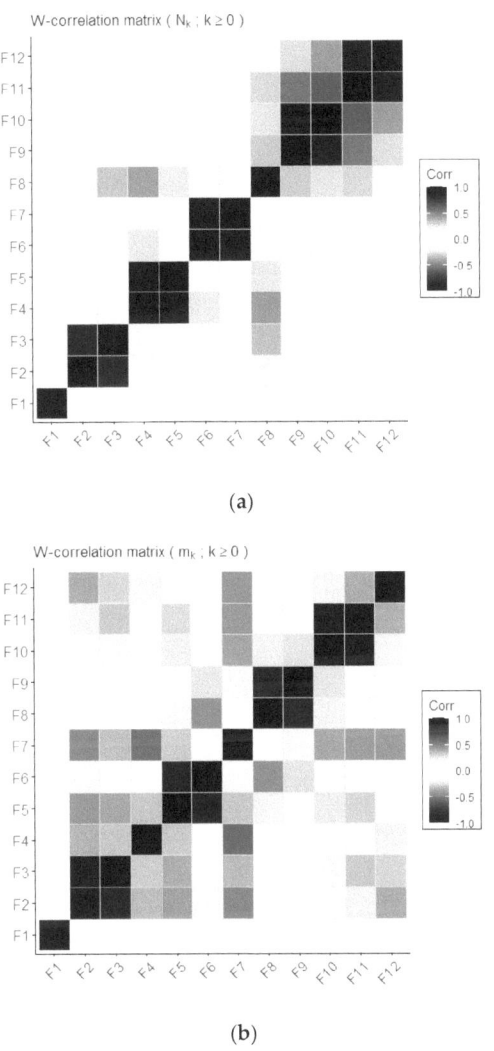

Figure 8. W-correlation matrix plots for the first 12 components of the earthquake number series (**a**) and the annual maximum magnitude series (**b**).

The first group is composed of solely the first component, which is uncorrelated to the other components. Because the second and third components are highly correlated, the pair (2,3) forms the second group. After linking the components from 4 to 8, it is shown that the fourth component has a correlation with the fifth, sixth and eighth components. In addition, the sixth component has a high correlation with the seventh component. Thus, the pairs (4,5) and (6,7), as well as the eighth component, configure the last group.

Therefore, the rest of components in $\{N_k; k \geq 0\}$ series correspond to the noise. For $\{m_k, k \geq 0\}$ series, according to the w-correlation matrix in Figure 8b, two groups can be used in the reconstruction of the original series. The first group consists of mainly the first component, whereas the second group consists of Components 2–8 and Component 12, which are all correlated with one another. As a result, all of the other components form the noise in the $\{m_k, k \geq 0\}$ series. It is worth noting that the first component in both matrices that is uncorrelated with the other component corresponds to the trend component in both series. Therefore, the reconstruction parameters in this case are fixed to 3 and 2 for the $\{N_k; k \geq 0\}$ and $\{m_k, k \geq 0\}$ time series, respectively.

Table 2 presents the RMSE value of the candidate SSA models for the studied series. According to the results given in Table 2, the best SSA models for $\{N_k; k \geq 0\}$ and $\{m_k, k \geq 0\}$ are the SSA (24,3) and SSA (12,2) models, respectively. Figure 9 depicts the independent main component extracted from the $\{N_k; k \geq 0\}$ (a) and $\{m_k, k \geq 0\}$ (b) series, representing the trend, seasonality and noise components.

Table 2. The SSA chosen model based on the RMSE of the analyzed time series.

Series	Model	RMSE
Earthq_Num	SSA (12,2)	3.847
	SSA (24,3)	3.048
	SSA (36,2)	3.426
Max_Mag	SSA (12,2)	0.314
	SSA (24,2)	0.365
	SSA (36,2)	0.395

Finally, the RMSE value is used to compare the different approaches. Table 3 displays the RMSE values of the ARIMA and SSA models for the $\{N_k; k \geq 0\}$ and $\{m_k, k \geq 0\}$ time series, with the smaller RMSE value indicating the better model.

Table 3. Best model selected based on the RMSE value for the two considered time series.

Series	ARIMA (p,d,q) RMSE	SSA (L,r) RMSE
Earthq_Num	(2,1,1) 3.317	(24,3) 3.048
Max_Mag	(2,1,2) 0.374	(12,2) 0.314

As a result, the SSA (24,3) and SSA (12,2) models are the best ones for describing the number of earthquakes and the maximum magnitude series, respectively. Table 4 also shows the forecasted values from 2020 to 2030 using the selected SSA models. Finally, Figure 10 depicts the original (grey dashed line) and forecasted (red dashed line) series, where a stationary behavior can be observed in both time series from 2020 to 2030.

Table 4. Forecasted annual earthquake number and annual maximum magnitude time series from 2020 to 2030 from the selected SSA model.

| Years | Series | |
	Earthq_Num	Max_Mag
2020	5	4.9
2021	6	5.1
2022	5	4.8
2023	5	4.9
2024	5	5.1
2025	4	5.0
2026	5	4.9
2027	6	5.0
2028	4	5.1
2029	4	5.0
2030	5	5.1

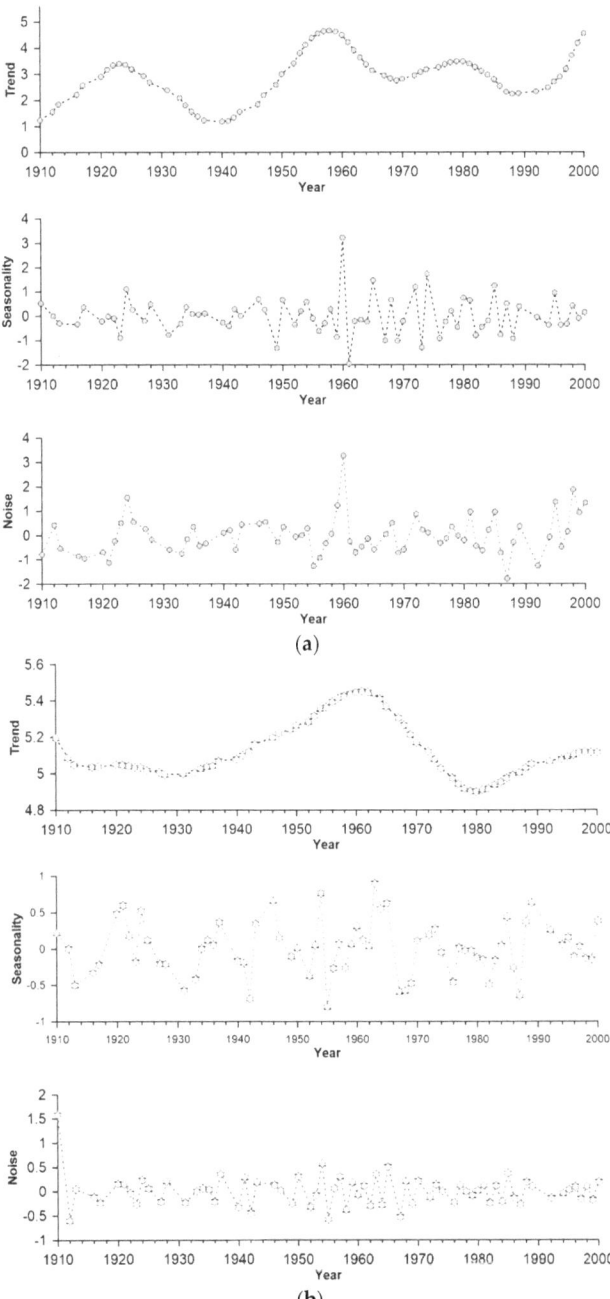

Figure 9. Trend, seasonality and noise components for the annual earthquake number (**a**) and maximum annual magnitude (**b**) series.

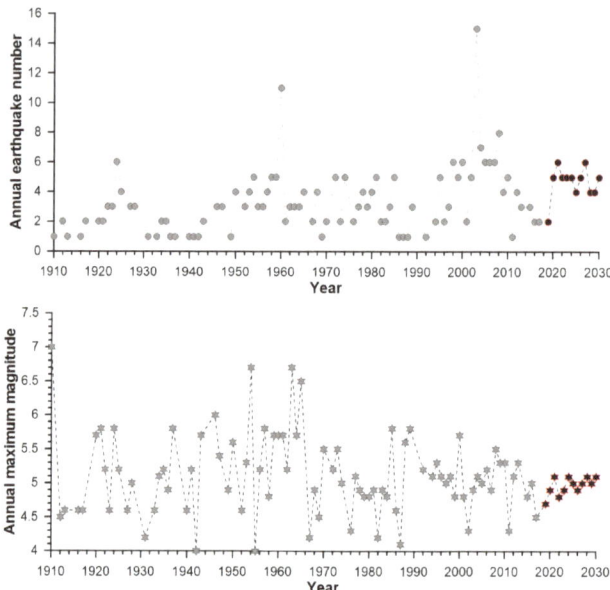

Figure 10. Observed and forecasted (in red) values for the number of earthquakes (top) and the annual maximum magnitude (bottom) using the SSA model.

5. Validation of the Procedure

After a certain earthquake forecast method has been developed using training data and set up by best fit on real data, and before any practical implementation, it must be validated [105].

The SSA method is used to perform forecasting analysis of the earthquake data file from 1910 to 2015, with the purpose of generating forecast values and comparing them to observed values from 2016 to 2019. As previously stated, the time series are divided into two sets, the first of which includes 80% of the data used as training data [74] and encompasses the years 1910 to 1997, while the remaining 20% covers the years 1998 to 2015, considered as testing data.

The stationarity and the normality of the studied series in the considered training period are tested again using the ADF and the SW tests. The derived ADF values are 0.34 and 0.077 for the annual earthquake number and maximum magnitude, respectively, whereas the obtained SW values are 2.0×10^{-7} and 0.035 for the two investigated series, respectively. The ADF test results for the two series are higher than 5%, showing that the two series are non-stationary during the training period. Moreover, the two series are not normally distributed and exhibit a non-stationary behaviour as a result of the computed SW values. Therefore, as proceeded initially, and in order to achieve the stationarity in the data, the differentiated series of $\{N_k; k \geq 0\}$ and $\{m_k, k \geq 0\}$ are computed.

Considering the d parameter of the ARIMA model equal to 1, the ACF and PACF functions of the resultant series are used to select the p and q parameters. Thus, ARIMA (2,1,2) and ARIMA (2,1,3) are the model-candidates for the time series $\{N_k; k \geq 0\}$, and ARIMA (2,1,2) and ARIMA (3,1,2) for the time series $\{m_k, k \geq 0\}$, derived during the training period 1910–1997. Analyzing the annual earthquake number series, AIC values equal to 3.99 and 4.00 are obtained for the ARIMA (2,1,2) and ARIMA (2,1,3) models, respectively, whereas BIC values equal to 4.20 and 4.24 are obtained for the same model candidates, respectively. In addition, analyzing the annual maximum magnitude time series, the obtained AIC values are equal to 2.21 and 2.23 for the ARIMA (2,1,2) and ARIMA (3,1,2) models, respectively. For the same model-candidates, the BIC values are equal to 2.41 and 2.16. Thus, on the base of AIC and BIC criteria, the ARIMA (2,1,2) model is considered the best one to describe the annual earthquake number and the annual maximum magnitude during the training period.

The parameters of the SSA model are then obtained, as previously proceeded, by testing several window lengths (12, 24 and 36 samples). The best model is also derived using the RMSE criterion. Analyzing the annual earthquake number time series, the lower RMSE value equal to 3.62 is derived for the model SSA (24,2), whereas for the models SSA (12, 2) and SSA (36,2), the values are equal to 4.40 and 3.89, respectively. Concerning the annual maximum magnitude time series, the lower RMSE is derived for the model SSA (36,2), whereas for the models SSA (12,2) and SSA (36,2), the values are equal to 0.379 and 0.375, respectively. Finally, for the two considered time series, SSA (24,2) is considered the best model.

Then, using the previously described procedure, the chosen models ARIMA (2,1,2) and SSA (24,2) are used to forecast the annual number of earthquakes and the annual maximum magnitude from 2016 to 2019. Uncommonly, no events with magnitudes greater than Mw 4.0 occurred in the studied region in 2018, whereas two events with magnitudes greater than Mw 4.0 occurred in 2016, 2017 and 2019. Then, the period from 2016–2019 appears as a low seismicity epoch. That being the case, the forecasted values using the model ARIMA (2,1,2) are greater than real ones. In 2016 and 2019, about four events were predicted, and three events were predicted in 2017.

On the other hand, values found using the SSA (24,2) model are of the order of 3 for each year, and hence closer to the observed values. Regarding the annual maximum magnitude, similar values are obtained using the ARIMA (2,1,2) and SSA (24,2) models, of the order of Mw 5.0 for 2016, 2017 and 2019. These forecasted values are in agreement with the observed ones, which are equal to Mw 5.0, 4.5 and 4.7 for 2016, 2017 and 2019, respectively.

Thus, clearly the SSA (24,2) model makes it possible to find realistic results corroborating the observed data.

A statistical test is used to assess the consistency of the results obtained using the SSA algorithm in the period from 2016 to 2019. According to Schorlemmer et al. [19], to take into account the uncertainty, the likelihood test, named L-test, can be conducted by simulating the observed events. In the current study, we focus on the statistical N-test [42], which consists to test the rate forecast. The N-test is intended to measure, in a probabilistic manner, how the forecasted number of events will match the observed number of earthquakes.

Then, the N-test [19,42,106] is implemented. The N-test takes into account two linked quantile scores, δ_1 and δ_2, reflecting whether the produced sequences produced forecasted event numbers N_{fore} that were higher or lower than the observed values N_{obs}, as given in the equations

$$\delta_1 = 1 - P\Big((N_{obs}-1)\Big|N_{fore}\Big) \qquad (15)$$

$$\delta_2 = P\Big(N_{obs}\Big|N_{fore}\Big) \qquad (16)$$

bearing in mind that $P(\omega|\lambda) = \frac{\lambda^\omega}{\omega!}exp(-\lambda)$.

The quantity δ_1 is the probability of observing at least N_{obs}, and δ_2 is the probability of observing at most N_{obs}. Both the overall forecast rate and observed number of events are assumed to be Poissonian and described by N_{fore} and N_{obs}, respectively. The quantity δ_2 describes the right-continuous Poisson cumulative distribution with the expectation N_{fore} at corresponding N_{obs} at the times evaluated. This score describes the fraction of forecast expectations smaller than the observed events. The probability that more than N_{obs} events are forecasted is given by $(1-\delta_2)$. The problem with this approach is addressed in [42]. Instead, the δ_1 probability was added in addition to the original N-test to describe at least N_{obs}, in which the user only needs to be concerned about low probability values [19,42].

The quantile scores in this statistical N-test assess if the number of forecasted occurrences is inconsistent with N_{obs}. A small δ_1 indicates that the forecast underestimates the observed sequence, whereas a small δ_2 suggests that the forecast overestimates the number of occurrences. The forecast can thus be rejected if the probabilities of δ_1 and δ_2 are less than the effective significance level [42]. The effective significance threshold for the one-sided N-tests was set at 2.5% to coincide with a single quantile score, which corresponds to a 5% error rate for the test [42,107].

Table 5 presents the obtained results, the observed N_{obs} and the forecasted number of earthquakes N_{fore}, and the quantile scores δ_1 and δ_2. The N-test performance can be interpreted by observing whether the quantile scores δ_1 and δ_2 fall the region between 0.025 and 1. In Figure 11, we can observe that high δ_1 scores tend to correspond to low δ_2 scores.

Table 5. Observed and forecasted earthquake number using the selected SSA model quantile score δ_1 and δ_2.

Year	N Observed	N Forecasted	N-Test δ_1	N-Test δ_2
2016	2	3.0	0.8506	0.2240
2017	2	3.2	0.8705	0.2079
2018	0	3.5	1	0.0302
2019	2	3.4	0.8865	0.1929

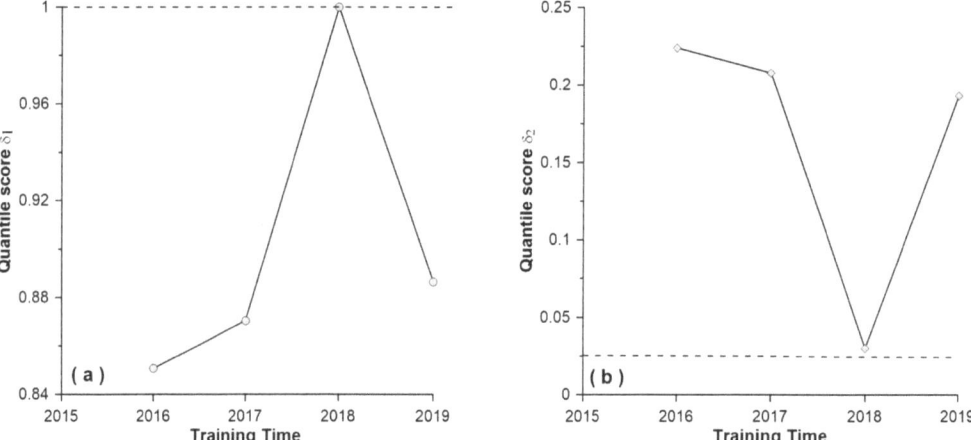

Figure 11. N-test values for (**a**) δ_1 index and (**b**) δ_2 index.

6. Discussion and Conclusions

The SSA technique is a well-known and effective time series analysis tool. On the studied earthquake magnitude time series, the forecasting capabilities of the SSA method were evaluated and compared with those of the standard ARIMA one, which is recognized to have a more suitable structure for forecasting.

The results of this study show that the SSA technique could be effectively applied as an algorithm for forecasting earthquake number and sizes.

According to Abacha et al. [61], the seismicity in the studied area is continuous and moderate. Several swarm sequences occurred in the recent past, showing intense activity with low magnitudes and limited time. An analysis of the series covering the years 1910 to 2015 is performed in order to validate the method employed in the current study by forecasting for the years 2016 to 2019. The forecasting values agree very well with the observed events both for the frequency and the annual maximum magnitude. Moreover, according to the recent recorded seismicity in the studied area, the forecasted magnitudes computed in the current study agree very well with the recorded seismicity during the years 2020 and 2021. The recorded magnitude events during these two years are lower than the maximum forecasted magnitudes, equal to 4.9 and 5.1, respectively. These results should to be considered as the maximum magnitude that is not exceeded.

The SSA model successfully modelled the considered data file and provided an accurate forecast of future earthquake magnitudes. Furthermore, the SSA model's trend component is a clear deterministic component for estimating earthquake magnitude.

The N-test was employed in this study to assess the consistency between the observation and forecasting in terms of the total number of events. The results were given in terms of quantile scores δ_1 and δ_2. According to the results, the test is passed, which validates the suggested model.

The results also show that, while significant parts of the variability in those seismological time series do not appear to have an adequate time structure to be forecasted, the key components may still be identified and forecasted using the SSA model.

It is worth noting that the data file used in this study, which spans the years 1910 to the end of 2019, including events with magnitudes greater than Mw 4.0, could be modelled by an inhomogeneous Poisson process with a variable activity rate (Figure 2). A future study could forecast the number of earthquakes using such an inhomogeneous Poisson process, while the annual maximum magnitude could also be forecasted using, for instance, the extreme probability statistics [25]. An issue that appears to be a weakness of these procedures, and deserves special attention in the future, is the assessment of uncertainties of the forecasted values.

Author Contributions: Conceptualization, M.M., M.H. and J.A.P.; methodology, M.H., M.M. and J.A.P.; validation, M.H., M.M., J.A.P., and J.H.; formal analysis, M.H., M.M. and J.A.P. and T.M.; investigation, M.H., M.M., J.A.P., J.H. and T.M.; resources, M.H.; data curation, M.H., M.M., and J.A.P.; writing-original draft preparation, M.H., M.M., and J.A.P.; writing-review and editing, M.H., M.M., J.A.P., J.H. and T.M.; visualization, M.H., M.M., J.A.P., J.H., and T.M; supervision, M.H., M.M., J.A.P., J.H. and T.M.; project administration, M.H. All authors have read and agreed to the published version of the manuscript.

Funding: This research received no external funding.

Institutional Review Board Statement: Not applicable.

Informed Consent Statement: Not applicable.

Data Availability Statement: The data used in this study are available on request from the corresponding author.

Conflicts of Interest: The authors declare no conflict of interest.

References

1. DeMets, C.; Gordon, R.G.; Argus, D.F.; Stein, S. Current plate motions. *Geophys. J. Int.* **1990**, *101*, 425–478. [CrossRef]
2. Calais, E.; Demets, C.; Nocquet, J.M. Evidence for a post-3.16 Ma change in Nubia-Eurasia plate motion. *Earth Planet. Sci. Lett.* **2003**, *216*, 81–92. [CrossRef]
3. Serpelloni, E.; Vannucci, G.; Pondrelli, S.; Argnani, A.; Casula, G.; Anzidei, M.; Baldi, P.; Gasperini, P. Kinematics of the western Africa-Eurasia plate boundary from focal mechanisms and GPS data. *Geophys. J. Int.* **2007**, *169*, 1180–1200. [CrossRef]
4. EERI-Earthquake Engineering Research Institute. El-Asnam. In *Algeria Earthquake of October 10, 1980: A Reconnaissance and Engineering Report*; National Academy of Sciences: Washington, DC, USA, 1983.
5. Hamdache, M.; Peláez, J.A.; Yelles-Chauche, A.K. The Algiers, Algeria earthquake (Mw 6.8) of 21 May 2003: Preliminary report. *Seismol. Res. Lett.* **2004**, *75*, 360–367. [CrossRef]
6. ASCE-American Society of Civil Engineers. *Zemmouri, Algiers, Mw 6.8 Earthquake of May 21, 2003*; Report to the Technical Council on Lifeline Earthquake Engineering Monograph No. 27; American Society of Civil Engineers: Reston, VA, USA, 2004.
7. Hamdache, M.; Peláez, J.A.; Talbi, A.; López Casado, C. A Unified Catalog of Main Earthquakes for Northern Algeria from A.D. 856 to 2008. *Seismol. Res. Lett.* **2010**, *81*, 732–739. [CrossRef]
8. Keilis-Borok, V.I. What comes next in the dynamics of lithosphere and earthquake prediction? *Phys. Earth Planet. Inter.* **1999**, *111*, 179–185. [CrossRef]
9. Orihara, Y.; Noda, Y.; Nagao, T.; Uyeda, S. A possible case of SES selectivity at Kozushima Island, Japan. *J. Geodyn.* **2002**, *33*, 425–432. [CrossRef]
10. Tiampo, K.F.; Rundle, J.B.; McGinnis, S.; Gross, S.J.; Klein, W. Eigenpatterns in southern California seismicity. *J. Geophys. Res.* **2002**, *107*, ESE 8-1–ESE 8-17. [CrossRef]
11. Tiampo, K.F.; Rundle, J.B.; Mcginnis, S.; Klein, W. Pattern dynamics and forecast methods in seismically active regions. *Pure Appl. Geophys.* **2002**, *159*, 2429–2467. [CrossRef]

12. Kanamori, H. Earthquake prediction: An overview. In *International Handbook of Earthquake and Engineering Seismology*; Lee, W.H.K., Kanamori, H., Jennings, P.C., Kisslinger, C., Eds.; Academic Press: Amsterdam, The Netherlands, 2003; pp. 1205–1216.
13. Evison, F.F.; Rhoades, D.A. Demarkation and scaling of long-term seismogenesis. *Pure Appl. Geophys.* **2004**, *161*, 21–45. [CrossRef]
14. Holliday, J.; Chen, C.; Tiampo, K.F.; Rundle, J.B.; Turcotte, D.L. A RELM earthquake forecast based on pattern informatics. *Seismol. Res. Lett.* **2007**, *78*, 87–93. [CrossRef]
15. Kagan, Y. On Earthquake Predictability Measurement: Information Score and Error Diagram. *Pure Appl. Geophys.* **2007**, *164*, 1947–1962. [CrossRef]
16. Papazachos, B.C.; Karakaisis, G.F.; Papazachos, C.B.; Scordilis, E.M. Evaluation of the results for an intermediate-term prediction of the 8 January 2006 Mw $\frac{1}{4}$ 6.9 Cythera earthquake in the Southwestern Aegean. *Bull. Seismol. Soc. Am.* **2007**, *97*, 347–352. [CrossRef]
17. Mignan, A. The stress accumulation model: Accelerating moment release and seismic hazard. *Adv. Geophys.* **2008**, *49*, 67–191. [CrossRef]
18. Field, E.H. Overview of the working group for the development of regional earthquake likelihood models (RELM). *Seismol. Res. Lett.* **2007**, *78*, 7–16. [CrossRef]
19. Schorlemmer, D.; Gerstenberger, M.C.; Wiemer, S.; Jackson, D.D.; Rhoades, D.A. Earthquake likelihood model testing. *Seismol. Res. Lett.* **2007**, *78*, 17–29. [CrossRef]
20. Schorlemmer, D.; Zechar, J.D.; Werner, M.J.; Field, E.H.; Jackson, D.D.; Jordan, T.H.; Relm Working Group. First Results of the regional earthquake likelihood models experiment. *Pure Appl. Geophys.* **2010**, *167*, 859–876. [CrossRef]
21. Zechar, J.D.; Schorlemmer, D.; Werner, M.J.; Gerstenberger, M.C.; Rhoades, D.A.; Jordan, T.H. Regional earthquake likelihood models I: First-order results. *Bull. Seismol. Soc. Am.* **2013**, *103*, 787–798. [CrossRef]
22. DeVries, P.M.R.; Viégas, F.; Wattenberg, M.; Meade, B.J. Deep learning of aftershock patterns following large earthquakes. *Nature* **2018**, *560*, 632–634. [CrossRef]
23. Lippiello, E.; Petrillo, G.; Godano, C.; Tramelli, A.; Papadimitriou, E.; Karakostas, V. Forecasting of the first hour aftershocks by means of the perceived magnitude. *Nat. Commun.* **2019**, *10*, 2953. [CrossRef]
24. Gutenberg, B.; Richter, C.F. Frequency of earthquakes in California. *Bull. Seismol. Soc. Am.* **1944**, *34*, 185–188. [CrossRef]
25. Dargahi-Noubary, G.R. A method for predicting future large earthquakes using extreme order statistics. *Phys. Earth Planet. Inter.* **1986**, *42*, 241–245. [CrossRef]
26. Kagan, Y. Statistics of characteristic earthquakes. *Bull. Seismol. Soc. Am.* **1993**, *83*, 7–24.
27. Firuzan, E. Statistical Earthquake Frequency Analysis for Western Anatolia. *Turk. J. Earth Sci.* **2008**, *17*, 741–762.
28. Özel, G.; Inal, C. The probability function of the compound Poisson process and an application to aftershock sequence in Turkey. *Environmetrics* **2008**, *19*, 79–85. [CrossRef]
29. Özel, G. A bivariate compound Poisson model for the occurrence of foreshock and aftershock sequences in Turkey. *Environmetrics* **2011**, *22*, 847–856. [CrossRef]
30. Jackson, D.D.; Kagan, Y.Y. The 2004 Parkfield earthquake, the 1985 prediction, and characteristic earthquakes: Lessons for the future. *Bull. Seismol. Soc. Am.* **2006**, *96*, S397–S409. [CrossRef]
31. Helmstetter, A.; Sornette, D. Importance of direct and indirect triggered seismicity in the ETAS model of seismicity. *Geophys. Res. Lett.* **2003**, *30*, 1576. [CrossRef]
32. Ogata, Y. Statistics of Earthquake Activity: Models and Methods for Earthquake Predictability Studies. *Annu. Rev. Earth Planet. Sci.* **2017**, *45*, 497–527. [CrossRef]
33. Zhu, F. Modelling over dispersed or under dispersed count data with generalized Poisson integer-valued GARCH models. *J. Math. Anal. Appl.* **2012**, *389*, 58–71. [CrossRef]
34. Shishegaran, A.; Taghavizade, H.; Bigdeli, A.; Shishegaran, A. Predicting the earthquake magnitude along zagros fault using time series and ensemble model. *J. Soft Comput. Civ. Eng.* **2019**, *3*, 67–77. [CrossRef]
35. Serita, A.; Hattor, K.; Yoshino, C.; Hayakawa, M.; Isezaki, N. Principal component analysis and singular spectrum analysis of ULF geomagnetic data associated with earthquakes. *Nat. Hazards Earth Syst. Sci.* **2005**, *5*, 685–689. [CrossRef]
36. Guo, J.; Shi, K.; Liu, X.; Sun, Y.; Li, W.; Kong, Q. Singular spectrum analysis of ionospheric anomalies preceding great earthquakes: Case studies of Kaikoura and Fukushima earthquakes. *J. Geodyn.* **2019**, *124*, 1–13. [CrossRef]
37. Cekim, H.O.; Tekin, S.; Özel, G. Prediction of the earthquake magnitude by time series methods along the East Anatolian Fault, Turkey. *Earth Sci. Inform.* **2021**, *14*, 1339–1348. [CrossRef]
38. Silva, E.S.; Hassani, H.; Heravi, S. Modelling European industrial production with multivariate singular spectrum analysis: A cross industry analysis. *J. Forecast.* **2018**, *37*, 371–384. [CrossRef]
39. Hassani, H.; Yeganegi, M.R.; Khan, A.; Silva, E.S. The Effect of Data Transformation on Singular Spectrum Analysis for Forecasting. *Signals* **2020**, *1*, 4-25. [CrossRef]
40. Rabaute, A.; Chamot-Rooke, N. Active Inversion Tectonics from Algiers to Sicily. In *On Significant Applications of Geophysical Methods, Proceedings of the 1st Springer Conference of the Arabian Journal of Geosciences (CAJG 2018), Hammamet, Tunisia, 12–15 November 2018*; Sundararajan, N., Eshagh, M., Saibi, H., Meghraoui, M., Al-Garni, M., Giroux, B., Eds.; Springer: Cham, Switzerland, 2019; pp. 249–251. [CrossRef]

41. Peláez, J.A.; Hamdache, M.; Sanz de Galdeano, C.; Sawires, R.; García Hernández, M.T. Forecasting moderate earthquakes in Northern Algeria and Morocco. In *Earthquakes and Their Impact on Society*; Springer Natural Hazards Series; D'Amico, S., Ed.; Springer: Berlin/Heidelberg, Germany, 2016; pp. 81–95.
42. Zechar, J.D.; Gerstenberger, M.C.; Rhoades, D.A. Likelihood-based tests for evaluating space-rate-magnitude earthquake forecasts. *Bull. Seismol. Soc. Am.* **2010**, *100*, 1184–1195.
43. Nanjo, K.Z.; Tsuruoka, H.; Yokoi, S.; Ogata, Y.; Falcone, G.; Hirata, N.; Ishigaki, Y.; Jordan, T.H.; Kasahara, K.; Obara, K.; et al. Predictability study on the aftershock sequence following the 2011 Tohoku-Oki, Japan, earthquake: First results. *Geophys. J. Int.* **2012**, *191*, 653–658. [CrossRef]
44. Peláez, J.A.; Henares, J.; Hamdache, M.; Sanz de Galdeano, C. A seismogenic zone model for seismic hazard studies. In *Northwestern Africa in Moment Tensor Solutions. A Useful Tool for Seismotectonics*; Springer Natural Hazards Series; D'Amico, S., Ed.; Springer: Berlin/Heidelberg, Germany, 2018; pp. 643–680.
45. Peláez, J.A.; Henares, J.; Hamdache, M.; Sanz de Galdeano, C. An updated seismic model for the northwestern Africa. In Proceedings of the 16th European Conference (EECE), Thessaloniki, Greece, 18–21 June 2018.
46. Morel, J.L.; Meghraoui, M. The Goringe Alboran-Tell (Galtel) tectonic zone: A transpression system along the Africa-Eurasia plate boundary. *Geology* **1996**, *24*, 755–758.
47. Déverchère, J.; Yelles, K.; Domzig, A.; Mercier de Lépinay, B.; Bouillin, J.P.; Gaullier, V.; Bracène, R.; Calais, E.; Savoye, B.; Kherroubi, A.; et al. Active thrust faulting offshore Boumerdès Algeria, and its relations to the 2003 Mw 6.9 earthquake. *Geophys. Res. Lett.* **2005**, *32*, L04311. [CrossRef]
48. Nocquet, J.M.; Calais, E. Crustal velocity field of western Europe from permanent GPS array solutions, 1996–2001. *Geophys. J. Int.* **2003**, *154*, 72–88. [CrossRef]
49. Nocquet, J.M.; Calais, E. Geodetic measurements of crustal deformation in the western Mediterranean and Europe. *Pure Appl. Geophys.* **2004**, *161*, 661–681. [CrossRef]
50. Sparacino, F.; Palano, M.; Peláez, J.A.; Fernández, J. Geodetic deformation versus seismic crustal moment-rates: Insights from the Ibero-Maghrebian region. *Remote Sens.* **2020**, *12*, 952. [CrossRef]
51. Harbi, A.; Benouar, D.; Benhallou, H. Re-appraisal of seismicity and seismotectonics in the north-eastern Algeria. Part I: Review of historical seismicity. *J. Seismol.* **2003**, *7*, 115–136. [CrossRef]
52. Adams, R.D.; Barazangi, M. Seismotectonics and seismology in the Arab region: A brief summary and future plans. *Bull. Seismol. Soc. Am.* **1984**, *74*, 1011–1030.
53. Yelles-Chaouche, A.; Kherroubi, A.; Beldjoudi, H. The large Algerian earthquakes (267 A.D.-2017). *Fís. Tierra* **2017**, *29*, 159–182. [CrossRef]
54. Deschamps, A.; Gaudemer, Y.; Cisternas, A. The El Asnam, Algeria, earthquake of 10 October 1980: Multiple-source mechanism determined from long-period records. *Bull. Seismol. Soc. Am.* **1982**, *72*, 1111–1128. [CrossRef]
55. Meghraoui, M.; Philip, H.; Albarede, F.; Cisternas, A. Trench investigations through the trace of the 1980 El Asnam thrust fault: Evidence for paleoseismicity. *Bull. Seismol. Soc. Am.* **1988**, *78*, 979–999. [CrossRef]
56. Bezzeghoud, M.; Dimitrov, D.; Ruegg, J.C.; Lammali, K. Faulting mechanism of the El Asnamn (Algeria) 1954 and 1980 earthquakes from modelling of vertical movements. *Tectonophysics* **1995**, *249*, 249–266. [CrossRef]
57. Harbi, A.; Maouche, S.; Vaccari, F.; Aoudia, A.; Oussadou, F.; Panza, G.F.; Benouar, D. Seismicity, seismic input and site effects in the Sahel-Algiers region (North Algeria). *Soil Dyn. Earthq. Eng.* **2007**, *27*, 427–447. [CrossRef]
58. Boulahia, O.; Abacha, I.; Yelles-Chaouche, A.; Bendjama, H.; Kherroubi, A.; Mohammedi, Y.; Aidi, C.; Chami, A. Recent Seismic Activity in the Bejaia-Babors Region (Northeastern Algeria): The case of the 2012–2013 Bejaia earthquake sequences. *Pure Appl. Geophys.* **2021**, *178*, 1253–1279. [CrossRef]
59. Boulahia, O.; Abacha, I.; Yelles-Chaouche, A.; Bendjama, H.; Kherroubi, A. Analysis of the Bejaia Seismic Sequence of 2012–2013, Northeastern, Algeria. In *Advances in Geophysics, Tectonics and Petroleum Geosciences, Proceedings of the 2nd Springer Conference of the Arabian Journal of Geosciences (CAJG 2019), Sousse, Tunisia, 25–28 November 2019*; Meghraoui, M., Ed.; Springer: Cham, Switzerland, 2022; pp. 135–139. [CrossRef]
60. Bendjama, H.; Yelles-Chaouche, A.; Boulahia, O.; Abacha, I.; Mohammedi, Y.; Beldjoudi, H.; Rahmani, S.T.E.; Belheouane, O. The March 2017 earthquake sequence along the E-W trending Mcid Aïcha-Debbagh Fault, northeast Algeria. *Geosci. J.* **2021**, *25*, 697–713. [CrossRef]
61. Abacha, I.; Yelles-Chaouche, A.; Boulahia, O. Statistical Study of Earthquake Swarms in North-eastern Algeria with Special Reference to the Ain Azel Swarm; Hodna Chain, 2015. In *Advances in Geophysics, Tectonics and Petroleum Geosciences, Proceedings of the 2nd Springer Conference of the Arabian Journal of Geosciences (CAJG 2019), Sousse, Tunisia, 25–28 November 2019*; Meghraoui, M., Ed.; Springer: Cham, Switzerland, 2022; pp. 145–148. [CrossRef]
62. Yelles-Chaouche, A.; Abacha, I.; Boulahia, O.; Aidi, C.; Chami, A.; Belheouane, A.; Rahmani, S.T.E.; Roubeche, K. The 13 July 2019 Mw 5.0 Jijel Earthquake, northern Algeria: An indicator of active deformation along the eastern Algerian margin. *J. Afr. Earth Sci.* **2021**, *177*, 104149. [CrossRef]
63. Frohlich, C. Triangle diagrams: Ternary graphs to display similarity and diversity of earthquake focal mechanisms. *Phys. Earth Planet. Inter.* **1992**, *75*, 193–198. [CrossRef]
64. Zoback, M.L. First and second order patterns of stress in the lithosphere: The world stress map project. *J. Geophys. Res.* **1992**, *97*, 11703–11728. [CrossRef]

65. Henares, J.; López Casado, C.; Sanz de Galdeano, C.; Delgado, J.; Peláez, J.A. Stress fields in the Ibero-Maghrebian region. *J. Seismol.* **2003**, *7*, 65–78. [CrossRef]
66. Cornell, A. Engineering seismic risk analysis. *Bull. Seismol. Soc. Am.* **1968**, *58*, 1583–1606. [CrossRef]
67. Esteva, L. Seismicity prediction: A Bayesian approach. In Proceedings of the Fourth World Conference on Earthquake Engineering, Santiago, Chile, 13–18 January 1969; Volume 1, pp. 172–184.
68. Esteva, L. Seismic risk and seismic design decisions. In *Seismic Design for Nuclear Power Plants*; Hansen, R.J., Ed.; MIT Press: Cambridge, MA, USA, 1970; pp. 142–182.
69. McGuire, R.K. *FORTRAN Computer Program for Seismic Risk Analysis*; Open-File Report 76-67; U.S. Geological Survey: Reston, VA, USA, 1976.
70. Gardner, J.K.; Knopoff, L. Is the sequence of earthquakes in Southern California, with aftershocks removed, Poissonian? *Bull. Seismol. Soc. Am.* **1974**, *64*, 1363–1367. [CrossRef]
71. EPRI-Electric Power Research Institute. *Seismic Hazard Methodology for the Central and Eastern United States*; EPRI Report NP-4726; U.S. Department of Energy Office of Scientific and Technical Information: Oak Ridge, TN, USA, 1986.
72. Peláez, J.A.; Hamdache, M.; López Casado, C. Seismic Hazard in Northern Algeria Using Spatially-smoothed Seismicity. Results for Peak Ground Acceleration. *Tectonophysics* **2003**, *372*, 105–119. [CrossRef]
73. Box, G.E.P.; Pierce, D.A. Distribution of Residual Autocorrelations in Autoregressive-Integrated Moving Average Time Series Models. *J. Am. Stat. Assoc.* **1970**, *65*, 1509–1526. [CrossRef]
74. Hyndman, R.J.; Athanasopoulos, G. *Forecasting: Principles and Practice*, 2nd ed.; OTexts: Melbourne, Australia, 2018.
75. Box, G.E.P.; Jenkins, G.M. *Time Series Analysis: Forecasting and Control*; Holden-Day: San Francisco, CA, USA, 1976.
76. Lai, Y.; Dzombak, D.A. Use of the Autoregressive Integrated Moving Average (ARIMA) Model to Forecast Near-Term Regional Temperature and Precipitation. *Weather Forecast.* **2020**, *35*, 959–976. [CrossRef]
77. Cowpertwait, P.S.P.; Metcalfe, A.V. *Introductory Time Series with R*; Springer: New York, NY, USA, 2009. [CrossRef]
78. Akaike, H. A new look at the statistical model identification. *IEEE Trans. Autom. Control* **1974**, *19*, 716–723. [CrossRef]
79. Schwarz, G. Estimating the dimension of a model. *Ann. Stat.* **1978**, *6*, 461–464. [CrossRef]
80. Fabozzi, F.J.; Focardi, S.M.; Rachev, S.T.; Arshanapalli, B.G.; Markus, H. *The Basics of Financial Econometrics. Tools, Concepts, and Asset Management Applications*; John Wiley and Sons, Inc.: Hoboken, NJ, USA, 2014.
81. Kullback, S.; Leibler, R.A. On Information and Sufficiency. *Ann. Math. Stat.* **1951**, *22*, 79–86. [CrossRef]
82. Hurvich, C.M.; Tsai, C.L. Regression and Time Series Model Selection in Small Samples. *Biometrika* **1989**, *76*, 297–307. [CrossRef]
83. Kumaresan, R.; Tufts, D.W. Data-adaptive principal component signal processing. In Proceedings of the 1980 19th IEEE Conference on Decision and Control including the Symposium on Adaptive Processes, Albuquerque, NM, USA, 10–12 December 1980; pp. 949–954.
84. Broomhead, D.S.; King, G.P. Extracting qualitative dynamics from experimental data. *Phys. D Nonlinear Phenom.* **1986**, *20*, 217–236. [CrossRef]
85. Fraedrich, K. Estimating the dimensions of weather and climate attractors. *J. Atmos. Sci.* **1986**, *43*, 419–432. [CrossRef]
86. Vautard, R.; Ghil, M. Singular spectrum analysis in nonlinear dynamics, with applications to paleoclimatic time series. *Phys. D Nonlinear Phenom.* **1989**, *35*, 395–424. [CrossRef]
87. Ghil, M.; Vautard, R. Interdecadal oscillations and the warming trend in global temperature time series. *Nature* **1991**, *350*, 324–327. [CrossRef]
88. Yiou, P.; Baert, E.; Loutre, M.F. Spectral analysis of climate data. *Surv. Geophys.* **1996**, *17*, 619–663. [CrossRef]
89. Pereira de Albuquerque, W.C.; Maciel, C.D. Performance of ultrasound echo decomposition using singular spectrum analysis. *Ultrasound Med. Biol.* **2001**, *27*, 1231–1238. [CrossRef] [PubMed]
90. Moskvina, V.; Zhigljavsky, A. An algorithm based on singular spectrum analysis for change-point detection. *Commun. Stat.-Simul. Comput.* **2003**, *32*, 319–352. [CrossRef]
91. Sivapragasam, C.; Liong, S.Y.; Pasha, M.F.K. Rainfall and runoff forecasting with SSA-SVM approach. *J. Hydroinform.* **2001**, *3*, 141–152. [CrossRef]
92. Deng, C. Time Series Decomposition Using Singular Spectrum Analysis. Master's Thesis, East Tennessee State University, Johnson City, TN, USA, 2014.
93. Golyandina, N.; Zhigljavsky, A. *Singular Spectrum Analysis for Time Series*; Springer: Berlin/Heidelberg, Germany, 2013.
94. Golyandina, N.; Nekrutkin, V.; Zhigljavsky, A. *Analysis of Time Series Structure: SSA and Related Techniques*, 1st ed.; Chapman & Hall/CRC: New York, NY, USA, 2001.
95. Gao, W.; Guo, J.; Zhou, M.Y.H.; Chen, X.; Ji, B. Gravity tides extracted from SSA-denoised superconducting gravity data with the harmonic analysis: A case study at Wuhan station, China. *Acta Geod. Geophys.* **2020**, *55*, 609–625. [CrossRef]
96. Golyandina, N.; Korobeynikov, A.; Zhigljavsky, A. *Singular Spectrum Analysis with R*; Springer: Berlin/Heidelberg, Germany, 2018. [CrossRef]
97. Goulet, V. Introduction à la Programmation en R, 5th ed.École D'actuariat, Université Laval: Québec, QC, Canada, 2016.
98. Korobeynikov, A. Computation- and space-efficient implementation of SSA. *Stat. Its Interface* **2010**, *3*, 357–368. [CrossRef]
99. Shumway, R.H.; Stoffer, D.S. *Time Series Analysis and Its Applications*; Springer: Cham, Switzerland, 2017. [CrossRef]
100. Elliott, G.; Stock, J.H.; Rothenberg, T.J. Efficient Tests for an Autoregressive Unit Root. *Econometrica* **1996**, *64*, 813–836. [CrossRef]
101. Shapiro, S.; Wilk, M.B. An analysis of variance test for normality (complete samples). *Biometrika* **1965**, *52*, 591–611. [CrossRef]

102. Baddeley, A.; Turner, R.; Moller, J.; Hazelton, M. Residual analysis for spatial point processes. *J. R. Stat. Soc. Ser. B* **2005**, *67*, 617–666. [CrossRef]
103. Andersen, A.J.; Dennison, J. An Introduction to Quantile-Quantile Plots for the Experimental Physicist. *Am. J. Phys.* **2019**, *87*, 1–4.
104. Hassani, H. Singular spectrum analysis: Methodology and comparison. *J. Data Sci.* **2007**, *5*, 239–257. [CrossRef]
105. Console, R. Testing earthquake forecast hypotheses. *Tectonophysics* **2001**, *338*, 261–268. [CrossRef]
106. Shcherbakov, R. Statistics and forecasting of aftershocks during the 2019 Ridgecrest, California, earthquake sequence. *J. Geophys. Res. Solid Earth* **2021**, *126*, e2020JB020887. [CrossRef]
107. Taroni, M.; Marzocchi, W.; Schorlemmer, D.; Werner, M.J.; Wiemer, S.; Zechar, J.D.; Heiniger, L.; Euchner, F. Prospective CSEP Evaluation of 1-Day, 3-Month, and 5-Yr Earthquake Forecasts for Italy. *Seismol. Res. Lett.* **2018**, *89*, 1251–1261. [CrossRef]

Disclaimer/Publisher's Note: The statements, opinions and data contained in all publications are solely those of the individual author(s) and contributor(s) and not of MDPI and/or the editor(s). MDPI and/or the editor(s) disclaim responsibility for any injury to people or property resulting from any ideas, methods, instructions or products referred to in the content.

Article

The Cut-Off Frequency of High-Pass Filtering of Strong-Motion Records Based on Transfer Learning

Bo Liu [1,2], Baofeng Zhou [1,2,*], Jingchang Kong [3,*], Xiaomin Wang [1,2] and Chunhui Liu [3]

1. Key Laboratory of Earthquake Engineering and Engineering Vibration, Institute of Engineering Mechanics, China Earthquake Administration, Harbin 150080, China
2. Key Laboratory of Earthquake Disaster Mitigation, Ministry of Emergency Management, Harbin 150080, China
3. School of Civil Engineering, Yantai University, Yantai 264005, China
* Correspondence: zbf166@iem.ac.cn (B.Z.); kjch8811@126.com (J.K.)

Abstract: A high-pass cut-off frequency in filtering is critical to processing strong-motion records. The various processing procedures available nowadays are based on their own needs and are not universal. Regardless of the methods, a visual inspection of the filtered acceleration integration to displacement is required to determine if the selected filter passband is appropriate. A better method is to use a traversal search combined with visual inspection to determine the cut-off frequency, which is the traditional method. However, this method is inefficient and unsuitable for processing massive strong-motion records. In this study, convolutional neural networks (CNNs) were used to replace visual inspection to achieve the automatic judgment of the reasonableness of the filtered displacement time series. This paper chose the pre-trained deep neural network (DNN) models VGG19, ResNet50, InceptionV3, and InceptionResNetV2 for transfer learning, which are only trained in the fully connected layer or in all network layers. The effect of adding probability constraints on the results when predicting categories was analyzed as well. The results obtained through the VGG19 model, in which all network layers are trained and probability constraints are added to the prediction, have the lowest errors compared to the other models. The coefficient of determination (R^2), root mean square error (RMSE), mean absolute error (MAE), and mean absolute percentage error (MAPE) are 0.82, 0.038, 0.026, and 2.99%, respectively.

Keywords: cut-off frequency of high-pass filtering of strong-motion records; transfer learning; convolutional neural networks (CNNs)

1. Introduction

Strong-motion records provide important primary data for scientific research and engineering practice in earthquake engineering. Strong-motion records usually need to be processed scientifically and reasonably to obtain correct analysis results. Data processing is indispensable in many research subjects such as site effect analysis [1–3], studies on the attenuation relation of ground motion [4–7], structural design and seismic performance assessment [8,9], and seismic resilience assessment [10,11]. In structural dynamic time history analysis, appropriate natural ground motion input can effectively reduce the uncertainty in the analysis results [12,13]. However, slight baseline drift and noise in strong-motion-acceleration records will lead to significant shifts in velocity and displacement time history, which do not correspond with the physical meaning of practical earthquake events and are not appropriate for engineering input and research analysis. Therefore, it is necessary to carry out proper strong-motion records processing in earthquake engineering research.

Various methods have been proposed worldwide to process strong-motion records. The data processing method presented by the NGA strong-motion database [14,15] is firstly to remove the instrument response and zero-line offset from the acceleration time series and then to reduce the noise interference by filtering. The processing flow of the

Reference database for seismic ground-motion in Europe (RESORCE) [16] is: (i) the zero-line adjustment of the acceleration time series; (ii) filtering via a fourth-order non-causal filter; (iii) polynomially fitting the baseline of the displacement time series; (iv) subtracting the second derivative of the baseline with the filtered acceleration. For the Chilean strong-motion database [17], the trigger type of all records is determined, and different methods are applied for the normal trigger and post-trigger records to taper strong-motion records before calculating the Fourier Amplitude Spectrum (FAS). The subsequent filtering process is similar to RESORCE. The data processing method proposed by the European Strong Motion Engineering Database (ESM) [18] and the Italian Strong Motion Database (ITACA) [19] is similar to the one described above. However, the zero-line correction, the taper length, the filter order, and other parameters are different, and post-processing after obtaining the filtered acceleration time series is added.

In the above processing of strong-motion records, the effects of noise are all removed by filtering, in which the high-pass and low-pass cut-off frequencies are essential parameters. For the Internet Site for European Strong-Motion Data (ISESD) [20], two constant values (0.25 Hz and 25 Hz) are used as high-pass and low-pass cut-off frequencies in band-pass filtering. In the NGA strong-motion database [14], the high-pass cut-off frequency is determined by visually examining the FAS and the integrated displacements, while the high-pass and low-pass cut-off frequencies are both determined via the visual inspection of FAS in the ESM [18] and ITACA [19]. Furthermore, in RESORCE [16], the high-pass cut-off frequency is selected by referring to the theoretical corner frequencies of the double-corner source spectrum [21], and the low-pass cut-off frequency is determined based on the recommendations of Douglas et al. [22]. In addition, the signal-to-noise ratio (SNR) can also be used to calculate the high-pass and low-pass cut-off frequencies. In the Chilean strong-motion database [17], the high-pass cut-off frequency is determined by limiting the SNR to be greater than 3.0, while the Nyquist frequency is selected as the low-pass cut-off frequency. The high-pass and low-pass cut-off frequencies were determined by limiting the SNR to be greater than 3 by Parker et al. [23]. Bahrampouri et al. [24] determined the high-pass cut-off frequency by limiting the SNR to be greater than 2, and choosing the low-pass cut-off frequency requires an SNR to be greater than 1. Edwards et al. [25] used the point at which the linear trend of the recorded FAS decays more slowly than the theoretical spectrum [26] to define the high-pass cut-off frequency. An SNR equal to 3 was taken as the lower limit of the low-pass cut-off frequency. A better method is to filter by using a high-pass cut-off frequency from small to large and to determine the rationality and accuracy of the selected high-pass cut-off frequency by visually inspecting the effect of integral displacement after filtering.

Unfortunately, low-frequency noise sometimes cannot be effectively and accurately filtered using the method above of determining the filter passband of strong-motion records. At present, a better way to ensure a high-pass cut-off frequency is to determine the rationality and accuracy of the selected cut-off frequency by visually inspecting the effect of the integral displacement after filtering, which is the traditional method [27]. If the mean value at the end of the filtered displacement time series is close to zero and the fitted straight line at the end of the range remains horizontal, the time series curve is considered qualified. A new filtered passband must be selected for filtering if it is not considered qualified. However, the efficiency of the traditional method is extremely low, and it is not suitable for processing massive strong-motion records. It is necessary to visually inspect the integral displacement after filtering to determine whether the results are acceptable.

According to Xie [28] and Zhou [29], the low-pass cut-off frequency has little effect on the baseline offset of displacement time series for strong-motion records. The low-pass cut-off frequency in this paper is taken as 35 Hz (where the sampling frequency is 100 Hz) or 20 Hz (where the sampling frequency is 50 Hz). Generally, in the traditional method, people must subjectively inspect the acceptability of the filtering result by classifying the integral displacement time series curve into qualified or unqualified. However, there is no uniform classification standard in traditional artificial identification for the integral displacement time series qualification.

Computer vision has been applied to image classification with uniform criteria and a faster speed. Convolutional neural networks (CNNs) that can automatically extract higher-dimensional features of data can significantly improve the accuracy of computer vision tasks [30,31]. However, deep neural networks (DNNs) [32] are slower to converge due to their large number of parameters. Transfer learning [33] enables the model to converge quickly by fine-tuning the pre-trained weights of the model. In this way, pre-trained network models can be better adapted to new data sets to achieve higher performance and reduce training time.

In this paper, to address the shortcomings of the traditional method, deep CNNs were used to replace visual inspection to achieve the automatic judgment of the reasonableness of a filtered displacement time series in processing massive strong-motion records. The pre-trained neural network models VGG19 [34], ResNet50 [35], InceptionV3 [36], and InceptionResNetV2 [37] were adopted for transfer learning to classify the filtered displacement time series as qualified or unqualified. The classification performance of the models that only train the fully connected layer was compared with the models in which all layers are trained. Moreover, the model with higher classification performance was applied to the traversal search of the high-pass cut-off frequency. Finally, the high-pass cut-off frequencies determined using traditional methods were used as accurate values, and four metrics widely used in past investigations (i.e., the coefficient of determination, root mean square error, mean absolute error, and mean absolute percentage error) were used to evaluate the results obtained using each model. The effect of adding a probability constraint to the predictive classification for the final results was also compared and analyzed.

2. Database

Raw ground motion records, supplied by the Center for Engineering Strong Motion Data (CESMD) [38], were adopted in this work. A total of 4461 raw records in V1c format were selected for this paper. The traditional method was applied to these raw records to obtain the appropriate high-pass cut-off frequency for each record.

2.1. Traditional Method

The procession of the traditional method to determine the high-pass cut-off frequency of strong-motion records is shown in Figure 1, which consists of four crucial steps, as follows:

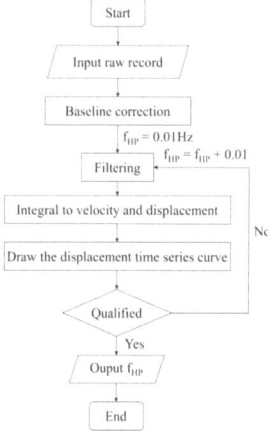

Figure 1. The process of obtaining the high-pass cut-off frequency (f_{HP} is the high-pass cut-off frequency).

Step 1: The baseline correction of raw records. The method used here is to remove the first-order function fitted by the record.

Step 2: The selection of the appropriate high-pass cut-off frequency for filtering to remove the low-frequency noise, starting from 0.01 Hz and increasing the high-pass cut-off frequency with every step of 0.01 Hz.

Step 3: The integration of filtered acceleration time series into velocity and displacement time series.

Step 4: The artificial identification of displacement time series curves that are qualified; if they are not, skip to step 2; if they are qualified, output the cut-off frequency.

2.2. Data Pre-Processing

Yao et al. [39] showed that the causal filtering method does not produce interference signals in the noise segment before the seismic signal arrives, while acausal filtering causes interference vibration before the signal arrives. Moreover, the order of the filter is an important factor for filtering, and a higher-order filter will lead to more oscillation at both ends of the filtered record [40]. Therefore, the fourth-order Butterworth causal filter, a widely used filter [14,16,17,24,29], was used in this paper. The traditional method was used to find the high-pass cut-off frequencies of 4461 records, and 3065 records could only obtain qualified displacement time series curves only through band-pass filtering. Observing the processed records from CESMD showed that the cut-off frequencies were selected in a "one-size-fits-all" manner, i.e., the same cut-off frequency was adopted for all three components of the same record (Figure 2a). However, the velocity and displacement time series curves obtained in this way appeared to be qualified but may have had too much valid information filtered out, because the noise affecting the three components of the same record was not necessarily the same. Therefore, it was essential to find the high-pass cut-off frequency for every record. The high-pass cut-off frequencies corresponding to the 3065 records obtained using the traditional method were taken as the accurate values. The scatter plot of these values is shown in Figure 2b.

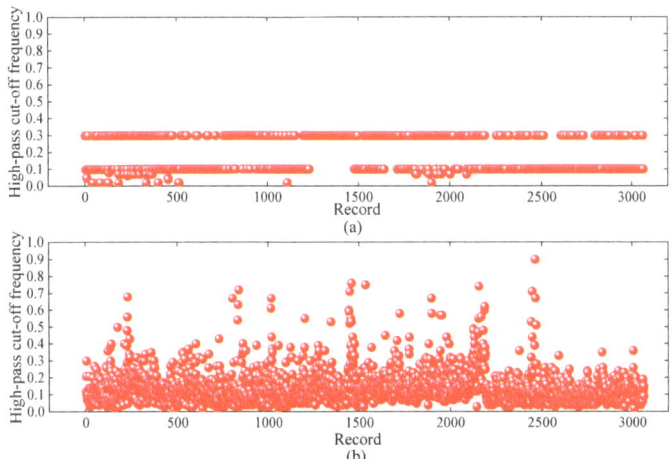

Figure 2. The high-pass cut-off frequency for each record. (**a**) CESMD; (**b**) traditional method.

The partial acceleration, velocity, and displacement time series curves of record AKBAW–n.0212o88mof.BNE after filtering with different high-pass cut-off frequencies are shown in Figure 3. It was observed that the displacement time series curves obtained via filtering with the value before the accurate value as the cut-off frequency were all unqualified, and the ones after that were all qualified.

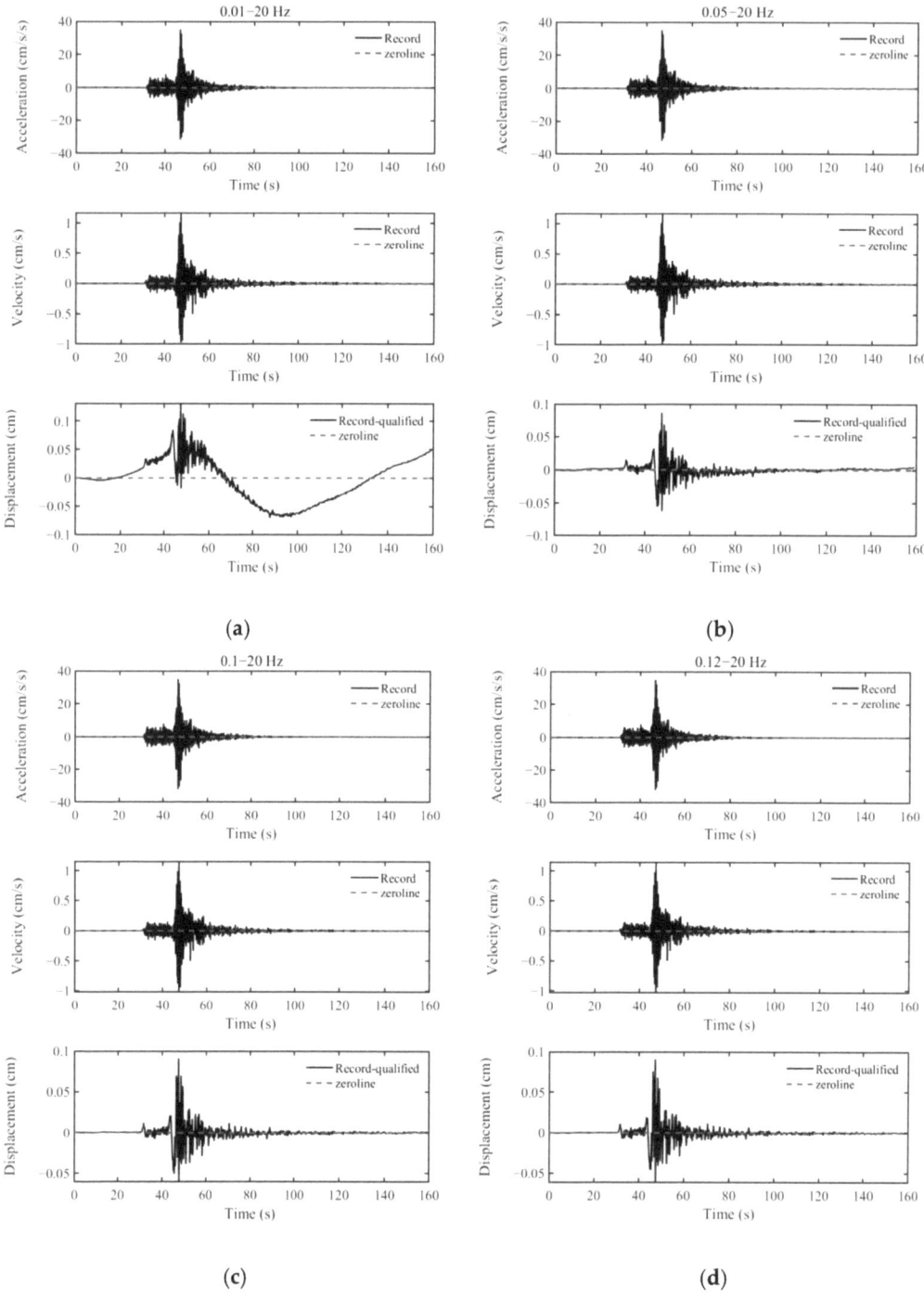

Figure 3. Cont.

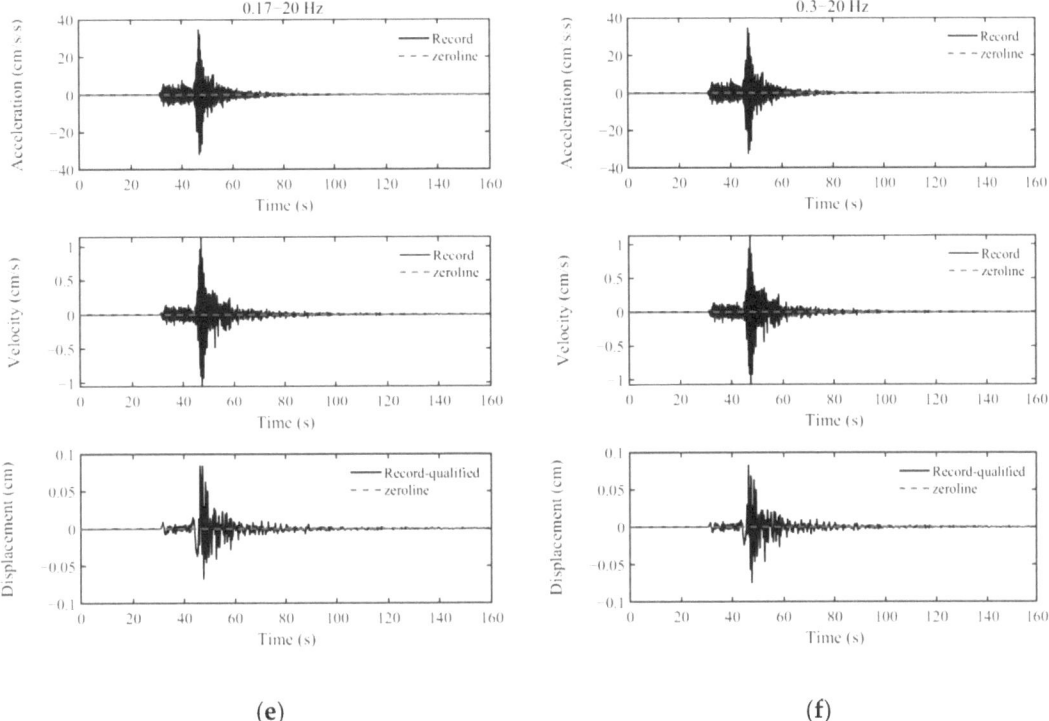

Figure 3. The post-filtering time series curve of record AKBAW–n.0212o88mof.BNE (**d**) and subsequent images are considered qualified, where figure f is the filtered time series curve using the frequency given by CESMD). (**a**) 0.01 Hz; (**b**) 0.05 Hz; (**c**) 0.10 Hz; (**d**) 0.12 Hz; (**e**) 0.17 Hz; (**f**) 0.30 Hz.

For each strong-motion record, up to six filtered displacement time series curves were selected for the purpose of building the database. These included three unqualified curves and three qualified curves. The three qualified displacement curves were obtained by filtering using the accurate value and two frequency values after it as the high-pass cut-off frequency. There was little difference between the displacement curves after filtering with two adjacent frequencies. The unqualified displacement curves were obtained by filtering with 0.01 Hz, 0.03 Hz, and 0.05 Hz as high-pass cut-off frequencies. The exact value of some records did not reach 0.05 Hz, so the frequency value of the unqualified time series curve was only 0.01 Hz and 0.03 Hz. A total of 8866 unqualified displacement curves and 9195 qualified displacement curves were obtained through the above method. Ultimately, 18,061 displacement curves were used as the dataset. Additionally, 80% of the data were input into the CNN as the training set, and the test and validation set was 10%; the dataset was divided randomly.

The zero line was used as a reference in the artificial identification of the drift of the displacement curve, and to facilitate machine differentiation, the zero line was represented by a solid red line. To avoid the influence of axes and legends on model training, all graphs were cropped so that the CNN could only see the displacement curve. To meet the input requirement of the networks in this paper, the image was resized to 224 × 224 × 3. The result of the image resizing is shown in Figure 4.

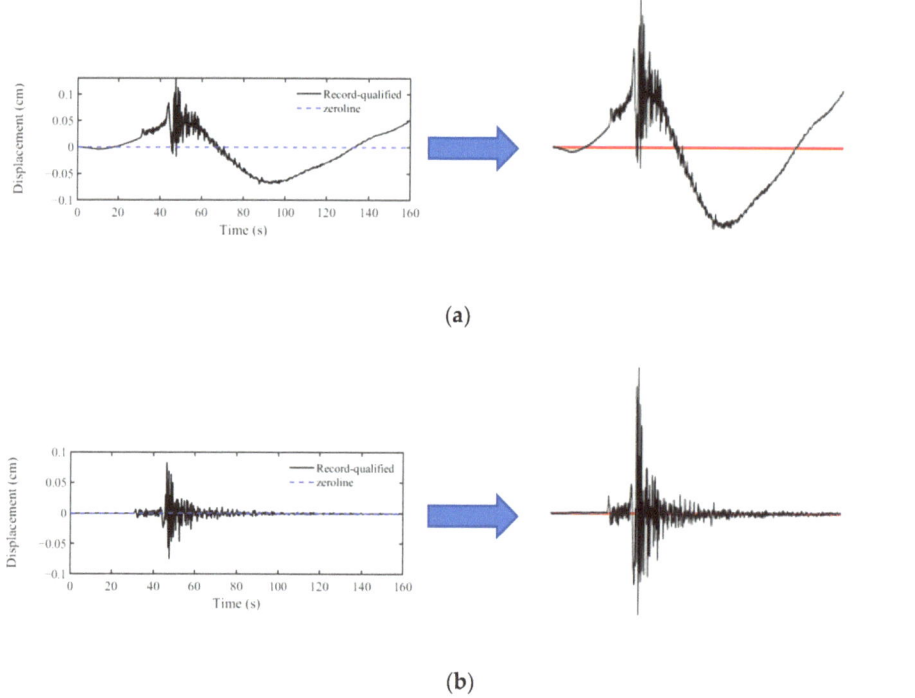

Figure 4. The processing of displacement diagram. (**a**) Unqualified displacement time series curve; (**b**) qualified displacement time series curve.

3. Deep Neural Networks (DNNs)

In the classification of data, convolutional neural networks (CNNs) are widely used. However, it is difficult to extract high-dimensional abstract data features in a CNN with simple architecture, and this leads to under-fitting problems. In order to achieve more effective data character extraction and classification, a more complex network model is needed. Complex network structures often have a large number of parameters, and the model takes a long time to converge. Therefore, model-based transfer learning [33] was adopted in this study to solve the above problems. Previous research [41] has shown that trained models can be adapted to other datasets or tasks by simply fine-tuning them. Fine-tuning allows the pre-trained parameters of the model to fit the new dataset better, which can improve classification performance and save training time.

3.1. Transfer Learning Model

In this paper, the VGG19 [34], ResNet50 [35], InceptionV3 [36] and InceptionResNetV2 [37] pre-trained network models were adopted for transfer learning, and the corresponding network architectures are shown in Figure 5. The parameter information regarding these models is shown in Table 1. It can be seen that the VGG19 network model has a minor depth but the most significant number of parameters. There are two large fully connected layers (4096 neurons) after the backbone model. Resnet50 has a global average pooling layer which dramatically reduces the size of output from the model. On the other hand, the InceptionV3 and InceptionResNetV2 models reduce the number of parameters in the model by using parallel modules and concatenating small convolutions instead of large convolutions and using a global average pooling layer.

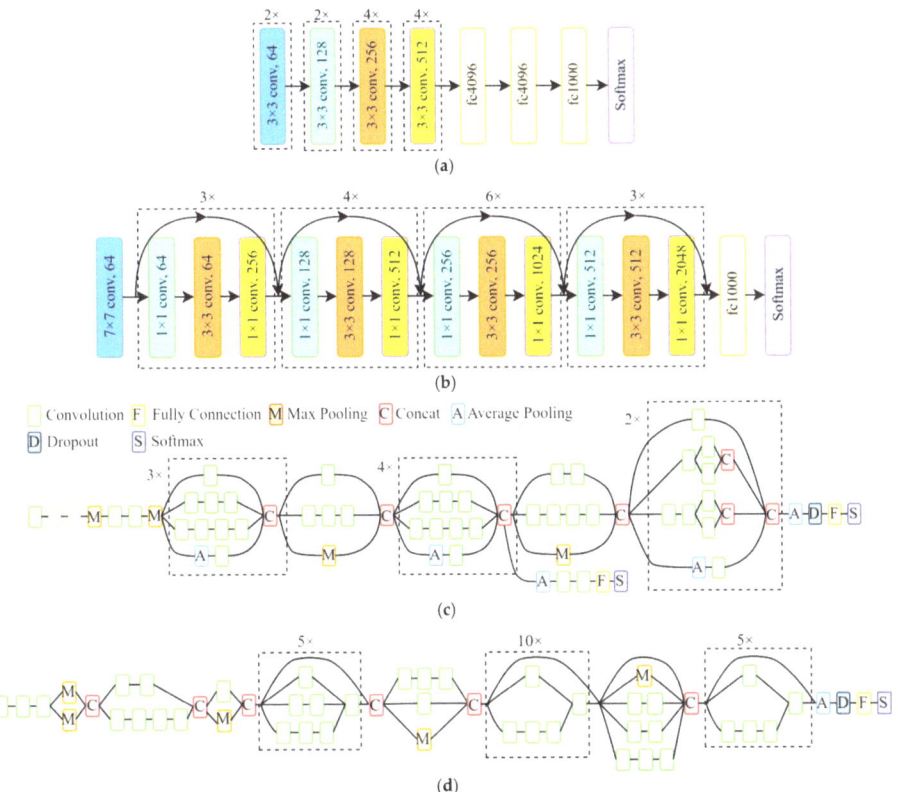

Figure 5. Architectures of typical deep neural networks. (**a**) VGG19; (**b**) ResNet50; (**c**) InceptionV3; (**d**) InceptionResNetV2.

Table 1. The parameter information regarding network models.

Model	Size (MB)	Depth	Number of Parameters (Million)
VGG19 [34]	549	26	144
ResNet50 [35]	98	168	25.6
InceptionV3 [36]	92	159	23.9
InceptionResNetV2 [37]	215	572	55.9

3.2. Training and Evaluation Methods

In this paper, the training of the network model was divided into two parts. On the one hand, only the fully connected layers were trained, and the weights of all the other layers were frozen. On the other hand, all the network layers were unfrozen, and the parameters of all the network layers were fine-tuned. Additionally, all the models were trained for 50 epochs. Furthermore, Python 3.8 [42] with Tensorflow 2.8 [43] and Keras 2.8 [44] deep learning frameworks were used as the training environment. Adam [45] optimizer was used to improve the accuracy of the model. Binary cross-entropy was used as the loss function (Equation (1)). The cross-entropy function is widely used in deep learning classification, which is based on maximum likelihood estimation to fit a model. It minimizes the distance between two probability distributions (predicted and actual). Combined with the activation function in the output layer (such as sigmoid or softmax), it can accelerate the training of deep learning models faster via logarithmic operations.

Additionally, the evaluation metric $Perf$ [46] (Equation (2)) was selected to compare the performance of different models, and both training and validation performance were considered in the method.

$$\text{Loss} = -\frac{1}{N}\sum_{i=1}^{N} y_i \times \log(p(y_i)) + (1-y_i) \times \log(1-p(y_i)) \quad (1)$$

$$Perf = \mu_{train} \times \frac{acc_{train}}{loss_{train}} + \mu_{vaild} \times \frac{acc_{valid}}{loss_{valid}} \quad (2)$$

where N is the total number of samples, y_i is the binary label 0 or 1, and $p(y_i)$ is the probability of the output y_i label. μ_{train} and μ_{vaild} are the weights of the training and validation results, respectively; the values are 0.1 and 0.9, respectively. The acc_{train} and $loss_{train}$ are the accuracy and loss of the training results, and acc_{valid} and $loss_{valid}$ are the accuracy and loss of the validation results. Here, the mean value of the last 10 epochs is presented.

3.3. Training and Evaluation Results

Figure 6 presents the detailed training process for the four network models. The solid and dashed lines are the training and validation results, respectively. Frozen denotes the models in which only the fully connected layers are trained, and unfrozen indicates the models in which all layers are trained. As shown in Figure 6, among the network models that only train fully connected layers, only the VGG19 model has higher accuracy and lower loss on the training and test sets. On the contrary, the remaining three models have relatively high losses and significantly lower and not converged accuracies. As the depth of the model increases, the accuracy of the model gets lower, and the loss gets higher and higher, indicating that the weights of other network layers except the fully connected layer are frozen so that the powerful feature extraction ability of the deep neural network has not been exerted. For the models in which all the network layers are trained, all four models achieve high accuracy in training and validation results, and the losses are close to zero and converge in the end. These results indicate that no overfitting occurred.

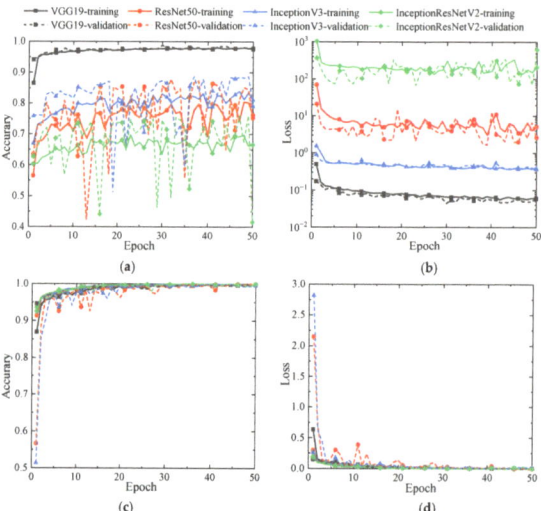

Figure 6. Detailed training process for deep neural networks. (**a**) Training and validation accuracies (frozen); (**b**) training and validation losses (frozen); (**c**) training and validation accuracies (unfrozen); (**d**) training and validation losses (unfrozen).

The performance of each model was evaluated using Equation (2), and the results are presented in Table 2. For the displacement curve classification problem in this paper, the $Perf$ of InceptionV3-frozen, ResNet50-frozen, and InceptionResNetV2-frozen is close to 0, which is not suitable for this paper. However, the $Perf$ of VGG19-frozen and the model with all the network layers trained is higher, with the InceptionResNetV2-unfrozen model reaching 40.43, and they are more suitable for the dichotomous classification problem in this paper.

Table 2. Performance evaluation of deep transfer neural networks.

DNN	VGG19– Frozen	VGG19– Unfrozen	InceptionV3– Frozen	InceptionV3– Unfrozen	ResNet50– Frozen	ResNet50– Unfrozen	InceptionResNetV2– Frozen	InceptionResNetV2– Unfrozen
acc_{train}	0.979	0.998	0.770	0.999	0.768	0.999	0.670	0.999
acc_{valid}	0.980	0.997	0.801	0.997	0.801	0.997	0.682	0.998
$loss_{train}$	0.061	0.008	4.804	0.004	42.364	0.004	212.492	0.003
$loss_{valid}$	0.052	0.010	3.356	0.011	30.580	0.009	214.860	0.009
$Perf$	3.479	23.04	0.043	37.40	0.004	36.07	0.000	40.43

3.4. Test Results

Finally, the test set was tested using the network model with the lowest loss and highest accuracies among the 50 epochs. The accuracy of various models was evaluated using confusion matrices, and the corresponding results are shown in Figure 7. Categories 0 and 1 represent the unqualified and qualified displacement time curves, respectively. The diagonal elements of the matrix represent the number of samples with the correct predicted class, and the other pieces represent the number of samples with the incorrectly predicted class. The third column of the third row of the matrix is the ratio of correctly classified samples to the total number of samples, which is the accuracy rate.

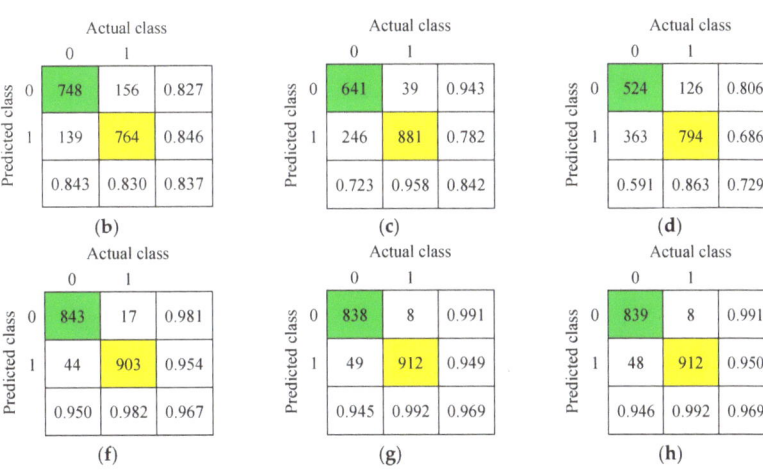

Figure 7. Confusion matrix of test set, where green and yellow represent the number of correctly classified samples with labels of 0 and 1, respectively. (**a**) VGG19–frozen; (**b**) ResNet50–frozen; (**c**) InceptionV3–frozen; (**d**) InceptionResNetV2–frozen; (**e**) VGG19–unfrozen; (**f**) ResNet50–unfrozen; (**g**) InceptionV3–unfrozen; (**h**) InceptionResNetV2–unfrozen.

As shown in Figure 7, the test results remained consistent with those in Table 2, and the InceptionResNetV2–unfrozen model performed the best with an overall accuracy of 96.9%. The five models that performed better had relatively high classification accuracies for qualified displacement curve images, with a maximum of 99.2%. For all the models, misclassifying unqualified displacement curve pictures as qualified was an essential factor affecting the overall accuracy.

In summary, among all the network models that only train the fully connected layer, the VGG19 network model has the best performance in the validation and testing process. Models with all the network layers trained can achieve good classification results. Therefore, in the following work of this paper, the VGG19–frozen model and the four models that train all the layers were chosen to identify whether the displacement curve was qualified.

4. Application of the Trained Network Models

In this section, the trained DNN models were used to identify whether the filtered displacement time curve was qualified. The artificial recognition of the displacement curve in the traditional method is replaced by a CNN, which saves a lot of time and improves work efficiency.

4.1. Filtering Results

In the filtering process of this paper, after filtering, the displacement curve changed from unqualified to qualified. When approaching the reasonable filtering frequency obtained using the traditional method, there was no significant difference in the displacement curve picture, so it would be judged as qualified prematurely. The conventional data binary classification problem considers that as long as the prediction probability is greater than 50%, it is considered to belong to the class. In order to avoid premature judgment as qualified, stricter criteria should be adopted. Therefore, probability restrictions were added to determine whether the filtered displacement curve was qualified using the deep network model. Only when a higher probability is judged to be qualified can it be considered qualified and not be the traditional 50%. After comparison, this paper argued that more than 99.9% of the probability being considered qualified is appropriate. Figures 8 and 9 show the relationship between the high-pass cut-off frequency obtained by considering the probability and not considering the probability and the high-pass cut-off frequency obtained by using the traditional method when judging whether the displacement after filtering is qualified.

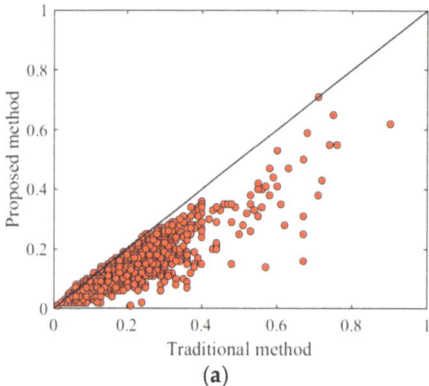
(a)

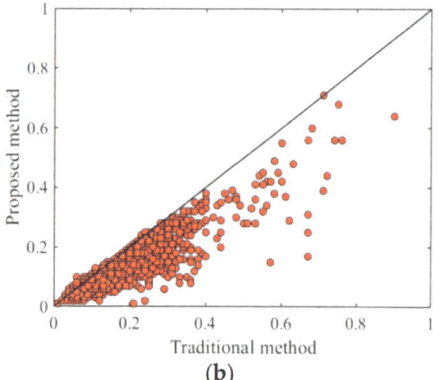
(b)

Figure 8. The high-pass cut-off frequency was obtained using a model that only trains the fully connected layer (unit: Hz). (**a**) The VGG19 when not considering probability; (**b**) the VGG19 when considering probability.

As seen from Figures 8 and 9, almost all of these scatter points were distributed below the black line, indicating that the values obtained using the method in this paper were generally smaller than those obtained using the traditional method, and the unqualified displacement curve was prematurely judged as qualified. The black line here was y = x; if two values were equal, they were distributed on the black line.

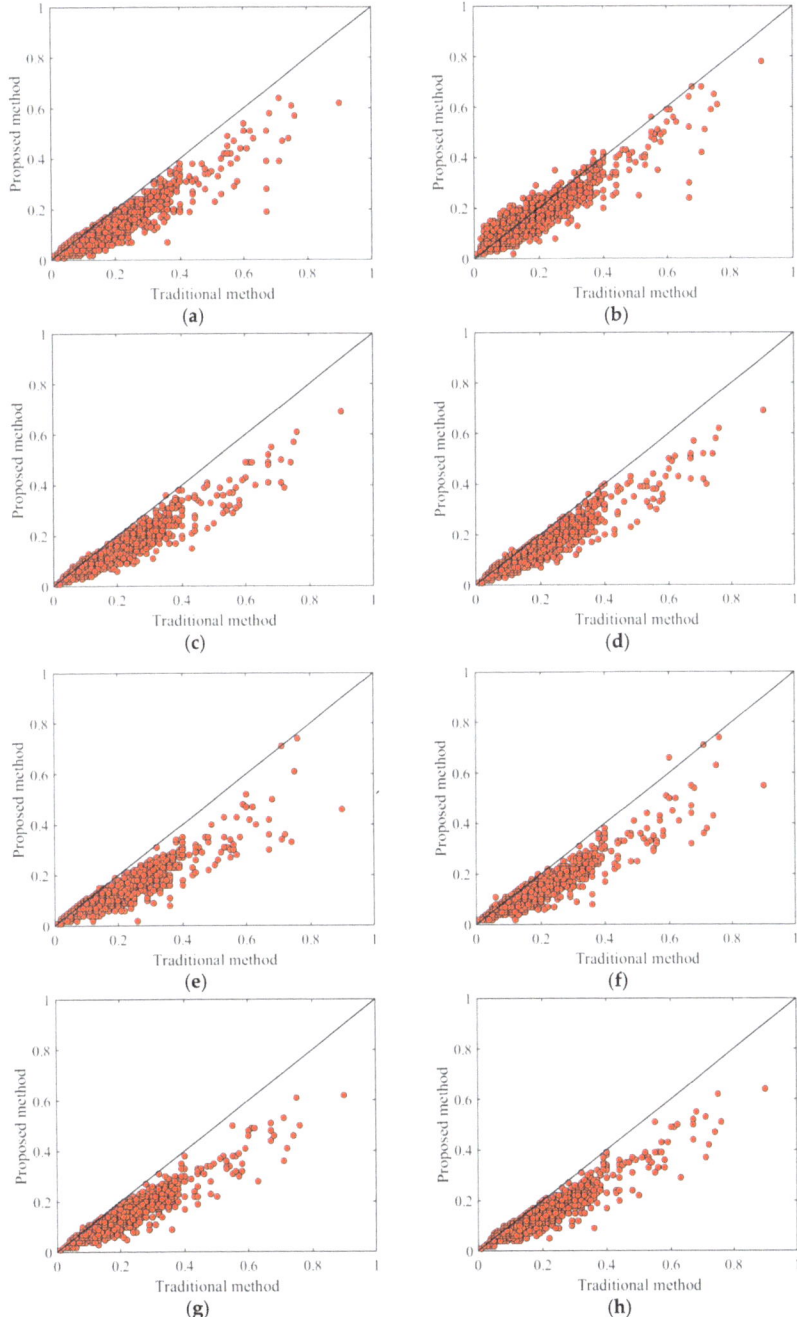

Figure 9. The high-pass cut-off frequency obtained by training the model of all layers (unit: Hz). (**a**,**c**,**e**,**g**) are the results of VGG19, ResNet50, InceptionV3, and InceptionResNetV2 when probabilities are not considered, respectively; (**b**,**d**,**f**,**h**) are the results of VGG19, ResNet50, InceptionV3, and InceptionResNetV2, respectively, when considering the probability.

4.2. Analysis of Filtering Results

To evaluate the accuracy of the high-pass cut-off frequencies obtained with different models, four error functions (Equations (3)–(6)) were applied to analyze the errors concerning the values obtained using the traditional method. The coefficient of determination R^2 is widely used in regression problems to estimate the degree of linear correlation between the true value and the predicted value. The closer R^2 is to 1, the better the performance of the model. The RMSE is used to measure the deviation between the predicted value and the true value. The MAE reflects the actual situation of the prediction error. The MAPE is the ratio of the prediction error to the true value. The closer these three values are to zero, the higher the performance of the model. The results of the calculations related to the four statistical parameters for each model are presented in Table 3.

$$R^2 = 1 - \frac{\sum_{i=1}^{n} (\hat{y}_i - y_i)^2}{\sum_{i=1}^{n} (y_i - \bar{y})^2} \qquad (3)$$

$$RMSE = \sqrt{\frac{1}{n} \sum_{i=1}^{n} (\hat{y}_i - y_i)^2} \qquad (4)$$

$$MAE = \frac{1}{n} \sum_{i=1}^{n} |\hat{y}_i - y_i| \qquad (5)$$

$$MAPE = \frac{100\%}{n} \sum_{i=1}^{n} \left| \frac{\hat{y}_i - y_i}{y_i} \right| \qquad (6)$$

where y and $\hat{y}$ are the high-pass cut-off frequencies obtained using the traditional method and the high-pass cut-off frequency obtained using the method of this paper, respectively, n represents the number of data samples, and $\bar{y}$ denotes the mean value of y.

Table 3. Analysis of results.

Model	Considering Probability?	R^2	RMSE	MAE	MAPE (%)
VGG19–frozen	Yes	0.64	0.054	0.035	21.03
	No	0.57	0.059	0.040	25.34
VGG19–unfrozen	Yes	0.82	0.038	0.026	2.99
	No	0.65	0.052	0.038	24.53
ResNet50–unfrozen	Yes	0.74	0.046	0.031	18.54
	No	0.68	0.050	0.035	21.63
InceptionV3–unfrozen	Yes	0.68	0.051	0.034	20.43
	No	0.59	0.057	0.039	24.40
InceptionResNetV2–unfrozen	Yes	0.69	0.050	0.034	20.49
	No	0.63	0.055	0.039	24.02

According to the analysis results in Table 3, using a CNN instead of artificial identification to judge whether a filtered displacement curve is qualified and thus obtain a high-pass cut-off frequency of strong-motion records can be satisfactory. The coefficient of determination R^2 reached a maximum of 0.82 and a minimum of 0.57. The RMSE ranged from a minimum of 0.038 to a maximum of 0.059. The MAE ranged from a minimum of 0.026 to a maximum of 0.040. The MAPE ranged from a maximum of 25.34% to a minimum of 2.99%. In comparison, the VGG19–unfrozen model considering probabilities was used to achieve the highest accuracy.

It can be concluded that the probability limit added to the prediction classification of the model enhanced its performance. R^2 was improved by an average of 14.41%, of which VGG19–unfrozen had the most improvement at 26.15%. The RMSE, MAE, and

MAPE were reduced by 12.6%, 16.23%, and 30.01% on average. Among them, the three parameters of VGG19–unfrozen were reduced the most by 26.92%, 31.58%, and 87.81%. The performance of the VGG19–unfrozen model was most significantly improved by adding probabilistic restrictions.

4.3. Comparison to Results of the SNR Method

As described in the introduction, the SNR method is widely used in obtaining high-pass cut-off frequencies of strong-motion records [17,23–26]. This section compares the high-pass cut-off frequencies obtained via the traditional method in this paper with those obtained using the SNR method. The method proposed by Bahrampouri et al. [24] was used to obtain a high pass cut-off frequency, and this paper used an SNR greater than 3. The strong-motion record before the arrival of the P-wave was used as a noise window (Figure 10). The P-wave arrival pickup algorithm proposed by Ma et al. [47] was used here. The FAS of strong-motion records and noise was smoothed (the Konno–Ohmachi method [48]), and the smoothed noise FAS was linearly scaled by 4 times (the green dotted line in Figure 11). The point where the zoomed noise smoothing FAS intersects the ground motion smoothing FAS was considered the high-pass cut-off frequency (indicated by an arrow in Figure 11). The choice of a scaling factor equal to four ((signal + noise)/noise) implied an SNR equal to three as the criterion for the choice of the high-pass cut-off frequency.

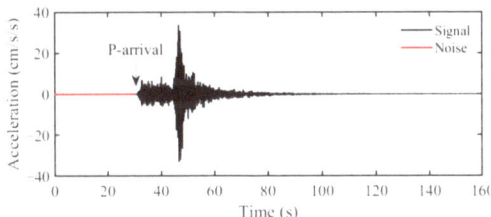

Figure 10. An example of recorded ground motion and noise (AKBAW–n.0212o88mof.BNE).

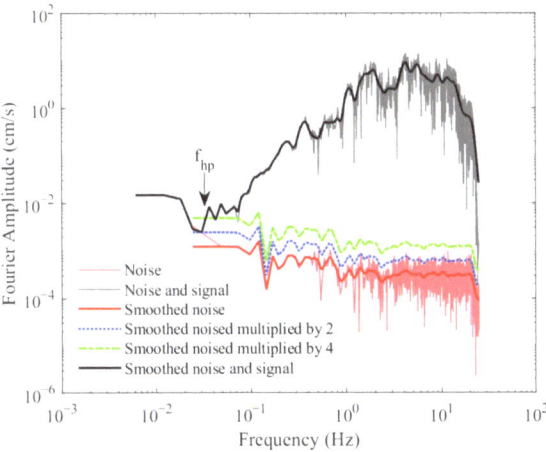

Figure 11. Illustrative plot for selecting filter corner frequencies.

Figure 12 shows the displacement curves for filtering at high-pass cut-off frequencies obtained using the traditional method, the method of this paper, and the SNR method, respectively. For this record, there was a significant drift in the filtered displacement curve using the high-pass cut-off frequency based on the SNR method, indicating that the high-pass cut-off frequency used was inappropriate.

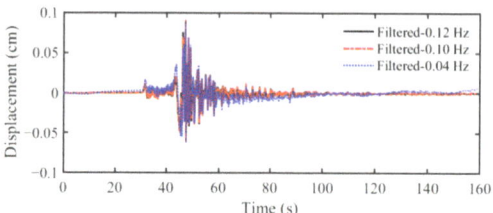

Figure 12. Displacement curves after filtering using different cut-off frequencies.

Then, 300 records were randomly selected from the strong-motion database in this paper, and the high-pass cut-off frequencies obtained using the traditional and SNR methods were compared. Records without intersections (at 0–1 Hz range, as shown in Figure 13) between noise smoothing FAS and record smoothing FAS were removed, and 184 records could be obtained with high-pass cut-off frequencies via the SNR method. Figure 14 shows the high-pass cut-off frequencies obtained via the SNR method for 184 records.

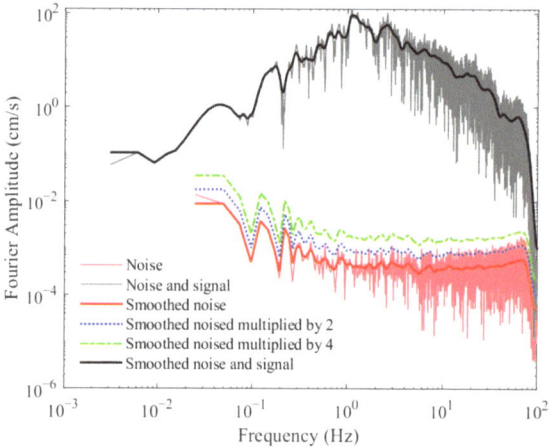

Figure 13. FAS of f_{HP} cannot be obtained via SNR method (AKPWL–n.1000hyfh.HNN.–.V1c).

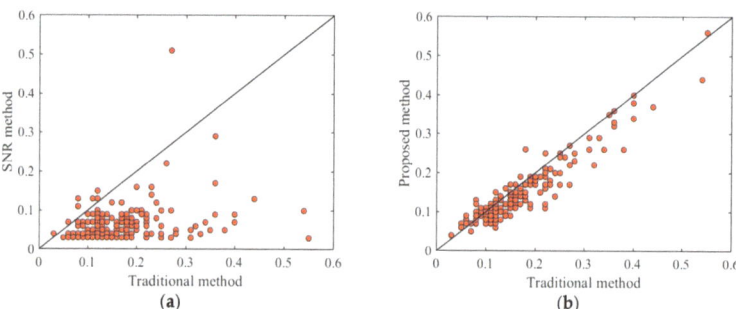

Figure 14. The obtained high-pass cut-off frequency (unit: Hz). (**a**) SNR method (**b**) Proposed method.

It can be seen from Figure 14 that the high-pass cut-off frequency obtained via the SNR method was generally smaller than that obtained using the traditional method. This indicates that the displacement time series curves obtained by filtering the high-pass cut-off frequency obtained using the SNR method were mostly unqualified. In contrast, most of the displacement time series curves obtained via filtering with high-pass cut-off frequency obtained using this paper's method were qualified.

5. Conclusions

This paper studied the rationality of using DNNs instead of artificially judging the displacement curve after filtering strong-motion records. The classification performances of the VGG19, ResNet50, InceptionV3, and InceptionResNetV2 deep transfer neural networks only training the fully connected layer and training all the layers were compared and analyzed. The trained model was then applied to high-pass cut-off frequency traverse searching. Additionally, a probability limit of 99.9% was added to the model's classification of the qualified displacement time series. The accuracy of the high-pass cut-off frequency obtained was analyzed by using the high-pass cut-off frequency obtained via the traditional method as the accurate value. Finally, the high-pass cut-off frequencies using the SNR method were also obtained and compared with the results of the proposed method.

The main conclusions are as follows:

1. Among the network models that only train the fully connected layer, only the VGG19 model could achieve satisfactory classification performance. In contrast, the rest of the models had higher losses, and the accuracies did not converge. All the trained models of all the network layers could achieve satisfactory classification performance, among which, InceptionResNetV2 had the highest performance with 99.9% and 99.8% accuracy in the training and validation sets, respectively, and 0.003 and 0.009 loss, respectively. The overall accuracy of the test set in the confusion matrix was 96.9%.
2. Considering probability when predicting categories can improve the classification performance of the model. R^2 increased by 14.41% on average, and the RMSE, MAE, and MAPE decreased by 12.6%, 16.23%, and 30.01% on average, respectively.
3. The VGG19 model with all the network layers being trained and the addition of probabilistic restrictions in predicting the category was more suitable for the high-pass cut-off frequency automatic search problem of strong-motion records in this paper. The results obtained using this model had the highest R^2 of 0.82 and the lowest RMSE, MAE, and MAPE of 0.038, 0.026, and 2.99%, respectively.
4. The high-pass cut-off frequency obtained using the SNR method was generally smaller than the accurate value. This also inspires authors to use this frequency instead of 0.01 Hz as the starting frequency in the search for high-pass cut-off frequencies to improve efficiency.

Author Contributions: Conceptualization, B.L., B.Z., J.K. and X.W.; methodology, B.L., J.K. and C.L.; software, B.L. and X.W.; validation, B.L., B.Z., X.W. and J.K.; formal analysis, B.L. and B.Z.; investigation, B.Z. and C.L.; resources, B.Z. and J.K.; data curation, B.Z. and C.L.; writing—original draft preparation, B.L. and X.W.; writing—review and editing, B.Z., J.K., X.W. and C.L; visualization, B.L.; supervision, J.K.; project administration, C.L.; funding acquisition, B.Z., J.K. and X.W. All authors have read and agreed to the published version of the manuscript.

Funding: This research was funded by the Scientific Research Fund of Institute of Engineering Mechanics, China Earthquake Administration (Nos. 2022C05), and the Natural Science Foundation of Heilongjiang Province (LH2022E120) and the National Key Research and Development Program of China (2018YFE0109800). This support is greatly appreciated.

Institutional Review Board Statement: Not applicable.

Informed Consent Statement: Not applicable.

Data Availability Statement: The data presented in this study are available on request from the corresponding author.

Acknowledgments: Grateful acknowledgment is given to Ruizhi Wen, Maosheng Gong, Qiang Ma, and Yefei Ren at the Institute of Engineering Mechanics, China Earthquake Administration, for their guidance and suggestions regarding theoretical analyses.

Conflicts of Interest: The authors declare no conflict of interest.

References

1. Rong, M.; Wang, Z.; Woolery, E.W.; Lyu, Y.; Li, X.; Li, S. Nonlinear site response from the strong ground-motion recordings in western China. *Soil Dyn. Earthq. Eng.* **2016**, *82*, 99–110. [CrossRef]
2. Ren, Y.; Zhou, Y.; Wang, H.; Wen, R. Source characteristics, site effects, and path attenuation from spectral analysis of strong-motion recordings in the 2016 Kaikōura earthquake sequence. *Bull. Seismol. Soc. Am.* **2018**, *108*, 1757–1773. [CrossRef]
3. Sandhu, M.; Sharma, B.; Mittal, H.; Chingtham, P. Analysis of the Site Effects in the North East Region of India Using the Recorded Strong Ground Motions from Moderate Earthquakes. *J. Earthq. Eng.* **2022**, *26*, 1480–1499. [CrossRef]
4. Wen, R.; Xu, P.; Wang, H.; Ren, Y. Single-Station Standard Deviation Using Strong-Motion Data from Sichuan Region, China. *Bull. Seismol. Soc. Am.* **2018**, *108*, 2237–2247. [CrossRef]
5. Shoushtari, A.V.; Adnan, A.B.; Zare, M. On the selection of ground–motion attenuation relations for seismic hazard assessment of the Peninsular Malaysia region due to distant Sumatran subduction intraslab earthquakes. *Soil Dyn. Earthq. Eng.* **2016**, *82*, 123–137. [CrossRef]
6. Guo, D.; He, C.; Xu, C.; Hamada, M. Analysis of the relations between slope failure distribution and seismic ground motion during the 2008 Wenchuan earthquake. *Soil Dyn. Earthq. Eng.* **2015**, *72*, 99–107. [CrossRef]
7. Si, H.; Midorikawa, S.; Kishida, T. Development of NGA-Sub ground-motion prediction equation of 5%-damped pseudo-spectral acceleration based on database of subduction earthquakes in Japan. *Earthq. Spectra* **2022**, *38*, 2682–2706. [CrossRef]
8. Wen, R.; Ji, K.; Ren, Y. Review on selection of strong ground motion input for structural time-history dynamic analysis. *Earthq. Eng. Eng. Dyn.* **2019**, *39*, 1–18. [CrossRef]
9. Ren, Y.; Yin, J.; Wen, R.; Ji, K. The impact of ground motion inputs on the uncertainty of structural collapse fragility. *Eng. Mech.* **2020**, *37*, 115–125. [CrossRef]
10. Aroquipa, H.; Hurtado, A. Seismic resilience assessment of buildings: A simplified methodological approach through conventional seismic risk assessment. *Int. J. Disaster Risk Reduct.* **2022**, *77*, 103047. [CrossRef]
11. Narjabadifam, P.; Hoseinpour, R.; Noori, M.; Altabey, W. Practical seismic resilience evaluation and crisis management planning through GIS-based vulnerability assessment of buildings. *Earthq. Eng. Eng. Vib.* **2021**, *20*, 25–37. [CrossRef]
12. Wang, W.; Ji, K.; Wen, R.; Ren, Y.; Yin, J. Impact of strong ground motion's process procedure on the structural nonlinear time-history analysis. *Eng. Mech.* **2020**, *37*, 42–52+62. [CrossRef]
13. Ji, K. Strong Ground Motion Selection for Multiple Levels of Seismic Fortification Demand in China. Doctor Thesis, Institute of Engineering Mechanics, China Earthquake Administration, Harbin, China, 2018.
14. Chiou, B.; Darragh, R.; Gregor, N.; Silva, W. NGA Project Strong-Motion Database. *Earthq. Spectra* **2019**, *24*, 23–44. [CrossRef]
15. PEER. PEER Ground Motion Database. Available online: https://ngawest2.berkeley.edu/ (accessed on 25 December 2017).
16. Akkar, S.; Sandıkkaya, M.A.; Şenyurt, M.; Azari Sisi, A.; Ay, B.Ö.; Traversa, P.; Douglas, J.; Cotton, F.; Luzi, L.; Hernandez, B.; et al. Reference database for seismic ground-motion in Europe (RESORCE). *Bull. Earthq. Eng.* **2013**, *12*, 311–339. [CrossRef]
17. Bastías, N.; Montalva, G.A. Chile Strong Ground Motion Flatfile. *Earthq. Spectra* **2016**, *32*, 2549–2566. [CrossRef]
18. Luzi, L.; Puglia, R.; Russo, E.; D'Amico, M.; Felicetta, C.; Pacor, F.; Lanzano, G.; Çeken, U.; Clinton, J.; Costa, G.; et al. The Engineering Strong-Motion Database: A Platform to Access Pan-European Accelerometric Data. *Seismol. Res. Lett.* **2016**, *87*, 987–997. [CrossRef]
19. Pacor, F.; Paolucci, R.; Ameri, G.; Massa, M.; Puglia, R. Italian strong motion records in ITACA: Overview and record processing. *Bull. Earthq. Eng.* **2011**, *9*, 1741–1759. [CrossRef]
20. Ambraseys, N.; Smit, P.; Douglas, J.; Margaris, B.; Sigbjörnsson, R.; Olafsson, S.; Suhadolc, P.; Costa, G. Internet site for European strong-motion data. *Boll. Geofis. Teor. Appl.* **2004**, *45*, 113–129.
21. Atkinson, G.M.; Silva, W. Stochastic modeling of California ground motions. *Bull. Seismol. Soc. Am.* **2000**, *90*, 255–274. [CrossRef]
22. Douglas, J.; Boore, D.M. High-frequency filtering of strong-motion records. *Bull. Earthq. Eng.* **2010**, *9*, 395–409. [CrossRef]
23. Parker, G.A.; Aagaard, B.T.; Hearne, M.G.; Moschetti, M.P.; Thompson, E.M.; Rekoske, J.M. The 2019 Ridgecrest, California, Earthquake Sequence Ground Motions: Processed Records and Derived Intensity Metrics. *Seismol. Res. Lett.* **2020**, *91*, 2010–2023. [CrossRef]
24. Bahrampouri, M.; Rodriguez-Marek, A.; Shahi, S.; Dawood, H. An updated database for ground motion parameters for KiK-net records. *Earthq. Spectra* **2020**, *37*, 505–522. [CrossRef]
25. Edwards, B.; Ntinalexis, M. Defining the usable bandwidth of weak-motion records: Application to induced seismicity in the Groningen Gas Field, the Netherlands. *J. Seismol.* **2021**, *25*, 1043–1059. [CrossRef]
26. Brune, J.N. Tectonic stress and the spectra of seismic shear waves from earthquakes. *J. Geophys. Res.* **1970**, *75*, 4997–5009. [CrossRef]
27. Yu, H.; Xu, X.; Zhang, T. Automatic Search Algorithm of Low Cut-off Frequency for Filtering Strong Motion Records. *Technol. Earthq. Disaster Prev.* **2018**, *13*, 65–74.
28. Xie, L.; Li, S.; Qian, Q.; Hu, C. Some characteristics of strong motion record processing and analysis methods in China. *Earthq. Eng. Eng. Dyn.* **1983**, *6*, 1–14. [CrossRef]
29. Zhou, B. Some Key Issues on the Strong Motion Observation. Doctor Thesis, Institute of Engineering Mechanics, China Earthquake Administration, Harbin, China, 2012.

30. Zhang, S.; Zhang, S.; Zhang, C.; Wang, X.; Shi, Y. Cucumber leaf disease identification with global pooling dilated convolutional neural network. *Comput. Electron. Agric.* **2019**, *162*, 422–430. [CrossRef]
31. Kozłowski, M.; Górecki, P.; Szczypiński, P.M. Varietal classification of barley by convolutional neural networks. *Biosyst. Eng.* **2019**, *184*, 155–165. [CrossRef]
32. Cottrell, G.W. New life for neural networks. *Science* **2006**, *313*, 454–455. [CrossRef]
33. Pan, S.J.; Yang, Q. A Survey on Transfer Learning. *IEEE Trans. Knowl. Data Eng.* **2010**, *22*, 1345–1359. [CrossRef]
34. Simonyan, K.; Zisserman, A. Very deep convolutional networks for large-scale image recognition. *arXiv* **2014**, arXiv:1409.1556. [CrossRef]
35. He, K.; Zhang, X.; Ren, S.; Sun, J. Identity mappings in deep residual networks. In Proceedings of the European Conference on Computer Vision, Amsterdam, Netherlands, 8–16 October 2016; pp. 630–645.
36. Szegedy, C.; Vanhoucke, V.; Ioffe, S.; Shlens, J.; Wojna, Z. Rethinking the inception architecture for computer vision. In Proceedings of the IEEE Conference on Computer Vision and Pattern Recognition, Las Vegas, NV, USA, 27–30 June 2016; pp. 2818–2826.
37. Szegedy, C.; Ioffe, S.; Vanhoucke, V.; Alemi, A.A. Inception-v4, inception-resnet and the impact of residual connections on learning. In Proceedings of the Thirty-First AAAI Conference on Artificial Intelligence, San Francisco, CA, USA, 4–9 February 2017.
38. CESMD. Center for Engineering Strong Motion Data. Available online: https://www.strongmotioncenter.org/index.html (accessed on 20 December 2021).
39. Yao, X.; Ren, Y.; Tadahiro, K.; Wen, R.; Wang, H.; Ji, K. The procedure of filtering the strong motion record: Denoising and filtering. *Eng. Mech.* **2022**, *39*, 320–329. [CrossRef]
40. Boore, D.M. On Pads and Filters: Processing Strong-Motion Data. *Bull. Seismol. Soc. Am.* **2005**, *95*, 745–750. [CrossRef]
41. Yanai, K.; Kawano, Y. Food image recognition using deep convolutional network with pre-training and fine-tuning. In Proceedings of the 2015 IEEE International Conference on Multimedia & Expo Workshops (ICMEW), Turin, Italy, 29 June–3 July 2015; pp. 1–6.
42. Python. Available online: https://www.python.org/ (accessed on 15 March 2022).
43. Abadi, M.; Barham, P.; Chen, J.; Chen, Z.; Davis, A.; Dean, J.; Devin, M.; Ghemawat, S.; Irving, G.; Isard, M. {TensorFlow}: A System for {Large-Scale} Machine Learning. In Proceedings of the 12th USENIX Symposium on Operating Systems Design and Implementation (OSDI 16), Savannah, GA, USA, 2–4 November 2016; pp. 265–283.
44. Keras. The Python Deep Learning Library. Available online: https://keras.io (accessed on 15 March 2022).
45. Kingma, D.P.; Ba, J. Adam: A method for stochastic optimization. *arXiv* **2014**, arXiv:1412.6980. [CrossRef]
46. Liao, W.; Chen, X.; Lu, X.; Huang, Y.; Tian, Y. Deep Transfer Learning and Time-Frequency Characteristics-Based Identification Method for Structural Seismic Response. *Front. Built Environ.* **2021**, *7*, 10. [CrossRef]
47. Ma, Q.; Jin, X.; Li, S.; Chen, F.; Liao, S.; Wei, Y. Automatic P-arrival detection for earthquake early warning. *Chin. J. Geophys.* **2013**, *56*, 2313–2321. [CrossRef]
48. Konno, K.; Ohmachi, T. Ground-motion characteristics estimated from spectral ratio between horizontal and vertical components of microtremor. *Bull. Seismol. Soc. Am.* **1998**, *88*, 228–241. [CrossRef]

Disclaimer/Publisher's Note: The statements, opinions and data contained in all publications are solely those of the individual author(s) and contributor(s) and not of MDPI and/or the editor(s). MDPI and/or the editor(s) disclaim responsibility for any injury to people or property resulting from any ideas, methods, instructions or products referred to in the content.

Article

Predicting Geotechnical Parameters from Seismic Wave Velocity Using Artificial Neural Networks

Fatema Tuz Johora [1,*], Craig J. Hickey [2,*] and Hakan Yasarer [1]

1 Civil Engineering Department, University of Mississippi, Oxford, MS 38677, USA
2 National Center for Physical Acoustics, Oxford, MS 38677, USA
* Correspondence: fatema.mist09@gmail.com (F.T.J.); chickey@olemiss.edu (C.J.H.)

Abstract: Geotechnical investigation plays an indispensable role in site characterization and provides necessary data for various construction projects. However, geotechnical measurements are time-consuming, point-based, and invasive. Non-destructive geophysical measurements (seismic wave velocity) can complement geotechnical measurements to save project money and time. However, correlations between geotechnical and seismic wave velocity are crucial in order to maximize the benefit of geophysical information. In this work, artificial neural networks (ANNs) models are developed to forecast geotechnical parameters from seismic wave velocity. Specifically, published seismic wave velocity, liquid limit, plastic limit, water content, and dry density from field and laboratory measurements are used to develop ANN models. Due to the small number of data, models are developed with and without the validation step in order to use more data for training. The results indicate that the performance of the models is improved by using more data for training. For example, predicting seismic wave velocity using more data for training improves the R^2 value from 0.50 to 0.78 and reduces the ASE from 0.0174 to 0.0075, and MARE from 30.75 to 18.53. The benefit of adding velocity as an input parameter for predicting water content and dry density is assessed by comparing models with and without velocity. Models incorporating the velocity information show better predictability in most cases. For example, predicting water content using field data including the velocity improves the R^2 from 0.75 to 0.85 and reduces the ASE from 0.0087 to 0.0051, and MARE from 10.68 to 7.78. A comparison indicates that ANN models outperformed multilinear regression models. For example, predicting seismic wave velocity using field plus lab data has an ANN derived R^2 value that is 81.39% higher than regression model.

Keywords: field measurement; laboratory measurement; multilinear regression analysis; artificial neural networks

1. Introduction

Seismic wave velocity is a practical, non-destructive, non-invasive, cost-effective measurement related to the inherent mechanical properties of geomaterials [1]. However, seismic wave velocity is not used directly in most designs of engineering structures. Developing correlations between seismic wave velocity and different engineering soil properties could facilitate the use of seismic information for designing engineering structures.

Researchers have extensively studied the correlation between seismic wave velocity and different soil properties. Dikmen developed correlations between shear wave velocity (V_s) and uncorrected Standard Penetration Test (SPT-N) values for sandy, silty, and clayey soils [2]. It was shown that SPT-N and shear wave velocity were strongly correlated but the type of soil had no significant effect on the estimation of V_s. Gautam established correlations between shear wave velocity and uncorrected standard penetration resistance [3]. This study used 500 measurements on various sand and silt soils. The coefficient of determination for silty and sandy soils was relatively low in comparison to using all soils together. He also compared his results with existing correlations from the literature and showed significant similarities with existing correlations. Hasancebi developed correlations between shear wave velocity and penetration resistance for sandy, clayey, and all soil (i.e., sandy and clay) using regression analysis [4]. Correlations between shear wave velocity and SPT-N were found to be significant. For sandy soil, the R-value was 0.65, for clayey soil the R-value was 0.75, and the combined data had an R-value of 0.73. Hasancebi also concluded that the blow count was a significant parameter for the correlation, but the soil type had no significant influence. A good correlation was established between S-wave velocity and the degradation factor (G_{PMT}/G_o), where G_{PMT} is intermediate strain shear modulus from the PMT and G_o is low strain modulus from S-wave velocity. However, the correlations between SPT-N and field measured S-wave velocity and P-wave velocity were poor. Correlations were also developed between shear wave velocity and cone penetration resistance. Mayne and Rix worked on field clay soil and found empirical correlations between shear wave velocity (V_s) and cone penetration tip resistance (q_c) [5]. An increasing trend in shear wave velocities with cone penetration resistance was observed with consistency from soft to stiff to hard clay materials. Log regression analysis returned a coefficient of regression of 0.736. Inazaki established correlations between S-wave velocity and SPT-N, bulk density, solidities as the complement of porosity, and mean grain size of surficial unconsolidated sediments [6]. S-wave velocities were measured in boreholes using the PS suspension logging tool. The results showed that it is possible to express N-values in terms of S-wave when N-value data have good accuracy. The correlation between S-wave velocities and solidities was good but was dependent on lithofacies and depositional age. The data also showed a good relationship between S-wave velocity and density but a weak relation between S-wave velocity and mean grain size. Even though most of the researchers found good correlations between S-wave velocity and N-values, studies by some researchers could not find out good correlations between S-wave velocity and N-values. A large number of researchers worked on developing correlation between shear wave velocity and SPT-N [7–21].

Some other researchers attempted to develop correlation between seismic wave velocity and other geotechnical parameters. Evans worked with sand and clay soils to establish correlations between geophysical and geotechnical parameters [22]. Seismic refraction surveys were performed to collect S-wave and P-wave velocities. Pressure Meter Test (PMT), SPT, Atterberg limit tests, and dry unit weight data were also collected from the Salt River Project (SRP) [23,24]. Heureux and Long developed correlations between S-wave velocity, cone penetration parameters, undrained shear strength, and 1-D compression parameters for Norwegian clay [25]. Data used for this research was collected from 29 sites; in south-eastern and mid-Norway. Regression analyses were performed to establish the correlation between in situ S-wave velocity (V_s) and cone net resistance (q_{net}), collected from the cone penetration test. The coefficient of determination R^2 was 0.73. The undrained shear strength values obtained from direct shear tests were correlated with V_s with a regression coefficient (R^2) of 0.91. Their analysis also showed a good correlation between pre-consolidation stress (P_c') and V_s with an R^2 value of 0.81. Johora developed ANN models to predict geotechnical parameters from S-wave and P-wave velocity separately using laboratory data for compacted clay and sandy clay soil [26]. The results indicated that P-wave velocity and S-wave velocity were more sensitive to dry density and void ratio than to saturation and water content. The performance of the ANN models to predict geotechnical parameters from soil mix proportion and either P-wave or S-wave velocity was better when multiple geotechnical parameters were predicted at a time. Empirical correlations were developed by Imai et al. between index properties and seismic velocities [27]. Foti and Lancellotta used velocity data published by Hunter and showed the dependency of porosity with S-wave and P-wave velocity [28,29]. Alshameri and Madun showed a direct positive linear correlation exists between seismic wave velocity and cohesion and shear strength for compacted sand-kaolin mixtures. They also attempted to establish correlation between seismic wave velocity and friction angle but found that it is insignificant [30]. Duan et al. developed correlations between shear wave velocity with vertical effective stress, unit weight, preconsolidation stress and undrained shear strength for clay type soil [31].

ANN is gaining popularity as a problem-solving tool in the field of civil engineering. Researchers are using ANN to predict concrete compressive strength [32–34], ultrasonic pulse velocity [35], slump of concrete [36–38]. Zeh showed the application of ANN to assess the nonlinear behavior of steel structures [39]. ANN was used to forecast flexure and initial stiffness of beam column joints [40]. In geotechnical engineering ANN was used to study slope stability [41], pile analysis [42,43], developing correlation between ER and geotechnical parameters [44], analysis of liquefaction potential [45,46]. In transportation engineering researchers applied ANN to develop transportation systems [47].

ANN can solve complex problems, but the performance depends on the size and accuracy of the data set. Using a big data set can help to train the network efficiently. In many fields big data sets are not always easily available. Researchers are working on developing ANN models using small data sets. Pasini described a particular neural network tool which is capable of handling small data sets and its application to a specific case study [48]. Feng et al. used deep neural network to predict material defects using small data set [49].

Literature contains a good number of correlations between seismic wave velocity and blow counts. There are fewer correlations with other important geotechnical parameters, such as water content, dry density, cohesion, angle of friction, saturation, void ratio, etc. More study is necessary to establish the correlation between seismic wave velocity and different types of geotechnical parameters. Many of the existing studies employ conventional regression methods to develop the correlations between geotechnical and seismic wave velocity, even though ANN was used in many fields of civil engineering In this study, multi regression analysis and the ANNs approach were used to develop the relationships between seismic wave velocity and geotechnical parameters or, conversely, to predict geotechnical parameters from seismic wave velocity and other geotechnical parameters using data from the literature. The performance of the ANN and regression analysis was compared. Two different ANN approaches with and without validations were also discussed to handle the small size data set.

2. Seismic Wave Velocity

Soil allows for the propagation of different types of seismic waves. Waves that deform the material through shear are referred to as shear waves, and those that produce volumetric deformations are referred to as compressional waves. These are often referred to as S-wave and P-wave, respectively. Seismic wave velocity is related to the maximum shear modulus, bulk modulus, Young's modulus, bulk density, and Poisson's ratio of the soil [50].

The longitudinal P-wave and the transverse S-wave velocity in an infinite elastic continuum are related to the elastic properties by

$$V_p = \sqrt{\frac{M}{\rho}} = \sqrt{\frac{B + \frac{4}{3}G}{\rho}} \quad \text{P-waves} \tag{1}$$

$$V_s = \sqrt{\frac{G}{\rho}} \quad \text{S-waves} \tag{2}$$

where M (Pa) is the constraint modulus, B (Pa) is the bulk modulus, G (Pa) is the shear modulus, and ρ (kg/m^3) is the mass density of the medium. Hence, the propagation velocity increases with the material stiffness and decreases with its mass density (inertia). Velocity of S-waves is always smaller than the velocity of P-waves [50].

For fluid-filled porous media, the effective bulk modulus is provided by Gassmann [50].

$$B_{eff} = B_{SK} + \frac{\left(1 - \frac{B_{SK}}{B_g}\right)^2}{\frac{\varphi}{B_f} + \frac{1-\varphi}{B_g} - \frac{B_{SK}}{B_g^2}} \qquad (3)$$

where B_{SK} (Pa) is the bulk modulus of the skeleton, B_g (Pa) is the bulk modulus of the grains, B_f (Pa) is the bulk modulus of the fluid phase, and φ is the porosity. In the Gassmann model, the shear modulus of the soil, G_{eff} (Pa) remains unaffected by the presence of the fluid at low excitation frequencies:

$$G_{eff} = G_{SK}. \qquad (4)$$

For partially saturated soils, the mass density of the mixture ρ_{mix}, changes due to the different densities of the saturating fluids. By ignoring granular effects, fluid substitution can be used to modify the expression for the effective bulk modulus of the soil. For soil with water saturation of S_w, the fluid bulk modulus in Equation (5) given by

$$\frac{1}{B_f} = \frac{S_w}{B_w} + \frac{1-S_w}{B_a} \qquad (5)$$

where B_w (Pa) is the bulk modulus of the liquid phase and B_a (Pa) is the bulk modulus of the air phase. Small volumes of air produce a large decrease in the modulus of the fluid phase. However, under dynamic loading, differences in inertia, shear stiffness, and bulk compressibility can add further complexity to the analysis.

Seismic wave propagation in granular soil materials is more complicated due to the complex behavior of the solid skeleton and the influence of capillary forces. The skeletons B_{SK} and G_{SK} depend on the "strength" of the grain contacts and are therefore dependent upon the applied effective stress. The concept of effective stress for soils at low saturation is still an area of active research because internal forces associated with capillary forces and electrical forces at the grain surface play an important role [50]. That is why empirical relationships are often necessary to predict seismic wave propagation in the partially saturated particulate medium.

There are numerous methods for measuring seismic wave velocity in the field and the laboratory. In the laboratory, the "time of flight" approach is common. A seismic wave is generated using a source in contact with one end of the sample, the disturbance passes through the soil and is detected by a receiver at the opposite end of the sample. Velocity is calculated by dividing the distance (sample length) by the measured travel time. The soil samples usually consist of remolded soil or a field sample with some degree of disturbance. The frequency of the seismic wave is usually in the 10–100 kHz range. Field measurements of seismic velocity can be performed using surface surveys such as refraction surveys or surface wave analysis. These approaches mitigate the problem of soil disturbance since no samples are required. However, they are less repeatable and have larger uncertainty in measure values. The frequency of the seismic wave is in the 10 Hz to several 100 Hz ranges. It should be noted that field-measured seismic velocities are usually lower than laboratory-measured velocities.

3. Data Collections

This study uses data from a report on seismic wave velocity (P wave) published by the Engineering Research Institute of Iowa State University, Ames, Iowa [51]. Field measurement of seismic wave velocity was conducted on highway embankments. The embankments were constructed with three types of soil namely, clay loam, silty clay (two weathering variations, gray and brown), and silty loam. For laboratory measurements, samples were collected from the side slope of the highway embankment adjacent to the field measurement location. One additional soil type was used for the laboratory measurements defined as loess. The types of soils investigated, and their liquid limit and plasticity index are shown in Table 1.

Table 1. Type of soil used for the tests.

Soil Type	Liquid Limit	Plasticity Index
Clay loam	23	9
Silty clay (gray)	30	13
Silty clay (brown)	40	18
Silty loam	32	6
Loess	32	6

Micro-seismic refraction tests were conducted at 34 different locations to measure seismic velocities in the field. The equipment consists of three components: an impact source, a receiving transducer, and a seismic timer. A model 217 Micro-Seismic Timer and a transducer were used for these micro-seismic refraction tests. A tack hammer was used as the impact source on a 5/8-inch diameter steel ball-bearing to transmit the energy into the ground. Seismic measurements were taken along a 2 ft line by moving the receiver in 3-in intervals. A total of 10 first-arrival measurements were collected at each station. The seismic wave velocities were calculated from slope of the distance-time plots. At the midpoint of the seismic line, a standard rubber balloon volumetric density measurement and an in situ water content measurement were performed [52]. The range of values associated with the field measurements is listed in Table 2.

Table 2. Parameters and ranges.

Type of Data	Parameters	Ranges	
		Max	Min
General	Plasticity Index	21.87	2.03
	LL (%)	45.43	17.39
Field	Dry density (kg/m^3)	2240.58	1465.69
	Water content (%)	18	3.87
	Velocity (m/s)	1128.99	67.12
Lab	Dry density (kg/m^3)	2240.58	1465.69
	Water content (%)	20.53	4.74
	Velocity (m/s)	1675.07	57.48
Field plus Lab	Dry density (kg/m^3)	2246.59	1484.71
	Water content (%)	20.96	3.13
	Velocity (m/s)	1705.07	7.23

In the laboratory, 35 different soils samples were compacted in 4-inch diameter by 4.58 inch high molds. Standard and modified AASHO compaction tests procedures were followed to prepare the samples. Water content, dry density of all the samples (total 35) were determined in lab. Liquid limit (LL), plasticity index (total 5 samples) were determined on for the different soil types. Seismic velocities were measured on all samples (total 35) using the pulse-transmission method.

4. Artificial Neural Networks Approach

During the past few years, artificial neural networks (ANNs) based modeling has been gaining popularity in the field of geotechnical engineering [53]. ANNs can learn complex nonlinear relationships between parameters from many data [54]. The methodology of ANN is based on the human brain activity of processing data. Much like the human brain, ANN has a large number of interconnected cells called neurons [55]. There are connection links between the neurons to transfer signals from one neuron to the other. ANN consists of three different layers (i.e., input layer, hidden layers, and output layer). Information is passed from the input layer through hidden layers to the output layer. The hidden layers process the received signals from the input layer then transmit the information to the output layer. The output layer receives the processed information from the hidden layer and executes the outputs. ANN is capable of learning highly complex relationships which are difficult to solve by traditional computational techniques. The performance of an ANN model depends on the quality and the size of the database. Erroneous and too small databases affect the accuracy of the model performance. ANN can be of different types, i.e., feed-forward neural networks, recurrent networks, and stochastic neural networks depending on the number of layers, the activation function and training algorithm [55]. The vital part of ANNs approach is the activation function, which introduces nonlinearity to the network to solve complex problems. Examples of different activation functions that can be used are linear, binary step, sigmoidal, and hyperbolic tangent sigmoid.

5. ANN Model Development

The architecture of an ANN model is determined based on the characteristics of the problem and knowledge of ANN. In this study, the feed-forward back propagation technique is used, and the nonlinear sigmoid function is chosen as the activation function. ANN models are usually developed following four different steps. In the first step, a database is divided into three different classes namely training, testing, and validation. Training sets include around 50% of the total data and are selected randomly, including minimum and maximum values of the input data. Testing and validation sets are also selected randomly and contain about 25% of the data in each set. In the second step, the optimum number of hidden nodes and iteration of the network is determined by training and testing the network. The three best-performing networks are chosen based on their statistics for comparison. In the third step, the three best networks are validated using a validation data set. For the final step, the selected three networks are re-trained using all the data to increase the prediction accuracy on the network structure that was determined in the previous step. The performance of the selected three networks is evaluated based on Mean Absolute Relative Error (MARE), Coefficient of Determination (R^2), and normalized Average Squared Error (ASE) and calculated using the following equations.

$$\text{MARE} = \frac{\sum_{i=1}^{N}(|X_i^P - X_i^A|)/X_i^A}{N} * 100 \tag{6}$$

$$R^2 = 1 - \frac{\sum_{i=1}^{N}\left(X_i^A - X_i^P\right)^2}{\sum_{i=1}^{N}\left(X_i^A - \overline{X_i}\right)^2} \tag{7}$$

$$\text{ASE} = \frac{\sum_{i=1}^{N}\left(X_i^A - X_i^P\right)^2}{N} \tag{8}$$

where, X_i^A = Actual value, X_i^P = Predicted value, $\overline{X_i}$ = Mean of X_i^A, N = Total number of data.

6. ANN Models

ANN models are developed to predict seismic wave velocity, water content, and dry density using the data from the lab and field experiments. Separate ANN models are developed using lab data, field data, and lab and field data combined. Since the number of data is limited, two different ANN approaches are used for predicting seismic wave velocity. The first approach is the typical approach, where the data is used for training, testing, and validation. Around 50% of data is used for training, 25% for testing, and 25% for validation. In the second approach, the validation stage is excluded so that 75% data is used for training and 25% for testing. The parameters used for developing models are shown in Table 2, along with their ranges.

6.1. ANN Models for Predicting Seismic Wave Velocity

Six different models are developed to predict seismic wave velocity. Models are using lab data, field data and both lab and field data together following the two approaches, with validation and without validation. Correlation matrix analysis was used before selecting the input and output parameters for prediction model development.

The best three networks selected based on the statistical measures and optimal hidden nodes to predict seismic velocity using field data from LI, plasticity index, water content, and dry density are presented in Table 3. The best model is the model which has lower the ASE, MARE and higher the R^2. The statistics show that ASE, MARE and R^2 of all three networks are very close to each other in training, testing, and all-trained. From these three networks, network 4_ (4_4_3100) _1 (where network structure is denoted as input_ (initial hidden nodes_final hidden nodes_iteration) _output) is chosen as the best model depending on the best statistics in testing. The predicted versus actual graph is shown in Figure 1a. The statistics and predicted versus actual graph indicate that the accuracy of predicting velocity is marginal. The best model for predicting velocity using field data without the validation stage is network 4_ (2_4_2900) _1. The predicted versus actual graph for network 4_ (2_4_2900) _1 is shown in Figure 1b. The statistics are presented in Table 4. The accuracy of predicting velocity is increased after omitting validation, but the overall performance is still marginal.

Table 3. Statistical accuracy measures of model for predicting seismic wave velocity using field data, with validation).

Model Architecture	4_ (1_1_2100) _1	4_ (2_2_2100) _1	4_ (4_4_3100) _1
Training			
ASE	0.0151	0.0152	0.0152
MARE	19.61	19.87	19.75
R^2	0.30	0.30	0.30
Testing			
ASE	0.0122	0.0121	0.0121
MARE	21.72	21.70	21.56
R^2	0.26	0.28	0.27
Validation			
ASE	0.0153	0.0149	0.0147
MARE	18.54	18.63	18.49
R^2	0.25	0.28	0.29
All			
ASE	0.0132	0.0132	0.0133
MARE	18.87	19.01	19.04
R^2	0.34	0.34	0.34

The best model using lab data to predict velocity is network 4_ (2_2_200) _1. The statistics in Table 4 and predicted versus actual graph shown in Figure 1c indicate that the accuracy of the velocity prediction is good. The best model to predict velocity without validation is network 4_ (1_5_100) _1. The predicted versus actual graph shown in Figure 1d and the statistics presented in Table 4 indicate that the accuracy of the velocity predictions is good. Again, excluding the validation helps to slightly minimize the errors and increases the R^2 values. The results also show that the errors are much lower, and the R^2 values are much higher for the networks trained using lab data in comparison to the network trained using field data.

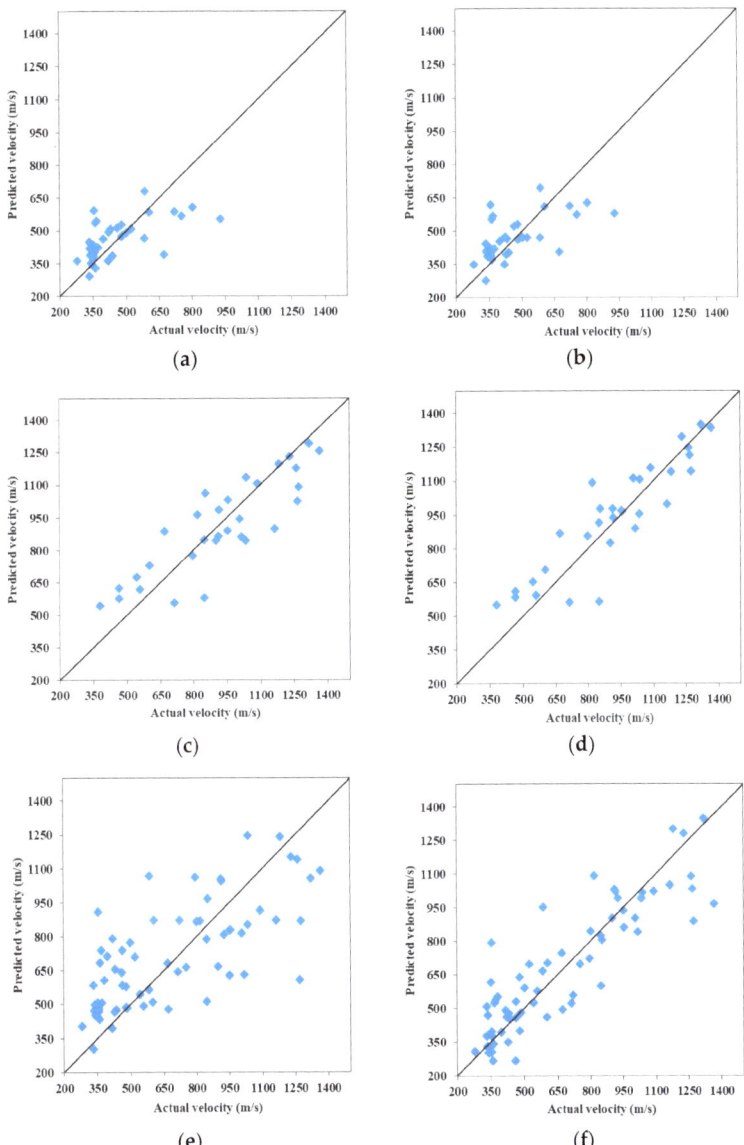

Figure 1. Graphical prediction accuracy of model for predicting seismic wave velocity, (**a**) field, with validation, (**b**) field, without validation, (**c**) lab, with validation, (**d**) lab, without validation, (**e**) field plus lab, with validation, (**f**) field plus lab, without validation.

Table 4. Comparing ANN models (predicting seismic wave velocity).

Source of Data	Model	Model Structure	ASE	MARE	R^2
Field	with validation	4_ (4_4_3100) _1	0.0133	19.04	0.34
	without validation	4_ (2_4_2900) _1	0.0128	19.34	0.37
Lab	with validation	4_ (2_2_200) _1	0.0079	14.86	0.71
	without validation	4_ (1_5_100) _1	0.0058	13.33	0.80
Field plus Lab	with validation	4_ (1_2_2900) _1	0.0174	30.75	0.50
	without validation	4_ (5_10_20000) _1	0.0075	18.53	0.78

The best model using field and lab data together to predict the seismic wave velocity is network 4_ (1_2_2900). The statistics are shown in Table 4. and the predicted versus actual graphs for the best network shown in Figure 1e. indicates that the accuracy is marginal. The ASE and MARE are higher after combining lab and field data in comparison to the models trained with lab and field data separately. The R^2 values are improve. The model developed without the validation stage is network 4_ (5_10_20000) _1 The statistics are shown in Table 4. and the predicted versus actual graphs for the best network shown in Figure 1f. indicates that the accuracy is good This model has significantly smaller errors and increased R^2 values compared to the model with validation.

In summary, of the results in Table 4 indicates that developing models without the validation stage in order to have more data for training results in slightly better models. The errors are lower and the R^2 values are higher for the network trained using lab data than using field data. The models using field data and lab data together perform in between models based solely on lab data or field data.

6.2. ANN Models for Predicting Water Content

Water content is an important index property of soil. The amount of water gives an indication of grading of soil and porosity. Soil compaction and strength is highly affected by water content. ANN models are developed to predict water content using lab and field data independently and in combination. Based on the previous models for velocity this analysis is developed without validation. Models are developed with and without velocity as input to evaluate if velocity helps in predicting water content. The statistics for the six different models are presented in Table 5.

Table 5. Comparing ANN models (predicting water content).

Source of Data	Model	Model Structure	ASE	MARE	R^2
Field	without velocity	3_ (2_3_1000) _1	0.0087	10.68	0.75
	with velocity	4_ (1_5_100) _1	0.0051	7.78	0.85
Lab	without velocity	3_ (4_4_100) _1	0.0051	7.69	0.82
	with velocity	4_ (3_3_100) _1	0.0043	6.63	0.89
Field plus Lab	without velocity	3_ (5_12_100) _1	0.006	10.69	0.74
	with velocity	4_ (3_3_1000) _1	0.0083	11.61	0.67

The best model to predict water content from LL, plasticity index, and dry density using field data is Network 3_ (2_3_1000) _1. The predicted versus actual graph for the best network is shown in Figure 2a indicates that the accuracy of predicting water content is good. Predicting water content from field data by including seismic wave velocity into the input parameters is Network 4_ (1_5_100). The predicted versus actual graph is shown in Figure 2b and the statistics indicate better accuracy in predicting water content. So, the results indicate that including seismic wave velocity improves the prediction of water content.

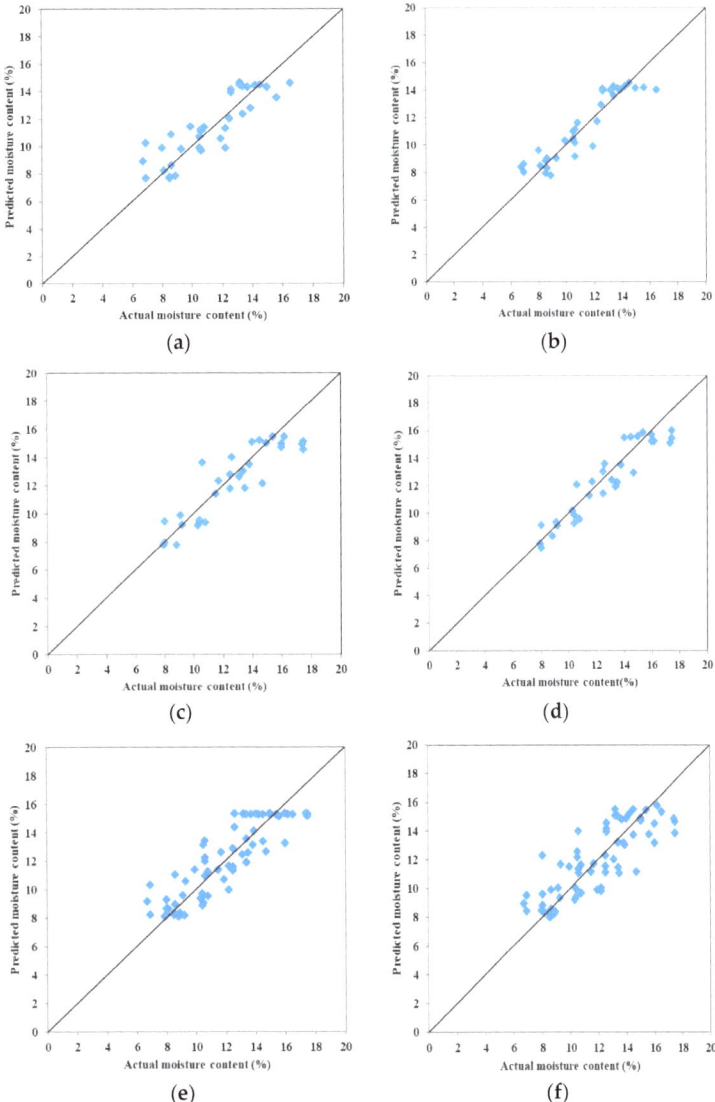

Figure 2. Graphical prediction accuracy of model for predicting moisture content, (**a**) field, without velocity, (**b**) field, with velocity, (**c**) lab, without velocity, (**d**) lab, with velocity, (**e**) field plus lab, without velocity, (**f**) field plus lab, with velocity.

Using lab data to predict water content from LL, plasticity index, and dry density is best for network 3_ (3_3_100) _1 The predicted versus actual graphs are shown in Figure 2c and statistics indicate that the accuracy of predicting moisture content is higher than the model derived from field data. Adding the velocity as additional input to traditional lab data results in network 4_ (3_3_100) _1 with even better accuracy. The predicted versus actual graph for this network is shown in Figure 2d and the statistics shown in Table 5 indicate this is the best model for predicting moisture content. In summary, the models for predicting moisture content are better using laboratory data than field data and the addition of seismic velocity information enhances the models

Combining lab and field data to develop ANN models to predict water content reduces the performance of the models. Network 3_ (5_12_100) _1 is the best network without the velocity. The predicted versus actual graph, is shown in Figure 2e. The statistics indicate that the errors are higher and the R^2 values are lower for the network built using field data and lab data together in comparison to the network built using lab data and field data separately. So combining field and lab data together lowers the performance of the model. The predicted versus actual graph for the best network 4_ (3_3_100) _1 including seismic wave velocity into the input parameters is shown in Figure 2f. Contrary to the previous models, based on solely lab or field data, the addition of velocity as input causes the ASE, MARE to increase and the R^2 to decrease. In summary, models for predicting water content are more accurate when using lab data than field data. Combining the data results in much poorer models. The addition of velocity as an input to either the lab or field data results in more accurate models. Adding velocity as in input to the combined lab and field data results in poorer models.

6.3. ANN Models for Predicting Dry Density

Soil dry density is used to determine the degree of compaction. The maximum dry density is very important to increase the soil ability to support the structure and to avoid excessive settlements. ANN models are developed to predict dry density using lab and field data independently and in combination. Based on the previous models for velocity this analysis is developed without validation. Models are developed with and without velocity as input to evaluate if velocity helps in predicting dry density. The statistics for the six different models are presented in Table 6.

Table 6. Comparing ANN models (predicting dry density).

Source of Data	Model	Model Structure	ASE	MARE	R^2
Field	without velocity	3_ (4_4_2000) _1	0.0068	2.90	0.80
	with velocity	4_ (3_5_100) _1	0.0032	1.81	0.91
Lab	without velocity	3_ (4_4_500) _1	0.0051	2.42	0.86
	with velocity	4_ (4_4_100) _1	0.0056	2.52	0.85
Field plus Lab	without velocity	3_ (3_11_19800) _1	0.0087	2.94	0.75
	with velocity	4_ (9_9_400) _1	0.0077	3.00	0.78

The best model to predict dry density from LL, plasticity index and water content using field data is Network 3_ (4_4_2000) _1. The predicted versus actual graph for the best network shown in Figure 3a indicates that the accuracy of predicting dry density is good. The best ANN model developed to predict dry density with the same number of classified data and ranges but including seismic wave velocity into the input parameters is network 4_ (3_5_100) _1. The predicted versus actual graph is shown in Figure 3b and the statistics indicate better accuracy in predicting dry density So, the results indicate that including seismic wave velocity improves the prediction of dry density. The best network using lab data to predict dry density from LL, plasticity index, and dry density is network 3_ (4_4_500) _1. The predicted versus actual graphs are shown in Figure 3c and statistics indicate that the accuracy of predicting dry density is lower than the model derived from similar field data. Adding the velocity as additional input to traditional lab data results in network 4_ (4_4_100) _1.

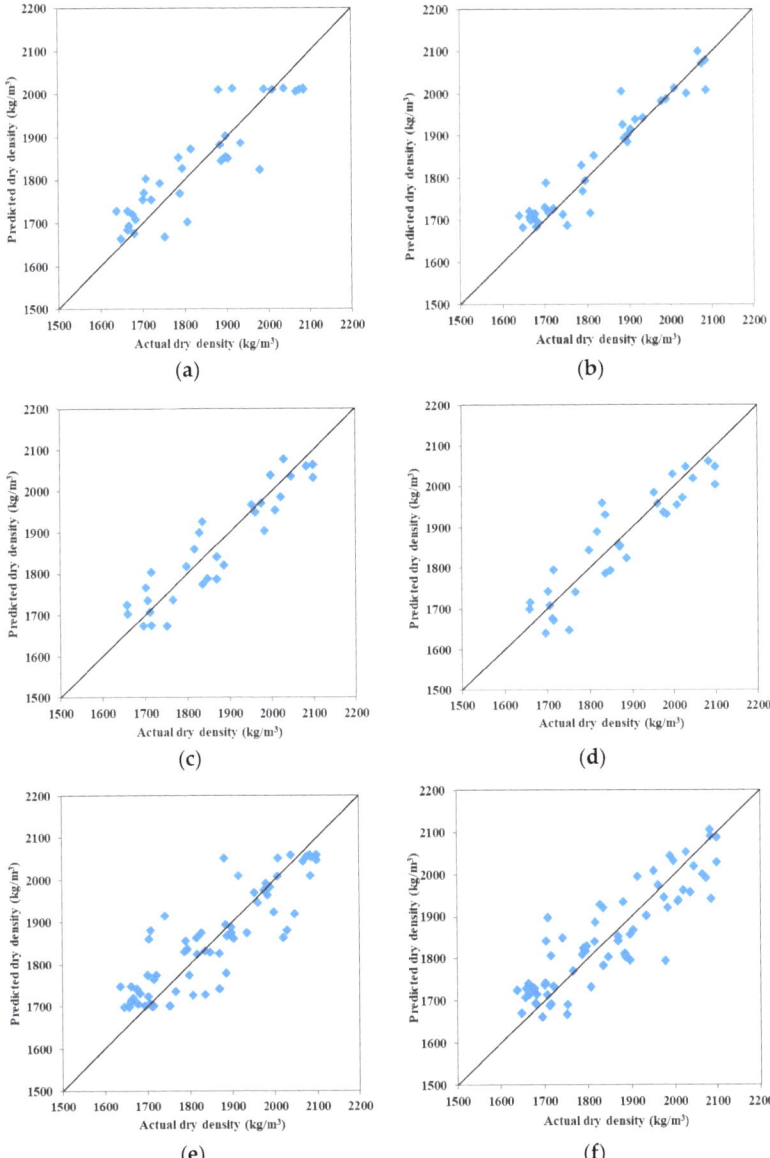

Figure 3. Graphical prediction accuracy of model for predicting dry density, (**a**) field, without velocity, (**b**) field, with velocity, (**c**) lab, without velocity, (**d**) lab, with velocity, (**e**) field plus lab, without velocity, (**f**) field plus lab, with velocity.

The predicted versus actual graph for this network is shown in Figure 3d and the statistics shown in Table 6 indicate the addition of velocity in the lab data did not help to improve the results.

The models for predicting dry density are better using field data than laboratory data. This is in contrast to the results for water content shown previously. Combining lab and field data to develop ANN models to predict dry density reduces the performance of the models. Network 3_ (3_11_19800) _1 is for without the velocity. The predicted versus actual graph is shown in Figure 3e. The statistics indicate that the errors are higher and the R^2 values are lower for this network in comparison to the networks built using lab data or field data. The predicted versus actual graph for the best network 4_ (9_9_400) _1 including seismic wave velocity into the input parameters is shown in Figure 3f. The addition of velocity as input causes the MARE to increase but the R^2 is higher, and ASE is lower. This suggests a slight to insignificant improvement of the model after adding velocity as an input.

In summary, models for predicting dry density are more accurate when using field data with velocity as an input. The model based on lab data is comparable to field data-based models without the additional of velocity. Combining the lab and field data results in much poorer models. The addition of velocity as an input to either field data and lab plus field data results in more accurate models but did not help to improve the accuracy of the model build using lab data.

7. Comparison between ANN and Regression Models

Regression analysis is a conventional way to determine the relationship between independent and dependent variables. It determines how strongly the independent variables affect the depended variables. Multiple-linear regression analyses are performed using the same databases used for the ANN models. The performance of the models is determined based on RMSE, MARE, unnormalized ASE and R^2. For predicting seismic wave velocity three different data set: lab data, field data and both lab and field data are used. Input parameters for predicting seismic wave velocity models are LL, plasticity index, water content and dry density.

For predicting water content LL, plasticity index, dry density and velocity are used as input parameters. Models are developed for lab, field and both lab and field data sets. For predicting dry density same type of data set and approach are used except the input parameters are LL, plasticity index, water content and seismic wave velocity. The results of regression analysis are shown in Table 7.

Table 7. Comparison of ANN and regression models.

Model	Source of Data	ANN				Regression			
		RMSE	ASE	MARE	R^2	RMSE	ASE	MARE	R^2
Predicting velocity	F	394	155,616	19.3	0.37	403	162,712	18.8	0.34
	L	403	162,650	13.3	0.80	465	216,368	15.4	0.72
	F + L	483	233,701	18.5	0.78	772	596,434	30.8	0.43
Predicting water content	F	1.0	1.0	7.7	0.85	1.5	2.3	12	0.66
	L	1.0	1.0	6.6	0.89	0.9	0.9	6.5	0.88
	F + L	1.6	2.6	11.6	0.67	1.6	2.7	12	0.66
Predicting dry density	F	2.7	7.5	1.8	0.91	4.9	24.2	3.3	0.69
	L	3.4	11.6	2.5	0.85	3.3	11.0	2.4	0.85
	F + L	4.1	17.5	3	0.78	4.4	19.5	3.1	0.75

Note: Field (F), Lab (L).

Table 7 presents the statistics for ANN (without validation) and regression models. To compare ANN models with regression models the unnormalized ASE is calculated using the unnormalized actual and predicted values. Additionally, root mean squared error (RMSE) is also calculated using.

$$\text{RMSE} = \sqrt{\frac{\sum_{i=1}^{N}\left(X_i^A - X_i^P\right)^2}{N}} \quad (9)$$

For predicting seismic wave velocity, the regression model using laboratory data showed the higher R^2 value and lower MARE but higher. ASE and RMSE than field data models. Combining the field and lab data increased errors and a R^2 value in between the models using individual lab and field data. For predicting water content, the regression models based on lab data also showed the best performance The performance of field data and field plus lab data are very close to each other. For predicting dry density, the best performance is also observed for the lab data model. The second-best model is field plus lab data and lowest performance is observed for the field data.

For all the cases, ANN models resulted in better R2 values in comparison to regression analysis. Significant improvements are observed for the case of field data for predicting water content, the R2 increases 22.35%, using field data for predicting dry density the R2 increase 24.18% and for using field & lab data for predicting seismic wave velocity the R2 increase 44.87%. Errors are lower for ANN models in comparison to regression models with some minor exceptions. ANN models showed significantly reduced errors than regression models using with field data for predicting water content RMSE decreases 50%, ASE decreases 130%, MARE decreases 55.84%, for predicting dry density the RMSE decreases 81.48%, ASE decreases 222.67%, 83.33%. The model build with field and lab data for predicting velocity the RMSE decreases 59.83%, ASE decreases 155.21% and MARE decreases 66.49%. So, it appears that ANN shows better accuracy in prediction when compared to regression analysis.

8. Conclusions

This study used ANN and regression analysis to predict geotechnical parameters from seismic wave velocity and other geotechnical parameters using a published data. The geotechnical parameters used here are plasticity index, LL, dry dry density, and water content. The aim was to evaluate the use of seismic wave velocity to predict geotechnical parameters so that it can save time and cost by minimizing the number of geotechnical tests.

From the analysis this can be concluded that seismic wave velocity helps to predict water content and dry density. This validates that seismic wave velocity is sensitive to change in water content and dry density. Combination of other geophysical parameters may increase the accuracy of the prediction model. The study shows that the performance of the prediction models is better when lab and filed data are used separately. However, combining lab and field data resulted in poorer models and requires further investigation. From the comparison of ANN and regression models it is proved that ANN can predict better with more accuracy than traditional regression analysis. This study showed the correlation between seismic wave velocity and water content, dry density for four types of soil using field and lab data. Other geotechnical parameters such as angle of friction, cohesion, saturation, void ratio can be considered for developing correlations. Correlations can also be developed for other soil types.

Author Contributions: F.T.J. was involved in drafting the manuscript, made substantial contributions to the conception, design, analysis and interpretation of data. C.J.H. was involved in the interpretation of data, revising it critically on important intellectual contents and gave final approval of the version to be published. H.Y. was involved in reviewing analysis of data and gave final approval of the version to be published. All authors have read and agreed to the published version of the manuscript.

Funding: This study was funded by U.S. Department of Agriculture under Non-Assistance Cooperative Agreement 58-6060-6-009. The authors have no relevant financial or non-financial interests to disclose.

Data Availability Statement: This study uses data from a report on seismic wave velocity (P wave) published by the Engineering Research Institute of Iowa State University, Ames, Iowa [13].

Acknowledgments: We thank the U.S. Department of Agriculture under Non-Assistance Cooperative Agreement 58-6060-6-009 for providing financial support. We also thank Yacoub Najjar, Department Chair and Professor, Civil Engineering Department, University of Mississippi for the ANN software, used for the analysis of this research.

Conflicts of Interest: The authors declare no conflict of interest.

References

1. Fam, M.; Santamarina, C. Study of geoprocesses with complementary mechanical and electromagnetic wave measurements in an oedometer. *Geotech. Test. J. ASTM* **1995**, *18*, 307–314.
2. Dikmen, U. Statistical correlations of shear wave velocity and penetration resistance for soils. *J. Geophys. Eng.* **2009**, *6*, 61–72. [CrossRef]
3. Gautam, D. Empirical correlation between uncorrected standard penetration resistance (N) and shear wave velocity (V_S) for Kathmandu valley, Nepal. *Geomat. Nat. Hazards Risk* **2017**, *8*, 496–508. [CrossRef]
4. Hasancebi, N. Empirical correlations between shear wave velocity and penetration resistance for ground shaking assessments. *Bull. Eng. Geol. Environ.* **2007**, *66*, 203–213. [CrossRef]
5. Mayne, P.W.; Rix, G.J. Correlations between shear wave velocity and cone tip resistance in natural clays. *Soils Found.* **1995**, *35*, 107–110. [CrossRef] [PubMed]
6. Inazaki, T. Relationship between S-wave velocities and geotechnical properties of alluvial sediments. In Proceedings of the Symposium on the Application of Geophysics to Engineering and Environmental Problem (SAGEEP), Seattle, WA, USA, 2–6 April 2006.
7. Campbell, K.; Duke, C. *Correlations among Seismic Velocity, Depth and Geology in the Los Angeles area Report ENG-7662*; University of California at Los Angeles School of Engineering and Applied Science: Los Angeles, CA, USA, 1976.
8. Athanasopoulos, G.A. Empirical Correlations Vso-NSPT for Soils of Greece: A Comparative Study of Reliability. In *Transactions on the Built Environment*; WIT Press: Southampton, UK, 1995; pp. 19–26.
9. Barrow, B.L.; Stokoe, K.E. Field Investigation of Liquefaction Sites in Northern California. Ph.D. Thesis, Civil Engineering Department, University of Texas at Austin, Austin, TX, USA, 1983.
10. Fujiwara, T. Estimation of ground movements in actual destructive earthquakes. In Proceedings of the 4th European Symp. Earthquake Engineering, London, UK, 5–7 September 1972; pp. 125–132.
11. Imai, T. P-and S-wave velocities of the ground in Japan. In Proceedings of the 9th International Conference on Soil Mechanics and Foundation Engineering, Tokyo, Japan, 10–15 July 1977; Volume 2, pp. 127–132.
12. Jafari, M.K.; Asghari, A.; Rahmani, I. Empirical correlation between shear wave velocity (Vs) and SPT-N value for south of Tehran soils. In Proceedings of the 4th International Conference on Civil Engineering, Tehran, Iran, 4–6 May 1997. (In Persian).
13. Jinan, Z. Correlation between seismic wave velocity and the number of blow of SPT and depth. *Chin. J. Geotech. Eng. (ASCE)* **1987**, 92–100.
14. Kiku, H.; Yoshida, N.; Yasuda, S.; Irisawa, T.; Nakazawa, H.; Shimizu, Y.; Ansal, A.; Erkan, A. In-situ penetration tests and soil profiling in Adapazarı, Turkey. In Proceedings of the ICSMGE/TC4 Satellite Conf. on Lessons Learned from Recent Strong Earthquakes, Istanbul, Turkey, 25 August 2001; pp. 259–265.
15. Lee, S.H. Regression models of shear wave velocities. *J. Chin. Inst. Eng.* **1990**, *13*, 519–532. [CrossRef]
16. Tamura, I.; Yamazaki, F. Estimation of S-wave velocity based on geological survey data for K-NET and Yokohama seismometer network. *J. Struct. Mech. Earthq. Eng.* **2002**, *2002*, 237–248.
17. Ohba, S.; Toriuma, I. Dynamic response characteristics of Osaka Plain. In Proceedings of the Annual Meeting AIJ, Tokyo, Japan, 5–7 December 1970.
18. Ohsaki, Y.; Iwasaki, R. On dynamic shear moduli and Poisson's ratio of soil deposits. *Soil Found* **1973**, *13*, 61–73. [CrossRef]
19. Ohta, T.; Hara, A.; Niwa, M.; Sakano, T. Elastic shear moduli as estimated from N-value. In Proceedings of the 7th Annual Convention of Japan Society of Soil Mechanics and Foundation Engineering, Tokyo, Japan, 10–15 July 1972; pp. 265–268.
20. Ohta, Y.; Goto, N. Empirical shear wave velocity equations in terms of characteristic soil indexes. *Earthq. Eng. Struct. Dyn.* **1978**, *6*, 167–187. [CrossRef]
21. Kanai, K. *Conference on Cone Penetrometer*; The Ministry of Public Works and Settlement: Ankara, Turkey, 1966.
22. Evans, A.E. Estimation of Pressure Meter Modulus from Shear Wave Velocity in the Sonoran Desert. Ph.D. Dissertation, Arizona State University, Tempe, AZ, USA, 2018.
23. SPR. Pinal West to Duke 500 KV Transmission Line: Final Geotechnical Investigation Report. Report No. CE, File No. AV-5031. 2012.
24. SPR. Duke to Pinal Central 500 KV Transmission Line: Final Geotechnical Investigation Report. Report No. CE-593, File No. AV-5051, 5056. 2012.
25. Heureux, J.S.; Long, M. Correlations between in Norwegian clays. In Proceedings of the 17th Nordic Geotechnic, Reykjavík, Iceland, 25–28 May 2016.
26. Johora, F.T. Forecasting Geotechnical Parameters from Electrical Resistivity and Seismic Wave Velocities Using Artificial Neural Network Models. Ph.D. Dissertation, University of Mississippi, Oxford, MS, USA, 2021.
27. Imai, T.; Fumoto, H.; Yokota, K. The Relation of Mechanical Properties of Soils to P and S-Wave Velocities in Japan Technical Note OYO Corporation. 1975. Available online: https://www.researchgate.net/institution/OYO_Corporation (accessed on 21 November 2022).
28. Foti, S.; Lancellotta, R. Soil porosities from seismic velocities. *Geotechnique* **2004**, *51*, 551–554. [CrossRef]
29. Hunter, J.A. Some observations of Vp, Vs, depth and porosity from boreholes in water-saturated unconsolidated sediments. *Proc. SAGEEP* **2003**, *2003*, 650–661.
30. Alshameri, B.; Madu, A. Compressive correlations between the Geotechnical and seismic data conducted via Bender element. *Geotech. Geol. Eng.* **2019**, *37*, 5077–5095. [CrossRef]

31. Duan, W.; Cai, G.; Liu, S.; Puppala, A.J. Correlations between shear wave velocity and Geotechnical parameters for Jiangsu clays of China. *Pure Appl. Geophys.* **2018**, *176*, 669–684. [CrossRef]
32. Wu, N.J. Predicting the compressive strength of concrete using an RBF-ANN model. *Appl. Sci.* **2021**, *11*, 6382. [CrossRef]
33. Lee, S.C. Prediction of concrete strength using artificial neural network. *Eng. Struct.* **2003**, *25*, 849–857. [CrossRef]
34. Shikha, A.; Marathe, S. Predicting the compressive strength of concrete using ANN in Matlab. *J. Constr. Eng. Technol. Manag.* **2020**, *10*, 3.
35. Johora, F.T.; Yasarer, H. Predicting concrete compressive strength and ultrasonic pulse velocity using artificial neural network technique. In Proceedings of the The Mississippi Academy of Sciences 83rd Annual Meeting, Hattiesburg, MS, USA, 21–22 February 2019.
36. Agrawal, V.; Sharma, A. Prediction of slump in concrete using artificial neural networks. *J. Civ. Environ. Eng.* **2010**, *45*, 25–32.
37. Badawi, Y.M.H.; Ahmed, Y.H. Prediction of concrete compressive strength & slump using artificial neural networks (ANN). *FES J. Eng. Sci.* **2021**, *9*, 84–89.
38. Kiran, M.; Mane, S.; Chavan, S.A.; Salokhe, P.A.; Nadgouda, S.T. Predicting slump values of concrete made by pozzolans and manufactured sand using ANN. *Int. J. Recent Technol. Eng.* **2022**, *10*, 66–72.
39. Tran, V.L.; Kim, J.K. Revealing the nonlinear behavior of steel flush endplate connections using ANN-based hybrid models. *J. Build. Eng.* **2022**, *57*, 104878. [CrossRef]
40. Lima, L.R.O.; Vellasco, P.C.; Andrade, S.A.L.; Silva, J.G.S.; Vellasco, M.M.B.R. Neural networks assessment of beam-to-column joints. *J. Braz. Soc. Mech. Sci. Eng.* **2005**, *27*, 314–324. [CrossRef]
41. Chakraborty, A.; Goswami, D. Slope stability prediction using artificial neural network (ANN). *Int. J. Eng. Comput. Sci.* **2017**, *6*, 21845–21848. [CrossRef]
42. Pham, T.A.; Ly, H.B.; Tran, V.Q.; Giap, L.V.; Vu, H.L.T.; Duong, H.A.T. Prediction of pile axial bearing capacity using artificial neural network and random forest. *Appl. Sci.* **2020**, *10*, 1871. [CrossRef]
43. Lee, Y.; Lee, S.; Bae, H.K. Design of jetty piles using artificial neural networks. *Sci. World J.* **2014**, *2014*, 405401. [CrossRef]
44. Johora, F.T.; Hickey, C.J.; Yasarer, H. Predicting geotechnical parameters from electric resistivity using artificial neural network. In Proceedings of the 33rd Symposium on the Application of Geophysics to Engineering and Environmental Problems, SAGEEP 2021, Online, 14–19 March 2021.
45. Shahri, A.A. Assessment and prediction of liquefaction potential using different artificial neural network models: A case study. *Geotech. Geol. Eng.* **2016**, *34*, 807–815. [CrossRef]
46. Mughieda, O.; Bani-Hani, K.A.; Safieh, B.A. Liquefaction assessment by artificial neural networks based on CPT. *Int. J. Geotech. Eng.* **2009**, *3*, 289–302. [CrossRef]
47. Gharehbaghi, K. Artificial neural network for transportation infrastructure systems. *MATEC Web Conf.* **2016**, *81*, 05001. [CrossRef]
48. Pasini, A. Artificial neural network for small dataset analysis. *J. Thorac. Dis.* **2015**, *7*, 953–960.
49. Feng, S.; Zhou, H.; Dong, H. Using deep neural network with small dataset to predict material defects. *Mater. Des.* **2019**, *162*, 300–310. [CrossRef]
50. Santamarina, J.C.; Klein, K.A.; Fam, M.A. *Soils and Waves, Particulate Materials Behavior, Characterization and Process Monitoring*; John Wiley and Sons, LTD: Hoboken, NJ, USA, 2001.
51. Hogan, J.M.; Handy, R.L. *Seismic Wave Velocity as a Means of in-Place Density Measurement Final Report-Part 2 of 2*; Engineering Research Institute, IOWA State University: Ames, IO, USA, 1996.
52. ASTM. *Annual Book of Standards, Volume 04.08, Soil and Rock*; ASTM: West Conshohocken, PA, USA, 1989.
53. Shahin, M.A.; Jaksa, M.B.; Maier, H.R. Recent advances and future challenges for artificial neural systems in geotechnical engineering applications. *Adv. Artif. Neural Syst.* **2009**, *2009*, 308239. [CrossRef]
54. Yasarer, H.; Najjar, M.Y. Characterizing the permeability of Kansas concrete mixes used in PCC pavements. *ASCE J.* **2014**, *14*, 1–8. [CrossRef]
55. Najjar, Y.M.; Huang, C. Simulating the stress-strain behavior of Georgia kaolin via recurrent neural approach. *Comput. Geotech.* **2007**, *34*, 346–361. [CrossRef]

Article

Early Earthquake Detection Using Batch Normalization Graph Convolutional Neural Network (BNGCNN)

Muhammad Atif Bilal [1,*], Yanju Ji [1], Yongzhi Wang [2,3,*], Muhammad Pervez Akhter [4] and Muhammad Yaqub [4]

[1] College of Instrumentation & Electrical Engineering, Jilin University, Changchun 130061, China; jiyj@jlu.edu.cn
[2] College of Geoexploration Science & Technology, Jilin University, Changchun 130061, China
[3] Institute of Integrated Information for Mineral Resources Prediction, Jilin University, Changchun 130026, China
[4] Riphah College of Computing, Riphah International University (Faisalabad Campus), Faisalabad 38000, Pakistan; pervezbcs@gmail.com (M.P.A.); myaqubciitswl@gmail.com (M.Y.)
* Correspondence: bilal6517@mails.jlu.edu.cn (M.A.B.); wangyongzhi@jlu.edu.cn (Y.W.)

Featured Application: Earthquake Detection, Earthquake Early Warning System (EEWS), Processing of Seismic data.

Abstract: Earthquake is a major hazard to humans, buildings, and infrastructure. Early warning systems should detect an earthquake and issue a warning with earthquake information such as location, magnitude, and depth. Earthquake detection from raw waveform data using deep learning models such as graph neural networks (GNN) is becoming an important research area. The multilayered structure of the GNN with a number of epochs takes more training time. It is also hard to train the model with saturating nonlinearities. The batch normalization technique is applied to each mini-batch to reduce epochs in training and obtain a steady distribution of activation values. It improves model training and prediction accuracy. This study proposes a deep learning model batch normalization graph convolutional neural network (BNGCNN) for early earthquake detection. It consists of two main components: CNN and GNN. Input to the CNN model is multi-station and three-component waveform data with magnitude $\geq$ 3.0 were collected from January 2000 to January 2015 for Southern California. The extracted features of CNN are appended with location information and input to GNN model for earthquake detection. After hyperparameter tuning of the BNGCNN, when testing and evaluating the model on the Southern California dataset, our method shows promising results to the baseline model GNN by obtaining a low error rate to predict the magnitude, depth, and location of an earthquake.

Keywords: batch normalization; deep learning; earthquake detection; graph convolution network; seismic network

1. Introduction

Earthquake is a major hazard to humans, buildings, and infrastructure. In recent years, for emergency response, early automatic detection of an earthquake from raw waveform data generated from the sensors of seismic stations is becoming an important research area [1]. For this purpose, the earthquake early warning (EEW) system generates an early warning on the targeted area a few seconds after the detection of earthquake waves without the intervention of an analyst [2]. Machine learning-based computational methods are stronger candidates for automatic earthquake detection.

Traditional machine learning and deep learning techniques have shown superior performance in many automated tasks such as text processing [3,4] image processing [5,6], and speech recognition [7,8]. Ref. [9] used an ANN-based MLP model to assess the safety of existing buildings. Results show that the model outperforms the others to classify concrete structure damage. Ref. [10] designed an earthquake early warning system using SVM to predict magnitude and peak ground velocity. The proposed system can effectively generate an alert at different levels from 0 to 3. The major drawback of machine learning techniques is their dependency on feature selection techniques. Several feature selection methods have been proposed in the past but several comparative studies show that there is no universal feature selection method that works well with all types of data. In contrast to traditional machine learning, convolutional filters in the convolutional layer extract feature automatically, and therefore, deep learning models outperform the traditional machine learning models on various tasks [11]. An important factor that can increase the performance of deep learning models is hyper-parameter tuning [12,13]. A model has several parameters such as batch size, dropout, learning rate, activation function, number of epochs, and number of convolutional filters. Finding the best value of these parameters (also called parameter tuning) is a time-consuming and resource-exhausting process. Batch normalization is a technique used for more stable and faster training of deep learning models [13,14].

Recently, deep learning techniques such as convolutional neural networks (CNN), graph neural networks (GNNs), and their ensemble models graph convolutional neural networks (GCNNs) have shown good performance for earthquake detection [15,16]. CNN has strong power to extract useful information from the seismic raw waveform data. Convolutional layers in the CNN model can extract contextual local features from input waveform data and by applying pooling operation it can learn global features. Combining these features with spatial information of stations helps for the accurate prediction of an earthquake. Adding batch normalization in CNN results in faster and more stable training of the model. GNNs have been designed particularly to process data arising from networks [17]. CNN with the GNN model has shown very good performance on seismic data processing in several studies [18].

Several past attempts for earthquake detection using deep learning techniques have some shortcomings. Ref. [18] used deep learning-based GNN method for seismic source characterization and appended latitude and longitude information with data to extract features from CNN. A graph partitioning method with CNN used for earthquake detection is proposed [15]. In this method, they did not use the actual GNN method but only classic graph theory was used. Recently, a study by [1] used GNN with CNN for seismic event classification from multiple stations but they did not use any spatial information or meta-information about stations.

Therefore, in this study, we propose a large-scale deep learning model batch normalization graph convolutional neural network (BNGCNN). The CNN part of the model extracts useful and relevant features from seismic raw waveform data collected from multiple stations and GNN processes spatial information and meta-information about multiple base stations. Batch normalization in CNN improves learning and reduces training time [13,14]. In this way, the proposed model effectively process seismic data obtained from multiple networks and can predict earthquake efficiently and correctly.

Our contributions to this study are summarized as follows:

- We propose a deep learning-based model BNGCNN model for the early prediction of an earthquake.
- For experiments, we use a seismological dataset having 1477 events collected from 187 stations. Event waveform data with location information have been collected from multiple seismic stations instead of a single station.
- The performance of our model has been systematically analyzed by fine-tuning its several hyper-parameters.
- We chose the model proposed in [18] as a baseline model to compare the results obtained from the proposed model. Results show the superiority of our model.

The rest of the paper is organized as follows: In Section 2, we discuss related work including seismic data, convolutional networks, and graph networks. Section 3 discusses the architecture of the proposed model and its parameters. A brief introduction of the seismic dataset, challenges, and statistics are given in Section 4. Section 5 includes the experimental results of the proposed model and the baseline models. Conclusion and future work are given in Section 6.

2. Related Work

Traditional machine learning requires user knowledge to extract meaningful features from the data. These feature selection or extraction methods heavily affect the performance of these models like decision trees, support vector machines, and naïve Bayes [19]. Ref. [10] designed an earthquake early warning system using SVM to predict magnitude and peak ground velocity. The proposed system can effectively generate an alert at different levels from 0 to 3. Further, applying feature selection methods to the raw data is time-consuming and more prone to errors. Deep learning models perform feature selection automatically using multiple hidden layers. These layers are also used for dimensionality reduction which makes deep learning models more powerful for processing nonlinear and complex data [20]. The architecture of deep learning models such as graph neural networks and multilayer perceptron represents effectively spatial information such as stations and their relationship [18].

Deep learning models have shown superior performance to traditional machine learning models on a variety of tasks such as image processing [21], text classification [22], blockchain, etc. Deep learning has three mainstream architectures CNN [23], GNN [5], and RNN which are inherited from the machine learning model known as multi-layer perceptron (MLP) [18]. MLP has a fully connected layered architecture that is powerful but because of its high computational time, the depth of the model is limited. The advanced architectures have multiple layers of different types (convolutional, pooling, dropout, softmax) to learn complex data and improve performance. Refs. [9,24] used an ANN-based MLP model to assess the safety of existing buildings. Results show that the model outperforms the others to classify concrete structure damage. Ref. [25] proposed a neural network-based forecasting model to predict earthquake intensity. Experiments show that DeepShake can effectively predict an earthquake five seconds before the event.

In some studies, CNN-based models have been used for seismic data processing, feature extraction, and classification. Ref. [16] investigated the CNN for rapid earthquake detection and epicenter classification from the single station waveform data. Experiments on three-component waveform data obtained from IRIS show that the proposed CNN-based model achieves 87% accuracy to predict earthquake sources over a broad range of distances and magnitudes. Ref. [16] used CNN to predict the ground shaking intensity of earthquake after 15–20 s after earthquake origin time. Ref. [23] proposed two CNN-based models to estimate the seismic response of the surface. Ref. [20] used a deep CNN model for earthquake detection and source region estimation. The proposed models predict fairly well the amplitude and the natural periods. All these studies used single-station waveform data and do not consider location information in prediction.

Recently, a hybrid deep learning model GCNN is becoming popular for earthquake detection using seismic data. Ref. [17] used the GNN model to show that along with the time series data sensor location information can be exploited using graph-based networks. Experimental results on two seismic datasets containing earthquake waveforms show promising results. Refs. [1,18] proposed a deep CNN and GNN model for earthquake events classification from multiple stations. CNN layers aggregate features from the waveform data and combining these features with spatial information of stations helps the GNN for accurate prediction of an earthquake. Ref. [15] proposed a graph partitioning-based model that uses both CNN and GNN for earthquake detection from seismic array data. They used data from multiple seismic stations but the spatial information of these stations was ignored completely.

Different events can be detected by multiple stations in different locations. Multiple stations enable a generation of heterogeneous data but there exists a relationship between the observations collected from multiple stations [1]. A single station enables the generation of a large amount of homogenous data. Therefore, earthquake detection from multiple station data is a more challenging task than single station data for deep learning models [17]. CNN-based models are often used for single-station datasets [26,27] while GCNN models are good to process multiple-station datasets [5,18].

A problem with deep learning models is the fine-tuning of their parameters. Batch normalization is a technique used for faster and stable training of a deep learning model [13,14]. In training, the objective of batch normalization is to normalize the layer output using the statistics of each mini-batch size. Recently, many studies used batch normalization in their proposed deep learning models to improve the model performance such as brain tumor detection [6], gas–liquid interface construction [28], and fault diagnosis of a machine [29]. Unfortunately, automatic earthquake detection from seismic data generated from multiple stations is deprived of the batch normalization technique.

A set of studies have been summarized in Table 1. It is seen that CNN-based studies only use single-station seismic data for earthquake detection and do not use geographical information of the station for prediction. The studies which use graph-based neural networks use the dataset where events have been collected from multiple seismic stations. Moreover, these studies include station geographical information that significantly increase model prediction. It is because GNNs are good to handle spatial information [30]. A few studies are based on other models such as transformers or RNN models such as LSTM or BiLSTM.

Table 1. A summary of the literature is discussed in this study. Most of the studies do not use spatial information about events.

Study	Model	Spatial Info	Year	Data	Station
[17]	GCNN	Yes	2022	Italy and California	Multiple
[18]	GCNN	Yes	2020	California	Multiple
[27]	CNN	No	2019	IRIS	Single
[16]	CNN	No	2021	Central Italy	Multiple
[1]	GCNN		2022	–	Multiple
[26]	SVMR	No	2018	Bogota, Colombia	Single
[31]	CNN + LSTM + BiLSTM + Transformer	No	2020	STEAD	Single
[15]	CNN and Graph	No	2021	MeSO-Net Japan	Multiple, Single
[23]	CNN	–	2021	NIED Japan	Single
[23]	Deep CNN	–	2021	CARABOBO	Single
[2]	CNN and Team. Transformer	Yes	2021	Japan, Italy	Multiple

3. Methods

There are several advantages of using CNN on seismic waveform data: (1) It operates directly on waveform data with little preprocessing and without feature extraction; (2) it is shifted invariant and not sensitive to the time position of the feature (P- or S-waves); and (3) it does not make explicit use of existing physics-based knowledge such as S-P difference, or seismic travel times. The proposed methodology used in this study is shown in Figure 1. First, three component wave-from data are downloaded from IRIS (Incorporated Research Institute for Seismology). After preprocessing, in the second step, we use a CNN to examine the waveforms of a specific station. The three-component waveform is processed by this CNN, and then a set of features is extracted from it. After that, the geographic location (latitude and longitude) of the seismic station is appended to the feature vector to create it. In the third step, this feature vector is used as an input by the second component, which is a GNN. This GNN will recombine the time series features with the station location to create a final station-specific feature vector. This procedure is carried out once for each of the stations that make up the network, utilizing the CNN and GNN components in the same way (i.e., the same operations are applied to each station individually). Only along the time axis are the processes that constitute the convolution carried out. Output is flattened and the final prediction about the magnitude, location, and depth is made finally. The architecture of the proposed model is given in detail in Figure 2.

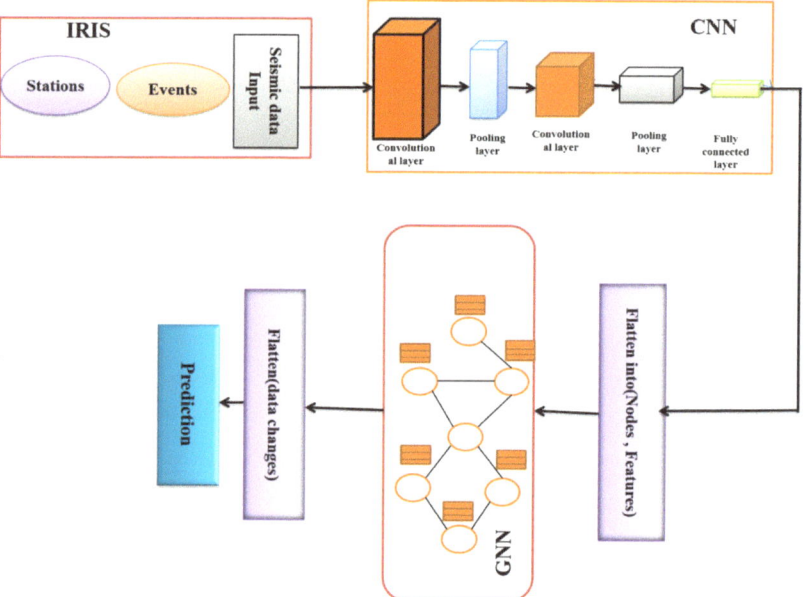

Figure 1. The proposed methodology consists of three components. First, data downloading and preprocessing. Second, CNN part to examine the data to extract the feature map. Third, use extracted future map and combine it with station location information to make a final prediction.

BNGCNN is derived from the model [18] to detect an earthquake event and predict its magnitude and location. We have modified the architecture and added CNN with a batch normalization layer for optimized training and to improve prediction accuracy. Input to the BNGCNN is an array size (50, N, 3) for all stations where the number of components in data is three, 50 is the number of stations and N is the number of samples with a sampling rate of 512 per second. As a result of the fact that seismic waveforms recorded at various stations have distinct biases, we preprocess the data in accordance with:

$$y_m = x_m - \frac{1}{M}\sum_{i=1}^{M} x_i \ , \ m = 1,\ldots, M \quad (1)$$

where x_m is the seismic waveform data, y_m is the converted seismic waveform data, and M is the total number of samples in the occurrence event, preprocessing has the effect of geometrically pushing the data center to the origin. The ordering of the stations is preserved and each waveform starts its origin time. We have normalized the waveform by its maximum value as it is recommended to improve CNN performance [16]. A stack of 5 feed-forward convolutional blocks where each block consists of 2-D convolution filters of size $1 \times 5 \times f_i$ where f = {4, 8, 16, 32, 64} is the number of filters in the ith block. Convolution is performed on the time-axis and recombined into the filters of the next layer. Convolutional operation is defined as:

$$y_i^{l+1}(j) = k_i^l * M^l(j) + b_i^l \quad (2)$$

where $y_i^{l+1}(j)$ denotes the input of the jth neuron in the feature map i of layer $l+1$. k_i^l the weights of the ith filter kernel in layer l, M^j the jth local region in the layer l and b_i^l the bias. After each convolutional layer, an activation function is employed to extract the nonlinear features. The rectified linear unit (ReLU) is a typical activation function used for this purpose and can be defined as:

$$\text{ReLU}(x) = max(0, x) \tag{3}$$

where x is the output of the convolutional layer. It is a piecewise linear function that returns a value of zero if the input is negative and if the input is positive, it will be output directly.

$$Tanh(x) = \frac{e^x - e^{-x}}{e^x + e^{-x}} = \frac{2}{1 + e^{-2x}} - 1 \in (-1 \text{ to } 1) \tag{4}$$

where e is Euler's constant. The advantage of this activation function is that it can return negative values which are useful if the desired output distribution contains negative values. If the value of the input is greater (more positive), then the value of the output will be closer to 1.0. On the other hand, if the value of the input is smaller (more negative), then the output will be closer to -1.0.

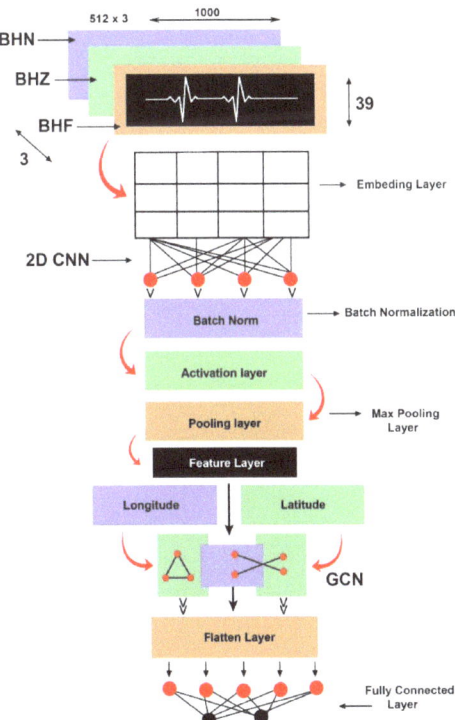

Figure 2. The proposed architecture of the batch normalization graph convolutional neural network. 3-channel data are fed into the model. Features are extracted by CNN and batch normalization is applied before pooling operation. Location information is added to the feature vector and the GNN part makes the final prediction.

Batch normalization is added before the activation function. ReLU introduced non-linearity followed by a spatial dropout of 15%. Data are reduced by 1×4 max-pooling with stride 1 after passing three convolutional layers. The last convolutional layer does not use any activation function. To preserve the extracted features, in the last layer of the final block, we use tanh activation function not followed by a dropout. The final max-pooling layer reduced the data from Ns × 32 × 64 to Ns × 1 × 64. Ns denotes the total number of stations. For each station from Ns, it produces a feature vector of size 64. This feature vector is then appended by spatial information (longitude, latitude) and yields a feature vector Ns × 2 × 66.

The second component of the BNGCNN is a multi-layer perceptron that recombines spatial information with time-series features. It has two hidden layers 128 neurons and ReLU activation function, and spatial dropout. It produces the data of Ns × 1 × 128 size and represents the collection of features of each node in the graph. This node feature vector is aggregated with the graph feature vector by performing max reduce operation along the station's dimension.

The final component is MLP with two hidden layers of 128 neurons. After activation using tanh, this component maps the graph feature vector into the model output of size 4 (depth, magnitude, latitude, longitude). The predicted output is mapped with the labels scaled between −1 and 1 through a mean absolute error (MAE) loss function. The loss can be expressed as the mean of the absolute differences between the actual values and those that were predicted, or it can be written as a formula as follows:

$$L(y, \hat{y}) = \frac{1}{N} \sum_{i=0}^{N} |y - \hat{y}| \tag{5}$$

where $\hat{y}$ is the predicted value by the model, and y is the actual value in the data. We used an Adam optimizer with initial learning rate 0.0001. All the components are directly connected and trained as a single model.

4. Results

4.1. Datasets

This study uses a dataset from Southern California. The area of study is important because it is the economic and social hub of the states. The dataset consists of three component raw waveforms (BHN, BHE, BHZ) recorded directly from seismic stations. N oriented north-west, E oriented west-east, and Z oriented vertically. We extracted 120 s long time windows that contained the onsets of both P- and S-wave arrivals for all the available events. An earthquake with a magnitude less than 3.0 with no depth cut-off was not considered. Each station provides a simultaneous sampling of three channels with a 24-bit resolution. Each waveform file is converted to a sac file using python libraries. Waves are filtered at a frequency range from 0.1–8.0 Hz and interpolate onto a time base $1 < t < 101$ s after the event origin time, over 512 evenly spaced time samples (5 Hz sampling frequency). We considered the waveform length starting from its origin time to 120 s after its end time.

We use a python library ObsPy to collect data for datasets [32,33]. ObsPy downloads the broadband inventory and earthquake catalog of the Southern California Seismic Network (SCSN (doi:10.7914/SN/CI)). In the dataset, there is a total of 1427 events collected from 187 stations from the period 31 January 2000 to 31 December 2015 (15 years). For both seismic stations and event locations, we set the limits for latitude from [32° to 36°] and longitude [−120° to −116°]. Maps of stations and events considered in this study are given in Figure 3. The locations of these seismic stations are shown as triangles in Figure 3a and the event locations are shown as dots in Figure 3b. Statistics of the dataset are given in Table 2.

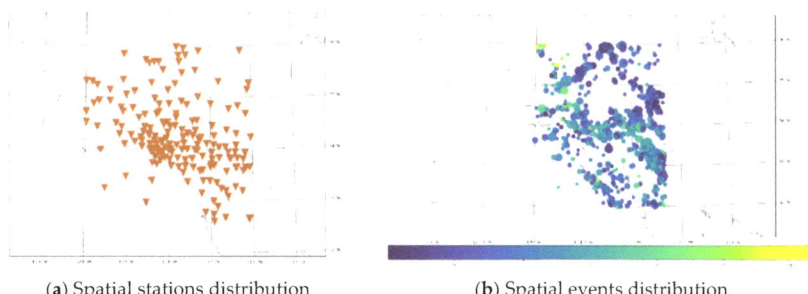

(a) Spatial stations distribution   (b) Spatial events distribution

Figure 3. (a) Shows the number of stations and their location for the Southern California region. (b) Event distribution for California. The depth and magnitude of an event are encoded by its color and size.

Table 2. A summary of the Southern California dataset used in this study.

Properties	Values	Properties	Values
Period	2000–2015	Min. and Max. Latitude	[32° to 36°]
No. of events	1427	Min and Max. Longitude	[−120° to 116°]
No. of stations	187	Minimum magnitude	3.0
Filter the waveform	0.1–8 Hz	Even spaced time sample	2048 Hz
No. of stations	187	Scaled Min. max. source depth	0 to 30 km
Scaled magnitude	3–6	Time-base	$1 < t < 101$

The magnitude distribution and depth distribution of each event are shown as Histograms in Figure 4a,b. Magnitude distribution shows that events are not equally distributed concerning the magnitude values. Half of the events in the dataset have magnitude ranges from 3.0 to 3.13. Only a few events have a magnitude greater than 3.9. The average magnitude value of all the events is 3.3. On the other side depth distribution, more than 60% of events have a depth range from 1.7 km to 10.2 km. Only a few events have a depth of more than 20.0 km. The average value of the depth in the dataset is 9.0 km.

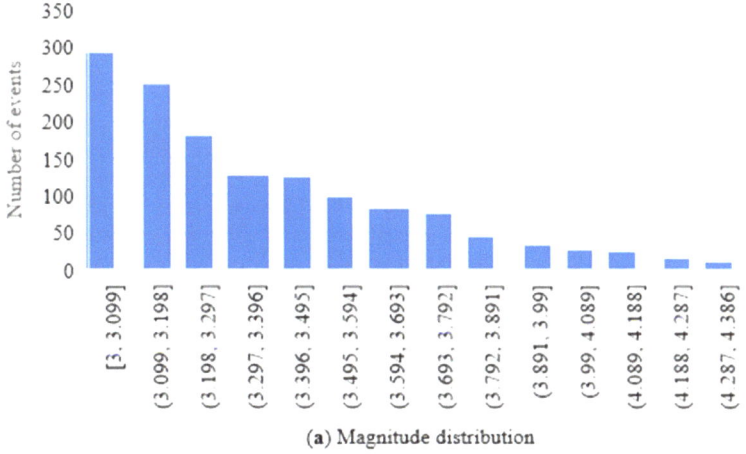

(a) Magnitude distribution

Figure 4. *Cont.*

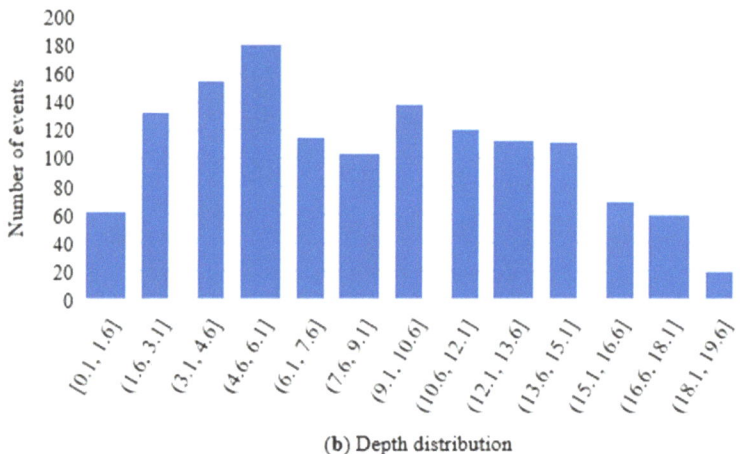

(b) Depth distribution

Figure 4. The histogram in (**a**) shows the magnitude distribution and the histogram in (**b**) shows the depth distribution of the events from the Southern California dataset used in experiments by the proposed model.

4.2. Experimentation

All of the experiments are carried out on an Intel Core i7-7700 processor running at 3.60 GHz with 16 GB of RAM, an NVIDIA GeForce GTX 1080 graphics card, Windows 10, and TensorFlow 2.3 with CUDA toolkit, respectively.

To optimize the network parameters, we started our model parameters as the parameters of the model [18]. The experiments are designed to compare two different types of neural network models, GNN and BNGCNN, with the ultimate goal of developing a generalized detection model as a result of the findings. A random 80/20 split is performed on the entire data set to create a training set and a validation set, respectively. Training set constitutes 80 percent of the whole data with 1140 out of 1427 events. This dataset is used for training the model. Remaining 20 percent data used as a validation set to validate the model performance with 287 out of 1427 events. We evaluate the performance of the trained model on both the training and validation data sets separately as [18]. Several models can be compared to one another with the use of an independent test set to determine which is the most efficient. In addition, it should be emphasized that k-Fold cross-validation would almost probably result in somewhat better-performing models with smaller sample sizes, but this has not been confirmed in this study.

Finding the optimal parameters for a model requires extensive training across a large number of epochs. The term "one epoch" refers to when a model passes through all of the examples once in a forward pass and once in a backward pass in a dataset or a batch of data. A large, complicated, and noisy dataset necessitates the use of more epochs by the model. To do this, early halting from evaluating validation performance is employed. A model may be trained for 30 epochs and then the best parameters are selected from the model with the highest validation performance, as an example. Positive class labels are less likely to be mislabeled in training data than negative class labels, hence models with higher accuracy on the positive class are preferred over models with higher accuracy on the negative class. Figure 5a shows the training loss and validation loss with a different number of epochs (50 to 500). A model's training loss reveals how well it fits the training data, whereas a model's validation loss tells how well it fits new data that was used for validation. Our model is showing the best performance over 400 epochs where the validation loss is minimum and the model best fits the new data.

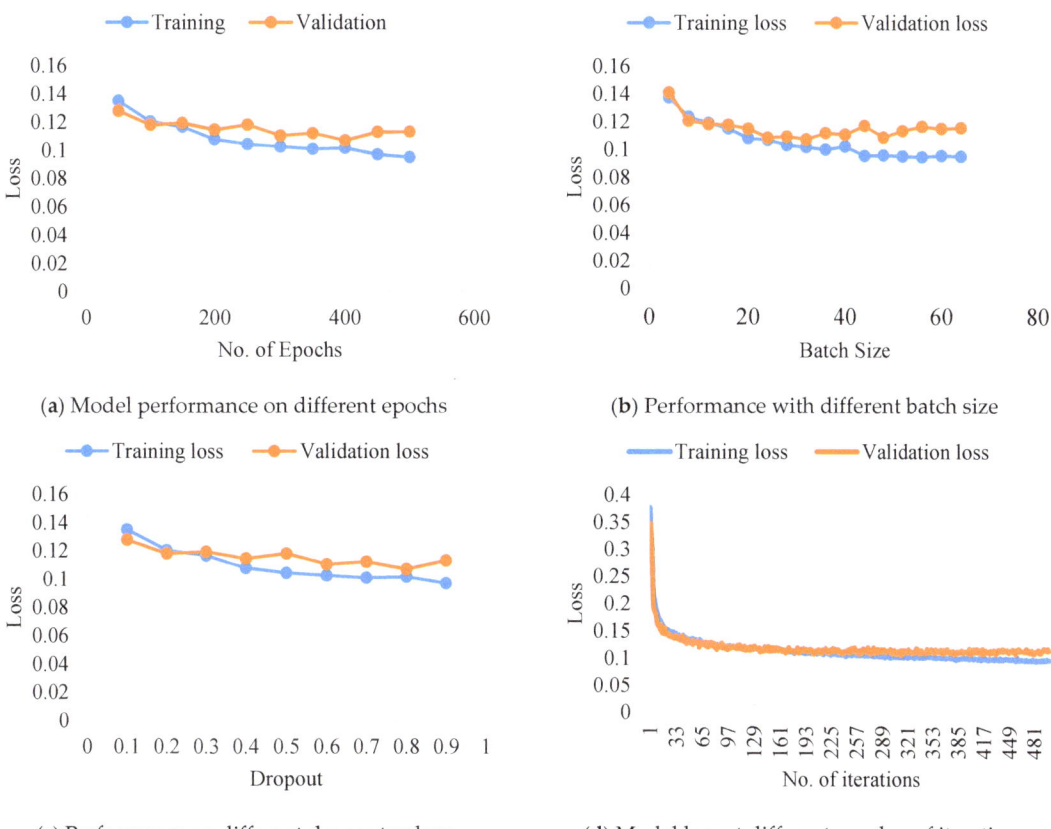

Figure 5. Model performance using different values of epochs in (**a**), batch size in (**b**), dropout in (**c**), and iterations in (**d**).

Batch size refers to the number of instances that are sent to the model at one time for processing in a single iteration of the model. A large batch would take more memory on the GPU, resulting in slower training operations. Figure 5b shows the performance of our model over different batches. We put our model through its paces on 16 different batches of varying sizes (4 to 64). The results demonstrate that a batch size of 32 produces superior results by obtaining the lowest validation loss value of 0.107, which is consistent with the findings of [6].

Figure 5c depicts the performance of our model when different dropout values are considered. To protect the network against noise and overfitting, dropouts are used. If the model is trained on an insufficient dataset, it may encounter the problem of overfitting. An alternative method would be to increase the dataset size or decrease the number of hidden units utilized for feature computation. Dropout is a model feature that deletes or deactivates inactive units in the model's hidden layer. These units are not included in the calculations for the following rounds of the algorithm. Figure 5c illustrates that the model gets the maximum accuracy on a 0.8 dropout value.

Tests are carried out with varying batch sizes, several epochs, dropout values, and other hyperparameters. Ultimately, the goal is to develop a generalized detection model that outperforms the competition in terms of prediction accuracy. There is a maximum number of training epochs allowed for each sample size; these values are determined by reviewing a large number of potential training scenarios with a small number of epochs and manually selecting the numbers from empirical evidence. It is preferable to train for an excessive amount of time since early stopping will select the highest performing model on the validation set, which is resistant to over-fitting.

When several further experiments have been conducted to analyze hyperparameters, the most ideal choices are made for executing the ensuing stated experiments and obtaining the resulting results. Figure 5d shows the performance of the proposed model with the best-performing network parameters. Take note of how the distance between validation and train loss narrows with each passing epoch. The reason for this is that while the network learns the data, it also reduces the regularization loss (model weights), resulting in a slight discrepancy between validation and train losses. On the training set, the model, on the other hand, is still more accurate.

5. Results and Discussion

In this section, we compare the performance of our proposed model with the GNN model [18] through experiments on the California dataset. Performance is evaluated separately for training and validation datasets. Charts of Figure 6 show the mean training error, mean validation error, and mean square error obtained from the GNN model for longitude, latitude, depth, and magnitude predictions. The mean absolute difference between the predicted values and the actual values in the catalog is less than 13 km for longitude and latitude, 3.3 km for depth, and 0.13 for magnitude. The experimental results for the proposed BNGCNN model are shown in Figure 7. The mean absolute difference between the predicted values and the actual values in the catalog is less than 10 km for longitude and latitude, 2.6 km for depth, and 0.09 for magnitude. It is visible from the comparison of both Figures 6 and 7 that the proposed model with batch normalization significantly reduces the error and improves accuracy.

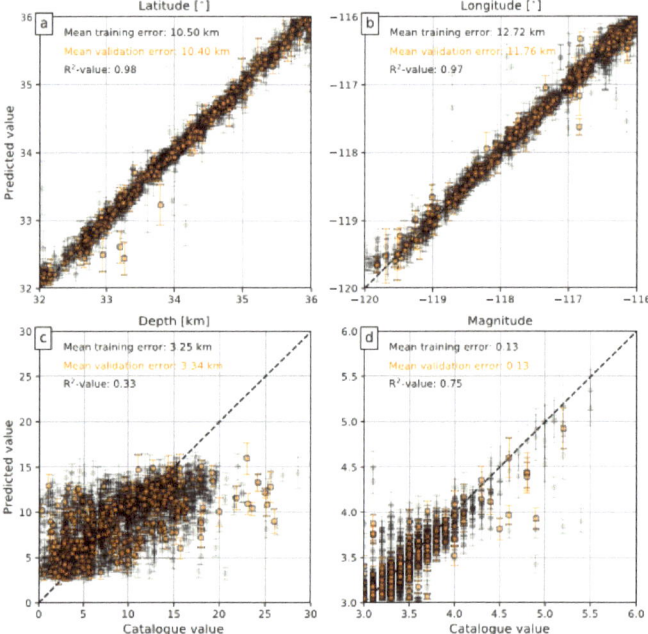

Figure 6. Mean absolute error for training and validation sets obtained from the California dataset. Predicted values by GNN model and the actual values for (**a**) latitude, (**b**) longitude, (**c**) depth, and (**d**) magnitude after inserting geographical information.

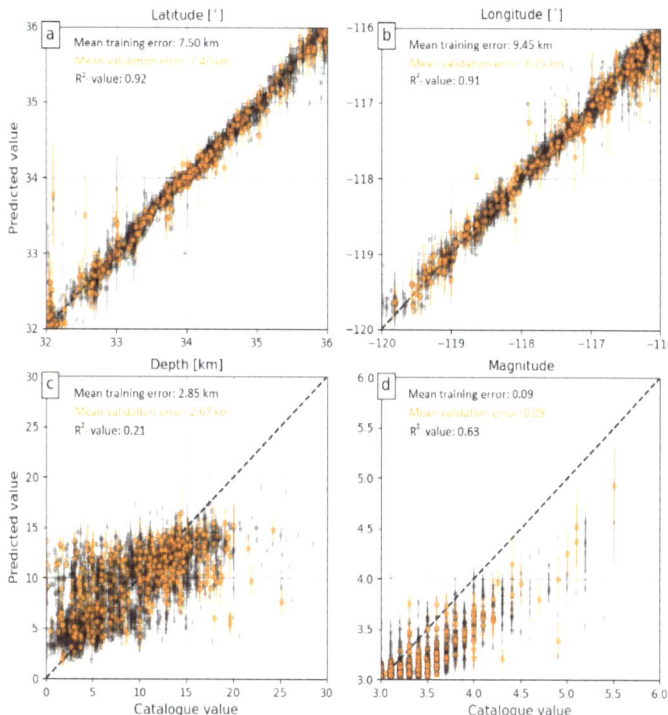

Figure 7. Mean absolute error for training and validation sets obtained from the California dataset. Predicted values by the BNGCNN model and the actual values for (**a**) latitude, (**b**) longitude, (**c**) depth, and (**d**) magnitude by inserting geographical information.

On the training and validation datasets, we examine the model's performance with and without station position information. The results are shown graphically in Figure 8a–d for the baseline model and Figure 8e–h for the BNGCNN model. The black color line shows the training error, the yellow line for validation error, and the blue line for errors when no station location information is used. The performance of the model when including the geographic locations of the stations is examined separately for both the train data set and the validation data set, and the results demonstrate minimal overfitting. The performance is evaluated using the combined data set even when the station locations are not included in the analysis. The model posterior is calculated by running inference 100 times on each event in the training and validation catalogs and determining the related mean and standard deviation while retaining dropout regularization. For GNN, both data sets produce similar results, indicating that overfitting on the training set is minimal. The mean absolute difference between catalog data and model projections is less than 0.13 for magnitude, 3.3 km for depth, and less than 0.11° (13 km) for latitude and longitude (which translates to a mean epicentral location error of 18 km). For the proposed BNGCNN model, averaging the latitude and longitude values from the catalog and model predictions, the mean absolute difference is less than 10 km in distance for the latitude and longitude (resulting in a mean epicentral location error of 18 km), 2.6 km in depth, and 0.09 in magnitude. The approach produces a respectable first-order estimate of location and magnitude that can be used as a starting point for further refinement using typical seismological instruments. The magnitude curve in Figure 8h illustrates some prominent peaks than Figure 8d. This is because of the scale and shift operations that a batch normalization layer uses [13]. Unlike the input layer, which requires all normalized values to have a zero mean and unit variance, Batch Norm allows its values to be shifted (to a different mean) and scaled (to a different variance). It does this by multiplying the normalized values by a factor, gamma, and adding to them a factor, beta. Therefore, the results in Figure 8b are different than Figure 8h.

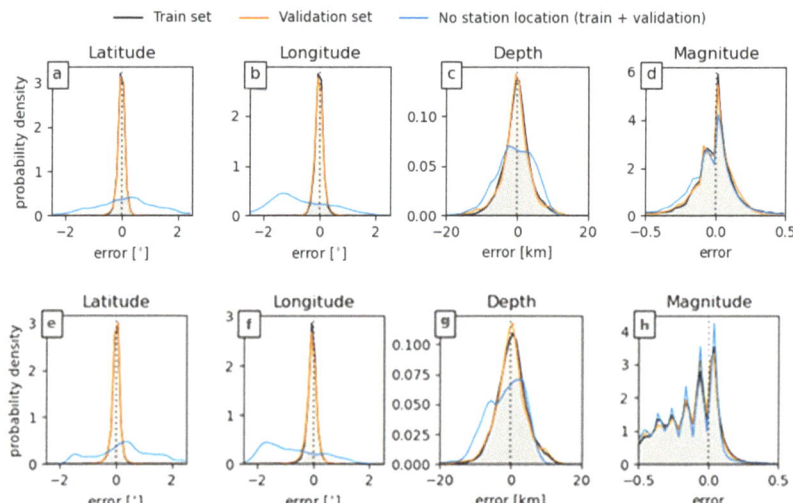

Figure 8. Prediction errors of the GNN from (**a**–**d**) and BNGCNN from (**e**–**h**) models to predict latitude, longitude, depth, and magnitude of a seismic event without and with using station location information. With station spatial information, the black line shows the training error on the training subset while the yellow line shows the validation error on the validation set. The blue line shows the prediction error on combined training and validation subsets without location information.

Figure 9a,b show the difference between the event's actual epicenter and the predicted epicenter of GNN and BNGCNN, respectively. Each arrow represents a single cataloged event, beginning from the predicted epicenter and pointing to the catalog epicenter. The colors represent the misfit ratio over the model posterior's 95 percent confidence interval. As a result, the blue color denotes that the catalog epicenter is within the 95 percent confidence interval, while the red color denotes that it is not. We can compare the posterior's confidence intervals with the actual epicenter location error because we can compute the posterior distribution for each event. A model error ratiometric, which measures the distance between predicted and observed epicenters, is used to illustrate the model uncertainty. This metric is normalized by the model posterior's 95% confidence interval. A score of 1 indicates that the genuine epicenter location falls within a 95 percent confidence interval, while a value of 0 indicates that the true epicenter location does not lie within the confidence interval at all. In most cases, the error ratio is less than one. This means that the model posterior distribution's expected aleatoric uncertainties are substantially smaller than the actual epistemic uncertainties.

Because regions with the highest density of seismic stations also have the lowest prediction error (see Figure 8), it appears that the spatially interpolated prediction error is somewhat related to the local density of seismic stations. The highest systematic errors are seen in the northwest and southeast corners of the selected region, where the station density is low and the model appears to be unable to obtain the boundary values of latitude and longitude. In this case, the behavior of the tanh activation function can be explained by the fact that it asymptotically approaches the value ± 1, which corresponds to the range of latitudes and longitudes represented by the training samples. As a result, ever greater activations are necessary to push the final location predictions toward the boundaries of the domain, resulting in findings that are biased toward the interior of the domain. This shows a basic trade-off between resolution (prediction accuracy) in the interior of the data domain and the greatest amplitude of the predictions (which also applies to linear activation functions).

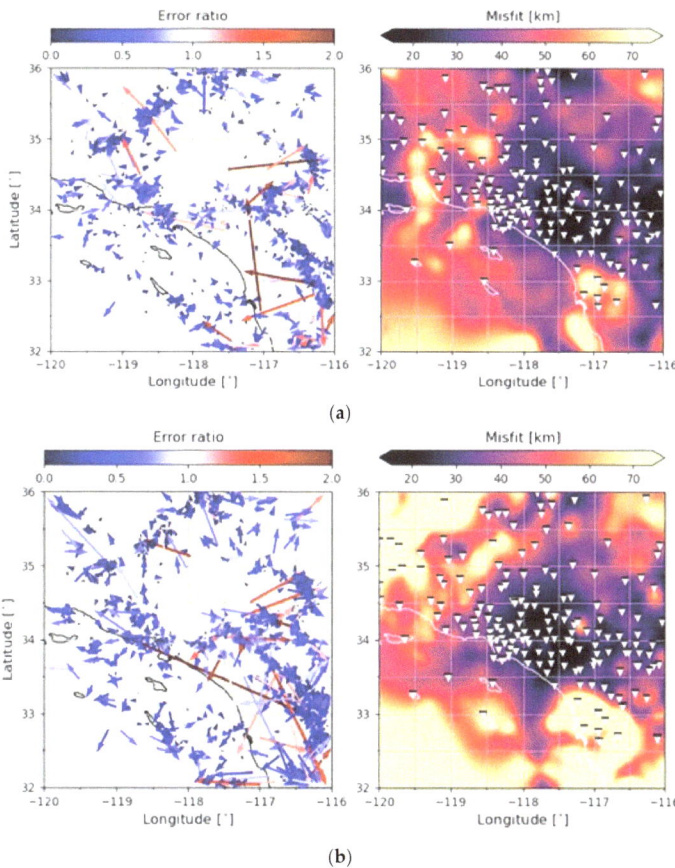

Figure 9. Residuals of the epicentral locations (in first column) and overlay of the locations of seismic stations (in second column) on the interpolated prediction error (in km) on the California dataset. (**a**) Residuals of the epicentral locations and overlay of the locations of seismic stations by GNN; (**b**) Epicentral residuals and an overlay of seismic station locations by BNGCNN.

6. Conclusions

In this study, we propose a BNGCNN model to predict earthquakes with satisfying accuracy adopting multistation and 3 channel waveform data consisting of 1477 events with magnitude 3 or more than 3 from 187 stations. After preprocessing the data, CNN of the proposed model with batch normalization before activation is applied to the input data. We found that it not only helps to extract valuable features but also improves training by reducing the number of epochs and reducing nonlinearity which helps in fast training and improves prediction accuracy. We also found that incorporating station location information in feature vectors and applying GNN on the feature vector also improves the prediction accuracy of our model. We have analyzed the performance of our proposed model by analyzing its different hyperparameters which help us to find the best values of the model parameters to reduce training error. Comparison with the baseline model proves the superiority of our model on the same dataset by reducing the error rate to 3 km, 0.7 km, and 0.04 for longitude and latitude, depth, and magnitude, respectively.

For future work, we aim to explore other variants of deep learning models such as GNN with attention layer mechanisms [34] and transformers [2,31]. We also aim to test deeply deep learning models on multiple datasets with sparse and dense stations with and without station location information. The proposed model can also be applied to assess the damage done by an earthquake [9].

Author Contributions: Conceptualization, Y.J. and Y.W.; Formal analysis, M.A.B., M.P.A. and M.Y.; Funding acquisition, Y.J. and Y.W.; Investigation, M.Y.; Methodology, M.P.A.; Software, M.A.B.; Supervision, Y.W.; Visualization, M.A.B.; Writing—original draft, M.A.B.; Writing—review & editing, M.P.A. All authors have read and agreed to the published version of the manuscript.

Funding: National Key R & D Plan: 2021YFC2901801.

Institutional Review Board Statement: Not applicable.

Informed Consent Statement: Not applicable.

Data Availability Statement: Not applicable.

Conflicts of Interest: The authors declare no conflict of interest.

References

1. Kim, G.; Ku, B.; Ahn, J.K.; Ko, H. Graph Convolution Networks for Seismic Events Classification Using Raw Waveform Data from Multiple Stations. *IEEE Geosci. Remote Sens. Lett.* **2022**, *19*, 1–5. [CrossRef]
2. Münchmeyer, J.; Bindi, D.; Leser, U.; Tilmann, F. The Transformer Earthquake Alerting Model: A New Versatile Approach to Earthquake Early Warning. *Geophys. J. Int.* **2021**, *225*, 646–656. [CrossRef]
3. Elnagar, A.; Al-Debsi, R.; Einea, O. Arabic Text Classification Using Deep Learning Models. *Inf. Process. Manag.* **2020**, *57*, 102121. [CrossRef]
4. Akhter, M.P.; Zheng, J.; Afzal, F.; Lin, H.; Riaz, S.; Mehmood, A. Supervised Ensemble Learning Methods towards Automatically Filtering Urdu Fake News within Social Media. *PeerJ Comput. Sci.* **2021**, *7*, e425. [CrossRef] [PubMed]
5. Zhou, J.; Cui, G.; Hu, S.; Zhang, Z.; Yang, C.; Liu, Z.; Wang, L.; Li, C.; Sun, M. Graph Neural Networks: A Review of Methods and Applications. *AI Open* **2020**, *1*, 57–81. [CrossRef]
6. Amin, J.; Sharif, M.; Anjum, M.A.; Raza, M.; Bukhari, S.A.C. Convolutional Neural Network with Batch Normalization for Glioma and Stroke Lesion Detection Using MRI. *Cogn. Syst. Res.* **2020**, *59*, 304–311. [CrossRef]
7. Park, T.J.; Kanda, N.; Dimitriadis, D.; Han, K.J.; Watanabe, S.; Narayanan, S. A Review of Speaker Diarization: Recent Advances with Deep Learning. *Comput. Speech Lang.* **2022**, *72*, 101317. [CrossRef]
8. Zia, T.; Zahid, U. Long Short-Term Memory Recurrent Neural Network Architectures for Urdu Acoustic Modeling. *Int. J. Speech Technol.* **2019**, *22*, 21–30. [CrossRef]
9. Harirchian, E.; Lahmer, T. Improved Rapid Assessment of Earthquake Hazard Safety of Structures via Artificial Neural Networks. *IOP Conf. Ser. Mater. Sci. Eng.* **2020**, *897*, 012014. [CrossRef]
10. Song, J.; Zhu, J.; Wang, Y.; Li, S. On-Site Alert-Level Earthquake Early Warning Using Machine-Learning-Based Prediction Equations. *Geophys. J. Int.* **2022**, *231*, 786–800. [CrossRef]
11. Audretsch, J. Earthquake Detection Using Deep Learning Based Approaches. Available online: https://repository.kaust.edu.sa/handle/10754/662251 (accessed on 17 March 2020).
12. Srivastava, N.; Hinton, G.; Krizhevsky, A.; Sutskever, I.; Salakhutdinov, R. Dropout: A Simple Way to Prevent Neural Networks from Overfitting. *J. Mach. Learn. Res.* **2014**, *15*, 1929–1958.
13. Santurkar, S.; Tsipras, D.; Ilyas, A.; Madry, A. How Does Batch Normalization Help Optimization? In Proceedings of the Advances in Neural Information Processing Systems, Montreal, ON, Canada, 3–8 December 2018.
14. Kalayeh, M.M.; Shah, M. Training Faster by Separating Modes of Variation in Batch-Normalized Models. *IEEE Trans. Pattern Anal. Mach. Intell.* **2020**, *42*, 1483–1500. [CrossRef] [PubMed]
15. Yano, K.; Shiina, T.; Kurata, S.; Kato, A.; Komaki, F.; Sakai, S.; Hirata, N. Graph-Partitioning Based Convolutional Neural Network for Earthquake Detection Using a Seismic Array. *J. Geophys. Res. Solid Earth* **2021**, *126*, 1–17. [CrossRef]
16. Jozinović, D.; Lomax, A.; Štajduhar, I.; Michelini, A. Rapid Prediction of Earthquake Ground Shaking Intensity Using Raw Waveform Data and a Convolutional Neural Network. *Geophys. J. Int.* **2021**, *222*, 1379–1389. [CrossRef]
17. Bloemheuvel, S.; van den Hoogen, J.; Jozinović, D.; Michelini, A.; Atzmueller, M. Multivariate Time Series Regression with Graph Neural Networks. *arxiv* **2022**, *2201*, 00818. [CrossRef]
18. van den Ende, M.P.A.; Ampuero, J.P. Automated Seismic Source Characterization Using Deep Graph Neural Networks. *Geophys. Res. Lett.* **2020**, *47*, 1–11. [CrossRef]
19. Mousavi, S.M.; Beroza, G.C. A Machine-Learning Approach for Earthquake Magnitude Estimation. *Geophys. Res. Lett.* **2020**, *47*, 1–7. [CrossRef]

20. Tous, R.; Alvarado, L.; Otero, B.; Cruz, L.; Rojas, O. Deep Neural Networks for Earthquake Detection and Source Region Estimation in North-Central Venezuela. *Bull. Seismol. Soc. Am.* **2020**, *110*, 2519–2529. [CrossRef]
21. Ahmad, J.; Farman, H.; Jan, Z. *Deep Learning Methods and Applications BT—Deep Learning: Convergence to Big Data Analytics*; Khan, M., Jan, B., Farman, H., Eds.; Springer: Singapore, 2019; pp. 31–42, ISBN 978-981-13-3459-7.
22. Akhter, M.P.; Jiangbin, Z.; Naqvi, I.R.; Abdelmajeed, M.; Fayyaz, M. Exploring Deep Learning Approaches for Urdu Text Classification in Product Manufacturing. *Enterp. Inf. Syst.* **2022**, *16*, 223–248. [CrossRef]
23. Hong, S.; Nguyen, H.T.; Jung, J.; Ahn, J. Seismic Ground Response Estimation Based on Convolutional Neural Networks (Cnn). *Appl. Sci.* **2021**, *11*, 10760. [CrossRef]
24. Harirchian, E.; Lahmer, T.; Rasulzade, S. Earthquake Hazard Safety Assessment of Existing Buildings Using Optimized Multi-Layer Perceptron Neural Network. *Energies* **2020**, *13*, 2060. [CrossRef]
25. Datta, A.; Wu, D.J.; Zhu, W.; Cai, M.; Ellsworth, W.L. DeepShake: Shaking Intensity Prediction Using Deep Spatiotemporal RNNs for Earthquake Early Warning. *Seismol. Res. Lett.* **2022**, *93*, 1636–1649. [CrossRef]
26. Ochoa, L.H.; Niño, L.F.; Vargas, C.A. Fast Magnitude Determination Using a Single Seismological Station Record Implementing Machine Learning Techniques. *Geod. Geodyn.* **2018**, *9*, 34–41. [CrossRef]
27. Lomax, A.; Michelini, A.; Jozinović, D. An Investigation of Rapid Earthquake Characterization Using Single-Station Waveforms and a Convolutional Neural Network. *Seismol. Res. Lett.* **2019**, *90*, 517–529. [CrossRef]
28. Tan, C.; Li, F.; Lv, S.; Yang, Y.; Dong, F. Gas-Liquid Two-Phase Stratified Flow Interface Reconstruction with Sparse Batch Normalization Convolutional Neural Network. *IEEE Sens. J.* **2021**, *21*, 17076–17084. [CrossRef]
29. Wang, J.; Li, S.; An, Z.; Jiang, X.; Qian, W.; Ji, S. Batch-Normalized Deep Neural Networks for Achieving Fast Intelligent Fault Diagnosis of Machines. *Neurocomputing* **2019**, *329*, 53–65. [CrossRef]
30. Bacciu, D.; Errica, F.; Micheli, A.; Podda, M. A Gentle Introduction to Deep Learning for Graphs. *Neural Netw.* **2020**, *129*, 203–221. [CrossRef]
31. Mousavi, S.M.; Ellsworth, W.L.; Zhu, W.; Chuang, L.Y.; Beroza, G.C. Earthquake Transformer—an Attentive Deep-Learning Model for Simultaneous Earthquake Detection and Phase Picking. *Nat. Commun.* **2020**, *11*, 1–12. [CrossRef]
32. Krischer, L.; Megies, T.; Barsch, R.; Beyreuther, M.; Lecocq, T.; Caudron, C.; Wassermann, J. ObsPy: A Bridge for Seismology into the Scientific Python Ecosystem. *Comput. Sci. Discov.* **2015**, *8*, 014003. [CrossRef]
33. Megies, T.; Beyreuther, M.; Barsch, R.; Krischer, L.; Wassermann, J. ObsPy—What Can It Do for Data Centers and Observatories? *Ann. Geophys.* **2011**, *54*, 47–58. [CrossRef]
34. Ku, B.; Kim, G.; Ahn, J.K.; Lee, J.; Ko, H. Attention-Based Convolutional Neural Network for Earthquake Event Classification. *IEEE Geosci. Remote Sens. Lett.* **2021**, *18*, 2057–2061. [CrossRef]

MDPI AG
Grosspeteranlage 5
4052 Basel
Switzerland
Tel.: +41 61 683 77 34

Applied Sciences Editorial Office
E-mail: applsci@mdpi.com
www.mdpi.com/journal/applsci

Disclaimer/Publisher's Note: The title and front matter of this reprint are at the discretion of the Guest Editors. The publisher is not responsible for their content or any associated concerns. The statements, opinions and data contained in all individual articles are solely those of the individual Editors and contributors and not of MDPI. MDPI disclaims responsibility for any injury to people or property resulting from any ideas, methods, instructions or products referred to in the content.

www.ingramcontent.com/pod-product-compliance
Lightning Source LLC
LaVergne TN
LVHW072324090526
838202LV00019B/2346